The Papers of
George Washington

The Papers of
George Washington

W. W. Abbot and Dorothy Twohig, *Editors*

Philander D. Chase and Beverly H. Runge, *Associate Editors*

Beverly S. Kirsch and Debra B. Kessler, *Assistant Editors*

Confederation Series
2

July 1784–May 1785

W. W. Abbot, *Editor*

UNIVERSITY PRESS OF VIRGINIA

CHARLOTTESVILLE AND LONDON

This edition has been prepared by the staff of
The Papers of George Washington
sponsored by
The Mount Vernon Ladies' Association of the Union
and the University of Virginia
with the support of
the National Endowment for the Humanities,
the Andrew W. Mellon Foundation,
and the J. Howard Pew Foundation Trust.

THE UNIVERSITY PRESS OF VIRGINIA
Copyright © 1992 by the Rector and Visitors
of the University of Virginia

First published 1992

Library of Congress Cataloging-in-Publication Data
Washington, George, 1732–1799.
    The papers of George Washington. Confederation series / W. W. Abbot and
Dorothy Twohig, editors; Philander D. Chase and Beverly H. Runge, associate
editors; Beverly S. Kirsch and Debra B. Kessler, assistant editors.
        p.   cm.
    Includes indexes.
    Contents: 1. January–July 1784 — 2. July 1784–May 1785
    ISBN 0-8139-1349-7 (v. 2)
    1. Washington, George, 1732–1799—Archives.   2. Presidents—United
States—Archives.   3. United States—History—Confederation,
1784–1788.   I. Abbot, W. W. (William Wright), 1922–
II. Twohig, Dorothy.   III. Title.   IV. Title: Confederation series.
E312.7   1992
973.4'1'092—dc20   91-3171
                                                                              CIP

Printed in the United States of America

Contents

NOTE: Volume numbers refer to the *Confederation Series*.

Editorial Apparatus	xxi
Symbols Designating Documents	xxii
Repository Symbols and Abbreviations	xxii
Short Title List	xxiv

1784

To Robert Townsend Hooe, 18 July	1
From Robert Townsend Hooe, 18 July	2
From David Parry, 18 July *see* 1:306	
From Jeremy Belknap, 19 July	2
To Walter Magowan, 20 July	3
From Edmund Randolph, 20 July	4
To Benjamin Harrison, 22 July	5
From Richard Henry Lee, 22 July	6
To William Skilling, 22 July	7
To William Fitzhugh, 23 July *see* 1:532-33	
To Benjamin Harrison, 23 July *see* 1:533	
From John Augustine Washington, c. 24 July	8
From George Augustine Washington, 25 July	9
From Henry Knox, 26 July	10
From Tench Tilghman, 27 July	11
To Wakelin Welch, 27 July	12
To Clement Biddle, 28 July	14
From William Skilling, 28 July	14
To Tench Tilghman, 29 July	15
From Jacob Read, 30 July	15
From Hugh Hughes, 31 July	17
From Gilbert Simpson, 31 July	18
From Thornton Washington, 1 August	20
To Charles Washington, 2 August	21
To Clement Biddle, 4 August	22
From Pierre-Charles L'Enfant, 4 August	22
To Tench Tilghman, 4 August	23
From John Ariss, 5 August	24
From Jacob Read, 6 August	25
From Warner Washington, 7 August	26
To John Ariss, 8 August	27

From Lafayette, 10 August   28
To Jacob Read, 11 August   29
To Tench Tilghman, 11 August   30
From George Augustine Washington, 11 August   31
From David Humphreys, 12 August   32
From James Madison, 12 August   *see* 1:482
From Francis Mentges, 12 August   34
From Jacob Read, 13 August   35
From William Smith, 13 August   37
From Jean Le Mayeur, 14 August   38
From George Augustine Washington, 14 August   39
From David Humphreys, 18 August   41
From Tench Tilghman, 18 August   42
To Chastellux, 20 August   44
To James Crane, 20 August   45
To William Drew, 20 August   45
To Duportail, 20 August   46
To La Luzerne, 20 August   47
To Rochambeau, 20 August   48
From Stephen Sayre, 20 August   49
To Hugh Hughes, 22 August   *see* 2:18
To Francis Mentges, 22 August   *see* 2:34
From George William Fairfax, 23 August   51
To Reuben Harvey, 25 August   55
To James Mercer, 25 August   56
To William Smith, 25 August   57
To Thomas Walker, 25 August   58
From Unzaga y Amézaga, 26 August   58
From Nathanael Greene, 29 August   59
To David Griffith, 29 August   61
From Thomas Walker, 29 August   62
From William Gordon, 30 August   63
To Jean Le Mayeur, 30 August   65
To Stephen Sayre, 1 September   65
From Joseph Wright, 1 September   66
To Daniel Morgan, 4 September   67
To Edward Snickers, 4 September   67
Certificate for James Rumsey, 7 September   69
From John Rumney, Jr., 8 September   70
From Rochambeau, 9 September   70
From Kersaint, 12 September   71
From La Luzerne, 12 September   72
From Battaile Muse, 12 September   73
From Lafayette, 15 September   *see* 2:492

From John Woddrop, 16 September 74
To Thomas Freeman, 23 September 78
From David Humphreys, 30 September 80
From Daniel Morgan, 30 September 82
From James Craik, 2 October 82
Table of Distances from Detroit to Montreal, 4 October
    see 2:97-98
From Lafayette, 8 October 84
To Benjamin Harrison, 10 October 86
From Stephen Sayre, 15 October 99
From Pusignan, 16 October 100
From James Rumsey, 19 October 101
To Sidney Lee, 20 October 102
From George Plater, 20 October 102
From Lafayette, 22 October 103
From Jacob Read, 22 October 104
To George Plater, 25 October 106
To George Rindfleisch, 25 October 110
From Walter Stewart, 26 October 110
From Melancton Smith, 27 October 111
To Stephen Bloomer Balch, 30 October 113
To Robert Anderson, 3 November 113
To Clement Biddle, 3 November 114
To Elias Boudinot, 3 November 115
To William Gordon, 3 November 116
To Battaile Muse, 3 November 117
To Jacob Read, 3 November 118
From John Preston, 6 November 123
From David Humphreys, 11 November 124
From Normand Bruce, 13 November 126
From Benjamin Harrison, 13 November 134
From Officials of the City of Richmond, 15 November
    see 2:135-36
To Officials of the City of Richmond, 15 November 135
To Virginia House of Delegates, 15 November 136
From Patrick Henry, 15 November   *see* 2:137
From Charles Washington, 16 November 137
From Henry Lee, Jr., 18 November 139
From Arthur Lee, 19 November 141
From Fontenille, 20 November 141
From Richard Henry Lee, 20 November 142
From Henry Knox, 23 November 143
To Henry Lee, Jr., 24 November 144
To George Clinton, 25 November 145

To Fock, 25 November   *see* 1 : 151
To David Humphreys, 25 November   149
To Kersaint, 25 November   *see* 2 : 72
To Anastasie de Lafayette, 25 November   150
To Adrienne, marquise de Lafayette, 25 November   150
To La Touche-Treville, 25 November   *see* 1 : 450
To Maithe, 25 November   *see* 1 : 399
To Joseph Mandrillon, 25 November   *see* 1 : 442
To Friedrich Anton Mesmer, 25 November   151
From William Roberts, 25 November   151
To Rochambeau, 25 November   *see* 2 : 71
To Vienne, 25 November   *see* 1 : 187-88
To William Washington, 25 November   153
To George Augustine Washington, 26 November   154
To James Madison, 28 November   155
From John Filson, 30 November   *see* 2 : 170
From Charles MacIver, November   157
From Nathanael Greene, 2 December   161
Certificate Making George Washington a Freeman of New
     York City, 2 December   *see* 2 : 188-89
Address from Officials of New York City, 2 December
     see 2 : 189-90
From William Carmichael, 3 December   163
   Enclosure: Floridablanca to William Carmichael, 24
     November   165
To James Madison, 3 December   165
From John Filson, 4 December   168
To Henry Knox, 5 December   170
To La Luzerne, 5 December   172
To George Clinton, 8 December   174
To Lafayette, 8 December   175
From Thomas Jefferson, 10 December   176
To George Plater, Charles Carroll, John Cadwalader,
     and Samuel Chase, 11 December   178
To George Mason, 13 December   180
To Richard Henry Lee, 14 December   181
To George Chapman, 15 December   183
To Richard Claiborne, 15 December   184
From Beverley Randolph, 15 December   185
From James Duane, 16 December   187
From Udny Hay, 16 December   190
From Joseph Palmer, 16 December   192
From Lafayette, 17 December   194
To Thomas Blackburn, 19 December   195

To William Paca, 19 December   195
From Thomas Blackburn, 20 December   196
To William Gordon, 20 December   196
To Alexander Henderson, 20 December   197
Lady Huntingdon's Scheme for Aiding the American
    Indians, 20 December   198
    I. From James Jay, 20 December   200
    II. From the Countess of Huntingdon, c. March   205
    III. From the Countess of Huntingdon, 20 March   208
    IV. From the Countess of Huntingdon, 8 April   210
    V. Lady Huntingdon's Plan for Settlement, 8 April   211
    VI. Lady Huntingdon's Circular Letter to the
        Governors of North Carolina, Virginia,
        Pennsylvania, and New York, c.8 April   216
    VII. James Jay's Copy of His Letter to the Governors
        of North Carolina, Virginia, Pennsylvania,
        and New York, c.20 December   218
From La Luzerne, 20 December   222
To Beverley Randolph, 20 December   223
To Melancton Smith, 20 December   223
From Benjamin Walker, 20 December   224
From Lafayette, 21 December   226
To Lafayette, 23 December   228
To Charles-Louis de Montesquieu, 23 December   *see* 2:524
From Horatio Gates, 24 December   229
From Richard Henry Lee, 26 December   230
To James Madison, 28 December   231
George Washington and Horatio Gates to the Virginia
    Legislature, 28 December   235
    Enclosure I: Report of the Maryland and Virginia
        Commissioners, 28 December   236
    Enclosure II: An Act for Opening and Extending the
        Navigation of Potowmack River   240
    Enclosure III: Resolutions of the Maryland
        Legislature, 28 December   245
From Aeneas Lamont, 31 December   246
From Charles Willson Peale, c. December   247
From a French Wine Merchant, 1784   247
From Richard Price, c.1784   *see* 2:271

1785
From James Madison, 1 January   248
From Robert Morris, 1 January   250
To Jeremy Belknap, 5 January   251

To Samuel Chase, 5 January   252
To Ebenezer Hazard, 5 January   *see* 2:251
To Henry Knox, 5 January   253
From Benjamin Harrison, 6 January   256
To George Augustine Washington, 6 January   258
From James Madison, 9 January   260
   Enclosure I: Resolution of the Virginia Assembly,
     28 December 1784   262
   Enclosure II: Resolution of the Virginia Assembly,
     1 January   263
   Enclosure III: Resolution of the Virginia Assembly,
     1 January   264
To Charles Carroll, 10 January   265
From William Gordon, 10 January   266
From Alexander Henderson, 11 January   267
From David Humphreys, 15 January   268
To John Filson, 16 January   269
From Richard Henry Lee, 16 January   271
To Samuel Chase, 17 January   272
To Thomas Johnson, 17 January   273
To John Fitzgerald and William Hartshorne, 18 January   273
From Hanna Moore, 20 January   275
From Samuel Brenton, 21 January   276
From John Fitzgerald and William Hartshorne, 21 January   277
To Matthew Campbell, 22 January   278
To William Grayson, 22 January   280
To Benjamin Harrison, 22 January   282
To Bushrod Washington, 22 January   284
From Jacob Gerhard Diriks, 24 January   285
From Otho Holland Williams, 24 January   287
From John Armstrong, 25 January   287
To Thomas Clarke, 25 January   290
To James Jay, 25 January   291
To Elias Boudinot, 26 January   294
From Samuel Hanway, 26 January   294
From Henry Knox, 26 January   295
From Melancton Smith, 26 January   295
From Thomas Stone, 28 January   297
From Clement Biddle, 29 January   298
From Abraham Hite, Jr., 29 January   298
To Joseph Wright, 30 January   299
To Patience Wright, 30 January   299
To Elias Boudinot, 31 January   300
To Udny Hay, 31 January   300

From Henry Knox, 31 January   301
To Aeneas Lamont, 31 January   *see* 2:319
To William Paca, 31 January   306
To Clement Biddle, 1 February   306
To Robert Morris, 1 February   309
From Edmund Richards, 1 February   315
To Robert Lewis & Sons, 1 February   317
To Clement Biddle, 2 February   318
To Otho Holland Williams, 2 February   319
From John Sullivan, 3 February   320
To John Beckley, 5 February   322
To Benjamin Lincoln, 5 February   323
To Battaile Muse, 5 February   324
To Benjamin Vaughan, 5 February   325
To Samuel Vaughan, 5 February   326
From Christopher Chamney, 8 February   326
From John Filson, 8 February   327
From Benjamin Harrison, 8 February   328
To Richard Henry Lee, 8 February   330
From Elias Boudinot, 9 February   333
From John Fitzgerald, 9 February   335
From Lafayette, 9 February   335
From John Rumney, Jr., 9 February   336
From Thomas Smith, 9 February   338
From James Keith, 10 February   359
From John Beckley, 11 February   360
From Richard Henry Lee, 14 February   361
To Lafayette, 15 February   363
From La Luzerne, 15 February   367
From Samuel Love, 15 February   368
From Charles Washington, 19 February   370
From Hugh Williamson, 19 February   371
To Charles Lee, 20 February   373
From Frederick Weissenfels, 21 February   375
To John Francis Mercer, 23 February   *see* 2:366
From Josiah Parker, 24-28 February   376
From Rochambeau, 24 February   378
To Thomas Jefferson, 25 February   379
From George Augustine Washington, 25 February   382
From Joseph Dashiell, 26 February   385
To George William Fairfax, 27 February   386
To Patrick Henry, 27 February   391
To the Countess of Huntingdon, 27 February   392
From Richard Henry Lee, 27 February   395

Certificate for James Sever, 28 February *see* 2:401
To Chastellux, 28 February *see* 2:401
From Daniel of St. Thomas Jenifer, 28 February   397
To Henry Knox, 28 February   398
To Hanna Moore, 28 February   401
To Rochambeau, 28 February *see* 2:401
From Charles MacIver, February   402
To Matthew Campbell, 1 March   402
To James Keith, 1 March   404
To Charles MacIver, 1 March   404
From John Boyle, Jr., 4 March   405
From Lebarbier, 4 March   406
From George Clinton, 5 March   408
From Patrick Henry, 5 March   409
From Clement Biddle, 7 March   410
To William Gordon, 8 March   411
To John Witherspoon, 8 March   414
From Jacob Read, 9 March   416
From James Duane, 10 March   418
From William Grayson, 10 March   419
From Alexander Hamilton, 10 March   424
From James Rumsey, 10 March   425
From Benjamin Walker, 11 March   429
From Patrick Henry, 12 March   430
From Henry Lee, Jr., 12 March   431
To Sarah Bomford, 15 March   431
To Mathew Carey, 15 March   433
From James Cross, 15 March   434
To Jacob Gerhard Diriks, 15 March   435
To John Filson, 15 March   436
To Arthur Lee, 15 March   436
To Richard Henry Lee, 15 March   437
To Frederick Weissenfels, 15 March   438
To Hugh Williamson, 15 March   439
From George William Fairfax, 19 March   441
To John Harvie, 19 March   442
From Patrick Henry, 19 March   447
From Lafayette, 19 March   449
To Edmund Randolph, 19 March   451
From William Blake, 20 March   451
To Patrick Henry, 20 March   452
To Edward Newenham, 20 March   453
From St. John de Crèvecoeur, 21 March   455
From John Craig, 22 March   455

From Elkanah Watson, 22 March ... 456
To William Hunter, 24 March ... 458
From Henry Knox, 24 March ... 458
Advertisement, 25 March *see* 2 : 475
From William Carmichael, 25 March ... 460
From La Luzerne, 25 March ... 461
To John Francis Mercer, 27 March ... 463
From Frederick Weissenfels, 27 March ... 464
From William Gordon, 28 March ... 465
From Reuben Harvey, 28 March ... 468
From Benjamin Lincoln, 28 March *see* 2 : 533
To John Craig, 29 March ... 469
From Robert Townsend Hooe, 29 March ... 470
From Robert Townsend Hooe, 29 March ... 470
From Henry Knox, 29 March *see* 2 : 533-34
From Christopher Ludwick, 29 March ... 471
From Josiah Parker, 29 March ... 472
From Benjamin Lincoln, 30 March *see* 2 : 533
To Lucretia Wilhemina van Winter, 30 March ... 472
From Daniel of St. Thomas Jenifer, 31 March ... 473
From Robert Townsend Hooe, 3 April ... 474
To Bushrod Washington, 3 April ... 474
From Patrick Henry, 4 April ... 476
To George Clinton, 5 April ... 477
From Sidney Lee, 5 April ... 478
From George Mason, 5 April ... 478
From Edmund Randolph, 5 April ... 479
From Robert Lewis & Sons, 5 April ... 480
To Charles Thomson, 5 April ... 482
From Robert Townsend Hooe, 6 April ... 483
To Christopher Richmond, 6 April ... 483
From George Crocker Fox & Sons, 8 April ... 484
From Christopher Richmond, 8 April ... 484
To James Duane, 10 April ... 485
To James Duane, 10 April *see* 2 : 487
To New York City Officials, 10 April *see* 2 : 487-88
To Thomas Walker, 10 April ... 488
To Frederick Weissenfels, 10 April *see* 2 : 465
To Thomas Freeman, 11 April ... 489
From Clement Biddle, 12 April ... 490
To Daniel of St. Thomas Jenifer, 12 April ... 491
To Lafayette, 12 April ... 492
To Robert Lewis & Sons, 12 April ... 493
To Charles Washington, 12 April ... 494

From John Harvie, 13 April   495
From Samuel Adams, 14 April   *see* 2:534
From John Dickinson, 14 April   *see* 2:508
From John Gardiner, 14 April   *see* 2:534
From William M. Roberts, 14 April   496
From John Witherspoon, 14 April   496
From William Grayson, 15 April   498
From Daniel of St. Thomas Jenifer, 15 April   501
From Adrienne, Marquise de Lafayette, 15 April   502
From Robert Morris, 15 April   *see* 2:508
From Lafayette, 16 April   503
From Henry Lee, 16 April   505
From Robert Morris, 17 April   506
From Clement Biddle, 19 April   507
From Francis Hopkinson, 19 April   507
To Mathew Carey, 20 April   509
To George Clinton, 20 April   509
From Otho Holland Williams, 20 April   512
From William Washington, 21 April   513
From John Harvie, 22 April   513
From Charles Thomson, 22 April   517
From Charles Thomson, 22 April   *see* 2:508-9
From Thomas McKean, 23 April   *see* 2:509
From Thomas Mifflin, 24 April   *see* 2:509
From John Baylor, 25 April   518
To William Grayson, 25 April   519
From Nathanael Greene, 25 April   521
From John Murray & Co., 25 April   523
From Charles-Louis de Montesquieu, 25 April   523
From Samuel Powel, 25 April   525
From Lyonel Bradstreet, 26 April   526
From Henry Hollyday, 30 April   526
From Thomas Ridout, 1 May   528
From William Fitzhugh, 2 May   529
From Jean-Baptiste de Montesquieu, 2 May   530
Resolutions of the Dismal Swamp Company, 2 May   530
From Richard Henry Lee, 3 May   532
From Thomas Bibby, 4 May   534
From William Grayson, c. 4-8 May   535
From Robert Howe, 4 May   538
From James Duane, 5 May   *see* 2:534
From William Grayson, 5 May   539
From Henry Knox, 5 May   539
From Ruthey Jones, 7 May   540

From Richard Henry Lee, 7 May 543
From Jacob Read, 8 May 544
From David Humphreys, 10 May 545
From Christopher Richmond, 10 May 547
From W. Symmes, 10 May 548
From Lafayette, 11 May   *see* 2:551
From Lafayette, 11 May 550
From Jacquelin Ambler, 12 May 552
To Lafayette, 12 May   *see* 2:553
To La Serre, 12 May 552
From Thomas Marshall, 12 May 553
From William Fitzhugh, 13 May 554
From John Harvie, 13 May 555
From Lafayette, 13 May 556
From John Swan, 13 May 559
From Tench Tilghman, 14 May 559
To Clement Biddle, 16 May 560
To John Dickinson, 16 May   *see* 2:562
To Francis Hopkinson, 16 May 561
To Thomas McKean, 16 May   *see* 2:562
From Stephen Moylan, 16 May   *see* 2:561
To Thomas Johnson and Thomas Sim Lee, 18 May 562
To Edward Lloyd, 18 May   *see* 2:567
To William Paca, 18 May   *see* 2:567
To Richard Sprigg, 18 May 566

Index 569

Editorial Apparatus

Transcription of the documents in the volumes of *The Papers of George Washington* has remained as close to a literal reproduction of the manuscript as possible. Punctuation, capitalization, paragraphing, and spelling of all words are retained as they appear in the original document. Dashes used as punctuation have been retained except when a period and a dash and another mark of punctutation appear together. The appropriate marks of punctuation have always been added at the end of a paragraph. When a tilde is used in the manuscript to indicate a double letter, the letter has been doubled. Washington and some of his correspondents occasionally used a tilde above an incorrectly spelled word to indicate an error in orthography. When this device is used the editors have corrected the word. In cases where a tilde has been inserted above an abbreviation or contraction, usually in letter-book copies, the word has been expanded. Otherwise, contractions and abbreviations have been retained as written except that a period has been inserted after an abbreviation when needed. Superscripts have been lowered. Editorial insertions or corrections in the text appear in square brackets. Angle brackets ⟨ ⟩ are used to indicate illegible or mutilated material. A space left blank in a manuscript by the writer is indicated by a square-bracketed gap in the text [ ]. Deletion of material by the author of a manuscript is ignored unless it contains substantive material, and then it appears in a footnote. If the intended location of marginal notations is clear from the text, they are inserted without comment; otherwise they are recorded in the notes. The ampersand has been retained and the thorn transcribed as "th." The symbol for per (℔) is used when it appears in the manuscript. The dateline has been placed at the head of a document regardless of where it occurs in the manuscript.

Since GW read no language other than English, incoming letters written to him in foreign languages generally were translated for his information. Where this contemporary translation has survived, it has been used as the text of the document and the original version has been included either in the notes or in the CD-ROM edition of the Papers. If there is no contemporary translation, the document in its original language has been used as the text. All of the documents printed in this volume, as well as other ancillary material (usually cited in the notes), may be found in the CD-ROM edition of Washington's Papers (CD-ROM:GW).

Individuals mentioned in the text have been identified whenever possible at their first substantive mention and will not be identified at length in future volumes. The index to each of the Confederation Series volumes indicates where an identification may be found in earlier volumes of the series.

Symbols Designating Documents

AD   Autograph Document
ADS   Autograph Document Signed
ADf   Autograph Draft
ADfS   Autograph Draft Signed
AL   Autograph Letter
ALS   Autograph Letter Signed
D   Document
DS   Document Signed
Df   Draft
DfS   Draft Signed
LS   Letter Signed
LB   Letter-Book Copy
[S]   Signature clipped (used with other symbols: e.g., AL[S], Df[S])

Repository Symbols and Abbreviations

CD-ROM:GW   See "Editorial Apparatus"
CSmH   Henry E. Huntington Library, San Marino, Calif.
CtY   Yale University, New Haven
DLC   Library of Congress
DLC:GW   George Washington Papers, Library of Congress
DNA   National Archives
DNA:PCC   Papers of the Continental Congress, National Archives
DSoCi   Society of the Cincinnati, Washington, D.C.

ICU	University of Chicago
MA	Amherst College, Amherst, Mass.
MAnP	Phillips Academy, Andover, Mass.
MdAA	Hall of Records, Archives, Annapolis
MdAN	U.S. Naval Academy, Annapolis
MdHi	Maryland Historical Society, Baltimore
MH	Harvard University, Cambridge, Mass.
MHi	Massachusetts Historical Society, Boston
MiD-B	Burton Historical Collection, Detroit Public Library
MiU-C	University of Michigan, Ann Arbor, William L. Clements Library
MnHi	Minnesota Historical Society, St. Paul
N	New York State Library, Albany
Nc-Ar	North Carolina State Department of Archives and History, Raleigh
NcD	Duke University, Durham, N.C.
NhD	Dartmouth College, Hanover, N.H.
NHi	New-York Historical Society, New York
NIC	Cornell University, Ithaca, N.Y.
NjHi	New Jersey Historical Society, Newark
NjP	Princeton University, Princeton, N.J.
NN	New York Public Library, New York
NNC	Columbia University, New York
NNPM	Pierpont Morgan Library, New York
PCarlD	Dickinson College, Carlisle, Pa.
PEL	Lafayette College, Easton, Pa.
PHi	Historical Society of Pennsylvania, Philadelphia
PPAmP	American Philosophical Society, Philadelphia
PPRF	Rosenbach Foundation, Philadelphia
PU	University of Pennsylvania, Philadelphia
PWacD	David Library of the American Revolution, Washington Crossing, Pa.
PWW	Washington and Jefferson College, Washington, Pa.
RG	Record Group (designating the location of documents in the National Archives)
RPJCB	John Carter Brown Library, Providence
Vi	Virginia State Library and Archives, Richmond
ViAlM	George Washington Masonic National Memorial Association, Alexandria, Va.
ViHi	Virginia Historical Society, Richmond
ViMtV	Mount Vernon Ladies' Association of the Union
VtHi	Vermont Historical Society, Montpelier
WHi	State Historical Society of Wisconsin, Madison

Short Title List

Belknap Papers.   Jeremy Belknap. *The Belknap Papers.* 3 vols. (1877–91).

Betts, *Jefferson's Garden Book.*   Edwin M. Betts, ed. *Thomas Jefferson's Garden Book, 1766–1824.* Philadelphia, 1944.

Bothwell, "The Astonishing Croghans."   Margaret Pearson Bothwell. "The Astonishing Croghans." *Western Pennsylvania Historical Magazine,* 48 (1965), 119–44.

Bowden, *Industrial Society in England.*   Witt Bowden. *Industrial Society in England, towards the End of the Eighteenth Century.* New York, 1925.

Boyd, *Jefferson Papers.*   Julian P. Boyd et al., eds. *The Papers of Thomas Jefferson.* 22 vols. to date. Princeton, N.J., 1950—.

Brackenridge, *Law Miscellanies.*   Hugh Henry Brackenridge. *Law Miscellanies: Containing an Introduction to the Study of the Law. . . .* 1814. Reprint. New York, 1972.

Crumrine, *Washington County.*   Boyd Crumrine. *History of Washington County, Pennsylvania, with Biographical Sketches of Many of the Pioneers and Prominent Men.* Philadelphia, 1882.

Diaries.   Donald Jackson and Dorothy Twohig, eds. *The Diaries of George Washington.* 6 vols. Charlottesville, Va., 1976–79.

Fabian, *Wright.*   Monroe H. Fabian. *Joseph Wright, American Artist, 1756–1793.* Washington, D.C., 1985.

Fitzpatrick, *Washington's Will.*   John C. Fitzpatrick, ed. *The Last Will and Testament of George Washington and Schedule of His Property.* Mount Vernon, Va., 1960.

Fitzpatrick, *Writings of Washington.*   John C. Fitzpatrick, ed. *The Writings of George Washington from the Original Manuscript Sources, 1745–1799.* 39 vols. Washington, D.C., 1931–44.

Ford, *Correspondence of Webb.*   Worthington Chauncey Ford, ed. *Correspondence and Journals of Samuel Blachley Webb.* 3 vols. New York, 1893–94.

Freeman, *Washington.*   Douglas Southall Freeman. *George Washington.* 7 vols. New York, 1949–57.

Griffin, *Boston Athenæum Collection.*   Appleton P. C. Griffin, comp. *A Catalogue of the Washington Collection in the Boston Athenæum.* Cambridge, Mass., 1897.

Haldimand Papers, *Michigan Pioneer and Historical Collections.*   *Collections and Researches Made by the Michigan Pioneer and Historical Society.* 5 vols. Lansing, Mich., 1886–92.

Hening.   William Waller Hening, ed. *The Statutes at Large; Being a Collection of All the Laws of Virginia from the First Session of the Legis-*

lature, in the Year 1619. 13 vols. 1819–23. Reprint. Charlottesville, Va., 1969.

House of Delegates Journal, 1781–1785.   *Journal of the House of Delegates of the Commonwealth of Virginia; Begun and Held in the Town of Richmond, in the County of Henrico, on Monday, the Seventh Day of May, in the Year of Our Lord One Thousand Seven Hundred and Eighty-One.* Richmond, 1828.

Hume, *Society of the Cincinnati.*   Edgar Erskine Hume, ed. *General Washington's Correspondence concerning the Society of the Cincinnati.* Baltimore, 1941.

Idzerda, *Lafayette Papers.*   Stanley J. Idzerda, Robert Crout, et al., eds. *Lafayette in the Age of the American Revolution: Selected Letters and Papers 1776–1790*. 5 vols. to date. Ithaca, N.Y., 1977—.

JCC.   Worthington C. Ford et al., eds. *Journals of the Continental Congress.* 34 vols. Washington, D.C., 1904–37.

Jeremy, *Transatlantic Industrial Revolution.*   David J. Jeremy. *Transatlantic Industrial Revolution: The Diffusion of Textile Technologies between Britain and America, 1790–1830s.* Cambridge, Mass., 1981.

Kappler, *Indian Treaties.*   Charles Joseph Kappler, ed. *Indian Affairs: Laws and Treaties.* 7 vols. Washington, D.C., 1903–41.

Konkle, *Thomas Smith.*   Burton Alva Konkle. *The Life and Times of Thomas Smith, 1745–1809.* Philadelphia, 1904.

Ledger B.   Manuscript Ledger in George Washington Papers, Library of Congress.

Ledger C.   Manuscript Ledger in Morristown National Historical Park, Morristown, N.J.

Mays, *Pendleton Letters.*   David John Mays, ed. *The Letters and Papers of Edmund Pendleton, 1734–1803.* 2 vols. Charlottesville, Va., 1967.

Md. House of Delegates Proceedings.   *Votes and Proceedings of the House of Delegates of the State of Maryland. November Session, 1784. Being the First Session of This Assembly.* N.p., n.d.

Md. Senate Proceedings.   *Votes and Proceedings of the Senate of the State of Maryland. May Session, 1781. Being the Second Session of This Assembly.* N.p., n.d.

Nancy Shippen Journal.   Ethel Armes, ed. *Nancy Shippen, Her Journal Book: The International Romance of a Young Lady of Fashion of Colonial Philadelphia with Letters to and about Her.* Philadelphia, 1935.

Papers, Colonial Series.   W. W. Abbot et al., eds. *The Papers of George Washington:* Colonial Series. 7 vols. to date. Charlottesville, Va., 1983—.

Rowe, *Thomas McKean.*   G. S. Rowe. *Thomas McKean: The Shaping of an American Republicanism.* Boulder, Colo., 1978.

Rutland, *Mason Papers.*   Robert A. Rutland, ed. *The Papers of*

George Mason, 1725–1792. 3 vols. Chapel Hill, N.C., 1970.

Rutland and Rachal, *Madison Papers.*   Robert A. Rutland, William M. E. Rachal, J. C. A. Stagg, et al., eds. *The Papers of James Madison.* 17 vols. Chicago and Charlottesville, Va., 1962–92.

Schoepf, *Travels in the Confederation.*   Johann David Schoepf. *Travels in the Confederation, 1783–1784,* trans. and ed. Alfred J. Morrison. 2 vols. Philadelphia, 1911.

Seilhamer, *American Theatre.*   George O. Seilhamer. *History of the American Theatre: During the Revolution and After.* 2 vols. Philadelphia, 1889.

Syrett, *Hamilton Papers.*   Harold C. Syrett et al., eds. *The Papers of Alexander Hamilton.* 27 vols. New York. 1961–87.

Wainwright, *Croghan.*   Nicholas B. Wainwright. *George Croghan, Wilderness Diplomat.* Chapel Hill, N.C., 1959.

Waterman, *Mansions of Virginia.*   Thomas Tileston Waterman. *The Mansions of Virginia, 1706–1776.* Chapel Hill, N.C., 1946.

Watson, *Men and Times of the Revolution.*   Winslow C. Watson, ed. *Men and Times of the Revolution; or, Memoirs of Elkanah Watson, Including Journals of Travels in Europe and America, from 1777 to 1842, with His Correspondence with Public Men and Reminiscences and Incidents of the Revolution.* New York, 1856.

Wharton, *Diplomatic Correspondence.*   Francis Wharton, ed. *The Revolutionary Diplomatic Correspondence of the United States.* 6 vols. Washington, D.C., 1889.

Wilkinson, "Land Policy and Speculation in Pennsylvania."   Norman B. Wilkinson. "Land Policy and Speculation in Pennsylvania, 1779–1800." Ph.D. diss., University of Pennsylvania, 1958.

Works of Humphreys.   David Humphreys. *The Miscellaneous Works of David Humphreys.* New York, 1804.

The Papers of George Washington
Confederation Series
Volume 2
July 1784–May 1785

To Robert Townsend Hooe

Sir,   Mount Vernon 18th July 1784.

Hearing that you have a Vessel bound to some port in Spain, I am induced to ask if it is safe & practicable to bring from thence a good Jack Ass, to breed from—The late Don Juan de Miralles, resident from the Court of Spain at Philadelphia, promised to procure one for me; but in his death I met a disappointment. Another Gentleman of his nation, not long since, has also given me a promise—but it is not yet fulfilled[1]—& as I am convinced that a good Jack would be a public benefit to this part of the country, as well as private convenience to myself, I am desireous of having more strings than one to my bow. I do not mean however to involve any person, or thing, in difficulty, to accomplish this end.[2]

Under this express declaration if you or your Partner Mr Harrison, could openly, fairly & upon easy terms, serve me, I should acknowledge the favor.[3] An ordinary Jack I do not desire; I will describe therefore such an one as I must have, if I get any—He must be at least fifteen hands high; well formed; in his prime; & one whose abilities for getting Colts can be ensured; for I have been informed, that except those which are designed to breed from; & more especially such as are suffered to be exported; they very frequently have their generative parts so injured by squeezing, as to render them as unfit for the purpose of begetting Colts, as castration would—when from a superficial view no imperfection appears. Whether the latter is founded in truth, or mere report, I do not vouch for; but as I would have a good Jack or none, I am induced to mention the circumstance. I am Sir &c.

G: Washington

LB, DLC:GW. For the problem with the dating of this letter to the Alexandria merchant, see Hooe's letter printed immediately below.

1. Don Juan de Miralles, the Cuban merchant and slave trader who acted as an agent of the king of Spain in the United States, was visiting GW at his headquarters in Morristown, N.J., when he died at noon on 28 April 1780. The other Spanish "Gentleman" has not been identified.

2. For GW's prolonged and eventually successful efforts to obtain Spanish jacks, see especially William Carmichael to GW, 3 Dec. 1784, n.1.

3. Richard Harrison, who later married Dr. James Craik's daughter Nancy, was a partner in the commercial firm of Harrison & Hooe in Alexandria. From 1780 to 1786 he acted as consul for the United States in Cadiz. See also Harrison to GW, 8 May 1789, n.1. Harrison asked for the help of the chargé d'affaires for the United States in Madrid, William Carmichael, who wrote GW on 3 Dec. about acquiring Spanish jacks for him.

From Robert Townsend Hooe

Sir—   Alexa[ndria, Va., 18 July 1784]
I am to acknowledge the honor of your letter of this day, and let me assure you that I will do every thing in my power to procure such a Spanish Jack as you describe[1]—Mr Harrison will with pleasure receive and execute the order and all will be done in that fair open and honorable manner you direct.

I could wish you had communicated your desire a few days Sooner that I might have given directions by one of our own Vessels—but we have a Ship lading flour at Balto. that I hope will Sail in a few days, and by her I will give the necessary orders. I have the honor to be sir Your most Aff. Hble servt
                                    R. Td Hooe

ALS, PHi: Dreer Collection; Sprague transcript, DLC:GW. This letter dated "July 17th 1784" by Hooe is in response to the letter from GW dated in GW's letter book 18 July. One or the other of the letters is misdated. The decision to change the date of Hooe's letter rather than GW's was arbitrary.

1. See GW to Hooe, this date.

From Jeremy Belknap

To General Washington: Dover, N.H. July 19th, 1784.
Great and Good Sir, After the multitude of addresses which have been presented to you in the course and at the conclusion of the late war, it would be needless for an obscure individual to repeat the voice of admiration and gratitude which has resounded from every part of America for the eminent services which you have rendered to this country. It shall be my part, Sir, to ask your acceptance of the first volume of a work, in which, you will see the early struggles and sufferings of one of those states which now claim the honor of being defended by

your sword. Though in the late arduous contest it has not been so much exposed as in former wars, yet, having long been a nursery of stern heroism, it has bred an hardy race of men, whose merits as soldiers are well known to their beloved general, and who will always glory in having assisted to plant the laurel which adorns his brow.

I am, Sir, with a degree of respect approaching to veneration, Your Excellency's most obedient servant,

J. B.

Life of Jeremy Belknap, D.D., the Historian of New Hampshire, with Selections from His Correspondence and Other Writings, Collected and Arranged by His Grand-Daughter (New York, 1847), 137.

Jeremy Belknap (1744–1798), a Congregational clergyman in Dover, N.H., published the first volume of his celebrated three-volume history of New Hampshire in 1784. Belknap's friend, Ebenezer Hazard, supervised its printing in Philadelphia, and on 24 May Belknap asked Hazard what he thought of "sending a copy to General Washington" (*Belknap Papers*, 1 : 345– 49). Hazard was enthusiastic: "I think it will be quite polite to present General Washington with a copy of your History, and it will produce a letter from him in *his own handwriting*, which will be worth preserving. I have several, which I intend to hand down carefully to posterity as highly valuable" (ibid., 355–57). Belknap sent Hazard this letter to GW for Hazard to send on to GW along with the volume of the *History*. On 31 July Hazard wrote that he would direct the printer, Robert Aitkin, "to bind one of your books neatly" and that he would "forward it with your letter" (ibid., 377–80). It was early winter, however, before Hazard sent Belknap's book and letter to GW (see GW to Belknap, 5 Jan. 1785).

To Walter Magowan

D. Sir   [Mount Vernon] 20th July 1784.

Not knowing of whom the vestry of Peccawaxon is composed—or that I have the honor of being acquainted with a single member of it; there would be I conceive, an impropriety in my addressing them on the subject of your application— otherwise I would with great pleasure join my recommendations of you to those of Majr Jenefer.[1] If my best wishes, however, can contribute to the success of your present movement, you have them very sincerely: or if my signifying, that from a long acquaintance with you, I can bear testimony to the truth of what Majr Jenefer has advanced in your behalf, will be of any avail, I would do it with pleasure. In the meanwhile such evidence thereof as this letter affords, you are at free liberty to make use of, because I have full conviction in my own breast, that if the choice of the vestry should light on you, you would make the Parish happy—With great truth & regard I am Dr Sir &c.

G: Washington

LB, DLC:GW.

Walter Magowan, a Scot, was the tutor for the Custis children at Mount Vernon from 1761 until 1767, when he went to London for his ordination in the Church of England. Upon his return to America, he became a probationer in St. James Parish, Herring Creek, in Anne Arundel County, Md., and in 1769 was made rector of the parish. He was holding that position when he asked GW to support his application for the living at William and Mary (Pickawaxon) Parish, Charles County, Maryland. He died in 1784, apparently while still rector at St. James.

1. Major Jenifer was Daniel of St. Thomas Jenifer (1723–1790), a native of Charles County, Md., but living at this time in Anne Arundel County, in or near Annapolis.

From Edmund Randolph

Dear Sir   Richmond [Va.] July 20. 1784.

Since my letter of the last week, I have inquired into the fruit of your chances in Colo. Byrd's lottery, from Mr James Buchanan, of this town, the only person, on whose information I can depend for such a subject.[1] No. 265, the prize of the ticket 4965 is a lot in Manchester; the value of which is unknown, and is therefore in all probability as yet of scarcely any. No's. 270, 138, 237, 257, the prizes of the tickets 3187, 3186, 5325, and 5519, lie in the town of Manchester. Mr Buchanan, (as you will perceive by his pencil memorandum inclosed) says that Colo. Richard Randolph sold the most valuable lot to Mr Trent.[2] No's. 823, 751, the prizes of the tickets 3193 and 5517 are 100 acre lots in Henrico, and were sold by Mr Mason.[3] I shall desire Mr Buchanan to make farther inquiry into the values and to inform you in my absence from hence; as I am about to go to Charlottesville on friday or saturday next. I am Dr Sir with great truth yr obliged & affte friend

Edm: Randolph

ALS, DLC:GW.

1. See GW to Randolph, 10 July 1784, and notes. When William Byrd advertised his lottery in 1767 (*Virginia Gazette* [Purdie and Dixon; Williams-

burg], 23 July 1767), James Buchanan (1737–1787) was one of those leasing land from Byrd, and he had holdings in Richmond as well. At the time of his death in Richmond in October 1787, Buchanan was called "the oldest merchant of this city" (*Virginia Independent Chronicle* [Richmond], 17 Oct. 1787).

2. James Buchanan's memorandum regarding the lottery tickets, dated 20 July, reads: "2 acre Lots—270, 138, 237, 257: All in the Town of Manchester—I recollect R[ichard] R[andolph] having sold the most valuable Lot to Mr Trent. having ⟨no⟩ Plan of Manchester, I say nothing of value of the other three, suppose them but indifferent, Or they would probably have been sold before this time.

"100 acres—No. 823, 751: I think were sold by Mr ⟨Mason.⟩ I heard R. R. complain of him.

"⟨G⟩W No. 265: Manchester, shall enquire the value" (DLC:GW). The memorandum is written in pencil, except for the word "no." Punctuation has been added. Richard Randolph of Henrico County and Alexander Trent of Chesterfield County were in 1769 among those named trustees of the town of Manchester being laid out at William Byrd's Rocky Ridge, on the south bank of the James at the falls. See 8 Hening 421–24.

3. Thomson Mason (1733–1785), George Mason's younger brother, placed the following advertisement, dated at Williamsburg, 7 Nov. 1769, in Purdie and Dixon's *Virginia Gazette*, 9 Nov. 1769: "*On* Friday *the 22d day of* December *next, will be sold, on the premises, to the highest bidder, for ready money,* THE LOTS in the town of *Shockoe*, at the falls of the *James* river, known by the name of *Younghusband's* tenements, lately drawn by the subscriber in the Honourable Col. Byrd's lottery. These lots consist of several acres of ground, very capable of being advantageously improved. There is at present on part of them a public warehouse, a large and commodious dwelling house, with other conveniences, well situated and adapted either for a merchant or public housekeeper." For the Byrd lottery and the drawings of 2 Nov. 1769, see Cash Accounts, May 1769, n.10.

To Benjamin Harrison

My Dr Sir,   Mount Vernon 22d July 1784
I have had the honor to receive your favor of the 2d—What you have asked of the Secretary at War, if obtained, is all I conceive essential to illucidate the accounts of the old & present impositions on the public—the rolls in the pay office might serve as checks to those of the Musters; but where all these are to be met with, I know not, as the Troops of Virginia were, by order of Congress, considered as a component part of the Southern army, and part of the time mentioned in your letter to the Secretary at war, were not under my direction. I do not however consider these as very necessary, as they & the Muster rolls (which for the purpose you want them must be sufficiently cor-

rect,) only act as checks upon each other. If however, in this, or any thing else, I can be of service to you, it will give me much pleasure to comply with your wishes.

It was my full intention to have made you a visit so soon as the Summers heat should be over; but the situation of my affairs, & attempts to take from me, the property I have in the back Country are such, that I am oblig'd to visit the latter in September, or suffer it, after all the expence I have been put to, to pass into other hands without compensation.[1] I am &c. &c.

G: Washington

LB, DLC:GW.

1. GW is referring to his Millers Run (Chartiers Creek) land in Pennsylvania. See editorial note in Thomas Smith to GW, 9 Feb. 1785.

From Richard Henry Lee

Dear Sir,   Chantilly [Va.] July the 22d 1784

The letter that you did me the honor to write to me on the 12th of June last, I did not receive until two days ago. I impute this to my having been obliged to leave the Assembly, by the ill state of my health, a fortnight before it was adjourned.[1]

The very great respect that I shall ever pay to your recommendations, would have been very sufficient to have procured my exertions in favor of Mr Paine, independent of his great public merits in our revolution.

I have a perfect knowledge of the extraordinary effects produced by that Gentlemans writings, effects of such an important nature, as would render it very unworthy of these States to let him suffer anywhere; but it would be culpable indeed to permit it under their own eye, and within their own limits. I had not the good fortune to be present when Mr Paines business was considered in the House of Delegates, or most certainly I should have exerted myself in his behalf. I have been told that a proposition in his favor miscarried from its being observed that he had shewn enmity to this State by having written a pamphlet injurious to our claim of Western Territory—It has ever appeared to me that this pamphlet was the consequence of Mr Paines being himself imposed upon and that it was rather the fault of the place than of the Man.[2]

This however, was but a trifle when compared with the great and essential services that his other writings have done for the

United States. I am with the most unfeigned esteem and re-gard, dear Sir Your most obedient & very humble servant

Richard Henry Lee

ALS, DLC:GW.

1. Richard Henry Lee (1732–1794) received permission to leave the house of delegates on 15 June; the bill to give land to Thomas Paine was not intro-duced in the house until 28 June. Lee went to Congress on 1 Nov. 1784 as a delegate from Virginia and on 30 Nov. was elected its president for the ensu-ing year.

2. For Madison's account of the failure of the house of delegates to make provisions for Thomas Paine, see Madison to GW, 2 July, and his letter of 12 Aug. 1784, printed as note 2 in that letter. Madison privately noted that the reversal by the house of its decision to give Paine land "was produced by prejudice against Mr. Paine, thrown into circulation by Arthur Lee" (Madison to GW, 2 July 1784, n.2, in Rutland and Rachal, *Madison Papers*, 8:91–92).

To William Skilling

Wm Skilling,   Mount Vernon 22d July 1784.

I have just received your letter of the [   ],[1] & this answer will be lodged on the road by Colo. Bassett. I cannot afford to give the wages you ask, nor can I find out the meaning of Mr Randolphs offering you Sterlg money, as it is altogether un-usual, & little understood by workmen—& subject to misunder-standings & disputes.

Colo. Bassett is sure there must be a mistake in the case—for that you only asked him thirty pounds & two pr of shoes per annum—& upon informing you that he stood in no need of your services, you desired him to mention the matter to others. In consequence, he spoke to Colo. Richd Randolph, & mentioned your terms, upon which he—(Colo. Randolph) wrote to you. How it should happen therefore that he should put in Sterling, he cannot conceive.

I am willing to allow you £30 curry estimating Dollars at 6/ — (& other specie in proportion)—& two pr of Shoes pr Ann. If you incline to take it, you may come as soon as it is convenient; but whether you do, or do not incline to take it, write me word immediately by the post, the Stage, or some safe hand, that I may know whether to look out elsewhere or not.[2]

You know perfectly what kind of living you will meet with here, & the advantages—I shall not therefore, enumerate them: nor shall I at this time point out the sort of work you will be employ'd in. It may be to ditch, to Garden, to level & remove Earth—to work alone, or with several others—& in the last case, to keep them closely employ'd as well as yourself—The work however will either be at the home house, or at the plantations adjoining; most probably ᴄne former—I again repeat the necessity there is for your letting me hear from you that I may know whether to look out elsewhere or not. I am &c.

G: Washington

LB, DLC:GW.

    1. The copyist left a blank where the date, 5 July, should have appeared.
    2. Skilling replied on 28 July.

From John Augustine Washington

        Bushfield [Westmoreland County, Va., c.24] July 1784
My dear Brother

Your favour of June the 30th came to hand on the 9th Instant, a Vessel saild the second day after for Alexandria the skipper promised to come too of[f] Mt Vernon and deliver a Letter I wrote you by his in answer to yours[1]—this will be handed to you by one of my Sons, the youngest comes to pay his respects to you for a few days, and Bushrod after spending a few days with you at Mt Vernon proposes to visit the springs to confirm his health and be in readyness to accompany you to the Westward[2]—by Corbin on his return I shall be happy to recieve a line from you, if I can possably meet with a water conveyance I will certainly come up to see you before you set of to the new Country—I want much to establish some lands there if it can be done to advantage by exchanging Negroes for Land— I have desired Bushrod to make the fullest inquiries as to the Soil, produce, Climate &c. &c. of the different parts of the western Country together with there advantages and disadvantages respecting the future prospects of trade, & also the likelyest way to obtain lands upon a certainty as to title—in these inquiries I shall be greatly oblige to you to furnish him with your observacions—Our Love and best wishes are for the health and happiness of yourself my Sister & the Family and am Dr Sir Your very affe & obt Brother

John Auge Washington

ALS, MH: Jared Sparks Collection. In an entry in his cash accounts dated 24 July (Ledger B, 199), GW records giving his nephew Corbin 24s. 6d., which indicates that Corbin must have been at Mount Vernon on or before 24 July. If Corbin and Bushrod Washington did indeed deliver this letter as their father said they would, it must have been written, in fact, before 24 July.

    1. John Augustine Washington's letter is dated 8 July.

    2. Bushrod Washington, the older son, did accompany GW on his trip to the frontier. No letter that GW might have sent to his brother by his nephew Corbin has been found.

From George Augustine Washington

Hond Uncle   Barbadoes July 25th 1784

    In my Letter to You, by the fair American, which was the first; and only conveyance I have had of writing, I intimated my apprehensions of this Climate, and the probability their was of my changeing it for that of Bermuda, which I very sincerely lament not having given the preferrence in the first instance, as I have experienced the utmost inconvenience, and I fear injury from this[1]—I have now been here about five Weeks, during which time (about that number of days excepted) I have been intirely confined to the House by incessant heavy rains; and the approaching season affording no hopes of its being better[.] am at this time imbarking in a Vessel for some of the Leeward Islands, with a hope should She not go to Bermuda (which their is a probability of) that some other conveyance may be met with, I shall have this to comfort me that their cannot be a more unfavorable Climate for my complaints, I belive in any part of the world, I find myself a good deal reduced by several severe fits of the Colic I have lately had—I hope to find Bermuda a more settled Climate where I shall be able to use some exercise, which I am sure is necessary, and which I am here totally deprived of—the expectation of finding Bermuda an agreeable Climate, induces me to hope that I shall derive the wished for advantages from it, I leave this here, to go by the Vessel in which I came; She goes for New York; but can hardly immagine She will arrive their sooner than I hope to reach Bermuda from whence I shall take the first opportunity of giving You full state of my situation which the hurry I am in at present (preparing for my departure and interupted by company,) must be my apology for this incorrect one[2]—not having time to write more, must beg the favor of You to offer my most affectionate love to Mrs Washington and Miss F. Bassett whose goodness will induce them to consider my situation as I can truely assure them inclination was not wanting—they, and other friends may expect to hear from me on my arrival—my prayers and sincerest good wishes attend You all—with sentiments of the purest regard and esteem I am Your affectionate Nephew

Geo: A. Washington

ALS, PPRF.

1. See George Augustine Washington to GW, 27 June 1784.

2. He arrived in Bermuda on 6 August. See George Augustine Washington to GW, 11 August.

From Henry Knox

My dear sir.   Dorchester [Mass.] July 26th 1784

A fear of intruding upon your more important concerns has prevented my writing to you since my return. I found here your kind favor of the 2d of June, with its enclosure for General Putnam which I delivered.

The measures taken by Congress respecting the western posts must defeat themselves by their own imbecillity. I cannot say but that I am well satisfied to be excluded from any responsibility in arrangements which it is impossible to execute. The attempt, to employ militia for twelve months in an arduous operation of conveying the Stores & making permanent establishments in that difficult country after the experience we have had of those kind of troops characterizes itself.[1]

Agreably to the orders of Congress I sent Colonel Hull to General Haldimand to request that he would immediately deliver up the posts on our frontiers. If he should comply and fix a short day, which it is probable for his convenience he would, we should be ridiculously embarrassed not having a man for that purpose.[2]

I presume that General Lincoln informed you the alterations of the Cincinnati are generally satisfactory in this state. The opposition to it is dead. One or two persons it is said however still grumble—Our State Society on the 4h of July was respectably full, and adopted it unanimous one vote excepted.[3]

General Lincoln, Mr Partridge, and mys[el]f are going at the

request of the Legislature of this State, to examine what en-
croachments have been made by the british on its eastern
boundary. We shall set out on this business in a few days.[4] Mrs
Knox joins me in presenting our affectionate respects to Mrs
Washington I am my dear General Your truly affectionate
Humble Servant

H. Knox

ALS, DLC:GW; LB, MHi: Henry Knox Papers.

1. On the day of its adjournment, 3 June, Congress voted to have Connecticut, New York, New Jersey, and Pennsylvania "furnish forthwith from their
militia to serve for 12 months" 700 men, for the purpose of "securing and
protecting the northwestern frontiers of the United States, and their Indian
friends and allies, and for garrisoning the posts soon to be evacuated by the
troops of his britannic Majesty" (*JCC*, 27:530). All of this was to be done
under the management of the secretary at war, to which post Knox was not
appointed until March 1785.

2. On 24 May Congress approved "the proposition of Major General Knox,
to send a field Officer into Canada, for the purpose of ascertaining with precision and expedition the time when the posts within the United States now occupied by the british troops, shall be evacuated; and endeavouring to effect
an exchange of the cannon and stores at those posts, agreeably to a resolution
of Congress of the 12th of May instant" (ibid., 420). General Knox's instructions to William Hull, lieutenant colonel of the 3d Massachusetts Regiment,
are dated 25 May. Lt. Gen. Frederick Haldimand (1718–1791), commander
in chief and governor of Canada since 1778, left his post in America in November 1784. Hull's mission was unsuccessful. Knox's letter to Haldimand
and the exchange of letters between Hull and Haldimand are in the Haldimand Papers, *Michigan Pioneer and Historical Collections*, 20:230, 238–39.

3. See Benjamin Lincoln to GW, 15 July.

4. Knox and Benjamin Lincoln did not sail to the Bay of Fundy until
late August. The third commissioner appointed by the Massachusetts legislature, George Partridge, did not accompany them. See Knox to GW, 31 Jan.
1785, n.1.

From Tench Tilghman

Dear Sir   Baltimore [Md.] 27th July 1784.
    Since I had the honor of writing to you a few days ago, I have
met with a House Joiner, in a Ship just arrived from Ireland—
He says much for himself, and the Captain says he is a well be-
haved Man. His price is £22.10/ Curry for 3 years and the Expences from hence to Alexandria by the Stage £1.14.8—I send
him to the Care of Colo. Fitzgerald—I could not get his Inden-

tures properly assigned in time to send with him, but you shall have them in a few days. His name is Branning.[1]

I was in treaty for a Brick layer, but he was prevailed upon to remain here—I am in hopes to get one of that Trade in a few Weeks, as Vessels are daily arriving.

I beg your Excellency to give yourself no trouble about an immediate remittance—desire Fitzgerald or some of your Freinds in Alexandria to put you up a draft upon this place whenever they find an opportunity.[2]

I hope you will have no occasion to repent of your Bargain. I have the honor to be with perfect Respect and Esteem Yr Excellency's Most Ob. and hble Servt

Tench Tilghman

ALS, DLC:GW.
    1. See Tilghman to GW, 15 July, and GW to Tilghman, 4 August. No record of anyone named Branning being in GW's employ has been found, but see GW to Tilghman, 4 August.
    2. For GW's proposal to Tilghman, see GW to Tilghman, 4 Aug., and Tilghman to GW, 18 August.

To Wakelin Welch

Sir,   Mount Vernon 27th July 1784
    Your letter of the 26th of Jany, & duplicate thereof, both coming by the way of James river, were long getting to hand.[1]

I return the Power of Attorney signed before the first Master & Mariners I could find, bound for the Port of London; and trust that no further difficulty will arise to prevent your drawing the money which had been deposited in the Bank, out of the same & placing it to my credit upon the most advantageous terms.[2]

I have not an ounce of Tobacco growing this year—whether I shall return to that species of Agriculture again, or not, will depend altogether upon the price that article is most likely to bear from the general State of the trade, of which, you who understand the matter better than I do, can best determine; & would do me a favor to signify for my information.

Not having, that I recollect, received the particulars of my Accot currt with your House; I should be glad to have it forwarded to me, together with that of the late Mr Custis's, as soon as convenient.[3] I am Sir &c.

G: Washington

LB, DLC:GW.

After GW's marriage to Martha Custis in 1759, the firm of Robert Cary & Co. served as his chief commercial agent in London. During the Revolutionary War two of the partners of the firm, Robert Cary and John Moory, died, leaving Welch as the sole surviving partner. By this time Wakelin Welch, Jr., had become a partner in the firm.

1. Letter not found.

2. When GW finally settled the estate of Daniel Parke Custis in 1761, Martha Parke Custis, GW's step-daughter, received, as part of her share of her father's estate, stock in the Bank of England valued at £1,650 sterling. Shortly after his young ward died, GW on 10 Nov. 1773 wrote to Robert Cary & Co. indicating a wish to sell the half of the shares of bank stock that had become a part of his wife's disposable property upon her daughter's death. On 1 June 1774 GW wrote Cary that he had "executed the Bond and other Papers necessary for the prerogative Court of Canterbury, in order to enable you to receive the Money in the Bank of England," but the stock remained unsold and the bank continued to pay dividends (see GW to Welch, July 1786). In 1783, after receiving a letter from Welch dated 31 May (not found), GW wrote Welch on 30 Oct. 1783 to complain about the failure of Robert Cary & Co. to sell the bank stock ten years before, and then he added: "As it now is, as it then was, my intention to apply this money towards payment of the Balle I owed your House, I would beg of you to take out such powers for the transfer, & give me such precise & ample directions for the execution as will admit of no doubt or delay—As the money will be for your benefit by its being applyed to the credit of your Ho. I wish you to have the negociating of the matter—The Letter of Admn power of Attorney or by whatever other name called may be made out in your name accordingly" (ALS, DLC:GW).

An entry in GW's account with Welch, dated 13 Jan. 1785, records £500 sterling "to my interest remaining in the Bank of England after you had sold as much as would discharge my debt to you, as appears by yr letter of this date—Making the residue subject to my Orders." GW continued to use Wakelin Welch's company as his agent in London, and on 7 Mar. 1787 he noted in the ledger "the sale of the above £500 Bank Stock in Novr last as appears by your letter of this date" (Ledger B, 234). See also GW to Lund Washington, 19 June 1775, n.2.

3. GW had asked for his account current with Robert Cary & Co. on 31 October. No copy of the account has been found, and there are no entries in the Cary account in Ledger B after the account was settled in August 1772. The account with Welch himself begins with the entry quoted in note 2. However, GW's account with the estate of John Parke Custis after Custis's death in 1781 indicates that Welch had sent GW a copy of the estate's account with Robert Cary & Co. See Ledger B, 217.

To Clement Biddle

Dear Sir,   Mount Vernon July 28th 1784

The Mulatto fellow William who has been with me all the War is attached (married he says) to one of his own colour a free woman, who, during the War was also of my family—She has been in an infirm state of health for sometime, and I had conceived that the connection between them had ceased—but I am mistaken—they are both applying to me to get her here, and tho' I never wished to see her more, yet I cannot refuse his request (if it can be complied with on reasonable terms) as he has lived with me so long & followed my fortunes through the War with fidility.[1]

After promising thus much, I have to beg the favor of you to procure her a passage to Alexandria either by Sea, by the passage Boats (if any there be) from the head of Elk, or in the Stage as you shall think cheapest & best, and circumstances may require—She is called Margaret Thomas als Lee (the name which he has assumed) and lives at Isaac & Hannah Sills, black people who frequently employ themselves in Cooking for families in the City of Phila.[2] I am—Dr Sir Yr Most Obedt Hble Servt

Go: Washington

ALS (photocopy), PU: Armstrong Photostats; LB, DLC:GW.

1. GW bought William (Will, Billy) Lee in 1768 from Mary Lee, the widow of Col. John Lee of Westmoreland County, Virginia. In April 1785 while surveying with GW, Lee broke his kneepan, and in 1788 a similar accident left him crippled for life. By his will, GW gave his old servant his freedom and an annuity of £30, with the right to remain at Mount Vernon if he wished. No evidence has been found that Margaret Thomas, or Margaret Lee, came to Mount Vernon.

2. No further information about Isaac Sills and his wife Hannah has been found.

From William Skilling

Sir   Caroline County [Va.] July 28th 1784

I Receivd your letter of the 22nd of July wherein you inform me that Col: Bassett thinks that mr Randolph made a mistake in offering me thirty pounds Sterling pr year. it could not be any mistake of the genleman, as he wrote me two different Letters—in the first he offerd me thirty pounds Currency & on my refusal he Sent me the other—Which I enclos'd to you in my firist letter—I am at present employ'd at a Dollar pr day & a pint of spirits and I am very well entertained and have as much worke as I can possibly do till the middle of November by that time I Shall finish the worke that I have Engag'd & if health permits you may then depend on my Coming as I should much rather serve you than any other[1]—from Sir Yr most obt Humle servt

William Skilling

ALS, DLC:GW.

1. On 6 April 1785 GW paid Skilling £6.4.0 "on Accot of Wages" (Ledger B), but later in the month Skilling became ill and, if he did survive, seems not to have continued to work for GW. See *Diaries*, 4 : 135–36.

To Tench Tilghman

Dear Sir,   Mount Vernon July 29th—84.

Your favor by Captn Bradstreet came to hand too late in the Afternoon of yesterday to send up for the Carpenter. The bearer now comes for him. Be so good as to let me know the amount of the expences you may have been at, on his acct, and I will thankfully repay them at meeting, or before, if an oppertunity presents.[1] With sincere esteem & regard I am—Dear Sir Yr Most Obedt Servt

Go: Washington

ALS, owned (1979) by Steven Alsberg, Skokie, Illinois.

1. See Tilghman to GW, 27 July, 18 Aug., and GW to Tilghman, 4, 11 August.

From Jacob Read

Sir   Annapolis [Md.] 30th July 1784

The very Short Stay the post makes at Annapolis precludes me the pleasure of acknowledging in the Manner I wou'd with the receipt of your favour of the 28th and of giving you the Information that an hours leizure might enable me to extract from the public dispatches &ca.

Having Several public Letters to finish for South Carolina & Which I must dispatch by this post I pray you'l be so good as pardon the hurry with Which this Letter will Necessarily be Stamped.

I beg your Acceptance of my grateful thanks for the kind reception given to the Gentlemen of my recommendation.[1]

This days post brings us dispatches from our Ministers abroad and a Copy of his Britannic Majesty's ratification of the Definitive Treaty. The Instruments of Ratification were exchanged on the 12th of May at passy[2]—we have also a New proclamation for regulating the West Indian trade of the U.S. I have not time to make any extract or Copy from this but you Shall have one (if on perusal worthy notice) by the next post.

The paper I do myself The Honour to Inclose you has the British King's Speech to his New Parliament. Almost An Unanimous Address in the Lords & 168 Majority for Pitts's Administration & Measures in the Commons.

I pray My Compliments to Mrs Washington I forwarded her Letter to Miss Sprigg immediately on the receipt by a careful Servant.[3]

I believe Mr Jay is arrived at New York as one of the public Letters was directed "by The Honourable John Jay" on the Cover—I again request you'l pardon the haste with Which I am obliged to finish this and believe me to be With the Utmost respect & regard Your Excellencys Most obedt & most Humle Sert

Jacob Read

ALS, DLC:GW.

1. Read wrote GW on 17 July a letter introducing Mark Prager.

2. See *JCC*, 27:615–24.

3. Sophia Sprigg (1766–1812) was the eldest daughter of Richard Sprigg of Annapolis. Thomas Jefferson wrote James Madison on 20 Feb. 1784 that Arthur Lee was "*courting Miss Sprig a young girl of seventeen* and of *thirty thousand pounds* expectation" (Boyd, *Jefferson Papers*, 6:546). Another Virginian, John Francis Mercer, married Sophia Sprigg on 3 Feb. 1785. Mercer at this time was one of the Virginia delegates to Congress.

From Hugh Hughes

Sir,   Philadelphia July 31st 1784

In Obedience to your Excellency's verbal Order, which was delivered to me by Colonel Joseph Trumbull, on the twenty seventh of August one Thousand seven Hundred and seventy six, the Quarter Master General acting, on that Day, as one of your Excellency's Aid de Camps, I impressed all the Sloops, Boats and Water Craft, from Spyghtenduyvel, in the Hudson, to Hellgate, in the Sound, by which Means many of them fell into the Hands of the Enemy, some of which have since been paid for, but others have not.

As I never expected to be prosecuted for obeying your Excellency's Orders that were evidently and eventually the Preservation of the Army, I never applied for a written Order, which is now demanded, and, in Case of a Non-Compliance, Prosecutions are directed to be immediately commenced against me.

In Justification of my Conduct, as above stated, I am compelled to solicit your Excellency to favour me with a written Order for that particular Service, or a Certificate of the verbal One, if more agreeable to your Excellency.[1]

And, should my other Services, whilst honoured with your Excellency's Commands, have generally met with your Approbation, I will thank your Excellency for such Sentiments con cer[n]ing them as your Candour may think that thc[y] mcrit. This I always intended to ask at the End of my Scrvicc, but was prevented from making the Application by a tedious Indispotion.

Colonel Pickering having very politely offered to frank this to your Excellency, it will be an additional Mark of your Favour if your Excellency will be pleased to order whatever may be intended for me, to be put under Cover to the Colonel, who has engaged to forward it to my Son in New York, as I have not yet returnd from Connecticut.

Your Excellency will be pleased to permit me, by this Opportunity, to offer my best Wishes for the Happiness of yourself and Lady. With the purest Respect and Esteem, I have the Honour to be, Sir, Your Excellency's most obedient, Humble, Servant

                                    Hugh Hughes

ALS, DLC:GW; LB, DLC: Papers of Hugh Hughes.

During the Revolution, Hugh Hughes (c.1727–1802), of New Jersey and New York, acted as a deputy quartermaster general under Joseph Trumbull (1737–1778), Thomas Mifflin, and Timothy Pickering, successively. In 1793, in an unsuccessful attempt to press his claims for payment for wartime services, Hughes presented a memorial to Congress to which he attached a copy of GW's letter of 22 Aug. (see note 1).

1. Hughes was acting as assistant commissary general to Trumbull when GW conducted the retreat of his army from Long Island to New York on the night of 29 Aug. 1776, ending the Battle of Long Island. The rivercraft commanded by Hughes were used to transport GW's soldiers across the river. GW responded to Hughes from Mount Vernon on 22 Aug. in these terms: "Sir, I have received your letter of the 31st Ulto from Philadelphia.

"My memory is not charged with the particulars of the verbal order which you say was delivered to you through Colonl Joseph Trumbull, on the 27th of August 1776, 'for impressing all the Sloops, Boats and Water Craft, from Spyghten Duyvel in the Hudson, to Helgate on the Sound.' I recollect very well that it was a day which required the greatest exertion, particularly in the Quarter Masters department, to accomplish the retreat which was intended under cover of the succeeding night; and that no delay, or ceremony could be admitted in the execution of the plan. I have no doubt therefore of your having received orders to the effect, and extent you have mentioned, & you are at liberty to adduce this letter in testimony thereof. It will, I presume, supply the place of a more formal certificate, and is more consonant with my recollection of the transactions of that day.

"It is with pleasure I add, that your conduct in the Quarter Masters line as far as it has come under my view, or to my knowledge was marked with zeal, activity & intelligence, and met my approbation accordingly. With grateful thanks for your good wishes, I remain—Sir Yr most obedt Hble Servt Go: Washington" (ALS, NHi: George and Martha Washington Papers).

From Gilbert Simpson

honoerd Sr   Washingtons Bottom [Pa.] July 31st—1784

This Comes to inform you that I Got Safely home the Saturday after I lef you and found Every thing well and undesturved thanks be to almighty God for his mercys which Remain So at this time and I have never felt much of that faintness only onst in my meadow when on a Sudden I had nearly falen of the top of the fens as I was setting on it loocking at my wheat—I have Saved more Grass than I have Ever had and in good order as there has been no Rane from the 9th of June untel 23th July which has almost don for our Corn our winter Crops are very lite tho the Grain as good as I Ever see—the villinious Robbers soon after my geting home had plundred on the frunttears and got a great number of horses and thre young Negros and a great deal of houshold goods and wheare there was a little money they got it and it is Said in the whole got a great deal of money but when they thought they had prety well featherd their nests they pushed over the ohio supposed to be makeing for detrote but our good well fixt fruntearmen happend to find what Cors they weare makeing and headed them in the indian Cuntry and took 2 men and 2 woman 13 head of horses 3 Negros and vast deal of other things one of the men taken of the name ⟨J⟩ones Sens dead by a bite of a Snake Supposed to one of the vilins that Robed the tresurry of Philladelpha there is one of there Confedrates taken sens and put in irons So I trust in God there helish Carings on is Stopt as there was one of them kiled whils I was down Sr I have planed of a boat for you and Shall have the plank and timbers got Reyday against you Com out and whilst you are Setteling your affairs heare and at Sur-tee[1] I Can get her put together I purpose to have her 30 feet by 10 which will be likely to Give Room Enuff—heare is one Charles Bradfored a good Survayer and a very jenteal plesent man that would Go down with you—hunters you may get plenty if you find powder and leed Give the Skins and a dram ur a grog at times and find bread and Salt I beleive they will Go on very Reasonable wayges I have mad in Quiry Concerning your geting Salt baycon but I beleive there is non to be had but as you Can kill a young beef heare and Salt it it will do untel your hunters Can Com in play: whiskey butter and Cheas you may likely get.

Sr I would be glad if you want any thing particular Concern-ing your voige down that has not been mentiond that you would wright me fwe lines and wheather you think the boat may be large Enuff or not a boat of that bulk will Carrey a great burden I would be glad of a fwe lines from you—Sir I am yours to Comd

Gilbt Simpson

ALS, DLC:GW.

1. GW arrived at Simpson's on 12 or 13 September. He went from there on 18 Sept. to look at his land on Millers Run, a branch of Chartiers (Shurtees) Creek. See *Diaries*, 4:18–31, and editorial note in Thomas Smith to GW, 9 Feb. 1785.

From Thornton Washington

Respeckted Sr   Stonehous [Va.] August the 1—1784

after my most respectkfool compliments to your self and lady I must beg lieave to lay before your considerashion A matter that interests me in A verry particular manner the plantashion whareon I now live sayd to contain two hundread acrees I purchast of my father for which I have his obligation for the mentaining me in the fool wright of. it is the land purchast of Colo. Phillup Pendleton I am informd was your property and that the title is still in your hands Mr James Nourse ferther informd me that he had wrought to you on that subjeckt and that you had informd him that you had nither ever recievd eany thing in considerashion of the sade land and that you had never past A deed or eany thing binding on you for the convayance of the sade lands[1] I have already been at the expence of refiting the hous and puting on the plantashion near twenty thousand new rales cheef of which I got of my one land without ever makeing eany considerable use of that part of my land more than pastureage I was Just going to put up A verry large barn for the resepshion of A crop of Tob. which will not admit of delay this is the reson of my wrighting[.] Cousin Bushrod Washington was at my hous yesterday who informd me of your intenshions of visiting this place in a short time though as I had workmen on expencees and all my timbers ready to hall togather and they got of the plantashion now in question I wood not wish to do one hands turn more untill I hear from you if I mentain the land I now live on it wood by no meens soot to put it on the other and if I am not to continue in posseshion of the above menshiond Land I wood wish to get amediately about a hous to remoove to as I wood not wish to be on rent or from doing some thing to wards makeing my removal comfortibble I most ernistly request of you that you will give me A final answar as I expeckt ferther to be at the sweet springs about the time of your comeing into this neighbourhood so that I shall not see you as thar is money now provideing for the payment of this land by my fathers Execkiters and I shall be payd for the Land if you should not make A convayance of the same I am intirely easy about it could I be on A certainty what to be at I think to set out to the springs in A few days I wood tharefore wish to set the to work on A dwelling hous before my departure I mus agane beg my Dr Sr that you will be positive in yor answar and if possubble lieave me no room to doubt wheather or not you meen to mentain the land I remain Sr with all duty and respeckt to your self and La[d]y your Verry obediant servant

Thornton Washington

ALS, ViMtV.

Thornton Washington (c.1760–1787) was the son of GW's dead brother, Samuel. Thornton lived at a house called Berry Hill, later Cedar Lawn, near his father's house, Harewood, in Berkeley County, Virginia.

1. For a full discussion of the property that GW sold to Pendleton and for which he never was paid, see GW to James Nourse, 22 Jan. 1784, n.3.

To Charles Washington

Dear Brother: Mount Vernon, August 2, 1784.

The enclosed came to my hands from Philadelphia last night. I am sorry to find by George's letter to me, that he had not received the benefit from the Sea Air he expected, but as his passage was not good and he in a manner but just landed, no Judgment at the time he wrote could be well formed of the effect the voyage would have upon his complaint; as he writes you himsclf there can be no doubt of his giving you an acc't of his health and present intentions, I shall add nothing further therefore on this subject.[1]

I still hold to my resolution of setting off the first of September for the Western Count[r]y, and if I am not obliged (in business) to go by the way of Fredericks Town in Maryland to the Springs, I shall most assuredly spend a night at[2] with you. Mrs. Washington joins me in best wishes for you, my sister and the family, and I am, etc.

Fitzpatrick, *Writings of Washington*, 27:452.

1. See George Augustine Washington to GW, 27 June 1784.

2. GW set out from Mount Vernon on 1 Sept. and spent the night of 3 Sept. at Happy Retreat. See *Diaries*, 4:1–5. Charles Washington recently had moved from Fredericksburg to Berkeley County and built his house, Happy Retreat, on Evitt's Run. Fitzpatrick inserted "Harewood" in brackets at this point. Harewood, also in Berkeley County, had been the home of another brother, Samuel Washington, until his death in 1783.

To Clement Biddle

Dear Sir,   Mount Vernon 4th August 1784
   Since my last to you, I have obtained from Baltimore (by means of Colo. Tilghman) a House-Joiner—and as the season for working in mortar will soon be over; & that of intermitants is approaching—I pray you to decline purchasing either the Joiner or Bricklayer formerly requested.[1] I am Dr Sir &c.
                                            G: Washington

LB, DLC:GW.
   1. See Tench Tilghman to GW, 27 July, and GW to Biddle, 30 June 1784.

From Pierre-Charles L'Enfant

your Excellency   philadelphia—august the 4th 1784
   having since my arrival at this place been informed that a number of foreigner claimes the Reight to be reconnised cincinnati, and being all so confident that many of those who applayed to the marquis de la fayette and whose demands were rejected by a colected body of members of the society as Expressed in my last account of our prociding.[1] and considering a great number of person which held commission in the continantal army must al since the begining of the war, and who without leave absented themselves, retourning to thier contry, or remaining in america on & trading way assuming now and then the character of officer watching for the opportunity of gething mony, or anny Rewards what so Ever, such as are due only to lasting services.
   I in the name of the comity held at the marquis de lafayette hotel on the ten day of march last, beg from the general assembly that no persons not comprehended in thier resolution of the same date, or not Especially recommanded by a majeur parts of the french members stil remaining in america, could Be admited in to the association if not suported by such an hotority, and if proveided with sufficient recommendation thier petition to Be presented By me to the assembly. Being directed to this by the mentioned comity, until a fixed numbers of thier representative be admited to set in the general assembly.

With great respect I have the honnour to be your Excellency most obeidient and humble servant

P. L'Enfant

ALS, DSoCi.

1. Pierre-Charles L'Enfant addressed letters to GW on 29 April and 10 and 17 May, the latter two of which are printed above as appendixes III and X in General Meeting of the Society of the Cincinnati, 4–18 May 1784.

To Tench Tilghman

Dear Sir,   Mount Vernon Augt 4th 1784.

The House Joiner you bought for me has arrived. I like his age, professions, and appearance very well and am obliged to you for procuring him. His Indentures may be sent at any time.[1]

As the Season for working in Mortar will soon be over, and that of intermittants is now approaching, I pray you unless a *very good* Bricklayer should offer, not to purchase one for me after the 15th of this month.

The Fan from Mr Thos Peters is also arrived, for which be so good as to thank him in my behalf. The handle of it is lost. Whether it did not get on board the Packet, was not delivered by the Master of it, or mislaid at Colo. Fitzgeralds is unknown as the Vessel had returned before I sent up and enquiry could be made.[2]

Enclosed are Bank notes for Ninety dollars, with which please to pay yourself and apply the overplus towards the payment for the Fan had of Mr Peters.[3] As the bill of cost did not accompany it, and my recollection of the price (if I ever heard it) has failed me, I do not know whether this Sum is sufficient for both purposes; if not, the balle shall be paid as soon as it is made known to Dr Sir Yr obedt Servt

Go: Washington

ALS, PHi: Gratz Collection; LB, DLC:GW.

1. See Tilghman to GW, 27 July, and GW to Tilghman, 11 August. GW seems to have acquired other indentured servants at this time. A document headed "A list of Servants & Redemptions that has been Free'd & Redeemed" (ViMtV), dated 1784, shows GW acquiring on 2 Aug. Farrell Slattery, a millwright, and Thomas Mahony, a "House Carpenter," each for £16 to work for

two years, and, on 4 Aug., Cornelius McDermott (McDermott Roe), also for two years.

2. See Tilghman to GW, 15 July, n.3.

3. See Tilghman to GW, 18 August. GW recorded on 4 Aug. in his cash accounts in Ledger B, 199, that he sent Tilghman "Bank Notes to pay for a H[ouse] Carpenter . . . & a Wheat Fan."

From John Ariss

Sir   Berkeley County [Va.] 5th Augst 1784

Permit me to Address your Excellency for a place to live at during Mrs Ariss and my Own Life. I am under the Necessity of Giving Up the place I now live at at the End of this Year, and have not as yet provided my Self with a place, nor do I know of any to be had in these parts, my Infirm Crazy Indisposition puts it Out of my Power to go any Great distance[.] Your Excellency may possibly Assist me with a place to live at. Mr Henry Whiting who is a Tenant on your Land on Bullskin Intends to make an offer of his Lease to your Excellency this Fall.[1] This place would Suit me provided it is to be Let out again. Indeed One half would be Sufficient but Rather than be Obliged to move to any Great Distance I would take the Whole I shall always make it a point to pay my Rent when it becomes due.[2] if This place is not to be had perhaps you may have Some other to let that may Suit me.[3] I am Sir Your Excellencys Most Obliged and Most Humble Servt

Jno. Ariss

ALS, DLC:GW.

John Ariss (d. 1799), originally of Westmoreland County, Va., moved in 1769 to the part of Frederick County that was soon to become Berkeley County. Ariss was perhaps the leading housebuilder in Virginia in the quarter of a century before the Revolution. Although literary evidence is almost entirely lacking, architectural historians have identified Ariss with such houses as John Carlyle's in Alexandria, Fielding Lewis's Kenmore in Fredericksburg, Samuel Washington's Harewood in Berkeley County, John Tayloe's Mount Airy in Richmond County, and Mann Page's Mannsfield in Spotsylvania County. It has also been said that he had some hand in the redesigning of Mount Vernon in the 1770s. See Waterman, *Mansions of Virginia*, 243 et seq.

1. Henry Whiting (1748–1786), the son of Francis Whiting and briefly, until her death in 1778, the husband of John Carlyle's daughter Anne, lived on the tract of GW's Bullskin lands in Berkeley County that GW first leased to the

father, Francis Whiting, in 1773 at £50 per annum. For Henry Whiting's decision to give up his lease and his final settlement with GW in the fall of 1784, see Warner Washington to GW, 7 Aug. 1784, n.1. See also GW to Battaile Muse, 3 Nov. 1784, n.3.

2. On 20 April 1786 Ariss leased from GW the tract on Bullskin that had been leased to the Whitings and agreed to pay £60 a year for the rent of 700 acres. The deed is in ViMtV. See also entry dated 17 Jan. 1786 in Battaile Muse's Account Book, NcD: Battaile Muse Papers.

3. See GW to Ariss, 8 Aug., n.1.

From Jacob Read

Sir   Annapolis [Md.] 6th August 1784

The Inclosed Copy of a Letter which I do myself the honour to inclose to you will perhaps give you some as Curious information as any you have had for a long time on the subject of Pollitics on the other side of the Water—The Intelligence is I believe to be relied on—You will do me the favour to return the ⟨sd⟩ Letter by next post and I must request you will not let it by any means transpire, I make the Communication to Your Excellency as Waranted by your general permission to see the Secret papers & Journals of Congress[.] as I shall destroy the Copy as soon as again in my possession I must also request that no Copy be taken[1]—the Proclamation mentioned in my last on the subject of the Trade of the U.S. with the West Indies is almost verbatim with those formerly issued & is fully explained in the Copy of the letter Inclosed.[2]

We shall loose the Two Gentlemen from New England in the next week their private affairs requiring their return to the Eastward[3] and as neither Deleware New York nor Connecticut Can be gotten to Attend I fear we shall have no more Committee of the States. this in the present Situation of European & Indian Affairs is really allarming—the delegates from Rhode Island always declared they woud not Attend.

If the Committee shoud dissolve or adjourn I shall go to Rhode Island where my mother is for her Health[4] and shall be happy to Execute any Commands you may have to the Eastward. I am with the sincerest regard & most perfect respect Sir your Excellency's most obliged & Most obedient Servt

Jacob Read

ALS, DLC:GW.

1. In his reply of 11 Aug., GW refers to "Mr Ls intelligence" in the enclosed letter from Read. The comments of both Read and GW on the letter make it clear that it is one written by Henry Laurens from London on April 24 to the president of Congress. In the letter, Laurens argues that a strong faction of politicians in Britain was "hoping in time to provoke a more hostile war and to improve upon what they call the errors of the last" (Wharton, *Diplomatic Correspondence*, 6:795–97).

2. See Read to GW, 30 July.

3. See Read to GW, 13 Aug., n.3.

4. Read's mother, Rebecca Bond Read, daughter of Jacob Bond of Hobcaw in Christ Church Parish, S.C., died in 1786.

From Warner Washington

Dear Sir   7th Augt 1784

At the request of Mr Henry Whiting a Neighbour and Relation of mine I write to you in his Name to beg you would be kind enough to allow Him to give up his Lease as the keeping it two Years longer would he says, be certain ruin to Him. He does not desire to make any advantage from it, either by selling or any other way neither does he make one farthing towards paying his Rent—I am informed Mr Ariss is desirous of taking the place and has wrote to you, should you think proper to let Him have it I am satisfied He would make you a better Tenant in every respect.[1]

I understand you intend up the begining of next Month, pray let us have the pleasure of seeing you—I am Dr Sir Yours Affectionately

Warner Washington

Mr Whiting will pay the whole Rent that will be due to you, this Fall.[2]

ALS, PHi: Gratz Collection.

1. Since the early 1770s Warner Washington, Sr. (1722–1790), had been living at Fairfield near the line between Frederick and Berkeley counties in that part of Frederick County later to become Clark County. Henry Whiting's sister Mary was married to Warner Washington, Jr. (1751–1829). John Ariss, who requested in his will, probated in 1800, that he be buried in the graveyard at Fairfield, may have been the builder of the house for Warner Washington.

2. GW saw both Warner Washington and Henry Whiting while at Charles Washington's house in Berkeley County on 3–4 September. See *Diaries*,

4:4–8. For Whiting's payment of his debt, see John Ariss to GW, 5 Aug., n.1, and GW to Ariss, 8 Aug., n.3.

To John Ariss

Sir,   Mount Vernon 8th Augt 1784

In answer to your letter of the 5th, I have to inform you that I have no untenanted Lands in the Counties of Berkley or Frederick, except two lotts Nos. 5 & 6—the first containing 346½ acres, & the 2d—224½—in the latter, which I bought at the Sale of Colo. George Mercers Estate, in the year 1774—& for which I have had many persons applying to become Tenants.[1] My intention was, after I had reviewed & laid those Lotts off into proper sized Tenements, to have appointed a day on the premises to let them.

If you choose to examine these Lots, & will, if either of them shou'd suit you, offer a good rent, it may (if I should not upon recollection find myself under a promise to give notice of the letting of them) supercede the necessity of this measure. I expect to be at my Brother's on my way to the Berkeley Springs, the 2d of next month (at night)—where you may deposit a letter, which shall receive an answer from thence, to any proposals you may incline to make.[2]

With respect to Mr Whiting, I know nothing of his intentions—unless they be, as it shou'd seem, to work my Lands as long as he will be permitted without paying rent. If the nonperformance of Covenants, on the part of the Tenant, can be construed into a forfeiture of his Lease—Mr Whiting I persuade myself will have candor enough to confess that his comes under this predicament.[3] I am &c.

                                              G: Washington

LB, DLC:GW.

1. The two tracts once belonging to George Mercer are near present-day Berryville, Virginia. For the sale of George Mercer's holdings in Virginia in 1774, see GW to Edward Snickers and GW to John Tayloe, both 30 Nov. 1774, and GW to James Mercer, 12 and 26 Dec. 1774.

2. GW does not mention in his diary having seen Ariss while at his brother Charles's Happy Retreat on 3–4 Sept., but in 1786 Ariss leased land from GW. See Ariss to GW, 5 Aug. 1784, n.2.

3. GW kept the record of Henry Whiting's payments of rent in the account that he set up in Ledger B for the original lessee, Francis Whiting, Henry's

father. The account shows that Henry Whiting paid £50.12 in cash on 3 Sept. 1784. A little over a year later, 5 Oct. 1785, GW records final payments of £199 plus £6.13.6 in interest "By Cash of Jas Crane for Henry Whiting's Rent up to Jany 1785 Judgemt thereon in Berkeley Court" (f. 113). For further details of Battaile Muse's settling this account for GW on 5 Oct. 1785, see NcD: Battaile Muse Papers.

Letter not found: to William Gordon, 10 Aug. 1784. On 30 Aug. Gordon wrote to GW: "Your obliging letter of the 10th instt was recd the last thursday."

From Lafayette

Philadelphia tuesday Evening [10 August 1784]
My dear General
I Have Already Had the pleasure to Acquaint You with My Arrival in America,[1] and am Endeavouring to Reach Mount Vernon as soon as possible—My first plan was only to Stay here two days, but the Affectionate Reception I Have met with in this City, and the Returning some Compliments to the Assembly Render it Necessary for me to Stay one day longer—on friday I will Be at the Head of elk—the next day at Baltimore, and By Sunday or Monday I Hope at last to be Blessed with a sight of My dear General—there is no Rest for me Untill I get to Mount vernon—I long for the pleasure to embrace you, My dear General, and the Happiness of Being once more with You will be so great that No words Can Ever Express it—Adieu, my dear General, in a few days I'll Be at Mount vernon, and I do already feel delighted with so charming a prospect[2]—My Best Respects wait Upon Mrs Washington, and not long after You Receive this, I shall tell You Myself How Respectfully and affectionately I Have the Honor to Be My dear General Your Most obedient Humble Servant

Lafayette

in Case Your Affairs Call You to the Spring I Beg leave either to go there after you or to Accompagny You in Your journey.[3]

ALS, anonymous donor.
    1. If Lafayette did in fact write GW from New York after his arrival there in early August, the letter has not been found.
    2. Lafayette wrote his wife on 20 Aug., three days after his arrival at Mount Vernon: "Though I do not know if my letter will reach you, my dear heart, I had to write you that I am at Mount Vernon and that I am reveling in the

happiness of finding my dear general again; and you know me too well for me to need to describe to you what I felt. Crossing the countryside very quickly, I arrived here on the seventeenth, and as the general, though he had been anticipating my arrival, did not expect me for several more days, I found him in the routine of his estate, where our meeting was very tender and our satisfaction completely mutual. I am not just turning a phrase when I assure you that in retirement General Washington is even greater than he was during the Revolution. His simplicity is truly sublime, and he is as completely involved with all the details of his lands and house as if he had always lived here. To describe to you the life that we lead here, I shall tell you that after breakfast the general and I chat together for some time. After having thoroughly discussed the past, the present, and the future, he withdraws to take care of his affairs and gives me things to read that have been written during my absence. Then we come down for dinner and find Mrs. Washington with visitors from the neighborhood. The conversation at table turns to the events of the war or to anecdotes that we are fond of recalling. After tea we resume our private conversations and pass the rest of the evening with the family" (Idzerda, *Lafayette Papers*, 5:237–38).

3. Lafayette made only a brief visit to Mount Vernon before GW left for his western trip on 1 Sept. and Lafayette left for Baltimore, Philadelphia, New York, Albany, and Boston. Lafayette returned to Virginia in November when he accompanied GW from Richmond for a second visit to Mount Vernon.

To Jacob Read

Dear Sir,   Mount Vernon Augt 11th 1784.
I return the letter you were so obliging as to send me & thank you for the perusal of it—no copy has been taken—nor will any part of its contents transpire from me.

Although Mr Ls intelligence may come from a man of information, and tho' it is undoubted, that the British Cabinet wish to recover the United States to a dependence on that government, yet I can scarcely think they ever expect to see it realized, or that they have any plan in contemplation by which it is to be attempted; unless *our* want of wisdom, and perseverence in error, should in their judgment render the effort certain.[1]

The Affairs of Ireland, if our accts from thence are to be relied on, are in too turbulent a state to suffer G. Britn to enter very soon into another War with America, even if her finances were on a more respectable footing than I believe them to be, and her prospect of success must diminish as our population encreases, and the governments become more consistent—without the last of which indeed, any thing may be apprehended.

It is however as necessary for the Sovereign in Council, as it is for a General in the field, not to despise information; but to hear all—compare all—combine them with other circumstances, and take measures accordingly—Nothing I acknowledge would sooner induce me to give credit to a hostile intention on the part of G. Britain than their continuing (without the shadow of reason, for I really see none they have) to withhold the Western Posts on the American side the line from us; and sending, as the Gazettes mention, Sir Guy Carleton over as Vice Roy to their possessions in America; which it seems is to undergo a new organization.

The opinion I have here given you will readily perceive is founded upon the idea I entertain of the temper of Ireland—the imbicility of G.B.—and her internal divisions; for it is with pain I add, that I think our Affairs are under wretched management—and that our conduct, if Great B: was in circumstances to take advantage of it, would bid her hope every thing; while other Powers might expect little from the wisdom, or exertion of these States.

I thank you for your proferred Services to the Eastward—I have nothing at this moment to trouble you with, but wishing you may find the air of Rhode Island salubrious & beneficial to your Mother I have the honor to be with Great Esteem—Sir Yr most Obedt and very Hble Servt

Go: Washington

ALS, NNPM; LB, DLC:GW.
    1. For Henry Laurens's "intelligence," see Read to GW, 6 Aug., n.1.

To Tench Tilghman

Dear Sir,   Mount Vernon Augt 11th—84.
    I shall essay the finishing of my Green Ho. this fall; but find that neither my own knowledge, or that of any person abt me, is competent to the business.
    Shall I, for this reason, ask the favor of you to give me a short detail of the internal construction of the Green House at Mrs Carrolls?[1]
    I am perswaded *now*, that I planned mine upon too contracted a Scale—My House is (of Brick) 40 feet by 24 in the outer dimensions—& half the width is disposed of for two rooms back of the part designed for the Green House; leaving

not more than about 37 by 10 in the clear for the latter. As there is no cover on the walls yet, I can raise them to any height.

The information I wish to receive is on the following points.

The dimensions of Mrs Carrolls Green House?

What kind of a floor is to it?

How high from *that* floor to the bottom of the Window frame?

What height the Windows are from bottom to top?

How high from the top to the Cieling?

Whether the Cieling is flat? or of what kind?

Whether the heat is conveyed by flues and a grate?

Whether the grate is on the out, or inside?

Whether the Flues run all round the House?

The size of them without, and in the hollow?

Whether they join the Wall, or are seperate from it?

If the latter, how far are they apart?

With any other suggestions which you may conceive it necessary to give.

I should be glad to hear from you on this subject soon, as I shall leave home on or before the first of Next Month on a journey to the Westward, and wish to give particular directions to the workmen before I go.[2] I hope you will excuse the trouble the solution of these enquiries will occasion. I am—Dr Sir Yr most Obedt Hble Servt

Go: Washington

P.S. I have received the Carpenters Indentures.[3]

ALS, RPJCB; LB, DLC:GW.

1. Margaret Tilghman (1742–1817) in 1763 became the wife of Charles Carroll, the barrister (1723–1783), who shared his wife's interest in horticulture. Mrs. Carroll's greenhouse was on the Carroll estate, Mount Clare, outside the town of Baltimore. Margaret Carroll was Tench Tilghman's first cousin and the older sister of Tilghman's wife.

2. Tilghman replied on 18 Aug. with a detailed description of the Carroll greenhouse, but GW did not complete work on his greenhouse until 1787.

3. For references to the carpenter Branning, see Tilghman to GW, 27 July, and GW to Tilghman, 4 August.

From George Augustine Washington

Honor'd Uncle   Bermuda Augt 11th 1784

Anxious to procure a conveyance to write my friends I called on the Naval Officer to make the inquiry, where I met with a

Capt. clearing out for Philadelphia but could not think of suffering Him to depart without informing You of my arrival tho'
I have only time to write a line—happy should I be could I inform You of my recovery, but the fatigues of my passage to the
West Indies and the inconvenience I experienced from the Climate and my passage to this place has greatly reduced and injured me, but this being a more settled climate than the West
Indies I flatter myself with the hope of experiencing relief from
it, but as yet I cannot judge as I arrived only the 6th Inst.—
nothing would afford me greater relief than to hear from You
and my friends—their is a Vessel which is expected to leave this
in eight or ten days for New York which will return, if Letters
were forwarded to the care of the Governor I should get them,
as I shall request the Capt. to call on Him, but to render it still
more certain if they were put under cover to Colo. Biddle as a
conveyance may offer from Philadelphia, if not to be forwarded to the Governor where I hope this Vessel will certainly
go. I will also beg a few lines to be forwarded to Norfolk as their
are often conveyances from that place—my anxiety to hear
from You and my friends will I hope apologise for the request—I shall write Mrs Washington and Miss Fanny Bassett by
the conveyance to Norfolk who with all other friends beg most
affectionately to be rememberd—my constant prayers attend
You all—most sincerely I am Your affectionate Nephew
                                   Geo: A. Washington

ALS, ViMtV.

From David Humphreys

L'Orient [France] Augst 12th 1784
Finding there was a Vessel in this port destined for Virginia, I
could not take my departure for Paris without informing my
dear General of my safe arrival in france after a most delightful
passage of twenty four days; and as I cannot give a better *discription* of the excellent accomodations & beautiful weather
which we have had during the whole of our voyage, than I have
already given in a Letter in verse to one of my poetical Correspondents, I take the liberty of enclosing a Copy of it for your
amusement.[1] Tho I believe your Excellency is not much at-

tached to Poetry, yet I conceive nothing to be indifferent to you, which is interesting to one who prides himself in having a share in your confidence & friendship; and who feels at the same time a conscious pleasure in doing justice to those laudable efforts which are made by the Officers & Subjects of His most Christian Majesty for strengthening the Amity which so happily subsists between the two Nations, as well as for removing any little prejudice which might still remain among our Countrymen with respect to the cleanliness & accomodations which are to be found on board of vessels in the service of france.

I have not been here long enough, to have acquired as yet any knowledge of Men & Manners, but I do not intend to be idle, and I hope to have the pleasure one day of communicating personally to your Excellency the result of some of my observations.

General Kosciuszko & myself are to set off in a Carriage together for Paris tomorrow—I am now going to see a french Comedy for the first time, & must therefore after offering my best wishes for the happiness of Mrs Washington & the family, take my leave of your Excellency for the present—I have the honor to be With every sentiment of friendship And veneration My dear General Your most Obedient & Most humble Servant

D. Humphreys.

Genl Kosciuszko desires his best respects may be presented to your Exy.

ALS, DLC:GW.

1. Humphreys addressed and sent the poem to his friend Timothy Dwight. The Dwight version is printed in *Works of Humphreys*, 211–15. Humphreys headed the copy of the poem that he sent to GW: "On board the Courier de L'Europe, in the Atlantic Ocean about 600 Leagues from New York July 30th 1784." It begins:

> From the wide watery waste, where nought but skies,
> And mingling waves salute the aching eyes;
> To thee my earliest friend, to thee dear
> Fond recollection turns, while thus I write—

And more than a hundred lines later, it ends:

> Amas'd with such few things, reclin'd at ease,
> While the swift barque glides thro' the summer Seas,
> Thus I (for past neglects to make amends)
> Now write to you, anon to other friends.

From Francis Mentges

Sir   Philadelphia. the 12th Augt 1784.

Having been in expectation of being appointed to command the Troops to be raised by this state[1] but the arrival of Colonel Harmar (who will get the appointment) disappointed my hopes[2]—I have now no other resource left but to return to Europe and Seek to be employed in the service of the Elector of Palatine or by the Emperor. I therefore take the liberty to request of your Excellency a testimony of my Services from the beginning of 76 to the end of the war which I shall esteem the greatest favour.[3] I have the honor to be with the Highest esteem Your Excellencys Most obt Servt

F. Mentges

Sprague transcript, DLC:GW.

Francis Mentges retired on 1 Jan. 1784 from the position of lieutenant colonel of the 5th Pennsylvania Regiment. Both he and Josiah Harmar (see note 2) were among the sixteen men who, as GW informed the president of Congress on 21 Dec. 1783, were "among the Officers of the Army who have been obliged to retire at the conclusion of the War" but "from various motives are desirous of being arranged on any Peace Establishment that may take place" (DNA:PCC, item 152).

1. See Knox to GW, 26 July, n.1.

2. Josiah Harmar, most recently colonel of the 1st Pennsylvania Regiment, became on this day commander of the little standing army authorized by Congress. He and Lt. Col. David S. Franks were chosen by Congress to take the approved treaty of peace to the American ministers in Paris, and he had just returned from France on board ship with Lafayette. Harmar retained command of the army, serving mostly in the West, until he was removed in March 1791 before resigning from the army.

3. There is a draft copy in GW's hand of a certificate for Mentges, with a covering letter that reads: "Enclosed you have a certificate of Service. for want of information respecting the dates of your appointments I could not be more particular—If this could be of any Service to you, it would give me pleasure—my best wishes will attend you, and I am Sir Yr most obedt Hble Servt." The text of the certificate is: "I certify that Francis Mentges Esqr. entered the Service of the United States of Am[eric]a in the Year 1776. and in the successive ranks of Captn Major and Lieutenant Col. & in the Contl army continued until dissolution in the year 1783. during which time his conduct as an Officer was brave zealous and intelligent—and as a Gentleman, unexceptionable & respectable. Given under my hand and Seal this 22d day of Augt 1784. Go: Washington, late Comr in chief Amn Army" (MHi: Jeremiah Colburn Papers).

From Jacob Read

Sir   Annapolis [Md.] 13th August 1784

This days post brought me your favour of the 11th, which I have the pleasure of Answering from Annapolis—having been prevented leaving Maryland by a Variety of Occurrencees in the last Week—I think however I Shall at all events get away in the Course of the next week & probably So early as to Compleat my Journey to Philadelphia.

I thank you for your Opinions, they Concur perfectly with my own Sentiments on those Subjects and I am Sorry to add there is too much truth in your Observation on the Management of our Affairs—Let the Blame fall where it ought, on those whose Attachment to State Views, State Interests & State prejudices is so great as to render them eternally opposed to every Measure that Can be divised for the public good.

The evil is not however as yet intirely incurable. I hope and trust the Next Congress will be more wise & be able to avert the Mischiefs, that appear to me to threaten the Union—If that Cannot be done we must look about & see if some more Efficient form of Government Cannot be divised—I have long entertained my doubts of the present form even if the States were all disposed to be honest & am sorry to say such a Conclusion wou'd however be against premises, I will determine nothing Rashly, & hope for the best. my most strenuous endeavours shall not be wanting to secure the peace & stability of the federal Union & the government as long as it is possible but I own I shall not hesitate to join in attempting another When I see from experience that we have instituted is not adequate to the purposes for which it was ordained—Congress either Has too little, or too much power. to be respected they must be enabled to enforce an Obedience to their Ordinances—else why the Farce of Enacting what no State is bound to Execute. If this is denied Congress is I think an Unnecessary & useless Burden & shoud not hold from the Individual States a great many powers, which they Cant exercise & had better be Remitted to the Individual Sovereignties—of this more at another time—I ask Your Excellencies pardon for so long trespassing on your patience at this time without treating the subject more Copiously & Conclusively.

Col. Hy Laurens is arrived at New York in 7 weeks from London & brings advices that the King & Ministry of great Britain are very favourably disposed towards the U/S & wish to have a liberal Commercial treaty.[1]

The Marquis de la Fayettee came to Philadelphia on the 9th Inst. advices from our Ministers abroad by his hands were by him delivered to Mr Mifflin at N. York & are not yet come to hand.

What think You of the State of New York undertaking to hold a Treaty of its own Authority with the Six Nations in defiance of our Resolves and the Clause of the Confederation Restricting the Individual States—The Governour is actually now at Albany for the purpose—Such a Step will Render all our Endeavours abortive & be attended with worse Consequences with Respect to the Indians than almost any other that State Cou'd take—tis said to be under an express Law of the State—If this Conduct is to be pursued our Commissioners are Rendered useless.[2]

As long as the Savages believe there are distinct Independent & perhaps Jealous powers to treat with them they will Certainly avail themselves of the Circumstance much to the disadvantage of the Union—New York has taken no Steps with Regard to the Troops Required for Garrisoning the N. Western frontier.

I beg my best Respects to your Lady & that you will always believe me to be with the greatest Regard & most perfect Esteem Sir Your Excellency's most obliged & most obedient Servant

Jacob Read

P.S. The Committee of the States is broken up, the Members from the Eastern States & from New Jersey having gone off on Wednesday in a most extraordinary manner.[3]

ALS, DLC:GW.
    1. Henry Laurens arrived in New York on 2 August.
    2. During the Revolutionary War most of the Iroquois sided with Britain. In the spring of 1784 both the state of New York and the Congress of the Confederation appointed commissioners to treat with the Six Nations and their confederates, each with a view to obtaining cessions of land. The New York commissioners met at Fort Stanwix at the beginning of September with Joseph Brant and other chieftains. The Indians declined to convey any land

to New York until they had first met with the commissioners appointed by Congress to treat with them. On 22 Oct. 1784 Congress's commissioners and leaders of the Six Nations agreed to the Treaty of Fort Stanwix by which the Indians renounced all claims to land west of Buffalo Creek and the Pennsylvania boundary.

3. Jonathan Blanchard of New Hampshire, Francis Dana of Massachusetts, and Samuel Dick of New Jersey left for their homes on 11 August.

From William Smith

Vienna, Eastern Shore of Maryland
Most worthy Sir   Augt 13th 1784

Being at this Place, on a Journey for the Purpose of collecting in the former Subscriptions, & raising some new Ones for our College, I met the Bearer, Mr David Arell, who lives at Alexandria, & gives me an Opportunity of enclosing & forwarding for your Perusal, the printed Account of Washington-College, the List of Subscribers & present State of the Seminary.[1] The Design of the Publication is obvious from the Title-Page &c. With the Advice of Govr *Paca* & others of the Visitors, we have also a *Lottery* on Foot, which may be at least an excusable Means of drawing some *Aid* from *some*, whose public Spirit might not otherwise induce them to subscribe. Enclosed is the Scheme of the *Lottery*, which we have Reason to hope may be full by Novr the Time mentioned. We have disposed of a considerable Number of Tickets in Baltimore, & on this Shore, the different Counties take their Proportion.[2]

If your Excellency could think of any friend to Learning in Alexandria, who might be engaged to dispose of some of the Tickets & would by Post, via Philada directed to me at Chester in Maryland, favor me with the Name, we would forward the Tickets by the Stage.[3]

Your Goodness, I know, will excuse this Trouble, which I would not dare to give you, if your Wishes for the Prosperity of this College were not publickly known—The Building rises fast, & will be covered in this Fall, if our Subscriptions can be tolerably collected. We have near forty Workmen employed, & our Expence is at about £100 pr Week, which occasions myself & some others a good Deal of Labor & Care, to keep all *afloat*. I

have the Honor to be with the most perfect Regard Your most
obedt humble Servt

William Smith

P.S. I shall be at Philada from the 24th Augt to 1st Septr. If you
should honor me with any answer, wch may reach Philada
about that Time, it may be sent to the Care of General St Clair
Philada.

ALS, DLC:GW.

1. William Smith had Joseph Cruickshank in Philadelphia print in 1784 *An
Account of Washington College in the State of Maryland*. It includes a list of nearly
three hundred subscribers who in 1782 pledged to contribute £9 or more to
the founding of Washington College. See Smith to GW, 5 May. David Arell
(d. 1792), formerly a captain in the 3d Virginia Regiment, was a lawyer in
Alexandria.

2. The Washington College Lottery offered 10,000 tickets for sale at four
dollars each. Of these, 3,187 were prizewinners: 3,000 paid 8 dollars and the
other 187 up to 4,000 dollars. See the announcement in the *Maryland Journal
and Baltimore Advertiser*, 3 Aug. 1784.

3. See GW to Smith, 25 August.

From Jean Le Mayeur

sir   new york august 14. 1784

among the many civilities I had the honor of reciving in your
Excellencys family[1] there was one which little master George
frequently showed in lending me his blue horse when I had occasion to ride—I have been so fortunate since my return to this
City as to meet with a little red horse which I beg to have the
pleasure of presenting to him as a token of my regard. this little
horse is just big Enough for the little house which master
George and myself built upon the side of the hill.

I shall always remember with singular pleasure and Gratitude the marks of a kind and generous regards which have
been Evident in the attentions I have had the honor of Experiencing from your Excellency and Lady washington.

I beg leave to present my most respectfull regards to Lady
washington to the amiable sutor to major washington of whom
I hope she has recived some newse, to mrs Stuede, Mr and Mrs
Leon washington.[2] I have the honor to be with parfect Respect
of your Excellency your most humble & obeisant serviteur

docr Le mayeur

ALS, DLC:GW.

1. For Le Mayeur's visit to Mount Vernon, see GW to Richard Varick, 22 Feb. 1784, n.4.

2. Le Mayeur is referring to Fanny Bassett, George Augustine Washington, Eleanor Calvert Custis Stewart, and to Lund Washington and his wife.

From George Augustine Washington

Honor'd Uncle   Bermuda Augt 14th 1784
On the 11th Inst. I wrote You a few lines by an accidental conveyance which left this for Philadelphia—You are before this I hope acquainted with my having left the West Indies destined for this place as I wrote You on the day of my departure.[1] I much lamented the necessity, as nothing was omit'ed to render my time agreeable, and I experinced as much pleasure as the situation of my health and absence from my freinds would permit, but a short time gave me reason to doubt, and daily experience then convinced me that no climate could be more improper, as I sensibly felt an increase of indisposition—from the 23d of June which was the time of my arrival untill my departure on the 25th Ulto (four or five days excepted) their fell powerful rains almost incessantly which interupted every persuit which could be conducive to health, my fealings urged me to leave it even sooner than I did, but inclination aided by the hope of a more favorable change induced me to continue—the present and two ensuing months being consider'd the most disagreeable, I could not hazard the consequences which experience convinced me would result from it—as yet (tho' I have been here but eight days) I have no cause to complain of the climate tho' I have been a part of the time much indisposed owing in some measure I hope to the fatigues of my passages from which I have experienced the contrary effects, to what I hoped, what with the fatigues of my passage to & from the West Indies, I am at present much reduced but a perfect relyance on divine Providence gives me the greatest hopes of restoration—the pain in my Breast, & sides, continue as heretofore intirely unattended with the symptoms usual in consumptive complaints, I theirfore divest myself of all apprehensions of that nature, and should I not derive such essential benefit from the climate, as to promise me the fairest prospects of recovery, I shall return in Novem-

ber,[2] as the ease and satisfaction I enjoy among my friends,
when compared with the many inconveniencies I have to encounter will I am persuaded render the climate of my own
Country equally efficatious, and was it not for a determination
of complying with the wishes of You and my friends which I
am convinced proceeded from the purest motives of affection,
I should not have hesitated to have returnd from the West
Indies—The difficulty of procuring fresh provision and the
prises are astonishing, the expences in the West Indies which I
thought could not be exceeded are not to be compair'd to this
place, it is seldom any thing is to be procured but Fowles—
Ducks which are more plentiful than any thing else are seldom
got for less than 2/6 and sometimes ½ Dollar and Dunghill
fowls ⅓ of Dollar and every thing in proportion—Horse hire
1 Dollar ⅌ day the Inhabitants are very hospitable and have
treated me very politely, and I hope the climate will prove
salubrious, which is all that can recommend the place, what I
have seen of it is in a perfect state of nature, and appears as
little favord by the hand of Providence as any place I ever saw—
during the hurricane Months conveyances from this are not
very frequent but shall not omit writing by any that may offer
could I but hear from You and my friends I should be greatly
relieved from many anxious thoughts that I cannot possibly de-
vest myself of—any letters that my friends may be so good as
to favor me with will probably meet with a conveyance if they
are recomd to the care of Saml Birks & Co: Norfolk who have
connections on this Island, their is also a conveyance which will
offer from New York that I mention'd in the few lines I wrote
You the other day by the way of Philadelphia—should my
worthy friend the Marquis be with You I beg to be rememberd
to him in the most friendly terms. I should have wrote Him but
apprehending from a peeice of information I recieved from a
person immediately from Philadelphia, that He had not accomplished His visit, He mentiond that accounts had been recieved
of His having saild but from a desaster that befel the Vessel He
was obliged to return[3]—to all inquiring friends I beg particularly to be rememberd—the sinceerest good wishes of a truely
grateful heart attend You—most sinceerly I am Your dutiful &
affectionate Nephew

Geo: A. Washington

P.S. If You wish a supply of Orange, Lemmon & Lime Trees for Your Green-House, I will procure what ever you wish and bring them with me.

ALS, PWacD: Sol Feinstone Collection, on deposit PPAmP.
    1. See his letter of 25 July.
    2. George Augustine Washington left Bermuda in the fall of 1784 and spent the winter in South Carolina as the guest of William Washington, not returning to Mount Vernon until 14 May 1785. See GW to William Washington, 25 Nov. 1784, to George Augustine Washington, 6 Jan. 1785, George Augustine Washington to GW, 25 Feb. 1785; and *Diaries*, 4:138.
    3. Lafayette was at Mount Vernon three days after George Augustine Washington wrote this letter.

From David Humphreys

Paris Augst 18th 1784.
    A direct opportunity for America having offered itself thro' the medium of Colo. Franks I again indulge myself in writing to my dear General; and take the most heartfelt satisfaction in acknowledging the receipt of the Dispatches which were so obligingly addressed for me to the care of Govr Jefferson—who arrived in this City about ten days before me. Tho I dare not undertake to say in this Letter how much I feel myself indebted to your goodness for these reiterated instances of your friendship, yet I may be allowed with the greatest truth to assert that I find myself under greater obligations than ever to support the character which your too great partiality has so ardently endeavoured to persuade the world I am entitled to.
    Franks is waiting—I have no time to add but by presenting my most affectionate regards to Mrs Washington & assuring you, that I have the honor to be My dear General Your Most Obedt Servt

D. Humphreys

ALS, DLC:GW.

Letter not found: from James Mercer, 18 Aug. 1784. On 25 Aug. GW wrote to Mercer: "My Sister handed me your favor of the 18th."

From Tench Tilghman

Dear Sir   Baltimore [Md.] 18th Augt 1784.

I have recd your Excellency's letters of the 4th and 11th. The first inclosing Bank Bills for 90 dollars which I beleive is more than sufficient—but Mr Peters has been so ill, that I have not been able to procure the Cost of the wheat Fan. My Clerk remembers shipping the Handle from hence.

I am glad your Carpenter is like to please you—Having not met with a Bricklayer, I shall desist looking further untill you may again direct me.

Inclosed you will find answers to your several Queries respecting the Green House in the order in which they were put,[1] and that you may the better understand the Construction of Mrs Carrolls, I have made a rough Plan of the Manner of conducting the Flues[2]—your Floor being 40 feet long, Mrs Carrol recommends two Flues to run up the Back Wall, because you may then increase the number of Flues which run under the Floor, and which she looks upon as essential—The Trees are by that mean kept warm at the Roots—she does not seem to think there is any occasion for the Heat to be conveyed all round the Walls by means of small Vacancies left in them. she has always found the Flues mark'd in the plan sufficient for her House.

She recommends it to you to have the upper parts of your Window sashes to fall down, as well as the lower ones to rise— you then give Air to the Tops of your Trees.

Your Ceiling she thinks ought to be Arched and at least 15 feet high—she has found the lowness of hers which is but 12 very inconvenient.

smooth stucco she thinks preferable to common Plaister because dryer.

The Door of the House to be as large as you can conveniently make it—otherwise when the Trees come to any size, the limbs are broken and the Fruit torn off in moving in and out.

It is the Custom in many Green Houses to set the Boxes upon Benches—But Mrs Carrol says they do better upon the Floor because they then receive the Heat from the Flues below to more advantage.

I recollect nothing more—I hope your Excellency will understand this imperfect description of a matter which I do not know much about myself—I am with true Regard Yr Excellency's very hble Servt

Tench Tilghman

ALS, DLC:GW.

1. Tilghman answered GW's queries in this way (DLC:GW):

	Qu:		Ansr
1st	dimensions of Mrs Carrolls Green House	1st	24 by 12
2d	What kind of Floor	2d	Tile
3d	How high from the floor to the Bottom of the Window frame	3d	16 Inches
4.	Height of the Windows from Bottom to Top.	4th	9 feet
5.	How high from Top of the Windows to the Ceiling	5th	18 Inches
6.	Whether the Ceiling is flat or Arched	6.	Flat—but Arches recommended
7.	Whether the heat is conveyed by Flues and a Grate	7th	Vid. Plan
8.	Whether the Grate is in the out or the Inside	8th	Vid. Plan
9th	Whether the Flues run all round the House	9th	Vid. Plan
10th	The Size of them without and in the Hollow	10th	2½ feet in the Clear as plan
11th	& 12th		Answered in the Foregoing.

2. In the enclosed sketch Tilghman draws an "A" on either side of the "S. E. Front in which are four Windows." Parallel to the two As, he has a line of three Bs. Perpendicular to the middle B, he has C and, at the back, D. His F is to the right of the As, at the right-hand wall of the greenhouse. On the left-hand wall he shows one "Window" and one "Door about 6 feet wide." He gives a key to his letters, A through E:

"A.A. Main Flue 2 feet wide. 2½ feet high. arches.
running the whole length of the House at about one foot from the Front Wall.

B.B.B. Flues issuing from the Main one and of the same dimensions

C. The place where all the Flues meet in order to carry the heat up the Back Wall—The dimensions of this place I could not ascertain as it is below Ground but it need be only sufficiently large to receive the mouths of the three Flues B.B.B.

D. The size of the Flue which runs up the Back Wall—which is one Foot Square in the Clear—it goes up thro' the Roof like a Chimney in order to give Vent to the Heat—and within the Green House is like the funnel of a Chimney without a Fire place—about three feet from the Floor of the

Green House there is an opening large eno. to receive an Iron pi⟨pe⟩ which slides in and out Horizontally. The use of this is to stop the ⟨*illegible*⟩ of the Heat from the Flues below when you want to warm the House quickly—you will observe that the Flue D. is nothing more than a continuation of the space C.

E. The Mouth of the Main Flue, which is without the House, and sun⟨k⟩ so low that the top of its Arch is sufficiently below the Floor of the Green House to allow a paving of Tile over it—It has an Iron Door The Wood is put in, in the Manner that the Brick Makers heat their Kilns—there is a small Building of Brick in the mouth of this Flue to prevent the Water from running into it" (DLC:GW).

To Chastellux

My Dr Sir,   Mount Vernon 20th Augt 1784

The Marqs de la Fayette, who I had been long looking for with the eyes of friendship and impatience, arrived here on Tuesday last[1] and presented me your favor of the 16th of June.[2]

I thank you My Dr Sir, for every testimony of your recollection of me, and every fresh assurance you give me of the continuation of your friendship is pleasing: it serves (to borrow an Indian phraze) to brighten the chain, & to convince me that you will not suffer moth or rust to injure or impair it. We talk of you often, and tho' we wish in vain to have you of our party, we do not fail to drink your health at Dinner every day. I will not give up the hope of seeing you at Mount Vernon, before I quit the stage of human action—the idea woud be too painful—I must indulge a contrary one.

As I have no communications at this time that are worthy of *your* attention, and a house full of company to claim *mine*. I shall, as the Ship by which I write has Spread her canvas wings, only add new assurances of what I hope you were before perfectly convinced, that I am with the greatest esteem & regard—My D. Sir Yrs &c. &c.

G: Washington

LB, DLC:GW; copy, DSoCi.

1. The following item appeared in the Alexandria newspaper: "Alexandria, *August* 19. *On Tuesday Morning* [17 Aug.] *the Marquis de la Fayette, accompanied by the Chevalier Caraman, Captain of Dragoons in the Army of France, passed through this Town, on their Way to his Excellency General Washington's Seat, Mount-Vernon*" (*Virginia Journal and Alexandria Advertiser*, 19 Aug. 1784).

2. The text of the translation of the letter from Chastellux to GW, dated "Paris. june. 16. 1784," is: "I have seen without jealousy the glory of my friend and cousin, the good marquess but when he enjoys the happiness to see again your excellency, I have neither philosophy nor friendship enough to guard my heart against envy. however it is upon him that I depend to console my sorrow. I hope he will be so generous to spare some of the delight full hours he will spend with you to review my attachment to your excellency. he, and he only, may express what he feels with me and as myself with the most sincer respect and attachment I have the honour to be dear general your most humble and obeedient servant" (DLC:GW). The ALS, in French, is in ViMtV; it is dated 17 June, not 16 June.

To James Crane

Sir,   Mount Vernon 20th Augt 1784

The enclosed letter which is left open for your perusal, will give you my sentiments respecting the sale of the Widow Bartletts Lease. Please to seal, before you send or deliver it. I shall have no objection to a transfer of the purchaser, if likely to fulfill the objects I had in view—& the conditions of the Lease are complied with.[1] I am Sir &c.

G: Washington

LB, DLC:GW.

James Crane of Berkeley County, Va. (now W.Va.), was deputy sheriff of the county during the Revolution and handled some affairs in the area for both George William Fairfax and GW. He by this time was sheriff of the county, and in 1786 he became one of the trustees named to establish Charles Town on Charles Washington's property in Berkeley County.

1. Mary Bartlett was Crane's sister. The enclosed letter was to William Drew, this date. See that letter, particularly note 1.

To William Drew

Sir,   Mount Vernon 20th Augt 1784

My inducements to lease Land were, to encourage emigration & to improve my property by planting industrious settlers on it; who, while they were working the soil would, for their own convenience, add value to the Tenements by buildings &c.—with this view I restrained the sale of my leases without my consent.

Having premised this, I wou'd next ask if you mean to build & reside on the Land, you express a wish to purchase from the widow Bartlett?[1] If you do, I should be happy in having you for a tenant. but if you intend it only for a quarter, under the management of an overseer, I must withhold my consent, because (tho' I am far from making any personal application) instead of improvements which wou'd add value to the Farm; I should expect, in such a case, to have it destroyed by incessant working; & rendered of no value by the time the lease might fall in— which would be defeating the principal objects I had in view from the grants of them, & injuring myself.[2] I am Sir &c.

G: Washington

LB, DLC:GW.

1. At his death in 1777, William Bartlett had a lease, for three lives (himself, his wife Mary, and his son William), for lot no. 5, probably 200 acres, of GW's Bullskin tract in Berkeley County. His widow Mary paid rent for GW to Deputy Sheriff James Crane until 1781 (undated receipts for taxes paid in 1779 and 1781, NcD: Battaile Muse Papers). On 1 Oct. 1783 Lund Washington was reporting on tenants when he wrote GW: "The Widdow of Wm Bartlett coud not inform me by what means she was to pay hers, she is Sister to the Actg Sheriff of Berkeley—a man of good Character (Mr [James] Crane) she said she woud talk to him and get him to dispose of part of her Estate so as to enable her to pay the Rents, but unless he coud point out some way of doing it, she coud not, she hope'd distress might not be made for some little time to come, for all shoud be done, that coud be done to get the Rents" (ViMtV).

2. Drew, who was county clerk, seems not to have rented this or any other land from GW. Mary Bartlett's lease was transferred to John Bryan on 5 July 1786 (NcD: Battaile Muse Papers).

To Duportail

Dear Sir,   Mount Vernon 20th Augt 1784

The Marqs de la Fayette who arrived at this place on tuesday last, gave me the pleasure of receiving your letter dated at Paris the 16th of June—& of learning from it, that you had not relinquished the idea of visiting a Country, on whose theatre you have acted a conspicuous part. Be assured Sir, that at whatever time, & under whatever circumstances this may happen, I shall be among the first to give you a welcome reception.

Several circumstances conspired to prevent my making the tour with the Chevr de la Luzerne, to the Great Cataract of Niagara; but that which had most weight with me, indeed which an insurmountable objection, was, the British (without even the colour of pretence), holding that, & the intermediate

Post of Oswego. I did not choose to make the trip upon curtesy; nor to place myself in a situation where either a denial or any indignity might be offered in the prosecution of it.

I pray you to offer my best wishes to any of the Gentlemen of your Corps with whom I have the pleasure of an acquaintance, when you see them. Mrs Washington thanks you for your kind remembrance of her, & begs you to accept her compliments. I am Dr Sir, with great esteem Yrs &c.

G: Washington

LB, DLC:GW.

To La Luzerne

Sir,   Mount Vernon 20th Augt 1784
The letter your Excellency did me the honor to write in the moment of your departure from this Country, conferred the highest honor upon me, & is not more flattering to my vanity, than it is productive of my gratitude.[1]

I shall ever reflect with pleasure Sir, on the readiness with which your communications to me have been made; & the dispatch & ability with which you have conducted business in the line to which I was called—and what will render these reflections more precious, is that you have accompanied them with marks of friendship & confidence which were as pleasing as they are honorable.

When I add Sir, that you have impressed me with sentiments of sincere respect and attachment, I do not speak the language of my own heart only; it is the universal voice, and your departure will always be regreted. The only consolation left us is, that you are gone to receive the smiles & approbation of a Prince, who knows full well how to distinguish, & how to reward merit.

It would give me great pleasure to make you a visit in France— to pay my respectful homage to a Sovereign to whom America is so much indebted—and to renew the friendships which I have had the honor to contract with so many respectable characters of your Nation. but I despair—my fortune has been injured by the war, & my private concerns are so much deranged, as to require more time to recover them than comports with the years of a man who is sliding down the stream of life as fast as I am—But whether I am in this or that Country, or wheresoever I may be, nothing will lessen the respect, or shake the attachment with which I have the honor to be Dr Sir Yrs &c. &c.

G: Washington

LB, DLC:GW.
1. La Luzerne wrote to GW from Philadelphia on 12 June.

To Rochambeau

My dear Count,   Mount Vernon Augt 20th 1784.

I thank you for your favor of the 16th of June by the Marquis de la Fayette, who arrived here three days ago—and for your other letter of the 4th of May which, also came safe. permit me to offer you my sincere congratulations on your appointment to the Government of Picardy. It is an honorable testimony of the approving smiles of your Prince, & a just reward for your Services & merit. Should fortune ever put it in my power to come to France, your being at Calais would be an irrisistable inducement for me to make it a visit.

My letters from Philadelphia (public & private) would give you a full acct of every matter & thing respecting the Society of the Cincinnati, and upon what footing all claims to the order were, thereafter, to be decided—to these referring, I shall save you the trouble of reading a repetition. Considering how recently the K—g of Sw-d-n has changed the form of the Constitution of that Country, it is not much to be wondered at that his *fears* should get the better of his *liberallity* at any thing which might have the semblance of *republicanism*. but considering further how few of his Nation had, or could have, a right to the Order, I think he might have suffered his complaisance to have superceded his apprehensions.[1]

I will not trouble you with a long letter at this time, because I have nothing worthy of communication. Mrs Washington who is always pleased with your remembrance of her, and glad to hear of your welfare, prays you to accept her Compliments & best wishes; mine are always sincere—and offered (tho' unknown) to Madame Rochambeau—the Viscount your Son—& any of the Officers of the army you commanded in America who may be with you, & with whom I have the honor of an acquaintance. With great esteem & regard I am My dear Genl Yr Most Obedt & Most Hble Servt

Go: Washington

ALS, DLC: Rochambeau Papers; LB, DLC:GW.
 1. See Rochambeau to GW, 16 June, n.1.

From Stephen Sayre

Sir   George Town [Md.] August 20th 1784
    The importance of clearing the river & the necessity of doing so immediatly induces me to offer Some thoughts on it to your Excellencys Consideration to prevent the Fatall consequ[e]nces of delay.[1] I wish any kind of Navigation or Mode of bringing down productions by Water May be adopted, that no time may be lost in removing prejudices, *which are worce than the Rocks in our way*, or advantages lost in application to bodies of Men who may Never agree—Governor Johnson & his friends, I am told, are more than Confident they Shall clear the Seneca Falls within a few weeks—let them do so—my opinion is that, with a few hundered pounds, the great & little Falls may be mead equally Navigable, to anything they will be able to do at the Seneca.[2] It is difficult, in a letter, to explain the Various things which different parts would require, but whereever the waters were too rapid anchors made to fill the Purpose by taking hold of Solid Rocks Chains & boats, Properly placed, & a few Bouys to direct the Channel would be all that is wanting except in two places, where Some part of the Rocks must be blown to make the decent Some what gradual, wide enough to let 2 Boats pass. the decending one to force up the other, which is infinitly more Simple & more certain of Perpetuall use then any Lock can be—If I am well informd as to the Shanadoah Falls, boats may assend & decend there without removing any Rocks; a force like this, on the same Simple plan, will then make them Navigable also.
    I am clearly of opinion that a practicable Navigation may be immediate, & done by a few Gentlemen as a Company—looking forward either to improve it or apply to the Legislatures of the two States to incorporate them, & others who may wish to do it on a more large & expencive Scale. If you have doubts as

to this being done—I mean a practical navigation. I should be hapy to attend you on the Spot, when I could point out the mode of doing it with great facility.

If your Excellency has no hops as to this expedient I offer the following thoughts, as to raising the Money. for the most extensive Improvements A board of respectable Trustees, being named & incorporated vacancies to be supplyd so as to make it perpetuall &c. &c. any given Sum will probably be subscribed by Classing People of the same age—The benifits or profits arising from the Toll to be paid annually to the Survivors of each Class in Proportion to their Stock.

For instance, suppose persons class'd as follows

50 from 35 to 40	at 250 dollars	each	Drs 12500
50 from 30 to 35	at 250	do	12500
50 from 25 to 30	at 250	do	12500
50 from 20 to 25	at 250	ditto	12500
50 from 15 to 20	at 250	do	12500
50 from 10 to 15	at 250	do	12500
50 from 5 to 10	at 250	do	12500
50 Children under 5 Years	at 250,	do	62500
Capital Stock in Dollars.			150000

The trustees to make no dividend for the first five years, & none to the Class of Children till after 15 Years; because children do not want it Sooner. & they are likely to lie longer on the Toll, which is to be liberated only on the death of all, but ought to be lightened as the Classes fall off—I should imagine that sixpence ℔ Ton on Goods would be a suffiecent inducement for subscribers, and that only one place of Payment, & that below the lowest fall ought to be established—I conceive the fund would fill rapidly from the great hops of a high Interest, its security, its certain encrease & from certain death, which must Soon double the Sum to the Survivor—The dead want no money—the living are sure of It. If any of the Capital remains, even after finishing the work, it may be apply'd to a further Navigation, or if the Trustees, looking forward to public Improvements, want money, they may open fresh Subscriptions & render many other parts of this vast Continent Solid & enviable Services—the act therefore ought to invest them with a power of doing so.

Your Excellencys good sense will decide as to the numbers of each Class, or whether it will not be necessary to have more Children—I think it would; for who would not wish to provide for a Child at the price proposed.

I should like to try the experiment of Subscription on condition that the States sanctify the measure, and am Sure if you will take the lead in it, with some respectable Gentlemen in the Neibourhood, no money would be wanting. I am with all possible respect & veneration most devotedly Your Excellencys very humble Servant

Stephen Sayre

ALS, DLC:GW.

1. GW must have discussed with Sayre the prospect of opening up to navigation the Potomac River above Alexandria and Georgetown. In his subsequent monthlong excursion into western Pennsylvania, GW worked out his ideas and plans for such an undertaking. See GW to Benjamin Harrison, 10 Oct. 1784, for a comprehensive statement of what GW had in mind for the Potomac after his return.

2. Thomas Johnson (1732–1819) of Frederick County, Md., who was governor of the state from 1777 to 1779, joined GW as one of the commissioners to conduct the affairs of the Potomac River Company after it was formed in early 1785 largely through GW's efforts. See editorial note in Harrison to GW, 10 Oct. 1784. Johnson also was the leader of the group of Marylanders who before the Revolution had joined forces with a number of Virginians, including GW, to form a company for improving the navigation of the Potomac (see, for instance, GW to Johnson, 20 July 1770).

From George William Fairfax

My Dear Sir,   Bath [England] August 23d 1784

Tho I had resolved to avoid being further troublesome to you an occasion has occur'd which obliges me to request that you'l be so good to look into my Deeds and over all my Papers (if they remain in your hands) for the Lord Proprietors discharge, for all arrears of Quitrents which He gave me the last time he was at Belvoir, just before I left Virginia. The importance of this small Scrip of paper will I trust plead my excuse for the trouble I am necessitated to give when I inform you that Mr G. Nicholas writes me that a demand has been made, by the late Lords Executors, for the arrears of Quitrents of all the Lands myself and Family hold,[1] a good return for the many Years service of my dear Father and self, for which neither of

Us ever received any recompence, except the remission of Quitrent & some Office Fees. I am very sensible that I have a just right to bring an Account against Doctor Martin now Fairfax's Estate, that would more than make me whole, but as I wish for nothing but Peace and retirement the remainder of my days, I would avoid Litigation, if not compelled to it in self defence.

In the extraordinary Will I acquiesed, tho' I was as well convinced that it was not the late Lords, as his Brother was who pressed me much to join in disputing it, which I thought I had nothing to do with, and that He was the only proper Person to do it, as Heir at Law.[2] When the honest old Man came down to take leave, and a last farewell of us, he appeard more Affectionate, open, and candid than he ever was before. as oft as he, my Wife, and self were alone, He entered upon the subject of Family affairs, talked of the fine Estates he had sold for a song in Yorkshire, laid the blame upon his Mother and Grandmother, who he said compelled him to do it to redeem the Culpeper Estates, assured me, he would do his Fathers family what Justice he could, and even named all the best things in his disposal also the sixth part of the Proprietary for them. the last named, he repeatedly said was the Fairfax's absolute right, as it was given to him as a bribe to the docking the Intails.[3] Excuse me my friend, nothing was further from my intention than troubling you with even these particulars, but I am hurt at this last peice of Iniquity, more upon my unfortunate Brothers & my Sisters Account than my own, as it is in my power to do myself justice.[4] I must intreat that provided you dont find Lord Fairfaxs acqu[i]ttal of Quitrents to my Family and self, that you'l be so good not to mention my having made the enquiry: it is possible it may be with my Papers in Yorkshire, where I have not a friend with whom I can take the liberty I've done with you, as I have not the same relyance upon them. if happily you should find the Paper, be pleased to deliver it to Mr Geo. Nicholas, or to Mr Randolph, the Attorney General.

Some time ago, I did myself the honor to send your Excellency a fine press Print, expressive of the great Oppressions and Calamities of America, also of the glorious Revolution with which it pleasd Heaven to terminate the infernal War. Heroic virtue, who heads up the train of help to weeping America was intended to represent your Excellency, and if your likeness could have been procured, it had been a fine portrait of your Person. Mr Pine the ingenious Allegorical designer and executor of that much admired peice lived very near us and did Mrs Fairfax & self the favor, to consult us oft in designing it. Poor Mr Pine is as true a "Son of Liberty["] as any Man can be, ever openly declared it, which with the great ⟨*illegible*⟩ of publishing the Piece, lost him business, and made so many Enemies in this selfish Nation, that he is compelled to go to America to seek bread in his profession, tho he is certainly one of the first Artists in this Isle. Give me leave to assure you Sir, that there is not a Person in England that merits a better reception in America than the unfortunate Gentn whose only fault was his good wishes to our Country. Therefore shall be ⟨greatly⟩ obliged to your Excellency, to honor Mr Pine with your Notice and if you will be so good to recommend him to your friends if he goes to Virginia, or continues in Philadelphia, it will be doing great Charity, for he has a very amiable Wife and six Daughters, women grown, a very heavy expence to a Man that has lost his great business through party zeal.[5]

We had lately the pleasure of hearing that you was very well at Philadelphia, from a Person that saw you at a Ball there, at the House of Mr Hills.[6] We hoped Dear good Mrs Washington, has recoverd her health. Mrs Fairfax and self most sincerely wish you both long to enjoy it and every felicity. We have had the happiest Summer we have known since we came over, in a sequestred Country Place, tho' the Weather has been very cold and wet, but our dear Country is in Peace, and that and retirement gives it to us. The mention of Peace reminds me to tell You that I have been assured by a Minr in the secrets of the Court, that nothing was less intended by the Cabinet than given Peace to America, even when the Treaty was in appearance far advanced. He added that I was to thank God for it, his situation would not allow him to say more. I trust and hope the Peace will not be broken by America, for I am convinced that nothing but the want of means for carrying on the War on the part of England continues the Peace. I should be sorry my name should be mentioned as the giver of this intelligence for my Friends sake, but I thought it necessary to inform you of it, and you'l please to make what aplication of it you judge proper. Adieu my Dear Sir, God bless, and preserve you long to America, and may you ever receive every mark of her gratitude, is the sincere wish of Dear Sir your faithful and ever Obliged humble Servt

Go: W: Fairfax

The Demand of the Arrears of Quitrent proceeds from Tom Martin. his Brother, who now calls himself Doctor Fairfax, disclaimes any knowledge of the matter, and has written to Tom to proceed no further in that business, and to let him know whence all this Arises, but I well know what representation to expect from that quarter. therefore it's necessary for me to prepare for Litigation, and I must collect all the Evidence and materials I can, for I am determined to Contest the matter to the last. Unless my Fathers family had been actual Servants to the Elder branch it could not be expected he was to dedicate our whole time to the Proprietary business, without proper compensation.[7]

ALS, DLC:GW. The commalike marks that Fairfax made at inappropriate places have been omitted.

Thomas Fairfax, sixth Baron Fairfax of Cameron, "the good old Lord" as GW called him, died in Frederick County, Va., on 9 Dec. 1781. Fairfax's title and five-sixths of his undivided interest in the Northern Neck Proprietary in Virginia went to his brother Robert, who lived in England, and the one-sixth undivided interest and most of the rest of his Virginia lands went to his oldest nephew, the Rev. Denny Martin, who also lived in England. Martin received his inheritance only after he had, by an act of Parliament, taken "upon him the name of Fairfax and coat of Arms." Denny Martin's younger brother, Thomas Bryan Martin, who, when George William Fairfax's father William Fairfax died in 1757, became manager of the land office of the Northern Neck Proprietary for Lord Fairfax, inherited 600 acres of land and all of the goods and stock at Greenway Court where Lord Fairfax had lived for many years, as well as one-fourth of Fairfax's ninety-seven slaves. (Lord Fairfax's will dated 8 Nov. 1777 is in the Frederick County Will Book.) Lord Fairfax left nothing to his cousin George William Fairfax who had been living in England since leaving Virginia in 1773 (see source note in George William Fairfax to GW, 10 June 1784).

1. GW wrote Fairfax in 1775 to give up his oversight of Fairfax's Virginia property (see source note in Fairfax to GW, 10 June 1784) and subsequently tried without success to turn over to Robert Carter Nicholas papers and records at Mount Vernon belonging to Fairfax (see GW to Fairfax, 30 June 1786, in which GW rehearses the history of his handling of Fairfax's affairs in Virginia after Fairfax's departure in 1773). On 5 Aug. 1773, before sailing from Yorktown, Fairfax wrote to GW in a postscript: "In looking over some of my Papers, I found the enclosed Papers, which ought to be left, and particu-

larly the Receipt from his Lordship the Proprieter for Arrears of Quit Rents, which I Think had better be Pasted on the inside cover of my Ledger for fear of accident." Not remembering this in 1784, GW searched at length before finding Lord Fairfax's receipt in George William Fairfax's ledger, "pasted on the cover of the Book" (GW to Fairfax, 30 June 1785). George Nicholas (c.1754–1799) was the son of Robert Carter Nicholas to whom Fairfax had looked during GW's absence after 1775 to keep an eye on his business affairs in Virginia.

2. For a discussion of the will of Thomas, the sixth Lord Fairfax, and the inheritance of his brother Robert who became the seventh Lord Fairfax, see source note and note 3.

3. At the age of 16, in 1710, Thomas, the sixth Lord Fairfax, inherited from his grandmother, Margaret, Lady Culpeper, one-sixth share in the Northern Neck Proprietary in Virginia. His mother Catherine, Lady Fairfax, controlled the other five-sixths of the proprietary until her death in 1719. By her will Catherine vested in the sixth Lord Fairfax, for life only, the five-sixths that had been hers. For a succinct history of the early years of the proprietary and of the Fairfax connection to it, see Appendix I-1, "The Northern Neck Proprietary to 1745," in Freeman, *Washington*, 1:447–513.

4. The only surviving siblings of George William Fairfax were Bryan Fairfax and Hannah Fairfax Washington, wife of Warner Washington.

5. See Fairfax to GW, 10 June 1784, n.1.

6. Fairfax was probably referring to the house of Henry Hill (1732–1798) on the Germantown Road near the Schuylkill Falls. GW had known Hill since 1773. GW was in Philadelphia in December 1783 and again for the meeting of the Society of the Cincinnati in May and June 1784.

7. See source note.

To Reuben Harvey

Sir,   Mount Vernon 25th Augt 1784

Captain Stickney has presented me with your favor of the 25th of May—together with the mess-beef & ox tongues, for which you will please to accept my best thanks.

I do not raise Tobacco on my Estate nor am I possessed of a pound at this time; otherwise I would with pleasure consign a few Hogsheads to your address, under full persuasion, that no person would do me more justice in the sale of them. Wheat or flour of the last year's produce, is either exported or consumed; that of the present year, is not yet got to market—what prices they will bear in this Country is not for me to say: but tho' I do not walk in the Mercantile line, except in wheat (which I manufacture into flour)—I should nevertheless, thank you for any information respecting the prices of these articles.[1] With very great esteem & regard I am Sir &c.

G: Washington

LB, DLC:GW. The same letter under the date of 30 Aug. is printed in the *Journal of the Cork Historical Archaelogical Society*, 2d ser., 2 (1896), 90. The only differences between the two copies are in the punctuation and in the wording of the closing. The printed version may have been taken from the receiver's copy.

1. See Harvey's reply, 28 Mar. 1785.

To James Mercer

Dear Sir,   Mount Vernon Augt 25th 1784.

My Sister handed me your favor of the 18th.[1] I thank you for the advice respecting the mode of conveying a title for the Lands I purchased at your Brother's Sale, & will pursue it; but necessity will oblige me to postpone the matter until I return from my Western jaunt; as, from Company & other circumstances, no leizure is left me to rummage for Papers before.

My letter to your Brother John Mercer,[2] would have informed you, that I apprehended there were omissions in the account I transmitted, to my prejudice, as I had not been able to make any statemt of my Books, or to assort my Papers (wch by frequent removals to get them out of the enemy's way, were in sad disorder) since my return. I am much obliged to you for the Memm taken from your journal, especially as I am in a way to be a considerable sufferer from my advances to obtain, & Survey the Grant of 200,000 Acres of Land under Dinwiddies proclamation. Many of the Grantees never having paid me a Shilling.

The enclosed letter will give you every information in my power respecting Vanbraam—when you have read it please to return it to me, as it has received no acknowledgement yet.[3] With very great esteem & regard I am—Dr Sir Yr most obt Servt

Go: Washington

ALS (photocopy), DLC:GW.
    1. Letter not found.
    2. See GW to John Francis Mercer, 8 July, and notes.
    3. The enclosed letter undoubtedly was the letter of Jacob Van Braam

(1725–1784) to GW, written "Au Chateau de Rouville, near Mallesherbes, France, Decbr 20th 1783." Van Braam was born in Holland and came to live in Fredericksburg, Va., in 1753. At GW's surrender at Fort Necessity, 3 July 1754, Captain Van Braam and Capt. Robert Stobo were taken hostages by the French. Van Braam remained a prisoner in Canada until his release in 1760. He then obtained a captain's commission in the Royal American Regiment and at the war's end retired on half-pay to Wales. Most of his letter to GW is taken up with an account of what had happened to him since his leaving America. Recalled to his regiment in 1775 over his protest, Van Braam had been sent to East Florida in 1776 and, as he wrote, had served unwillingly in the Georgia campaign before securing permission to sell his commission and return to England. His letter continues: "My sentiments in regard to the proceedings of the Ministry were too well known for me to remain in thier Army, and even in Devonshir where I retired for some time after; which determined me to leave England, and look for an retreat in this Country, and have luckly found in the nighbourhood of one of The most worthy caracters in Europe.

"No doubt but Monsieur de La Luserne has given Your Excellency an Account of his aimible and learned relation Monsieur de Mallesherbes. Amongst the many civilities I recieve from that Gentleman he was pleased to acquaint me that in a letter he had recieved from Monsieur De la Luzerne You had condesended to send Your complements to me" (DLC:GW).

Van Braam died in 1784, and there is no indication that GW responded to his letter. For GW's contact with Malesherbes, see Barbé-Marbois to GW, 8 June 1784.

To William Smith

revd Sir,   Mount Vernon 25th Augt 1784
Your letter of the 10th from Vienna, was more than ten days on its passage to me. It found me with company, & busily preparing for a journey which I am about to commence in a few days to the westward. I did not fail however to mention the purport of your wishes to Mr Arell who was the bearer of your packet to me. He offering his services to dispose of your lottery tickets—I do not know where two or three hundred could be better placed in Alexandria, & if you will send him that number, he has promised me that his ex[er]tion for the sale of them shall not be wanting.

I thank you for your printed account of Washington College. My best wishes will always attend it, and I am with great respect, Revd Sir Your mo: obedt humble Servt

G: Washington

LB, DLC:GW.

To Thomas Walker

Dr Sir,   Mount Vernon 25th Augt 1784
In April last I wrote you a letter, of which the enclosed is a copy—having received no reply to it, nor seen any meeting of the company summoned in the papers, I am lead to suspect it never got to hand—for this reason, and because I think a meeting of the company indispensably necessary, I have transmitted a copy.[1] I am upon the eve of a journey as far as the Kanhawa, from whence I may not be returned 'till sometime in Novr—but I would not wish to have the meeting delayed on that account. I am &c. &c.

G: Washington

LB, DLC:GW.
1. See GW to Walker, 10 April, and Walker's reply to that letter, which Walker did not write until 29 August.

From Unzaga y Amézaga

May it please your Excellency
Sir   Havana 26th August 1784.
Immediately after General Stewart's arrival here, he handed me your Excellency's esteem'd favor of the 5th Feby this Year recommending me this gallant Officer,[1] who remain'd here untill he finish'd settling his outstanding accts with the Inhabitants, wch without doubt were many, from the free Commerce carried on during the late War wth the Inhabitants of this Island.
I have procur'd General Stewart to be serv'd in all his Solicitations, & honor'd him all in my power, wch I have no doubt he will inform your Exy of, & repeating to your Exy the desire & wish I have of serving You—I remain &c.

Luis de Unzaga y Amezaga[2]

Translation, DLC:GW; L, DLC:GW; Df, Archivo General de Indias, Seville: Legajos de Cuba 1354.
1. GW enclosed his letter to Unzaga on behalf of Walter Stewart in his letter to Stewart of 5 February. It is printed as note 2 of that document.
2. Written below the signature is: "This is from the Govr of Havana."

From Nathanael Greene

Dear Sir   Charleston [S.C.] Augt 29th 1784

My ill health and the distressing situation of my private affairs for some time past has claimed too much of my Attention
to afford me either time or inclination to attend to any thing
else. At the time of the meeting of the Cincinnati in Philadelphia I had a dangerous and disagree[able] pain in my breast.
It had hung about me then upwards of two months; but by the
use of balsam of firr soon after I wrote you from Newport[1] I
got better of it. And the very day that Col. Ward returned from
the Meeting I set sail for Philadelphia upon some matters very
interesting to my Southern affairs; and was in hopes to have arrivd in time to have had the pleasure of seeing you—On my
return from Philadelphia and my stay was short I got information that my fortune was much exposed from the Situation of
sundry debts which I had guaranteed for the Contractors of the
Southern Army while I had the command in this Country. The
amount of the debts and the situation of the Contractors affairs
made it seriously alarming and brought me to this Country
without a moments hesitation notwithstanding the season and
climate.[2] I have been under great apprehensions of heavy
losses; but I have now got matters in so happy a train that I have
little to fear but from partial inconveniencies. It has given me
much pain and preyed heavily upon my spirits. My stay I expected would have been short in this Country; but from the peculiar situation of my concerns it will be protracted to a much
greater length than I wish or expected.

After the war I was in hopes of repose; but fortune will not
allow me what I most wish for. Some good natured Acts done
for individuals and the low state of public credit in this Country
has drawn me into many inconveniencies and some heavy
losses. By Baron Glaubeck whom Congress noticed for his conduct in Morgans affair I expect to loose a thousand dollars
having endorsed his bills and had them to settle.[3] And if I suffer
no loss by the Contractors, the uncertainty will hang over me
like a Cloud until the whole affair is closed.

While I feel much for my self I feel for you. You have had
your troubles since you left public life. The clamour raised

against the Cincinnati was far more extensive than I expected. I had no conception that it was so universal. I thought it had been confined to New England alone; but I found afterwards our Ministers abroad and all the Inhabitants in general throughout the United States were opposed to the order. I am happy you did not listen to my advice. The measures you took seemed to silence all the jealosies on the subject; but I wish the seeds of discontent may not break out under some other form. However it is hardly to be expected that perfect tranquility can return at once after so great a revolution: where the Minds of the people have been so long accustomed to conflicts and subjects of agitation. In this Country many discontents prevail, Committees are formed and correspondences going on, if not of a treasonable nature highly derogatory to the dignity of Government as well as subversive of the tranquility of the people. And I wish they may not break out into acts of violence and open rebellion against the Authority of the State—Nor am I without some apprehensions that the situation of our public credit at home and abroad and the general discontent of the public creditors may plunge us into new troubles. The obstinacy of Rhode Island and the tardiness of some other States seem to presage more Mischief. However I can but hope the good sense of the populace will correct our policy in time to avoid new convulsions— But many people secretly wish that every State should be completely independunt; and that as soon as our public debts are liquidated that Congress should be no more, a plan that would be as fatal to our interest at home as ruinous to it abroad. I see by the Northern Papers that the Marquis de la Fayette had arrived at New York and set out for Mount Vernon. Doubtless you will have a happy Meeting. It will be the feast of reason and the flow of soul. Present him my respectful compliments of congratulation upon his safe arrival in America and my affectionate regards to Mrs Washington. I am dear Sir with esteem & affection Your Most Obedt humble Sert

                                                    Nath. Green

ALS, DLC:GW; LB, CSmH: Greene Papers.
    1. See Greene to GW, 6 May.
    2. To secure essential supplies for his army in the winter of 1782–83, General Greene found it necessary to guarantee loans of more than £30,000 sterling for army contractors in South Carolina who were dealing with British

merchants in Charleston. At this time in 1784, Greene still believed that he could clear himself, through his own efforts, of liability for any remaining claims against the contractors. It was not until 22 Aug. 1785 that he petitioned Congress for indemnity in case of loss. By the time Alexander Hamilton made his report on the petition of Greene's widow at the end of 1791, the liability of Greene's estate was estimated at about eight thousand pounds sterling. For the details of Greene's transactions with the army contractors in 1783, see Hamilton's report with its attached documents and the editors' notes printed as Report on the Petition of Catharine Greene, 26 Dec. 1791, in Syrett, *Hamilton Papers*, 10:406–68.

3. In his letter to the president of Congress, 22 Aug. 1785, Greene wrote: "Another instance of private loss has attended my command, which, in many instances, has been rendered more difficult and distressing, than can be readily conceived. Baron Glusbeck, an officer created for special merit in the action at the Cowpens, was in Charleston, without money or means to get to the northward, and a foreigner and without credit. I had no money to advance him, and endorsed his bills, which were returned upon my hands with damages and interest, to the amount of near a thousand dollars, which I have been obliged to borrow the money to settle, and still owe it. My public station imposed this business upon me, and, although I would not have done it, if I had known the fellow to have been as great an imposter, as I have reason to believe him since, yet, at the same time, being commanding officer, I could not well refuse it" (ibid., 421–28).

To David Griffith

Dr Sir,   Mount Vernon 29th Augt 1784

Colo. Fitzhugh informs me that the Academy at George town is upon a good establishment—that the Gentn at the head of it is very capable, and clever in conducting of it—that the school is in high estimation, & that the terms are £25 for board, & £6.10 for teaching, Maryland Curry. Under these circumstances, let me pray you to inform Mr Nourse that I think it a desirable place to fix my Nephews at—Colo. Fitzhugh adds— that as Mr Balch is a particular friend of his, he will write to him on the subject as I should prefer having them boarded at his house to that of any other in town.[1] I am Dr Sir &c.

                                    G: Washington

LB, DLC:GW.

1. Colonel Fitzhugh was probably William Fitzhugh of Maryland. The two sons of the deceased Samuel Washington, George Steptoe and Lawrence Augustine whose ages were about 11 and 9, were enrolled in the academy of the Rev. Stephen Bloomer Balch in Georgetown, Md., and remained there for a

little over a year before GW deemed it too expensive and brought them back across the river to Alexandria. They lived only briefly in Balch's house. See GW to James Nourse, 22 Jan. 1784, and GW to Balch, 26 June, 22 Nov. 1785. GW placed the boys in the Rev. Alexander McWhir's academy in Alexandria in November 1785 and secured board and room for them first at Mrs. Parthenia Dade's and in January 1787 at Samuel Hanson's.

From Thomas Walker

Dear Sir   Castle Hill [Va.] August the 29th 1784
On the receipt of your favour dated April the 10th I wrote to Mr David Jameson inclosing a copy of the part [of] your letter relative to the swamp Company also copeys of the Honble Doctor Williamsons letter & the other proposal respecting the Canal, the originals & copy of Mr Jamasons answer are inclosed,[1] Mr Jameson has for several years had the cheif mannagment which induce'd me to expect that he could give a more satisfactory account than was in my power, what money the Company had is in the Loan office of Course chiefly lost. I intend to advertise a meeting in Richmd on the 16 of october, if this should come to yr hands in time I am satisfyed your doing it would have much greater effect. I shall inclose my advertisement to Mr Robert Bane Merchant in Richmond with orders not to publish it till the last of next Month & if you send one to publish yrs & destroy mine.[2]
I perfectly agree with you in the Sale of our partnership Lands,[3] Betsy is very well & most cordially joins in best wishes for your & Familys Healt and happiness with Dr Sr your most obliged Servt

Thomas Walker

ALS, ViMtV.
1. See Walker to GW, 24 Jan. 1784, nn.1 and 3. For Hugh Williamson's letter, see GW to Williamson, 31 Mar. 1784. In David Jameson's draft of a letter to Thomas Walker, dated 15 July 1784, he writes: "A few days ago I recd your favour of the 19h June wch is the only Letter I have recd from you since last November" (NcD: Dismal Swamp Land Company Papers).
2. After speaking of Dismal Swamp Company affairs and expressing his regret that the meeting called for November 1783 did not materialize, Jameson writes in the draft of his letter to Walker of 15 July 1784: "Could the great & good Genl Washington be prevailed on to appoint a time & place for Meeting the Members would suppose he intended to be there in person & I believe woud attend." Walker's notice, dated 20 Sept., appeared on 2 Oct. in

the *Virginia Gazette, or, the American Advertiser* (Richmond), calling for the "Members of the Dismal Swamp Company, of Virginia," to meet at Galt's tavern in Richmond on 16 Oct., "on business of great importance." Some of the members came to Richmond, but GW did not, and no formal meeting was held. See David Jameson to Thomas Walker, 25 Oct. 1784, to William Nelson, Jr., 4 Jan. 1785 (NcD: Dismal Swamp Land Company Papers), and GW to John de Neufville, 8 Sept. 1785. See also GW to Thomas Walker, 10 April 1785, n.1.

3. See GW to Thomas Walker, 10 April 1784.

From William Gordon

My dear Sir   Jamaica Plain [Mass.] Aut 30. 1784

Your obliging letter of the 10th instt was recd the last thursday.[1] With the greatest pleasure I read of the health & welfare of Self & family. I was glad, that the Boston Paper came regularly; & that you may be perfectly satisfied with its continuance, inform You that it costs me nothing being admitted to the benefit of clergy—that the very covers which save my using my own paper when I write you letters cost me the same, the printer refusing to take any thing for them—that I have no further service for it when I have lookt over it—& that Mumford the Postman takes it every monday at my door in his way to Providence. The sending it serves as an amusement & relaxation on a day when from the work of the preceeding I am unfitted for close application.

The Friendship You discover in your second paragraph, for with me it shall not pass for mere politeness, calls for the warmest returns; & added to the pleasure with which I was feasting my mind, in the contemplation that through the aide of a Boston Merchant fully conversant with the business I had procured a quintal of the best fish that Marblehead afforded, & which only waited an opportunity of being put on board for Alexandria for your Excellency's table. It is to go by the first ship that offers which I expect will be ere this can get to Mount Vernon. Whenever received view it as a small tribute, the mite of affection for services done to an insignificant individual, a rising & growing country, & the rights & liberties of mankind. I formed my purpose of thus expressing my gratitude, when I heard you while at dinner speak in praise of salt fish.[2]

Mrs McCauly Graham expressed her obligation to you, upon

reading the paragraph respecting her. Mrs Haley is at Newport.[3] You will have my wishes & prayers for your safety & success, whenever you put your pack saddles upon the beasts of burden & proceed upon your western expedition. That the class of settlers should pay more attention to convenience than right, is not to be so much wondered at, as that men in a superior form should have paid off their bonds to You for hard cash with depreciated notes at the rate of about a shilling in the pound, & at a period when You was hazarding your life for their liberties & property. But numbers have pretended great patriotism, while they have been destitute of common honesty, & were aiming only at private interest under the mask of public virtue. Thus it has been in all countries & in all ages; & the more the pity.

Your family, I judge, is increased by the presence of the Marquis. My most respectful compliments to him. You wished to get rid of all your Negroes, & the Marquis wisht that an end might be put to the slavery of all of them. I should rejoice beyond measure could your joint counsels & influence produce it, & thereby give the finishing stroke & the last polish to your political characters. Could it not be contrived that the industrious among them might be turned into copy-holders on the lands of their present masters, & by having a special interest in the produce of their labors be made ⟨*mutilated*⟩ more profit than at present? A⟨nd c⟩ould not this in its consequences excite the lazy to exertions ⟨tha⟩t might prove highly beneficial? I am not for letting them all loose upon the public; but am for gradually releasing them & their posterity from bonds, & incorporating them so in the states, that they may be a defence & not a danger upon any extraordinary occurrence.

Mrs Gordon unites in best wishes for your Excellency, your Lady, Dr Stewart & Lady, the grandchildren, Mr & Mrs L. Washington. When you see him pray remember me to Dr Craik. With the ⟨sincerest⟩ regard I remain my Dear Sir Your affectionate friend & humle Servt

William Gordon

ALS, DLC:GW.

1. Letter not found.

2. Gordon was at Mount Vernon earlier in the summer reading GW's papers. See source note, Gordon to GW, 8 Mar. 1784. On 6 Dec. 1785 GW

thanked Gordon for another "present of Fish," noting they had "a more successful passage than the last," which never arrived at Mount Vernon. See GW to Gordon, 20 Dec. 1784.

3. Catherine Sawbridge Macaulay Graham (1731–1791), author of the celebrated *History of England, from the Accession of James I to That of the Brunswick Line*, published in eight volumes between 1763 and 1783, visited Mount Vernon with her young husband in June 1785. Mary Haley was the widow of the London merchant George Haley.

To Jean Le Mayeur

Sir,   [Mount Vernon] 30th Augt 1784

Your letter of the 14th accompanying the horse for little Washington came safe. It is not in my power to describe his delight, which is the best proof of his thanks to you—he finds beauty in every part, & tho' shy at first, he begins now to ride with a degree of boldness which will soon do honor to his horsemanship.

Mrs Washington & all the family join me in best wishes for you. Mrs Lund Washington has added a daughter to her family—Miss Bassett is on a visit to her friends in the lower parts of this State—& I shall set off tomorrow on a tour to the Western Country. I shall always be happy to hear from you, & only wish for opportunities to make you amends for the attentions you have shewn me. This letter will be handed to you by the Marqs de la Fayette to whom I have mentioned you as one to whom I am under obligations. I am Sir, &c.

G: Washington

LB, DLC:GW.

To Stephen Sayre

Sir   Mount Vernon 1st Septemr 1784

The round of company in which I have constantly been, & other circumstances since I had the honor to receive your favor of the 20th ulto, induced me (indeed obliged me) to postpone from day to day, my answer, until the period has now arrived when I can do no more than give it a bare acknowledgment, being in the very act of setting out for the Western Country.[1] I could not depart however without thanking you for the sentiments you have conveyed respecting the mode for extending the inland navigation of Potomac. I have not time to be explicit in giving you mine—it shall be the subject of conversation when I return; in the mean while it would give me pleasure to hear that you are disposed to submit your plan to the public. My wish is that the public should be possessed of every scheme that has a promising tendency, that [they] may adopt the best, after a just comparison of them. The period is arrived when something ought, and I presume will be undertaken.[2] I am Sir &c. &c.

G: Washington

LB, DLC:GW.

1. GW left Mount Vernon with Dr. James Craik on 1 Sept. for his journey into Pennsylvania. There he visited his property at Washington's Bottom and at Chartiers Creek, or Millers Run, among other places, before giving up his plans to go down the Ohio in order to inspect his landholdings on that river and on the Great Kanawha. GW wrote very few letters during the trip, which lasted from 1 Sept. to 4 Oct., but he did keep a journal. The journal, with the editors' extensive notes, in *Diaries*, 4:1–71, provides a detailed record of GW's movements and activities. See also GW's cash accounts for September 1784 in Ledger B, 199–200. GW and Craik were joined by GW's nephew Bushrod Washington and by Craik's son William, who accompanied them into Pennsylvania.

2. GW is referring to Sayre's letter of 20 Aug., printed above.

From Joseph Wright

Phila. Septr 1st 84

J. Wrights respectful Compliments await Genrl Washington, and hopes he will not recollect how Long a Time has elapsed since this was to have been sent; as it was owing to its requiring some Alterations and there was no Bronze (the Stuff with which it is Covered) in America at that Time, He Begs Leave to assure Mrs Washington, that he has not forgot his Promise respecting the Large Bust, but hopes she will be as kind in excusing his delay, as she has been generous in her Frienship, and Promoting his Attempt.[1]

AL, DLC:GW.

1. GW wrote Wright on 30 Jan. 1785 that this card along with the bust did not arrive until December. During the summer of 1784 Wright worked on a full-size bust of GW for Congress as well as on the small one for GW. Under the terms of an act of Congress of 7 Aug. 1783 providing for a statue of GW, Wright had been commissioned to "take a resemblance" of the General. The

"resemblance" for Congress was cast in plaster, and on 5 Dec. 1784 Wright wrote Charles Thomson that he had "Compleated the Bust of his Excellency General Washington, without any further accident." He also told Thomson that for the sake of the public he had "with permission of the President, put it up in the Council room [in Philadelphia], in order that they may be gratified in Viewing it" (DNA:PCC, item 78). On 20 Jan. 1785, Wright presented Congress with a charge of fifty guineas for the completed work. See Wright to Charles Thomson, 20 Jan. and 28 Mar. 1785, and Thomson's report to Congress of 1 April, DNA:PCC, item 19. For the provenance and photographs of the busts of GW by Joseph Wright, see Fabian, *Wright*, 108–14.

To Daniel Morgan

Dr Sir,   [Berkeley County, Va.] 4th Septembr 1784.
  Colo. Kennedy has owed me £28 these many years. Enquiring yesterday where he lived—& into his circumstances—I was told that he had lately sold land or houses in Winchester, to you; & that it might be in your power to obtain the balance which appears upon the enclosed accot due to me.[1] If this should be the case, you would very much oblige me, as the money has been long due & I have always found it very difficult to get any from him. I am Dr Sir &c.

                                        G: Washington

LB, DLC:GW.
  1. GW arrived at Happy Retreat, the house of his brother Charles in Berkeley County, during the late morning on 3 September. The main purpose of his visit was to deal with his tenants in the county, with whom he had had no direct dealings since before the war. He also seized the opportunity to visit with the gentlemen in the neighborhood, including General Morgan, to discuss what should be done about improving navigation on the Potomac River. GW's tenant David Kennedy, who began renting a farm on GW's Bullskin land in 1766, had owed GW £28, one year's rent, since 1774 (see Cash Accounts, March 1767, n.4, and Ledger B, 22). The text of the note to Kennedy that GW enclosed is: "You would oblige me by paying the Balle of the enclosed Acct to General Morgan." Dated 4 Sept., it is in GW's hand and signed by him. It is privately owned. Morgan replied on 30 Sept. that he had paid Kennedy "long since" but would try to collect from him for GW. Kennedy did pay the £28 in October.

To Edward Snickers

Dr Sir,   Berckeley [Va.] 4th Septr 1784
  Several persons have been with me this day to rent the Land I bought at the sale of Colo. George Mercer's Estate; but I find it

is essential that some one, or more of them, should engage for the whole rent; or, that I should delay renting it until the Land can be divided to the best advantage—so as that each Lot may have water, & a proportionate quantity of good Land. for these reasons I mean to avail myself of the kind offer you made me yesterday, of letting the two Lots (I bought as above) to the best advantage on my behalf.[1]

Enclos'd is a plan of the Land wch may be some guide for you.[2] I have told Williams who is a liver on one of the lots, that I have no objection to his having an hundred acres or more, provided he will give as much as another, & the laying it off does not hurt the other part. As to the rents, I suppose the same which Mr Burwell has, must govern—to wit—ten pounds & the Taxes, for each 100 acres[3]—in other respects, my printed leases, one of which I enclose you, are to be shewn to the Tenants, & must be *your* rule & *their* terms[4]—I do not mean to give Leases for lives; indeed I do not incline to exceed ten years: but if it shou'd be thought by the tenants, & this should be your opinion also, that ten years is too short to make the buildings & other improvments which are required by the printed copy I send you, I would lengthen them to 14 years.

There is one thing I think it necessary to caution you upon: my object being to have my Lands improved by an industrious class of reputable people, I would not lease any of them to persons who do not mean to reside thereon; or to those who have lands adjoining—because in either case I should expect to have my land hard worked (perhaps totally ruined), without those aids or improvements which are to be expected from residents, whose convenience & comfort wou'd call for many things, which never would be furnished Negro Quarters.[5]

After you have done the needful, & hear of my return home, I shall thank you for information respecting this business. I am Dr Sir &c.

G: Washington

LB, DLC:GW; printed (incomplete), Maggs Brothers catalog, no. 576, item 169, 1932.

1. Lots 5 and 6 which GW bought at the Mercer sale in November 1774 were on the Shenandoah River near Snickers's home and ordinary. See Snickers to GW, 17 May 1784, n.3.

2. GW's "plan" has not been found.

3. John Williams on 16 Dec. 1785 signed a lease for 100 acres, the lease to run for twenty-six years from the beginning of 1782 at an annual rental of £10. See GW to Battaile Muse, 16 Dec. 1785. Nathaniel Burwell (1750–1814) of Carter's Grove, James City County, later built and lived in Carter Hall at Millwood in Berkeley County.

4. A number of GW's leases on printed forms have survived and are in DLC:GW.

5. This paragraph and the preceding one appear in the Maggs Brothers catalog. The only substantial difference between the printed and letter-book texts is that the printed text has "for Negro Plantations" instead of "Negro Quarters."

Certificate for James Rumsey

[Bath, Va., 7 September 1784]

I have seen the model of Mr Rumsey's Boats constructed to work against stream; have examined the power upon which it acts; have been an eye witness to an actual experiment in running water of some rapidity; & do give it as my opinion (altho' I had little faith before) that he has discovered the art of propelling Boats, by mechanism & small manual assistance, against rapid currents: that the discovery is of vast importance—may be of the greatest usefulness in our inland navigation—&, if it succeeds, of which I have no doubt, that the value of it is greatly enhanced by the simplicity of the works; which when seen & explained to, might be executed by the most common Mechanic's.[1]

Given under my hand at the town of Bath, county of Berkeley in the State of Virga this 7th day of September 1784.

G: Washington

LB, DLC:GW. Another copy of GW's original certificate, which Rumsey sent to Gov. Benjamin Harrison, is in Governor's Letter Book no. 5, Nc-Ar. A contemporary copy, now in MdAN, was printed on 9 Oct. 1784 in the *Virginia Gazette or, American Advertiser* (Richmond) with these words of introduction: "By the following Certificate it will appear, that our beloved General, in his retreat from the Glories of the Field, still continues to encourage, and pay attention to, such undertakings as are pregnant with great utility to his country."

1. In his journal on 6 Sept., GW describes at some length viewing the operation of James Rumsey's model at Bath in Frederick County (see *Diaries*, 4:9–10). A sketch of the mechanical boat that "walked on the bottom of shallow streams" is reproduced there on page 9. See also GW's correspondence with Rumsey in 1785.

From John Rumney, Jr.

Sir   Whitehaven [England] 8th Septr 1784
Having only arrivd a few Days ago, I have not opportunity of communicating to your Excellency as I could wish, the Particulars of the Enquiries you were pleas'd to honor me with. You may rely, Sir, on my Diligence in executing your Commission & giving you the earliest Advice. I have wrote to Newcastle abt a Bricklayer, that Place furnishing Mechanicks in that Branch preferable to any other in those Parts.[1] As we shall have a Ship sailing in Jany for Alexandria I hope to send both by her. I write this by the Hope Ct. Cragg a fine new Ship, which my Partners & I send out, to Potomack. in which Vessel my Friend & Partner Mr Robt Sanderson goes, I shall esteem it a particular Favor, your Excellency's honoring him with your Notice.[2] I sincerely thank *you*, Sir, & Mrs Washington for the genteel Present of Sea Stock sent me off by your Boat.[3] I remain with the greatest Esteem & Respect Your Excellency's most oblig'd & h'ble Servt

John Rumney

ALS, DLC:GW.
   1. For GW's request to Rumney to locate flagstones and artisans for him in England, see GW to Rumney, 3 July 1784.
   2. Robert Sanderson had dinner with GW at Mount Vernon as early as 12 June 1785 and last dined there a year later, on 4 June 1786, before crossing the Potomac "on his way to embark at Leonard town, Saint Marys, for England" (*Diaries*, 4:341).
   3. See GW to John Rumney, Sr., 5 July 1784.

From Rochambeau

My Dear General   Paris the 9th September 1784.
I have the honour of Sending to you the new promotion Which has been done lately for the order of Cincinnatus according to the resolutions of the last meeting of the general Society.[1] I also inclose in it the copy of a letter from M. le Mal de segur bearing the permission of his majesty for these new aggregated. you will See by it, at the Same time, that his majesty Stops all kind of farther demand, Which will disingage you, my Dear General, of great many demands Which certainly have been very troublesome to you.[2]

I profit With the liveliest pleasure of all—these opportunities for giving to you the new assurances of the respect and inviolable attachment With Which I am my Dear General, Your most obedient and Very humble servent

le cte de Rochambeau

the Prince henry, Brother of the King of Prussia Which has dined at my house has Seen your Picture with great pleasure.[3]

LS, DLC:GW. There are two signed copies of this letter, both in English and in the same hand, and two copies of each of the enclosed translations: (1) the "promotion" of new members of the Society of the Cincinnati and (2) the letter from Ségur to Rochambeau. The accent marks in Rochambeau's letter printed here have been omitted.

1. Rochambeau's "List of the officers Which have been promoted to the rank of Colonel since their Return from america" (DLC:GW) includes the names of twenty-three men, all of whom became original members of the French Society of the Cincinnati. See Hume, *Society of the Cincinnati*, 207–8.

2. The translation of Ségur's letter of 28 Aug. 1784 informed Rochambeau that Louis XVI "Will permit no more for the future that any of his subjects be yet admitted in it [the Cincinnati]. as it appears that you, Sir, and M. le Count d'Estaing have been look'd upon by the Général Washington as the chiefs of this Society in Europe, I refer it to you to make him an answer conform to the dispositions of his majesty" (DLC:GW).

3. GW gave the life-size, three-quarter-length portrait by Charles Willson Peale to Rochambeau before he returned to France in 1783. On 25 Nov. 1784 GW acknowledged from Mount Vernon the receipt of this letter from "my dear Count" in these terms: "Your favor of the 9th of Septr, enclosing the copy of a letter from the Marqs de Segar, is this moment received.

"The repeated instances of the honor, conferred on the Society of the Cincinnati by His most Christn Majesty's indulgent recognition of it, is highly flattering to the Order; and merits the most grateful acknowledgements of all its members.

"The pleasure with which you say Prince Henry of Prussia viewed my Picture at your house, is very flattering. I can never too often assure you of my affectionate regard . . ." (ALS, DLC: Rochambeau Papers). There is also a letter-book copy (DLC:GW).

From Kersaint

Sir   york. [Va.] 12 Sept. 1784

It is with every imaginable Regret that I renounce representing in person to your Excellency, the Lettre which I have the honor of addressing to you[1]—Charged by the King to visit these States at the head of a Squadron, I considered as the highest Satisfaction connected with this mission, that of finding myself within the reach of presenting to your Excellency the homage of the Military Marine of France, and my Respect, and my particular Admiration—Adverse causes oblidge me to quit this Bay without having enjoyed that honor,[2] and to quit America without having satisfied My most lively Desire, that of assuring your Excellency in Person of my Veneration & of the Respectful Sentiments with which I am Sir your Excellency's most Humble and most obt Servant—

Translation, DLC:GW; ALS, NHi: Naval History Society Collection. For a transcription of the ALS in French, see CD-ROM:GW.

1. Among these letters was one from Gimat, dated 12 July, introducing Kersaint to GW.

2. GW wrote from Mount Vernon on 25 Nov.: "I regret exceedingly that my absence from home should have happened at a time when you intended me the honor of a visit. I shall consider the tour I made, on that account, as unfortunate. If the orders of your Prince, or a desire to see these shores again, should ever bring you into this Country, I pray you to be assured of the pleasure I should feel in the honor of a visit from you. For the favourable sentiments you are pleased to express for me, you have a claim upon my gratitude" (LB, DLC:GW).

From La Luzerne

Sir. Paris September 12th 1784.

I flatter myself that the distance in which I live now from you has not lessened the esteem and Confidence with which you have been constantly pleased to honor me. I should think myself very fortunate if the future incidents of my Life could afford me an opportunity to receive new proofs of your Kindness and of your Friendship.

The first moments I passed with my Countrymen were employed in remembring the great events which have rendered your Excellency as dear to the French Nation as to your Fellow Citizens. The King, the Queen and the King's Brothers expressed their desire to be acquainted with the circumstances of a Life which has so much contributed to the liberty of your Country to whom we are sincerely attached. You may judge by this how happy these Princes would be to see you for some time at their Court. They wished that I would give them in this respect motives of greater expectation than those to which you have been pleased to authorise me and I really felt some pain to have it not in my power to gratify their anxiety.

I suppose that you receive too exactly the current European news as to render it necessary for me to entertain you of public affairs. Peace and tranquillity seem to be perfectly established, the Eastern troubles[1] are appeased at least for some time and I hope that we shall enjoy the fruits of the auspicious peace to which Your ability has so much contributed. England alone could interrupt this happy State of affairs but the interior dissensions in which she is involved must necessarily limit her ambition and I see in this moment no danger from her side.

I have met here with several of the French Officers who have served under your command. Their respect and esteem for you is unbounded. Their satisfaction would be perfect if they could see you in their Country. These are really the wishes of the French nation at large of which I am only the interpreter in repeating the general desire of my Countrymen. The advantage I have over them to have lived in your Society renders still more lively my desire to see you in France and to give you new assurances of the Sentiments of veneration and respect, with which I have the honor to be Sir Your Excellency's Most obedient and very humble servant,

                                        le che. de la luzerne

LS, DLC:GW.

1. La Luzerne is probably referring to the Turks' apparent acquiescence in the annexation of the Crimea by Catherine of Russia in 1783.

From Battaile Muse

Honorable Sir,   Sept. 12th 1784
I have been Informed that you have a Considerable Sum of money due in Berkeley Frederick and Fauquier Counties from your Tenants—altho a Very disagreeable Office—I beg leave to solicit your Favour in Leting me have the Collection It being Convenient with Colo. Fairfax's Collection As I attend the Courts and Sheriffs through which channel I expect some of the business will Pass[.] I am Oblig'd Frequently at Belvoir when I could make returns of the business.[1] Should you think Proper to Intrust me with the business I shall be Very Perticular

in attending to your Commands for a Proof of which I refur
you To your Brother Colo. Charles Washington the Two Mr
Mercers and my General Character in business of that nature. I
have the Honour to be Sir your Most Obedient Humble servant
                                                    B. Muse

ALS, DLC:GW.
    1. Although Muse gives no indication here of having received any commu-
nication from GW, a letter dated 4 Sept. 1784 from GW to Muse was advertised for sale in 1892 in Thomas Birch's catalog no. 683. A letter of that date
would have been written during the time that GW was seeing about his tenants in Berkeley County, where Muse was living. GW did not answer this letter of 12 Sept. until 3 Nov., explaining that it had not come to hand until "a
few days ago." At that time GW hired Muse who became GW's agent for his
tenanted lands in Frederick, Fauquier, Berkeley, and Loudoun counties.

From John Woddrop

                                            Glasgow [Scotland]
Sir,   Thursday the 16th day of September, 1784.
    I having done myself the honour for to write to your Excel-
lency on the 27th of July the last year, and to transmit along
therewith a list of the different Manufacturies in the linen
branch of bussiness in Scotland,[1] and as I did do so with a vow
to be of some use to the States of America, and also to serve the
Mississippi Company, of which Company my brother Robert
Woddrop, late factor & Merchant at Wiccocomica in Northum-
berland County in the State of Virginia, was a Member[2]—I now
do myself the honour to write to you at this time, and I do accompany the same with a letter from Thomas Ogden, Esquire,
a very a considerable trader in the Woollen Manufactury, which
Gentleman appearing to be very willing to be introduced into a
connection with your Excellency and with the other Gentlemen
who compose the Mississippi Company, and as I presume that a
person of Mr Ogdens General, & Fair, & Fine Charractor,
being of a very amiable & a just and most Honorable Char-
racter, as well as of great knowledge and of the most approven
abilities, & Competent in the line of the branch of the Woollen
&ca Manufactury, & whose house furnishes all the most approven & respectable houses in Great Britain with Woollen
Goods, and also foreign places, as will appear by his letter, now

sent to your Excellency herewith, which is dated the 4th of the last month,[3] and accompanying the same you have also a Number of Paterns of that Gentleman's Manufactury, and I presume that your Excellency, & your friends, will be the better able to form a true knowledge of which part of such paterns will answer with you, if this should be of any use to the States of America, in General, or to your own connections &ca and meet the Approbation thereof, I will hold myself happy in having done so.[4] At the same time, I am still ready to continue any farther tender of my services to the States of America, in General, & cheerfully, and most willingly to become a Citizen of these States, and if your Excellency & your friends approve of this offer, I will come out to these States in the Course of the next year, please God I am alive till then. I hope that neither that Country that Adopts me, nor that Country that give me birth, will ever need to be ashamed of me. The Manufacturers in the White Linen branch of bussiness and of the Lawn Muslin, Silk Gauze, & printed Linens, Fustains, &ca in this part of the Kingdom of Great Britain, and in many other places throughout Great Britain, are in a General ferment about the tax lately laid on these articles[.] Both the Master Manufacturers, Journymen, &ca and all who any manner or wise have their dependance on that branch of bussiness, cry down the tax, & all parts in this Country, wherein any Connection is with such a bussiness, are actually forming Committees to procure redress and a repail of that cursed tax, as they do all of them term it at Manchester in England, &ca. They are in a similar case & condition, and all of them reprobating the East India Compy whom they are naming the blood Suckers of the Poor in all parts of this country.[5] There Cursed tea, they say, shed the blood of our American friends &ca, and that having done all they could to extirpate millions of the Natives in the Regions of the East, they want to Compleat their Murders by a Starvation of many thousand of English & Scotch Weavers &ca. Theory is, in General, Anihilate that most abominable East India Company. Or Else let them be conveyed over to their brave friends & Country Men in America. I have Conversed with many of them since the Wednesday Evening of the twenty Eight day of July last, this very present year, on which evening a Great and a numerous multitude of these manufacturers did assemble in the Park, or the Green, of this City, but our Lord Provost, (Patrick Colquhoun, Esqr.) found means to pacify them on that evening. In this Country there is appearance of a plentiful harvest, but it's thought it will be late about this part of our Country.[6]

Any answer to this letter your Excellency may think proper for to send to me from your Most Worthy & Most Inestimable Person, or any otherwise you do me the honour to hear from your Excellency, will be received by me with all the due respectfulness such a honour is intitled to. With due respect, I have the honour to be, Sir, your Most obedient, And your Most Humble Servant

John Woddrop.

ALS, DLC:GW. The numerous and meaningless commalike marks in the manuscript have been omitted. Woddrop enclosed this letter and a letter to Francis Lightfoot Lee in a letter to Charles Thomson, secretary of Congress, on 6 Oct. 1784 (DLC:GW). Woddrop listed thirty-nine Marylanders and Virginians, former members of the Mississippi Company, to any of whom the letters could be delivered if Lee and GW were dead. On 30 Oct. 1784 Woddrop wrote Charles Thomson that in a letter to Thomson of 25 Oct. he had sent "some inclosures" for GW, which have not been found (DNA:PCC, item 78).

John Woddrop was a longtime tobacco merchant living at Springbank outside Glasgow.

1. The letter of 27 July 1783 has not been found. Only two other letters from Woddrop to GW, those of 25 Aug. 1785 and 29 Oct. 1788, are known to have survived, even though, as those two letters indicate, Woddrop often wrote GW in the 1780s about Scottish products and Scottish emigration to America. No letter from GW to Woddrop has been found, and no evidence has been found that he did respond to any letter from Woddrop, which would have been uncharacteristic.

2. For the Mississippi Land Company, see Mississippi Land Company Articles of Agreement, 3 June 1763, and Mississippi Land Company's Memorial to the King, 9 Sept. 1763, both printed above. GW and John Woddrop's brother Robert (d. 1767) were among the organizers of the company in Virginia in 1763.

3. Thomas Ogden's letter to John Woddrop of 4 Aug. 1784, written from Sarum, England, reads in part: "I am much obliged for your kind intention towards me in the Glove-way, they was articles We never dealt in—the best Market I should suppose Worcester ⟨*illegible*⟩ in Somersetshire—I shall be happy to serve you, in getting Information, and as I should be proud to unite with so respectable a Company, with that great worthy, & inestimable Character Genl Washington, at the head. I beg leave to offer my Services in any line & permit me to say it is in no Mans Power in the Kingdom, to do Business so in the *general* way, better and in the *woollen* branch in particular *so well*[.] The

Patterns, which I hope ere this you have recd will be suffict to shew You their quality & fitness for the Connection You are engaged in—Our American Connection, is principally in the north part. Messrs Smiths, Broad Street, have apply'd to Us for a Philadelphia Connection—Kirkman Holmes for New York. 3 Weeks ago We sent a large Cargo for Halifax Nova Scotia. We have another large Order to send off this Week. Sr Jas Harris, Ambassadr to the Hague, We have every Reason to hope will serve Us in holland.

"Just at the breaking out of the American War—I was made Agent for a Company at New York, Jersey &c. Robt Ogden, Esqr.[,] Amos Ogden, Esqr. late Colonel of the Jersey Corps, (He was in England, with me some time) Mr Stewart &c., at the head of it, which the accursed War by which I have lost 5,000, settled Acres in Florida put an end to. I had the Honor of Mr Hancocks Brother in law—Mr Langston Delegate for Portsmouth, Mason ⟨and his agent⟩, at my house for some days, during the War. I have good Connections likewise in the East & West Indies—His Excellency the Governor of Barbados—did me the Honor to appoint me his Secretary—and still continues his Sollicitations, in short, I may say no Person hath a more *universal* acquaintance & Connection; & I have the vanity to think, few Persons are more universally esteemed, and if I have the pleasure of being connected with Mr Woddropp & Co: I shall in every transaction study to deserve their good opinion" (DLC:GW).

4. In an enclosed memorandum Woddrop wrote: "Four Papers, containing Paterns, are put up, & inclosed herein, vizt: No. 1—Contains 25 Paterns of cloth, 27 & 29 inches Broad.

"No. 2—Contains 5 Paterns of Swan downs, & Clothes.

"No. 3—Contains 18 Paterns of Superfine Salisbury Flannels, 14 Nails Broad.

"No. 4—Contains 2 Paterns.

"In all 50 different Paterns."

One small sample of the cloth survives in DLC:GW.

5. Between 1781 and 1784 reform of the East India Company was a major issue in parliamentary politics. Warren Hastings would soon give up his position as governor of the company and return to Britain.

6. Patrick Colquhoun (1745–1820) returned to Scotland in 1766 from Virginia where for six years he had been engaged in trade. He settled in Glasgow, and in 1782 and 1783 he was elected lord provost of the city. Colquhoun was an effective champion of Glasgow trade and of cotton manufactures. In 1789 he moved to London and became a noted publicist and reformer.

Letter not found: from Benjamin Harrison, 17 Sept. 1784. On 10 Oct. GW wrote Harrison: "I had the pleasure to receive your favor of the 17th ulto."

To Thomas Freeman

Sir,   [23 September 1784]
   The situation of my affairs on the Western Waters in the State
of Pennsylvania & Virginia, requireing a Superintendant; &
you having been pleased to accept the appointment, I must beg
leave to point out to you the performance of such duties as are
particularly necessary.
   These will be to settle Tenants upon my Land; collect the
rents which will arise therefrom—the Debts which will proceed
from the sale of my copartnership effects—such others as may
be due to me from persons living as above; and in general, to
act & do (where no particular instruction is given) in the same
manner as you would for yourself under like circumstances;
endeavouring in all cases by fair & lawful means to promote my
interest in this Country.
   My Land on the Ohio & Great Kanhawa will be rented on the
terms contained in a printed advertisement herewith given
you; & as my disbursements will be great, I should prefer the
last mentioned therein, to the other two—as the *immediate*
profit arising therefrom is greatest[1]—It is my *wish* also that
each tract cou'd be rented on the same tenure, tho' I do not *bind*
you thereto.
   The remainder of my untenanted Lands in the tract commonly called & distinguished by the name of Washington's bottom, may be rented on the best terms you can obtain, until the
close of the year one thousand seven hundred and ninety
four—and no longer.[2] Less than what I am to get from the
other Tenants on the same tract (after allowing them three
years free from the payment of rent) I should not incline to
take: More I think ought to be had, & may be got.
   My tract at the Great Meadows may be rented for the most
you can get, for the term of ten years: there is a house on the
premises—arable land in culture, & meadow inclosed; much of
the latter may be reclaimed at a very moderate expence; which,
and its being an excellent stand for an Inn-keeper, must render
it valuable.[3]
   All my rents are to be fixed in specie Dollars (Spanish coin);
but may be discharged in any Gold or Silver coin of equivalent
value: the Tenants in all cases are to pay the Land-tax, which, to

prevent disputes, is to be expressed in the Leases; and it will be a necessary part of your duty to visit them at proper & convenient periods, to see that the Covenants, to the performance of which they are bound, are strictly fulfilled & complied with.

Where acts of providence interfere to disable a Tenant, I would be lenient in the exaction of rent; but when the cases are otherwise, I will not be put off; because it is on these that my own expenditures depend—& because an accumulation of undischarged rents is a real injury to the Tenant.

In laying off & dividing any of the Lands herein mentioned into Lots & tenements; particular care must be had that they are accurately surveyed—properly bounded—& so distributed as to do equal justice to the several Grantees, & to the Grantor—that a few may not injure the whole; & spoil the market of them.

If you should not have offers in a short time for the hire of my Mill alone, or for the Mill with 150 acres of land adjoining; I think it adviseable in that case to let it on shares; to build a good & substantial Dam of Stone where the old one stood—& to erect a proper forebay in place of the trunk which now conducts the water to the wheel—and, in a word, to put the House in proper repair. If you should be driven to this for want of a tenant; let public notice thereof be given, & the work let to the lowest bidder; the undertaker finding himself, & giving Bond & security for the performance of his contract. The charge of these things must be paid out of the first monies you receive for rent, or otherwise.

If I could get fifteen hundred pounds for the Mill & one hundred acres of Land most convenient thereto, I would let it go for that money.[4]

As a compensation for the faithful performance of all these services, I agree to allow you five pr Ct for all the money which shall be collected & paid to me, or for my use; whether arising from rents, Bonds, Notes or open accounts; or from the sale of wheat or Flour taken for rents & converted into cash. Also twenty shillings Pennsa Curcy for every Tenant which shall be fixed on any of my Land, & who shall receive a Lease for the same on the terms mentioned: and the further sum of two dollars for every Lott which you shall lay off for such Tenants, together with such reasonable expences as may be incurred thereby. Given under my hand at the plantation of Mr Gilbert Simpson this 23d day of Septembr 1784.

G: Washington

Note—There are four stacks of Hay on the Plantation,[5] my sole property; & half of the grain to be disposed of for, & on my behalf—as also a young Stallion whose covering, or final sale I am to be benefitted by.

G: Washington

LB, DLC:GW. This document is out of place in the letter book.

GW wrote in his travel journal on 17 Sept., while at Gilbert Simpson's, that he had "Agreed this day with a Major Thomas Freeman to superintend my business over the Mountains, upon terms to be inserted in his Instructions" (*Diaries*, 4:25). Freeman, who was living at Red Stone in Pennsylvania, continued as GW's land agent in that region until he left for Kentucky in 1787 (see Freeman to GW, 18 Dec. 1786, and Ledger B, 233).

1. See GW's Advertisement: Ohio Lands, 10 Mar. 1784, printed above. For the advertisement of the land at Washington's Bottom, see GW to Thomas Richardson, 5 July 1784, n.3.

2. On 17 Sept. GW ended his partnership with Gilbert Simpson at Washington's Bottom. Tenants were living on a part of the land, but a renter, or renters, needed to be found for Simpson's own farm and for the mill.

3. For GW's holdings at Great Meadows in Pennsylvania, see GW to Thomas Richardson, 5 July 1784, n.3.

4. See note 2.

5. The "Plantation" is the farm that Gilbert Simpson developed and lived on.

From David Humphreys

My dear General   Paris Septr 30, 1784

I was obliged to close my last Letter of the 18th of Augst so abruptly that I had not even time to tell you how much satisfaction it would afford me, should I be able by my communications to contribute in any degree to your amusement or information, as you were pleased to intimate—permit me now to assure you, that the delightful employment of thus conversing with my dearest General, under the restrictions which his prudence has had the precaution to suggest, will always be my highest gratification—and permit me at the same time to request that the following preliminaries may be understood: that my inclination as well as duty will prompt me to the fullest disclosure of my feelings & observations which may consist with propriety & prudence; that you will not, however, in this correspondence

expect too much entertainment from Letters which must sometimes be written in haste & perhaps on nugatory subjects; that
you will in reading rather consider the intentions of the heart
which dictates than the abilities of the hand that writes; and
that you will impose it as a law upon yourself, not to be particular or to take any trouble in answering them but only by sometimes just repeating in three plain words that you still retain the
same sentiment of *friendship for me*, which your actions as well as
your words have taught me to believe existed in your breast.

And now that I am speaking of friendship, I will take the liberty of adding a few observations upon it—It seems to me that
purity of heart, congeniality of disposition, sympathy of feelings, & an ardent desire to promote the happiness of the parties
concerned are the constituents of this amiable passion; from
thence it follows that these requisites being in the mind, in-
equality of age or circumstances is by no means an insurmountable obstacle to the existence of it. On the contrary those who
have no objects of emulation or envy to obstruct the natural
current of affections may expect to meet more candor, more
disinterestedness, & more sincerity in each other; than those
who are rivals in the various pursuits of life, whose views & interests often counteract each other, & who must in consequence
view each others success with a jealous eye—happily nothing of
this kind can ever take place between us—your course of glory
is accomplished—you are safely landed in Port—& conscious I
am, that influenced by friendship alone, it is the first wish of my
heart to see some writer assume the pen, who is capable of placing your actions in the true point of light in which posterity
ought to view them. That there is no one better able to perform
this task than yourself, I am more & more convinced by reflecting on the subject myself as well from hearing the sentiments of
others upon it—I have even gone so far as to revolve in my own
mind the manner in which such a plan could be most happily
executed. This I think would be by arranging the various
Events into Campaigns, or particular Epochs—selecting from
your Orders, Letters & Documents, everything that is the most
interesting concerning these Events, either by extracting the
substance or inserting the whole of such Papers as tended most
to elucidate the Subject.[1] I am my Dear Genl with every sentiment of affection Your friend

D. Humphreys.

ALS, DLC:GW; ADf, CtY: Humphreys-Marvin-Olmsted Collection.
    1. For Humphreys' interest and subsequent involvement in the preparation of a biography of GW, see particularly Humphreys to GW, 15 July 1784, n.3.

From Daniel Morgan

Dr Sir   30th Septr 1784
    I was Honored with your letter Enclosing an accompt against David Keneday. He had drawn every Shilling from me Long since, and I fear the debt is in a bad way.[1] However I have kept the accompt & order, and If I can get by any barter or turn over so much in my hands I will secure it for you, and shall at the same time be happy to have it in my power to serve you and shall in future think myself Honored by any commands you chose to lay upon me. I have the honor to be with great regard your obedt Hble servt

                                            Danl Morgan

ALS, DLC:GW.
    1. See GW to Morgan, 4 September.

Letter not found: to John Preston, 1 Oct. 1784. On 6 Nov. Preston wrote GW: "In consequence of receiving your Excellency's favour dated Rockingham Octr 1st 84. . . ."

From James Craik

                        Mount Vernon Octr 2d 1784
    I have thought it might be more satisfactory to leave you the different Accounts I received respecting the Communication between the waters of the Yoheogany & the North Branch of Potowmack, that you might from a view of the whole Collect an opinion for yourself[1]—it appears to me that the land Carriage from the Forks of Yoheogany to Cumberland which from a variety of Accounts will not be more than thirty miles is to be preferred to Sixty miles of difficult Navigation up the little Crossing, and twenty miles land Carriage afterwards, which is the distance from the little Crossing on the Turkey foot Road to Cumberland—If the Communication is to be carried on by the little Crossing, the Turkey Foot Road is to be preferred to Braddocks old Road, as it is infinitely better and above two

miles shorter. Indeed I found the whole Turkey foot Road across the mountains much better & nearer than Braddocks Road, that if there were good entertainment no one could hesitate in the choice.

I delivered your letter to Colo. Stenson, who informed me he had a few day's before engaged his mare to Captn Tauneyhill, but offered me a horse Colt far above its value. He says he expects to be at Alexandria this month when he will endeavour to let you have some money. Colo. Bell will also be down & has promised to go and view the Falls of Yoheogany and report to you particularly on them[2]—On my arrival at Colo. Warner Washingtons I wrote to your Brother Charles who next day called on Mr Gaunt, when he informed him that he was still in the mind of purchasing the Land and requested that you would leave your terms in writing and that if they were not very high he would take the land upon your word he said he knew what you gave for it[3]—As you attend your Rout down I desird Bushrod to request him to come down to you as Soon as possible, which was his first intention. I have the Honour to be with the utmost Respect & affectn your Excellys Most obedt huml. Sert

Jas Craik

P.S. I have recd of Mr Lund Washington Twelve Pounds Seven Shillings & Sixpence being the Expences down, the General Account of Expences must be defer'ed untill I have the pleasure of Seeing you.

ALS, MnHi.

1. GW and Bushrod Washington parted from James Craik and his son William on 21 Sept., intending to rejoin them at Warner Washington's house in Frederick County. On 29 Sept. GW decided to return to Mount Vernon by way of Staunton in Augusta County and sent his nephew to tell Craik that he would not come to Warner Washington's. Craik then proceeded to Mount Vernon and left this letter there pending GW's return on 4 October.

2. The letter to John Stephenson, William Crawford's half brother, has not been found. Captain Tauneyhill may be John Tannehill who was living in Washington County, Pa., when the census was taken in 1790. Colonel Bell has not been identified.

3. This is probably John Gaunt of Berkeley County, who was named a justice of the peace for the county in the first state commission of 9 Dec. 1776.

Letter not found: from Edward Newenham, 2 Oct. 1784. On 20 Mar. 1785 GW wrote to Newenham: "I regret very much that your letters of the 2d & 13th of October should have been detained."

Letter not found: from Sarah Bomford, 8 Oct. 1784. On 15 Mar. 1785 GW wrote to her: "I have had the honor to receive your favor, & duplicate, of the 8th of Octor."

From Lafayette

My dear General   Albany October the 8th 1784

Every where I Have Met with delays—but so Agreable were they in their Nature that I Cannot Complain of them—it is not Quite the Case with the Indian treaty—Altho' the Hope to Be Useful Has kept me there longer than I Had Expected—my presence at the oppening of it Had Been desired—Many Circumstances kept it off—at last it Began, and My influence with the indians was found Greater than I myself Could Expect—I was therefore desired to Speak—to Hearken to Answers—I took the liberty to Caution the Commissioners Upon Such Points as You Had Mentionned me—and did not leave the Ground Untill they thought they Had No farther Occasion for me—But as the Business is just Begining, I Cannot Give you any farther Intelligence, But that Grat deal of intrigue is Carried on By some tory indians of Brant party, and that the Whigg and tory distinctions Are kept up Among those tribes to an Amazing degree of private Animosities.[1]

This day, My dear General, I am Going towards Hartfort, Boston, and Newport where the french ships Now are—and (as, if I went By land, I would Be So much kept of By my friends as to Be very late on our Appointed Meeting,) I intend Submitting Myself to the little Inconvenience of Going By Water from Rhode island to Williamsburg where I Hope to Be About the 26th and where I Will Be Happy to Receive the orders of My dear General.[2]

Waiting Upon the Assembly in Richmond, and Visiting frederisburg on My way to Mount Vernon would Be My plan—But Expect Your orders to know where I am to Meet You—it is possible You Had Rather Not Go to Richmond—in a word, My dear General, as Your Paternal goodness to me Cannot Stand Upon any Kind of Ceremony, Give me Your orders—tell me what I Had Best to do—and I Shall Be As You well know Happy to obey them.

One thing, My dear General, I Very much wish You Might

grant Me—as the time of my stay in Virginia will depend Upon Your Advice Respecting french letters which I am to Receive there, as it will Be then a last Visit for this American trip of Mine—I Will Be Happy My dear General, if without Inconvenience to Yourself You may Come with me So far, at least, as Philadelphia where Your friends depend Upon me to Have an Opportunity to See You.

Could You Pay the Virginia Visits With me, Could I meet You Some where, or Frederisburg I Suppose, where in that Case I would Go Before I visit Richmond, it Should be to me a most Heartfelt Happiness.

I Beg Your Pardon, My Beloved General, But I want to See You, and No Heart Can Better feel the pleasure to Be with You than the filial Heart of Your Respectfull and affectionate friend

lafayette

the chevalier Begs leave to Be most Respectfully presented to you[3]—We unite in Respects to Mrs Washington and Compliments to Mr Washington and Children—if you Hear from George, I Beg You will let me know it.

ALS, PEL. The reading of Lafayette's capitalization generally follows that in Idzerda, *Lafayette Papers*, 5:264–65.

1. For the peace congress that commissioners from Congress held at Fort Stanwix this month with representatives of the Six Nations, see Jacob Read to GW, 13 Aug. 1784, n.2.

2. Lafayette sailed in early November from Boston to Yorktown in Virginia aboard the French frigate *Nymphe*. See Lafayette to GW, 22 Oct., and notes.

3. The chevalier Maurice Riquet de Caraman was Lafayette's traveling companion.

Letter not found: from George Augustine Washington, 9 Oct. 1784. On 25 Nov. GW wrote to William Washington: "From a letter dated the 9th of last month from my Nephew Geo: Augte Washington. . . ."

To Benjamin Harrison

[10 October 1784]

EDITORIAL NOTE

GW's letter to Governor Harrison marks his return to public life as the leader of a movement to form a public company for improving the navigation of the upper Potomac and linking it with the waters of the Ohio. He first became deeply involved in schemes for opening up the Potomac in the early 1770s (see particularly the source note and its references in Thomas Johnson to GW, 18 June 1770). His determination to use the Potomac to tie the burgeoning transmontane West to the states along the Atlantic seaboard was renewed in the spring of 1784 after his return to Mount Vernon in his exchange of letters with Thomas Jefferson (see Jefferson to GW, 15 Mar., and GW to Jefferson, 29 Mar. 1784, and notes). One of the main purposes of GW's recent trip into Pennsylvania had been to confirm the feasibility of making the upper Potomac navigable and of linking it by means of short land portages with navigable streams flowing into the Ohio (see *Diaries*, 4:1−71). After writing this letter to Harrison on his return from the West, GW in the next few weeks also corresponded about the Potomac with, among others, Stephen Sayre, George Plater, Jacob Read, and Normand Bruce (see Sayre to GW, 15 Oct., Plater to GW, 20 Oct., GW to Plater, 25 Oct., GW to Read, 3 Nov., and Bruce to GW, 13 Nov.). On 2 Nov., presumably on GW's initiative, a notice was printed in the Alexandria newspaper calling for any gentlemen living "contiguous to Potomack" in both Virginia and Maryland who "wish to see an attempt made to open and extend the navigation of that River" to meet in Alexandria on 15 Nov. (the notice is quoted in note 4, GW to Read, 3 Nov.).

Before the meeting was held, at Lomax's tavern in Alexandria, GW left for Richmond, arriving there on 14 November. The purpose of his trip to the capital was to meet Lafayette and to persuade key members of the house of delegates, then in session, to adopt a scheme for forming a Potomac River company. (For GW's reception in Richmond, see the notes in GW's address to the Officials of the City of Richmond and to the Virginia House of Delegates, both 15 Nov.). Governor Harrison probably had given GW's letter of 10 Oct. to the house of delegates at the opening of its session, on 1 or 2 Nov., but there is no indication in its journals that the house took any action on the letter before GW's arrival (see Harrison to GW,

13 Nov., n.1). While in Richmond, GW discussed the Potomac River project with the leader of the house of delegates, James Madison, and with other members. He left on 21 or 22 Nov. with Lafayette for Mount Vernon.

A letter that Henry Lee wrote to GW from Alexandria on 15 Nov., the day of the "very numerous and respectable Meeting of the Gentlemen of this State and Maryland," has not been found, and Lee's letter of 18 Nov. enclosing the meeting's petition to the Virginia and Maryland legislature and its draft of a bill for forming a Potomac River company did not reach GW before he left Richmond. (A report on the meeting in Alexandria which appeared in the *Virginia Journal and Alexandria Advertiser* on 25 Nov. is printed in note 1, Lee to GW, 18 Nov.). After Lee's letter and the enclosed documents finally caught up with him at Mount Vernon, GW on 28 Nov. forwarded to Madison the draft bill and petition, neither of which has been found (see GW to Madison, 28 Nov., and particularly note 1 of that document).

Immediately after writing Madison on 28 Nov., GW left Mount Vernon with Lafayette for Annapolis where he conversed "with some of the leading characters in the different branches of the Legislature of Maryland, on the subject of inland navigation, and the benefits which might arise from a commercial intercourse with the Western Territory." GW "was happy to find them so forcibly struck with the importance of these objects; and that there appeared the most favorable disposition to give encouragement to them" (GW to Madison, 3 Dec.). His conversations with the leaders of the Maryland and Virginia legislatures confirmed GW in his opinion that he could not look to public funds to finance his great Potomac project, and so after his return from Annapolis on 2 Dec., he wrote Madison to urge that one or more members of the Virginia legislature be appointed to meet with a man or men chosen by the Maryland legislature for the purpose of devising a bill for creating a Potomac River company composed of private investors. The bill would be one that each of the legislatures could consider simultaneously and hence adopt before adjournment (see GW to Madison, 28 Nov., n.1, and 3 Dec.).

In the meantime, Madison had received GW's letter of 28 Nov. with the enclosed draft of a bill, and a committee of the house of delegates had begun work on a Potomac River bill, presumably based upon the (missing) bill drawn up by the Alexandria meeting on 15 November. The house canceled a scheduled debate on the committee's bill (also missing) after Madison received GW's letter of 3 Dec., and on 13 Dec.

the delegates adopted GW's suggestion that the legislature appoint commissioners to meet with Maryland commissioners and draft a Potomac River bill that could be immediately enacted by both legislatures (see GW to Madison, 28 Nov., n.1, and GW to Madison, 3 Dec., and notes).

The acting governor of Virginia, Beverley Randolph, wrote GW on 15 Dec. sending him resolutions of the Virginia legislature supporting the establishment of a Potomac River company and naming GW one of three commissioners to meet with Maryland commissioners to draft a Potomac River company bill (see note 1 in Beverley Randolph's letter). On 19 Dec. GW forwarded a letter to Gov. William Paca of Maryland about the proposed meeting, which Randolph had enclosed in his letter. GW also informed the other Virginia commissioners that the meeting with their Maryland counterparts in Annapolis had been set for 22 Dec. (see GW to Paca, 19 Dec., n.2, GW to Beverly Randolph, 20 Dec., and Thomas Blackburn to GW, 20 Dec.). GW met, alone for most of the time, with the four Marylanders, and in six days they drafted a Potomac River bill which GW forwarded to James Madison on 28 Dec. (see GW to Madison, 28 Dec., and notes, and GW and Horatio Gates to the Virginia Legislature, 28 Dec., and its three enclosures and notes).

GW's report of the proceedings in Annapolis and the drafted bill were given to the Virginia house of delegates on 31 Dec., and the next day William Grayson introduced in the house GW's Potomac River Company bill. The bill received its final passage on 4 Jan. (see Madison to GW, 1 Jan. 1785, and notes). An identical bill had been introduced on 27 Dec. in the Maryland legislature where it passed on 28 Dec. (see GW to Madison, 28 Dec., n.6). On 9 Jan., Madison wrote GW to inform him of the passage of the act creating the Potomac River Company and of a similar act creating the James River Company. He also enclosed a copy of the Potomac River Company act and copies of "several kindred measures" adopted by the Virginia legislature (see Madison's letter and notes and enclosures).

Upon the receipt on 17 Jan. of Madison's copy of the Potomac River Company act, GW had the two men who were named in the act to serve as managers in Alexandria; they were to compare the texts of the Virginia and Maryland acts and to have one hundred copies of the act printed (see GW to John Fitzgerald and William Hartshorne, 18 Jan. 1785, and Fitzgerald and Hartshorne to GW, 21 Jan. 1785). GW by this time also had received, to his dismay, notice from Speaker Benjamin Harrison and from Gov. Patrick Henry that the Virginia legislature had voted to give him fifty shares in the Potomac River

Company and one hundred in the James River Company (see note 1 and its references, Harrison to GW, 6 Jan. 1785). Before the end of the month, fearing that Gov. William Paca of Maryland had not been properly informed of the actions taken by Virginia with regard to the Potomac River Company, GW took it upon himself to write Paca and to send him a copy of the Virginia act (see GW to Paca, 31 Jan.).

At its first meeting in Alexandria on 17 May 1785, the Potomac River Company elected GW its president, a position he held until his election to the presidency of the United States under the new constitution in 1789. (An account of the meeting of May 1785 and of the action that its shareholders took is printed in note 1, GW to Thomas Johnson and Thomas Sim Lee, 18 May 1785). GW was to devote a great deal of time and attention for the next four years to the management of the company, the actual work of which got underway in the summer of 1785 (see GW to James Rumsey, 3 Aug. 1785, and *Diaries*, 4:170–81, and references).

Dear Sir,   Mount Vernon 10th October 1784

Upon my return from the western Country a few days ago, I had the pleasure to receive your favor of the 17th ulto[1]—It has always been my intention to pay my respects to you before the chance of *another* early & hard winter should make a warm fire side too comfortable to be relinquished. and I shall feel an additional pleasure in offering this tribute of friendship & respect to you, by having the company of the Marqs de la Fayette, when he shall have revisited this place from his Eastern tour; now, every day to be expected.[2]

I shall take the liberty now, my dear sir, to suggest a matter, which would (if I am not too short sighted a politician) mark your administration as an important œra in the Annals of this Country, if it should be recommended by you, & adopted by the Assembly.

It has been long my decided opinion, that the shortest, easiest & least expensive communication with the invaluable & extensive Country back of us, would be by one, or both of the rivers of this State which have their sources in the apalachian mountains.[3] Nor am I singular in this opinion—Evans, in his Map and Analysis of the middle Colonies which (considering the early period at which they were given to the public) are done with amazing exactness. And Hutchins since, in his topographical description of the Western Country, (good part of which is from actual surveys)—are decidedly of the same sentiments; as indeed are all others who have had opportunities, & have been at the pains to investigate, & consider the subject.[4]

But that this may not stand as mere matter of opinion or assertion, unsupported by facts (such at least as the best Maps now extant, compared with the oral testimony, which my opportunities in the course of the war have enabled me to obtain); I shall give you the different routs & distances from Detroit, by which all the trade of the North Western parts of the United territory, must pass;[5] unless the Spaniards, contrary to their present policy, should engage part of it; or the British should attempt to force nature by carrying the trade of the upper Lakes by the river Outawaies into Canada, which I scarsely think they will or could effect. Taking Detroit then (which is putting ourselves in as unfavourable a point of view as we can be well placed, because it is upon the line of the British territory) as a point by which, as I have already observed, all that part of the trade must come, it appears from the statement enclosed, that the tide waters of this State are nearer to it by 168 miles than that of the river St Lawrence; or than that of the Hudson at Albany by 176 miles.

Maryland stands upon similar ground with Virginia. Pennsylvania altho' the Susquehanna is an unfriendly water, much impeded it is said with rocks & rapids, & nowhere communicating with those which lead to her capital; have it in contemplation to open a communication between Toby's Creek (which empties into the Alleghany river, 95 miles above Fort Pitt) & the west branch of Susquehanna; & to cut a Canal between the waters of the latter, & the Schuylkill; the expence of which is easier to be conceived than estimated or described by me. A people however, who are possessed of the spirit of Commerce—who see, & who will pursue their advantages, may atchieve almost anything. In the meantime, under the uncertainty of these undertakings, they are smoothing the roads & paving the ways for the trade of that Western World. That New York will do the same so soon as the British Garrisons are removed; which are at present insurmountable obstacles in *their* way, no person who knows the temper, genius & policy of those people as well as I do, can harbour the smallest doubt.

Thus much with respect to rival States—let me now take a short view of our own; & being aware of the objections which are in the way; I will enumerate, in order to contrast them with the advantages.

The first & principal one is, the *unfortunate Jealousy*, which ever has & it is to be feared ever will prevail, lest one part of the State should obtain an advantage over the other part (as if the benefits of trade were not diffusive & beneficial to all)—then follow a train of difficulties viz:—that our people are already heavily taxed—that we have no money; that the advantages of this trade are remote; that the most *direct* rout for it is thro' *other* States, over whom we have no controul; that the routs over which we have controul, are as distant as either of those which lead to Philadelphia, Albany or Montreal; that a sufficient spirit of commerce does not pervade the Citizens of this Commonwealth; that we are in fact doing for others, what they ought to do for themselves.

Without going into the investigation of a question, which has employed the pens of able politicians, namely, whether trade with Foreigners is an advantage or disadvantage to a country. This State as a part of the confederated States (all of whom have the spirit of it very strongly working within them) must adopt it, or submit to the evils arising therefrom without receiving its benefits—common policy therefore points clearly & strongly, to the propriety of our enjoying all the advantages which nature & our local situation afford us; and evinces clearly that unless this spirit could be totally eradicated in other States, as well as in this, and every man made to become either a cultivator of the Land, or a manufacturer of such articles as are prompted by necessity, such stimulas should be employed as will *force* this spirit; by shewing to our Countrymen the superior advantages we possess beyond others; & the importance of being upon a footing with our Neighbours.

If this is fair reasoning, it ought to follow as a consequence, that we should do our part towards opening the communication with the fur & peltry trade of the Lakes; & for the produce of the Country which lies within; & which will, so soon as matters are settled with the Indians, & the terms on which Congress mean to dispose of the Land, & found to be favourable, are announced[6]—settle faster than any other ever did, or any one would imagine. This then when considered in an interested point of view, is alone sufficient to excite our endeavours; but in my opinion, there is a political consideration for so doing, which is of still greater importance.

I need not remark to you Sir, that the flanks & rear of the United States are possessed by other powers—& formidable ones, too; nor, how necessary it is to apply the cement of interest, to bind all parts of the Union together by indissoluble bonds—especially that part of it, which lies immediately west of us, with the middle States. For, what ties, let me ask, shou'd we have upon those people? How entirely unconnected with them shall we be, and what troubles may we not apprehend, if the Spaniards on their right, & Gt Britain on their left, instead of throwing stumbling blocks in their way as they now do, should hold out lures for their trade and alliance. What, when they get strength, which will be sooner than most people conceive (from the emigration of foreigners who will have no particular predilection towards us, as well as from the removal of our own Citizens) will be the consequence of their having formed close connexions with both, or either of those powers in a commercial way? It needs not, in my opinion, the gift of prophecy to foretell.

The Western settlers, (I speak now from my own observation) stand as it were upon a pivot—the touch of a feather, would turn them any way—They have look'd down the Mississippi, until the Spaniards (very impoliticly I think, for themselves) threw difficulties in their way; & they looked that way for no other reason, than because they could glide gently down the stream; without considering perhaps, the fatigues of the voyage back again, & the time necessary to perform it in: & because they have no other means of coming to us but by a long Land transportation & unimproved roads. These causes have hitherto checked the industry of the present settlers; for except the demand for provisions, occasioned by the increase of population, & a little flour which the necessities of Spaniards compel them to buy, they have no excitements to labour. But smooth the road once, & make easy the way for them, & then see what an influx of articles will be poured in upon us—how amazingly our exports will be encreased by them, & how amply we shall be compensated for any trouble & expence we may encounter to effect it.

A combination of circumstances makes the present conjuncture more favourable for Virginia, than for any other State in the Union, to fix these matters. The jealous & untoward disposition of the Spaniards on one hand, & the private views of some individuals, coinciding with the general policy of the Court of Great Britain, on the other, to retain as long as possible the Posts of Detroit, Niagara, Oswego &c. (which, tho' they are done under the letter of the Treaty, is certainly an infraction of the spirit of it, & injurious to the union) may be improved to the greatest advantage by this State; if she would open her avenues to the trade of that Country, & embrace the present moment to establish it—It only wants a beginning—the Western Inhabitants wou'd do their part towards its execution. weak as they are, they would meet us at least half way, rather than be *driven* into the arms of, or be made dependant upon foreigners; which would, eventually, either bring on a separation of them from us, or a War between the United States & one or the other of those powers—most probably with the Spaniards. The preliminary steps to the attainment of this great object, would be attended with very little expence; & might, at the same time that it served to attract the attention of the Western Country, & to convince the wavering Inhabitants thereof of our disposition to connect ourselves with them & to facilitate their commerce with us, would be a mean of removing those jealousies which otherwise might take place among ourselves.

These, in my opinion, are; to appoint Commissioners, who from their situation, integrity & abilities, can be under no suspicion of prejudice or predilection to one part more than to another. Let these Commissioners make an actual survey of James River & Potomack from tide water to their respective sources—Note with great accuracy the kind of navigation, & the obstructions in it; the difficulty & expence attending the removal of these obstructions; the distances from place to place thro' the whole extent; and the nearest & best Portages between these waters & the Streams capable of improvment which run into the Ohio; traverse these in like manner to *their* junction with the Ohio, & with equal accuracy—The navigation of this river (i.e. the ohio) being well known, they will have less to do in the examination of it; but nevertheless, let the courses & distances of it be taken to the mouth of the Muskingum, & up that river (notwithstanding it is in the ceded lands) to the carrying place with Cayahoga—down Cayahoga to Lake Erie, & thence to Detroit. Let them do the same with big Bever creek, although part of it is in the State of Pennsylvania; and with the Scioto also—In a word, let the Waters East & West of the Ohio, which invite our notice by their proximity, & the ease with which Land transportation may be had between them & the Lakes on one side, & the rivers Potomac & James on the other, be explored—accurately delineated, & a correct & connected Map of the whole be presented to the public. These things being done, I shall be mistaken if prejudice does not yield to facts; jealousy to candour—& finally, that reason & nature thus aided, will dictate what is right & proper to be done.

In the mean while, if it should be thought that the lapse of time which is necessary to effect this work, may be attended with injurious consequences, could not there be a sum of money granted towards opening *the best*, or if it should be deemed *more eligible*, two of the nearest communications, one to the Northward & another to the Southward, with the settlements to the westward? And an act be passed (if there should not appear a manifest disposition in the Assembly to make it a public undertaking) to incorporate, & encourage private Adventurers if any should associate & sollicit the same, for the purpose of extending the navigation of Potomac or James river? and, in the former case, to request the concurrence of Maryland in the measure—It will appear from my statement of the different routs (and as far as my means of information have extended, I have done it with the utmost candour) that all the produce of the settlements about Fort Pitt, can be brought to Alexandria by the Yohoghaney in 304 Miles; whereof only 31 is land transportation. And by the Monongahela and Cheat river in 360 miles; 20 only of which are land carriage. Whereas the common road from Fort Pitt to Philadelphia is 320 Miles, all Land transportation; or 476 miles, if the Ohio, Toby's Creek, Susquehanna & Schuylkill are made use of for this purpose: how much of this by land, I know not; but from the nature of

the Country it must be very considerable. How much the interests & feelings of people thus circumstanced would be engaged
to promote it, requires no illustration.

For my own part, I think it highly probable, that upon the
strictest scrutiny (if the Falls of the Great Kanhawa can be made
navigable, or a short portage had there)—it will be found of
equal importance & convenience to improve the navigation of
both the James & Potomac. The latter I am fully persuaded affords the nearest communication with the Lakes; but James
river may be more convenient for all the settlers below the
mouth of the Gt Kanhawa, & for some distance perhaps above,
& west of it: for I have *no* expectation that any part of the trade
above the falls of the Ohio will go down that river & the Mississippi, much less that the returns will ever come up them; unless
our want of foresight & good management is the occasion of it.
Or upon trial, if it should be found that these rivers, from the
before-mentioned Falls, will admit the descent of Sea vessels; in
which case, & the navigation of the former's becoming free, it is
probable that both vessels & cargoes will be carried to foreign
markets & sold; but the returns for them will never in the natural course of things, ascend the long & rapid current of that
river; which with the Ohio to the Falls, in their meanderings, is
little if any short of 2000 miles. Upon the whole, the object, in
my estimation is of vast commercial and political importance: in
these lights I think posterity will consider it, & regret (if our
conduct should give them cause) that the present favourable
moment to secure so great a blessing for them, was neglected.

One thing more remains, which I had like to have forgot, and
that is the supposed difficulty of obtaining a passage thro' the
State of Pennsylvania. How an application to its Legislature
would be relished, in the first instance, I will not undertake to
decide; but of one thing I am almost certain, such an application would place that body in a very delicate situation. There is
in the State of Pennsylvania at least 100,000 souls west of the
Laurel hill, who are groaning under the inconveniencies of a
long land transportation; they are wishing, indeed they are
looking for the improvement & extension of inland navigation;
& if this cannot be made easy for them, to Philada (at any rate it
must be lengthy), they will seek a Mart elsewhere—the conse-

quence of which would be, that the State, tho' contrary to the policy & interests of its Sea-ports, must submit to the loss of so much of its trade, or hazard not only the trade but the loss of the Settlement also: for an opposition on the part of Government to the extension of water transportation, so consonant with the essential interests of a large body of people, or any extraordinary impositions upon the exports or imports to, or from another State, would ultimately bring on a separation between its Eastern & Western Settlements—towards which, there is not wanting a disposition at this moment in that part of it, which is beyond the mountains.

I consider Rumsey's discovery for working Boats against stream, by mechanical powers (principally) as not only a very fortunate invention for these States in general, but as one of those circumstances which have combined to render the present epocha favourable above all others for fixing, if we are disposed to avail ourselves of them, a large portion of the trade of the Western Country in the bosom of this State irrevocably.[7]

Lengthy as this letter is, I intended to have written a fuller & more digested one, upon this important subject, but have met with so many interruptions since my return home, as almost to have precluded my writing at all—what I now give is crude; but if you are in sentiment with me, I have said enough; if there is not an accordance of opinion I have said too much, & all I pray in the latter case is, that you will do me the justice to believe my motives are pure, however erroneous my judgment may be on this matter, & that I am with the most perfect esteem & friendship Dr Sir Yrs &c. &c. &c.

G: Washington

LB, DLC:GW. The incomplete copy in CSmH may be a contemporary one.

In the weeks and months that follow, GW often repeats, modifies, or elaborates upon the points that he makes here, to the governor of Virginia, regarding his vision of the role that the Potomac should play in the future of the transmontane West. See, in particular, his letters to a member of Congress, Jacob Read, 3 Nov.; to the president of the Maryland senate, George Plater, 25 Oct.; and to the old financier Robert Morris, 1 Feb. 1785.

1. Letter not found.
2. See Lafayette to GW, 22 Oct., n.2.
3. GW is referring to the Potomac and the James.
4. For those publications of Lewis Evans and Thomas Hutchins to which GW is referring, see GW to John Witherspoon, 10 Mar. 1784, n.3.

5. GW sent copies of his table of distances to several people. The copy printed here, most of it in GW's hand, is in the Dartmouth College Library:

Table of Distances From Detroit To Montreal
is

	Miles	
To the North end of Lake Erie	350	
Fort Niagara (18 of wch is Land Transpn)	30	380
North end of Lake Ontario	225	
Oswegatche	60	
Montreal—very rapid	110	395
		775
To Quebec	180	
Total		955

From Detroit to Albany
is

To Fort Niagara as above	380	
Oswego	175	
Fall of Onondago River	12	
Portage	1	
Oneida Lake—by water	40	
Length of Do. to Wood Creek	18	
Wood Creek—very crooked	25	
Portage to the Mohawk Rivr	1	
Rapid in Ditto	60	
Portage	1	
Schenectady	55	
Portage to Albany	15	783
City of New York		160
In all	943	

From Detroit to the tide Water of Potomack
is

To Cayahoga River (of Lake Erie)	125	
Up Ditto to the Portage	60	
Portage to big bevr Creek	8	
Down Bever Creek to the Ohio	85	
Up the Ohio to Fort Pitt	25	303
The Mouth of Yohiogany	15	
Fall of Ditto	50	
Portage	1	
The 3 forks or Turkey foot	8	
Portage to Fort Cumberld	30	
To tide water	200	304
In all	607	

another rout

To Fort Pitt as above	303	
The Mouth of Cheat River	75	
The Dunker bottom	25	
Portage to the No. bra. Potomk	20	
Fort Cumberland	40	
to tide Water	200	663

Another avoiding Pensylvania—is

To the Mouth of Cayahoga as before	125
Up Do to the Carrying place between it & Muskingham	54
Portage	1
The Mouth of Muskingham	192
Down the Ohio to the little Kanhawa	12
Up the little Kanhawa .	40
Portage to the West bra. of Monongahela	10
Down Do to the Mouth of Cheat*	80

*The Pensylvania Line takes in about 2 miles up the River Cheat—but if it should be found necessary an easy portage may be had from the Monongahela above

Up Cheat to the Dunkr Bottom	25
Portage to Potomack	20
Fort Cumberland	40
To tide Water of Do	200

In all   799

Note, It appears, and the fact is, that the most direct, and easy communication is through the State of Pensylvania—and all that part of it which is to the westward of the Laurel hill are deeply interested in opening of it, but how far such a measure would meet the approbation of the State remains to be decided.

rout by Susquehanna

From Fort Pitt up the Allegany to Kiskemenatas	30
up Kiskemenetas to Conemack old Town	60
Portage from Conemack old to Canoe place on Juniata	25
N.B. The Head Waters of Comenack a branch of Kiskemi- natas nearly interlock with those of Juniata & might be joined by a Canal on the middle ground—from the Ca- noe place by Huntingdon down Juniata to its ⟨*illegible*⟩ on Susquehanna	90
To Middle Town on Susquehanna	25
To tide water	50
	280

6. See Jacob Read to GW, 13 Aug. 1784, n.2.

7. See GW's Certificate for John Rumsey, 7 Sept. 1784, printed above.

Letter not found: from Edward Newenham, 13 Oct. 1784. On 20 Mar. 1785 GW wrote to Newenham: "I regret very much that your letters of the 2d and 13th of October should have been detained."

Letter not found: from Robert Anderson, 15 Oct. 1784. On 3 Nov. GW wrote to Anderson: "Your letter of the 15th of Octor is at hand."

From Stephen Sayre

Sir   Georgetown [Md.] 15th Octo. 1784

When I did myself the honor of laying before your Excellency such thoughts as then occur'd to my imagination on the importantance of opening this River, it was not my Intention to have given you the trouble of a Reply; but I am not ashamed to acknowledge myself happy in the honorable Correspondence.[1]

It is my wish, that every Idea, leading to accomplish the great Object may be made public, and have reason to beleive the money may sooner be raised by Tontine, than in any other way, not only from the success such a mode has generally met with in Europe, but from the approbation of every Individual I have conversed with on the subject. Nor is there any other method which so fairly discharges posterity from the Toll, doing equal Justice to Creditors. I conceive also, that the early profits or enviable payments which the Toll will make to the Lenders will create an ardent disposition in the public to see Inland navigation extended to its utmost stage of improvement. It is reported, and I hope truly, that your Excellency will be at Annapolis; about the 1t of novr[2] I propose being there also at the same time, when I shall, unreservedly communicate my Ideas, and I trust, prove to conviction, that as to the work, nothing is more practicable than a good, safe, & convenient navigation thro the great & Little Falls, without a *single Lock*—to my understanding, all Idea of Locks ought to be renounced & exploded forever—perhaps in all cases of navigation; but surely in this River.[3] The single difficulty, in case the two States agree, is to raise the Funds. I am clearly persuaded that £50000 Maryland Cury would make a good navigation, & upon a plan that would never require repairs. I am, most respectfully Yours &c. &c.

Stephen Sayre

ALS, DLC:GW.

1. Sayre wrote to GW on 20 Aug., and GW responded on 1 September.

2. GW accompanied Lafayette to Annapolis at the end of November, at which time he consulted with members of the Maryland legislature about

forming a company to improve navigation on the Potomac. See particularly GW to Joseph Jones and James Madison, 3 Dec. 1784. Although there is no diary record of his movements after his return from his journey to the West, it is almost certain that GW did not make an earlier trip to Annapolis in the fall (see his cash accounts, Ledger B, 201).

3. In hopes of adding "Vigor to the great Design of improving our inland Navigation," the *Virginia Journal and Alexandria Advertiser* on 16 Dec. 1784 printed an "Extract of a Letter from London, dated September 20, to Stephen Sayre . . . from a Character, who is consulted in all Europe on all Objects of public Improvements." The letter begins: "I like your Description of America—What an amazing Country—what noble Rivers—I am glad you recommended, and pray insist in advising G. W. to sink or deepen upper levels . . . Discourage Locks—Encourage Ballast Work—deepening Shallows, and removing Rocks. . . ."

From Pusignan

Sir,   Roan in the Forest 16th October 1784

Anxious to partake of the military honors, with the Officers of your Country, where I served under Count Rochambeau, during the stay of the French Army in America; I addressed myself to Doctor Franklin, persuaded you had commissioned him to admit into the Order of Cincinnatus, those who were entitled to it. He told me I must apply to you, the President of the Order—I should not Sir, have sollicited this honor of you, if I had not seen it conferred on so many French Officers. I must inform you truly Sir, that I was not a Captain when wounded at Yorck—But this consideration has not operated so, as to withold the Kings favors from me, as you will observe by the Ministers letter; which I must entreat your Excellency to return to me[1]—Immediately after the Siege however, my Captain went to France, and the Command of the Company, of the Brigade of Soissonois devolved on me, and the care of eight field pieces—On my arrival in France, I was immediately made a Captain. I have so much confidence in your goodness, as to hope, you will not exclude me from the honor I ask—I am with the greatest respect, Your Hble & Obt Sert

De Surignan, Captain of the
regiment of Auxerne of the Royal Corps of Artillery.[2]

Translation, in the hand of David Stuart, DLC:GW; ALS, DLC:GW. GW wrote Pusignan on 25 Sept. 1785: "It is not fourteen days since I was honored with your letter of 16th of last Octr." For a transcription of the ALS, see CD-ROM:GW.

1. David Stuart's translation of the enclosed letter to Pusignan from Ségur, dated 5 Dec. 1781 at Versailles, reads: "I am just come Sir, from giving the King an account of your merit and long services, as well as the new proofs you have given of your zeal and bravery at the siege of Yorck, and the wound you recieved there—His Majesty has been graciously pleased in consequence, to confer on you the honor of Chevalier of the royal & military order of St Louis, and a gratification besides of five hundred livres—it is with pleasure I give you this information" (DLC:GW).

2. The original letter is signed "de Pusignan," not "Surignan," and the regiment is Auxonne, not "Auxerne."

Letter not found: from William Gordon, 18 Oct. 1784. On 3 Nov. GW wrote to Gordon: "The last post brought me your favor of the 18th ulto."

Letter not found: from Benjamin Lincoln, 18 Oct. 1784. On 5 Feb. 1785 GW wrote to Lincoln: "Not until these few days have I been favored with your letter of the 18th of Octr."

From James Rumsey

Dear General   Alexandria [Va.] octr 19th 1784
    I have been geting of Mr Herbert a few Coarse Clothes for my workman, and A Few materials towards Building, and has Taken the Liberty to Draw on you in his favour, for forty pounds Curencey payable at twenty Days Sight.[1] I thought It my Duty to give you notice of it—The honor you Did me at Bath by giveing me So ample a Certificate I Shall Eve[r] most greatfully acknowledge[2] It Convicts almost Every person that Sees it and puts Quite a new face on my Scheme I Long to have the Opertunity of Convinceing those that Remain Unbeleivers that you are not mistaken in your opinion I am with perfect Esteem your Obt hbe Servt

                                           James Rumsey

ALS, DLC:GW.
    1. At Alexandria on 18 Oct. 1784 James Rumsey wrote: "Sir[,] At twenty days Sight, please to pay Herbert & Potts forty pounds Curr[enc]y Value in Acct with them & place the same to Acct with Sir, your Most Hble Servt James Rumsey" (DLC:GW). William Herbert and John Potts, Jr. (1760–1809), were business partners who had a store in Alexandria.
    2. GW's Certificate for James Rumsey, dated 7 Sept., is printed above.

To Sidney Lee

Madam, Mount Vernon in Virginia 20th Octobr 1784.

The letter you did me the honor to write to me on the 23d of May last, came to my hands in the moment of my departure for our Western territory. Knowing that I should be in the walks of Mr White, and intending if I did not see him, to write to him on the subject of your letter, I thought it best to decline giving you any trouble until one of those events should have happened.

Fortunately I saw Mr White, who informed me, that tho' appearances were against him, he had not been unmindful either of your commands, or his own promises; for, tho' long before he could get matters in such a train as to give a precise account of the state of the trust reposed in him, he had, nevertheless, done it some little time before; and would leave nothing unattempted to settle the business in the best manner he was able, and that circumstances would admit.

He marked the parts of your letter to me, which required his attention; and promised me that he would address you on the Subject of them.[1]

For the favorable wishes you have been pleased to bestow on this young Country—and for the flattering sentiments you have expressed for me—my warmest acknowledgements are due. I have the honor to be with great respect. Madam Yr Most Obt Hble Servt

Go: Washington

ALS, NNPM; LB, DLC:GW.

1. For references to GW's correspondence regarding Charles Lee's will, see notes 1 and 2 in GW to William Drew, 13 Feb. 1784.

From George Plater

Dear Sir Oct. 20th 1784

Since I had the Honor of visiting you I have been revolving in my Head the Subject of our Conversation respecting the opening the Potowmack, Advancing the Trade of the back & new settled Countries [in] this these middle States & the more I consider it, the more I am impressed with the Utility & Advantages resulting therefrom[1]—So much so, that I am determined to press the Measure in our Assembly, which will soon meet, & I hope we shall be joined by Virginia[2]—To enable me to do it with more Effect, I take the Liberty to entreat the Favor of you, in some Leisure Moment, to give me as concisely as you please, some Description of the Waters in the back Country, the Land Carriage unavoidably necessary, & what other Information you may deem important—Your Letter sent to Mrs Digges will come safe to Hand[3]—Mrs Plater joins me in warmest Respects to your Lady & you, & I have the honor to be with the highest Regard & Esteem—Dear Sir—Yr most aff: & obt hume Servt

Geo. Plater

ALS, DLC:GW.

George Plater (1735–1792) of Sotterly, St. Mary's County, Md., was married to Elizabeth Frisby (d. 1789), stepdaughter of GW's friend William Fitzhugh. Plater at this time was president of the Maryland senate, and at the time of his death he was governor of the state.

1. It is not known when Plater visited Mount Vernon, but the tone and content of GW's lengthy response of 25 Oct. suggest that the visit was perhaps made before rather than after GW's western journey in September.

2. Plater was active in support of GW's successful efforts to secure the passage of his Potomac River Company bill by the Maryland legislature in January 1785.

3. See GW's letter to Plater, 25 October. Mrs. Digges may be the widow of William Digges (1713–1783), who lived at Warburton Manor, directly across the river from Mount Vernon and upriver from Sotterly.

From Lafayette

My dear General   Boston octobr the 22d 1784

On My Arrival at Boston I Have Been So kindly Received that No Words Can Express My lively, Affectionate Gratitude— to those Enjoyements I Have added the Heartfelt pleasure to Contemplate the Effect, a Sudden Appearance of your picture, Had Upon a people whose love to You is as Great at least as in Any part of the World[1]—Circumstanced as I am Here, I Could not with Any propriety set out So Soon as I expected—I am Sorry our Meeting Again is differd—But When You are absent, I Endeavour to Guess What You Would Have Advised me to do—and then to do it—I am sure You Would advise My staying Here some time longer—I therefore Will not go Untill the first or Second of next Month—and then I embark from Boston in the Nimph frigat to Go to York—monsieur de grandchain Who Commands Her Begs to Be Most Respectfully Remembered to You, and as He expects Reaching York about the 8th or tenth, He Will in Compagny with me Wait upon You whereever You May be found—the Bearer I Send to Mount vernon in order I may Receive Your Commands at the Moment I Arrive—So late in the Season, I think You Will Advise my Going immediately to Richmond—I Hope you Will let me know where We are to Meet[2]—and I also Hope, My dear general, You will not deny My affectionate pressing Request to induce Your Visiting with me our friends in philadelphia—the chev.'s respects and Mine wait upon mrs Washington and Wish to Be Remembered to all the family—Adieu, My dear General, With the Most Affectionate and devoted Sentiments of filial love and Respect I Have the Honor to Be Your

Lafayette

ALS, PEL.

1. Joseph Barrell wrote Samuel B. Webb from Boston on 21 Oct. 1784: "The Marquiss is with us, & has been treated with a friendship *unknown* by the dishonest. . . . I did not draw the Acct, but was one of the Managers of the Entertainment, & the Sole Contriver of Introducg Gen. Washington, when his health was Drank. The Contrivance was unknown to every one but the Managers, & the Effect was as I conjectured, exceedingly great. Many were the friendly Tears, that involuntarily Started from the Company" (Ford, *Correspondence of Webb*, 3:40).

2. GW arrived in Richmond on Sunday, 14 Nov., and Lafayette came into the town on 18 November. Grandchain de Sémerville was captain of the frigate *Nymphe* in which Lafayette sailed from Boston to Yorktown in November and in which he was to sail from New York for France in late December.

From Jacob Read

Sir   New York 22nd Octr 1784

Having met with the Little Tract a Copy of which I do myself the honour to inclose to you in this City[1] and Conceiving it possesses Some Merit I Seize the occasion it affords me of addressing a few Lines to you and of making inquiries of Your health & that of your most amiable Lady.

I hope Your late Tour Westward has been Attended with every pleasure & advantage you promised Yourself and as I conclude you are by this time returned home may I expect the pleasure of hearing from You & to be favoured with Any observations that may be Essential towards my forming a proper Judgment in Any Measures Congress may have in View respecting the Western Territory, Posts, or in General on Indian Affairs.[2]

Since the last time I had the Honour of addressing myself to you by Letter I have made a Tour to New Hamshire & am just returned much pleased with my Journey—the season proved most uncommonly favourable.[3] I am delighted with the Country & tho the people throughout appear to be in Very Indifferent Circumstances they do not however Seem to want a Competency & what is most desirable of all sublunary Enjoyements they appear to possess Contentment.

We hear nothing here (Authentically) of the proceedings of our Indian Commissioners But report says that nothing further will take place at the present Meeting than An Agreement for a Cessation of Hostilities for One Year, We are told that Brandt Woud not Attend—I fear this was a Consequence of the Treaty by the Commissioners for this state[.] People in power deny an Actual Treaty but the Governours think it in itself a sufficient Evidence of the fact. So glaring a Violation of the federal Compact by this state is to Me Allarming.[4]

When I left Boston the Marquis de La Fayette was expected there, a French Frigate of Forty Guns had also arrived from St Pierre de Miquelon on purpose to conduct him to France he is however expected to attend Congress at their meeting on the 30th Inst. when I have a hope all the states will be represented.[5]

Do me the Honour to present my most respectful Compliments to Mrs Washington & believe me to be with the greatest Esteem & regard Sir Your Excellency's most obedt and most Humle Servt

Jacob Read

ALS, DLC:GW.

1. The "Little Tract," which GW acknowledges receipt of on 3 Nov., has not been identified.

2. See GW to Read, 3 November.

3. Jacob Read, who was a member of Congress from South Carolina, wrote on 6 Aug. that he was going to New England to visit his mother who had gone north from South Carolina for her health.

4. See note 2 in Read's letter of 13 Aug. 1784.

5. See Lafayette to GW, this date, n.2.

To George Plater

Dear Sir,   Mount Vernon 25th Oct. 1784

Your letter of the 20th did not reach me until yesterday afternoon. I am now set down to acknowledge it, and shall be happy if from any information I can give, you should derive satisfaction, or the public benefit.

To describe the usefulness of water transportation, would be a mere waste of time. every man who has considered the difference of expence between it, & land transportation, and the prodigeous saving in the article of draught cattle, requires no arguments in proof of it. and to point out the advantages which the back Inhabitants of Virginia and Maryland would derive from an extension of the inland navigation of the river Potomk, (even supposing our views did not extend beyond the Apalachian Mountains) would be equally nugatory.

But I consider this business in a far more extensive point of view—and the more I have revolved it, the more important it appears to me; not only as it respects our commerce, but our political interests, and the well being, & strength of the Union also.[1]

It has long been my opinion, that the shortest, easiest, and least expensive communication with the invaluable and extensive Country back of us, would be by the river Potomack; and in this opinion I am not singular; Evans in his map and analysis of the middle Colonies, which (considering the early period at which they were given to the public) are done with surprizing exactness—and Hutchins since, in his topographical description of the Western Country (some parts of which are from actual Surveys) are of the same sentimts; as indeed all others who have had opportunities, & taken the pains to investigate & consider the subject, also are.

But that this may not appear a European scheme, or as an opinion unsupports by facts, I will give you the different routs & distances from *Detroit*, by which the Fur & Peltry trade of the lakes, even as far as that of the Wood, must pass; unless the Spaniards contrary to their present policy should open their Ports to it—or Great Britain, to divert it from us, should endeavor to *force* nature by carrying it along the river Outawaies into Canada, which I scarcely think they will attempt, or could effect if they did, as the Lakes are as open to our Traders as theirs, and the way easier from them.

These routs and distances are given from the best maps extant, corrected by actual Surveys in many instances, and by such oral testimony as my opportunities during the war have enabled me to obtain.

Taking Detroit then (which is putting ourselves in as distant a point of view as we can be placed, because it is on the North-western line of the United territory) it appears from the enclosed statement, that the tide water of Potomack is nearer to it, by 168 Miles than that of the river St Lawrence—or that of the Hudson at Albany, by 176 Miles.[2]

Maryland as it respects the navigation of Potomack stands upon similar ground with Virginia—Pensylvania, altho' the Susquehanna is said to be an unfriendly water, much impeded by rocks & rapids, and disgorging itself into Chesapeak bay, have it, I am told, in contemplation to open a communication between Tobys Creek (which emptys into the Alligany river 95 Miles above Fort Pitt) and the West branch thereof; and to cut a canal between the latter, that is the Susquehanna, and the Schuylkill—the expence of which is more easy to be conceived than estimated or described. but a people possessed of the spirit of Commerce—who sec--and who will resolve to pursue advantages, may atchieve almost any thing. In the meanwhile, under the uncertainty of these undertakings, they are smoothing (as I have been informed) the roads, and paving the ways for the trade of that western world, to their capitol—That New York will do the same, so soon as the British Garrisons are removed, which at present are insuperable obstacles in their way, none who are as well acquainted with the genious & policy of those people as I am, can harbour the smallest doubt—any more than they will of the difficulty of diverting trade, after connections are once formed, & it has flowed for any length of time in one channel into that of another.

I am not for discouraging the exertion of any State to draw the Commerce of the Western Country to its Seaports. The more communications are opened to it, the closer we bind that rising world (for indeed it may be so called) to our interests; and the greater strength shall we acquire by it. Those to whom nature affords the best communication, will, if they are wise &

politic, enjoy the greatest share of the trade. all I would be understood to mean therefore, is, that the gifts of Providence may not be neglected, or slighted. These when viewed upon a commercial scale, are alone sufficient to excite our endeavors; but the political object is, in my estimation, immense.

I need not remark to you Sir, that the flanks and rear of the United territory are possessed by other powers, and formidable ones too. nor how necessary it is to apply the cement of interest, to bind the several parts of it together; for what ties let me ask, should we have upon those people, and how entirely unconnected shall we be with them, if the Spaniards on their right, or Great Britain on their left, instead of throwing stumbling blocks in their way as they now do, should envite their trade, & seek alliances with them? what, when they get strength, which will be sooner than is generally imagined (from the emigration of foreigners, who can have no predeliction for us, as well as from the removal of our Citizens) may be the consequence of their having formed close connections with both, or either of those powers in a Commercial way? needs not the gift of prophecy to foretell.

The Western settlers—I speak now from my own observations—stand as it were upon a pivet; the touch of a feather would almost incline them any way—they looked down the Mississipi until the Spaniards (very impoliticly I think for themselves) threw difficulties in their way; & for no other reason that I can devise, than because they glided gently down the stream without considering perhaps the length of the voyage, & the time necessary to perform it in. & because they had no other means of coming to us, but by a long land transportation, and unimproved roads.

These causes have hitherto checked the industry of the present Settlers, for except the demand for provisions, occasioned by the encrease of population; and the little flour which the necessities of the Spaniards have compelled them to buy; they have no excitements to labour—But open the road once, & make easy the way for these, and see what an influx of articles will be poured in upon us. how amazingly our exports will be encreased by them, and how amply we shall be compensated for any trouble and expence we may encounter to effect it.

A combination of circumstances make the present con-

juncture more favorable than any other, to fix these matters—
The crusty & untoward disposition of the Spaniards on one
side, and the private views of some individuals coinciding with
the policy of the Court of G. Britain on the other, to retain the
Posts of Oswego, Niagara, Dretroit &ca (which though they are
done under the letter of the treaty, is certainly an infraction of
the spirit of it, and injurious to the Union) may be improved to
the greatest advantage by the States of Virginia & Maryland if
they would open their arms, and embrace the means which are
necessary to establish the trade—It wants but a beginning—the
Western Inhabitants would do their part towards its execution.
Weak as they are at present, they would meet us half way rather
than be *driven* into the arms of, or be dependent upon, foreigners; the consequence of which would be, a seperation or a
war—the way to avoid both, fortunately for us, is, to do that,
which our most essential interests prompts us to; and which, at
a very small comparitive expence, is to be effected. that is, to
open a wide door to their commerce, & make the communication as easy as possible for their produce.

This, in my judgment, would dry up the other sources, or
if any part should flow down the Mississipi from the Falls of
the Ohio, by means of Vessels built for the sea, & sold with
their Cargoes, the returns for them, I conceive, would go back
this way.

I consider Rumseys discovery for working Boats against the
stream, by mechanical powers principally, as not only a very
fortunate invention for these States in general, but as one of
those circumstances which have combined to render the present epocha favorable above all others, for fixing, if we are disposed to avail ourselves of them, a large portion of the Peltry &
Fur trade of the lakes, and the commerce within, irrecoverably,
to these two states.

Lengthy as this letter is, I might have enlarged, but company
prevents me—If there are any ideas in it which may be improved upon, I shall feel happy in having obeyed your commands. if there are not, your request must be my apology for
having troubled you with these observations. My best respects,
in which Mrs Washington joins me, are tendered to Mrs Plater.
and I am—Dear Sir Yr Most Obedt Hble Servt

Go: Washington

ALS (photocopy), MiD-B; LB, DLC:GW; contemporary copy (incomplete), DLC:GW. The spelling and punctuation in this letter are more erratic than is usual in those letters of this period that are written in GW's hand.

1. GW uses in this letter much of the material contained in his letter to Benjamin Harrison, 10 October.

2. For GW's table of distances from Detroit, see note 5 in his letter to Harrison.

To George Rindfleisch

Sir,   Mount Vernon 25th Octor 1784

Herewith is a copy of the Plat you desired. Permit me to remind you that this tract, & my other Lands in the neighbourhood of it, have been offered to be leased, and may soon, in part, be engaged.

The sooner therefore you determine whether to take it or not, the better chance there will be of having it wholly for your own use, or the benefit of your friends, which, no doubt would be more agreeable to you, or them, than to be mixed with strangers. I am Sir Yr most Obt Servt

G: Washington

LB, DLC:GW.

GW probably talked to George Rindfleisch at some time during his trip in September to Frederick and Berkeley counties and into western Pennsylvania. No other mention of Rindfleisch has been found in GW's papers and accounts, and no one of his surname appears in the 1790 census in either Virginia or Pennsylvania. The Library of Congress's catalog of GW's papers supplies Rindfleisch's first name.

From Walter Stewart

Dear Sir,   Philadelphia Octr 26th 1784

Not meeting with an Opportunity of forwarding Your Excellency a Letter has been the only Cause of my not writing since my return from the Havannah.

I have in the most sincere manner to thank Your Excellency for the kind Introduction You gave me to the Governor, it was paid every Attention to I could Possibly wish, and was the Cause in a great measure of my getting the business on which I went Effected.[1]

My detention Exceeded every Idea I had when I left America, it was Occasion'd by a difference which has long Existed between the Governor, Admiral, and Intendant; Individually they wish'd to do every thing in their power for me, but Collectively they Could not Agree on the mode.

I was fortunate in setling an Account of near twelve thousand Dollars with our Agent there.[2] He has return'd to America where his losses and other distresses has reduced him to the Necessity of Calling his Creditors together; they have granted Him a length of time to settle his affairs and pay his debts.

The Season got so far Advanced before I return'd, that our friends have persuaded us not to go to Ireland untill the Spring; Indeed matters are becoming more and more Serious in that Quarter every day, And by that time I think We must Ascertain what is Meant by each Party.

The Marquis la fayette is at the Indian Treaty Where he made a Speech to those who had met, I am informed that the number was by no means equal to what was Expected, or could be wished & it is fear'd nothing of Consequence will be done.[3]

Mrs Stewart Joins in respectful Compliments to your Excellency and Mrs Washington, and in hopes that you both enjoy perfect Health.

Inclos'd I forward a Letter from Governor Unzaga And Am Dr sir With the greatest respect & Esteem Yr Excellency's Most Obedt Servant

Walter Stewart

ALS, DLC:GW.

1. Colonel Stewart, a Philadelphia merchant, wrote GW on 26 Jan. 1784 asking for a letter of introduction to the governor of Havana. GW answered on 5 Feb., enclosing a letter to the governor, Luis de Unzaga y Amézaga, which is printed as note 2 in GW's letter to Stewart.

2. The agent was Oliver Pollock. See Beauregard & Bourgeois to GW, 14 Oct. 1789, source note.

3. For the peace conference with the Iroquois, see Jacob Read to GW, 13 Aug. 1784, n.2.

From Melancton Smith

Sir   New York Octr 27th 1784

I have the honor of inclosing you a Copy of an Invoice of plate &c., shipped from London by order of Daniel Parker Esqr. Mr Parker before he left Philadelphia authorized me to receive them, and forward them to you. They arrived here the

Latter part of Summer, since which no oppurtunity has offered to Ship them to you. A Friend of mine now Ships a number of Goods to go to Alexandria by way of Philadephia and by this way I have sent the Case, and wish it safe to hand. Inclosed is an Accot of the Freight & other charges paid on the Case—The amount of the cost and charges Mr Parker requested you will send to me. As I am to make remittances to Messrs Joy & Hopkins for them. If it would be convenient to send it in a good Bill of Exchange upon London, it would best suit me.[1]

Mr Henry Wyckoff and myself have entered into business in this place under the firm of Smith & Wyckoff, & should you have any business to transact here in the mercantile line we should be happy to execute it with fidelity & dispatch. I am with the highest respect Your Obed. Sert

Malancton Smith

ALS, DLC:GW. The letter is addressed to GW at "Mount Vernon near Alexandria Virginia ⟨℗⟩ Brigantine Greenwich with a Box." For the additional notation on the cover, see GW to Smith, 20 Dec. 1784, n.1.

Melancton Smith (1744–1798), who is remembered mostly for his fight against the ratification of the federal Constitution in New York, had recently moved from Dutchess County, where he had been a successful merchant, into New York City. In the city, he thrived as a lawyer as well as a merchant.

1. For GW's dealings with Daniel Parker regarding the silver articles listed in the invoice that Smith sent GW, see Daniel Parker to GW, 21 June 1784, and the note in that document. See also GW to Melancton Smith, 20 Dec. 1784. The enclosed invoice showed a charge by the English firm of Joy & Hopkins of £56.18.4 sterling for the silver and for their handling of it and also Smith's own charges of £3.15.7, New York currency, for freight and storage. The pieces of silverware included:

1 large plain beaded plated Gallon Tea Urn		7. 7.0
1 ditto Coffee Pot to match		2.14.
2 beaded chaised Tea Pots		5.16.
2 Ea. sugr & cream pails with Ladles & Glasses		4.15.
4 plain beaded Waiters		8.
engraving the above with crests & Arms		1.16.4
a large inlaid Tea Board best kind		3.10.
a Tea Caddy to match do		3.
a Mahogony Plate Chest best wood lined with green Cloth		
& Clumped with Brass		16.10.
	Case	.12.
		£54. .4

A transcript of the invoice is in CD-ROM:GW. At GW's request of 20 Dec., Smith provided a copy of GW's account with the new firm of Smith & Wyckoff.

To Stephen Bloomer Balch

Sir,   [Mount Vernon] 30th Octr 1784.
    If you will *now*, or at any other time, furnish me with an account of the expences which have been incurred for schooling, boarding & clothing of my Nephews, I will transmit you the money. Such of the latter as are proper for them, I hope will be obtained on the best terms, as the cost of them shall be regularly paid.[1]
    I think it would be very proper to have them taught the French language & such parts of the Mathematics as will bring them acquainted with practical Surveying, which is useful to every man who has landed property. As they are fatherless & motherless children, I commit them to your benevolent care & protection. I am Sir &c.

                                        G: Washington

LB, DLC:GW.
    1. See GW to David Griffith, 29 Aug. 1784, n.1, and Charles Washington to GW, 16 Nov. 1784, nn.1 and 2.

Letter not found: from Benjamin Vaughan, 31 Oct. 1784. On 5 Feb. 1785 GW wrote to Vaughan: "I pray you to accept my acknowledgement of your polite letter of 31st of October."

To Robert Anderson

Sir,   Mount Vernon 3d Novr 1784.
    Your letter of the 15th of Octor is at hand, & is the first I have ever received from you. Persons as well acquainted with Husbandry, in its various branches, as you profess yourself to be, & have credentials of, must no doubt be an acquisition to any Country, & meet with encouragement in this. I should be glad to employ a Man who has a perfect knowledge of Agriculture— skilled in the rotation of crops, & who understands feeding horses, Cattle, sheep &c. But before I would be under any legal, or honorary engagement, or put you to the trouble or expence of coming this way, I should be glad to know precisely your terms, wages &c. To which I wou'd give you an answer by the return of the Post. It may not be amiss to inform you, that it is a head or Director only I want; hands I could furnish from my

own Estate to occupy any farm I have unengaged at present.[1] I
am Sir &c.

G: Washington

LB, DLC:GW.
    1. Robert Anderson's letter has not been found, nor is there any evidence
of further correspondence with him. On 30 June 1785 GW wrote George
William Fairfax for help in finding a farmer to manage the farming at Mount
Vernon. It was through Fairfax's agency that GW hired the English farmer,
James Bloxham, who arrived at Mount Vernon in April 1786.

To Clement Biddle

Dear Sir,   Mount Vernon Nov. 3rd 1784
    I have not yet received a statement of my Acct with you. It
would give me pleasure to have it at full length—and soon.
    I wish you would add to it 100 lbs. of fresh & good (red)
clover seed, to be sent by the first vessel to Alexandria, as I
should be glad to receive it before Ice may impede the navigation of this or Delaware river.
    I requested the favor of Mr Bourdinot (late president of
Congress[)][1] to send me from New Jersey as much of the Orchard grass seed as would sow ten acres; and if no opportunity
should offer from New York immediately to Alexandria to address it to your care, should the latter be the case I pray you to
forward it by the first conveyance after its arrival.[2]
    Last spring you were unable to get me English grass seed, but
if it is to be had now, it would be very convenient for me to receive as much as would sow five acres (say 50 lbs.) The grass I
mean has different names, which may be a reason of your unsuccessful enquiries before. By some it is called English Grass,
by others Goose Grass, By others spear grass, but the kind I
want is that which affords the best turf for walks and lawns, and
is the purpose for which I want it. Could these seeds be had
from a Farmer, or of the growth of the country there would be
more certainty of its coming up. Imported seeds even (when no
pranks are played with them) often get heated in the ship &
vegetation thereby destroyed.[3]
    At what prices pray could good Ticklenburg be had in Phila-
delphia, Nails, Paints, and in short course goods, are goods in

general cheap or dear with you.[4] I am Dr Sir Yr most Obedt Servt

G. Washington

LB, PHi: Washington-Biddle Correspondence; LB, DLC:GW. For the only significant difference between the copies in the Biddle letter book and GW's letter book, see note 1.

1. Elias Boudinot's name is not misspelled in GW's letter book, nor is he thus identified.

2. See GW's letter to Boudinot of this date. On 26 Jan. 1785 GW wrote Boudinot, again asking for "as much of the Orchard grass seed as would sew about ten Acres of Land." Three days later, on 29 Jan., Biddle wrote GW that he had recently sent to Alexandria two bags of grass seed gotten from Boudinot. In his reply to GW's letter of 26 Jan., Boudinot wrote on 9 Feb. that upon receiving GW's letter of 3 Nov. he had been able to get six or seven bushels of the desired grass seed which he had immediately forwarded to Biddle and that he had recently found 3½ bushels more which he would also send along to Biddle. On 7 Mar. Biddle wrote that he had received another barrel of grass seed from Boudinot, which he would send to Alexandria.

3. Biddle was unable to obtain the English, or goose, grass for GW. See his letter of 29 Jan. 1785.

4. The punctuation of this passage in GW's letter book makes the meaning of this passage clearer: "At what prices could good Tichenburg be had in Philadelphia—nails—paint—&ca in short course goods? Are goods in general cheap or dear with you?" Perhaps GW intended to write, or did write, "coarse" instead of "course." No response to GW's queries has been found.

To Elias Boudinot

Dr Sir,   Mount Vernon 3d Novr 1784.

Mrs Washington & I have heard with great pleasure of Miss Boudinot's restoration to health, & change of condition; on both which events we join in sincere compliments of congratulation to you, Mrs Boudinot & the young couple.[1]

Will you permit me my good Sir, to request the favor of you (if it should not be attended with inconvenience) to purchase as much of the Orchard grass seed for me, as will sow about ten acres of Land, & forward it by any Vessel which may be coming from New York to Alexandria—or if opportunities from thence are rare—to Colo. Biddle in Philadelphia, with a request to forward it to me without delay, that I may be certain of getting it for early seeding in the Spring. You would add to the favor if the Seed should be accompanied by the direction of a good farmer, with respect to the quantity which should be given to an Acre, & the manner of sowing it. I will remit the price of the Seed with thanks, so soon as you shall inform me of the cost of it.[2]

You were so obliging some years ago as to furnish me with a little of this seed; but like most other things which belonged to me it was neglected. I want to try it now under my own management. With very great esteem & regard, I am Dr Sir, Yrs &c. &c.

G: Washington

LB, DLC:GW.

1. The Boudinot's only child, Susan Vergereau Boudinot, in 1784 became the wife of Col. William Bradford (1755–1795), attorney general of Pennsylvania and, in 1794–95, attorney general of the United States.

2. See GW to Clement Biddle, this date, n.2.

To William Gordon

Dear sir,   Mount Vernon 3d Novr 1784

The last post brought me your favor of the 18th ulto, & gave me the pleasure to hear you were well.[1]

My return from our Western territory was sooner than I expected when I left home. The Indians from accounts were in too discontented a mood to have rendered an interview with them agreeable, if chance should have thrown us together. I therefore returned from the Neighbourhood of Fort Pitt, where I found part of my property (Lands) in possession of others, & myself under the necessity of bringing ejectments for the recovery of it.[2] To that which was more remote I did not go, for the reason above. Another year—& I may find it in like predicament. But as the *Land* cannot be removed, I did not think any attempts which might be made in the meanwhile, sufficient inducement to expose myself to the insults of Savages; & having no other objects in view, I returned three weeks sooner than I expected when I set out on the tour.

In my absence I had a very sickly family, but no deaths—Mrs Washington has been very unwell—Miss Custis very ill—and your friend *Tub* a good deal reduced by a diarrhaea—he has got perfectly well, & is as fat & saucy as ever. Mrs Washington is pretty well recovered, but Miss Custis remains in a puny state. The family unite in best wishes for you, & I am &c. &c.

G: Washington

LB, DLC:GW.
1. Letter not found.
2. See editorial note in Thomas Smith to GW, 9 Feb. 1785.

To Battaile Muse

Sir,   Mount Vernon 3d Novr 1784.

Your letter of the 12th of Septr only came to my hands a few days ago. You can best tell how far the collection of my Rents in Berkeley, Frederick, Fauquier & Loudoun would interfere with the business you have to execute for Colo. Fairfax.[1] If it can be made to comport with his, and the Gentleman who employed you to look after it would signify as much I should be very willing to commit my smaller matters to your care—and would then, as soon as it should be in my power, transmit you a Rental of the Sums (as far as I can ascertain them) which arc due.[2]

At any rate, as Mr Whiting is about to quit the tenement he holds of mine—as he is a good deal in arre⟨ars⟩ of rent—as common fame not only denomin⟨a⟩tes him a bad manager but one who is very much involved; which may occasion me a good deal of trouble if not loss, if his effects are suffered to be removed before the Sum which he owes me for rent is secured—I have to request that you will cause distress to be made before this event takes place unless he will give indubitable security for the payment of it in Six Months.

You will readily perceive by this, that my meaning on the one hand is not to loose the hold which the law gives me of his property on the premises unless he will secure me in some other manner—and on the other hand, not to distress him beyond what a prudent regard to my own interest & that security which justice requires makes absolutely necessary.

Enclosed you have a statement of the Acct between us. On the 25th of Decr next another rent will become due (making in the whole £199.8.0) the securing of which is also necessary.[3] I am Sir Yr Very Hble Servt

Go: Washington

ALS, NjHi; LB, DLC:GW. The letter was addressed to Muse "in Berkeley County," and GW wrote on the cover, "recommended to the care of Colo. Warner Washington." The parts of two words torn from the manuscript are enclosed in angle brackets.

1. When George William Fairfax left Belvoir in the summer of 1773 and went with his wife to live in England, GW assumed general supervision of Fairfax's business affairs in Virginia, which Fairfax had left under the immediate management of a steward and rent collector. See George William Fairfax to GW, 10 June 1784, and notes. See also GW's letter to Fairfax of 30 June 1786 in which GW reviews the history of his involvement, and lack of involvement, in Fairfax's affairs since 1773. At the outbreak of the Revolution, Robert Carter Nicholas took over from GW the supervision of Fairfax's American interests, and at Nicholas's death in 1780, his son George replaced him. Muse at this time was the collector of Fairfax's rents for George Nicholas.

2. GW had difficulty establishing his rent rolls, and it was not until 18 Sept. 1785 that he sent Muse a list of his tenants in Fauquier and Loudoun counties. See GW's letter to Muse of that date in which there is an enclosure identifying his tenants in all four counties—Frederick, Berkeley, Fauquier, and Loudoun.

3. Henry Whiting had been renting a tract of GW's Bullskin lands since the death in 1775 of his father, Francis Whiting. See John Ariss to GW, 5 Aug. 1784, n.1. More than a year before GW wrote this letter to Muse, Lund Washington reported to GW: "Your Tenaments over the Ridge are clever and in good order with Fine Crops growing on them, White[in]gs excepted and that I think has the appearance of decay . . . your Brother Charles told me he thought it woud be no bad plan to secure Whitegs Rents, for he was thought to be in but bad cercumstances" (1 Oct. 1783, ViMtV). By August 1784 Whiting was talking of giving up his lease. On 20 Aug. Whiting wrote GW a letter enclosing a statement of rents paid and owed. Neither the letter nor the enclosure has been located. When GW was at Charles Washington's on 3 and 4 Sept., Whiting came to the house and paid GW £50.12, one year's rent. This left him in arrears £149.8. In October 1785 Whiting paid £205.13.6 to settle his account. See GW to Warner Washington, 7 Aug. 1784, n.1, and to John Ariss, 8 Aug. 1784, n.3. See also Muse to GW, 15 June, 19 July, 16 Aug., and 6 Sept. 1785, and GW to Muse, 28 July 1785.

To Jacob Read

Sir,   Mount Vernon Novr 3d 1784.

The last Post gave me the honor of your letter of the 22d Ulto from New York and the little Tract which it enclosed. for both, you have my thanks.

My tour to the Westward, was less extensive than I intended. The Indians, it was said, were in too discontented a mood, for me to expose myself to their insults; as I had no object in contemplation which could justify any risk; my property in that Country having, previously, undergone every species of attack and diminution, that the nature of it would admit. To see the condition of my Lands which were nearest, & settled—and to dispose of those which were more remote, & unsettled, was all I had in view. The first I accomplished. The other I could not; and returned three weeks sooner than I expected.

You are pleased, my good Sir, to request that I would furnish you with such observations as I might have made in this tour, respecting "the Western Territory, Posts, or in general on Indian Affairs." with respect to the first and last, I had abundant reason to convince me, that the predictions of a letter, which I wrote on the 7th of Septr 1783 to a Committee of Congress, (at their request) in part, are already verified—and that the rest, if the treaty which is now depending with the Indians, does not avert them, are upon the point of being so. And with respect to the Posts—two other letters of mine—the first on the 2d of May last year, the other of the 8th of Septr following—addressed (by desire) to the Committee appointed to form a Peace establishment for the Union, contain my Sentiments on that Subject; fully, & clearly.

As these letters were addressed to Committees, at their own request, 'tis possible the members *only* of them, may have seen them— this must be my apology therefore for the reference, instead of a recital.

What may be the result of the Indian Treaty I pretend not to say; equally unacquainted am I with the Instructions, or Powers of the Commissioners; but if a large cession of territory is expected from them, a disappointment I think will ensue; for the Indians, I have been told, will not yield to the proposal. Nor can I see wherein lyes the advantages of it, if they would—at a first purchase—unless a *number* of States, tho' thinly Inhabited, would be more than a counterpoize in the *political* Scale, for progressive & compact settlements.[1]

Such is the rage for speculating in, and forestalling of Lands on the No. West side of the Ohio, that scarce a valuable spot within any tolerable distance of it, is left without a claimant. Men in these times, talk with as much facility of fifty, a hundred, and even 500,000 Acres as a Gentleman formerly would do of 1000 acres. In defiance of the proclamation of Congress, they roam over the Country on the Indian side of the Ohio— mark out Lands—Survey—and even settle them. This gives great discontent to the Indians, and will unless measures are taken in time to prevent it, inevitably produce a war with the western Tribes. To avoid which, there appears to me to be only these ways. Purchase, if possible, as much Land of them immediately back of us, as would make one or two States, according to the extent Congress design, or would wish to have them of; and which may be fully adequate to all our *present* purposes. Fix such a price upon the Lands, so purchased, as would not be too exorbitant & burthensome for real occupiers, but high enough to discourage monopolizers. Declare all steps, heretofore taken to procure Lands on the No. Wt side of the Ohio, contrary to the prohibition of Congress, to be null & void. and that any person thereafter, who shall presume to mark—Survey—or settle Lands beyond the limits of the New States, & purchased Lands, shall not only be considered as outlaws, but fit subjects for Indian vengeance.

If these, or similar measures are adopted, I have no doubt of Congress's deriving a very considerable revenue from the Western territory; but Land, like other commodities, rise or fall in proportion to the quantity at market. consequently a higher price may be obtained by the acre, for as much as will constitute one or two States, than can be had if ten States were offered for Sale at the sametime, besides extending the benefits, and deriving all the advantages of Law & Government from them at once; neither of which can be done in sparse settlements, where nothing is thought of but scrambling for Land, which more than probably would involve confusion & bloodshed.

It is much to be regretted, that the slow determinations of Congress involve many evils. It is much easier to avoid mischiefs, than to apply remedies after they have happened. Had Congress paid an earlier attention to, or decided sooner on Indian Affairs, matters would have been in a more favorable train than they now are—and if they are longer delayed, they will grow worse. Twelve months ago the Indians would have listened to propositions of *any kind* with more readiness than they will do now. The terms of Peace frightened them, and they were disgusted with Great Britn for making such. Bribery, and every address which British art could devise have been practiced since to sooth them—to estrange them from us—and to secure their Trade.

To what other causes can be ascribed, their holding our Western Posts so long, after the ratification of the Treaty, contrary to the spirit tho they do it under the letter of it. To remove their Garrisons and Stores is not the work of a week; for if report be true, they have only to shift them to the opposite side of the line. but it is now more than a year since I foretold what has happened; & I shall not be surprized if they leave us *no* Posts to occupy; for if they *mean* to surrender them *at all*, they may fix upon a *season*, or appoint a *short* day perhaps for the evacuation, which would preclude all relief—especially as I beleive you are in no condition to possess them—To do it properly, requires time; ordnance, stores, Provisions, and other articles, no more than Garrisons, are to be established in a moment; even where Boats & other conveniences (of which I dare say you are deficient) are at hand to transplant them. Supposing this to be the case, their will be an interregnum, during which the works will be left without guards, and being obnoxious to British policy, & Indian prejudices, will, by *accidental* fires, or Indian Drunkeness end in conflagration.

There is a matter which tho' it does not come before Congress wholly, is in my opinion, of great political importance, and ought to be attended to in time. It is to prevent the trade of the Western territory from settling in the hands, either of the Spaniards or British.[2] if either of these happen, there is a line of seperation at once drawn between the Eastern & Western Country. The consequences of which may be fatal. To tell any man of information, how fast the latter is settling—how much more rapidly it will settle, by means of foreign emigrants, who can have no particular predeliction for us; of the vast fertility of the Soil—and the population the Country is competent to, would be futile—and equally nugatory to observe that it is by the cement of inte⟨rest⟩ only, we can be held together. If then the trade of that Country should flow through the Mississipi or St Lawrence—If the Inhabitants thereof should form commercial connexions, which lead, we know, to intercourse of other kinds—they would in a few years be as unconnected with us, indeed more so, than we are with South America; and wd soon be alienated from us.

It may be asked how we are to prevent this? Happily for us the way is plain—and our *immediate* Interests, as well as remote political advantages, points to it; whilst a combination of circumstances renders the present Epocha more favorable than any other, to accomplish them—Extend the inland navigation of the Eastern waters—communicate them as near as possible (by excellent Roads) with those which run to the Westward. open these to the Ohio—and such others as extend from the Ohio towards Lake Erie; and we shall not only draw the produce of the Western Settlers, but the Fur & peltry trade of the lakes also, to our Ports (being the nearest, & easiest of transportation) to the amazing encrease of our Exports, while we bind those people to us by a chain which never can be broken.

This is no Utopean Scheme—it can be demonstrated as fully as facts can ascertain any thing—that not only the produce of the Ohio & its waters, at least to the falls, but those of the lakes also, as far even as that of the Wood,[3] may be brought to the Sea Ports of the United States by routs shorter, easier, and less expensive than they can be carried to Montreal or New Orleans. if we would be at a little trouble and expence to open them. I will acknowledge that the most essential part of this business comes more properly before individual States than the Union;[4] but there is one part of it, which lyes altogether with the latter— and that is, to have actual Surveys of the Western territory; more especially of the Rivers which empty into the Ohio on the North West side thereof, which have the easiest & best communications with Lake Erie—reporting the nature of these waters—the practicability of their navigation, & expence in opening of them. This, in my opinion, is an important business, and admits of no delay—it would shew the value of those Lands more clearly—it would attract the attention of the Settlers, and the Traders—it would give the Ton[e], & fix ideas that at present are as floating as chaos.

You see Sir I have obeyed your commands—my sentiments are delivered with freedom—the worst construction they will admit of, is, that they are errors of judgment; for sure I am, I have no private views that can be promoted by the adoption of them. Mrs Washington thanks you for your polite remembrance of her, and joins me in best respects. I am with esteem & regard Dr Sir Yr most Obt Hble Servt

Go: Washington

ALS (photocopy), DLC:GW; LB, DLC:GW.

1. For the recently concluded conference with the Iroquois leading to the signing of a peace treaty with the United States at Fort Stanwix on 22 Oct., see Read's letter of 13 August.

2. The remainder of the letter echoes what GW wrote Benjamin Harrison on 10 October.

3. The Treaty of Paris of 1783 identified the Lake of the Woods as the northwest corner of the United States.

4. The first public move toward creating a company for extending navigation up the Potomac and to the Ohio had already been taken in Virginia. The following announcement dated at Alexandria, 2 Nov. 1784, appeared in the *Virginia Journal and Alexandria Advertiser* on 4 November. Whether the meeting was called at GW's instigation or only with his blessing has not been determined.

"A Meeting is proposed of the Gentlemen of the States of Virginia and Maryland, especially those who live contiguous to Potomack, and wish to see an attempt made to open and extend the navigation of that River.—The objects of this meeting will be to form a company, and determine on the propriety of preferring a petition to their respective Assemblies, praying to be incorporated and favoured with such immunities, as to them may seem proper for such an undertaking—The advantages which both States must derive from the completion of this work, are so numerous and so obvious, that it is hoped this notice will be generally attended to, and that Gentlemen will come prepared to offer such advice and support, as the importance of the plan requires.—The meeting is to be at Mr. LOMAX's on Monday, the 15th inst. at 10 o'clock, A.M."

For an account of the meeting at Alexandria on 15 Nov., see Henry Lee to GW, 18 Nov., n.1. For a summary account of GW's role in the establishment of the Potomac River Company, see the editorial note in GW to Benjamin Harrison, 10 October.

From John Preston

Hond Sir   Novr 6th 1784.

In consequence of receiving your Excellency's favour dated Rockingham Octr 1st 84,[1] I gave the necessary attention due to your business, & have examined all the records of my Office deligently, but find nothing relating to your Lands only the enclosed Warrent of 2000 Acres, a copy of the entry & survey thereon:[2] All warrents granted by Lord Dunmore agreeable to the Proclamation of 1763, Which were recd into the Surveyors Office of Fincastle, where immediately registered; among those I have search'd for yours of 5000 Acres, but cannot find it, which gives me reason to suppose this War[ran]t was neglected or miscarried & never came into my Fathers hands:[3] Possibly it was put into the care of some of the deputies acting under my Father, who not finding suitable Lands to locate it on, never lodged it in the Office, but still kept it in their possession, This is only a bare supposition of my own, & have no grounds for it: But if the person to whom you delivered it could be known, he might give some satisfaction on this head, & such Information as would make known where the War[ran]t is & a line from you on this subject I shall endeavour to procure it, & transmitt it you immediately.

Your apoligy for any trouble you can give me is wholly unecessary, for be assured in this or any other request wherein I can be servicable to you, I shall most chearfully comply. I am with the utmost respect Your Excellencys most Obt Servt

J. Preston

ALS, DLC:GW.

John Preston succeeded his father, William Preston, as surveyor of Montgomery County after his father's death in 1783.

1. Letter not found. GW was at Gabriel Jones's house in Rockingham County on 1 October. See *Diaries*, 4:54–56.

2. John Preston returned to GW his copy of a warrant of survey for 2,000 acres issued by the governor, Lord Dunmore, on 25 Nov. 1773. Dunmore's warrant states that under the terms of the Royal Proclamation of 17 Oct. 1763 Charles Mynn Thruston was entitled to 2,000 acres of land and that Thruston had conveyed his right of survey to GW (DLC:GW). For further information on this 2,000-acre tract on the Great Kanawha, see GW to Thomas Lewis, 1 Feb. 1784, n.6. Preston also enclosed in this letter of 6 Nov. a copy of the survey on the Great Kanawha, which was entered in Fincastle County on 18 April 1774 by his father, the Fincastle County surveyor.

3. William Preston was successively the first surveyor of the counties of Botetourt, from 1769, of Fincastle, from 1772, and of Montgomery, from 1776. The warrant for the 5,000 acres that GW received under the proclamation of 1763 for his own service in the French and Indian War was directed to the surveyor of Botetourt County, not Fincastle where William Preston had become surveyor in 1772. See GW to Samuel Lewis, 1 Feb. 1784, source note and n.1, GW to William Preston, 28 Feb. 1774, and GW to Andrew Lewis, 27 Mar. 1775.

From David Humphreys

My dear General   Paris Novr 11th 1784.

Colonel le Maire who is this moment Setting off for Virginia affords an opportunity for communicating the latest & most important intelligence respecting European politics.[1]

The Emperor & the Dutch have gone so far in their quarrel

about the navigation of the Scheld that there is hardly a possibility that either should recede—indeed the act of recalling their Ministers amounts in the estimation of the world to a declaration of war—besides this, each party is making every hostile preparation; and the Emperor is said to have put 60,000 men in motion towards the quarter which must be the theatre of action: on the other hand, it is supposed the Dutch must have been morally certain of receiving Succour from this nation & from Prussia, or that they would not have proceeded to such lengths as they have done.

Prince Henry the Brother of the King of Prussia has been here some time, his visit is thought to involve some political objects in it—two days ago it was reported he had a private rendevouz with the King at Fontainbleau—it is also rumored that a Camp of 50,000 Men is immediately to be formed in this Kingdom; & that Mr de Vergennes will probably go out of office. but these I give as reports only.

If the war should commence it is likely that almost all Europe will first or last be engaged in it. How happy that our local situation does not require that we should become a party in the quarrels of other nations. And what a wonder that Britain could not have conjured up such a storm before our frail Bark had safely arrived in Port!

In Ireland the troubles do not seem to have subsided—Notwithstanding the interference in Dublin to prevent the election of Members to attend the National Congress, the election has taken place, & Sir E. Newenham who is one, writes Dr Franklin that the Congress will certainly convene[2]—I have the honor to be my Dr Sir your most obedt Servt

D. Humphreys

ALS, DLC:GW.

1. Jacques Le Maire de Gimel (b. 1749), colonel of artillery, whom the Virginia legislature sent back to France on a mission in 1778 and 1779 to secure aid for the state, arrived in Virginia, on this later trip, early in 1785 and then journeyed into Kentucky.

2. See GW's letter to Edward Newenham, 10 June 1784. The letter from Newenham to Benjamin Franklin to which Humphreys is referring is probably the one dated 12 October.

Letter not found: from George Clinton, 12 Nov. 1784. On 25 Nov. GW wrote to Clinton: "A few days ago I had the pleasure to receive your favor of the 12th Instt."

From Normand Bruce

Sir   Washington Cou[n]ty [Md.] 13 Novembr 1784
   There being many reasons to believe that our Specie has
been much lessened not only during the War but ever since the
Peace—It is not however to be doubted, but that much has
been also imported during these periods, but it cannot bear any
proportion to the Exports—Not only the difference of Exchange, which has uniformly since the Peace, been so far above
Par, but, the large Exportations of Specie which still continues,
seems to demonstrate the Ballance to be much against us, and
in favour of all the Manufacturing Countrys with which we
Trade—But notwithstanding these reasons as well as the many
great and obvious inconveniences evidently arrising from the
scarcity of a Circulating Medium amongst us, it is urged by
many that our Complaints on this head are imaginary, main-
taining that there is more specie amongst us at present, than
ever there was at any one Period before—The principle argument aduced in support of this opinion is, it seems, the liberal Prices given for our Comodities, which is by no means
conclusive—it may be owing to very different Causes a scarcity of Produce here, but most probably a brisk demand and
high prices at the Market of Consumption—However admitting that we have as much specie as before the War—yet when
we consider the large quantity of Paper then in Circulation, but
now so much wanted, Our present distress will in a great measure be accounted for—Nor is it probable, that the worst is
over—The insignificance of our Trade at the time of calling
our late large emissions of Paper out of circulation, and for a
considerable time after, the Indulgence of paying Taxes in
produce, and above all the Laws screening Debtors from Suits,
hath hitherto prevented many bad consequences which yet may
be dreaded—In short Sir it must appear evident, to every impartial enquirer, particularly from the embarrassed situation of
the People, and the uncultivated state of our Lands, without the
means of relief usual in all other trading Countrys as well as
heretofore in this, that an addition to our Medium, would not
only be of general benefite by promoting Industry but so Critical seems our situation, that without some speedy and adequate
remedy, we must infallibly be deprived of many of those essen-

tial benefits we had reason to expect from a Peace so very favourable—It therefore certainly becomes an enquiry of the utmost consequence to the Trade & Cultivation of these States, how far the Evil may admit of a speedy and effectual cure.

As it seems impracticable under our present circumstances to procure Specie either by Loan or other ways, adequate to our Exigences & encreasing Business⟨,⟩ Paper seems the only resource left us—I am well aware of the strong prejudices imbibed by many against a paper medium, and during the continuance of the War there might be Reason, but since the Peace we surely have it more in our Power than ever to Emit it on Solid & sufficient funds, and having previous to the Revolution experienced (and most other Civilized Nations still experience) Very Salutary Effects flowing from a Prudent use of it, and surely because we may have been nearly Phisecked to death by the unskilfull application of a Medicine, it by no means follows that we should entirely reject it, when convinced that a Moderate Portion thereof, judiciously administer'd, is the only remedy left us for our disorder—The Benefits arising to any State more particularly to such, circumstanced as we are, uncultivated and unimproved, from Public Emissions are apparent, *and* past Expereince proves the great Advantages flowing therefrom to the Public—a part may be Circulated in discharging Internal Debts, whilst the remainder is lent out in small Sums to Induviduals able to procure Securety for the repayment therof, the annual Interest of which, would not only add to the Public Revenue, but the Sums so lent would give Scope to Industry & Agriculture, the best and surest means of keeping the little specie we have or may hereafter get amongst us, for thereby our Exports would be increased and our Commerce augmented, and a Ballance finally obtained against Those Nations who at present have it against us—For these obvious reasons Public Emissions ought to be preffered by every well wisher of his Country: But the inffluence which some men seems to possess in our Councils, who pretending a Dread of they know not what, have deprived the Public of this benefite and Induviduals of the only seeming rational means of assistance, without it is Emitted on such terms as must Evidently check its Circulation and give the Creditors a very unfair advantage over their Debtors—As therefore we have but little hopes left of seeing Public Emissions the following proposition for Circulating a very small Sum on Private Security, and for Establishing a Bank is submited to your private consideration wether it may admit of such amendment or additions as to be rendered practicable and of Service to the Comunity.

Proposal, That provided the Legislatures of Virginia & Maryland will Emit the Sum of 500,000 Dollars, which they will grant upon Loan to the Subscribers or otherways Vest them with the Priveledge of Emitting and of Circulating such a Sum for and during the term of Ten Years from the date of the Grant or Emission—In consideration whereof they will engage to expend the Sum of [   ] Dollars within the Space of [   ] Years from the date of such Grant towards rendering Potowmack River Navigable from Tide Water, towards its Source, or as far up, as to the nearest convenient Landing for the Westren Waters.

That the said Sum of 500,000 dollars shall be subscribed for and divided into (either 125 or 250) Shares (which will make each share amount to 4000 or 2000 Dollars) and that no Subscription shall be received for more than [   ] Shares nor for less than ¼ Share.

That every Subscriber shall be entitled to a Loan of one half of the Sum Subscribed by him, upon giving Bond with Sufficient Security for the repayment thereof with Interest Annually.

That the other Moiety or Residue of the Money excepting a Sum not exceeding [   ] Dollars shall be lent out upon Satisfactory Security in Sums not exceeding [   ] Dollars to any one Person at the Annual Interest of 5 prCt.

That one half of the Amount of the Proposed Emissions shall be redeemed and paid off in the year 179[   ] and the other Moiety in the year following; and for the certain and effectual redemption whereof the Subscribers &c. to be liable.

That the Subscribers &c. shall be incorporated by the Name of the Potowmack Company with such other further necessary Priveledges as the respective Legislatures may judge proper for their encouragement and for the effectual securing the repayment of Money lent by them.

That the Proprietors shall meet on the [   ] day of [   ] next and on the same day annually at Alexandria there to Elect by Ballot a Governour [   ] Directors [   ] Treasurer & Secratary.

That the Governour with a Majority of Directors shall meet Quarterly and be empowered to make such further Appointments as may be found necessary, make Contracts fix the Price of Wages, Draw on the Treasurer and give such directions from time to time as may be necessary for executing with Delegence & frugality, the intended Navigation in a Manner which shall be deemed of the greatest Public Utility.

The Treasurer shall give approved Security for a faithfull discharge of Trust reposed in him.

A fair Record shall be kept of all proceedings by the Secratary who shall regularly attend the Annual meetings of the Proprietors and at All meetings of the Governour & Directors.

Every Subscriber or Subscribers of each share shall only have a Vote in the Proceedings and may Vote by Proxy Authorized under Hand & Seal & lodged with the Secretary Previous to Voting.

And to Establish a fund upon which to Circulate Notes payable on demand, Similar to Bank Notes.

That every Subscriber do pay unto the [   ] in Gold or Silver or in Good Bills of Exchange (payable in Europe) on or before the first day of [   ] next a Sum equal to ⅒ of their Subscriptions—the like Sum, at the expiration of [   ] Months from that time, and so on untill half the Amount of the Subscriptions are paid in.

That the Governour & Directors shall be empowred to receive new Subscriptions towards encreasing the Capital Stock on such terms as they may judge Proper.

That Notes shall be Emitted from time to time, not to exceed the Proportion of [   ] Dollars for one Received, as the Payments are made.

That Cash Accounts shall be opened by which every Person upon giving approved Security shall be advanced Cash to a certain Extent, at such times and in such Proportions as he may order, for which [   ] prCt is to be charged from the time the Money is advanced—He also having the liberty of returning such Sums (not less however than [   ] Dollars at a time) as it may suit him, on which the like Interest will be allowed whilst in Bank.

A supposed State agreeable to the above out Lines

		Virga	Curry
Sum proposed to St⟨rick⟩ 500.000 Dollars		6/.	£150.000
10 Years Interest at 5 prCt on £150,000		is	£ 75.000
To Be expended on Potowmack supports	£40000		
10 years Salery to Secratary Treasurer	1500		
Governour, Directors, Expences & on			
Business for 10 years—say	7500		
Clerks Overseers &c. Wages for 10 years	7500		56 000

By this state there remains a Ballance of £18 500 out of which however is to be deducted loss by bad debts &c. It seems unecessary to enter into any further Comment on the Benefits arising from the Circulation even of this small Sum—doubtless many Industrious Persons might therefrom be furnished with the means of Prosecuting their Improvements and shall only observe that the Sum being so Small in Comparison to the Trade of Potowmack even in its present State and the number of People who are closely interested in the success of this Beneficial Undertaking, which can never be executed upon more advantageous terms to them selves and Posterity it is but reasonable to Presume that notwithstanding our Prejudices against Paper, there can be no doubt but that this Money will Circulate freely.

As the Nature of Banking may not have come under your Consideration, I thought that a few observations on that Subject might not be construed as an intrusion on Your Patience but at Present I am unavoidably called off, and altho after this delay it seems strangely ridiculous to offer an excuse for the hurry and incorrectness with which this is wrote yet such has been my case that this is the first day of rest I have enjoy'd not having been two days in a Place since I had the pleasure of seeing you—I trust that I shall not from the freedom which I have taken in communicating my Sentiments incure Your Censure as a Projector—The Profit which the Public might reap from the Circulation of Paper is apparently considerable, I have therefore ever thought that the States only ought to possess these Advantages and enjoy the Monopoly, But as there is reason to fear that the Public Benefite may be overlooked amidst that encreasing eagarness with which Induviduals amongst us seems to prosecute their Particular Interests, I have therefore been induced to trouble you, hoping that as the Sum here intended to be Circulated is so trifling and the services proposed to be rendered of such Public Advantage & Utility that this Money would be received with avidity and Circulated freely in which case it might also prove a means of effacing our prejudices against Paper and pave the way for future Emission should you however Sir deem the proposal in consistant I have inclosed the outlines of another mode of Executing this important Business upon the same principles, that Works of this kind are most commonly undertaken and executed[1]—I remain, most Worthy Sir with perfect Respect and Esteem your very Obdt Servt

Normd Bruce

ALS, MnHi.

Normand Bruce (d. 1811), a Scot by birth, lived in Frederick County, Maryland. He had large landholdings in that county and also in Montgomery, Prince George's, and Washington counties, Maryland. In 1783 the Maryland legislature had him and Charles Beatty look into and report on the feasibility of "opening, clearing, and making navigable the River Potomack" to the Maryland line (*Md. Senate Proceedings*, 443; see also GW's notes on the Bruce-Beatty report in note 1). When at Bath in September 1784, GW talked at length with Bruce about connecting the upper reaches of the Potomac to the Ohio River by means of other streams and short land portages. GW also had access to the Bruce-Beatty report of 1783, on which he made notes (see *Diaries*, 4:11–14).

1. The text of Bruce's alternate plan is: "Proposals of opening the Navigation of Potowmack for which purpose the Sum of 150,000 dollars shall be subscribed & divided into Seventy five Shares of 2000 dollars each.

"No Subscription shall be taken for more than [   ] Shares nor less than ¼ of a Share.

"The Subscribers to be incorporated by Acts of the Virga and Maryld Legislatures by name of the Potomack Company with an Exclusive right to them, their Heirs, Assigns &c. to all the Water they may think propper to collect into their Canals and the Lands through which the same may run shall be condemned for their use and that they shall have power to Levy on all Boats Rafts &c. Passing thru their Cannals a Toll not exceeding [   ] pr Ton.

"The Proprietors shall meet on the [   ] Day of [   ] next at Alexandria and on the same day Annually and then Elect by a Majority of Votes a Governour and [   ] Directors a Treasurer Secretary for the year.

"The Governour with a Majority of Directors shall have Power to make Contracts fix the Price of Wages and Employ such Persons to direct & Oversee the Work as they shall find necessary & Draw on the Treasurer for Money.

"The Treasurer shall give Security for discharge of Trust.

"The Company to be impowed by the Legislature of the Two States to Emit & Circulate a Sum not exceeding Sixty thousand Dollars which shall pass & be receivd in payment of Taxes & Public dues untill the year [   ] when the sum shall be called in & paid off by the Compy.

"Each Subscriber shall pay into the Hands of the Treasurer such parts of his share and at such times as the Governour & Directors shall order.

"The Holder or Holders of each share shall only have a Vote in the Proceedings & May Vote by Proxy Authorized under the Hand & Seal & Lodged with the Secratary Previous to receiving such Votes.

"The Secratary shall attend the Meetings of the Proprietors & of the Governour & Directors & keep a fair Record of all their Proceedings and Lay the Same before the meetings of the Proprietors.

"P.S. The above Estimate is made upon a supposition that 150,000 dolls. is component for the work—It exceeds the Sum mentioned in the Returns of C. Beatty & myself to the assembly of this State—but the manner in which we were obliged to make the Survey rendered much of the Value of the Business to be done Guess Work" (AD, MnHi).

To compare Bruce's two alternate plans for a Potomac River company with the one adopted by the Virginia and Maryland legislatures in December 1784 and January 1785, see Enclosure I in Beverly Randolph to GW, 15 December. Bruce also enclosed a map that he had drawn, which GW docketed: "Sketch of the Country between the Waters of the Potomack—And those of Yohiogany—& Monongahe[la]."

It is not known whether it was before or after receiving Bruce's letter that GW made the following notes on the report that Bruce and Charles Beatty made to the Maryland legislature in 1783, which GW heads: "Taken from Messrs Charles Beatty, and Normd Bruces report & estimate, respecting the opening the Navigation of the River Patomack from Fort Cumberland to tide water":

"No actual Survey of the River has been made by them.

"The North branch of the River may easily be made Navigable a considerable distance above Fort Cumberland.

"The object would be, to shorten the Portage between it and the western waters.

"These are yet to be explored—& the communication between.

"The Estimate therefore is from Fort Cumberland only.

"The River Potomack runs over a hard firm bottom & penetrates many mountains & ridges of Land which occasion Falls & Rapids.

"All of which may be rendered safely navigable except at three places in the Channel of the Rivr.

"Viz. at the Shannondoah Falls—which from the Beginning thereof to Harpers Ferry about one Mile is 20 feet. 2 Locks on the Virginia Side; a narrow space to cut through, none on the Maryld side, the Mountn butting close down. Shannondoah Rivr coming in here, the channel of the River (Potk) must be used till it is passed—Then in another mile 10 feet fall requiring one Lock on the Maryland Shore. but removing some obstructions, & swelling the water in other places this last may be made Navigable for Batteaus & Rafts— The estimated distance of these falls from Fort Cumberland—is about 110 or 20 miles.

"The Seneca Falls, distant from these about 60 Miles continues about a mile; & is nearly 10 feet, the principal channel much encumbered with rieffs of Rocks but by means of some Islds on the Virginia side may easily be made navigable & with safety, without a Lock.

"The great Falls distant from the last about 6 miles, & only a trifling impediment in the way, is about 80 feet in the course of a mile—and requires 8 Locks on the Virginia Side.

"From hence to the lower Falls is abt 6 miles in wch distance there are several Rapids, but wch may be easily made passable as it only requires to remove stones wch are thickly intersperced in the bed of the River in a detached manner.

"From the upper end of the rapids at the lower falls to tide water may be about 2 miles—and 40 feet fall requiring 4 locks on the Maryld shore to be taken out opposite the lower end of an Island above into a cove below at some distance below the flowing of the tide which is necessary for the security of the Locks against floods & Ice.

"The River between Fort Cumberland and the Shannondoah Falls is rapid & impetuous in places, yet, during the moderate floods admits rafts to pass with safety and is navigated in its pres[en]t state by small Vessels in the Spring, & beginning of Summer. afterwards, the Waters getting low & spreading over a wide bed become too shallow.

"There are also several Rapids between the Shannondoah & Seneca falls which are not easily passed in dry weather—the most considerable of them is the Catoctan which are dangerous in their *present* state, but may easily be renderd navigable.

"Vessels of 6, & not exceeding 10 Tons burthen, are recommended tho' the Canals should be made to suit larger Vessels, & Rafts drawing 3 feet water & 60 feet long.

"It appears very difficult to them to render this river navigable for heavy Vessels from the many rapids.

"Are of opinion (under all circumstances) that the navigation from Fort Cumberland to the great falls may be completed in two years.

"Recommends the beginning with this part of the river for several reasons "Three years more might finish the remainder of the work—to tide water.

"Expence	Dollars
From Fort Cumberland to the Shannonh Falls	12,000
Cutting a Canal at Do 1 mile long & 20 feet wide 3½ feet deep	4,000
Making 2 Locks in ditto	6,000
Removing Rocks, swelling the water &ca in sundry places betwn Harpers Ferry & the Seneca Falls	4,000
At the Seneca falls	3,000
Total, from Ft Cumbd to the Gt Falls	29,000
Cutting a Canal 1 Mile long at the G. Falls	8,000
Erecting 8 Locks—difficult grd	26,000
	·34,000
Betwn the Great & little Falls	6,000
Cutting a Canal at the little Falls 3 Miles long	9,000
4 Locks 16 feet wide, 3½ deep, & 60 feet in length	11,000
Makg a Dam & ca to regul[at]e the Water	3,000
	23,000
Whole amount	92,000"

(AD, MHi: Jeremiah Colburn Papers).

From Benjamin Harrison

My Dear Sir,   Rich[mon]d [Va.] Novr 13th 1784

I was in great hopes of seeing you here before this that I might have acknowledged the rect of your favor of the 10th of last month in person, and have told you how much I approve your plan for opening the navigation of the western waters. The letter was so much more explicit than I could be that I took the liberty to lay it before the assembly, who appear so impress'd with the utility of the measure that I dare say they will order the survey you propose immediately and will at their next sitting proceed to carry the plan into execution.[1]

My time of service is so near expiring that I must remove my family and effects next week or my successor will elbow me out perhaps which would not be quite so comfortable, indeed there is a vacancy for an assembly man in Chs city and I shall endeavour to fill it and it seems there is such opposition to me that unless I go down a few days before the election there is a probability of my being disappointed.[2] Mrs Harrison joins me in compliments to your good lady, who she had hopes of seeing here when last down to have renew'd an acquaintance of very long standing but which has been so much interruped of late years.[3] I am with every sentiment of esteem and regard Dr Sir your affect. and obedt servt

Benj. Harrison

ALS, DLC:GW.

1. Governor Harrison wrote the Virginia house of assembly early in the session, on both 1 and 2 Nov., enclosing "sundry letters and papers." There is no indication in the assembly's journal that GW's proposals for opening up the Potomac were discussed on the floor of the house before his arrival in Richmond on 14 November. For GW's role in the enactment of the Potomac River Company bill in both the Virginia and Maryland legislatures, see editorial note: GW and the Potomac River Company, in GW to Harrison, 10 October.

2. Henry Southall, not Harrison, became in 1785 a delegate from Charles City County in place of William Green Munford who seems not to have attended either the spring or the fall session of the legislature in 1784. Edmund Pendleton reported to Richard Henry Lee on 18 April 1785 that Governor Harrison had "lost his election in Charles City, which he imputes I hear, to the intrigues of his old friend the speaker and is, as usual, very angry, that he should meet with this reward from the people, for thirty-six years faithful service" (Mays, *Pendleton Letters*, 2:479–80). Harrison went to the house of delegates from Surry County in the fall of 1785 and shortly replaced as speaker the other delegate from Charles City County, John Tyler.

3. Harrison's wife Elizabeth was the sister of Martha Washington's brother-in-law, Burwell Bassett. Mrs. Washington and Mrs. Harrison saw one another frequently in the prewar years when both their husbands regularly attended the meetings of the House of Burgesses in Williamsburg.

Letter not found: from Henry Lee, 15 Nov. 1784. On 18 Nov. Lee wrote to GW: "I did myself the pleasure of writing to you on the 15th."

To Officials of the City of Richmond

[Richmond, Va., 15 November 1784]
To—The Worshipful the Mayor, Recorder, Aldermen, & Common Council of the City of Richmond.
Gentlemen,

I derive great honor from your congratulatory address; the language of which, is too flattering not to have excited my utmost gratitude.[1]

To the Smiles of Heaven—to a virtuous & gallant Army—and to the exertions of my fellow Citizens of the Union—(not to superior talents of mine) are to be ascribed the blessings of that liberty, Independence, & Peace, of wch we are all now in the enjoyment. Whilst these are afforded us, & while the advantages of commerce are not only offered but are solliciting our acceptance, it must be our own fault indeed if we do not make them productive of a rich & plenteous harvest—and of that National honor & glory, which should be characteristic of a young, & rising Empire.

That this growing City may enjoy all the benefits which are to be derived from them, in the fullest extent—that it may improve such as nature has bestowed—and that it may soon be ranked among the first in the Union for population, commerce & wealth is my sincere and fervent wish.

Go: Washington

ADfS, DLC:GW; LB, DLC:GW. The differences between GW's draft copy and letter-book copy are slight. The letter-book copy is dated "15th Novembr 1784."

1. The *Virginia Journal and Alexandria Advertiser* on 2 Dec. carried the following item from Richmond, dated 20 Nov.: "On Sunday last [14 Nov.] arrived in this city, our worthy and beloved late Commander in Chief. His arrival was announced by the discharge of cannon; and on the evening following, the citizens, wishing to show every mark of respect to so illustrious a character, illuminated their houses in a most elegant manner.

"On the Thursday following, the Marquis la Fayette, attended by two French Gentlemen of distinction, also arrived. His services in the late revolution, and particularly in this State, are too well known to need encomiums.

"Same day, the merchants of the city, entertained them with a sumptuous dinner, at Mr. Trower's tavern; where also were present, the Members of the General Assembly, the Governor, Members of the Council of State, and the principal Gentlemen of the city.

"And Yesterday evening, a ball at the capital, by the common Hall."

This is followed by extensive excerpts from the journal of the house of delegates (see GW to House of Delegates, 15 Nov., n.1), ending with GW's reply to the address from the officials of the city of Richmond. The text of the city's address, dated 15 Nov. at Richmond, is: "Actuated by every Sentiment which can inspire a grateful People, the Mayor, Recorder, Alderman & Common Council of the City of Richmond, embrace this long wished for Opportunity of congratulating you on your Return to the Bosom of Peace and Retirement in your native Country, after so many years honourably spent amidst the Toils and Tumults of a War, which, thro' the Smiles of Heaven on your Exertions, has been productive of Liberty, Glory, & Independence to an extensive Empire.

"On seeing you Sir, in this City, we feel all that Men can feel, who are indebted to you for every social Enjoyment, and who are deeply impressed with a Conviction, that, if the late illustrious Leader of the Armies of America, had not possessed and exercised, every Talent, and every Virtue, which can dignify the Hero and the Patriot, we might not at this Day have dared to speak the Language of free born Citizens, nor would we have seen Commerce & Navigation with their fruitful Train, liberated from their Shackles, inviting the Inhabitants of distant Nations to seek an Asylum and a Residence Among us.

"When in the Review of a few Past years, we behold you not only forming Soldiers, but also teaching them to Conquer, when we contemplate that Prudence, Courage & magnanimity, which surmounting every Difficulty, regardless of every Danger; and Contemning every Reward, excited not only the veneration of your Country, but even commanding the Admiration and Applause of her Enemies, & spread the Fame of America, in the remotest Corners of the world, giving his Rank & Consequence among the Kingdoms of the Earth, and when we think what we might have been if Washington had not existed our Hearts expand with Emotions too strong for utterance, and we can only pray that the supreme giver of all Victory may crown you with his choicest Blessings—here and with never fading glory hereafter. Signed by order of the Common Hall" (DLC:GW).

To Virginia House of Delegates

Gentlemen   [Richmond, Va., 15 November 1784]

My sensibility is deeply affected by this distinguished mark of the affectionate regard of your honble House. I lament upon this occasion that my powers of utterance will not do justice to my feelings; and shall rely upon your indulgent report to supply the defect; at the sametime I pray you to present for me the strongest assurances of unalterable affection & gratitude for this last pleasing & flattering attention of my Country.[1]

ADf, DLC:GW; LB, DLC:GW. The differences between the draft and letter-book copies are minimal; for the difference in wording of the version printed in the journals of the house for 16 Nov. 1784, see note 1.

1. There is the following entry in the journal of the house of delegates for 15 Nov.: "The House being informed of the arrival of Gen. Washington, in this city;

"*Resolved, nemine contra dicente,* That as a mark of their reverence for his character, and affection of his person, a committee of five members be appointed to wait upon him, with the respectful regards of this House, to express to him the satisfaction they feel in the opportunity afforded, by his presence, of offering this tribute to his merits; and to assure him, that, as they not only retain the most lasting impressions of the transcendent services rendered in his late public character, but have, since his return to private life, experienced proofs, that no change of situation can turn his thoughts from the welfare of his country, so his happiness can never cease to be an object of their most devout wishes and fervent supplications.

"And a committee was appointed, of Messrs. [Patrick] Henry, [Joseph] Jones of King George, [James] Madison, Carter Henry Harrison, and [Edward] Carrington" (*House of Delegates Journal, 1781–1785*).

Later in the day ("Monday"), Patrick Henry wrote GW: "Having the Honour to be one of a Committee who are charged with the inclosed Resolution of the House of Delegates, I beg to know when it will be agreable for the Committee to wait on you? Some of the Gentlemen have mentioned tomorrow 10'o'clock, but I am very sure they will take the greatest pleasure in conform ing to your Wishes as to Time & Place. I beg Leave to assure you I am with the greatest possible Regards Dear sir your most obedient Servant" (DLC:GW).

On 16 Nov. "Mr. Henry reported, from the committee appointed to wait upon General Washington, with the resolution of this House, of yesterday, that the committee had, according to order, waited upon the General, and presented him with the said resolution, to which he was pleased to return the following answer." The text of GW's response in the journal of the house has wording different from the draft and the letter-book version in the first clause of the second sentence, which in the journal reads: "I lament, upon this occasion, the want of those powers, which would enable me to do justice to my feelings" (*House of Delegates Journal, 1781–1785*).

From Charles Washington

Dear Brother,   Berkeley [Va.] Novr 16th 1784
    The Death of Mr Nourse, renders it Necesary, for some Person to Succeed him in the guardian Ship of the two Little Boys,

who I understand are at School at George Town.¹ wishing them not to be Neglected, am Prevailed upon by my Brother John, to undertake that Office. but the distance being great, aded to some Infurmatives which I labour under, makes it very Inconveniant for me [to] Ride that distance—this fa[vo]re I would beg of you (if not Disagreable) through The Assistance of Mr Lund Washington, when Conveniant, to make Inquiry into there Necesary Wants and those to be Supply'd, as well as other Demands against them—I would by know means wish you to be in advance on there Acct, as there Annual Income will greatly overgo there Expenditures, and therefore would Deposet, so much Money in your Hands, so as to answer every purpose— Should this be disagreble or Inconveniant to you, I would then beg your advice, whether you would think it Prudent to remoove them to Mr Booths Academy, which at present stands in the highest Reputation, and from the great Regard he Expreses for our Family, I know the greatest justice wou'd be done them. Aded to this I have my Own Little Son there, which of Course calls upon me to see every Attention paid to him, and therefore the same Trouble wou'd do for the three.²

A few Lines Lodged in the Post Office at Alexandria, Directed to the Care of Capt. Benjn Beeler (A Nabour of mine) & where the Post mak a Stage will Come safe and soon to hand Should you of hear'd any thing from my Son since I had the pleasure of seeing you, shall take it kind³ of you to let me know, by the last Letter I had from him I had reason to believe he wou'd been in this State by this Time, which gives me reason to Believe his state of Health is the Cause of it.⁴ I am Dear Sir with the Greatest Regard And Esteem your Affecte Brother

Chas Washington

ALS, MH: Jared Sparks Collection.

1. For GW's dealings with James Nourse regarding the care of his nephews, George Steptoe and Lawrence Augustine Washington, see GW to Nourse, 22 Jan. 1784, and nn.1–3. Nourse died at Annapolis on 10 October.

2. The boys, who until recently had been under the care of the Rev. David Griffith in Alexandria, at this time were being schooled by the Rev. Stephen Bloomer Balch across the river in Georgetown. See GW to Griffith, 29 Aug. 1784, n.1. They remained with Balch until the end of 1786 when GW gave the charge of them to Samuel Hanson of Samuel in Alexandria (see Hanson to GW, 27 Jan. 1787). Booth of "Mr Booths Academy" was probably William Booth, a fairly frequent visitor at Mount Vernon. Before 1773, Colonel Booth moved from his plantation in Westmoreland County, across Nomini Creek

from John Augustine Washington's place, to Frederick County where he was living near Charles Washington at this time.

3. He wrote "king" instead of "kind."

4. GW's response to his brother's letter has not been found, but see Charles Washington to GW, 19 Feb. 1785, and GW to Charles Washington, 12 April 1785. See also GW to George Augustine Washington, 26 Nov. 1784.

Letter not found: from Richard Claiborne, 17 Nov. 1784. On 15 Dec. GW wrote to Claiborne: "I have received your letter of the 17th ulto."

From Henry Lee, Jr.

My dear Genl   Alexand[ri]a [Va.] Novr 18th 84.

I did myself the pleasure of writing to you on the 15th Since which the meeting have concluded their business.[1] they determined to send the petition to the representatives of this county, I beleive, & to trouble you with their bill for perusal, & then to place it in proper hands. However the express who will deliver this, is sent purposely by the meeting with our papers, & will bear a letr to you from the chairman.[2] Thus you will receive the matter fully explained. This would have superceded the necessity of any communication from me, did I not think it proper to suggest to you two changes in the bill which appear to many, unsurmountable objections—if they strike you so, it would be well to communicate them, that they may be altered—the one is, the taxing the company with recompensing individuals for all new damages which may arise from or by means of the canal locks &c.—the 2d is the authorizing the company to purchase & erect mill seats water works &c.—the first of these will prevent subscriptions—the 2d permits monopoly, which is disgusting— as the tolls are in the first of the bills decided to be adequate compensation for the expence & in accomplishing the object, it appears mercenary to pray the addition of extra privileges— However the changes will speak for themselves.[3]

The hurry which attended the whole business subjects the bill to many grammatical errors & omissions—this can easily be amended by the gentlemen to whom it may be entrusted. I hope it may strike the assembly in the same manner, the inhabitants of this country view it, & that success may attend the plan in every stage of it. I am my dear Genl with unalterable respect & affection Your friend & ob. servt

Henry Lee Junr

ALS, ICU.

Henry Lee (1756–1818), known as Light-Horse Harry, was deeply interested in the Potomac River Company from its inception. In 1782, Lee married Matilda Lee, the heiress to Stratford Hall in Westmoreland County where he at this time was living.

1. Lee's letter written on 15 Nov., which was the day interested gentlemen from Maryland and Virginia met at Alexandria to lay plans for forming a company to improve the navigation of the Potomac (see GW to Jacob Read, 3 Nov., n.4), has not been found. See also the editorial note in GW to Benjamin Harrison, 10 October. The following report of the meeting appeared in the Alexandria newspaper on 25 Nov.: "On Monday the 15th Instant, at a very numerous and respectable Meeting of the Gentlemen of this State and Maryland, convened by public Advertisement at Mr Lomax's Tavern, to deliberate and consult on the vast, great, political and commercial Object, *the rendering navigable the River Potomack from Tide Water*—It was unanimously Resolved, That every possible Effort ought to be exerted to render these waters navigable to their utmost Sources. In consequence Petitions to the respective Honorable Assemblies were prepared, praying to form a Company, with such Immunities as might seem meet to them to grant. The Patriotism and Zeal of the Meeting, make it a Matter of little Doubt, but that the respective Honorable Assemblies will most cheerfully grant the Prayer of the Petitions, and render every possible Assistance to complete so great a national Concern.

"The opening of the Navigation of Potomack is, perhaps, a Work of more political than commercial Consequence, as it will be one of the grandest Chains for preserving the federal Union, the Western world will have free Access to us, and we shall be one and the same People, whatever System of European Politics may be adopted.—In short, it is a Work so big, that the intellectual Faculties cannot take it at a View.

"The Company in their Plan, have engaged to accomplish the Navigation from the Source to the Upper Falls in Three Years, about Two Hundred Miles from us, and to make it complete to Tide-Water in Ten Years.—The Commerce and Riches that must of Necessity pour down upon us, are too obvious to mention" (*Virginia Journal and Alexandria Advertiser*). More or less the same account appeared in the *Virginia Gazette, or, the American Advertiser* (Richmond) on 4 December.

2. GW went from Mount Vernon to Richmond shortly before the meeting was held in Alexandria, arriving in the capital on Sunday, 14 Nov., and remaining there until he and Lafayette departed for Mount Vernon about a week later. One of the Fairfax County representatives, Thomas West, did not take his seat in the house of delegates in Richmond until 10 Nov., and he had left by 6 Dec.; the other delegate, Alexander Henderson, did not arrive at the capitol until 18 December. Most of the important decisions regarding the proposed Potomac River Company were made when neither of these men were present. The draft of the bill for creating a Potomac River company with a covering letter and probably a copy of the petition of the Alexandria meeting to the two state legislatures did not reach GW until after his return to Mount Vernon from Richmond. He at that time, on 28 Nov., forwarded the documents to James Madison (see GW to Madison, 28 Nov.).

3. One may infer from Lee's discussion here of the original draft of the Potomac River bill, as is in any case most likely, that GW had already been made familiar with the bill's contents, or even participated in its drafting, before he left for Richmond.

From Arthur Lee

Dear Sir   Carlisle [Pa.] Novr 19th 1784
I have the pleasure of enclosing you a Copy of the treaty lately concluded with the Six Nations, in which the carrying place & the fort of Niagara, together with a competent district round Oswego are securd to the U.S. By attempting a speedier rout down the Susquehannah, we have been thrown greatly back as to the time appointed for the 2d treaty. But I hope we shall have compleated that by the middle of next month; so that the laying off of that Country may commence in the Spring.[1]

I beg to have my very best respects presented to Mrs Washington—& have the honor to be, with the most entire esteem, Dear Sir Yr most Obedt Servt

Arthur Lee

ALS, DLC:GW.
1. For the negotiation of the treaty of Fort Stanwix, 22 Oct. 1784, see Jacob Read to GW, 13 Aug., n.2. The text of this treaty of peace with the Iroquois is in Kappler, *Indian Treaties*, 2:5 6. A later treaty with "The Wiondot, Delaware, Chippewa, and Ottowa Nations" was concluded at Fort McIntosh on 21 Jan. 1785 (ibid., 6–8). Arthur Lee was one of the commissioners appointed by Congress to treat with the Indians. The copy of the treaty of Fort Stanwix that Lee enclosed is in Arthur Lee's hand. The second copy of the treaty in DLC:GW is probably the one sent to GW on 20 Nov. by Richard Henry Lee.

From Fontenille

My General,   Paris 20 Ner—1784.
I am to Sensibly affected at the gratefull hommage you so Justly receive from the state of Virginia to resist the desire of Expressing you My Joye upon this occasion; the good fortune I have had of being able to Say you mine Will engage you, I hope My General, to Excuse the Liberty I take to Congratulate upon this Opportunity, and of assuring you, that the Gratitude and Admiration I am Penetrated of for you are as strongly impressed in My heart as Your Glory in America.[1]

Will you be Kind Enough to Excuse the Broken inglish I make Me of to Express the Respectfull sentiments With Which I have the honour to be My General Your Most Obedient servant

M[arqu]is de fontenilles

I have the honour to Present My Respectfull Compliments to Milady Washington.

ALS, DLC:GW.
  1. Fontenille may be referring to the resolution of the Virginia legislature of 22 June 1784 providing for having a statue of GW made. See Thomas Jefferson to GW, 10 Dec. 1784. Fontenille visited Mount Vernon in April (see GW to Thomas Mifflin, 4 April 1784, nn.2 and 3).

From Richard Henry Lee

Dear Sir,   Trenton in N. Jersey Novr 20. 1784
  I should sooner have done myself the honor of writing to you, if it had been in my power to have communicated any thing agreeable—But I could only have informed you that we had not, have not, nor can we say when, Members enough will be assembled to make a Congress. As yet we have but four States convened. This lassitude in our public councils must afflict our friends, and encourage the hopes of our Trans-Atlantic foes, who look at us with an evil eye. Mr Wolcott arrived here yesterday with the Treaty made at Fort Stanwix with the Six Nations, and he informs us that the other two Commissioners have proceeded to Pittsburg to treat with the western Tribes. He thinks (from the satisfaction that appeared among some Shawanese Chiefs who were at Fort Stanwix) that the Commissioners will not find much difficulty in their treaty with the western Indians. I have the honor to inclose you a copy of the Northern treaty, and shall be happy to know your opinion of it.[1]
  I understand from Mr Wolcott, that the Commissioners of the United States met many difficulties thrown in their way by N. York, which they overcame at last by firmness and perseverance. It is unfortunate when individual views obstruct general measures, and more especially when a State becomes opposed to the States; because it seems to confirm the predictions of those who wish us not well, and who cherish hopes

from a discord that may arise from different interests. Colo. Monroe, of our delegation, who is lately returned from a Tour to Montreal, Niagara, and Lake Erie, informs us that he learnt in his journey, that the western posts were to be detained from us; and that the reason assigned was, because of the conduct of N. York and Virginia. The former for pushing the law of confiscation beyond the terms of peace, and Virginia for not repealing the laws that impede the recovery of British debts. The Governor of N. York told Colo. Monroe, that it was a mistaken charge upon them, for that they had not confiscated since the provisional articles. It is to be lamented that any pretext should be furnished for injuring us in the essential manner that the detention of these posts will do.[2] The Parliament, it seems, is prorogued without touching the subject of their trade with us, altho a committee of the privy Council upon the petition of the West India merchants and planters, had reported an approbation of all the silly, malign principles of Lord Sheffield respecting our trade with the B.W. Indies. This book of Lord Sheffields has been ably answerd by several writers in G. Britain.[3] My respects, if you please, to your Lady—I hope that she has recoverd her health. I have the honor to be dear Sir your most obedient and very humble servant

Richard Henry Lee

ALS, PHi: Gratz Collection.
   1. See Arthur Lee to GW, 19 Nov., n.1.
   2. See GW's response of 14 December.
   3. John Baker Holroyd (1735–1821), who in 1781 was made an Irish peer, Baron Sheffield of Dunamore, published in 1783 his *Observations on the Commerce of the American States*, which went into its sixth edition in 1784. He wrote his treatise for the purpose of opposing Charles James Fox's move to relax Britain's trade restrictions affecting the United States.

From Henry Knox

Dorchester near Boston [Mass.] 23 Novr 1784
   Heaven forbid my dear Sir, that you should measure my affection for you by the frequency of my letters. I have been absent from this place, a considerable part of the summer and upon my return I learned that you had gone to the Western Waters, and would not return untill the beginning of this

month.[1] There is another reason which I confess has had its influence. I considered you as overwhelmed with letters from every body, and upon every subject, and that it would be unreasonable in me to add to your vexation. I have contented myself with preserving that pure and sincere attachment which I shall carry to my grave.

Our dear friend the Marquis de la Fayette is probably now in Virginia. We have had the happiness of having him here, and I think he was well pleased with his reception. We have had reports that it was your intention to come this way. whenever you shall find it convenient to make the journey, you will experience with how much ardor the people love and respect you.[2]

On the 4th of this month, Mrs Knox presented me with another. She and her children are in perfect health, and she unites wth [me] in her affectionate compliments to you and Mrs Washington.

We have no politics. Indeed I do not know of any that are in operation on the continent—excepting those creeping principles of self or local politics which are the reverse of what ought to actuate us in the present moment, and which can neither form the dignity nor strength of a great nation. I am my Dear Sir with great respect and attachment Your truly affectionate

H. Knox

ALS, DLC:GW.

1. On 5 Dec. GW made an almost identical apology to Knox; their letters must have crossed. Knox's most recent letter to GW is dated 26 July and GW's is dated 2 June.

2. See Lafayette to GW, 22 Oct., n.1. Lafayette or someone else seems to have given the impression that GW would travel north with Lafayette when Lafayette left Mount Vernon. See, in particular, the letters of James Duane and Udny Hay of 16 Dec. and that of Benjamin Walker of 20 December. See also Lafayette to GW, 22 October.

To Henry Lee, Jr.

Mount Vernon Wednesday Afternoon.
Dr Sir,   24th Novr [1784]

Accompanied by the Marquis de la Fayette, Captn Grancheau & the Chevr Caraman, I am just arrived at this place.[1] The Marquis joins me in wishes to see you—come then to Dinner tomorrow, or as soon as you can make it convenient.

I have heard since I came home, indeed at Dumfries, of some dispatches which went down for me from the Commee; but none have yet got to hand.[2] I should be glad to receive duplicates. it may be necessary. I am, Yrs affectionately

G. Washington

P.S. Come prepared to stay a few days.

If Mr Fendal is disengaged I should be glad if he would accompany you.[3] G.W.

ALS, CSmH.
1. GW and Lafayette remained in Richmond until as late as 20 November. See GW to the Officials of the City of Richmond, 15 Nov., n.1. GW's cash accounts for 22 Nov. indicate that he paid the expenses of his guests on their journey from Richmond to Mount Vernon: "By Exp[ense]s at Hanno[ver] Ct House £1.13.1, at Bowl[in]g Green £3.15. . . . By D[itt]o at Fredericksburgh £3.76, at Staff[or]d Ct H[ou]s[e] £3.5.6. . . . By D[itt]o at Dumfries 1.10.1, Servts on the journey 13/10. . . ."
2. See Henry Lee to GW, 18 Nov., n.2.
3. Philip Richard Fendall moved from Stratford Hall in 1782 with his wife, Ann Steptoe Lee, the widow of Philip Ludwell Lee. The Fendalls lived in Alexandria at this time.

To George Clinton

Dear Sir,   Mount Vernon 25th Novr 1784

A few days ago I had the pleasure to receive your favor of the 12th Instt. Altho' I felt pain from your Silence, I should have imputed it to any cause rather than a diminution of friendship. The warmth of which I feel too sensibly *for* you, to harbour a suspicion of the want of it *in* you, without being conscious of having given cause for the change—having ever flatterd myself that our regards were reciprocal.[1]

It gives me great pleasure to learn from yourself, that the State over which you preside is tranquil. Would to God it may ever remain so, and that all others would follow the example. Internal dissentions, and jarring with our Neighbours, are not only productive of mischievous consequences, as it respects ourselves, but has a tendency to lessen our national character, & importance in the eyes of European powers. If any thing can, this will expose us to their intrieguing politics, & may shake the Union.

It has been my avowed & uniform opinion, ever since the interview between Baron de Steuben & Genl Haldimand last year, that whilst a pretext could be found, the Western Posts would be withheld from us; and I do not think I should hazard a false prediction, were I to add, that they never will come into our hands in the condition they now are. When pretexts can no longer put on a decent garb, a season may be named for the surrender, in which it would be impracticable for us to plant a garrison, or transport provisions & stores. an interregnum would then follow, during which the Indians by innuendos, may reduce them to ashes. I wish it may be otherwise, but these are my opinions.

I am sorry we have been disappointed in our expectation of the Mineral Spring at Saratoga—and of the purchase of that part of the Oeriskeny tract on which Fort Schuyler stands; but I am glad you have succeeded upon such advantageous terms in the purchase of 6,000 acres adjoining—for you certainly have obtained it amazingly cheap. Be so good, my dear Sir, along with the other information you have kindly promised me, to signify whether you have any prospect of borrowing (on interest) money for the payment of my moiety (as was talked of between us) or whether I am to provide it in any other manner; that I may take measures accordingly.[2] The time is also come for the payment of interest due on the old score—and I shall do it with as little delay as possible.[3]

It gave great pain to Mrs Washington and myself, to hear of Mrs Clintons indisposition, and of the sickness and accidents with which your little flock have been afflicted—our best, and sincere wishes are offered for them; and we hope, shortly, to hear of their perfect restoration; for we have a most affectionate regard for them all, & feel ourselves interested in every thing which concerns them.

Give me leave now, my dear Sir, to thank you for your recollection, and attention to the small articles which I begged you to provide for me. Whenever you conceive the season is proper, and an oppertunity offers, I shall hope to receive the Balsam trees; or any others which you may think curious, and exoticks with us; as I am endeavouring to improve the grounds about my house in this way.[4] If perchance the Sloop Pilgrim is not yet Sailed from your Port, you would add to the favor you mean to confer on me, by causing a number of grape vines sent me by an Uncle of the Chevr de la Luzernes—brought over by Captn Williamos—and deposited by him in the Garden of a Mr Beakman near the City, to be forwarded by that Vessel. They consist of a variety of the most valuable eating grapes of France—a list of the kinds, & distinction of them, no doubt accompanied the Sets. I pray you to take some of each sort for your own use, & request Mr Beakman to do the same—with my thanks for his care of them.[5]

I thank you for the interest you take in the welfare of my Nephew, and for his letter which you were so obliging as to send me—Poor young fellow! his pursuit after health is, I fear, altogether fruitless. Ever since the Month of May he has been traversing the Seas, from Island to Island, to very little purpose—When he last wrote he was about to Sail for Charleston, where he proposed to spend the Winter; and if no salutary effects resulted from it, to come hither & resign himself to his fate, in the Spring.[6] Mrs Washington unites with me in every kind & affectionate regard for you, Mrs Clinton & family—and with sentiments of warmest friendship and respect I am My dear Sir Yr most obedt & obliged

Go. Washington

P.S. Tell Walker that Mrs Washington & I not only congratulate him on his matrimonial connexion, but wish him all the joy & comfort which is to be derived from a good wife.

ALS, NHi: George and Martha Washington Papers; LB, DLC:GW.

1. Clinton's letter of 12 Nov. has not been found, but it was written apparently in response to a missing letter from GW. See note 4. No letter from GW in response to Clinton's letter of 27 Feb. 1784 has been found, but see GW's letter to Clinton's secretary, Benjamin Walker, 24 Mar. 1784, and Walker's responses of 3 and 6 April.

2. In a statement of GW's account with George Clinton, there is this undated notation in Benjamin Walker's hand: "To the amount of one half of 6071 Acres of Land in the Townships of Coxeborough & Carolana in Montgomery Co. State of New York purchased of Mar[inu]s Willet Esqre @ 7/ ℔ acre payable in Depreciation Certificates—1062.5" (N). In 1793, GW wrote in his account with Clinton in Ledger C: "To my moiety of 6053 Acres of Land purchased in partnership with him on the Mohawk River in Coxburgh. Which said land he was empowerd to sell as a joint concern, & part thereof

actually hath been sold as will appear by his letter of 18th Decr 1793—accompanied by an acct, of which the following is an exact copy—viz." (f. 2). Clinton's letter of 18 Dec. 1793 with the enclosed account has not been found, but GW lists in his ledger the lots sold, giving the dates they were sold, the acreage, the name of the purchasers, and the price of the lots in New York currency. Between 1 May 1788 and 9 Oct. 1793, Clinton sold seventeen lots totaling 4,034 acres for a total price of £3,400.2, New York currency. GW also lists in the ledger the cash that Clinton had actually received by 1793 for each tract sold, all but one at six dollars an acre; and, finally, he lists the nine unsold lots with a total acreage of 2,019. In his will, GW lists "abt." 1,000 acres on the Mohawk River in New York, as his "moiety" of the unsold portion of the land that he and Clinton bought together from Marinus Willett (Fitzpatrick, *Washington's Will*, 46). GW was not able to pay for his half of the Mohawk Valley land until 1787 (see GW to Clinton, 5 Nov. 1786, 9 June 1787, and notes). Clinton sent a copy of the deed to the property in a letter to GW of 26 Dec. 1784, which is missing (see Clinton to GW, 5 Mar. 1785).

3. For GW's debt to Clinton incurred in December 1782, see Clinton to GW, 27 Feb. 1784, source note. GW paid most of what he owed on this earlier debt at the beginning of 1785 (see GW to Clinton, 5 and 20 April 1785, and notes).

4. GW at some point asked Clinton to give him plants for the "walks, groves, & Wildernesses" that he was creating at Mount Vernon (*Diaries*, 4:75), and Clinton must have promised in his missing letter of 12 Nov. to provide them. Benjamin Walker wrote GW on 20 Dec. that he had sent to Norfolk "Pease . . . a Tierce of Nuts & a small bundle of Trees" from Clinton for GW. Clinton confirmed this in his missing letter of 26 Dec. (see Clinton to GW, 5 Mar. 1785), and on 18 Feb. 1785 GW recorded in his diary planting "four Lime or Linden Trees, sent me by Govr. Clinton of New York, which must have been out of the ground since the middle of Novr. without any dirt about the Roots" (*Diaries*, 4:92). On 20 April 1785 GW acknowledged receipt of the trees, saying that he did not expect any of them to live.

5. The vines were sent in the spring of 1784 by Chrétien-Guillaume Lamoignon de Malesherbes (1721–1794), one of the luminaries of the French Enlightenment who was among other things a distinguished *naturaliste*. On 6 April 1784 Benjamin Walker wrote GW that Charles Williamos had arrived in New York with the grape cuttings for him. GW also was sent by someone a letter from Malesherbes in Paris to Barbé-Marbois in America, dated 7 Jan. 1784, which David Stuart translated for him. The translation includes this passage: "We will now speak of the vine plants for General Washington—I understood by one of your preceding letters, that the General only wishes for such vines as produce a good grape for eating; and in consequence of this I addressed myself to the Abbé Nolin, who has made the most complete assortment of such that it is possible to have. We have been happy in meeting with Mr Williamos an old Colonist, who is on his return to America. & he will take charge of these plants and deliver you & the Chevalier my letters—He is himself a cultivator of the vine, and of course can take better

care of the plants, than any one; a circumstance very necessary in a long passage."

Malesherbes went on to say: "At present, you tell me the General would wish to have both for him & for a friend, some of the vine plants, that are most proper for making wine—Here is my answer to that." There follows a long disquisition on the need to send across the Atlantic plants rather than cuttings and on the efforts he intended to make to get GW plants from the various regions of France. He ends by asking Barbé-Marbois to tell GW not to "be surprised at the arrival of a box of plants, with a letter of advice from a Frenchman [M. Dupré] he knows nothing of" (DLC:GW).

Clinton wrote GW on 5 Mar. 1785 that after receiving GW's letter he had inquired of James Beekman (1732–1807) about the grapevines only to learn that they had all died.

6. GW undoubtedly is referring to George Augustine Washington's letter of 9 Nov. 1784, which is missing. See GW to William Washington, 25 Nov. 1784.

To David Humphreys

My dear Humphreys   Mount Vernon 25th Novr 84.

I have had the pleasure to receive two letters from you since your arrival in France,[1] and cannot let the Marquis de la Fayette depart without an acknowledgement of them, altho' his doing it is Sudden, & I at the same time am surrounded with Company.[2]

When I have a little more leizure (if that ever should be) I will give you all the occurrences of this quarter that have come under my view & recollection—at present I shall content myself with informing you, that we are all very well, & join very sincerely in every wish for your health, welfare & happiness; and that I am with the most affectionate esteem & regard Dr Sir Yr sincere friend & Obedt Servt

Go: Washington

ALS, CSmH; LB, DLC:GW.

1. GW is referring to Humphreys' letters of 12 and 18 August. By this time Humphreys had written two more letters, dated 30 Sept. and 11 Nov., which GW had not yet received.

2. With Lafayette soon to depart from Mount Vernon for his return to France, GW on 25 Nov. took the opportunity to acknowledge a number of letters written to him from France. In addition to the letters printed here, he wrote on this day letters to Fock, Kersaint, La Touche, Maithe, Mandrillon, Rochambeau, Vienne, and perhaps others. See table of contents, 25 November.

To Anastasie de Lafayette

[Mount Vernon] 25th Novr 1784.

Permit me to thank my dear little correspondent for the favor of her letter of the 18th of June last, & to impress her with the idea of the pleasure I shall derive in a continuation of them. Her Papa is restored to her with all the good health, paternal affection & honors, her tender heart could wish.

He will carry a kiss to her from me, (which might be more agreeable from a pretty boy) & give her assurances of the affectionate regard with which I have the pleasure of being her well wisher,

G: W——n

LB, DLC:GW.

To Adrienne, Marquise de Lafayette

Madam,   Mount Vernon 25th Novr 1784

If my expression was equal to my sensibility, I should in more elegant language than I am Master of, declare to you my sense of the obligation I am under for the letter you did me the honor to write me by the Marqs de la Fayette, & thanks for this flattering instance of your regard.[1] The pleasure I received in once more embracing my friend could only have been encreased by your presence, & that opportunity I should thereby have had of paying, in my own house, the homage of my respectful attachment to his better half. I have obtained a promise which the Marqs has ratified to Mrs Washington, that he will use his influence to bring you with him to this Country, whenever he shall visit it again. When the weight of so powerful an advocate is on our side, will you My Dr Marchioness deny us the pleasure of accompanying him to the shores of Columbia? In offering our mite, we can only assure you that endeavours shall not be wanting on our part to make this New World as agreeable to you as rural scenes & peaceful retirement are competent to. The Marquis returns to you with all the warmth & ardour of a newly inspired lover—We restore him to you in good health, crowned with wreaths of love & respect from every part of the Union. That his meeting with you, his family & friends, may be propitious, & as happy as your wishes can make it—that you may long live together revered & beloved—& that you may transmit to a numerous progeny the virtue which you both possess—is consonant with the vow & fervent wish of your devoted & most respectful Humble Servant

G: Washington

N.B. In every good wish for you Mrs Washington sincerely joins me.

LB, DLC:GW.
   1. See her letter of 18 June.

To Friedrich Anton Mesmer

Sir,   Mount Vernon 25th Novr 1784
   The Marqs de la Fayette did me the honor of presenting to me your favor of the 16th of June; & of entering into some explanation of the Powers of Magnetism—the discovery of which, if it should prove as extensively beneficial as it is said, must be fortunate indeed for Mankind, & redound very highly to the honor of that genius to whom it owes its birth. For the confidence reposed in me by the Society which you have formed for the purpose of diffusing & deriving from it, all the advantages expected; & for your favourable sentiments of me, I pray you to receive my gratitude, & the assurances of the respect & esteem with which I have the honor to be Sir, Yr most obedt humble servt

G: Washington

LB, DLC:GW.

From William Roberts

Sir   Mount Vernon Mills Novr the 25th 1784
   This is to acquint your Exsellency that I maid Aplacation to Mr Lund Washington Near three Months ago to Know if I was to Stay a nother Year in your Imploy or not, his Reply was that he New Nothing to the Contrary that He Amagend I was to Contenew As you had Said Nothing Conserning My Going Away, Which Caused me to Rest Quiet—But to acquint your

Exsellency that in your Absence to Richmon My Wife & I have had a Most unhapy falling out Which I Shall not Troble you with the Proticlers of No farther than this, I hapned To Git to Drinking one night as She thought Two much, & From one Cross Questune to a nother Matters were Carred to the Langth it has been Which Mr Lund Washington will Inform you For My part I am hartely Sorry in my Sole My wife appares to me to be the Same & I am of Apinion that we Shall Live More Happy than we have Dun for the fewter But My Time is Now Run out & Mr Washington Says hel Not Imploy Me any More for fare it Shold be against your Inclanation—Sir. I Shold think it hard to be Turnd out of Dors at this Seson of the year without the Lest Notes—Howaver I Shall Leve it to your Exsellencys Goodness as I have had no Notes to Git Into other Imploy Whather to Imploy Me one year More or Not—if you Mean to Imploy Me Pray Send me A Line As I may be out of pane For I Raly Doe Not want to Leve you, As I Have Livd So Long in the Imploy Without Flatery it has Caused Me to have A Real Regard for your Salf & Famaly[1]—For the many past Favours that you have Dun Me a My first Comming to Virgenia. From Sir, your Exsellencys Most obt Servt

W:M. Roberts

ALS, DLC:GW.

1. William Roberts of Pennsylvania had been GW's miller since 1770 when GW hired him to operate his new gristmill on Dogue Run. After Roberts had been miller and millwright at Mount Vernon for nearly eight years, Lund Washington wrote to GW, on 2 Sept. 1778 from Mount Vernon, that he and Roberts had had "some talk about his continuing here longer." Lund goes on for several pages about Roberts's virtues and vices. After noting that "Roberts has Faults—he is fond of Drinkg too much & when in Liquor is apt to be ill natured" and conceding that "he is a strange temperd man," Lund concludes that "there are few millers so good as he is." Five years later, in September 1783, GW made his first move to replace Roberts. He wrote to a Phildalphia mercantile firm: "My present Miller . . . who perhaps understands the manufacture of wheat, as well as any miller upon the Continent; and who, I believe, is also an honest man; is become so unfit for the trust reposed in him by his addiction to liquor . . . that however reluctantly I do it, I shall be induced to part with him," provided that he could find a suitable replacement (GW to Robert Lewis & Sons, 6 Sept. 1783; see also GW to Lewis & Sons, 16, 31 Oct. 1783). On 1 Feb. 1785, two months after receiving this letter from Roberts, GW wrote Robert Lewis again, saying that Roberts had "now become such an intolerable sot, and when drunk so great a madman" that he must find a new

miller. GW fired Roberts in April 1785 and through the agency of Robert Lewis & Sons acquired Joseph Davenport to take his place (see particularly Robert Lewis & Sons to GW, 5 April 1785, and GW to Lewis, 12 April 1785). As late as 2 Sept. 1787 Roberts was still trying to persuade GW to let him return to Mount Vernon as miller.

To William Washington

Dear sir,   Mount Vernon 25th Novr 1784.
From a letter dated the 9th of last month from my Nephew Geo: Augte Washington then at Burmuda, I have reason to believe he is 'ere this at Charleston.[1] The poor fellow is travelling about in pursuit of health, which, it is to be feared he will never obtain. His determination at the time he wrote to me was, to procure a passage, which he thought might happen in a fortnight or three weeks, for Turks Island[2]—thence to your City, where he proposed to stay during the inclemency of the winter.
He writes to me for some winter cloaths which he left here; but as I know of no direct or safe conveyance and as I presume his finances may be somewhat reduced, you would oblige me by procuring him a credit for such sums as he may want for this & other purposes, & I will see that due payment is made. I beg leave to recommend him to your patronage & kind offices whilst he remains in So. Carolina—he is a very amiable young man, and one for whom I have an entire affection and regard.
I saw your Brother, well, the other day at Richmond. It is said he is on the point of Matrimony; but of this & other matters of family concern, I presume you receive regular & better advice than I can give.[3] tho' unknown I beg leave to offer my best respects to your Lady. Mrs Washington joins me in it, & in complimts to yourself. I am Dr Sir &c. &c.

G: Washington

LB, DLC:GW.
William Washington (1752–1810), a distant cousin of GW's who was a hero of the Battle of Cowpens, remained in South Carolina after the war. Through his marriage in April 1782 to Jane Elliott, he gained control of the plantation, Sandy Hill, where he now lived.
1. Letter not found, but see George Augustine Washington to GW, 25 Feb. 1785.
2. Turks Island is the Bahama island most distant from the United States mainland.

3. William Washington had two brothers, Bailey Washington (1753–1814), who inherited his father's plantation in Stafford County, and John (b. 1756).

To George Augustine Washington

Dear George,   Mount Vernon Novr 26th 1784

I have received two letters from you at Barbadoes, & three from Burmuda.[1] The last informing me of your intention to embark for Charleston, which I much approve of.

I have not wrote to you since you left Mount Vernon, first because I did not know where to direct to you & next because I was on the Western waters when your first letters from Burmuda came to this place. My best wishes however have constantly attended you; and such aids of fresh provisions & other articles would have been sent you, as you appear to have stood in need of, had I returned in time from the back Country, & could have met with any conveyance.

I flatter myself the eruption in your Neck—the Season which followed—your voyage to South Carolina—and stay there the Winter, will restore you to health—Your friends sincerely wish it, but none more than myself. March is a disagreeable Month to travel in, either by Land or Water, I think therefore you had better let it pass over before you commence your Journey for this place.[2]

I am just returned from Richmond, where I saw Fanny Bassett. She has not escaped the Fall fever (which has been very prevalent in all parts of Virginia & indeed in the neigbouring States also)—but she was pretty well at the time I left her; and will, as soon as her father can be spared from the Assembly, come up here & stay with Mrs Washington. In my way up I saw (at Fredericksburgh) Colo. Ball who informed me that your Sister was well—She has lost one, & got another Child lately, a boy;[3] Your father, Mother, and family were well a few days ago—My Brother John & family who came from Berkeley a few days since, brought this acct—Bushrod, who I left at Richmond, is also well.

The Marquis La Fayette with whom I was at Richmond & with whom I returned on Wednesday last, is now here; but sets out on Monday next on his return to France; via New York. He is in good health, and speaks of you affectionately.

I would gladly send the cloathing you require, if there was any direct way of doing it; but this not being likely, you had better get a fresh supply—and for this and other purposes for which you may want money (as I presume your finances must, by this, have run low) I have requested my namesake Colo. Wm Washington to obtain you a credit & I will see it answered.[4] I am much hurried in dispatching many letters before the Marquis leaves this which, and having few things interesting to add I must conclude—Mrs Washington, Mrs Stuart and the little folks are all well at this time tho' most of them have been Sick—they all cordially join in best wishes for your perfect restoration to health & your friends with Dr George Yr Most Affecte

Go: Washington

ALS, ViMtV.

1. George Augustine Washington's letters of 27 June and 25 July from Barbados and 11 and 14 Aug. from Bermuda are printed above, but his letter of 9 Oct. from Bermuda (see GW to William Washington, 25 Nov.) has not been found.

2. George Augustine Washington finally reached Mount Vernon on 14 May 1785.

3. Col. Burgess Ball (1749–1800) was married to George Augustine's sister, Frances Washington (1763–1815).

4. See GW to William Washington, 25 November.

To James Madison

Gentlemen,   Mount Vernon 28th Novr 84

After the several conversations we have had on the subject of inland navigation; and the benefits which would, probably, be derived from a commercial intercourse with the Western territory; I shall make no apology for giving you the trouble of the enclosed.[1]

It is matter of regret to me, however, that I cannot accompany them with some explanations & observations. It was intended these Papers should have met me at Richmond. They missed me on the road thither—travelled back to Baltimore—returned—and were put into my hands at the moment I was setting off for Annapolis; to which place I mean to accompany the Marqs de la Fayette on his return to New York where he expects to embark, about the middle of next month, for France.[2]

I could not think of withholding these Papers until my return, as I shall probably accompany the Marquis from Annapolis to Baltimore. Therefore, in the order I receive, I send them to you. Your own judgments in this business will be the best guide. but in one word, it should seem to me, that if the public cannot take it up with efficient funds, & without those delays which might be involved by a limping conduct, it had better be placed in the hands of a corporate Company—What encouragements, and what powers, to give this Company, deserves all that consideration which I persuade myself you, Gentlemen, will bestow.

The Maryland Assembly is now sitting—If I should return in time, I will have the honor of writing to you again on this Subject[3]—in the meanwhile, if your leizure will permit, I should be glad to know your Sentimts on, and what will be the issue of, this business—With very sincere esteem and regard I have the honor to be Gentn Yr most Obedt Hble Servt

Go: Washington

P.S. As your Assembly are upon a Militia Law, I send you the thoughts of the Baron de Steuben which I found here upon my return from Richmond.[4] G.W.

ALS, NNC. GW addressed the letter to "James Madison Esquire—or in his absence Joseph Jones Esquire At Richmond." The letter was docketed by Madison, who probably had received it by 3 Dec. (see Madison to James Monroe, 4 Dec. 1784, in Rutland and Rachal, *Madison Papers*, 8:175–76). Joseph Jones (1727–1805), delegate from King George County, was shortly after this elected to the council of state and so was not active in the house of delegates when the Potomac River Company was under consideration and finally incorporated in December.

1. The "conversations" took place while GW was in Richmond the week of 15 November. GW enclosed both a draft of a bill for creating a Potomac River company, which the meeting at Alexandria adopted on 15 Nov., and a covering letter from the chairman of the meeting, along with, perhaps, a copy of the petition that the Alexandria meeting drew up to present to the legislatures of Virginia and Maryland. See Henry Lee to GW, 18 Nov., and note 1 of that document. None of these enclosures has been found, but on 4 Dec. the clerk of the house of delegates noted in the house journals: "A petition of sundry inhabitants of the State of Maryland, and also of this State, was presented to the House, and read; setting forth, that they conceive it would greatly contribute to the extension of commerce, and the improvement of agriculture, if the river Potomac was made navigable from the falls, and a communication opened by that means with the western country; and praying that

an act may pass establishing a company, to be invested with full powers for that purpose" (*House of Delegates Journal, 1781–1785*). The Virginia house ordered that the petition be referred to "the committee of the whole House on the state of the Commonwealth" for its consideration on 7 December. On the seventh, the committee of the whole reported and the house agreed: "That an act ought to pass, for opening and extending the navigation of the river Potomac." Two days later, a committee composed of Carter Henry Harrison, Thomas Matthews, and William Grayson reported to the house a bill for "establishing a company for opening and extending the navigation of the river Potomac." The committee had access to the drafted bill that GW sent to Madison in this letter and to a greater or lesser extent based its bill on it, but as no copy of either the Alexandria draft of the bill or the delegates' bill has been found, it cannot be determined just how closely the house bill followed the wording of the Alexandria bill. However, Madison wrote Richard Henry Lee on 11 Dec.: "The scheme for opening the navigation of the Potomac, which has been settled between the Maryland and [the Virginia] gentlemen, is before the House of Delegates, and will be favoured, as far as the objectionable amount of the tolls will admit. As the concurrence of Maryland in this scheme is necessary, some difficulties will attend its progress" (Rutland and Rachal, *Madison Papers*, 8:180–81). Madison also wrote GW a letter on 11 Nov., which has not been found. Madison in his missing letter may have been responding to GW's letter of 3 Dec., which see, and he undoubtedly reported on these developments with regard to the Potomac River Company bill. In any case, the house bill, which was scheduled for debate in the committee of the whole on 14 Dec., was dropped; on 13 Dec. the house of delegates adopted the suggestion GW made in his letter to Madison of 3 Dec. that the Virginia assembly appoint commissioners to meet with commissioners of the Maryland legislature to draft a single bill for creating a Potomac River company acceptable to both state bodies. See GW to Madison, 3 Dec., n.5.

2. See Henry Lee to GW, 18 Nov., and note 2 of that document. It was probably on this day, 28 Nov., that GW and Lafayette left Mount Vernon for Annapolis. For the duration of their stay in Annapolis, see GW to Madison, 3 Dec., n.1.

3. See GW to Madison, 3 December.

4. GW was probably referring to Steuben's *A Letter on the Subject of an Established Militia, and Military Arrangements, Addressed to the Inhabitants of the United States* (1784). For GW's earlier involvement in the composition of Steuben's pamphlet, see GW to Steuben, 15 Mar. 1784, and notes. In this session, the Virginia legislature replaced the colonial and wartime statutes governing the state's militia with a new comprehensive statute (see 11 Hening 476–94).

From Charles MacIver

Sir   Alexandria [November 1784]

If Affairs of infinite Consequence had not engaged your Excellency's Time & Attention an Address on the following Subject would probably have been directed to you at an earlier Period. Had I the Honour of your Acquaintance, most probably it would have first sought your Patronage.

Your Excellency will now give me Leave to acquaint you that I was early imbued with certain Principles repugnant to Oppression and Tyranny, and one of the most forward & zealous Instigators of Emigration from the Highlands of Scotland. My Designs were benevolent and hazardous. They proved unfortunate. I incurred the Resentment of the opulent Part of my Countrymen and Relations, (as well as of the British Tories in general[)], and received no Support nor Patronage on this Side. I regret still more that many of the Emigrants revolted from that Freedom they formerly courted, and that neither the one nor the other received the Benefit intended. On these Accounts I entertained Doubts whether I should ever take Concern in such Matters again. Instead of a Kind of circular Letters, I at last confined my Advices to one Gentleman, whose Age & Infirmities, concurring with other Circumstances, will retard his usual Activity among his oppressed Countrymen. Four young Gentlemen, of natural Influence and personal Popularity, accompanied with an enthusiastic Ardour in the Cause of Freedom, individually bid fair to outstrip him in Exertion and Success. Their Letters on Emigration are not directed to me, because the Accounts they received of me during the latter Part of the War were uncertain. They refer me to later Emigrants, and to some new Comers; none of whom has overcome national Prejudices. In short, they are all averse to Emigration, and will probably discourage it with Success, unless some powerful Patronage is discovered. Without the Aid of such, I shall lay still, as I have for several Years. Is it not natural for one who desires to know what may be expected in this Way, to wish for the Honour of Access to your Excellency, for Information?

The young Gentlemen above-mentioned represent that Oppression is reduced to a System, and are ready to imbarque their own little Property in an approved Plan of Emigration. Repeatedly and cordially have they congratulated the Americans, first on the near Prospect, and since on the actual Enjoyment of Liberty and Independence. Three of them are Clergymen, and being so well disposed to this Country, seem to merit Encouragement in a Settlement of Highlanders; especially, as they detest the Principles of the Scotch Aristocracy, and will oppose their influence against any Man who may dare to advance them in a Land of equal Liberty. But these Gentlemen are not wealthy, & consequently cannot support the thousands who will wish to accompany them, and the thousands who will wish to follow them. The Number of poor Emigrants will probably be very great. It is submitted whether they merit the Patronage of Men of publick Spirit, who should make it a Point to with-draw them from every Degree of Aristocratical Influence. If Landmongers of great Property could be recompenced in Land, clear of Taxes for a limited Time, they might support very beneficial undertakings in this Way. Population would keep Pace with Commerce, & Debts nobly incurred would be honourably discharged. Tho the Success of any Part I may take in this Business may depend on total Silence till the Expiration of the accompanying Tour, and I have accordingly exercised great Caution on the Subject of late Years, yet have I discovered Reason to suppose that your Excellency could not want respectable Associates to second any Designs of this Sort you may think proper to patronize. Your Excellency's Humanity will lead you to consider how far the Benefit of the Emigrants, the Benefit of their Patrons, & the Benefit of the Publick may be made to coincide. The same Disposition will lead you to consider whether the Risques & Trouble of Emigration will be amply recompenced to the Emigrants by any Amendment of their Condition on this Side: And whether our Constitutions promise them more ample and permanent Privileges than they already enjoy: or, in other Words, whether the Powers of Government are more properly bounded, & the Liberties of the People better secured by our Constitutions, than in their own Country.

Tho I lost most of my Mss. & Letters, since the Year 1773, I have now some before me, mostly Scrolls and short Memorandums wrote in 1774, & since; political Hints, some of which were printed and approved; a large Ms. which was intended for the Press; a Lecture intended to promote the Honour, Happiness and Security of the united States, including a close and interesting Application to the present Circumstances and future Prospects of this new World.

These Writings consist of several Hundred Pages, which the

Circumstances of my Health & Affairs will not allow me to transmit; especially as they consist of first Thoughts, often irregularly disposed, amidst the Distractions of a laborious Business. Even on the Subject of Emigration, to which I have such Ambition to draw your Excellency's Attention, I am stinted, for Health and Time, to send the present.

Almost every Thing in Ms. No. 25, containing near 100 folio Pages, was a vain Attempt to secure the most shining Members of the Minority of the British Parliament in our Interest. I have Reason to think it contributed to prolong the Opposition of a few Individuals. When no Hopes of Peace or Reconciliation remained, I suspended all attempts of this Sort, & was provoked to attempt a political Pamphlet, including, among numerous Topics, an attempt to explain the Resources of America to support a War, and inculcating the great, & almost evident, Probability of foreign Assistance.

In Order to be honest & intelligent, as well as confident, during the British Part of the accompanying Tour, the Promoter of Emigrations should be well acquainted with the Quality of Lands, Usages, political Institutions, & all Matters of Importance respecting this Country. With the Support of an easy Patronage, for a short Time, I should hope to acquire the necessary Information in this Way.

Tho I have been accustomed to expect the greatest Crouds from the Highlands, yet I little doubt of procuring valuable Individuals in the Rest of my British Tour, and contributing to promote a Spirit of Emigration, which promises to increase the Wealth & Population of the united States. Some Highlanders who acted on the Highlands in Consequence of my Letters, brought many Passengers also from Ireland, & other Parts.

I shall be very happy and highly honoured in knowing your Excellency's Opinion on this Matter, or hearing that you will consider of it, & send me your Opinion with all convenient Speed. It is evident that my Plans must undergo a very great, if not a total Change, if I should revise them myself. But, under your Excellency's Patronage, they might be rendered perfectly correct & consistent. After what I have said of the Advantage of keeping my Concern in the Matter a Secret till a proper Opportunity, I need add no more at this Time, than that I am, with the most profound Respect, Your Excellency's most devoted humble Servant

Chas MacIver at the Printing-office in Alexandria.

ALS, DLC:GW. In a letter to GW written before 1 Mar. 1785, MacIver refers to this letter as written "last November."

It is not to be wondered that GW made no immediate response to this cryptic and disjointed letter. After MacIver wrote again, probably in February, asking GW to drop him "a Line" expressing his "opinion of the Practicability or Expedience" of his "Proposals," GW apologized and declared that while he did "not clearly comprehend" MacIver's "plan," he would be glad to talk to him about it and would give him his "sentiments with freedom & candor" when he "more fully" understood it (1 Mar. 1785). MacIver did not act on GW's suggestion that they meet, but a month later, on 31 Mar., MacIver placed the following notice in the *Virginia Journal and Alexandria Advertiser*: "The Subscriber, in expectation of a meeting of the Town Council, deferred certain proposals so long as to leave no room for their publication in this Week's Journal. They will be published soon, if necessary. In the meantime they may be seen at the Printing-Office, or in the public's most Humble Servant CHARLES M'IVER." MacIver must have decided that it was not "necessary" to print his proposals, for there is nothing in the paper about them during the next three months. He renewed his correspondence with GW the following year when on 5 June 1786 he wrote GW to complain of the treatment he had received from others and to ask for GW's "Countenance on the Subject of the Proposal irregularly laid before you in the inclosed Papers." Two days later, GW returned the unidentified enclosures, saying that he was pleased with "any attempts made towards improving literature & science." He declined, however, to give MacIver "the encouragement" he desired, on the grounds that there were others in Alexandria better acquainted with MacIver's "character & abilities." This ended the exchange between MacIver and GW except for a bizarre letter MacIver wrote ten days later with a long, rambling account of a dress, or dresses, having been stolen from his wife by one of GW's servants and of an ensuing quarrel.

MacIver seems to have owned a ferry at Alexandria during the Revolution and to have had a school in the town before becoming ill sometime in 1784. In both this letter and his letter of 5 June 1786, MacIver refers to himself as a Scottish Highlander and alludes to his writing before and during the Revolution in support of the American cause.

From Nathanael Greene

Dear Sir   Newport [R.I.] Decem. 2d 1784

Mr Watson by whom this will be handed you having some things for you brought with him from England and having it in

contemplation to call at Mount Vernon it gives me an opportunity to inform you of my safe arrival with my family.[1] I found
Mrs Greene and the children all in good health.

I hope the Marquis arrivd safe in Virginia. A report prevails
here that his Frigate is cast away near the Hook; but this must
have happened if true since the Marquis landed in Virginia.[2] I
wish to see him before he returns to France and would meet
him in New York if he embarks from that place. I hope he will
return to France well pleasd with the reception he has met with
in America and advocate our cause tho we little deserve it in
many respects. Congress are dilatory in meeting and I fear little
will be done to restore public credit. I have not been at home
long enough to learn the present temper of the people of this
State. Many begin to be alarmed at the proposition of Connecticut; and I can but hope if Congress persist in the Plan of finance it will finally succeed. However we are such a heteroge-
neous body that it is difficult to draw conclusions from any
general principles which influence human conduct.

Mrs Greene joins me ⟨*mutilated*⟩ affectionate complemen⟨ts⟩
to you and Mrs Washington to Doctor Steward and his Lady—I
am dear Sir with esteem & regard Your Most Obedt humble
Serv.

Nath. Greene

ALS, DLC:GW.

1. Elkanah Watson (1758–1842) was sent to France in 1779 by the great
Rhode Island merchant John Brown of Providence and became a merchant
on his own in Nantes. Watson records in his memoirs that shortly before re-
turning to Rhode Island in October 1784 he conversed in England with that
"noble enthusiast in the cause of African emancipation and colonization,"
Granville Sharpe, who "confided two bundles of books to my care, embracing
his entire publication on emancipation and other congenial topics, directed to
Washington" (Watson, *Men and Times of the Revolution*, 233). Watson arrived at
Mount Vernon on 19 Jan. 1785 with this letter from Greene, another from
John Fitzgerald, and Sharpe's books. He then spent with GW what he calls,
and describes in some detail, "two of the richest days of my life" (ibid.,
243–46; see also *Diaries*, 4:78). Eight pamphlets by Granville Sharpe, published between 1771 and 1780, are listed as belonging to GW in Griffin, *Boston
Athenæum Collection*, 179–82.

2. In his letter of 23 Dec., GW refers to the grounding of the frigate
Nymphe while she was en route to New York to take aboard Lafayette and his
two companions for their passage to France.

Letter not found: from Richard Varick, 2 December. On 26 Sept. 1785 GW wrote Varick: "I have received your other letter of the 2d of December."

From William Carmichael

Sir   Madrid 3d Decr 1784

In the course of the last month I recd a letter from Mr Richard Harrison established at Cadiz requesting me to use my endeavours to procure the permission to extract a Jack Ass of the best breed, which you wished to import into America.[1] In consequence of this application, I mentioned in a Conversation with his Excy the Ct de Florida Blanca the Minister of State, my desire to render you this Little Service. The Abovementioned Minister seemed pleased to have this occasion of proving his esteem for a character which is not less dear to his Countrymen, than it is revered by Foreigners. Actuated by this Sentiment he wrote me the note of which I have now the honor to transmit you the Copy & the Translation.[2] I must confess sincerely that I shall be uneasy until I have your Approbation. The glory that you have acquired needs not the attention of a Monarch to augment it. But you are now a Citizen of the United States and as such will interest yourself in the Smallest circumstance that can contribute to its prosperity. This Mark of Attention to the Late Cheif of the Union, considered in this point of view, will while it adds another proof to the Many you have recd of General approbation, evince the desire of the head of a Nation, of which we are the Neighbour, to cultivate their good will, by paying that attention, (which his own fellow Citizens accord) to the Person whose services rendered their Country Independant. I inclose this Letter to the Marquis de la Fayette[.] The Share that I had in making him known to you is a much better claim to interest a heart like yours in my favor, than any assurances that I can make you of the high respect & affection with which I have the honor to be Sir Your Most Obedt & Most Humble Sert[3]

                                                    Wm Carmichael

ALS, DLC:GW. The original and an earlier copy of this letter from Carmichael, which were sent under cover to Lafayette who had sailed from New York for France before the letter arrived, have not been found. Carmichael later sent a second copy of the letter, the one printed here, with a long postscript dated 25 Mar. 1785. The postscript is printed below as a separate letter. GW wrote Carmichael on 10 June acknowledging the receipt of the 25 Mar. copy of this letter and saying that he had received neither the original nor the first copy of it sent to Lafayette.

William Carmichael (d. 1795), a native of Queen Anne's County, Md., was the U.S. chargé d'affaires at the Spanish court at this time. He finally was recalled on 5 June 1794 but died on 9 Feb. 1795 before leaving Spain.

1. GW had for long wished to have a Spanish jackass, thought to be the best in the world, to begin breeding mules in Virginia. He was convinced that mules would prove superior as draft animals to horses and oxen. It was at his behest that Robert Townsend Hooe wrote to his business partner Richard Harrison in Cadiz asking him to try to obtain one or more jacks for GW (see GW to Hooe and Hooe's reply, both 18 July 1784). GW also spoke to Lafayette during Lafayette's visit to Mount Vernon in November about his wish to have a jack. After GW learned from Harrison through Hooe how much a Spanish jack might cost, which in any case could be got only by permission of the king of Spain, GW told both Hooe and Lafayette to discontinue their efforts on his behalf (see GW to Lafayette, 15 Feb. 1785). When acknowledging on 10 June 1785 Carmichael's "favour of the 25th of March covering a triplicate of your letter of 3d December" (see source note), GW expressed in elaborate terms his appreciation for the king's intended gift of two jackasses. For the remainder of the summer and early fall he anxiously awaited the arrival of the animals (see GW to William Fitzhugh, 21 May 1785, and GW to Lafayette, 25 July, 1 Sept. 1785). GW finally heard from Thomas Cushing, the lieutenant governor of Massachusetts, on 7 Oct. 1785, that one of the jacks was safely ashore in Boston. (The other one was lost at sea.) GW promptly sent John Fairfax, one of his overseers, to Boston to conduct the jack and his Spanish caretaker back to Mount Vernon (see GW to Cushing and GW to John Fairfax, both 26 Oct. 1785, and Cushing to GW, 6, 9, and 16 Nov. 1785). To GW's satisfaction, Fairfax arrived safely with his charges on the evening of 5 Dec. 1785 (see GW to Carmichael, to Floridablanca, and to Francisco Rendon, all 19 Dec. 1785, and *Diaries*, 4:244). For GW's full description of the Spanish jack, which GW named Royal Gift, see GW's newspaper advertisement, dated 23 Feb. 1786 and printed below, offering the jack's services. Unknown to GW, Lafayette also acquired in 1785 two jacks for GW, which also were shipped to America in two different ships. One of them again was lost at sea. For the arrival of Lafayette's present, the Knight of Malta, in 1786, see Lafayette to GW, 16 April 1785, n.4.

2. See enclosure.

3. Carmichael's letter to Lafayette is not listed in Idzerda, *Lafayette Papers*, volume 5. Carmichael as Silas Deane's secretary helped arrange Lafayette's departure for America in 1777 (see Carmichael to Richard Henry Lee, 17 Mar. 1777, n.2, ibid., 1:34–37).

Enclosure
Floridablanca to William Carmichael

Sir   S[a]n Lorenzo 24th Novr 1784

The King has not only condescended with pleasure to permit the extraction of the Jack Ass which you sollicit on acct of General Washington But further his Majesty desirous that this Commission should be executed to the entire Satisfaction of so distinguished a personage, has ordered me to look out for & place at your orders two of the best of those Animals, in case that an accident should happen to one on the passage.[1] I shall advise you when they are ready, & in the mean time I renew my Desires to be of use to you & pray God to preserve you many years. I am & &c.

(Signed) Count of Florida Blanca

Translation, DLC:GW; ALS, in Spanish, DLC:GW.

José Monino y Redondonde, conde de Floridablanca, was the Spanish foreign minister.

1. See Carmichael to GW, 3 Dec. 1784, n.1. The king of Spain was Charles III.

To James Madison

Mount Vernon 3d December, 1784.

Gentlemen: I returned yesterday from Annapolis, having conducted the Marquis La Fayette that far on his way to New York, and left him proceeding on the road to Baltimore, on Wednesday last.[1]

This trip afforded me opportunities of conversing with some of the leading characters in the different branches of the Legislature of Maryland, on the subject of inland navigation, and the benefits which might arise from a commercial intercourse with the Western Territory.—I was happy to find them so forcibly struck with the importance of these objects; and that there appeared the most favorable disposition to give encouragement to them.[2]

Like us, they have two interests prevailing in their assembly—or rather in the present instance like ourselves have two ways by which the *same* interest is to be effected. The ill-grounded jealousies arising therefrom serves in some degree to embarrass this measure of public utility. The Baltimore interest has already obtained an act to encourage, and to empower a corporate company to remove the obstructions in that part of the Susquehanna, which lie within the territory of Maryland.— And this, I perceive, is all that can be obtained in behalf of Potomac, from that quarter.[3]

As no public money, therefore, is likely to be obtained from that State, and as little chance perhaps of getting it from this— should not the wisdom of both assemblies be exerted without delay to hit upon such a happy medium as will not on the one hand, vest two much power and profit in a private company;— and on the other to hold out sufficient inducements to engage men to hazard their fortunes in an arduous undertaking?—If the act does not effect this the object of it is defeated; and the business of course is suspended; which, in my opinion, would be injurious; as the present moment is important, favorable, and critical; and the spirit for enterprize greater now than it may ever be hereafter.

It is to be apprehended the money lenders among the class of private gentlemen are but few; resort, therefore, must be had to mercantile funds, from whence nothing can be extracted if there is not a prospect of great gain, present or future—but to you gentlemen, these observations are unnecessary, as you are better acquainted with public funds, and the circumstances of individuals than I am; and I am sure are not to learn that the motives which predominate most in human affairs is self-love and self-interest.

The bill I sent you is exceptionable in some parts, and gives discontent in others—so I am informed,—for it came to my hands at a moment when I could not read, much less consider it.[4] Would it not be highly expedient, therefore, as the session of both assemblies must soon draw to a close, for each to depute one or more members to meet at some intermediate place, and agree, (first knowing the sentiments of the respective assemblies,) upon an adequate bill to be adopted by both States? This would prevent dissimilar proceedings, as unproductive as no bill—save time—and bring matters at once to a point. A measure of this kind is consonant, I know, with the ideas of some of the leading members of the Maryland Assembly, who requested me to suggest it to my friends in our assembly, and inform them of the result.[5]

From what I can learn, there was in the meeting held at Alexandria too great a leaning to local advantages on one part, and too much compliance on the other part, to obtain general approbation of the bill which proceeded from it—I shall not pronounce on either side, but imperfections, if they really exist, at the meetings proposed, may be rectified; and a liberal plan adopted which shall have no eye to the interested views of a few individuals to the prejudice of the majority; who rather than damp the spirit which was up, resolved, it is said, to submit, to *any* plan, rather than impede the undertaking.[6]

At such a meeting as has been suggested, of delegates from the two assemblies of Virginia and Maryland, might it not prove a politic step for them to agree upon a representation to be made by their respective Assemblies *to the State of* Pennsylvania, *of the political advantages which would flow from a close connection with the Western Territory; and to request their concurrence to make the communication through their State* As Easy And As Diffusive As Possible?—*pointing to the consequences which in the course of things must follow, if we do not open doors for their produce and trade. That State has many Delegates in the Assembly who would relish such a proposition highly.*—It would on our parts, appear attentive and respectful; and if rejected on theirs, place them (at least in the eyes of those people) in the wrong—and excite their reiterated applications, which most assuredly would effect it.[7]

Another thing, in my opinion, should also be the object of this meeting, and that is to agree upon a sum, to be advanced by the States of *Virginia and Maryland*, for the purpose of opening a road between the Eastern and Western Waters.—The Company, (if one should be formed,) and the bill, having nothing to do with this—and the Western settlers are not in circumstances to effect it themselves.[8] With very great esteem and regard, I am, gentlemen, Your most obedient humble servant,

G.W.

Printed, *House Reports*, 1st Sess., 19th Cong., no. 228. The letter was directed to Joseph Jones as well as to Madison.

1. Wednesday last was 1 December. On 28 Nov. GW wrote Madison that he was "at the moment" of "setting off for Annapolis" with Lafayette. GW ar-

rived back at Mount Vernon on 2 December. On 8 Dec. GW wrote Lafayette that he got home before dinner on the day after they parted, indicating that they left Annapolis on 1 December.

2. For GW's role in the forming of the Potomac River Company by the states of Virginia and Maryland, see editorial note in GW to Benjamin Harrison, 10 Oct. 1784.

3. On 9 Dec. George Digges of Prince George's County introduced in the Maryland legislature a bill "to prevent the obstruction of the navigation of the eastern and north-west branches of the river Patowmack" (*Md. House of Delegates Proceedings*), which the governor signed into law on 22 Jan. 1785.

4. For the disposition of the bill drafted by the Alexandria meeting of 15 Nov. and forwarded to Madison by GW on 28 Nov., see GW to Madison, 28 Nov., n.1.

5. On 13 Dec. the Virginia house adopted GW's suggestion that it appoint commissioners to meet with the Marylanders, and it named GW to be one of the three to act for Virginia. See Beverley Randolph to GW, 15 Dec., and note 1 of that document.

6. For Henry Lee's analysis of the bill's weakness as amended and adopted by the Alexandria meeting, see his letter to GW of 18 November. See also GW to Madison, 28 Nov., n.1.

7. The Virginia house of delegates on 28 Dec. voted to join with Maryland to inform Pennsylvania of their plans for the Potomac and to ask that the state of Pennsylvania place no impediment on measures that Virginia and Maryland might take to link the Potomac and the Ohio by means of navigable streams and the roads through Pennsylvania. See Enclosure I in James Madison to GW, 9 Jan. 1785.

8. When on 13 Dec. the Virginia house of delegates voted to send three commissioners to confer with the Marylanders to form a Potomac River company, it also voted to have the Virginia commissioners "concert" with the Marylanders about the opening of a proper road from the head of navigation on the Potomac to "the most convenient western waters." See Beverley Randolph to GW, 15 Dec. 1784, n.1; Enclosure III in George Washington and Horatio Gates to the Virginia Legislature, 28 Dec. 1784; and Enclosure II in James Madison to GW, 9 Jan. 1785.

From John Filson

Sir   Philadelphia Decr 4th 1784

Permit me by these lines to express the sentiments of a grateful heart, in testifying the happiness I sensibly feel in addressing your Excelly. I am not So happy as to have a personal acquaintance with you Sir, and hope you will excuse the freedom of my pen.[1] I inform You Sir, that I have the pleasure to be the author of a late publication in Substance a Narrative and Map of Kentucke; I made bold to dedicate the map to the honour-

able Congress, and Your Excelly, which I presume You will
chearfully patronise. I have desired Mr John Page of Rosewel to
whom I consigned a number, to present you with a book and
map from me, which I expect you will do me the honour to receive.[2] This impression of 1500 have in the Course of a few
weeks met with a rapid sale, which encourages me to offer the
publick a Second edition of this book, which I intend in the
Course of this winter. I lately had the pleasure to be acquainted
with Mr Claybourn a gentleman from Richmond, with whom I
supose you are acquainted; I informed him of my intentions, at
which Mr Claybourn expressed his Sattisfaction, desireing me
to write requesting you Sir, to form your sentiments in a letter
indicative of the probability and Convenience of a Communication in trade, with the eastern & western waters, by the Sources
of Potowmac, and the waters that form the Aleghany, particularly Cheat river; a publication of this Nature he said would
Certainly be Sattisfactory to you,[3] I therefore request you Sir, if
agreeable, to be explicit on the subject and Send it to me at
Dunlaps printing office in this City, with all Convenient expedition, which you may depend I Shall add in your own Sentiments to this my second edition of the Kentucke history, which
I intend Commiting to the press about Christmas, perhaps I
may delay a few days for your letter if it Comes not before that
time. I wrote you a letter with the books, I Sent to Colo. Harvey,
and Mr Page, a few days ago: I expect Mr Page will soon receive
the books if they arrive safe at Richmond. This request Sir I
Sincerely desire you will grant, your Compliance will do me
honour, and Verry much oblige your humble Servt

John Filson

P.S. Your particular acquaintance with the Counties between
Fayatte in Kentucke, and the pensylvania line, will enable you to
give me the Natural & topographical history of them also Com-
prehensively which I request in the letter. J. F——

ALS, DLC:GW.
    John Filson (c.1747–1788) went from Pennsylvania to Kentucky in 1783.
There he took up land and perhaps briefly taught school. Filson returned east
in 1784 to have his book, *The Discovery, Settlement, and Present State of Kentucke*,
printed in Wilmington, Delaware. The book included his celebrated map of
Kentucky, which he undertook to have printed separately as well. Filson returned to Kentucky in 1785 and thereafter occasionally wrote to GW.

1. GW wrote Filson on 16 Jan. 1785 that he had received Filson's letter of 4 Dec. 1784 before receiving his earlier letter of 30 November. The substance of the short letter of 30 Nov. is repeated here on 4 Dec., in virtually identical language, beginning: "I inform you Sir"; and ending, "do me the honour to receive." The earlier letter contains the additional information that Filson had also sent "a number" of copies of his publication to John Harvie in Richmond.

2. Filson chose John Page (1744–1808) of Rosewell, Gloucester County, to be one of the distributors of his work perhaps because Page was president in Virginia of the more or less moribund Philosophical Society for the Advancement of Useful Knowledge.

3. Mr. Clayborne is Richard Claiborne. See GW's letter to him, 15 December. GW's detailed letter to Gov. Benjamin Harrison of 10 Oct. 1784 regarding the navigation of the Potomac and opening of the West received wide circulation (see Harrison to GW, 13 Nov.). GW wrote Filson on 16 Jan. 1785, expressing approval of Filson's undertaking but declining to contribute to his proposed publication.

To Henry Knox

My Dr sir,   Mt Vernon 5th Decr 1784.

Apologies are idle things: I will not trouble you with them— that I am your debtor in the epistolary way I acknowledge— and that appearances indicate a disposition to remain so, I cannot deny; but I have neither the inclination nor the effrontary to follow the example of Great Men or St—s to withhold payment altogether. To whatever other causes therefore my silence may be attributed, ascribe it not I beseech you to a want of friendship, for in this, neither time nor absence can occasion a diminution; & I regret that fortune has placed us in different States & distant climes, where an interchange of sentiments can only be by letter.[1]

When your letter of the 26th of July came here, I was upon the eve of a tour to the Westward which ended in the neighbourhood of Fort Pit, altho' my original plan took in the Great Kanhawa. I found from information, that the Indians were in too discontented a mood to render it prudent for me to run the risk of insult: to see the condition of the property I had in that Country, & the quality of my Lands, were all the objects I had in view. Those in the vicinity of Fort Pitt (for which I have had patents more than ten years) I found in possession of people who set me at defiance, under the claim of pre-occupancy. Another

year, & I may find the rest seized under the like pretext; but as
the land cannot be removed, altho' the property may be
changed, I thought it better to return, than to make a bad matter worse by hazarding abuse from the Savages of the Country.[2]

I am now endeavoring to stimulate my Countrymen to the
extension of the inland navigation of the rivers Potomac and
James—thereby, & a short land transportation, to connect the
Western Territory by strong commercial bands with this—I
hope I shall succeed, more on account of its political importance—than the commercial advantages which would result
from it, altho' the latter is an immense object: for if this Country, which will settle faster than any other ever did (and chiefly
by foreigners who can have no particular predilection for *us*),
cannot, by an easy communication be drawn this way, but are
suffered to form commercial intercourses (which lead we all
know to others) with the Spaniards on their right & rear, or the
British on their left, they will become a distinct people from
us—have different views—different interests, & instead of
adding strength to the Union, may in case of a rupture with either of those powers, be a formidable & dangerous neighbour.[3]

After much time spent (charity directs us to suppose in duly
considering the matter) a treaty has at length been held With
the Six Nations at Fort Stanwix: much to the advantage it is said
of the United States, but to the great disquiet of that of New
York: fruitlessly, it is added by some, who assert that the Deputies on the part of the Indians were not properly authorized to
treat—How true this may be, I will not pretend to decide; but
certain it is in my opinion, that there is a kind of fatality attending all our public measures—inconceivable delays—particular
States counteracting the plans of the United States when submitted to them—opposing each other upon all occasions—torn
by internal disputes, or supinely negligent & inattentive to
every thing which is not local & self interestg & very often short
sighted in these, make up our system of conduct. Would to God
our own Countrymen, who are entrusted with the management
of the political machine, could view things by that large & extensive scale upon which it is measured by foreigners, & by the
State[s]men of Europe, who see what we might be, & predict
what we shall come to. In fact, our fœderal Government is a
name without substance: No State is longer bound by its edicts,

than it suits *present* purposes, without looking to the consequences. How then can we fail in a little time, becoming the
sport of European politics, & the victims of our own folly.

I met the Marqs de la Fayette at Richmond—brought him to
this place—conducted him to Annapolis—saw him on the road
to Baltimore, and returned. About the middle of this month he
expected to embark at New York for France—He tells us that
Mrs Knox was about to add to your family—We hope 'ere this
we may congratulate you both on a son, or daughter, according
to your desires. Mrs Washington joins me in every good wish
for you & Mrs Knox; & with every sentiment of esteem, regard
& friendship, I am My D. Sir &c. &c.

G: Washington

P.S. Had you an agreeable tour to the Eastward? Are the State-
societies in the New England Governments making any moves
towards obtaining Charters?[4] If they are, with what success?

LB, DLC:GW.

1. For reference to the correspondence between Knox and GW in 1784, see
Knox to GW, 23 Nov. 1784, n.1. By "St—s" GW probably means "States."

2. For GW's western journey in September, see particularly *Diaries*,
4:1–71.

3. These are the views on which GW expanded in his letter to Gov. Benjamin Harrison, 10 Oct. 1784.

4. For the trip Henry Knox and Benjamin Lincoln made into Maine in August, see Knox to GW, 26 July 1784, and, particularly, 31 Jan. 1785, n.1.

To La Luzerne

Sir,   Mount Vernon 5th Decr 1784

Your early attention to me after your arrival at the Court of
Versailles, amidst scenes of gaiety & the gratulations of friends,
does me great honor & excites my warmest acknowledgments.
That your august Sovereign, his amiable consort, & the Princes
his brothers, should deign to interest themselves in, & wish to
be acquainted with the circumstances of my life, is one of the
most flattering incidents of it; & affects my sensibility beyond
any expression I have of my feelings. If any thing could overcome the present difficulties which impede my desires to pay
my respectful homage at your Court, it would be the wish
which you say these august personages have been pleased to ex-

press to see me there, & the welcome reception I should meet from the nation at large, especially from those characters to whom I have the honor of a personal acquaintance; but I fear my vows & earnest wishes are the only tribute of respect I shall ever have it in my power to offer them in return.

It gave me great pleasure to learn from your letter (of the 12th of Septr) that the sword which had been so lately sheathed, was likely to remain in the scabbard for some time— other information according with appearances, seemed rather to indicate an approaching storm in the United Netherlands; which, in its consequences, might touch the torch, which would kindle the flames of a general war in Europe. How far British policy may yield to Irish claims, is not for me to determine. The first, it should seem, have had too much of civil contentions to engage, without some respite, in fresh broils; & the other is too near, & too much divided among themselves, to oppose effectually without foreign aid—especially maritime. But I know not enough of their politics, or their expectations, to hazard an opinion respecting the issue of their disputes. That they slumbered during the favourable moment, none I think can deny, & favourable moments in war, as in love, once lost are seldom regained.

We have lately held a treaty with the Six Nations at Fort Stanwix, advantageously it is said for the United States, tho' the issue of it is not pleasing to that of New York—The Commissioners were by the last accounts, proceeding via Fort Pitt, to Cayahoga to a meeting of the Western Tribes, who every now & then have bickerings with our Settlers on the Ohio, in which lives and property have been lost. At the eclaircissement which is about to be had with them, it is to be hoped a proper understanding will take place—the causes of discontent removed, & peace & amity perfectly reestablished.

The honor of your correspondance I shall ever set a high value upon, & shall thank you for the continuation of it—the occurances of Europe cannot come thro' a better informed channel, nor from a more pleasing pen. Such returns as can flow from the cottage of retirement, I will make you: these indeed will be inadequate; but to a mind generous as yours is, there is more pleasure in conferring than in receiving an obligation.

If sir, the name of your Sovereign has been committed to your letter by his approbation or authority, you will know how far my respectful acknowledgments are due, & can be offered with propriety. I wish not to obtrude myself; nor to step over that line which custom has drawn—altho' feeling more respect & veneration for the King & Queen of France than I have powers to utter, I should in that case rest more on your abilities & their goodness to disclose them, than upon my own faint endeavours. To the military characters with whom I have the honor of an acquaintance, I present my best wishes & affectionate regards, at the same time that I never can too often repeat to you the assurances of the esteem & attachment with which I have the honor to be sir Yr Most Obedt and most hble servt

G: Washington

LB, DLC:GW.

To George Clinton

Dear Sir,   Mount Vernon 8th Decr 1784.
When the Marqs de la Fayette left this place, he expected to embark abt the 14th or 15th Instt on board the Nymph frigate, at New York, for France. Therefore, as this event may have taken place before this letter gets that far, I take the liberty of putting the enclosed packet under cover to you, with a request, if he should have Sailed to forward it by the first French Packet which follows.[1]

In looking into Millers Gardeners Dictionary, I find, besides transplanting, that the Pine-tree and evergreens of all kinds, are to be raised from the Seed. As this may be an easier way of helping me to the balm of Gilead—Spruce—White pine—or Hemlock, than by Stocks. I would thank your Excellency when it may be convenient (if not too late in the Season for it) to forward me some of these Seeds—especially the first, extracted from the Cone, & put in Sand—a thimbleful or two of each would suffice, & this might, at any time, come by the Stage—first to the care of Colo. Biddle in Philadelphia—who would forward it to me.[2] Mrs Washington joins me in best wishes for Mrs Clinton, yourself & all the family—With great truth & sincerity I am—Dr Sir Yr Most Obedt & Affecte Servt

Go: Washington

ALS (photocopy), DLC:GW; LB, DLC:GW.

1. The packet included GW's letters to La Luzerne of 5 Dec. and to Lafayette of 8 December. See Lafayette to GW, 21 Dec. 1784, and La Luzerne to GW, 15 Feb. 1785.

2. No record of Clinton's having sent the seed has been found, but for his sending GW trees, see GW to Clinton, 25 Nov. 1784. He also sent GW peas and corn (see Benjamin Walker to GW, 20 Dec. 1784, Clinton to GW, 5 Mar. 1785, GW to Clinton, 20 April 1785, and entry of 19 Mar. 1785 in *Diaries*, 4:104).

To Lafayette

My Dr Marqs,   Mount Vernon 8th Decr 1784.

The peregrination of the day in which I parted with you, ended at Marlbro': the next day, bad as it was, I got home before dinner.[1]

In the moment of our separation upon the road as I travelled, & every hour since—I felt all that love, respect & attachment for you, with which length of years, close connexion & your merits, have inspired me. I often asked myself, as our Carriages distended, whether that was the last sight, I ever should have of you? And tho' I wished to say no—my fears answered yes. I called to mind the days of my youth, & found they had long since fled to return no more; that I was now descending the hill, I had been 52 years climbing—& that tho' I was blessed with a good constitution, I was of a short lived family—and might soon expect to be entombed in the dreary mansions of my father's—These things darkened the shades & gave a gloom to the picture, consequently to my prospects of seeing you again: but I will not repine—I have had my day.

Nothing of importance has occurred since I parted with you; I found my family well—& am now immersed in company, notwithstanding which, I have in haste, produced a few more letters to give you the trouble of—rather inclining to commit them to your care, than to pass them thro' many & unknown hands.[2]

It is unnecessary, I persude myself to repeat to you my Dr Marqs the sincerity of my regards & friendship—nor have I words which could express my affection for you, were I to attempt it. My fervent prayers are offered for your safe & pleasant passage—happy meeting with Madame la Fayette & family, the completion of every wish of your heart—in all which Mrs

Washington joins me, as she does in complimts to Capt. Grand-cheau & the Chevr of whom little Washn often speaks—With every sentimt wch is propitious & endearing—I am &c. &c. &c.

G: Washington

LB, DLC:GW.

1. GW got back to Mount Vernon on Saturday, 2 December. See GW to Joseph Jones and James Madison, 3 Dec., n.1.

2. See note 1 in GW to George Clinton, this date. See also Lafayette to GW, 17 December.

Letter not found: to George Augustine Washington, 8 Dec. 1784. On 25 Feb. 1785 George Augustine wrote to GW: "I received with inexpressible pleasure Your two friendly Letters of the 26th of Novr, and 8th of Decr."

From Thomas Jefferson

Dear Sir   Paris Dec. 10. 1784.

Every thing on this side the water seems to indicate a certainty of war. the Emperor seems decided in not receding from the right to navigate the Scheld; & the Dutch as determined not to yeild it. I suppose that this court & that of Berlin will take part with the Dutch. the Turks of course become parties in a war against the Emperor: & it seems as probable that the Empress of Russia will join him. there are many who beleive he will yet retract: but every public appearance is against this supposition. I own myself astonished he should have gone so far: but I should be more so were he now to retire. he is indeed in a perillous predicament. if he recedes, his character, which his public acts have placed on very high ground, dwindles to that of a petty bully, & is marked, as his enemies denote it, with eccentricity & inconsistence: if he persists, the probable combination against him seems to threaten his ruin. when the season arrives for opening a campaign we shall know decidedly & probably not before.[1]

The disposition of Gr. Britain does not seem very favourable to us. all information from thence represents the people & still more the merchants as extremely hostile. I think it probable we shall take a trip to that court in order to bring their intentions to a decisive issue. it seems probable also that Spain will refuse to treat at this place, & oblige us to visit Madrid. I had lately a letter from mr Carmichael at Madrid. he informs me that a mr Harrison of Cadiz had on your behalf applied to him to procure permission to send you a Jack of the best race; and that on his making the application the king had ordered two of the very best to be procured & sent you as a mark of his respect. besides the pleasure I receive from every testimonial of this kind, I view this present as likely to be of great public utility. I had before intended to endeavor to procure a male of that race: but shall now change my object to the procuring one or more females, that we may be enabled to propagate & preserve the breed. should I go to Spain, I shall surely be able to effect this.[2]

The executive of our state have remitted to Dr Franklin & myself the care of having the statue made which the assembly directed as a mark of their gratitude to you.[3] I was unwell when I received the letter & have not yet been able to see & confer with Doctr Franklin on the subject. I find that a Monsr Houdon of this place possesses the reputation of being the first statuary in the world. I sent for him & had some conversation with him on the subject. he thinks it cannot be perfectly done from a picture, & is so enthusiastically fond of being the executor of this work that he offers to go himself to America for the purpose of forming your bust from the life, leaving all his business here in the mean time. he thinks that being three weeks with you would suffice to make his model of plaister, with which he will return here, & the work will employ him three years. if Dr Franklin concurs with me, we shall send him over, not having time to ask your permission & await your answer. I trust that having given to your country so much of your time heretofore, you will add the short space which this operation will require to enable them to transmit to posterity the form of the person whose actions will be delivered to them by History. Monsr Houdon is at present engaged in making a statue of the king of France. a bust of Voltaire executed by him is said to be one of the first in the world.[4]

I beg leave to present my respectful compliments to Mrs Washington & to assure yourself of the high esteem & veneration with which I have the honour to be Dr Sir your most obedient and most humble servt

Th: Jefferson

ALS, DLC:GW.

1. In 1785 the French arbitrated the dispute of four years between Joseph II of Austria and the Dutch over the navigation of the River Scheldt.

2. See William Carmichael to GW, 3 Dec. 1784, and notes. Carmichael wrote to Jefferson on 25 Nov. 1784: "You will be pleased to hear, that the Kings Attention has been extended to General Washington; Mr. Harrison, of Alexandria in Virginia, but now settled in Cadiz, having had recourse to me, to obtain permission for the Extraction of a Jack Ass of the best breed in Spain, which the General had directed him to purchase, I was obliged to have recourse to the Minister for it, as without the Kings express permission these animals cannot be sent out of the Kingdom. His Majesty, being informed for whom it was intended, Directed the Ct. de Florida Blanca to procure two of the best, that can be found in Spain, to be sent as a proof of his esteem for so distinguished a character. They are sold for, from three to four hundred pistoles a peice, when they are of the best breed. I am apprehensive that the Generals delicacy may be wounded, but I flatter myself when he shall see the manner in which I have acted on this occasion, he will do me the justice to beleive that I could not have done otherwise" (Boyd, *Jefferson Papers*, 7:548–50).

3. See doc. I in Virginia General Assembly and George Washington, 15 May–15 July 1784, printed above.

4. Jean-Antoine Houdon (1741–1828) did not arrive at Mount Vernon until 2 Oct. 1785, when he formed the life mask from which he made his famous statue and busts of GW. The reason for the delay was Houdon's illness (see Jefferson to GW, 10 July 1785).

Letter not found: from James Madison, 11 Dec. 1784. On 28 Dec. GW wrote to Madison: "I have been favored with your letter of the 11th."

To George Plater, Charles Carroll, John Cadwalader, and Samuel Chase

Sir,   Mt Vernon 11th Decr 1784

The Gentn who will have the honor of presenting this letter to you, is a Nephew of mine, heir to my Brother who was one of the Partners in the Principio Company, and to whose Will I was appointed an Executor, though circumstances put it out of my power to qualify.

He is about to offer a petition to your honble Assembly, from the Execrs of my Brother, to obtain the Estates proportion of the property belonging to the company and sold by Commissioners, appointed under the Act, for confiscating British property[1]—The petition is explanatory of the Justice on which it is founded, and so full that it Leaves nothing for me to add, further, than as it was by misconception or misinformation, that the Estates proportion of the Bonds, got into the hands of the Intendant, so I am persuaded it only requires to be known, to obtain an order for the Assignment of them to the Exectrs, as the Act of your Assembly reserved the Estates interest therein, absolutely and clearly; and only a punctilio of the Intendant could possible be the cause of the delay, which, for the reasons assign'd in the petition, is exceedingly distressing to the Execrs & injurious to my Nephew, you will excuse me I hope, for the freedom of this address, and do me the justice to believe that I am Sir Yr most obt & very Hble Sert

Go: Washington

LS, PPAmP: Bradford Family Papers, directed to John Cadwalader; ADS, PWacD: Sol Feinstone Collection, on deposit PPAmP.

George Plater (1735–1792), Charles Carroll of Carrollton (1737–1832), John Cadwalader (Cadwallader; 1742–1786), and Samuel Chase (1741–1811) were all leading figures in Maryland. At this time, Plater and Carroll were members of the Maryland senate, and Cadwalader and Chase were in the Maryland house. In 1725 GW's father, Augustine Washington (1694–1743), reached an agreement with the Principio Iron Company of London, which had ironworks in Maryland, whereby he received stock in the iron company in return for the iron found on the lands that he held on Accokeek Creek in Virginia. For a full account of Augustine Washington's involvement in the Principio Iron Company, see Freeman, *Washington*, 1:37–42. At Augustine Washington's death, his Principio stock passed to his oldest son Lawrence (1718–1752), then from Lawrence to Lawrence's brother Augustine (1720–1762), and finally, from Augustine to Augustine's son William Augustine Washington (1757–1810), the nephew to whom GW is referring here. In 1780, the Maryland legislature confiscated Loyalist property, including that of the Principio ironworks. In ordering the sale of the Principio property, the act noted that "a certain Mr Washington, a subject of the State of Virginia, is entitled to one individual one-twelfth ($\frac{1}{12}$) part thereof." No further correspondence on the matter has been found, but GW may have received a satisfactory response when he met with the Maryland legislature in Annapolis later this month.

1. This sentence in the LB copy, after the word "Assembly," reads: "for his part of the Sales of the property of that company." On 15 Dec. the speaker of the Maryland house of delegates received from the Maryland senate "a petition from the executors of Augustine Washington, deceased, respecting the assignment of certain bonds" (*Md. House of Delegates Proceedings*). No record of either house having taken action on the petition in this session has been found.

Letter not found: from Chastellux, 12 Dec. 1784. On 5 Sept. 1785 GW wrote Chastellux: "I am your debtor for two letters—one of the 12th of Decemr."

To George Mason

Dr Sir,   [Mount Vernon] 13th Decr 1784.

My brother John is much in want of four, five or six hundred pounds which he is desirous of borrowing on Interest. If it is in your power to supply him, I will become security for the fulfilment of his agreement. He seems to have little expectation that money in these times, can be had at the common interest; & his own words will best express what he is willing to allow.

"I believe I mentioned to you before" (when he was last up) "that I was willing to receive ninety pounds for an hundred, & pay interest for the latter sum from the date, provided I could be allowed to retain the principal two years. If I could receive 4, 5, or 6 hundred pounds on these terms, it would be a real convenience & happiness for me; because it would enable me to observe that punctuality in dealing I always wished to do, & without which I am miserable. If you cou'd prevail upon Colo. Mason, or any other Gentleman to furnish me with the above sum on these terms, you would confer a very great favor, and I would attend at a time to be appointed to give Bond & receive the money."[1]

To this, I can add nothing but my wishes for his success, & an expression of my own inclination to have supplied his want, if I had been in circumstances to have done it. I am Dr Sir Your most obedt & very humble servt

G: Washington

LB, DLC:GW.

1. The letter from John Augustine Washington, from which presumably this quotation is taken, has not been found. The most recent known visit of John Augustine Washington to Mount Vernon was in June 1784 (see John Augustine Washington to GW, 4 April 1784, n.3). What response Mason made to the application for a loan has not been determined.

Letter not found: from Elias Boudinot, 14 Dec. 1784. On 31 Jan. 1785 GW wrote to Boudinot: "I was honored with your favor of the 14th of last Month."

To Richard Henry Lee

Dear Sir,   Mount Vernon 14th Decr 84

The letter which you did me the honor to write to me on the 20th of last Month, only came to my hands by the Post preceeding the date of this.

For the copy of the treaty held with the Six Nations at Fort Stanwix, you will please to accept my thanks. These people have given, I think, all that the United States could reasonably have asked of them; more perhaps than the State of New York conceive ought to have been required from them, by any other, than their own Legislature. I wish they were better satisfied. Individual States opposing the measures of the United States—encroaching upon the territory of one another—and setting up old and obsolete claims, is verifying the predictions of our enemies; and, in reallity, is truly unfortunate. If the Western tribes are as well disposed to treat with us as the Northern Indians have been, & will cede a competent district of Country North West of the Ohio, to answer our present purposes, it would be a circumstance as unexpected, as pleasing to me; for it was apprehended, if they agreed to the latter at all, it would be reluctantly. but the example of the Six Nations who (if they have not relinquished their claim) have pretensions to a large part of those Lands, may have a powerful influence on the Western gentry, & smooth the way for the Commissioners, who have proceeded to Fort Pitt.

It gave me pleasure to find by the last Gazettes, that a sufficient number of States had Assembled to form a Congress, and that you had been placed in the Chair of it—On this event, permit me to offer my Compliments of congratulation. To whatever causes the delay of this meeting may have been ascribed, it most certainly has an unfavorable aspect—contributes to lessen—(already too low)—the dignity and importance of the fœderal government. and is hurtful to our National character, in the eyes of Europe.

It is said (how founded I know not) that our Assembly have repealed their former act respecting British debts.[2] If this be true, & the State of New York have not acted repugnant to the terms of the treaty, the British government can no longer hold the western posts under that cover; but I shall be mistaken if they do not intrench themselves behind some other expedient, to effect it; or, will appoint a time for surrendering them, of which we cannot avail ourselves—the probable consequence whereof will be, the destruction of the Works.

The Assemblies of Virginia and Maryland have now under consideration the extension of the inland navigation of the rivers Potomack & James; and opening a communication between them, and the Western Waters. They seem fully impressed with the political, as well as the commercial advantages which would result from the accomplishment of these great objects; & I hope will embrace the present moment to put them in a train for execution—Would it not at the same time, be worthy the wisdom, & attention of Congress to have the Western Waters well explored; the Navigation of them fully ascertained; accurately laid down; and a complete & perfect Map made of the Country; at least as far Westerly—as the Miamies, running into the Ohio & Lake Erie; and to see how the Waters of these communicates with the river St Joseph, which emptys into the Lake Michigan, & with the Wabash? for I cannot forbear observing that the Miami village in Hutchins Map, if it and the Waters are laid down with accuracy points to a very important Post for the Union—The expence attending such an undertaking could not be great—the advantages would be unbounded—for sure I am Nature has made such a display of her bounties in those regions that the more the Country is explored the more it will rise in estimation—consequently greater will the revenue be, to the Union.

Would there be any impropriety do you think Sir, in reserving for special Sale, all Mines, Minerals & Salt Springs in the general grants of land, from the United States? The public, instead of the few knowing ones might, in that case, receive the benefits which would proceed from the Sale of them; without infringing any rule of justice that occurs to me, or their own laws—but on the contrary, inflict just punishment upon those who, in defiance of the latter, have dared to create enemies to disturb the public tranquility, by roaming over the Country marking & Surveying the valuable spots in it, to the great disquiet of the Western tribes of Indians, who have viewed these proceedings with jealous indignation.

To hit upon a happy medium price for the Western Lands,

for the prevention of Monopoly on one hand—and not discouraging useful Settlers on the other, will, no doubt, require consideration; but ought not in my opinion to employ too much time before the terms are announced. The Spirit of emigration is great—People have got impatient—and tho' you cannot stop the road, it is yet in your power to mark the way; a little while, & you will not be able to do either—It is easier to prevent, than to remedy an evil.[3]

I shall be very happy in the continuation of your corrispondence—& with sentiments of great esteem & respect I have the honor to be Dr Sir Yr Most Obedt Hble Servt

Go: Washington

ALS, PPAmP: Correspondence of Richard Henry Lee and Arthur Lee; LB, DLC:GW.

1. The copyist corrected this in the letter book to read "Cayahuga" instead of Fort Pitt.

2. The bill "for enabling the British merchants to recover their debts from the Citizens of the Commonwealth" failed to gain final passage before adjournment of the Virginia house of assembly on 7 Jan. 1785 (*House of Delegates Journal, 1781–1785*, 5 Jan. 1785). On what was intended to be the last day of the session, Wednesday, 5 Jan., and for the next two days, the delegates were unable to muster a quorum so that they could take a final vote on the bill. Because of the ice in the James River, members on the opposite side were unable, or unwilling, to cross over into Richmond. See James Madison to James Monroe, 8 Jan. 1785, in Rutland and Rachal, *Madison Papers*, 8:220–22.

3. GW wrote on 3 Nov. to Jacob Read about what policy Congress ought to adopt for the disposition of the western land becoming available for settlement as the result of the negotiations with the Iroquois and the Indians in the Ohio country. For the Indian treaties, see Arthur Lee to GW, 19 Nov. 1784, n.1.

To George Chapman

Sir,   Mount Vernon 15th Decr 1784.

Not until within a few days have I been honor'd with your favor of the 27th of Septr 1783 accompanying your treatise on Education.

My sentiments are perfectly in unison with yours sir, that the best means of forming a manly, virtuous and happy people, will be found in the right education of youth. Without *this* foundation, every other means, in my opinion, must fail; & it gives me pleasure to find that Gentlemen of your abilities are devoting their time & attention in pointing out the way. For your lucubrations on this subject which you have been so obliging as to send me, I pray you to accept my thanks, & an expression of the pleasure I felt at the declaration of your intention to devote a further portion of your time in so useful a study.

Of the importance of education our Assemblies, happily, seem fully impressed; they establishing new, & giving further endowments to the old Seminaries of learning, and I persuade myself will leave nothing unessayed to cultivate literature & useful knowledge, for the purpose of qualifying the rising generation for patrons of good government, virtue & happiness. I have the honor to be &c.

G: Washington

LB, DLC:GW.

George Chapman (1723–1806) in 1774 gave up the position of headmaster of the grammar school in Dumfries in his native Scotland because of ill health. At this time, in 1784, he had a small school in his house near Banff. Chapman wrote GW from there on 27 Sept. 1783 and sent a copy of the second edition of his *A Treatise on Education with a Sketch of the Author's Method of Instruction While He Taught the School of Dumfries and a View of Other Books on Education*, first printed in 1773. GW was sufficiently impressed that, more than two years after Chapman sent the pamphlet and a year after having received it, he sent George William Fairfax a letter for Chapman in which he asked Chapman to recommend someone to be tutor to Martha Washington's two grandchildren at Mount Vernon, Eleanor Parke ("Nelly") Custis and George Washington Parke Custis, ages 5 and 3 (see GW to George William Fairfax, 11 Nov. 1785, n.2).

To Richard Claiborne

Sir,   Mount Vernon 15th Decr 1784

I have received your letter of the 17th ulto.[1] It would interfere with no views of mine, to give you a field to speculate in, if I was sufficiently master of the business, & had leisure for these kind of communications: but the truth is, I do not turn my thoughts to matters of that sort, & if I did, the business in which you want to be informed is too much in embryo—& depends too much on contingencies, to speak to with any degree of certainty at this time. First, because Acts of the Assemblies of Virginia & Maryland, must be obtained to incorporate private adventurers to undertake the business—2d the Company must be formed before anything can be done—3d an actual survey of the waters, by skilful Engineers, (or persons in that line) must take place & be approved before the points at which the navigation on the different waters can be ascertained, as proper to end, or commence the water transportation. From Fort Cumberland to the Yohioghany is one of the Portages in contemplation—& from some place higher up the Yo. river, most convenient to the navigable part, or such part as can be made so, of the Cheat river, is another portage talked of; but whether either, neither or both may be attempted does not lie with me to determine, & therefore I should be unwilling to mislead any one by hazarding an opinion, as my knowledge of that Country goes more to the general view of it—& to general principles—than to the investigation of local spots for interested purposes. I am Sir &c.

G: Washington

LB, DLC:GW.

Richard Claiborne during the war served on Gen. Nathanael Greene's staff and from 1781 to 1783 was an assistant deputy quartermaster general for Virginia. In 1783, he was awarded 3,555 acres of bounty land in the Ohio country. The interest in the West and western land which he betrays here continued for the rest of his life. He also became closely associated with James Rumsey in Rumsey's efforts to develop mechanically driven boats for river transportation. After living several years in London in the late 1780s and early 1790s, where he was engaged in a number of speculative enterprises, Claiborne returned to the United States, eventually settling in the Louisiana territory and becoming one of its most prominent citizens.

1. Claiborne's letter has not been found, but see the reference to him in John Filson's letter of 4 December. It would appear from GW's letter that Claiborne had inquired about the points at which land portage would become necessary between navigable streams running into the Potomac and the Ohio.

From Beverley Randolph

Sir   In Council Decr 15th 1784.

I have the Honour to Inclose you Several Resolutions of the General Assembly, relative to the Opening the Navigation of the River Potomack; by which you are Appointed One of the Commissioners on the part of this State to meet those who may be Appointed on the Part of Maryland to Concert Such regulations as may be best Adapted to Attain this important Object:[1] the Letter Addressed to the Governor of Maryland is inclosed Open to you with a Blank which the Executive request you will fill up with the time at which it will be Convenient for yourself and the Other Commissioners to meet at Annapolis.[2] It may be requisite to Observe that the Day shou'd be as early a One as Possible, the Assembly being Anxious to receive your report so that they may Adopt the Necessary Measures During their Present Session. you will be Pleased after filling up the Blank, to forward the Letter to Mr Paca by the Express who will Deliver you this.[3] with the Greatest respect I am Sir Yr Very Obt Servt

B. Randolph

ALS, ICU; LB, Vi: Executive Letter Book.

Although Patrick Henry's new term as governor of Virginia began on 30 Nov., he did not appear in the council to assume office until 21 December. Until then, Beverley Randolph (1734–1797) as lieutenant governor acted in his stead.

1. These particular copies of the resolutions implementing GW's suggestions to Madison of 3 Dec. regarding cooperation between Virginia and Maryland to form a Potomac River company and to build a road in Pennsylvania from the Potomac to the waters of the Ohio have not been found. The texts of the resolutions, however, are printed in the journal of the Virginia house of delegates for 13 Dec.: "Whereas, the opening and extending the inland navigation of this Commonwealth, will greatly contribute to the interest of individuals, and to the prosperity of the whole State; and a memorial has been presented to the present General Assembly, by sundry inhabitants of this State and of the State of Maryland, representing the particular advantages which would flow from the establishment of a company under the authority of two States, for the purpose of opening and improving the navigation of the river Potomac, from tide water, up the said river, as far as the same can be carried; and praying that an act may be passed by the present General Assembly, for establishing such a company: And whereas, the prayer of the said memorial is deemed reasonable; but it appearing to this House, that acts passed without previous communication between the two States, may be dissimilar and productive of much delay;

"*Resolved*, That George Washington, Horatio Gates and Thomas Blackburne, Esquires, or any two of them be, and they are hereby appointed, forthwith to meet such persons as may be appointed by the State of Maryland, and to concert with them the regulations under which a company ought to be established for the purpose aforesaid; and that they immediately report the result of such conference to the General Assembly.

"And whereas, one material advantage to be derived to the two States, from the opening and improving the navigation of the river Potomac as aforesaid, will consist in the progress and facility it will afford towards a commercial intercourse with the western country;

"*Resolved*, That the said commissioners, or any two of them be, and they are hereby authorised and instructed to concert with the persons who may be appointed on the part of Maryland, a plan, for opening a proper road between the waters of the Potomac and the most convenient western waters, together with the just proportions of money which ought to be supplied by the two States for that purpose; and that the said commissioners also report the result of their proceedings herein, to the General Assembly.

"*Resolved*, That these resolutions be transmitted by express to the State of Maryland, by the Executive, with propositions for the time and place of meeting the persons who may be deputed on the part of Maryland" (*House of Delegates Journal, 1781–1785*).

2. GW forwarded Lieutenant Governor Randolph's letter to Gov. William Paca under cover of a letter dated 19 December. For the text of Randolph's letter to Paca, see note 1 in GW to Paca, 19 December. GW set the date for the meeting with the Marylanders at Annapolis on 22 Dec. (see GW to Randolph, 20 Dec., and Enclosure I in George Washington and Horatio Gates to the Virginia Legislature, 28 Dec., printed below). Thomas Blackburn did not go to Annapolis and General Gates became ill during the meeting, leaving GW to act alone for Virginia (see Blackburn to GW, 20 Dec., Gates to GW, 24 Dec., and GW to James Madison, 28 Dec.).

3. The "express," or messenger, was named Daniel Thompson. See GW to Randolph, 20 Dec., n.1.

From James Duane

Dear Sir   Trenton [N.J.] 16th Decemr 1784

I entertained the pleasing hope of meeting you at this place; on no better authority indeed than report; and yet I feel the disappointment in proportion to my affection for your Person, my gratitude for your publick Services, and the kind attention with which you have always indulged me.[1]

Be pleased to take in good part the Address which I have the honor to transmit with the Freedom of our City in a golden box.[2] It can add nothing to your Glory; but we flatter ourselves it may not be unacceptable as a permanent Testimony of the Esteem and Gratitude of Citizens who, of all others, have been most distinguished by your Care and Sollicitude.

I once flatterd myself that the Dignity of our Government would have born some proportion to the illustrious atchievements by which it was succesfully established—but it is to be deplored that fœderal attachment, and a sense of national obligation, continue to give place to vain prejudices in favour of the Independance and Sovereignty of the individual States. I have endeavourd, in pursuance of the great Motive which induced me to continue in publick life, to inculcate more enlarged and liberal principles; but the Spirit of the times seems opposed to My feeble efforts, and I have lost credit with our Assembly, tho' I hope not with the world. If opportunity offers I shall take the liberty to submit to your perusal the Judgement pronounced in the Court where I preside which has produced the Censure promulgated in the papers—"in effect that we had the presumption to controul the operation of an act of the Legislature from a respect to the Treaty of peace and the Law of Nations."

I trust you know me too well to think that I can be otherwise concerned for this Event than as it may injure the reputation of my native State, of which I have so long been a faithful and confidential Servant.

Mr Jay, Mr Dickenson, and other great men, from publick Considerations, have honor'd us with the highest Approbation. Their comments are calculated for the publick Eye, and will appear when they can do the greatest good.[3]

I have too long been indulged in writing to you with unreserved freedom and confidence to suppress this detail, and if it was ever so immaterial your Goodness wou'd pardon it.

Do me the honor to make my most respectful Compliments acceptable to Mrs Washington and to assure her that in the Circle of her numerous Friends there are none who remember her with more sincere regard than Mrs Duane and all the branches of our Family. With every Sentiment of the most perfect and affectionate attachment—I have the honor to be—Dear Sir your most obedient and very humble Servant

Jas Duane

ALS, DLC:GW; ADfS, NHi: Duane Papers. Duane seems to have delayed sending this letter and its enclosure until 10 Mar. 1785, at which time he enclosed both in a letter of that date.

1. See Henry Knox to GW, 23 Nov. 1784, n.2.

2. The certificate making GW a freeman of New York City and the address from the officials of the city are both dated 2 Dec. 1784 and both are signed by Duane as mayor. GW's responses are printed in GW to Duane, 10 April 1785. The certificate reads: "By James Duane Esqr. Mayor and the Recorder & Alderman of the City of New York:

"To all to whom these presents shall come or concern Greeting:

"Whereas his Excellency George Washington late Commander in Chief of the Armies of the United States of America by a Series of the most illustrious Services is entitled to the respect gratitude and applause of every heart which is truly american: And as none can have greater reason to cherish the most honorable and affectionate Sentiments towards him than the Citizens of the State of New York: So we have the fullest Confidence that there is no State in which they are more generally and emphatically felt: Flattering ourselves that convinced of this truth, his Excellency may be present to have his name enrolled among the Citizens of a Metropolis for the Recovery of which so much of his Care and Solicitude have been employed: Now therefore Know Ye that we considering that the Effusions of public esteem are the most welcome Tribute to a patriot Mind have admitted and received and by these presents Do admit and receive his said Excellency to be a Freeman and Citizen of the said City To Hold exercise and enjoy all the rights priviledges and immunities to the Freedom and Citizenship of the said City incident and appurtaining As a permanent Proof of the Admiration we feel for his exalted Virtues, for the wisdom Fortitude and Magnanimity which he hath so gloriously displayed, thro' all the Vicissitudes and embarrasments, thro' all the alternate Scenes of prosperous and adverse fortune produced in the progress of an arduous and difficult War: And finally for that patriotic heroism which after having been an essential Instrument in giving, by the divine Blessing, Liberty and Independence to thirteen Republics hath led him to retire with chearfulness from the head of a Victorious Army to the modest Station of a private Citizen.

"In Testimony of these Truths and to perpetuate them to our remotest Posterity we the said Mayor Recorder and Alderman have caused these presents to be entered on our public Records and our common Seal of the said City enclosed in a Golden box to be here unto affixed: Witness James Duane Esquire Mayor of the said City this second day of [Dec]ember in the Year of our Lord 1784 and of the Independence of the State the ninth" (DLC:GW).

The address reads: "When this City immediately after its restoration, had the honor of your Excellencys presence, it was regretted that the arrangement of its Institutions suspended those public Testimonials of respect, gratitude, and applause which every heart truly american is sollicitous to pay to your distinguished merits and services. The Corporation, since organized, resolved to embrace a proper opportunity to manifest the exalted Sense which they entertain of both, and are happy that your Approach to the Vicinity of this State will put it in their power to carry that Resolution into effect.

"The effusions of public Esteem are the most welcome Tribute to a patriot Mind, and as none can have greater reason to cherish the most honorable and affectionate Sentiments toward you than the Citizens of the State of New York. So we have the fullest Confidence that there is no State in which they are more generally and emphatically felt. Flattering ourselves that you are convinced of this truth we are led to hope that it may not be displeasing to you to have your name enrolled among the Citizens of a Metropolis for the Recovery of which so much of your Care and Sollicitude have been employed.

"On the present Occasion we would wish to convey to your Excellency a just Idea of the admiration we feel for the Virtues you have displayed in the late Revolution; but justice to the illustrious part you have acted would oblige us to adopt that strong language of Panegyric which we fear might wound the Delicacy for which you are conspicuous. We shall therefore only indulge ourselves so far as to observe that it is your glory, thro' all the vicissitudes and embarrasments of a Revolution, thro' alternate Scenes of prosperous and adverse Fortune never to have known a Moment when you did not possess the full confidence and esteem of your Country; and after having, by the divine Favor most essentially contributed to establish the Liberty and Independence of thirteen republics, it is your peculiar Glory to have chearfully retired from the Head of a Victorious Army to the modest Station, of a private Citizen.

"Permit us to add our fervent Prayers that your Excellency in just reward of such eminent Services and Virtues may be crowned with every Blessing which a grateful Country and indulgent Heaven can bestow. By order of the Corporation" (DLC:GW).

3. Duane is referring to the famous case, *Rutgers v. Waddington*, which was ordered in Duane's mayor's court on 29 June 1784. Elizabeth Rutgers, an elderly widow and Patriot, entered a suit early in 1784 against Joseph Waddington, agent of the British merchants who had taken over Mrs. Rutgers's brewery during the British occupation of the city, for £8,000 unpaid rent. The lawyers for the plaintiff, led by Attorney General Egbert Benson, argued for the validity of the Trespass Act passed by the New York legislature on 17 Mar. 1783, under the terms of which Mrs. Waddington would be paid. The lawyers for the defense, led by Alexander Hamilton, argued that the law of nations and the terms of the treaty of peace barred Mrs. Rutgers from collecting rent for her brewery. In a finely drawn decision, Duane delivered the opinion of the court on 27 Aug. 1784. It held that for the three years, from 1780 to 1783, when the two merchants controlled the brewery under the authority of the British commander, the law of nations transferred the right to the rent to the British commander, which the two had paid in accordance with the commander's directions. This left the defendants liable for the payments to Mrs. Rutgers in 1778 and 1779 when they held the brewery under orders from the commissary and paid no rent. *Rutgers v. Waddington*, in its contemporary context, receives full and authoritative treatment in Julius Goebel, Jr., ed., *The Law Practice of Alexander Hamilton: Documents and Commentary*, 1 (New York, 1964), 282–419.

From Udny Hay

Sir,   New York 16th December 1784

In the fullest confidence that your Excellencys love of Justice will induce you to forgive the trouble of this Letter, I shall without further hesitation enter at once on the subject thereof.

My Brother Charles Hay was, with some circumstances of extreme rigour, confined in Canada in a common Jail upwards of three years on suspicion of treasonable Practices; When Governour Haldeman was by the Secretary of State in England ordered either to release or exhibit specifick charges against him, the three following were transmitted by the Governours order, viz:

⟨1⟩st That he was suspected of corresponding with the Rebels by message or otherwise.

⟨2⟩nd That he was formerly connected in trade with a Brother who was now in high office with the Rebels.

⟨3⟩d That he was known to be an arrant Rebel at his Heart.[1]

As my Brother is determined to seek redress in England, and as none but the first of these charges can possibly be supposed to have any weight even with a prejudiced Jury, he being at the same time conscious that this charge, if attempted to be supported at all, can only be so either by Witnesses of a known infamous Character or by very slender circumstantial Evidence, he has been advised to counteract such an attempt by the best negative proof which the nature of the case will admit of. I have therefore made an affidavit and Governour Clinton and General Greene have been so oblidging as give certificates Copies of all which I have enclosed for your perusal,[2] and must now take the liberty of requesting your Excellency will be so good as add one from yourself and transmit it to Charles Hay at Mr John Thompsons Merchant, Cheswick, near London.[3]

Permit me to wish that your Excellency and Lady may long enjoy that tranquillity and domestick happiness, without the smallest interruption, which the world seems pleased in your having already tasted, and which even your late public Enemies do not hesitate to confess you have so justly merit a continuation of, and believe at same time that I am with the most sincere and Heart-felt Gratitude, Your Excellencys, most obedient and most humble Servant

Udney Hay

ALS, DLC:GW.

In December 1775 Udny and Charles Hay, Scottish brothers living in Canada, left Quebec City on the approach of Gen. Richard Montgomery. Charles Hay returned in 1776, but his brother first joined Moses Hazen's 2d Canadian Regiment in the American army and subsequently transferred to the commissary department, reaching the rank of lieutenant colonel and the office of deputy quartermaster general by the war's end. During the 1780s Udny Hay was in charge of settling Canadian refugees on land on Lake Champlain in New York (see the note in Clement Gosselin to GW, 18 Sept. 1789).

1. Gov. Sir Frederick Haldimand arrested Charles Hay at Quebec on 15 April 1780 on grounds that Hay was involved in supplying information to a

Patriot spy. Hay's wife acted vigorously on his behalf, and apparently it was due to her efforts that Haldimand was ordered to justify Hay's arrest. Haldimand wrote Shelburne on 16 July 1782, giving his account of Hay's arrest and imprisonment. Hay was released on 2 May 1783. The numbers 1, 2, and 3 have been torn off the page.

2. Udny Hay's affidavit was made on 16 Dec. 1784 in the presence of Richard Varick, recorder of the city of New York. The copy of George Clinton's certificate is dated 17 Dec. and that of Nathanael Greene's is dated 18 December. The copies of all three documents are in DLC:GW.

3. Under the cover of a letter to Udny Hay of 31 Jan. 1785, GW sent a certificate dated 1 Feb. 1785 stating that he had no knowledge of any information about the British forces having been received from Charles Hay during the war.

From Joseph Palmer

Dear Sir   Germantown [Mass.] 16th Decr 1784.

I sincerely congratulate you on having Seen an end to the late destructive War, in which you have acted so conspicuous a part; so much to your own honor, & the honor & benefit of these States. And I thank God for having endow'd you with Such a high degree of Wisdom, courage & prudence; & preserving your life to this time. May you be still eminent for private & public Virtue; & die in peace, in a good old Age, ripe for immortal Glory.

The known goodness of your Heart, & extensive knowledge of the internal parts of the Country, lead me to request of your Exellency, to inform me of any Salt Springs; or ⟨fossile⟩ Salt; in any parts of these States; where Situated; whether to be purchased, or not; if to be Sold, at what rate, & how to apply; with all such other circumstances as you shall judge useful.

This application arises from the ruin brought upon myself & Son by the operations of the late War; a concise sketch of which follows. Previous to the War, I had large concern in the manufacture of Spermaceti Candles, in which my *all* was involved; & that War put an end to the business. I then employ'd all my powers, in the support of our common Cause; & indeed had done so for several preceding years. The Resolves of the County of Suffolk, before the War commenced, Show that I was early engaged. In the course of the war, I sunk much money, in the investigation of the Salt Manufactures; & brought the manufacture of white Salt, to a greater degree of perfection, as

I think, than is known in Europe; & had, as I suppose, the largest Boilery in America; & produced as good Epsom Salts, as any imported. And from a full conviction of the propriety or raising, & manufacturing, within ourselves, all things necessary for support & defence, in order to being truly independent, I not only encouraged the White Salt business, but also, Manufacturing in general, & that of Bay Salt in particular; but the latter wanted public encouragement, which cou'd not, then, be obtain'd. I also sank large Money, in the Support of the Credit of our paper Currency. But what compleated our ruin was the Resolve of Congress, recinding a former Resolve for drawing Bills on Europe at 25 for one; this sunk its Thousands. And now, at about 66, or 67 years of age, with a weakly family, & little to set out with, I am to begin the World again; either in the spermaceti manufacture; or ⟨in⟩ the Salt way. The first will require, perhaps 7 or 8000£ Stock; which probably will be out of my p⟨ower⟩ to obtain, as I have little besides my character to build upon: And the latter, to me, & mine, under ⟨pres⟩ent circumstances, must yeild a gloomy prospect, especially if in the Wilderness; but if driven to that, & can set up the works, on a good Spring, or, where there is plenty of Sal Gemma; & a sufficient demand for the Salt; & safety from the Indians; we may obtain a comfortable living, especially as the annual Stock will cost but little. The Maps mention Salt Springs at Kentucky; also 50, or 60 miles NW from Fort Pitt. And also in the onondago Country. Whose is the property, I know not. Wherever arc Salt Licks, there is Salt, either Rock-Salt, or Springs.

You will doubtless consider the manufacturing of Salt, in any considerable quantities, in the internal parts of the Country, as an object, a matter of public utility. And you will wish to relieve, in some degree, the distresses of those who have been *thus* ruin'd. These considerations will doubtless lead your Excellency to reply to this, as soon as conveniently may be, & will excuse my application.

You will please to present my very respectful Compts to Mrs Washington, & assure her that our best wishes always attend her. You will please to direct for Joseph Palmer, at Germantown, near Boston, & it will come Safe to your Sincere friend & most humle Servt

J: Palmer

ALS, DLC:GW.

Joseph Palmer (1716–1788) arrived in Boston from England in 1746. He gives here an accurate summary of his career in Massachusetts as a manufacturer of candles and salt and of his role as a Patriot during the Revolution. Having quarreled bitterly with John Hancock, to whom he was heavily indebted, Palmer left Germantown shortly after writing this letter and set up new factories in Dorchester, where he remained until his death. No acknowledgment of this letter by GW has been found.

From Lafayette

New York 17th Decr 1784

I Shou'd think myself much Obliged to Your encellency if through Your Means Some of the Following Seeds might be Procured From KentucKé for the Use of the King's Garden— Viz., The Seeds of the *Coffe Tree* which Resembles the Black oak

Do of the *Pappa Tree*

Do of the *Cucumber Tree*

Do *Black berry Tree*

Do *Wild Cherry Tree*

Do *Buck-Eye Tree*

Do of *Wild Rye, Buffalo Grass—Shawanese Salad—Wild Lettuce—Crown Imperial[—]Cardinal Flower—the Tulip-bearing Laurel Tree—*& the Seeds of Every thing else Curious which that Famed Country Producs.[1]

It wou'd be Necessary Your Encellency Wou'd order the whole to be Carefully Sent to the Care of the director of the French Pacquets at New York, that it might be Transmitted to Paris.

God Bless you, my dear General, I am Requested By Mr St John to sign this, and do it with the Greater pleasure as these seeds and trees will be very wellcome in france.

Lafayette

LS, PEL. The closing of this letter is in Lafayette's hand; the body of the letter does not seem to be in St. John Crèvecoeur's hand, but presumably it was he who presented it to Lafayette for his signature.

1. The trees may be identified as the Kentucky coffee tree (*Gymnocladus dioica*), papaw (*Asimina triloba*), cucumber tree (*Magnolia acuminata*), perhaps black alder or winterberry (*Prunus virginiana*), buckeye or horse chestnut (*Aesculus hippocastanum*), and, probably, tulip poplar (*Liliodendron tulipifera*). The flowering plants, crown imperial and cardinal flower, are *Imperialis coronata* and *Lobelia cardinalis*. GW wrote Lafayette about the seed on 15 Feb. and 25 July 1785.

To Thomas Blackburn

Dr Sir, Mount Vernon 19th Decr 1784.
The Express who brought me the resolves of our Assembly, & is going to Annapolis with dispatches for Govr Paca, informs me that he deliver'd others to you[1]—It only remains therefore for me to add, that Thursday next, the 23d is the day appointed for the commissioners to meet at Annapolis.[2] I shall go to our Court tomorrow, & proceed from thence. I am Dr Sir &c.

G: Washington

LB, DLC:GW.
Thomas Blackburn, who represented Prince William County, Va., in several of the Revolutionary conventions of the 1770s, lived at Rippon Hall on Occoquan Creek.

1. Blackburn was one of the three men chosen by the Virginia assembly to go to Maryland and secure the passage of a bill creating the Potomac River Company, but he did not accompany GW and Horatio Gates. See Beverley Randolph to GW, 15 Dec. 1784, and notes 1 and 2 of that document.

2. See Blackburn's response of 20 December. GW set 22 Dec., not 23 Dec., as the date for the meeting. Perhaps it was the copyist who wrote "23" by mistake.

To William Paca

sir, Mount Vernon 19th Decr 1784.
The enclosed letter came under cover to me, after Sun-down this evening; I have the honor to inform your Excellency that I propose to be at Annapolis at the time appointed.[1] Genl Gates will also attend, & I will give Colo. Blackburn notice of the appointed time. I have the honor to be &c.

G: Washington

LB, DLC:GW.
William Paca (1740–1799), a well-to-do Maryland lawyer and planter, at this time was governor of the state.

1. See Beverley Randolph to GW, 15 Dec. 1784, and notes 1 and 2 of that document.

2. The text of the enclosed letter from Lt. Gov. Beverley Randolph, 15 Dec., as it appears in the governor's letter book is: "I do myself the honor to enclose to your Excy several resolutions of the general assembly of this State, which I request you will lay before the Legislature of Maryland. The importance of the object will I flatter myself insure the earliest attention of yr Excy.

"The Commissioners appointed on the part of this State will meet those that may be appointed by your State at Annapolis on the [   ] Day of [   ] in order to concert the most effectual measures for obtang the end proposed" (Vi).

From Thomas Blackburn

Dear Sir!   Rippon Lodge [Va.] Decr 20th 1784.
    Your Favor of Yesterday's Date came to Hand this Morning.
    I intended to have done myself the Honor to have waited on You Today, to confer with You on the Subject of the Dispatches I received by Yesterday's Express; but the Intervention of your Letter, & the Badness of the Weather, will excuse me.[1]
    I am sorry to inform You, that it is not in my power to attend the Meeting of the Commrs on the Day You mention, being engaged, as an Administrator, in the Sale of the late revd James Scott's personal Estate, in a few Days after; which I must, of Necessity, attend.[2]
    I am informed that Genl Gates is with You, and can have no Doubt of his Attendance on this Business; I am happy to think it will not be retarded by my Inability to attend. I am, most respectfully, Dr Sir Yr most obt humble Servt
                                    T. Blackburn.

ALS, MnHi.
    1. See GW to Blackburn, 19 Dec., nn.1 and 2. A copy of Lt. Gov. Beverley Randolph's letters to Blackburn and Horatio Gates appointing them commissioners to go to Annapolis and copies of the enclosed resolution of the Virginia legislature of 15 Dec. regarding this are in the governor's letter book, Vi.
    2. The Rev. James Scott of Dettingen Parish, Prince William County, Va., died in 1782. His son William was Blackburn's brother-in-law.

To William Gordon

Dear sir,   Mount Vernon 20th Decr 1784.
    I am indebted to you for several letters; & am as much so for the Fish you kindly intended, as if it had actually arrived, & I was in the act of paying my respects to it at table—the chance, however, of doing this would be greater, was it at Boston, than in York-town in this State, where, I am informed it was landed at the time the Marqs de la Fayette did; who proceeded from thence to richmond, where I met him, & conducted him to An-

napolis on his way to New York; the place of his intended embarkation for France, about the middle of this month.[1]

I am glad to hear that my old acquaintance Colo. Ward is yet under the influence of vigorous passions—I will not ascribe the intrepidity of his late enterprize to a mere *flash* of desires, because, in his military career he would have learnt how to distinguish between false alarms & a serious movement. Charity therefore induces me to suppose that like a prudent general, he had reviewed his *strength*, his arms, & ammunition before he got involved in an action—But if these have been neglected, & he has been precipitated into the measure, let me advise him to make the *first* onset upon his fair del Tobosa, with vigor, that the impression may be deep, if it cannot be lasting, or frequently renewed.[2]

We are all well at this time except Miss Custis, who still feels the effect, & sometimes the return of her fever—Mrs Lund Washington has added a daughter to her family—She, child and husband are well, & become house keepers at the distance of about four miles from this place.[3]

We have a dearth of News, but the fine weather keeps us busy, & we have leisure for cogitation. All join in best wishes for you. Doctr & Mrs Stuart are of those who do it. I am Dr sir yrs &c.

G: Washington

LB, DLC:GW.

1. Gordon wrote GW on 30 Aug. that "by the first ship that offers," he was sending "a quintal of the best fish that Marblehead afforded."

2. Early in the war Joseph Ward was Gen. Artemas Ward's aide-de-camp, and after 1777 he was colonel and commissary general of musters, and then of prisoners, in the Continental army. Ward was 47 years old at the time of his marriage.

3. Lund Washington (1737–1796) became manager of GW's Mount Vernon estate in 1765. He and his wife Elizabeth Foote Washington had recently moved to Hayfield, which he built on land south of Alexandria. Lund continued as GW's manager through 1785.

To Alexander Henderson

Dr Sir   [Mount Vernon] 20th Decr 1784.

I will thank you for presenting the enclosed. If it is not immediately paid, or a moral certainty that it will be before you leave

the Assembly: be so good as to return it to Mr Rumsey if in richmond, or to me if he is not, by Post[1]—I persuade myself you
will excuse this trouble, & believe that I am &c.

G: Washington

LB, DLC:GW.

Alexander Henderson, a merchant in Colchester, was in Richmond attending the session of the Virginia general assembly as a delegate from Fairfax
County.

1. The enclosed was a note for £50 due GW from James Rumsey and transferred by Rumsey to a man named Dennis Ryan. Unable to track Ryan down,
Henderson returned the note undelivered (see Henderson to GW, 11 Jan.
1785). In a letter to GW of 10 Mar. 1785, Rumsey explains at length why instead of receiving from Rumsey the £50 that Rumsey owed him, GW found
himself stuck with "the note of a shuffling player" named Ryan. GW accepted
Rumsey's explanation and sent Ryan's note to Rumsey (see GW to Rumsey, 5
June 1785). See also GW to Bushrod Washington, 22 Jan. 1785, GW to Edmund Randolph, 19 Mar. 1785, and Edmund Randolph to GW, 5 April 1785.

In September 1782 Dennis Ryan and his wife, probably Irish players,
joined a theater company in Baltimore as leading actors. Ryan assumed management of the company in February 1783. At the end of the season, Ryan
took the company to New York to play there during the summer but was back
in Baltimore for the 1783–84 season. Ryan may have been attempting to arrange for his company to play in Richmond when he fled from his creditors in
the fall of 1784. In any case, he at some point returned to Baltimore, where
he died in 1786. See Seilhamer, *American Theatre*, chaps. 6–9.

Lady Huntingdon's Scheme for Aiding
the American Indians

[20 December 1784]

I.   From James Jay, 20 December
II.   From the Countess of Huntingdon, c.March
III.   From the Countess of Huntingdon, 20 March
IV.   From the Countess of Huntingdon, 8 April
V.   Lady Huntingdon's Plan for Settlement, 8 April
VI.   Lady Huntingdon's Circular Letter to the Governors of
        North Carolina, Virginia, Pennsylvania, and New
        York, c.8 April
VII.   James Jay's Copy of His Letter to the Governors of
        North Carolina, Virginia, Pennsylvania, and New
        York, c.20 December

EDITORIAL NOTE

With the aid of Sir James Jay, Lady Huntingdon in 1784 developed a proposal to send out from Britain at her expense pious men and women to settle on the American frontier. There, by example and by their efforts, they would convert the Indians to Christianity and at the same time improve the conditions in which the Indians lived. Even before she developed this plan, Lady Huntingdon had sought to involve GW in bringing help to the Indians. On 20 Feb. 1783 she wrote a letter to GW, to be conveyed to him by Henry Laurens, in which she informed GW that she had taken the liberty of naming him "one of my Executors for establishing a foundation in America principally intended as a college for a Mission to the Indian nations." She went on to say that she had "a claim to your acceptance of this as done to a relation in which you certainly stand connected with me—Washington Earl Ferrers being my Father, whose mother was a Washington." (The quotations are from a draft of the letter in the manuscript collections in Chestnut College, Cambridge.) In his reply of 10 Aug. 1783, GW assured her ladyship that "so far as my general Superintendence, or incidental attention can contribute to the promotion of your Establishment, you may command my assistance." He also conceded that his "Ancestry being derived from Yorkshire in England," it was indeed likely that they were kin.

GW, however, did not learn of Lady Huntingdon's specific plans for western settlement until 17 Jan. 1785 when he received James Jay's letter of 20 Dec. 1784 (doc. I). Jay enclosed in this letter of 20 Dec. a letter from Lady Huntingdon of 8 April (doc. III) with its enclosed copies of both her plan (doc. V) and her circular letter to the governors of North Carolina, Virginia, Pennsylvania, and New York (doc. VI). GW wrote Jay on 25 Jan. 1785 expressing approval of Lady Huntingdon's scheme. He pointed out that of the four states that she was approaching, only New York held extensive unsettled lands in close proximity to the Indians. He suggested that land held by the United States beyond the Ohio would best serve her purposes.

On 8 Feb. 1785 GW sent Lady Huntingdon's letter of 8 April 1784 and its enclosures to the president of Congress, Richard Henry Lee, expressing his hope that Congress would set aside land for Lady Huntingdon's use north of the Ohio. He then wrote Lady Huntingdon (on 27 Feb.) to tell her of his support of her project and of what he had done with regard to Congress. He also suggested to her that as a "dernier resort" she might consider taking his own land south of the Ohio for her people. On the same day, Richard Henry Lee wrote GW to tell him of the rejection by Congress of the plan, explaining that Congress could dispose of land only to secure revenue and that, in any case, it was opposed to placing on the frontier "those religious people" who "were remarkable in the late war for an unanimous and bitter enmity to the American cause." None of the four states made land available for Lady Huntingdon's settlers, and the scheme came to nothing.

Selena Hastings, the countess of Huntingdon (1707–1791), daughter of Washington Shirley, Earl Ferrers, was an early convert to Methodism and became a close associate of Charles and John Wesley. Upon George Whitefield's return from America in 1744, she became Whitefield's patron and chief sponsor in his ministry to the aristocracy. At his death in 1770, Whitefield left to the countess his school and orphanage in Savannah, called Bethesda. It was this that first engaged her in mission work in America. Her friend James Jay (1732–1815) of New York, the brother of John Jay and a medical doctor trained at Edinburgh, was knighted in 1763 for his success in raising money in London for the benefit of King's College (later Columbia) in New York. Jay returned to America in 1778 from England, where he had been living, but he was captured by the British in 1782 in New Jersey, by prearrangement, and taken back to England. In the summer of 1784, he returned to New Jersey, where he lived until the time of his death.

I

From James Jay

Sir   New York Decr 20. 1784.

I would have sent you, before now, the Papers enclosed with this letter, if I had not been in expectation that I should have the pleasure of delivering them in person to you in Virginia; and of conversing with you on the subjects of them.[1] I still entertain some expectation of the kind, but it becomes more uncertain whether I shall be able to realize it. I have suffered so much by an unbounded zeal for the public welfare; and by an implicit confidence in the public faith; that the situation of my affairs, or to speak more plainly, the situation of my finances, too often supercedes my intentions—Thus circumstanced, I think it improper to delay any longer the transmitting the Papers to you.

The subjects involved in those papers, appear to be of great importance. The pious and humane Design set forth in them, needs no illustration. There are other things which require explanation, and seem to deserve very serious consideration.

I have known Lady Huntingdon upwards of twenty years. I well know the Line of her Connexions, and the nature of her influence. Both are extensive and great. Animated, even to Enthusiasm, with a desire to convert and civilize the Indians of North America, She was at a Loss how to proceed in order to accomplish that favorite Object. Whitfield had left her the Orphan House, the College or Schools, and all the other property he had in Georgia. Her Design was to have Indian & white children educated in those Seminaries, to serve as Missionaries and Schoolmasters among the Indians. She communicated her intentions to me. On considering the matter in various lights, its connexions and consequences, and knowing the materials in her power for a truly great Undertaking; and being convinced that those materials could be brought forth to accomplish such an Undertaking; I helped her to work her ideas into the Plan now sent to you.[2] Besides the reasons detailed in her papers in favour of the plan, others, of a political nature, had their weight with me. Some of those reasons, such as the forming a good Frontier, increasing our Indian interest, and our Indian Trade, &c. will readily occur to you Sir. But there is another Object which I had in view that does not appear in her Ladyship's papers; and may not, though a consequence of her Design, present itself to gentlemen who have not paid peculiar attention to the subject in Europe. It appears however to me so worthy the consideration of the States, that I thought it proper to enlarge upon it in a letter I have written, and shall send by this opportunity, to the Governors of the respective States to whom her Ladyship has applied on the business. For the same reason, I take the Liberty to trouble you with the following Extract, or, as it may rather be called, Copy of that letter.

[At this point, Jay copied his letter to the four governors, which is printed here as doc. VII.]

Thus much for the Extract. I have been so much taken up with my own Affairs, and so much out of the way of learning the State of Continental Affairs, that I am unable to judge whether the Plan should be laid before Congress, and made a Continental Object. I should be glad to know your sentiments on that head, and on every part of the plan, and on every thing relative to it. If you should be of opinion that it ought to be laid before Congress, I beg you would do it. By that means, time will not only be saved, but the sanction of your approbation will ensure it due attention.[3]

I shall send, by this Post, her Ladyship's papers, with a Copy of the letter of which I have given you so long an Extract, to the Govr of your State.[4] I think it proper to acquaint you with this circumstance, that you may, if the plan meets your ideas, be better able to take measures in favour of it.

You will observe, Sir, in perusing her Ladyship's Papers, that neither the number nor the occupations of the intended Settlers are specified. General, indefinite expressions only are used. This was purposely done, in order to avoid raising alarms in England, in case the particulars were mentioned, and a copy of the Papers, as it probably would do, should find its way to that Country. I shall however be explicit with you, and leave it to your discretion to communicate the information to such persons as you may think proper. The number of Settlers from England, Scotland, & Ireland, will be very great indeed. I am clear that in five years we may get over above ten thousand people; in five years more a much greater number. Besides farmers and common labourers, it will be in our power to get a great number of Mechanics & Manufacturers in any branch we please. These are the people I had chiefly in view, and in regard to whom the above precaution was taken. Difficult as it may now appear to you, and any other gentleman, to get over such a number of people, particularly the Mechanics & Manufacturers, considering the Laws in England to prevent it,[5] you would readily see it is very feasible, did you but know the Connexions and ways & means there are for executing that part of the Plan. I candidly informed her Ladyship, that though I wished well to her peculiar Objects in the Plan, I was as much induced to promote it for the advantages which the States would derive from it in a political way, and particulary for the opportunity it would afford of getting over a number of Mechanics & Manufacturers, and establishing several useful Manufactures in the Country. Notwithstanding I frequently talked to her in the same frank manner, I am persuaded she does not see to what a length this matter of getting over Workmen, and establishing manufactures, may be carried by us by the means proposed for executing her own Design.

Should the Plan be adopted and vigorously pursued, it would soon prove very beneficial to our Country. It would soon lessen the importation of several Articles from Europe. In a few years, it would not only put a stop to the importation of such articles, but enable us to export them. Manufactures may be brought forwards expeditiously as well as Plants. In several of the States, we have Iron equal to any in the world. We have or can produce many other raw materials as cheap as they are to be had in Britain. Cotton, the manufactures of which are so convenient & are so much in use, thrives, as I have been informed, very well in the Southern States. Consider a moment, Sir, that many things in Manufacturing, which are generally thought to be performed by manual labour, are done by Machines; and that it is chiefly owing to those mechanic contrivances, not merely, as is commonly thought, to the cheapness of manual labour in England, that they can afford their goods at so cheap a rate. The manufacture of Cotton is an instance of the truth of this observation. They have a Machine which goes by water, and is attended by one or two persons, that cards as much as a dozen women can do in the same time in the common way. Their method of spinning Cotton is nearly equally advantageous. These things are in general use. Within a few years, they have likewise invented a Machine which goes by water, and both cards & spins, and in some cases, even weaves. There are not above 3 or 4 of these Machines in England: The proprietors of them taking great care to conceal their structure, and having a Patent to secure the invention to themselves. This Machine spins faster than can be done in any other way yet known: and the threads spun by it, are much more even than can be done by the hand.[6] When we know they have such Contrivances, can we be surprised at the cheapness of their Cotton goods? Knowing they employ similar Machinery in other branches of manufactury, is it astonishing that they can supply not only us with many Articles cheaper than we can make them, but also several Countries in Europe where labour is lower, and the raw materials cheaper, than in England? In those manufactures therefore where machinery is so advantageously employed, may we not hope for success? Considering the greater cheapness of some raw materials, the superior cheapness of provisions in America than in England, the expence of freight, Commissions, Insurance &c. attending the importation of foreign manufactured goods, may we not even advantageously introduce and establish such Manufactures among ourselves; and thereby keep in the States the money annually sent out of them for such commodities?

The idea held by some gentlemen, that manufactures can only suceed in populous Countries, where there are more hands than can be employed in Agriculture, and where labour is therefore cheap; and that our Country should be well peopled before we attempt to introduce Manufacturies, appears to be ill founded. It seems even contrary to fact. France is as populous as England, and labour there is cheaper, yet France is certainly far behind England in Manufactures. Ireland is extremely populous, labour is also lower there than in England, but excepting the Linnen manufactury, there is none of consequence in the country. This perhaps may be thought to be owing to the restraints and discouragements that kingdom has been laid under by England; but if that be admitted, how has it happened that Scotland, which since the Union has been free from such restraints and discouragements, and where labor is likewise cheaper than in England, hath made, comparatively speaking, so little progress in manufacture? Holland, on the other hand, is, in proportion to its extent, more populous than England, and labour in general is dearer than in England, yet it abounds in Manufactures. If we look through Europe, we shall find that cheapness of labour and of provisions are insufficient, of themselves, to give rise to, or to support, various and great manufacturies in a Country.

It is almost impossible that such a combination of circumstances as concur at present, in consequence of Lady Huntingdon's very peculiar situation and influence, to favour our introducing sundry Manufactures into America, should ever happen again. Should She die before the Plan is adopted, and some leading Measures taken to carry it into execution, we should lose the advantage of this combination. But should her death happen soon after such steps are taken, it will make no material difference. She is old and declining, yet possesses a strong and active mind. If we therefore enter soon on the business, in a way agreeable to her, every thing could be put into a train that would ensure success, even if we should lose her shortly afterwards.

I beg my best respects to Mrs Washington: and wishing you both the Compts of the approaching season, I remain, Sir Your Most Obedt & Very humble Servt

James Jay

ALS, DLC:GW.

1. Jay enclosed the letter of Selena, Lady Huntingdon, to GW of 8 April 1784 and its enclosures, which included Lady Huntingdon's plan for western settlements and her circular letter to the governors. See docs. IV, V, and VI.

2. See doc. II, apparently the work of Jay. Lady Huntingdon's letter to GW of 20 Mar. (doc. III) and 8 April (doc. IV) are based on this draft.

3. See GW to Jay, 25 Jan. 1785, GW to Richard Henry Lee, 8 Feb. 1785, and Lee to GW, 27 Feb. 1785.

4. For reference to the action Gov. Patrick Henry took upon receiving Lady Huntingdon's proposal, see Richard Henry Lee to GW, 27 Feb. 1785, n.1.

5. Recognizing the value of Britain's new mechanical inventions in foreign trade, Parliament passed numerous laws prohibiting the exportation of certain machinery and the emigration of artisans from Great Britain. A 1750 law forbade the exportation of machinery used in silk or wool manufacturing, prohibited the emigration of any skilled worker, and mandated strict fines and imprisonment for anyone, especially ship captains and customs officers, who induced or aided the emigration of artisans. In 1774 a second act expanded the previous law to include cotton textile manufacturing. See Witt Bowden, *Industrial Society in England*, 129–31.

6. In the years after 1770 the innovations of such men as James Hargreaves, Richard Arkwright, and Samuel Crompton revolutionized the carding, spinning, and weaving of cotton, enormously increasing the production of cotton cloth. Individual British artisans in America during the 1770s and 1780s were able to build these new machines, but in 1790 "the United States operated fewer than two thousand jenny spindles in about ten cotton manufactories" as compared to nearly two and one-half million machine spindles in Britain (Jeremy, *Transatlantic Industrial Revolution*, 19).

II
From the Countess of Huntingdon

[c.March 1784]

I have long looked with pain and compassion on the unhappy condition of the poor Indians in America; a people destitute of religion or addicted to Idolatry; given to revenge, bloodshed, and cruelty. I have often regretted that so little pains have been taken to bring them from darkness to light, to make them Christians, and good and useful Citizens. I rejoice to think that something may now be done towards accomplishing those desirable ends. Justice & humanity interested me warmly in favour of America. I trust in god that religion & benevolence will interest the Rulers of America in behalf of those poor Savages. One great & good effect of the late revolution I hope will be, to open a way for this conversion and civilization. It seems to me, that the changes which have taken place in the Government & political situation of America, will greatly facilitate Undertakings for those benevolent purposes. I enclose you the Outlines of a Plan which I have much at heart to attain those Objects.[1] There is a happy circumstance in it. With the conversion & civilization of the Indians, it combines the liberty & welfare of great numbers of good, religious people in these kingdoms, who have all along been the friends, and would be glad to become Citizens of America. To doubt that any State, or that even any individual in America would be backward to encourage & cooperate in a great and solid plan for these purposes, would be to doubt their attachment to the great Cause of Universal liberty, the glory of their Country, as well as to the precepts of our holy religion & the dictates of humanity. I have no such doubt. I am persuaded of the contrary, and in that persuasion, I feel no difficulty in sending a Copy of the Plan, & in freely & sincerely explaining myself further on the subject, to the Governors & Legislative Bodies of those States which appear to me, from their local circumstances, to have it greatly in their power to encourage and cooperate in the Plan. My design in addressing myself to several States, and not to one only, is to acquire the fullest information, and to induce an extensive cooperation. From their opinion and advice, and the degree of encouragement they may severally be disposed to give to the Undertaking, I shall be able to judge, better than I now can do, whether it will be best to plant all the Settlers in one large Settlement in one of the States, or to divide them into lesser Settlements in several States. I wish to act in a way that will be most effectual, and of the most general utility, and I make no doubt but every benevolent person, whether in a public or private station, will take up the matter in the same large way, and act accordingly.[2]

Though you have apprized me of your intention to retire from public life; and though I, like thousands more, acquiesce for your own sake in what we cannot, for the general welfare, but regret; I am confident the Design will not want any assistance you can give it. I am confident of this, because I am confident that the man who is the Christian & the Soldier cannot be insensible to the duty and to the glory of extending the knowledge of religion and Civil Life to heathen & savage Nations; and of making useful Arts and peaceable industry flourish where ignorance & barbarity now prevail. I have requested Sr J.J. to take an active part in this business, and he has candidly promised me to do it as far as his own Affairs will permit. I have desired him to forward this to you; and to send a letter from me, containing a Copy of the enclosed paper, to the Governors of North Carolina, Virginia, Pennsylvania & New York.[3] I have desired him to correspond with you Sir and with the Govrs of the above States, and if it be possible for him, to confer with you & them & the Members of the several Legislatures on the Subject. I have desired him also to take the opinions of judicious Individuals; and to acquaint me with the result of the application to the States & of his own Enquiries. I rely much on his activity & judgment. The knowlege he has of both Countries must render him very useful in combining a variety of circumstances in this Country & in America into a solid & useful Plan. We have often conversed on the Subject. The Outlines I send you, is the product of our joint deliberations. He knows my views, & I have given him all the necessary information; so that he can judge very well of what may be done in these kingdoms. He also knows my mind so well in regard to the Land & other Matters depending on America, that I am inclined to think that whatever may be offered on these heads by any of the States and should appear proper to him, will meet my approbation & consent. I beg therefore that you would freely consult & communicate with him on this great business.

Df, Great Britain: Chestnut College, Cambridge. This draft of a letter to GW was drawn up for Lady Huntingdon probably by James Jay. "Gen: Washington" is at the top of the page, followed by: "After addressing him on other subjects, perhaps something to the following purpose may not be improper." Lady Huntingdon drew on this for her letters to GW, particularly that of 20 Mar. (doc. III), and, perhaps, for her circular letter to the governors (doc. VI).

1. See doc. V.

2. At this point, Lady Huntingdon indicated that there should be inserted here something she wrote on the reverse side of the sheet of paper, where she first notes: "G. W. did not acquainte *Me* in particular that to retire from publick life was his Intention." Her insertion reads: "being informed of his Intentions & like thousands more ⟨does⟩ Justly Lament the loss the Publick of America must sustain⟨.⟩ Yet the certain universal good ⟨*mutilated*⟩ by this undertaking will not fa⟨il *mutilated*⟩adorer & Intrest."

3. The circular letter is doc. VI.

III
From the Countess of Huntingdon

Sr   Bath [England] March 20 1784

I should lament the want of expression extremily did I believe it could convey with the exactness of truth the sensibility your most polite kind & friendly letter afforded me—any degree of your consideration for the most interesting views of my Heart which stands so connected with the service of the Indian nations eminently demands my perpetual thanks[1]—no compliments can be accepted by you, the wise providence of God haveing called you to, & so honoured you in, a situation far above many of your Equals, & as one mark of his favour to his servants of old Has given, "The Nations to your sword & as the driven Stubble to your Bow"; allow me then to follow the comparison till that character shall as eminently belong to you—"He was called the Friend of God"—may therefore the Blessings obtained for the Poor so unite the Temporal with the eternal good of those miserable neglected and despised nations that they may be enabled to Bless you in future ages whose fatherly hand has yielded to their present & everlasting comfort—I am obliged to say that no early or intemperate zeal under a religious character, or those various superstitious impositions, too Generally taken up for Christian piety, does in any measure prevail with my passions for this end—to raise an altar for the Knowledge of the true God & Jesus Christ whom He hath sent—Where Ignorance alike of him & of themselves so evidently appears is my only object, & thus to convey the united Blessings of this Life, with the Lively Evidence of an eternity founded on the sure & only wise Testimony of Immutible truth, is all my wants or wishes in this matter & my poor unworthy prayers are for those providences of God that may best prepare the way to so rational & great an end—I have been Induced from this great object before me to accept the oblige-ing offers of Sr James Jay (who was upon the point of embark-ing for America) to convey the outline of my design to each of the Governors[2] of those states in which from nearest access to the Indian Nations & from Soil & Climate a situation for many Hundred familys for the ⟨services⟩ of the Indians & the estab-lishment of a people connected with me, should appear best— & whose objects would be to support the Gospel, & render those missionarys sent by me for the Indians, & their various ministrations among themselvs, the most consistently usefull for all—Should I be able to obtain a sufficient Quantity of Land suitable for such purposes, my Intentions would be to transfer both my trust estate with all my own property in Georgia for this more extensive prospect, of which from the extreme Heat of the Climate renders the labours of missionaries there of little advantage—this with the poor & little all I have to give on earth has been long devoted to God—Should ever so happy a Period arrive as in his tender mercy to us. We might be made the fortu-nate & honoured Instruments in that great day approaching for calling the Heathen Nations, as his Inheritance, to the Glo-rious Light of the Gospel, or should this appear any little prelude to so important an event the hearts of all men for this purpose will be made subject & as certainly no Intrested motives can ap-pear but, on the contrary, a ready willingness to do & suffer his rightious will as his servants, so none can feel any effect from the accomplishment of this design but the increase of order, wealth, & the pure protestant faith carrying the Glad Tydings of Peace & Christian Love over the Earth—I indulge myself with the Hope of your forgiveness for an openness so due to you on a subject that interesting in its views to me & also consid-ering it as so great an honour done me by your admitting a rep-resentation for your attention tho but for an hour—My kind & most excellent friend Mr Fairfax[3] undertakes the care of this packet for me—His noble Just & Equitable mind renders him the friend of my highest regard & his ever willing & important services engage me as one under the greatest obligations to him & who on all occasions has my first confidence—you must yet

bear with me by the liberty I take in Sending the copy of the
letter to the Govern[or]s & outlines of the Plan,[4] as no Reserves
to you on the Subject is compatable with the Just honour & respect you must ever claim from me—could my best compliments & best wishes to Mrs Washington be rendered acceptable
she would help to Plead my Pardon with you for this unreasonable long letter but which does certainly contain in meaning the
truest & most faithfull regard from Sr, yours & Her most devoted obedient & most Humble Sert

S: Huntingdon

ALS, DLC:GW. The countess begins many words with small capital letters;
these have been transcribed as lowercase letters. When GW wrote George
William Fairfax on 27 Feb. 1785, he had not received this letter.

    1. Lady Huntingdon is referring to GW's letter of 10 Aug. 1783. See Edi-
torial Note.
    2. James Jay delayed his departure until summer.
    3. She is referring to George William Fairfax.
    4. See docs. V and VI.

IV
From the Countess of Huntingdon

Sr   Bath [England] Apl 8 1784
    I live in hopes that before this you must have Received, by
the means of our mutual & most excellent friend Mr Fairfax,
the gratefull acknowledgements of my heart for your most Polite, & to my feelings the yet more Welcome Testimony of your
kind & Friendly letter[1]—an excuse therefore for this further
Trouble must be due, & which arises from the Kindness of Sr
James Jay's offering to take the Charge of My Packets to the several Governors of these States of America to Whom I have applied relative to my most anxious wishs for the poor Indians, &
I felt it quite impossible to let any thing go out of my hands that
did not mean to Communicate my Intentions to You Previous
to all others—I have in Consequence of this taken the liberty of
sending you with this—a Copy of my letter to the Governer of
each of those States together with the Plan, or rather outlines
thrown together, to Convey some Idea of my views upon this
subject, & which in my other letter to you is rendred so much
more Intelligable for your most Just & wise Consideration as

only now to occasion me to beg your forgiveness & with my very
best Compts to Mrs Washington I remain with the greatest respect & esteem Dr Sr Your most obligd Friend & most Faithfull
& obedient Humble Sert

S: Huntingdon

ALS, PHi: Gratz Collection. This letter with its enclosures (docs. V and VI)
were forwarded by James Jay on 20 Dec. (doc. I) and received by GW on 17
Jan. 1785.

1. See her letter of 20 Mar. 1784 (doc. III).

V
Lady Huntingdon's Plan for Settlement

8 April 1784

To the Friends of Religion and Humanity, in America the
Address of Selina Countess of Huntingdon.

To introduce the benevolent Religion of our blessed Re-
deemer among Heathen & Savage Nations; to lead them from
Violence & Barbarity, to the Duties of Humanity and the arts of
civil Life; to provide a Refuge for pious, industrious People,
who wish to withdraw themselves from scenes of Vice and irre-
ligion, to a Country where they may spend their Days in the
pursuits of honest Industry, and in the practice of Religion and
Virtue. These are Objects, in which the Glory of the Almighty,
and the happiness of a great Number of our fellow Creatures
are so eminently combined, that I trust you will chearfully concur and assist in a design expressly formed for the attainment
of them.

Experience has shewn, that the sending a few Missionaries,
and establishing a few Schools among the Indians of America,
have been very inadequate to the great Object of their Conversion & Civilization. It is reasonable to think that no great Progress can be made in converting a Savage People, thinly scattered
over an extensive Country, & often wandering, in single Families or small Bodies, to distant places, until they can be brought
to live in a more settled and social manner; or, unless the works
of Conversion and Civilization can be made to go Hand in Hand.

It is a peculiar Happiness therefore, that these different Objects of Converting and Civilizing the Indians, and of providing

Settlements for orderly Religious People, so perfectly coincide, that there is the greatest Reason to think we shall succeed better in our endeavours to attain both, if we unite them into one great Concern, and proceed accordingly than if we were, to undertake & pursue them each independently of the other.

The People I wish to provide a Settlement for, are not loose idle Vagabonds, but decent, industrious, Religious People, of exemplary Lives and Manners, and attached to the cause of Liberty. If these People can be settled in a proper place among the Indians, where they and the Indians may have a free and easy intercourse, they may not improperly be considered as so many Missionaries and School-Masters among them. From a Sense of Religious Duty, they will kindly entertain those poor ignorant People; they will do them every good Office; they will take pains to gain their Esteem & Affection and to cultivate a good Correspondence with them. Their more comfortable way of living, their inoffensive & friendly Manners, their Modes of Cultivation and their Mechanic Arts, will be constant Examples to them. Some part of these things may be gradually, though insensibly, imbibed. Reason tells us, that little change is to be expected in a Savage Indian, while he is able to pursue his wonted course of Life. Yet even in that case, something may engage his Attention, and excite his imitation. On those Indians who are past enjoying the active Scenes of Life, or are restrained therefrom by Infirmity or Accident, greater impressions may be made. But it is not unreasonable to think that the Women and Children may be induced to mix more in Society with the Settlers, to join with them occasionally in some little work of Agriculture, or of the Mechanic kind, if it be only to amuse themselves and pass away time. When People are neither compelled nor confined to work, but on the other hand, are at liberty to leave off at pleasure, and are encouraged to go on, or to return another time to the same or a similar Employment; they are less averse to Labour. Frequent practice may become habitual, and insensibly induce habits of useful Industry under the notion of amusement. The Progress that would naturally be made in this way, would gradually soften their manners, influence their Morals and lead them into social Life.

Several worthy Clergymen, of well known Character for Religious Zeal and Integrity of Manners, will accompany the

Settlers. Their Duty will be, according to their Talents and Personal Health & Strength, to keep up the Spirit of Religion and Piety among their own People; and by means of Interpreters, to Preach the glad Tidings of Salvation in the Wilderness, to bring the Inhabitants of those benighted Regions from Darkness to Light, to the Knowledge of the true God, and of Jesus Christ.

Schools will also be established. Children will be Educated in them to Religion and Virtue, in a liberal manner, agreeably to that great principle of Christianity, Love to God, Universal Charity and Good will to all Mankind. They will also be instructed in useful knowledge, so that they may become good Christians, and useful Members of the Community. One great Object will be, to endeavour to induce the Indians to suffer their Children to go to such Schools; and to permit them, for the greater Convenience, to live in such Families of our People, as the Parents or the Children themselves shall chuse. Regulations will be made, on the most solid Footing in regard to the Clergy, and the Schools; but independently of regular Arrangements for those Purposes; as there will be among the Settlers, several discreet People of good Understanding, Clergy and others, zealous in the cause of Religion, great hopes are entertain'd, that every Measure will be taken, which good Sense, Zeal, and Industry can employ, to accomplish the important Objects in view.

To carry the Plan into Execution it will be necessary that a quantity of Land, answerable to the Magnitude of the Undertaking, be granted for the Purpose in one or more of the united States: that the Land be among the Indians, or very near to them, and so situated, in regard to the bulk of the more distant Indian Nations, that there may be an easy communication by Water with those Nations, in Order that the Clergy may, with tolerable ease, and without loss of time, go among them; and that the Indians may be tempted, by the facility of the communication, to have frequent Intercourse with the Settlements.

As I have no other view in the Undertaking than what I have frankly declared—as I mean not to have any property myself in the Land to be granted, nor that any Person should acquire any in it, except in the same way, and on the same Conditions, which shall be laid down for all Settlers upon it: as I heartily wish to guard against every abuse and departure from the true

Spirit of the Undertaking: it is my earnest desire, that the Land be granted on such Terms, and under such Restrictions and Precautions, as the Legislature of the State which shall make the Grant, shall think best suited to promote the Design, and to prevent all abuses. My Idea of the Matter is in general this; that a Tract of Land be laid out for a considerable Number of Families, that Protestants of all denominations be admitted to settle upon it; that no Persons shall settle upon it, but such as shall severally bring a Certificate & Recommendation from Me or from the Trustees which I shall appoint in England, Scotland, and Ireland; so that the Settlers shall not be liable to have bad People obtrude upon them; That one or more Persons be appointed by the State to grant Warrants of Settlement to People having such Certificates; that the Persons so to be appointed by the States, shall be Residents in the State and shall be accountable to the Legislature, that no Settlers shall, on any Account or pretence, have a Warrant for more than 500 Acres: that no Person shall have a right to sell his Land, without the consent of the Person appointed by the Legislature to issue Warrants of Settlements unless he shall have resided [   ] Years upon the said Land; and that no Person be permitted to purchase such Lands, except such Persons, who have obtained Certificates as above mentioned; that the Tract or Tracts be laid out in Townships by the Persons I shall appoint to Survey and lay out the same; that they set a part places for one or more Cities or Towns; that the residue of the Lands be divided into Farms of different sizes to accomodate greater or lesser Families: that the Places for Cities or Towns be laid out in streets and Lots of certain Dimensions for Public and private Uses; that the Farms be subjected to pay, after being settled a certain Number of Years, a moderate acknowledgement per Acre Annually to the State: that the Lots in the City be granted by Certificate and Warrant in the same manner as the Farms; that they also pay an annual acknowledgement to the State; that the acknowledgement commence [   ] Years after the Grant: that no Person have a grant for a Second or Third Lot, until the former has a Dwelling House that is inhabited, or a Work Shop that is used upon it: that from the Farms which shall not be settled by the Number of People for which they were granted within Three Years after the Warrants were issued a proportionable Number of Acres shall be deducted: that those deducted Acres, and all Farms which shall not be settled, and all Lots which shall not be built upon within the same Period shall revert to common Stock; that a certain number of Farms & City lots, as many as the Legislature shall think sufficient, be reserved as an Estate, to be let out & improved, for the purpose of supporting Public Schools, the Clergy, and other public Establishments.

As it is impossible that For my Friends in this Kingdom who are Strangers to the local Circumstances of America, can immediately fix on a suitable Spot or Spots of Land, and form a compleat Plan for the Execution of this great Work, I wish to have the most Authentic and ample Information on this Subject, from the Friends of Religion and Humanity in America. The most eligible Method of obtaining that, appears to be, to lay the Design before the Legislature of these States which seem to lay most convenient for the Purpose. I have requested Sir James Jay to perform this Office for me, to lay these Outlines of the Plan before them, to learn their Sentiments of it, their Disposition to encourage it, and to communicate the result to me.

When one contemplates the Revolution which Providence hath wrought in favor of the American States, that great Work seems but a prelude to the completion of yet more gracious Purposes of Love to Mankind. This Idea fills the Soul with joy, and raises it to the most solemn Devotion. Yet it is not for us frail Mortals, to determine on the Councils of the most High. With humble submission to the Divine Will, let us do our Duty. Let us endeavour to spread his Name among the Heathen: let us endeavour to obey his Divine Precepts, and to follow his gracious Example of Benignity to mankind.

Unite with me then my Friends, in this glorious Cause; you who have seen and felt the mercy and goodness of the Almighty, who have been supported by him in the Days of Trial and Adversity; and were at last delivered from Bondage; and raised to Liberty and Glory.

S: Huntingdon

DS, DLC:GW. There are two copies of this in DLC:GW, both in the same clerk's hand. One is signed and dated by Lady Huntingdon and the other signed by her and undated. Presumably the copy dated 8 April, printed here, was the one enclosed in her letter of that date and sent to GW by James Jay on 20 Dec. 1784.

VI
Lady Huntingdon's Circular Letter
to the Governors
of North Carolina, Virginia, Pennsylvania,
and New York

Sir.   [c.8 April 1784]

When a Person has no other Object in applying to the Supreme Authority of a State, than to interest the State in an extensive Design, expressly formed to promote the great Cause of Religion and Humanity, there can be no doubt but such an application will be favourably received, though the circumstances of the Country should not permit it to engage in the Undertaking, or to contribute largely to the carrying it on. With this general Sentiment, I entertain that Opinion of the Piety & benevolence of America, that I feel no difficulty, Sir, to address myself to your Excellency on the important Subject; and to request that you will communicate this Letter to the other Branches of the Legislature of the State over which you preside. If I err in the manner & form of this application, I humbly beg it may be imputed to Ignorance, not to want of respect.

The Object of my Application is great. I have long reflected with pain on the condition, both in a Religious and civil light, of the Indian Nations in North America. With a mind untinctured with Fanaticism or illiberality, I have long wished that some great and solid Plan for their Conversion and Civilization, for making them good Christians and useful Citizens, could be fallen upon. I rejoice in thinking that the late Revolution opens a way to this great work. I rejoice in the Hope that the Piety and Humanity of the Americans, will encourage a rational undertaking to attain those important ends. I rejoice in the firm expectation that they will cordially unite with me in such an Undertaking; and I fervently implore the Divine Being to crown our joint Endeavours with Success.

The enclosed Outlines of a Plan will give you an Idea of my Design. My views are so extensive, the means in some respects so great, that in Order to be able to concert Measures suitable to the largeness of the Design, I think it necessary to communicate these Outlines of a Plan to several of the States, which, from their situation, seem to have it more especially in their Power to give energy and facility to such an Undertaking. What one State cannot do, another may. If one alone should be unable to grant as much Land as will be necessary, they may severally contribute what on the whole will be sufficient. The States I propose to apply to are those of North Carolina, Virginia, Pennsylvania and New York.

I most respectfully request that the Legislature of your State will take the matter into th⟨eir⟩ serious consideration. Should the general Ideas I have given of the Design meet with approbation, it would give me infinate pleasure to be informed in what matter you & they think those Ideas could best be carried into Effect. As I have no view to private interest myself in the Design, so I earnestly wish that every precaution should be taken to guard against the selfishness of others, and against all abuses whatever. Whether therefore the plan should finally be—to make a great Settlement in one State, or to establish lesser Settlements in different States, I shall most chearfully concur in every provision which the State or States may think necessary to prevent fraudulent practices, and to preserve the true Spirit of the Undertaking. It cannot escape your Excellency that independently of other circumstances, the countenance and encouragement which the States may respectively be disposed to give to this Design, must be an important consideration in finally settling the Plan. It will in particular, be necessary that I should know what quantity of Land a state may be disposed to grant—what Quit-rent will be required, and what length of time the Settlers will be exempted from Taxes. The knowledge of these particulars is so essential to the coming to a proper determination, that I am persuaded your Excellency will immediately see the propriety of my requesting to be informed what your State is disposed to do in regard to them. I beg leave to mention here a circumstance which ought to have been inserted in the Outlines of the Plan vizt that the intended States have been hearty friends to the Rights and Liberties of America from the beginning of its controversy to the conclusion of it.

I have requested Sir James Jay to assist me in this weighty Business. He has promised to do it, as far as his own Affairs will permit. I have fully explained my views & intentions to him. We have often conversed on the Subject. The Outlines I enclose you, are the result of our joint deliberations. His long residence and personal knowledge of things in these Kingdoms, and his aquaintance with America, render him very fit to assist in forming a Plan in which many circumstances in each Country are to be combined. I have long known Sir James; and I rely much on his prudence and judgment. Besides, he knows my Mind so well, that I am inclined to think, the State should be disposed to grant Land for this Design and he should be consulted on the Subject, he will be able to say pretty nearly, Whether the Tract proposed would, in point of situation & terms of Settlement, be likely to meet my Ideas. I request therefore that he may be advised with on the occasion. It will facilitate Matters; and may prevent the delay and loss of time which repeated Explanations by Letter, at so great a distance as that between America and this Country, would necessarily occasion. When I know the dispositions and determinations of the States, & have obtained all the information I hope to receive; I shall be able to come to a final conclusion on every part of the Design. I hope, with the blessing of Heaven, that a solid Plan may then be formed for effectually answering the great ends in view. I have the honor to be With great respect Your Excellency's.

D, DLC:GW. There are two virtually identical copies in DLC:GW, one of which was presumably enclosed in Lady Huntingdon's letter of 8 April (doc. IV) and forwarded by James Jay on 20 Dec. (doc. I).

VII
James Jay's Copy of His Letter to the Governors of North Carolina, Virginia, Pennsylvania, and New York

[c.20 December 1784]

If the Plan be adopted, it will give us an opportunity of getting over, with the other Setlers, a number of good manufacturers in any branch of manufactury we please: and of course it will enable us to introduce and establish such manufacturies among us, as the circumstances of our Country will admit of doing with success and advantage.

It is an obvious Truth, that a Nation, in order to be independent, safe, and happy, ought to have, within itself, the means of furnishing its Citizens with every Article that is *indispensably necessary* to those Ends. To depend on Foreigners for every *such necessary* article that can be as well and as cheaply made in the Country, is a palpable absurdity. The policy of Britain subjected us to that hardship in many instances; and employed every method to entail it upon us. It is still the interest of the manufacturing nations in Europe to keep us in that state; but it evidently is our interest to emancipate ourselves, with the utmost expedition, from a dependence that is both injurious and disgraceful to us.

Every article, *indispensably necessary*, that is imported among us, but which can be as advantageously made in our own Country, may justly be considered as a Tax upon every person in the country; a Tax which no œconomy or frugality can avoid; a Tax laid upon us by foreigners for their own sole benefit; and which constantly works a detriment to the Country in proportion to the demand for such Articles. Were we to consider, Sir, the prodigious quantity of common *necessary* Clothing, and also of the common *necessary* articles of Iron & Steel, that is annually imported among us, it would give us some idea of the magnitude of the Evil, and evince the necessity of using our best endeavours to lessen it.

The preceeding observations lead us to a question of great importance, vizt—whether it is possible for us to introduce and establish manufactures for any of the above Articles? This is a Question that no man can decide properly upon, unless he has a competent knowledge of the method of fabricating the particular Article which may come under discussion. I do not mean a knowledge of the way of making any such article in this Country; but of the method in which great Manufactures for the purpose are carried on in Europe; and by which the Europeans are able to undersel us in our own country with every advantage in our favour. I am aware, Sir, that a general objection may at this moment occur to you: vizt—that the price of labor being so much dearer among us than in Europe, is an insurmountable Obstacle to any undertaking of the kind. Allow me to observe, Sir, that the objection is true in many respects, but that, like other general positions or general rules, it has its exceptions. There are indeed many exceptions in the present Case.

This assertion cannot be directly proved, without entering into a minute consideration of each manufacture to which the Objection is not applicable. But there is a circumstance which furnishes very substantial and satisfactory Evidence in favour of it; evidence the more to be regarded, because it is a tacit confession of the Parties interested against us, and who are, unquestionably, competent Judges in the Case. The Parliament of England have from time to time passed Acts which tended, directly or indirectly, to prevent and discourage manufacturing in America: and it may be fairly presumed they would not have taken those measures, unless they were well satisfied that we could manufacture sundry Articles as cheap as was done in Britain, or even cheaper, and to so great an amount as materially to injure their Trade with us. But, Sir, in asserting the practicability of establishing certain useful manufactures with advantage in this Country, I speak not at random. A fondness for mechanic Arts & manufactures, led me to embrace every favorable opportunity of enquiring into them. A long residence and much travelling in Europe, furnished me with frequent opportunities to indulge my taste; and it is from information derived from those Sources that I form my opinion.

There is reason to think that in some of those parts of the Country to which the Plan has respect, the establishment of Manufactures will greatly tend, if not be absolutely necessary, to make those Districts flourish, and render them more beneficial to the Nation at large than they otherwise are likely to be. If, for instance, some of the back Lands I allude to, shoud be inhabited merely or principally by Farmers, population will indeed increase, but those remote Citizens will, comparatively speaking, contribute but little, in other respects, to the general weal. The difficulty & expence of bringing the produce of their farms to market, will discourage their raising more than will be requisite for their own use. Experience shews that manufactures, unless where Measures are taken to introduce and establish them, spring up but slowly in any Country, that at first they are but few in number, and that it is a long time before they exceed the wants of the neighbourhood, and supply matter for internal or foreign Commerce. But where the difficulty and expence of carrying country produce to a distant market, is a discouragement to cultivation and commerce, would it not be sound policy to create a market for it on the spot? And what better method can be fallen upon for that purpose, than the planting a number of Manufacturers upon it? They would flourish themselves, and make the farmers flourish also. The productions of the manufacturer, are, in general, more valuable, in proportion to their bulk, than the produce of the Land, and can therefore better support the expence of transportation. In a fertile District, where the Farmer has a difficult or expensive transportation, provisions will be cheap; but where provisions are cheap, the price of labor is moderate; and where these two circumstances concur, and there is a sufficient demand, either in the way of home consumption or foreign exportation, for manufactured goods, Manufactures will flourish: because, as more money will be got by manufacturing than by farming, the people will naturally go into the former instead of the latter. In the well setled parts of this State, where grain and other country produce can be carried to market at little expence, the farmer can afford to pay a journeyman manufacturer as much for laboring on his farm, as the man could earn by working at his own trade; and therefore it becomes a matter of indifference to the hired person, whether he works at his Trade or in the field. The same thing may perhaps obtain, under similar circumstances, in other States. Hence arises the difficulty so frequently met with, of keeping journeymen Mechanics to their proper work; a circumstance which has proved, and must for a long time prove, an impediment to the regularly and advantageously carrying on any manufactury in such parts of the Country. But where Agriculture labours under the preceeding disadvantages, and depends solely on the consumption on the spot, a laboring person will earn more, and support his family better, by working at Manufacture than at Agriculture; and of course will find it his interest to follow his own Trade.

These general observations on Cultivation & Manufacture, may, I think, be regarded as general Truths. The application of them however is another Matter; and can only be judiciously done by those who are well acquainted with the local circumstances of a Country. For this reason, I presume not to be a competent Judge whether it would be proper for your State to adopt the principles laid down, and to attempt to carry them into effect. It seems pretty evident however, that the State would lose or risque nothing by coming into her Ladyship's proposals, because it may be provided that all the Land which shall not be setled within the time limitted, shall revert to the State.

Copy, DLC:GW. Jay made this copy of his letter to the four governors in the body of his letter to GW of 20 Dec. (doc. I). Jay's copy is printed here as a separate document for the sake of clarity.

From La Luzerne

Sir.   Paris December 20th 1784.
    Mr de Chateaufort, Consul of France for the State of So. Carolina, intends, on his Journey from Newyorck to Charlestown, to wait upon Your Excellency and to present You this letter.[1] Permit me to recommend him to your attention. He is quite a stranger in America, but he belongs to a nation for whom You have always shewn the greatest partiality, and his personal merit will, I doubt not, render him worthy of your notice. Permit me to thanck You beforehand for the Kind reception you will be pleased to honor him with.
    Since my arrival in France I have had the honor to address to Your Excellency several letters and I hope that at least one of them is come to your hand.[2] I shall therefore only repeat here that I shall always be happy in an opportunity to convince you of the respectful and inviolable attachment with which I have the honor to be Sir Your Excellency's Most obedient and very humble Servant,

le che. de la Luzerne

LS, DLC:GW.
    1. Louis XVI's appointment of the chevalier d'Aristay de Châteaufort to the post of consul for the Carolinas and Georgia is dated 25 April 1784. GW wrote Châteaufort on 15 June 1785 to say he would take "great pleasure in seeing you at this Seat on your way to Charleston," but Châteaufort was unable to visit Mount Vernon (see GW to Viomenil, 5 Sept. 1785). He had arrived in New York on 30 Mar. and sailed from Philadelphia on about 1 June, landing at Charleston after eighteen days at sea. Châteaufort was probably the grandson of Gen. Pierre de Boyseau who became the marquis de Châteaufort in 1728.
    2. The only letter from La Luzerne written after his return to France in the summer which has been found is that of 12 September.

To Beverley Randolph

Sir   Alexandria 20th Decr 1784

The letter you did me the honor to write to me the 15th Inst. was not delivered until late yesterday Evening—I filled the Blank in the letter to Govr Paca and forwarded it; and am now on my way to annapolis. I named the 22d, which at the rate your Express travels,[1] is as soon as the Govr can lay your letter before the Assembly of Maryland and Commrs be appointed to meet those from this State—Genl Gates will attend; & I have given Colo. Blackburne notice of the time & place.

As soon as the business of the meeting is finished a report shall be made. I have the honr to be Sir Yr most obt Servt

Go: W.

ADfS, ICU. The ALS was advertised for sale in 1890 in McKay catalog 3819, item 592.

1. Randolph's messenger, Daniel Thompson, signed with his mark at Annapolis, 25 Dec.: "Received from G. Washington two Guineas to defray my expences in this place & back to Richmond" (Vi).

To Melancton Smith

Sir,   Mt Vernon 20th Decr 1784

Your letter of the 27th of October came to my hands the 14th inst: the box of Plate is not yet arrived.[1]

It would have been very obliging in you, & would have done me an essential kindness, had you as soon as this Box arrived at New York (which you say was the latter part of summer) given me notice thereof by Post; altho' there might have been no opportunity at that time, or in any short time thereafter to forward the package to me: for having been assured by Mr Parker (before I left New York last year) that I might look for this Plate in the Spring; having, in answer to a letter I wrote to him early in the summer, been informed of some disappointment to his expectation of it; & having heard soon after, that that Gentlen was under peculiar embarrassment, and not a word from him since[2]—I gave up every idea of having my commission complied with by him, & supplied myself, not fourteen days ago, in another way.[3] I now have both setts, neither of which can be disposed of, one having been used, & the other having my Crest & arms on it.

When I was at New York, altho' I could not get Mr Parker, from his then hurry, to render me a full and complete transcript of my Accots; yet he gave me a short statement of the debit & credit of my dealings with him, by which there is a balance of £65.5.4 York Curry due to me—this sum I left in his hands declaredly and by agreement to be applied towards payment for the Plate his brother was to get for me. If you will be pleased (if Mr Parkers books are in your possession) to examine into this matter—or if they are not, will make out an account with this credit, at the current exchange, I will cause it to be paid. To do it in Alexandria, if you have any agent or correspondent there, would be more convenient for me, as I have no dealings either in New York or London at this time. In this case I shou'd be glad to have the original Bill sent with the accot. If the business cannot be closed in this manner I will endeavour to accommodate myself to your wishes in any other way I am able.[4] I am Sir &c.

G: Washington

LB, DLC:GW.

1. In addition to the address, Smith's letter of 27 Oct. had these notations: "Philida December 10th 1784 received from New York and forwarded Sir your most respectful servt ⟨George⟩ Frazier"; and "⟨Alexa. Decr 15th *illegible*⟩ forwarded by Sir your very ⟨*illegible*⟩ servant Thos Porter." See Smith to GW, 26 Jan. 1785.

2. For GW's dealing with Daniel Parker in purchasing silver, see Daniel Parker to GW, 21 June 1784, and note. For the silver that Smith sent GW, see Smith to GW, 27 Oct., n.1.

3. What silver GW bought "not fourteen days ago" and from whom he bought it has not been determined. See Kathryn C. Buhler, *Mount Vernon Silver* (Mount Vernon, 1957), 42–45.

4. See note 1 and Smith's response of 26 Jan. 1785, in which Smith encloses a statement of GW's account with his new firm, Smith & Wyckoff.

From Benjamin Walker

Dear Sir,   New York Decr 20. 1784

My very good friend Governor Clinton has doubtless informed you long since of his intention to ship you some seed Corn & Pease—the former he was disappointed in by the Person who promised to send it to him—the Pease together with a Teirce of Nuts & a small bundle of Trees he gave me in charge and after waiting a long time in vain for a direct Opportunity to Alexandria I thought it best to ship them to Norfolk—& if as I hope the opportunities from thence to your river are frequent they will soon be forwarded to you by Messrs Hartshorne & Lindley to whom I addressed them—before the Vessell saild for Norfolk a ship was put up for Alexandria but I could not get them back.[1]

It was supposed that on the return of the Marquis we might flatter ourselves with the hope of seeing your Excellency in this City or at least at Philadelphia,[2] in either case I should have been happy in the Opportunity of once more paying you my respects & acknowledging the many obligations I feel myself under for your kind countenance of me whilst in the Army. Since I last had the pleasure to address you I have fulfilled an Engagement of a very long standing with an amiable Girl with whom I enjoy all that comfort your Excellency is so Kind as to wish me in your letter to the Governor[3]—I have also quitted the place of Secretary to the Governor which offered no prospect—and have entered into Trade—in this channell I feel myself best calculated to push thro' life & my prospects in it are not unfavorable was not my means so very small as to disable me from carrying it on, with ease & satisfaction either to my self or those who favor me with their Commissions—the inability of the public to fulfill their engagements presses harder on none, than on those who have served her most faithfully.

I would write your Excellency the politics of the day but paying all my attention to my little business I scarce know what passes in the great world—Congress are to set here the 11 Jany & are then I am told to make their appointments of Ministers &c.—Mr Jay—Secretary for foreign affairs—Mr Livingston is talk'd of for the Court of London—Genls Knox—Green—Gates—the Baron & Colo. Pickering are all mentioned for Secretary at War—my friend the Baron lives about five miles from this City. Keeps very little company but lives retired I fear his situation is rather desponding.[4]

I pray your Excellency to tender my Respectfull Compliments to Mrs Washington and to believe me with every sentiment of Respect Dr Sr Your most obliged & Obedient humble Servt

Ben. Walker

ALS, DLC:GW.

1. See GW to George Clinton, 25 Nov. 1784, n.4. See also Clinton to GW, 5 Mar. 1785, and Walker to GW, 11 Mar. 1785. William Hartshorne was a merchant in Alexandria. In his letter of 5 Mar. 1785, Clinton refers to his letter to GW of 26 Dec., which has not been found. Lindley has not been identified.

2. See Henry Knox to GW, 23 Nov., n.2.

3. Benjamin Walker married a Quaker who was called Polly.

4. Walker was aide-de-camp to Steuben before becoming GW's aide in January 1782.

Letter not found: from Ebenezer Hazard, 21 Dec. 1784. On 5 Jan. 1785 GW wrote to Hazard: "A few days ago I was favored with your Letter of the 21st ulto." GW's letter is printed in GW to Jeremy Belknap, 5 Jan. 1785, n.1.

From Lafayette

On Board the Nimph Newyork Harbour
My dear General   december the 21st 1784
I Have Received Your Affectionate letter Of the 8th inst., and from the known Sentiments of My Heart to You, You will Easely guess what My feelings Have Been in perusing the tender Expressions of Your friendship—No, my Beloved General, our late parting was Not By Any Means a last interview—My whole Soul Revolts at the idea—and Could I Harbour it an instant, indeed, my dear General, it would make me Miserable—I well see You Never will go to france—the Unexpressible pleasure of Embracing You in My own House, of wellcoming You in a family where Your name is adored, I do not much Expect to Experience—But to You, I shall Return, and within the walls of Mount vernon we shall Yet often Speack of old times—my firm plan is to visit now and then My friends on this Side of the Atlantick, and the Most Beloved of all friends I Ever Had, or ever will Have Any where, is too Strong an inducement for me to Return to Him, nor to think that, when Ever it is possible, I will Renew my So pleasing visits to Mount vernon.

Since I Have left you, My dear General, we Have past through philadelphia to trenton, where I was Happy to find a Numerous and well Choosen Congress—their testimonies of kindness to me, and My Answer to them You will see in the Newspapers—as to My Services abroad—it Has Been (on Motion Respecting what I told You) Universally decided that public Confidence in me was a Matter of Course—a doubt of which ought not to be Expressed—But as I know the Sense of Congress, and as M. jay Has accepted and Mr jefferson will be Minister in france, My Situation in that Respect will Be very Agreable.[1]

Orders Have Been Sent to Canada to Reinforce the posts, put the lake vessels in Commission, and Repel force By force—But I think that, if once Congress Have the trade to Regulate, Mercantile interdictions will Set those people to Rights—altho' party Spirit Have a little Subsided in Newyork, yet that City is not By Any Means Settled—How far from Boston!

Altho' your Nephew is not Arrived, I Still Hope for the pleasure to See Him in paris[2]—Gnl greene was in Hartfort when the Letter Reached Him, from where He Came to Newyork, and I Had the pleasure to Spend Some days with Him—inclosed I Send You a Small Cypher—should any public political Business Require a fuller one, I will write to You by a Complete Cypher I Have Had long Ago with mr jay's present departement.[3]

M. Cary printer of the Volunteer journal Has Been obliged to fly for His life, and now lives at mr Sutter's Hatter front Street in philadelphia where He is Going to Set up a paper—a Letter from You, Becoming a Subscriber, and telling Him I Have Mentioned it to You, will the More oblige me as I Have promised Him to Recommend Him to My friends—He Now is an *American* and we Have nothing to do with His quarrel with the duke of Rutland—which disputes By the Bye seem to Subside and Vanish into Nothing—the french packet is not yet Arrived.[4]

Chev. de Caraman and Captain Grandchain Beg leave to offer their Respects to You, Mrs Washington, and all the family—My most affectionate tender Respects wait Upon Mrs Washington—I Beg she will give a kiss for me to the little girls, my friend tub—and I Beg mrs Stuart, the docter, mr lund Washington, and all our friends to Receive My Best Compliments—I Hope mr Harrison will Be Soon appointed, and I wish His Cousin may know it.[5]

Adieu, adieu, My dear General, it is with Unexpressible pain that I feel I am Going to be Severed from You By the atlantick—Every thing that Admiration, Respect, Gratitude, friendship, and filial love Can inspire, is Combined in my Affectionate Heart to devote me most tenderly to You—in your friendship I find a Delight which words Cannot Express—adieu, my dear general, it is not without Emotion that I write this word—altho' I know I shall Soon visit You Again—Be attentive to Your Health—let me Hear from You Every month—adieu, adieu.

l.f.

ALS, PEL.

1. Although GW complained to Clement Biddle on 1 Feb. 1785 of the paper's irregular delivery, GW may have read notices of Lafayette's progress northward in Claypoole's *Pennsylvania Packet and Daily Advertiser* (Philadelphia), 7, 8, and 23 December. On 11 Dec. a committee of Congress formally assured Lafayette of Congress's appreciation of and support for his efforts on behalf of the "commercial and other interests" of the United States (*JCC*, 27:673, 683–85).

2. Bushrod Washington was unable to take Lafayette up on his invitation to visit Paris. See GW to Lafayette, 15 Feb. 1785.

3. Lafayette and GW seem rarely to have used the code, but for an example of Lafayette's doing so, see his letter of 11 May 1785.

4. Mathew Carey (1760–1839) fled Ireland on 25 Sept. 1784 to Philadelphia, where he remained the rest of his life. Lafayette first had contact with Carey when the young Irishman was living in exile at Passy near Paris in the years 1779 to 1783. Carey returned to Dublin in 1783 and with the help of his father, Christopher Carey, began publishing his *Volunteer's Journal*. His attacks in the *Journal* on the leaders of the Irish government and his participation in a demonstration against the duke of Rutland, lord lieutenant of Ireland, led to his arrest and imprisonment in Newgate for a month, just before he left for America. Lafayette, in his brief stop in Philadelphia earlier this month after leaving GW at Annapolis, met with Carey and gave him four hundred dollars. The money from Lafayette helped make it possible for Carey to publish the first issue of the *Pennsylvania Herald*, launching his long and distinguished career in Philadelphia as an editor, writer, and bookseller.

5. Lafayette probably was referring to Richard Harrison, Robert Townsend Hooe's business associate who was in Spain at this time and became United States consul at Cadiz. The "Cousin" was probably Robert Hanson Harrison.

To Lafayette

My Dr Marqs   Annapolis [Md.] 23d Decr 1784.

You would scarcely expect to receive a letter from me at this place: a few hours before I set out for it, I as little expected to cross the Potomac again this winter, or even to be fifteen miles from home before the first of April, as I did to make you a visit in an air Balloon in France.

I am here however, with Genl Gates, at the request of the Assembly of Virginia, to fix matters with the Assembly of this State respecting the extension of the inland navigation of Potomac, & the communication between it and the Western waters; & hope a plan will be agreed upon to the mutual satisfaction of both States, & to the advantage of the Union at large.

It gave me pain to hear that the Frigate la Nymph, grounded in her passage to New York—we have various accots of this unlucky accident but I hope she has received no damage, & that your embarkation is not delay'd by it.

The enclosed came to my hands under cover of the letter which accompanies it, & which is explanatory of the delay it has met with.[1] I can only repeat to you assurances of my best wishes for an agreeable passage & happy meeting with Madame la Fayette & your family, & of the sincere attachment & affection with which—I am My Dr Marqs &c. &c.

Go: Washington

P.S. You & your heirs, Male, are made Citizens of this State by an Act of Assembly—You will have an Official Accot of it—this is by the by.[2]

LB, DLC:GW.

1. When Lafayette writes on 19 Mar. 1785 to acknowledge the receipt of this letter forwarded to him in Paris, he gives no clue to what was enclosed, but an editor of Lafayette's letters suggests that the enclosure included a letter of introduction for Thomas Ridout (Idzerda, *Lafayette Papers*, 5 : 290; see also Montesquieu to GW, 25 April 1785, n.1).

2. By "this State" GW means Maryland. On 22 Jan. 1785 Gov. William Paca signed "An act to naturalize major-general the marquis de la Fayette and his heirs male for ever" (*Md. House of Delegates Proceedings*).

From Horatio Gates

Rihmonds [Md.] Fryday Evening [24 Dec. 1784]
Believe me Sir were I in Health fit to attend the Committee this Evening I would on no account fail to do it but I feel I must go to bed instead of going to Mans.[1] You are so perfectly Master of the Business, that my Assent to your Opinions is all I have to

say upon the Subject; this you may be sure of having, whenever that is called for—when a Vote must Decide, I will get a Coach, & come at all Hazzards to Mans. Your Obedt Hble Servt

Horatio Gates

ALS, DLC:GW.

1. See note 2, Beverley Randolph to GW, 15 December. George Mann (1753–1795) operated Mann's tavern in Annapolis.

Letter not found: from George Clinton, 26 Dec. 1784. On 5 April 1785 GW wrote to Clinton: "Your other letter of the 26th of December came duely to hand."

From Richard Henry Lee

Dear Sir,   Trenton [N.J.] december 26th 1784

I had the honor to receive your obliging letter, of the 14th instant, seven days after its date and I thank you Sir for its friendly contents and sensible communications. Your ideas concerning the western country are wise and just. They will certainly have great weight when that business shall be discussed in Congress: and that will probably be the case soon after we know the success of our commissioners at Cayahoga.

Much time hath been taken up in debate upon the permanent and temporary residence of Congress, and finally it is determined that the former shall be on the banks of the Delaware, not exceeding eight miles above or below this place, and on either side of the river that may be fixt upon by commissioners to be appointed for the purpose of superintending the fœderal buildings. New York is to be the temporary residence, and Congress stands now adjourned to meet in that City on the 11th of January next—when I hope that we shall diligently put forward the public business.[1] Spain seems determined to possess the exclusive navigation of the Mississippi, which, with the bickerings that appear already on that quarter, will oblige Congress to send an able Minister to Madrid. And one also to the Court of London, that we may, if possible, negotiate commencing differences, before they have proceeded too far. The western Posts are with-held, and an encroachment already made on our north-eastern boundary. An ambiguity in the Treaty arising from there being two rivers named St Croix that empty into

Passamaquady Bay has encouraged the British to settle the country between them—thus determining in their own favor the right to an extensive and valuable country—The fact is, that the eastermost of these rivers is the true St Croix⟨,⟩ the same name having been of late date only, applied to the westermost of these waters. The very unfriendly commercial principles entertained by the B. Ministry and the disputes concerning debts and removed Negroes, are points of consequence also; which together form a field for able and ample negotiation.

The Marquis Fayette had embarked for Europe before the letter for him that you enclosed came to my hands.[2] I should be glad to know your pleasure concerning it—whether I am to send it on to France after him, or return it to you?

My respectful compliments attend your Lady, and wishing you and her the compliments of the season, I am, with very great esteem and regard, dear Sir your most obedient and very humble servant

Richard Henry Lee

ALS, DLC:GW.

1. After considerable debate Congress on 23 Dec., the day before it adjourned, adopted an ordinance providing for the appointment of three commissioners "to lay out a district, of not less than two nor exceeding three miles square, on the banks of either side of the Delaware, not more than eight miles above or below the lower falls thereof, for a fœderal town" (*JCC*, 27:704).

2. The only letters that GW is known to have written to Lafayette in December are the one of 8 Dec., which Lafayette did receive before sailing on 21 or 22 Dec., and the one dated 23 Dec., which he did not receive before sailing. As the letter of the twenty-third could not have been "enclosed" in GW's letter to Lee of 14 Dec., it may be that GW wrote a third letter to Lafayette in December which Lafayette did not receive and which has not been found. See also Lafayette to GW, 19 Mar. 1785.

To James Madison

Dear Sir,   Annapolis [Md.] 28th Decr 1784.

I have been favored with your letter of the 11th.[1]

The proceedings of the conference, and the Act & resolutions of this Legislature consequent thereupon (herewith transmitted to the Assembly)[2] are so full, & explanatory of the motives which governed in this business, that it is scarcely necessary for me to say any thing in addition to them; except that, this State seem highly impressed with the importance of the objects wch we have had under consideration, and are very desirous of seeing them accomplished.

We have reduced most of the Tolls from what they were in the first Bill, and have added something to a few others.[3] upon the whole, we have made them as low as we conceived from the best information before us, and such estimates as we had means to calculate upon, as they can be fixed, without hazarding the plan altogether. We made the value of the commodity the governing principle in the establishment of the Tolls; but having had an eye to some bulky articles of produce, & to the encouragement of the growth & Manufacture of some others, as well as to prevent a tedeous enumeration of the different species of all, we departed from the genl rule in many instances.

The rates of tollage as now fixed, may still appear high to some of the southern Gentlemen, when they compare them with those on James River; but as there is no comparison in the expence & risk of the two undertakings, so neither ought there to be in the Tolls. I am fully perswaded that the Gentlemen who were appointed, and have had this matter under consideration, were actuated by no other motives than to hit (if they could do so) upon such a happy medium as would not be burthensome to indivls or give jealousy to the public on one hand, nor discouragement to adventurers on the other. To secure success, and to give vigor to the undertaking, it was judged advisable for each State to contribute (upon the terms of private subscribers) to the expence of it;[4] especially as it might have a happy influence on the Minds of the western settlers. and it may be observed here, that only part of this money can be called for immediately, provided the work goes on—and afterwards, only in the proportion of its progression.

Though there is no obligation upon the State to adopt this (if it is inconvenient, or repugnant to their wishes) yet I should be highly pleased to hear that they had done so—(our advantages will, most assuredly, be equal to those of Maryland and our public spirit ought not, in my opinion, to be less)—as also the resolutions respecting the roads of Communication;[5] both of which, tho they look in some degree to different objects, are both very important; that by the Yohiogany (thro' Pensylvania) is particularly so for the Fur & Peltry of the Lakes, because it is the most direct rout by which they can be transported; whilst it is exceedingly convenient to the people who inhabit the Ohio (or Alligany) above Fort Pitt—the lower part of the Mononga-hela—and all the Yohiogany.

Matters might perhaps have been better digested if more time had been taken, but the fear of not getting the report to Richmond before the Assembly would have risen, occasioned more hurry than accuracy—or even real dispatch. But to alter the Act now, further than to accomodate it to circumstances where it is essential; or to remedy an obvious error if any should be discovered will not do. The Bill passed this Assembly with only 9 dissenting voices—and got thro' both Houses in a day, so earnest were the members of getting it to you in time.[6]

It is now near 12 at night, and I am writing with an Aching head, having been constantly employed in this business since the 22d without assistance from my Colleagues—Genl Gates having been sick the whole time, & Colo. Blackburn not attend-ing—But for this I would be more explicit. I am—with great esteem & regard—Dr Sir Yr Most Obedt Servt

Go: Washington

I am ashamed to send such a letter, but cannot give you a fairer one. G.W.

ALS (photocopy), ViMtV; LB, DLC: Madison Papers; ADfS, VtHi. There are no material differences between the three copies of the letter.

1. Letter not found. In a letter of 11 Dec. Madison wrote Richard Henry Lee about the Potomac River Company bill. See GW to Madison, 28 Nov., n.1.

2. The proceedings, the act, and the resolutions are printed below as enclosures I, II, and III in George Washington and Horatio Gates to the Virginia Legislature, 28 December. The journals of the Virginia house of delegates record on 31 Dec. that the governor gave the speaker GW's report, which included the three enclosures. No letter from GW transmitting his report to Gov. Beverley Randolph and none from the governor acknowledging its receipt has been found.

3. When the commissioners began their deliberations, they had before them the schedule of tolls contained in the bill that the Virginia and Maryland gentlemen drafted at Alexandria on 15 November. See Henry Lee to GW, 18 Nov., and notes. If the Virginia house of delegates in its consideration of their Potomac River Company bill in early December made changes in the toll charges, the commissioners may have had that schedule of tolls as well. On at least two separate occasions, GW himself drew up schedules of tolls. In one of these, which is labeled "Memo of Tolls" (ICU), he lists most of the same items in roughly the same order, often using similar or identical language, as ap-

pears in the schedule in the bill adopted at the Annapolis conference and subsequently enacted into law by both the Maryland and the Virginia legislatures. A significant difference is that GW gives the rates in Virginia currency with the tolls to be collected "at the lower Falls" and at "the Shan[andoa]h Falls," whereas the Potomac River Company act gives the rates in sterling and sets the collection points at "the mouth of the South Branch," at "Payne's Falls," and at "the Great Falls" (11 Hening 510–25). Attached to GW's memorandum is GW's "Estimate of proceeds of tolls" (ICU), which reads: "Suppose the labour of 10,000 People to be water borne to Alexandria & George Town. Will not this amount to

5000 Hhds of Tobacco @ 4/	1000.0.0
300,000 Bushls of wheat @ 2d.	
or	
50000 Barrls of Flour 1/	2500——
150,000 Bushls of Indian corn 1d.	625——
Hemp, Iron, Flax Seed, Pork[,] Beef[,] Potash, Coals, Ores of	
drift kinds, Lime Plank, Timber, Lumber—Stone &c. say	1000——
	5125.0.0″

The second schedule of tolls in GW's hand represents his attempt to compare the rates of the "Potomac Compa. Bill" with those that had been projected before the war for collection on the Potomac, James, and Susquehanna rivers. For GW's involvement in earlier efforts to improve the navigation of the Potomac, see the source note in GW to a Participant in the Potomac River Enterprise, 1762. The high rates set for the new Potomac River Company in both these schedules, far higher than those set in the acts passed by the Maryland and Virginia legislatures in late December or early January, indicate that GW drew up the two schedules earlier, in the process either of drafting or of promoting the original Potomac River bill of 15 November. The fact that labels on the cover of all three of these memoranda seem to be in Madison's hand suggests that GW either gave them to Madison when he went from Mount Vernon to Richmond in mid-November or sent them along to Madison with the copy of the proposed Potomac River Company bill on 28 November.

4. Article XX in the act provided in the one instance that the state of Maryland would purchase fifty shares and in the other that Virginia would buy fifty. See Enclosure II in George Washington and Horatio Gates to the Virginia Legislature, this date.

5. At the same time that the Maryland legislature passed the act to create the Potomac River Company, it adopted a resolution calling for the building of a road in Pennsylvania to help connect the Potomac and Ohio. Its resolution is printed as Enclosure III in George Washington and Horatio Gates to the Virginia Legislature, 28 December.

6. The Potomac River Company bill was introduced in the Maryland house on 27 Dec. and passed both houses on 28 December. After adopting the bill and the resolution regarding the Pennsylvania road, the house approved the following resolution received from the Maryland senate: "RESOLVED, that an attested copy of the act to establish a company for opening and extending the

navigation of the river Patowmack, and of the resolves respecting the opening a road to form a communication with the western country, be transmitted to general Washington and general Gates, commissioners for Virginia; and that the president and speaker, by a joint letter, inform those gentlemen, that the form of affixing the seal of the state, and signing by the governor, follows of course, to acts passed by the two houses, and that this will be complied with when the governor returns to town" (*Md. House of Delegates Proceedings*).

George Washington and Horatio Gates to the Virginia Legislature

Annapolis [Md.] December 28th 1784.
To the Honorable the General Assembly of the Commonwealth of Virginia

Pursuant to the resolves of the Honble the Senate & House of Delegates, and conformably to the direction of the Executive authority of the State, we repaired to the City of Annapolis, and held a Conference with Gentlemen appointed by the Legislature of Maryland—the result of which is contained in the Inclosure, No. 1.

In consequence of the opinion given by the Conferrees, the Legislature of Maryland have passed the Act inclosed, No. 2 and the Resolves No. 3.[1]

It may be necessary for us to explain the reason for the provision in the Act "that if Subscriptions should be taken in, or a meeting of Subscribers directed by the Legislature of Virginia at times different from those in the Act, then there should be a meeting at the time appointed by Virginia; and Subscriptions made at times by them appointed, should be received"—It was thought by the Conferrees to be most proper to appoint certain times in the Act, but as it was doubtful whether the Act would get to Virginia in time to be adopted at the present Session of the Assembly, it was judged necessary to make a provision to accomodate the Scheme to an Act to be passed by Virginia, at the next Session of their Assembly, without the necessity of having recourse again to the Legislature of Maryland; but it is the opinion of the Conferrees, that an Act upon similar principles to that passed by Maryland ought, if possible, to be passed by the Assembly of Virginia at this Session. This would give a speedy beginning to the work, and an oppertunity of embracing the present favorable state of things for accomplishing the views of the two States.

The Act appears to us from every consideration we can give it to be founded on just & proper principles, and to be calculated to answer in every respect the purpose for which it is designed—we conceive it our duty therefore to declare, that it meets our entire approbation.

The reasons why this Act has not the Signature of the chief Magistrate are, because he is not present—and because it wants not this formality to give it validity.

We should do injustice to our feelings, were we not to add that, we have been happy in meeting Gentlemen of liberallity & candour—impressed with the importance of accelerating the purposes of the Legislature of Virginia of opening a free and easy intercourse with the Western territory, and the extension of the inland Navigation of the Eastern Waters—and that, there has been a perfect accordance of Sentiment in the Legislature of the State.

Submitted, respectfully, by

Go: Washington
Horatio Gates.

ADS, in GW's hand, Vi; ADfS, in GW's hand, MiU-C; LB, DLC:GW. There are no material differences between GW's draft and his final version, but the letter-book copy, which is misdated 1785, is quite different, with the enclosures numbered differently (see CD-ROM:GW).

1. The proceedings of the Annapolis conference are printed as Enclosure I; the Potomac River Company act is printed in part as Enclosure II; and the resolutions regarding the road in Pennsylvania are printed as Enclosure III.

Enclosure I
Report of the Maryland and Virginia Commissioners

Annapolis [28 December 1784]

At a Meeting, at the City of Annapolis on the 22d day of December 1784, of the Commissioners appointed by the Commonwealth of Virginia to confer with persons authorised on the part of the State of Maryland upon the Subject of opening and improving the Navigation of the River Potomack and concerting a plan for the opening a proper Road between the Waters of the Potomack and the most convenient Western Waters.

And a Committee appointed by the Senate and House of Delegates of Maryland to meet the Commissioners of Virginia for the purposes aforesaid. Were present

General Washington and General Gates from Virginia.

The Honble Thomas Stone, Samuel Hughes, and Charles Carroll of Carrollton, of the Senate.

And John Cadwallader, Samuel Chase, John Debutts, George Digges, Philip Key, Gustavus Scott, and Joseph Dashiell Esquires, of the House of Delegates.

General Washington in the Chair.

Randolph B. Latimer appointed Clerk.

The Conference proceeded to take the Subject Matters to them referred into their considerations, and thereupon came to the following resolutions.

That it is the Opinion of this Conference, That the removing the obstructions in the River Potomack and the making the same capable of Navigation from Tide Water as far up the North Branch of the said River as may be convenient and practicable will increase the Commerce of the Commonwealth of Virginia and State of Maryland, and greatly promote the political Interests of the United States, by forming a free and easy Communication and Connexion with the people settled on the Western Waters, already very considerable in their Numbers and rapidly encreasing from the Mildness of the Climate and the fertility of the Soil.

That it is the Opinion of the Conference, That the proposal to establish a Company for opening the River Potomack merits the Approbation of, and deserves to be patronised by Virginia and Maryland, and that a similar Law ought to be passed by the Legislatures of the two Governments to promote and encourage so laudable an Undertaking.

That it is the Opinion of this Conference that it would be proper for Virginia and Maryland each to become Subscribers to the Amount of Fifty Shares, and that such subscription would evince to the Public the opinion of the Legislatures of the practicability and great Utility of the Plan, and that the example would encourage Individuals to embark in the Measure, give Vigor and Security to so important an Undertaking and be a substantial proof to our Brethren of the Western Territory of our disposition to connect ourselves with them by the strongest Bonds of Friendship and mutual Interest.

That it is the Opinion of this Conference, That an Act of Assembly of Virginia for opening and extending the Navigation of the River Potomack from Fort Cumberland to Tide Water ought to be repealed.[1]

That it is the Opinion of this Conference, from the best information they have obtained, That a Road to begin about the Mouth of Stoney river may be carried in about 20 or 22 Miles to the Dunker Bottom on Cheat River, from whence this Conference are of opinion, That Batteau Navigation may be made, though perhaps at considerable expence: that if such Navigation cannot be effected, by continuing the road about 20 Miles further, it would intersect the Monongahela where the Navigation is good and has been long practiced.

That a Road from Fort Cumberland to Turkey Foot would be about thirty three Miles from whence an Improvement of the Youghigeny River would be necessary, though probably it might be done at less expence then the Navigation of the Cheat River could be rendered convenient from the Dunker Bottom.

That it is a general Opinion, that the Navigation on Potomack may be extended to the most convenient point below or even above the Mouth of Stoney River, from whence to set off a road to Cheat River; and this Conference is satisfied that that road from the Nature of the Country through which it may pass, wholly through Virginia and Maryland will be much better than a Road can be made at any reasonable expence from Fort Cumberland to the Youghigeny which must be carried partly through Pennsylvania.

That it is the Opinion of this Conference, That if the Navigation on Potomack should be carried to about the Mouth of the Stoney River, a communication with the Western Waters through a road from thence extended even to the Monongahela would be preferable in most points of view to that, by road from Fort Cumberland to Turkey Foot, the only other Way practicable, and in any great degree useful. That the Communication by a Road from Fort Cumberland to the present navigable part of the Youghigeny and thence through that river; though in the opinion of this Conference a second Object only would facilitate the Intercourse with a very respectable Number of the Western Settlers, contribute much to their convenience and accomodation, and that the Benefits resulting therefrom to these States would compensate the expence of improving that road.

This Conference therefore recommend that the Legislatures of Virginia and Maryland appoint skilful persons to view and accurately examine and survey Potomack from Fort Cumberland to the Mouth of Stoney River, and the River Cheat, from about the Dunker Bottom to the present navigable part thereof, and if they judge the Navigation can be extended to a convenient distance above Fort Cumberland that they from thence survey, lay off, and mark a road to the Cheat river, or continue the same to the navigation as they may think will most effectually establish the communication between the said Eastern and Western Waters. And that the said road be cut and cleared not less than eighty feet and properly improved and maintained in repair, not less than Forty nor more than Fifty Feet wide at the joint expence of both States. And your Conferees beg leave to recommend that each State appropriate three thousand three hundred and thirty three Dollars and one third for the purpose; And this Conference are further of Opinion, that the States of Virginia and Maryland request permission of the State of Pennsylvania to lay out and improve a Road through such part of that State as may be necessary in the best and most proper direction from Fort Cumberland to the navigable part of the Youghigeny and on such permission being obtained that proper persons be appointed to survey, mark, clear and improve such Road at the equal expence of Virginia and Maryland.[2] Which are submitted to the Consideration of the Legislatures of Virginia and Maryland.

By Order R.B. Latimer Ck

D, MnHi; printed, *Md. House of Delegates Proceedings.* This is the first of five documents from the Minnesota Historical Society dated either 28 Dec. 1784 or 1 Jan. 1785 which are printed here. For the other four, see Enclosure III below and enclosures I, II, and III in Madison to GW, 9 January. They are among a number of documents of GW's relating to the various Potomac River companies that came into the hands of George Mason's son John. John Mason lent them to a Pennsylvania congressman named Andrew Stewart for his use in preparing a report on the Chesapeake and Ohio Canal (*House Report*, 19th Congress, 1st session, no. 228); see "Washington and the Potomac: Manuscripts of the Minnesota Historical Society, 1769–1796," *American Historical Review*, 28 (1923), 499–519, 705–22. This document and the resolution of the Maryland house of delegates, printed below as Enclosure III, were copied by the same clerk. This copy of the document was later docketed by one of GW's clerks, probably Tobias Lear: "Conference of the Commissioners For clearing the Potomack—Annapolis 24h Decr 1784 & making a Road from the Waters of the Potomac to those of Monogalia."

On 22 Dec. Charles Carroll of Carrollton from the Maryland senate delivered to the speaker of the Maryland house of delegates GW's letter of 19 Dec. to William Paca and the letter from Gov. Beverley Randolph of 15 Dec. which GW had forwarded, "enclosing sundry resolutions of the general assembly of the commonwealth of Virginia" (*Md. House of Delegates Proceedings*). The initial resolutions of the Virginia legislature regarding the Potomac River Company and the road in Pennsylvania are printed in note 1, Beverley Randolph to GW, 15 December. Upon receiving the letters and the enclosed resolutions, the Maryland house adopted the following resolution: "WE consider the petition for opening and extending the navigation of the rivers Patowmack, and the resolution of the general assembly of Virginia on that subject, to be of great importance, and worthy the immediate consideration of this government, and therefore we wish the senate would appoint some of its members to join the gentlemen nominated by this house, to meet and confer with the commissioners by the state of Virginia, respecting the regulations and provisions under which a company ought to be established for the purpose of carrying into execution a plan for opening the navigation of Patowmack, and a road between the said river and the most convenient western waters. This house have appointed Mr [John] Cadwalader, Mr [Samuel] Chase, Mr [John] De Butts, Mr [George] Digges, Mr [Phillip] Key, Mr G[ustavas] Scott, and Mr Joseph Dashiell, to join such members of the senate as they may be pleased to appoint" (ibid.). The commissioners, who met at Mann's tavern in Annapolis, began work on 22 Dec., and Cadwalader delivered this report to the Maryland house of delegates on 27 December.

1. At the time the Virginia house of delegates voted to send GW and the two other men to consult with the Marylanders about the Potomac River Company, its original bill creating the company had already had its second reading and was scheduled to be committed to the committee of the whole for debate. The house journal gives no indication that any further action was taken on this earlier bill.

2. For the actions taken by the Maryland and Virginia legislatures to initiate action on building a road from the Potomac in Pennsylvania, see Enclosure III below and Enclosure II in James Madison to GW, 9 Jan. 1785.

Enclosure II
An Act for Opening and Extending the Navigation of Potowmack River

Richmond, 18 October 1784. I. WHEREAS the extension of the navigation of Potowmack river, from tide water to the highest place practicable on the North branch, will be of great public utility, and many persons are willing to subscribe large sums of money to effect so laudable and beneficial a work; and it is just and proper that they, their heirs, and assigns, should be empowered to receive reasonable tolls forever, in satisfaction for the money advanced by them in carrying the work into execution, and the risk they run: And whereas it may be necessary to cut canals and erect locks and other works on both sides of the river, and the legislatures of Maryland and Virginia, impressed with the importance of the object, are desirous of encouraging so useful an undertaking: Therefore,

II. *Be it enacted by the General Assembly of Virginia,* That it shall and may be lawful to open books in the city of Richmond, towns of Alexandria and Winchester in this state, for receiving and entering subscriptions for the said undertaking, under the management of Jaquelin Ambler and John Beckley at the city of Richmond, of John Fitzgerald and William Hartshorne at the town of Alexandria, and of Joseph Holmes and Edward Smith at the town of Winchester, and under the management of such persons and at such places in Maryland as have been appointed by the state of Maryland, . . . that the said books shall be opened for receiving subscriptions on the eighth day of February next, and continue open for this purpose until the tenth day of May next, inclusive; and on the seventeenth day of the said month of May, there shall be a general meeting of the subscribers at the town of Alexandria. . . . [The managers were to "lay before" the meeting their books. If less than one-half the capital prescribed had been subscribed, the managers should reopen their books. If more than 222,222⅔ dollars had been subscribed, the managers were to reduce the capital to that amount and divide it into 500 shares. If subscriptions for at least one-half this amount could not be secured, all subscriptions would be void.]

III. *And be it enacted,* That in case one half of the said capital, or a greater sum, shall be subscribed . . . the said subscribers . . . shall be . . . incorporated into a company, by the name of the "Potowmack Company," . . . and such of the said subscribers as shall be present at the said meeting . . . are hereby empowered and required to elect a president and four directors, for conducting the said undertaking, and managing all the said company's business and concerns, for and during such time, not exceeding three years, as the said subscribers, or a majority of them, shall think fit. . . .

IV. *And be enacted,* That the said president and directors . . . shall have full power and authority, to agree with any person or persons, on behalf of the said company, to cut such canals, and erect such locks, and perform such other works as they shall judge necessary for opening, improving, and extending the navigation of the said river above tide water, to the highest part of the North Branch, to which navigation can be extended, . . . and out of the money arising from the subscriptions and the tolls, and other aids herein after given, to pay for the same, and to repair and keep in order the said canals, locks, and other works necessary thereto, and to defray all incidental charges; and also to appoint a treasurer, clerk, and such other officers, toll gatherers, managers, and servants, as they shall judge requisite, and to agree for and settle their respective wages or allowances, and settle, pass and sign their accounts; and also to make and establish rules of proceeding, and to transact all the other business and concerns of the said company, in and during the intervals between the general meetings of the same; and they shall be allowed as a satisfaction for their trouble therein, such sum of money as shall, by a general meeting of the subscribers, be determined. . . .

V. *And be it enacted,* That the said president and directors . . . shall have full power and authority, from time to time, as money shall be wanting, to make and sign orders for that purpose, and direct at what time, and in what proportion the proprietors shall advance and pay off the sums subscribed. . . . And if any of the said proprietors shall refuse or neglect to pay their said proportions, within one month after the same so ordered and advertised, as aforesaid, the said president and directors, or a majority of them, may sell at auction, and convey to the purchaser, the share or shares of such proprietor so refusing or neglecting payment. . . .

VI. *Be it enacted,* That from time to time . . . the proprietors of the said company, at the next general meeting, shall either continue the said president and directors, or any of them, or shall choose others in their stead. . . .

VII. *And be it enacted,* That every president and director, before he acts as such, shall take an oath or affirmation, for the due execution of his office.

VIII. *And be it enacted,* That the presence of proprietors, having one hundred shares at the least, shall be necessary to constitute a general meeting; and that there be a general meeting of proprieters on the first Monday of August, in every year, at such convenient town as shall from time to time, be appointed by the said general meeting; . . . to which meeting the president and directors shall make report, and render distinct and just accounts of all their proceedings, . . . and at such yearly general meetings, after leaving in the hands of the treasurer, such sum as the proprietors . . . shall judge necessary for repairs and contingent charges, an equal dividend of all the neat profits, arising from the tolls hereby granted, shall be ordered and made to . . . all the proprietors of the said company, in proportion to their several shares. . . .

IX. *And be it further enacted,* That for and in consideration of the expences the said proprietors will be at, . . . the said canals and works, with all their profits, shall be . . . vested in the said proprietors . . . in proportion to their respective shares, and the same shall be deemed real estate, and be forever exempt from payment of any tax . . . whatsoever; and it shall . . . be lawful for the said president and directors . . . to demand and receive at the nearest convenient place below the mouth of the South branch, and at or near Payne's falls, and at or above the great falls of the river Potowmack, and every of these places separately, for all commodities transported through either of them respectively, tolls according to the following table and rates, to wit; [There follows here the table of tolls for enumerated articles to be paid at the three named points.]

X. *And be it enacted,* That the said river and the works to be erected thereon in virtue of this act, when completed, shall forever thereafter be esteemed and taken to be navigable as a public highway, free for the transportation of all goods, commodities, or produce whatsoever, on payment of the tolls imposed by this act. . . .

XI. *Be it enacted,* That it shall be . . . lawful for the said president and directors . . . to agree with the owners of any land, through which the said canal is intended to pass, for the purchase thereof. . . . [The act describes procedures for acquisition of land when no agreement can be reached between the owner and the company.]

XII. *And be it enacted,* That the said president and directors . . . are hereby authorized to agree with the proprietors for the purchase of a quantity of land, not exceeding one acre, at or near each of the said places of receipt of tolls aforesaid, for the purpose of erecting necessary buildings. . . .

XIII. *Be it enacted,* That the water or any part thereof, conveyed through any canal or cut made by the said company, shall not be used for any purpose but navigation, unless the consent of the proprietors of the land through which the same be led, be first had. . . .

XIV. *And be it enacted,* That it shall and may be lawful for every of the said proprietors to transfer his share or shares, by deed executed before two witnesses, and registered after proof of the execution thereof, in the said company's books, and not otherwise, except by devise. . . .

XV. *Be it therefore enacted,* That the said president and directors . . . are hereby empowered to receive and take in subscriptions, upon the said condition, and upon the said works being completed and carried into execution, according to the true intent and meaning of this act. . . .

XVI. *And be it enacted,* That if the said capital, and the other aids already granted by this act, shall prove insufficient, it shall and may be lawful for the said company, from time to time, to increase the said capital by the addition of so many more whole shares, as shall be judged necessary by the said proprietors or a majority of them, holding at least three hundred shares, present at any general meeting of the said company. . . .

XVII. *And it is hereby declared and enacted*, That the tolls herein before allowed, to be demanded and received at the nearest convenient place below the mouth of the South Branch, are granted, and shall be paid on condition only, That the said Potowmack company shall make the river well capable of being navigated in dry seasons, by vessels drawing one foot water from the place on the North Branch, at which a road shall set off to the Cheat river, agreeably to the determination of the assemblies of Virginia and Maryland, to and through the place which may be fixed on, below the mouth of the South Branch, for receipt of the tolls aforesaid. . . . That the tolls . . . to be demanded . . . near Payne's falls, . . . shall be payable on condition only, that the said Potowmack Company shall make the river well capable of being navigated in dry seasons, by vessels drawing one foot water, from the said place of collection, near the mouth of the South Branch, to and through Payne's falls as aforesaid. That the tolls . . . received at the Great Falls . . . shall be payable on condition only, that the said Potowmack Company shall make the river well capable of being navigated in dry seasons, from Payne's falls to the Great falls, by vessels drawing one foot water, and from the Great falls to tide water, and shall at or near the Great falls make a cut or canal, twenty-five feet wide, and four feet deep, with sufficient locks, if necessary, each of eighty feet in length, sixteen feet in breadth, and capable of conveying vessels or rafts drawing four feet water at the least, and shall make at or near the Little falls such canal and locks, if necessary, as will be sufficient and proper to let vessels and rafts aforesaid, into tide water, or render the said river navigable in the natural course.

XVIII. *And it is hereby provided and enacted*, That in case the said company shall not begin the said work within one year after the company shall be formed, or if the navigation shall not be made and improved between the Great falls and Fort-Cumberland, in the manner herein before mentioned, within three years . . . the said company shall not be entitled to any benefit, privilege, or advantage, under this act: And in case the said company shall not complete the navigation through and from the Great falls to tide water . . . within ten years . . . then shall all interest of the said company and all preference in their favor, as to the navigation and tolls, at, through, and from the Great falls to tide water, be forfeited and cease.

XIX. *And be it enacted*, That all commodities of the produce of either of the said states, or of the western country; which may be carried or transported through the said locks, canals, and river, may be landed, sold, or otherwise disposed of free from any other duties, impositions, regulations, or restrictions, of any kind, than the like commodities of the produce of the state in which the same may happen to be so landed, sold, shipped or disposed of.

XX. *And be it further enacted,* That the treasurer of this commonwealth shall be authorized and directed to subscribe to the amount of fifty shares in behalf of the same. . . .

XXI. *And be it further enacted,* That so much of every act and acts within the purview of this act . . . is hereby repealed.

Printed, 11 Hening 510–25. For GW's extract of the bill in which he lists the powers and duties of the president of the Potomac River Company and the trustees, see GW to Thomas Johnson and Thomas Sim Lee, 18 May 1785, n.2.

Enclosure III
Resolutions of the Maryland Legislature

Annapolis, [28 December 1784]

By the House of Delegates Decr 28th 1784. Resolved That three thousand three hundred and thirty three and one third Dollars be appropriated to defray one half of the expence of examining surveying cutting clearing improving and keeping in repair a proposed road from the Waters of Potomack river to the River Cheat, and if necessary to the Monongahela, and that the Intendant of the revenue be authorised and directed to pay the said Money to the Use aforesaid, And that Mr Francis Deakins be appointed to join and act with such person or persons as may be nominated by the Common Wealth of Virginia to execute the Trust, and that the Money aforesaid be subject to their Order, and if the said Francis Deakins shall decline to act that his Excellency the Governor be authorised and requested to appoint another in his place.

Resolved, That his Excellency the Governor be requested to write to the Legislature of Pennsylvania to request permission to lay out and improve a Road through such part of that State as may be necessary in the best and most proper direction from Fort Cumberland to the navigable part of the Youghigeny.[1]

D, MnHi. See source line of Enclosure I. Docketed by Tobias Lear: "A Resolve of the House of Delegates of the State of Maryland respecting the Potomack Co. Decr 1784."

1. For GW's suggestion that Virginia and Maryland make preparations to

build a road in Pennsylvania, see GW to James Madison, 3 December. For the Virginia legislature's initial resolution advocating the building of the road, see Beverley Randolph to GW, 15 Dec., n.1. For the actions the Virginia legislature took in this matter, see Enclosure II in Madison to GW, 9 Jan. 1785.

Letter not found: from Samuel Chase, 31 Dec. 1784. On 5 Jan. 1785 GW wrote to Chase: "Receive my thanks for your favor of the 31st ulto."

From Aeneas Lamont

Sir,   Philadelphia 31st December 1784

Perhaps you will be surprized at receiving a letter from a person entirely unknown to you, and more so, I fear, at the liberty I have already taken with your name: Altho' I cannot attempt to Justifie this impertinance, yet I consider it some liquidation of my offence that I am not the first man of genius (or immaginary genius) that have succoured their efforts by the influence of the *great*.

The little world, whose thoughts and pursuits are busied in necessary and domestic employments, seldome pay attention to those who flatter the *Muses*—they often laugh at their simplicity, tho' seldom contribute for their amusement—But, believe me, great Sir, whatever bauble or toy contributes to a mans happiness—wo be to the heart that can revile against the acquisition, he is but a dunce in the school of nature!

If you can forgive a transgression which politeness would not excuse, my best ambition shall be to merit so much goodness. I am, Sir, With every sentiment of respect, your Devoted Humble Servant,

                                                    AEneas Lamont
My address is at Edward Jones's, Esqr. Walnut St[r]eet, Philadelphia.

ALS, PHi: Washington-Biddle Correspondence.

GW wrote to Lamont on 31 Jan. 1785, sending the letter to Clement Biddle with a request that Biddle deliver it if Lamont was "a man of decent deportment, & his productions deserving encouragement." Biddle wrote on 7 Mar. 1785 that he had not yet been able to get information about "the Author of the Poems," and on 12 April he informed GW that he had shown Thomas Paine GW's letter and that Paine's advice was not to forward it to Lamont. No record has been found of Lamont's publishing a book of poems. GW's letter to Lamont of 31 Jan. is printed in note 2, GW to Biddle, 2 Feb. 1785.

From Charles Willson Peale

Dear Sir   [c.December 1784]

   since my writing by the last Post I have recd the Twenty five
Guineas which you sent by Monsr Loyetta. your Manner of
Spelling the Name led me into a difficulty of finding out the
Gentleman and I am under some obligation to Mr Marboye the
Minister's Secy, for his assistance in the affair. I am Dear Sir
your most obedient humble Servt

                                                                  C.P.

ADf, PPAmP: Charles Willson Peale Papers.
   1. Loyetta (1756–1830) is probably Anne-Philippe-Dieudonné de Loyanté
whom the state of Virginia employed briefly in 1778 as inspector general of its
fortifications and military stores. He subsequently was made a lieutenant colonel and served under Steuben as a volunteer. It has not been determined
when Loyanté returned to France, and it is possible that he remained in the
United States as late as December 1784. Peale's recent letter has not been
found. It is not clear why GW sent him twenty-five guineas.

From a French Wine Merchant

                                                                [1784]
   I have addressed this hamper (which is in a double hamper to
prevent its being touched) to Mess. Rob. & Chas Garvey of
Rouen with request that they would forward it by first Vessell[.]
Before tasting this Wine it must rest five or six Days in a good
Cellar—I have 1800 of this sort which is of 1779 if your Excellencys friends should want any the price is 45 Lous—there is
one bottle with a ticket of 1781—40 Lous[.] of this I have
2400[.] I have 2000 of another sort à 35 Lous.
   As these Wines may be sent from here in September it is necessary to receive the Orders in July or August to send them that
fall or next spring[.] they may be orderd in hampers of fifty—
Sixty or 75 bottles—being more easy to Load on board than
those of 100 bottles—I can furnish of all sorts even the Mountain Red—in bottles[.] the white of 1782—has not turned out
so well which makes the Old preferred—If your Excelly will
give me Orders or your friends I will serve them with the greatest attention and on the best terms—being from the first
hand.—'Tis seldom they wax the bottles[.] the hamper is

marked M.WASG=/=OW= The bottles are Waxed with a red-dish Wax.

I am told the Mousseux Wines do not suit in your Country on account of the heat which bursts them—I could furnish very good.

I do not know if you love those which are *Liquoreux* (Li-quorish) the great Connoisseurs prefer those which are *Senés*—Champagne produces but very rarely of the 1st sort and those who pretend to furnish of it every Year are to be suspected—If this Year should produce any excellent I shall be able to furnish even Eail De perdrix. When this does not succeed—I do not offer it but only the Old and best.

L (translation), DLC:GW. The original letter, of which this is an undated and unsigned translation, has not been identified.

From James Madison

Dear Sir   Richmond [Va.] Jany 1. 1785

I was yesterday honored with your favor of the 28 Ult. ac-companying the report of the Conferees &c. &c. The latter have been laid before the H. of Delegates, and a Com[mitte]e appd to report a bill & Resolutions corresponding with those of Maryland.[1] The only danger of miscarriage arises from the im-patience of the members to depart, & the bare competency of the present number. By great efforts only they have been de-tained thus long. I am not without hopes however that the busi-ness of the Potowmac at least will be provided for before the adjourment, and some provision now depending be comple-ated in favor of James River. Before the rect of your dispatches a bill had been passed by the H. of D. for surveying the former as well as the latter river on a plan, which we shall endeavour by concert with the Senate, to accomodate to the provisions of Maryland.[2] A Resolution has passed both Houses instructing the Commissrs appd in June last to settle with Maryd Com-missrs the jurisdiction & navigation of the Potowmac, to join in a representation to Pena on the subject of the Waters of the Ohio within her limits This instruction ought rather to have been committed to the late Conference; but when the Commis-sion under which you attended it passed, I was confined to my room & it did not occur to any other member. And indeed if I had been well the haste which necessarily prevailed might have precluded me from comprehending the object within your Mission, especially as I had not previously digested my ideas on the subject nor accurately examined the text of the Confederation.[3] It were to be wished too I think that the application to P[ennsyl-vani]a on the subject of the Road cd have been blended with that of the River. As it is it will I think be best to refer it after the example of Maryld to the Executive.[4] I beg you Sir to excuse the brevity which our hurry has imposed upon me. As soon as I have leisure I will endeavour to make amends for it by a fuller communication on this subject remaining in the mean time with the most perfect esteem & the sincerest regard Yr Obedt & humble servt

J. Madison Jr

ALS, DLC:GW; ALS, DLC: Madison Papers. The letter in the Madison Papers is Madison's retained copy.

In this letter of 1 Jan., Madison is writing to GW of measures relating to the proposed Potomac River Company that the Virginia legislature adopted during GW's absence in Annapolis and before it received his report on 31 January. These are: (1) "an act, for opening and extending the navigation of James River," passed on 24 Dec.; (2) a resolution to join with Maryland in arranging with Pennsylvania for the free passage of goods and traffic on the Ohio and other streams to and from the Potomac, adopted on 28 Dec.; and (3) a bill "for taking the survey of the rivers James and Potomac, and of the nearest western waters to the head branches of the same, that may be rendered navigable," passed by the house on 30 Dec. (*House of Delegates Journal, 1781–1785*). Numbers 2 and 3 in particular were consequences of GW's urging (see GW to Madison, 28 Nov. and 3 Dec.); but as Madison indicates in both this letter and the one of 9 Jan., adjustments had to be made in these measures to bring them into conformity with the provisions of Maryland's Potomac River Company act and other measures adopted in Annapolis, about which GW had informed them in his report of 28 December. After receiving GW's report on 31 Dec., the Virginia legislature not only brought in a new James River Company bill to replace the one that had just passed, but the house, refusing to accept the senate's amendments to its bill providing for a survey of the upper reaches of the James and Potomac rivers, also substituted for its bill a resolution calling for a survey only of the James and Elizabeth rivers. The senate approved the resolution, and it is printed below as Enclosure III in James Madison to GW, 9 Jan. 1785.

1. GW's letter of 28 Dec. covered the letter of that date from him and Horatio Gates to the Virginia legislature with its three enclosures, one of which was the Potomac River Company act. On 31 Dec. the speaker "laid before the [Virginia] House a letter from the Governor, enclosing the report of

the commissioners appointed to confer with commissioners appointed by the Legislature of Maryland, respecting the opening and extending the navigation of the river Potomac." The Maryland bill was read and referred to a committee composed of William Grayson, James Madison, and Mann Page, with orders to bring in a bill. Grayson brought in a bill identical to the Maryland bill on 1 January. The bill received final passage in both houses on 4 Jan., without amendment.

2. This bill was dropped in favor of a resolution adopted on 1 January. See source note.

3. On 9 Jan., Madison sent GW a copy of this resolution of the Virginia assembly out of which came the Mount Vernon conference in March 1785, which in turn led to the Annapolis Convention of 1786 and the Constitutional Convention of 1787. The resolution is printed as Enclosure I in Madison to GW, 9 January.

4. The house of delegates on this day adopted a resolution regarding the building of a road in Pennsylvania from the Potomac to a navigable "part of the River Cheat or of the River Monongalia" similar to that adopted by the Maryland legislature. The Virginia resolution is printed as Enclosure II in Madison to GW, 9 Jan., and the Maryland resolution is Enclosure III in George Washington and Horatio Gates to the Virginia Legislature, 28 Dec. 1784.

From Robert Morris

Dear Sir   Philadelphia January 1st 178[5]

The Gentlemen who will have the honor to deliver you this Letter are from the West Indias they were Recommended to me by an old acquaintance and I find them very Genteel agreable Men. The Brilliancy of your Character attracts the attention of the World, they cannot pass to the Southward without gratifying their Wishes by an interview with the first Man of the Age and I am sure they will meet a kind reception.

May the present Year be as propitious to you as the last was, and may you long live to enjoy a succession of them is the sincere Wish of Dear Sir Your most obedient & very humble Servant

                                                            Robt Morris

by Messrs Scott, Colby & Gilpin.[1]

LS, DLC:GW. The year is mistakenly given as 1784 in the dateline.

1. Scott and "Doctor" Gilpin, "two West India Gentlemen," arrived for dinner at Mount Vernon on Tuesday, 25 Jan. (*Diaries*, 4:80). Colby fell ill and remained behind in Baltimore (see GW to Morris, 1 Feb.).

To Jeremy Belknap

Revd Sir,   Mount Vernon 5th Jan. 1785.
A few days ago, under cover from Mr Hazard of Philadelp[hi]a, I was honored with your favor of the 19th of July; and the first volume of your History of New Hampshire.[1] For both, I pray you to accept my thanks—but my acknowledgments are more particularly due, for your favorable expression in the former, of my past endeavors to support the Cause of liberty.

The proof you have given of your approbation of this, is interesting—I receive it with gratitude—and am with great respect Revd Sir, Yr Most Obedt Hble Servt

Go: Washington

ALS, MHi: Belknap Papers; LB, DLC:GW.
1. After writing his letter to GW on 19 July 1784, Belknap sent it to his friend Ebenezer Hazard in Philadelphia. Hazard, who had been supervising the printing of Belknap's first volume of his history of New Hampshire, wished to send to GW a properly bound copy of the *History* along with Belknap's letter (see Belknap's letter of 19 July and notes). On 13 Nov. 1784 Hazard wrote Belknap: "I have been waiting all this time to have one of your books *neatly bound* for General Washington; but Mr [Robert] Aitken cannot get a binder. . . . I have now concluded to send the General one in boards, with an apology for not sending him one sooner. The date of your letter will shew that *your* attention to him was seasonable" (*Belknap Papers*, 1:405–7). Finally, on 21 Dec. 1784, Hazard sent Belknap's letter and book to GW, who responded on 5 Jan. 1785: "A few days ago I was favored with your Letter of the 21st ulto enclosing the first Volume of the history of New Hampshire, & a letter from the Author, the revd Mr Belknap. I thank you for your attention in this matter—& pray you to be at the trouble of forwarding the enclosed to that Gentln for whose pleasing remembrance of me, I feel myself obliged" (LB, DLC:GW). Hazard's letter has not been found, nor has the letter by which he forwarded GW's letter to Belknap. Upon receiving GW's letter forwarded to him by Hazard, Belknap wrote Hazard on 11 Feb. 1785: "After very long but *not patient* waiting, I was so happy *last night* as to get yours of the 17th ult., enclosing one from General Washington, which, I suppose, from the character I have formed of him in my mind, though it is short and expresses but little, means something very pertinent and interesting. I shall, as you guess, rank it among my valuables" (*Belknap Papers*, 1:412–15).
In the inventory of GW's library taken after his death, the first volume as well as a three-volume set of Belknap's *History of New Hampshire* were listed.

To Samuel Chase

Dear Sir,   Mount Vernon 5th Jany 1785.

Receive my thanks for your favor of 31st ulto, & for the copies therewith enclosed: they will answer my purposes equally with the fairest that could be made.[1]

When I found your Express at Mount Pleasant, & was unable to procure another in Marlbro', I commenced one myself—got home before dinner, & dispatched one of my servants to Hooes ferry immediately. He placed the packet into the hands of the Express there waiting, before nine o'Clock next morning: on Friday with ease the business might have been laid before the Assembly of this State, yet sitting I believe. When I hear from thence, I will with pleasure communicate the result.[2]

The attention which your Assembly is giving to the establishment of public schools, for the encouragement of literature, does them great honor: to accomplish this, ought to be one of our first endeavours; I know of no object more interesting.[3] We want something to expand the mind, & make us think with more liberallity—& act with sounder policy, than most of the States do. We should consider that we are not now in leading strings. It behooves us therefore to look well to our ways. My best wishes attend the Ladies of your family.[4] I am, Dr Sir Yr mo. obt Servt

G: Washington

LB, DLC:GW.

1. Letter not found. Samuel Chase (1741–1811), who was one of the Maryland commissioners with whom GW had been meeting, may have sent copies of one or more of the documents relating to their proceedings (see George Washington and Horatio Gates to the Virginia Legislature, 28 Dec. 1784, and its enclosures).

2. GW returned to Mount Vernon from Annapolis probably on Thursday, 28 December. The packet he sent to Richmond included his letter to James Madison of 28 Dec. and his report to the Virginia legislature, 28 Dec., and its enclosures. GW's report with its enclosures was indeed presented to the house of delegates on Friday, 31 December.

3. The bill that became "An act for founding a college on the western shore of this state, and constituting the same, together with Washington college on the eastern shore, into one university, by the name of The University of Maryland" was introduced, debated, and passed in the Maryland house of delegates on 30 Dec. before being sent to the senate for its approval on 31 Dec. (*Md. House of Delegates Proceedings*).

4. Chase married his second wife Hannah Kitty Giles in 1784. He had one daughter named Matilda born to his first wife in 1763.

To Henry Knox

My dear Sir,   Mount Vernon 5th Jan. 1785

About the beginning of last month I wrote you a pretty long letter, & soon after, received your favor of the 23d of November.[1] It is not the letters from my friends which give me trouble—or adds ought to my perplexity. I receive them with pleasure, and pay as much attention to them as my avocations will admit. It is references of old matters with which I have nothing to do. Applications, which oftentimes cannot be complied with. Enquiries, which would employ the pen of a historian to satisfy. Letters of compliment, as unmeaning perhaps as they are troublesome, but which must be attended to. And the commonplace business, which employs my pen & my time; often disagreeably.

Indeed, these with company, deprive me of exercise, and unless I can obtain relief, may be productive of disagreeable consequences—I already begin to feel the effect. Heavy, & painful oppressions of the head, and other disagreeable sensations, often trouble me. I am determined therefore to employ some person who shall ease me of the drudgery of this business.[2] At *any rate*, if the whole of it is thereby suspended, I am resolved to use exercise. My private concerns also, require infinitely more attention than I have given, or can give, under present circumstances. They can no longer be neglected without involving my ruin.

This, my dear Sir, is a friendly communication—I give it in testimony of my unreservedness with you—& not for the purpose of discouraging your letters; for be assured that, to corrispond with those I love is among my highest gratifications, and I perswade myself you will not doubt my sincerity when I assure you, I place you among the foremost of this class. Letters of friendship require no study, the communications are easy, and allowances are expected, & made. This is not the case with those which require re-searches—consideration—recollection—and the de—l knows what, to prevent error, and to answer the ends for which they are written.

In my last I informed you that I was endeavouring to stimulate my Countrymen to the extension of the inland Navigation of our rivers; and to the opening of the best and easiest communication for Land transportation between them and the Western waters. I am just returned from Annapolis to which place I was requested to go by our Assembly (with my bosom friend Genl G—tes, who being at Richmond contrived to edge himself into the Commission)[3] for the purpose of arranging matters, and forming a Law which should be similar in both States, so far as it respected the river Potomack, which seperates them. I met the most perfect accordance in that legislature; & the matter is now reported to ours, for its concurrence.

The two Assemblies (not being in Circumstances to undertake this business *wholly* at the public expence) propose to incorporate such private Adventurers as shall associate for the purpose of extending the navigation of the River from tide water as far up as it will admit Craft of ten Tons burthen, & to allow them a per[pe]tual toll & other emoluments to induce them to subscribe freely to a Work of such magnitude; whilst they have agreed (or, I should rather say, probably will agree, as the matter is not yet concluded in the Virginia Assembly) to open, at the public expence, the communication with the Western territory. To do this will be a great political work—May be immensely extensive in a commercial point—and beyond all question, will be exceedingly beneficial for those who advance the money for the purpose of extending the Navigation of the river, as the tolls arising therefrom are to be held in perpetuity, & will encrease every year.

Rents have got to such an amazing height in Alexandria, that (having an unimproved lot or two there) I have thoughts, if my finances will support me in the measure, of building a House, or Houses thereon for the purpose of letting.[4] In humble imitation of the wise man, I have set me down to count the cost; and among other heavy articles of expenditure, I find lime is not the smallest. Stone lime with us, owing to the length of (Land) transportation comes very high at that place. Shell lime, from its weakness, & the consequent quantity used, is far from being low—These considerations added to a report that this article may be had from your State by way of Ballast, upon terms much easier than either can be bought here, inclines me without making an apology, to give you the trouble of enquiring from those who might be disposed to enter into a contract therefor, & can ascertain the fact with precision.

1st—At what price by the Bushel, a quantity of slaked stone lime could be delivered at one of the Wharves at Alexandria (freight & every incidental charge included), or to a Lighter opposite to my own House.

2d—At what price burnt lime stone, but unslaked (if it be safe to bring such) could be delivered as above.

3d—At what price unburnt lime stone, could be delivered at the latter place.

In the last case, it might I should suppose, come as Ballast very low. In the second, it might also come as Ballast, and (tho' higher than the former, yet) comparatively, cheap, if the danger of Waters getting to it, and its slaking & heating in the Hold, would not be too great—In the first case, their would be no certainty of its goodness, because lime from the late judicious experiments of a Mr Higgens,[5] should be used as soon as it slaked; and would be still better, if it was so, immediately after burning; as air as well as water, according to his observations, weakens & injures it. Your information upon these points from those who might incline to Contract, and on whom dependance could be placed, would much oblige me—and the sooner I get it the better, as my determination is suspended.[6]

Our amiable young friend the Marquis de la Fayette could not be other wise than well pleased with his reception in America. Every testimony of respect, affection & gratitude has been shewn him, wherever he went; if his heart therefore has not been impressed with these expressions (which I am far from supposing) the political consequence which he will derive from them must bear them in his remembrance, & point to the advantages wch must flow.

You informed me that Mrs Knox had got another—but left me to guess, boy or girl. On the birth of either Mrs Washington & I sincerely congratulate you both; & offer our best wishes for you all—hoping the good health which Mrs Knox & the Children enjoyed at the time your letter was written, may be of long continuance.

The report of my coming to Boston was without foundation—I do not, at this time, know when, or whether ever, I may have it in my power to do this, altho' to see my compatriots in War, would be great gratification to my mind.[7] with every sentiment of esteem and friendship, I am, My dear Sir, Yr Most Obedt, & Affece Ser.

Go: Washington

ALS, MHi: Knox Papers; LB, DLC:GW.

1. GW wrote on 5 Dec. 1784.

2. By May 1785 GW was making a concerted effort to find a clerk. See particularly GW to Tench Tilghman, 2 June 1785. He finally employed William Shaw, who began work in late July and remained for a little longer than a year.

3. In this aside, GW takes one of his rare digs, in writing, at someone of his own circle in Virginia.

4. GW had owned since 1764 two lots in Alexandria. Between 1769 and 1771, builders had erected a small house for him on the lot at the corner of Cameron and Pitt streets. See *Diaries*, 2:182–83. He decided against putting up a building at this time on the other lot at Pitt and Prince streets (see GW to Knox, 28 Feb. 1785).

5. GW borrowed a copy of Benjamin Higgins's *Experiments and Observations in Cement* (London, 1780) from Samuel Vaughan in Philadelphia in 1783 and made extracts from it. See GW to Vaughan, 14 Jan. 1784.

6. Knox answered GW's queries about lime on 31 Jan., saying that he thought he could secure it cheap "upon an Estate which belonged to Mrs Knox's family." GW wrote on 28 Feb. that although he had decided against proceeding with his "projected building in Alexandria," he still would like some lime if it could be got cheap. Knox wrote on 24 Mar. that he hoped to get the lime for GW in June, and GW wrote on 18 June to remind him of this. Knox, however, was not able to get lime for his friend in 1785. On 22 Nov. he wrote GW that he was "mortified and chagrined beyond bearance" by his failure to get the lime, despite all his efforts to do so. See also GW to Knox, 11 Dec. 1785.

7. For reference to the reports that GW planned to travel to the Northeast in the fall of 1784, see note 2 in Knox to GW, 23 Nov. 1784.

From Benjamin Harrison

My Dear Sir   Rich[mon]d [Va.] Jany 6th 178[5]

It gives me great pleasure to inform that the assembly yesterday without a discenting voice complimented you with fifty shares in the potowmack company and one hundred in the James River company. of which I give you this early notice to stop your subscribing on your own account. As this compliment is intended by your country in commemoration of your assiduous ⟨cares⟩ to promote her interest I hope you will have no scruples in accepting the present and thereby gratifying them in their most earnest wishes[1]—I most sincerely tender you and your good lady the compliments of the season and many happy renewals of it and am Dr Sir your affet. Servt

Benj. Harrison

ALS, DLC:GW.

1. Gov. Patrick Henry sent GW on 5 Jan., in a letter now missing, official notification of the vote of the Virginia general assembly to vest in GW 50 shares in the Potomac Company and 100 shares in the James River Company. Harrison enclosed a copy of "An act for vesting in George Washington, esq. a certain interest in the companies established for opening and extending the navigation of Powtowmack and James rivers" (11 Hening 525–26). After receiving notice of the action of the assembly from Harrison and Henry, and from others as well, GW began writing to friends and former associates expressing in agonizing terms his doubts about the propriety of his accepting the shares and of his uncertainty in what manner he should reject the gift if he became certain that is what he should do. See, for examples, GW to William Grayson and to Benjamin Harrison, both 22 Jan.; to Lafayette, 15 Feb.; to Thomas Jefferson, 25 Feb.; to George William Fairfax and Patrick Henry, both 27 Feb.; and to Henry Knox, 28 Feb. 1785. On 25 April GW wrote William Grayson that his "present determination" was "to hold the shares . . . in trust for the use & benefit" of the public, and he confirmed this in more formal terms with further explanation in a letter to Edmund Randolph on 30 July. It was not, however, until 29 Oct. 1785, early in the fall session of the Virginia legislature, that GW made his formal response to Governor Henry. After offering his "fervent acknowledgements to the Legislature for their very kind sentiments and intentions," he asked that "their Act, so far as it has for its object my personal emolument, may not have its effect." Instead, the legislature would, he hoped, "turn the destination of the fund vested in me from my private emoluments, to objects of a public nature." The ensuing act of the legislature, which included a copy of GW's letter to the governor, provided: "That the said shares with the tolls and profits hereafter accruing therefrom, shall stand appropriated to such objects of a public nature, in such manner, and under such distributions, as the said George Washington, esq. by deed during his life, or by his last will and testament, shall direct and appoint" (12 Hening 42–44).

Letter not found: to Josiah Parker, 6 Jan. 1785. On 24 Feb. Josiah Parker wrote to GW: "I feel myself much honored with your very friendly polite letter of the 6th Ultimo."

To George Augustine Washington

Dear George, Mount Vernon 6th Jan. 1785.

As soon as I got your letter announcing your intention of spending the Winter at Charleston I wrote you by Post, under cover to Colo. Willm Washington—& sometime after by Mr Laurens—by whom also I forwarded the articles of clothing you desired might be sent to you—there can be little doubt (as the Post now goes regularly) of both getting to hand.[1] I need not therefore repeat any part of the contents of those Letters. I had the pleasure to hear yesterday—from Colo. Parker of Norfolk—that you had left the Island of Burmuda with encreased health. I flatter myself the mildness of a Southern Winter will perfectly restore you—in addition to this, a trip in the Packet to Philadelphia when you determine to return to Virginia, may be of Service—this, at a proper Season wd be, I conceive, the easiest, cheapest, and best method of getting back, as the Stage from Philadelphia comes to Alexandria twice a week regularly—You would by this means avoid the dreary roads, & bad accomodation, which is to be encountered I am told, all through North Carolina.

Since my last Colo. Basset has been here & brought up Fanny, who is now with us.[2] She has been unwell all the Fall, as most others in this Country have been—she is not yet recovered, but the change of air & exercise will soon give her health.

We have nothing new in this Quarter—our Assembly has been sitting since the middle, or last of October—but we have little information of what they have done—A plan is now on foot for improving & extending the Navigation of the River by private Subscription, & opening a good road between it and the nearest western waters—I hope it will succeed; as the Assemblies of this State & Maryld seem disposed to give it their Countenance.

If it is not too late in the Season to obtain them, I wish you would procure for me in So. Carolina a few of the acorns of the live Oak—and the Seeds of the Ever-green Magnolia—this latter is called in Millers Gardeners dictionary greater Magnolia—it rises according to his Acct to the height of Eighty feet or more—flowers early, & is a beautiful tree; there is another Spe-

cies of the Magnolia of which I wish to get the Seeds—it is
called the Umbrella tree. but unless these Seeds grow in cones,
& the Cones are now on the Trees, there is no chance of obtaining them at this Season; in which case prevail on Colo. Washington, or some acquaintance on whom you can depend, to
supply me next Seed time. The Acorns, & Seeds of every kind,
should be put in dry sand as soon as they are gathered: and the
box which contains them might (if no oppertunity offers to Alexandria) be sent either to Mr Newton of Norfolk, or to Colo.
Biddle of Philadelphia, with a request to forward it safely, & by
the first oppertunity, to me. If there are any other trees (not
natives with us) which would be ornamental in a grove or forest, and would stand our climate, I should be glad to procure
the Seeds of them in the way abovementioned.[3] All here unite
in best wishes for you; and Mrs Washington joins me in compliments to Colo. Washington and Lady; & other friends of our
Acquainte. With great esteem & regard I am—Dr George yr
Affecte friend

                                        Go: Washington

P.S. Your Father and family were well some little time ago—& I
have heard nothing to the contrary since. G.W.

ALS, owned (1990) by Mr. H. Bart Cox, Washington, D.C.

1. George Augustine Washington's letter of 9 Oct. 1784 announcing his intention to return to South Carolina from Bermuda has not been found, nor
has GW's letter of 8 Dec. sent by Henry Laurens. GW's letter sent under cover
to William Washington is dated 26 Nov. 1784. See also George Augustine
Washington to GW, 25 Feb. 1785.

2. Burwell Bassett and his daughter arrived on 24 December. Fanny
Bassett came to make her home at Mount Vernon, where she remained after
her marriage to George Augustine Washington on 15 Oct. 1785. Josiah
Parker (1751–1810), of Macclesfield, Isle of Wight County, who for the last
two years of the war had been commander of the Virginia militia south of the
James, was at this time naval officer and collector for the port of Portsmouth,
Virginia. Neither Parker's letter to GW nor GW's letter of this date to him has
been found. See Parker to GW, 24–28 Feb. 1785.

3. George Augustine Washington wrote GW on 25 Feb. from William
Washington's place, Sandy Hill, S.C., saying that it was not the time of the year
to collect acorns and seed but that he was sending two boxes of small plants,
one of magnolia (*Magnolia grandiflora*) and one of live oak (*Quercus virginiana*). These GW received on 21 May, along with other plants and seed, including those sent by William Blake (1739–1803), a South Carolina planter

(see *Diaries*, 4:143–44, and Blake to GW, 20 Mar. 1785). In December 1785 William Washington sent GW, among other things, a box of acorns from live oaks and water oaks in South Carolina (see William Washington to GW, 18 Dec.). The merchant Thomas Newton, Jr. (1742–1807), often handled business matters in Norfolk for GW.

From James Madison

Dear Sir   Richmond [Va.] Jany 9th 1785

I have now the pleasure of confirming the expectations hinted in my last concerning the result of the measures which have been favoured with your patronage.[1] The Bill for opening the Potowmac has passed precisely on the model transmitted from Maryland, the last conditional clause in the latter being rendered absolute by a clause in the former which engages this State for fifty shares in the Company.[2] Before the receipt of your despatches, some progress had been made in a bill for James River founded on different principle. After the receipt of them, the bill was exchanged for one on the Potowmac principle which has passed into a law with the same rapidity & unanimity which attended the other. The circumstancial variations with respect to James River are. 1. that the Sum to be aimed at in the first instance is 100,000 Dollars, only. 2. the shares are fixed at 200 Dollars and the number of public shares at 500. 3. the tolls are reduced to one half of those granted on Potowmac. 4. in case the falls at this place, where alone tolls are to be paid shall be first opened, the Company are permitted to receive them immediately and to continue to do so until the lapse of ten years, within which period all the works are to be compleated under the same penalties as are specified in the case of the other River. 5. a pre-emption is reserved to the public on all sales and transfers of shares. We endeavoured to preserve an equal eye in this business to the interests of the two Rivers, and to regulate the dates in the two bills in such a manner as to allow the members of each Company to participate in the transactions of the other. The excessive hurry however and the length of the bills may have produced inaccuracies in these as well as in other respects.[3]

The Assembly have likewise taken several kindred measures in the form of Resolutions, of which copies are herewith inclosed.[4] No. 3 was meant to carry into effect an idea suggested in your letter to the late Governour & explained in conversations with which several members were honoured during your visit to Richmond. It had passed before the recept of your report from Annapolis. I observed in my last that the subject of it ought to have made a part of your negociation with Maryland, and mentioned the circumstances which prevented it. I regret the omission the more, as the task devolved on Gentlemen to a notification of whose appointment and object, no answer I am informed has yet been vouchsafed to the Governour by Maryland, and whose commission it may be presumed is not altogether palatable to that State. Taking a more candid supposition, that the Silence of the latter is the effect of some miscarriage, the delay or the necessity of a separate representation to Pennsylvania, are inconveniences still to be regretted.[5] As this goes by Col: Grayson who means to pay his respects to Mount Vernon on his way to Trenton,[6] I forbear to anticipate farther, communications which he can more fully make, and beg leave to subscribe myself with all possible respect and regard Sir Your Obedient & most humble Servt

J. Madison Jr

ALS, ICU.

1. See Madison to GW, 1 January.

2. For the reception and passage of the Potomac River Company bill, see Madison to GW, 1 Jan. 1785, n.1.

3. The first James River Company bill was introduced in the Virginia house by Madison on 18 December. It passed the house on 24 Dec. and the senate on 31 December. It was at that point that the Virginia assembly received GW's communications from Annapolis with a copy of the Maryland Potomac River Company bill. The next day, 1 Jan., the speaker ordered Madison and Alexander Henderson to bring in a new James River Company bill. Madison's new bill received final approval on 5 Jan., the last day of the assembly's session. The text of "An act for clearing and improving the navigation of James river" is in 11 Hening 450–62.

4. See enclosures I, II, III.

5. Madison is referring to GW's letter to Gov. Benjamin Harrison of 10 Oct. 1784 and to GW's visit to Richmond in November. Resolution "No. 3" is printed below as Enclosure I (see Madison's explanation for its adoption in his letter to GW of 1 Jan.).

6. GW received Madison's letter and its enclosures on 17 January. See GW to John Fitzgerald and William Hartshorne, 18 Jan., and GW to William Grayson, 22 January.

Enclosure I
Resolution of the Virginia Assembly

[Richmond] December the 28th 1784

Resolved that the Commissioners or any two of them appointed on the 28th day of June last to concert with Commissioners on the part of Maryland regulations touching the navigation and jurisdiction of the Potowmack,[1] be further authorized to unite with the said Commissioners in representing to the State of Pensylvania that it is in contemplation of the said two states to promote the clearing and extending the navigation of Potowmack from tide Water upwards as far as the same may be found practicable: to open a convenient road from the head of such navigation to the Waters running into the Ohio, and to render these Waters navigable as far as may be necessary and proper: that the said Works will require great expence, which may not be repaid unless a free use be secured to the said States and their Citizens of the Waters of the Ohio and its branches as far as the same lie withing the limits of Pensylvania: that as essential advantages will accrue from such works to a considerable portion of the said State it is thought reasonable that the Legislature thereof should by some previous act engage that for the encouragement of the said Works, all articles of produce or Merchandize which may be conveyed to or from either of the said two States through either of the said Rivers within the limits of Pensylvania to or from any place without the said limits shall pass throughout free from all duties or tolls whatsoever, other than such tolls as may be established and be necessary for reimbursing expences incurred by the said State or its Citizens in clearing, or for defraying the expence of preserving the navigation of the said Rivers: and that no articles imported into the State of Pensylvania through the Channel or Channels or any part thereof to be opened as aforesaid, and vended or used within the said State shall be subject to any duties or imposts, other than such articles would be subject to, if imported into the said State through any other Channel whatsoever; and it is further Resolved that in case a joint representation in behalf of this State and of Maryland shall be rendered by circumstances unattainable, the said Commissioners or any two of them may of themselves make such representations on the subject to the State of Pensylvania as may in such event become proper, and that in either event they report their proceedings to the next General Assembly.

Resolved that a Copy of the above resolutions be transmitted forthwith by the Executive to the State of Maryland.

D, MnHi; printed, *House of Delegates Journal, 1781–1785*. See the source line in Enclosure I in George Washington and Horatio Gates to the Virginia Legislature, 28 December. This document and the two documents printed below as enclosures II and III are copies made by the same clerk. They are all certified by John Beckley, clerk of the Virginia house of delegates. This particular document also has the notation: "1784 December the 30th. Agreed to by the Senate Will: Drew C[lerk] S[enate]."

1. On 28 June 1784 the Virginia house adopted the following resolution: "Whereas, great inconveniences are found to result from the want of some concerted regulations between this State and the State of Maryland, touching the jurisdiction and navigation of the river Potomac; *Resolved*, That George Mason, Edmund Randolph, James Madison, jun. and Alexander Henderson, Esquires, be appointed commissioners; and that they, or any three of them, do meet such commissioners as may be appointed on the part of Maryland; and, in concert with them, frame such liberal and equitable regulations concerning the said river, as may be mutually advatangeous to the two States; and that they make report thereof, to the General Assembly.

"*Resolved*, That the Executive be requested to notify the above appointment with the object of it, to the State of Maryland and desire its concurrence in the proposition" (*House of Delegates Journal, 1781–1785*). See also Madison to GW, 1 Jan. 1785, n.3, and Enclosure III in George Washington and Horatio Gates to the Virginia Legislature, 28 Dec. 1784.

Enclosure II
Resolution of the Virginia Assembly

[Richmond] The 1st of January 1785

Resolved that Thomas Massey Esqr.,[1] or in case of his death or failing to act through other cause, such other person as shall be appointed by the Executive in his stead, be authorized in conjunction with the person appointed or to be appointed on the part of Maryland, to open and keep in repair a convenient Road from such part of the Waters of the Potowmack, to such part of the River Cheat or of the River Monongalia, as on examination they shall Judge most eligible; and that the sum of three thousand three hundred thirty three and one third Dollars, arising from the Taxes of the year 1784, out of the Money subject to the votes of the General Assembly, be paid by the

Treasurer, on the joint Order of the Persons to be appointed as aforesaid, to be by them applied together with a like sum voted by the State of Maryland to the purpose aforesaid.

Resolved that the Governor be desired to write to the State of Pensylvania, requesting permission to lay out and improve a Road through such part of the said States, as may be necessary in the best and most proper direction from Fort Cumberland to the navigable part of the River Yohogania.[2]

D, MnHi; printed, *House of Delegates Journal, 1781–1785*. See the source line in Enclosure I, above. William Drew, clerk of the senate, attests that this resolution was agreed to by the Virginia senate on 5 January. Madison was the author of the resolution.

1. Thomas Massie (Massey; 1748–1834) was aide-de-camp to Thomas Nelson during the Revolution.

2. See the resolution of the Maryland legislature to the same effect, printed above as Enclosure III in George Washington and Horatio Gates to the Virginia Legislature, 28 Dec. 1784. See also Madison's comments in his letter of 1 Jan. and the source note and note 4 of that document.

Enclosure III
Resolution of the Virginia Assembly

[Richmond] 1st of January 1785

Resolved that the Executive be authorized to appoint three Persons, who or any two of whom shall make an accurate examination and survey of James River from Lynch's Ferry in Campbell County upwards, of the most convenient course for a Road from the highest navigable part of the said River to the nearest navigable part of the Waters running into the Ohio, and of the said Waters running into the Ohio: that they report to the next General Assembly a full Account of such examination and survey, with an estimate of the expence necessary for opening and improving the navigation of the said Waters of James River, and of the Western Waters and of clearing the said Road; that they be authorized to call on the Lieutenant of the County of Green Brier for a Guard of Militia not exceeding fifty Men in case they shall Judge such Guard to be necessary, which the said Lieutenant is hereby ordered to furnish, and which shall be paid by the Treasurer on Order of the Executive out of the Revenue for the year one thousand seven hundred and eighty four subject to be appropriated by votes of the General Assembly; that the Persons so appointed shall be furnished out of the said Fund with such sum, not exceeding two hundred pounds, as the Executive may Judge necessary: and shall each of them be allowed for his services the sum of twenty shillings for each day he shall be employed therein.[1]

Resolved, that the Executive be further authorized to appoint three other Commissioners who, or any two of whom shall carefully examine and fix on the most convenient course for a Canal from the Waters of Elizabeth River in this State, to those passing through the State of North Carolina, and report their proceedings herein with an Estimate of the expence necessary for opening such Canal to the next General Assembly. And in case they shall find that the best course for such Canal will require the concurrence of the State of North Carolina in the opening thereof, they are further authorized and instructed to signify the same to the said State and to concert with any Person or Persons who may be appointed on the part thereof, the most convenient and equitable plan for the execution of such Work, and to report the result to the next General Assembly. The said Commissioners shall be entitled to the same allowance and be paid in the same manner as those to be appointed under the preceeding Resolution.[2]

Resolved that the same allowance, to be paid in the same manner, be made to Thomas Massey for the service, which he is appointed to perform in conjunction with a Commissioner appointed or to be appointed by the State of Maryland.[3]

D, MnHi; printed, *House of Delegates Journal, 1781–1785*. See source line in Enclosure I, above. The senate agreed to the resolution on 5 January. For references to the genesis of these resolutions, see the source note in James Madison to GW, 1 January.

1. For the passage of the James River Company bill, see Madison to GW, 9 Jan., n.3.

2. See "An act for cutting a navigable canal from the waters of Elizabeth river to the waters of North river" (11 Hening 332–34), enacted in the October 1783 session.

3. See Enclosure II.

To Charles Carroll

Sir,   [Mount Vernon] 10th Jany 1785.

Immediately after my return from Annapolis, I wrote to some Gentlemen of my acquaintance in the Assembly of this State, suggesting the expediency of a conference between Delegates of their Body & yours, on the extension of the inland navigation of the river Potomac, & its communication with the Western waters.[1] When I receive an answer, I will communicate the contents of it to you. I am &c.

G: Washington

P.S. Are you likely Sir, to ascertain soon, to whom I am to pay the balance which is due for the land I bought of the deceas'd Mr Clifton under the decree of our high Court of Chancery?[2]

LB, DLC:GW. GW's clerk dated the letter-book copy of this letter 10 Jan. 1785, but its contents indicate that GW wrote it between 3 and 19 Dec. 1784: i.e., between the time he wrote his letter to James Madison on 3 Dec., the day after returning from Annapolis, in which he called for a meeting between Maryland and Virginia delegates on Potomac matters, and the time that he got notice from Lt. Gov. Beverley Randolph, on 19 Dec., that he was to be one of the Virginia commissioners to meet with members of the Maryland legislature. He could not have written it in January 1785.

1. See GW to Madison, 3 Dec. 1784.

2. When GW in 1760 bought from William Clifton the neck of land containing 1,806 acres across Little Hunting Creek at Mount Vernon, Charles Carroll (1702–1782) of Annapolis, the father of Charles Carroll of Carrollton, was one among several prominent Marylanders who held a mortgage on Clifton's Neck dating back to 1747. The elder Charles Carroll refused to accept the settlement that GW reached with the other mortgage holders after he had bought the tract at public sale in May 1760, and it was not until 1791 that the younger Charles Carroll and his sister Mary Carroll Digges gave GW clear title to the land. For a full summary of the negotiations in GW's purchase of Clifton's Neck, see note 1 in GW to Benjamin Waller, 2 April 1760.

From William Gordon

My dear Sir   Jamaica Plain [Mass.] Jany 10. 1785

In arranging the intelligence obtained from the inspection of your papers, I found that an extract from the private letters Vol. 1st dated Oct. 22. 1779, which alluded to one of the most important events of the late war, was not so complete as I wish. It relates to the capture of Fort Washington, which I apprehend ought now to be placed in its true light, as the public cannot suffer from its being done. The extract I have made, begins— When I came to Fort Lee, & found no measures towards an evacuation in *consequence of the order aforementioned*.[1] I have omitted taking *the order aforementioned*, which is material. If it will not trespass too much upon your Excellency's time, Shall reckon it a great favour to have that order transmitted with the place from whence, & the date when given.[2] With renewed & affectionate respects to Self & Family I remain with great esteem Your Excellency's sincere Friend & very humble Servant

William Gordon

ALS, DLC:GW.

1. William Gordon spent several weeks at Mount Vernon in early summer going through GW's Revolutionary War papers in preparation of his history of the Revolution. The letter from GW to Joseph Reed to which Gordon is referring is the letter of 22 Aug. 1779 and not the one dated 22 Oct. 1779. In that letter of 22 Aug., which is printed in Fitzpatrick, *Writings of Washington*, 16:150–54, GW attempts to explain, and to defend, the decisions he made in the days leading up to the surrender of Fort Washington on the Hudson in November 1776 and to the evacuation of Fort Lee across the river a few days later. See also his response to Gordon, 8 Mar. 1785.

2. In his letter to Reed of 22 Aug. 1779, GW refers to his order to Gen. Nathanael Greene of 8 Nov. 1776 in these terms: " . . . a non-compliance in General Greene with an order sent him from White-plains before I marched for the Western-side of Hudsons River to withdraw the Artillery Stores, &ca from the Fort; allowing him however some latitude for the exercise of his own Judgment as he was upon the spot & could decide better from appearances and circumstances than I, the propriety of a total evacuation." GW enclosed a copy of his orders to Greene in his letter to Gordon of 8 Mar. 1785.

From Alexander Henderson

Dear Sir   Dumfries [Va.] 11th Janry 1785

Your favour of the 20th came duly to hand, neither Ryan nor Mr Rumsey were in Richmond while I was there, Ryan was sick at Petersburgh.

The acts for opening the Navigation of Patowmack and James river passed all the forms fortunately the day before the hard weather obliged the assembly to separate—Resolutions similar to those in Maryland have also passed both Houses—of these Copies will be brought up by Mr Grayson,[1] I do myself the pleasure to inclose a Copy of one other Act passed during the present Session.[2] I have the honor to be with the greatest Esteem Sir Your obedt Sert

Alexr Henderson

You have inclosed Ryans Note[3]—and some of the proceedings of the Assembly.

ALS, DLC:GW.

1. For the passage of the Potomac River Company act and the adoption of ancillary resolutions, see James Madison to GW, 9 Jan., and enclosures. GW received Madison's letter and enclosures and William Grayson's missing letter with its enclosures on 17 Jan. (see GW to John Fitzgerald and William Hartshorne, 18 Jan.).

2. On 24 Dec. 1784 the Virginia house of delegates voted 45 to 38 to postpone further consideration of a bill for "establishing a provision for the teachers of the christian religion" until "the fourth Thursday in November next." The delegates then decided: "That the engrossed bill . . . together with the names of the ayes and noes . . . be published in hand-bills, and twelve copies thereof delivered to each member of the General Assembly, to be distributed in their respective counties; and that the people thereof be requested to signify their opinion respecting the adoption of such a bill, to the next session of Assembly" (*House of Delegates Journal, 1781–1785*). Henderson voted against deferral. The enclosed broadside of the bill and a broadside of reports on public accounts as printed in the *House of Delgates Journal* for 28 and 29 Dec. are in DLC:GW.

3. See note 1 in GW to Henderson, 20 Dec. 1784.

Letter not found: from Battaile Muse, 14 Jan. 1785. On 5 Feb. GW wrote to Muse: "I have lately received two letters from you, one of the 14th & the other of the 25th of last month."

From David Humphreys

My dear General   Paris Janry 15th 1785
There is no great alteration in the complexion of the political world since I had the honour of addressing you last, except that there appears to be more probability that the contest between the Emperor & the Dutch will be accomodated without bloodshed, than there did at that period—preparations for war are however continued, & the Count de Maillebois—Leiut. Gen. in the Armies of France, now appointed Commander in Chief of the Dutch forces, is to depart this week to assume his new command.

As to the state of our own politicks I can only say (and that for your ear alone) that the Treaties in contemplation which extend to all the commercial powers of Europe, tho' progressive, still they go slowly on; insomuch that I have had occasion to remark that there is no Sovereign in Europe but the King of Prussia who seems to do his business himself or even to know that it is done at all.

I have expressed in several of my letters to you, my dear General, my ardent desire to see a good history of the Revolution, or at least of those scenes in which you have been principally concerned—I have suggested your undertaking it yourself; and I cannot help repeating, that to travel over again those feilds of activity at leisure in your study would be a rational amusement, or if the task should be too labourious, it might be called a noble & truly philosophic employment.

Such a work, by having truth, instruction & public utility for its objects, would make the evening of your days more precious as well as more illustrious in the eyes of future ages, than they have appeared in the midst of glory & conquest in their meridian splendor. If however you should decline the task: & if ever I shall have leisure & opportunity, I shall be strongly tempted to enter on it more with the design of rescuing the materials from improper hands or from oblivion, than from an idea of being able to execute it in the manner it ought to be done[1]—With perfect esteem & friendship I have the honor to be your Exys most Obedt hble Servt

D. Humphreys

LS, DLC:GW.
1. Humphreys seems to have first broached the subject of GW's autobiography, or biography, in his letter to GW of 15 July 1784. For GW's enthusiastic response to the suggestion that Humphreys himself should undertake the project, see GW to Humphreys, 25 July.

To John Filson

Sir,   Mt Vernon 16th Jan: 1785.
I have been favored with two letters from you: that which was first written came last to hand, & neither of them long since.[1] Your history & map of Kentucke I have not yet seen. For the honor you have done me in the dedication of them, you will please to accept my acknowledgments; & for the favourable sentiments you have been so polite as to express for me in both your letters, you have my thanks.

It has long been my wish to see an extensive & accurate map of the Western Territory set on foot, & amply encouraged: but I would have this work founded upon actual surveys and careful observations—any thing short of these is, in my opinion, not only defective & of little use, but serve as often to mislead as to direct the examiner. My sentiments upon this subject are well known to many members of Congress, & to the Legislature of the State in which I have the honor to live: but what steps will be taken by both, or either, to accomplish this useful undertaking, is not for me to say.[2]

Altho' I possess a pretty general knowledge of the Ohio & its waters between Fort Pitt & the Gt Kanhawa, & have some parts of that Country laid down from actual surveys; yet they are not so connected, nor founded with such precision as to incline me to suffer my name to be given as the author of them, or any information in a Map or topographical description of the Country, that would not stand the test of future examination.

That the river Potomac communicates by short portages (which may be improved to great advantage) with the Yohoghaney & Cheat rivers, (branches of the Monongahela) for the countries East & West of the Apalachian mountains, as James river also does with the waters of the Great Kanhawa, none can deny: & that these will be the channels thro' which the trade of the Western Country will principally come, I have no more doubt of *myself*, than the States of Virga & Maryland had, when within these few days, they passed Laws for the purpose of extending & improving the navigation of those rivers, & opening roads of communication between them & the western waters.

Whenever business or inclination may bring you to this part of the country, it would give me pleasure to see you. I am Sir &c.

G: Washington

LB, DLC:GW.

1. Filson wrote GW on 30 Nov. and 4 Dec. 1784. See note 1 in the letter of 4 December.

2. GW wrote the governor of Virginia, Benjamin Harrison, on 10 Oct. 1784 about the state's making surveys in the West; on 3 Nov. 1784 he wrote Jacob Read, delegate to Congress from South Carolina, about the need for Congress to have such surveys made.

From Richard Henry Lee

Dear Sir, New York Jany 16. 1785

I had the honor of writing to you last by the post that left Trenton just before I quitted that place, and I should not so soon have troubled you again, if it were not to furnish you with the very excellent pamphlet that accompanies this letter—Doctor Price has lately sent over a few of those pamphlets to the President of Congress and left the disposal of them to him—I am very sure that I shall gratify the Doctors feelings as well as my own, when I request your acceptance of one of them[1]—We have no news here, except the account brought by the packet from England just arrived, and which is current in Town—That the war between the Emperor & Holland has certainly commenced[.] A small engagement, near Lillo upon the Scheldt, has taken place, in which a Dutch Regiment is said to have lost 20 or 30 Men—Prussia is said to have taken part with Holland, & the Empress of Russia with the Emperor—It is probable that this quarrel, if it proceeds, will embroil the greatest part of Europe—I hope Great Britain will find herself compelled to engage. My best respects attend your Lady. I am dear Sir, with the truest esteem & regard sincerely yours

Richard Henry Lee

ALS, DLC:GW.

1. GW received at least one other copy, and perhaps two, of Richard Price's pamphlet *Observations on the Importance of the American Revolution, and the Means of Making It a Benefit to the World*, published in London in 1784. Two copies from GW's library, one unbound, the other bound and with GW's autograph, are in the Boston Athenæum. On 5 Feb. 1785 GW thanks Benjamin Vaughan for sending him from London on 31 Oct. 1784 a copy of the Price tract, which he has "seen & read with much pleasure," and asks Vaughan to extend his thanks to Price for his "honorable mention" of himself. Either this copy from Vaughan or a third copy was the personal gift of Price, who sent with it these words of presentation: "To *George Washington* Esq. lately Commander in chief of the American Armies, but now retired to enjoy the happiness of private life after delivering his country and establishing a Revolution which may prove a blessing to the world, this pamphlet is presented by the Author as a Small testimony of the highest respect.

"While employ'd in writing this pamphlet the author has been animated more than he can well express by Genl Washington's excellent circular letter to the united States" (NjP).

GW's response, which his clerk placed in the letter book at the end of the correspondence dated in November 1785, was: "G: Washington presents his most respectful compliments to Dr Price. With much thankfulness he has received, & with the highest gratification he has read the Doctrs excellent observations on the importance of the American Revolution—& the means of making it a benefit to the world. Most devoutly is it to be wished that reasoning so sound should take deep root in the minds of the Revolutionists—But there is cause to apprehend that the inconveniences resulting from ill-founded jealousies & local politics must be *felt*, 'ere a more liberal system of fœderal Government is adopted. The latter I am persuaded *will happen*; but its progress may be slow—unless, as the Revolution itself was, it should be precipitated by the all grasping hand of [   ] or the illiberal & mistaken policy of other Nations.

"For the honorable notice of me in your address, I pray you to receive my warmest acknowledgments & the assurances of the sincere esteem & respect which I entertain for you" (LB, DLC:GW).

To Samuel Chase

Dear Sir,   Mt Vernon 17th Jan: 1785.

The irregularity of the post, occasioned by the frost, prevented my hearing with *certainty* what the Assembly of this State had done with the Potomac Bill until yesterday. I have now the pleasure to inform you that they have adopted the one which passed your Legislature, & come to similar resolutions respecting the road of communication with the river Cheat, & the application to the State of Pennsylvania for another to Yohioghaney—They have also passed a similar act for improving & extending the navigation of James river.[1]

As you expressed a desire to know what the Assembly of this State had done, or were about to do respecting an establishment for the teachers of religion[2]—I do myself the honor to enclose you a copy of their proceedings in that matter, & am &c.

                                        G: Washington

LB, DLC:GW.
    1. GW's letter to John Fitzgerald and William Hartshorne of 18 Jan. and his letter to William Grayson of 22 Jan. indicate that it was not until this day, 17 Jan., that he received the Potomac River Company act and the various resolutions of the Virginia assembly (see also James Madison to GW, 9 Jan., and Alexander Henderson to GW, 11 Jan.).
    2. See Alexander Henderson to GW, 11 Jan., n.1.

To Thomas Johnson

Dear Sir, Mount Vernon 17th Jan: 1785

Yesterday, & not before, I received authentic information, that the Assembly of this State had passed a similar Act & resolutions, with those of your Legislature, and have fixed upon the 8th of Feby to open Books for the purpose of receiving subscriptions in the City of Richmond & Towns of Alexandria & Winchester: which Books are to be kept open until the 10th day of May following.[1] They have granted equal sums towards the navigation & roads, with your Assembly.

I have pleasure in giving you this information—nothing remains now but to act with dispatch & vigor.

I presume official notice of the passing of this act, & attendant resolutions, will be made by the Executive of this State to your Governor; but lest thro' the hurry of business it may be delayed, I will take care that he shall have advice of it, as soon as copies can be taken; that if promulgation is necessary, & he thinks proper to act upon private information, it may not be wanted.

Our Assembly have passed a similar Law for the purpose of opening & improving the navigation of James river and a communication between it, and the nearest Western waters. With great esteem & regard I have the honor to be &c.

G: Washington

LB, DLC:GW.
1. See GW to Samuel Chase, this date, n.1.

To John Fitzgerald and William Hartshorne

Gentln Mount Vernon 18th Jany 1785.

At my return from Alexandria yesterday afternoon, I found the letters & papers herewith enclosed. I send the whole, as well private as public—the former for your satisfaction—the latter for you to act upon.[1]

As these, with the Maryland Act & resolutions which I left in the hands of Mr Lee for the purpose of communicating them to the Gentn in town (well wishers to the inland navigation of the river &c.) contain all the information on the subject, I could give, I beg leave to refer you to them.[2]

All the papers, except the Virginia Act, which are necessary for Mr Richards to strike printed copies from, I should be glad to have returned to me in the course of two or three days, as I shall have letters to write, & other matters to do, in consequence thereof.[3] It should be intimated to the printer that the Bill is an original paper, & spared indulgently from the Clerks office: great care therefore should be taken that no scratches or blots are suffered to be made thereon. The number of copies to be struck will depend upon you Gentlemn—the time for promulgation, & obtaining subscriptions is short—the former therefore should be as extensive & diffusive as the nature of the case will admit—With what materials the managers at the City of Richmond & town of Winchester are to commence their operations, does not seem very clear; it rests with you therefore, I conceive, to put things in motion, at least by opening a correspondence with the Gentlemen at these places, fixing a plan.

It appears to me also, that a notification of the passing of this Act & consequent resolutions should go immediately to the Executive of Maryland, from some quarter; otherwise that State may take umbrage, & think advantage on the score of subscriptions, is meant to be taken of her Citizens. From our Governor, such intimation *ought* in my opinion, to be given; but it does not appear by anything before us, that it either has been, or is intended to be done. Therefore as the Acts & resolutions of both Assemblies are now with you, if you will cause a comparative view to be taken of them, & note the alterations, that I may write with exactitude. I will communicate the matter to Govr Paca, lest there should be neglect or delay on the part of our Executive—or if you will do it, it may answer the same purpose.[4]

How far Mr Maddison might have intended the paper No. 3 for the public eye, I know not; I would have no copies therefore taken of it, as communication of its content might come better from those who are to act under it.[5] I have the honor to be, Gentn &c.

G: Washington

P.S. If a printed copy of the Virginia Act could be soon obtained, I would enclose one of them to the Governor of Maryland, & a copy of the correspondent resolutions of this State to that of Maryland; which would be the fullest & best information he could receive unofficially.

LB, DLC:GW.

1. When Bartholomew Dandridge, Jr., entered this letter in the letter book at some time after 1790 while he was one of GW's secretaries, he added the following notation below the letter, presumably taking it from what GW had written on the draft or original retained copy that Dandridge had before him: "Schedule of Papers sent to Jno. Fitzgerald & Wm Hartshorn Esqrs. 18th Jany 1785. Virginia Act. Colo. Graysons letter enclosing the James river Rate of Tolls. The cover from Mr Beckley Clerk of the H. D. containing his request.

"Mr Madisons letter enclosg No. 1—Similar resolutions respectg roads &c.—No. 2 Surveying James river, & Country between that & the western waters. No. 3 Respecting the Jurisdiction &c. of Potomac." Neither William Grayson's nor John Beckley's letter has been found, but see GW to Grayson, 22 Jan., and GW to Beckley, 5 February. See also James Madison to GW, 9 Jan., and its enclosures, and Fitzgerald and Hartshorne to GW, 21 January.

2. See George Washington and Horatio Gates to the Virginia Legislature, 28 Dec. 1784, and its enclosures.

3. George Richard was the publisher of the *Virginia Journal and Alexandria Advertiser*.

4. See GW's letter to Gov. William Paca, 31 January.

5. For James Madison's "paper No. 3," see Enclosure I, in Madison to GW, 9 January.

From Hanna Moore

Sir   Baltimore [Md.] January 20th 1785

An ardent desire for the Administration of the strictest Right in every Minutia which may fall under any inspection, added to that Respect due the preserver of a Country, influences me notwithstanding my repugnance to intrude, in advising you: That since my Mr Francis Moore Merchant at Baltimore exhibiting of a Testament made by Mrs Savage to you unattested, it has been transmitted to the Executors in Ireland, authenticated there, and by them with a Letter of Attorney remitted to him (now deceased) tho' not yet come to my hands;[1] from good information whereof, and too Conscious of the Immorality, Capacity and designs of Men, an Apprehension arrises that it probably might have been handed you by the bearer of it from Ireland named William Moore, or others, who may have thought proper to personate my deceased Husband—therefore should much esteem on Account of my friends in Ireland, and least they should presume my Husband or myself ne-

glectfull of their Interest, and that I may enter into further Enquiry, you wou'd by a single Line, or two, intimate, whether you
have received or heard of it; As I expect as soon as the Executors in Ireland are informed of my Husbands Decease, and my
Continuation they will send me Letters to act fully—Please to
direct under Cover to Zachariah Allen Esqre Baltimore[2]—I
have the Honor to be Your Excellency's Humble and Obedient
servant

Hanna Moore

ALS, DLC:GW.

1. GW became involved in Margaret Savage's affairs after the death of her
first husband, the Rev. Charles Green, in 1765, as a security for the deed of
trust made to Mrs. Green by her husband. When in 1767 Mrs. Green married
Dr. William Savage of Dumfries, Va., and in the next year went with him to
Ireland, GW and Bryan Fairfax found themselves faced with what proved to
be the impossible task of forcing Dr. Savage to pay his wife the £100 per annum which a trust obligated him to pay. For the details of GW's long and painful involvement in the Savage affair, see the note in Henry Lee and Daniel
Payne to GW, 24 April 1767. Margaret Savage died in 1781 and William Savage died shortly thereafter, whereupon the story of the interminable Savage
affair becomes that of suits by Mrs. Savage's heirs against the estate of Dr. Savage (see note 1 in John Dixon to GW, 5 Mar. 1789).

2. On 25 Sept. 1783 Hanna Moore's husband, Francis Moore, wrote GW
from Baltimore that he had in hand Margaret Savage's will which he wished
to turn over to GW. GW replied on 10 Oct. 1783, suggesting that Moore keep
the will until Moore could "deliver it to Mrs Washington as she passes through
Baltimore on her way to Virginia." In December 1783 when GW stopped in
Baltimore on his way to Mount Vernon, Moore gave him the will to send to
the executors in England but a few minutes later reclaimed it. GW wrote Mrs.
Moore on 28 Feb. 1785 that since then he had heard nothing further. See also
GW to Sarah Bomford, 15 Mar. 1785.

From Samuel Brenton

Sir   Newport [R.I.] the 21. January 1785
    I am Encouraged to address your Excellency from a Confi-
dence of your willingness to Overlook defects and from your
well known disposition to promote the happyness of others.
    You have Inclosd a Petition from the master wardens and
some of the members of the St Johns lodge of this City of which
I had the Honor of being master at the breaking out of the late
warr. the reasons assignd therein I hope will be found of Sufficient weight with your Excellency to grant us the prayer of the

petition which you will please to Observe is for the Revival of the Lodge St Johns or for putting it on Such a footing as that the Charter may Retain its Original powers—as by Virtue of that Charter the lodge St Johns purchasd a Real Estate for the accomodateing themselves with a building to be held by the master & wardens of Sd Lodge in Perpetuity. So that whether a new Constituted Lodge Can Claim the priviledge of the Charter Granted to the lodge St Johns in our Idea is doubt-full—Your Excellencys Knowledge in these matters will Set us right.[1] I have the Honor, to be with great Respect your Excellencys most Obedt Hble Servt

Samel Brenton

ALS, DLC:GW. GW docketed the letter "recd 30th April 1785."

1. The enclosed petition has not been found. If GW responded to this letter, he did not retain a copy of what he wrote. During GW's New England tour as president, it was the master, warden, and brethren of King David's Lodge, not St. John's Lodge, who presented an address at the synagogue in Newport in August 1790.

From John Fitzgerald and William Hartshorne

Sir   Alexandria [Va.] Jany 21st 1785

We are duly honor'd with your letter of 18th Inst. with the Virginia Bill & other enclosures the Bill we have put into the Printer's hands & order'd him to strike one Hundred Copies which we expect will be compleated by monday next at which time we intend to forward Copies to the Managers at Richmond & Winchester—Mr Richards has promis'd to be very carefull of the Original.

We now return you all the other papers & would wish to know how many of the printed Copies we shall send to you as we are fully of opinion that the notification to the executive of Maryland will come with greater propriety from you than us.

We have taken a full comparative view of the Bills pass'd in each State, & find no difference except what we have noted on the other side—some of which we are induced to believe have happen'd thro' mistake & the only one that appears essential is that respecting the width of Ground in which we are of opinion that the Maryland resolution is the most eligible.[1]

We have given the Bill *only* to the Printer, should you be of opinion that any of the resolutions sent by Mr Maddeson &

number'd 1. 2 & 3 should be printed you will please return such to us & they shall be added.

We have full confidence that through the course of this Business you will be pleased to assist us with your kind advice in any matters which may occur to you. We have the honor to be with the highest respect & Esteem Sir your mo. Obedt Servants

John Fitzgerald
Wm Hartshorne

LS, DLC:GW.

John Fitzgerald and William Hartshorne, merchants in Alexandria, were named by the Potomac River Company act to open the books of the company "for receiving and entering subscriptions" in Alexandria (11 Hening 510–25).

1. At the end of the letter, there is the following notation: "Differences between the Maryland & Virginia Bills.

"An Empty Boat not having come down the River is to pay at her going up by the Virga Act 2/6 2/6 & 5/ . This in the Maryland Act is left blank.

"Coin'd Silver in the Maryland Act valued @ 5/ 1¼ in the Virga @ 5/ 1¾ ℔ Penny weight.

"By the Maryland Law the Width of Ground to be condemn'd is not to exceed 200 feet—by the Virga Act 140."

To Matthew Campbell

Sir,   [Mount Vernon] 22d Jany 1785.

Understanding that Mr Wilson of Alexandria was empower'd to sell the plaister of Paris which you had sent to that place—I informed him by Mr L. W—— of the mistake under which a vessel Load of it had been landed at my wharf—but that, as it was there, I was willing to pay for it at the same rate as that which was in Alexandria should sell—To this, some considerable time after (if my memory serves) he answered, that the matter must be settled with you.[1]

It now remains for me sir, to bring you acquainted with the exact state of this matter, & on which you may depend—On my return from Richmond in Novr last, Mr Graham informed me that you had received (I think he said) about 50 tons of this stone, & asked if I wanted any of it. I answered that I might take a litt[l]e of it, at any rate, merely for experiment as a manure; but that taking a large quantity, would depend altogether upon the price of it, of which he was to know the lowest, & give me an account. Under this idea, & waiting for this information, I left no direction concerning this matter when I accompanied the Marquis de la Fayette to Annapolis; during my absence there, the plaister arrived: those about me not knowing what to do in this matter, & supposing, I presume, that I had ordered it, suffered it to be landed: which I most assuredly would not have done, had I been at home, at any thing like the price mentioned in Mr Grahams letter.[2]

The plaister is yet on my wharf in the order it was first landed, except that I had the powdered part of it, the virtue of which (if it ever possessed any as a manure) I presume must have been nearly exhausted, put into casks. I am yet willing to take it at whatever price that which is in Alexandria shall sell; or at any reasonable price to be agreed upon between ourselves, or by others on our behalf. More I think under the circumstances I have related, no person will think I ought to pay— Twelve Dollars per ton, I never can consent to give; nor do I think you would desire it, when I inform you that before the war, I got all I wanted from Fitzhughs in Maryland for digging out of the Bank; and that it never was, nor can be considered as of much more value than lime-stone—being of the nature of it.[3] I am &c.

G: Washington

LB, DLC:GW.

Matthew Campbell may be the son of Matthew Campbell (d. 1782), agent for the partnership of Carlyle & Adam of Alexandria and subsequently a partner in Robert Adam & Co., with both of which GW had extensive business dealings before the war.

1. William Wilson and his brother James arrived in Alexandria during the Revolution and at this time were partners there in a mercantile business based in Glasgow, Scotland. No correspondence between GW and the Wilsons has been found; the exchange between them regarding the plaster of paris presumably was conducted orally through Lund Washington ("Mr L. W——").

2. Graham is probably Richard Graham, a merchant in Dumfries, Virginia. GW went to Annapolis with Lafayette at the end of November. Graham's letter, which GW forwarded to Campbell on 1 Mar., has not been found. See GW to Campbell, 1 Mar. 1785.

3. GW is probably referring to William Fitzhugh (1721–1798) of Maryland.

To William Grayson

Dear Sir,   Mount Vernon 22d Jany 1785
   Your letter, with the Books, Potomac bill & other papers, did
not reach this until past eleven o'Clock on monday forenoon; at
which hour having set off for Alexandria—I did not receive the
dispatches until my return in the evening. The next morning I
forwarded the Bill to Messrs Fitzgerald & Hartshorn to act
upon, & to get a number of copies struck for promulgation, &
the benefit of those who might wish to become subscribers. For
the trouble you have had with the Books & for your care of the
letters & papers which accompanied them, you will please to accept my thanks.[1]
   It would have given me much satisfaction if, instead of pursuing the rout thro' Frederick, you had resolved to have taken
this road to the seat of Congress: besides the pleasure of seeing
you, I wished to have had some conversation with you on the
subject of the late generosity of the Assembly towards me; for I
will freely confess to you My dear sir, that no circumstance has
happened to me since I quited the walks of public life that has
given me more embarrassment, than the act vesting me with
150 shares in the tolls of each of the rivers Potomac & James.
On the one hand I consider this instance of the regard & attention of my native State as more than a mere compliment: this
evidence of her good opinion & wishes to serve me is *unequivocal & substantial*—it has impressed me with sentiments of the
deepest gratitude; & I should be hurt, if I could think that my
non-acceptance of her favors would be considered as an ostentatious display of public virtue, and disinterestedness—or disrespectful to the Country to slight her favors. On the other
hand it is my wish that my mind, and the actions resulting from
it, may be as free as Air—Not content therefore with the consciousness of having, in all this navigation business, acted upon
the clearest conviction of the political importance of it, I would
have every individual who shall hear that I had interested myself in the plan, be convinced that I had *no* other motive for giving it support than the happiness which I thought it wou'd be
productive of to the confederation in general & this State in
particular—by extending the commerce of the latter & affording convenience to its Citizens—& preparing an indissoluble

bond for the former. How would this matter stand then in the eye of the world, & what would be the opinion of it, when it comes to be related, that G.W. exerted himself to effect this work—& G.W. had received—gratuitously, 20,000 Dollars in the one—& £5,000 Sterling in the other, of the public money, as an interest therein—Would not this, (in their estimation—if I am entitled to any merit for the part I have acted—& without it there is no foundation for the donation) deprive me of the principal thing which is laudable in it? Would it not in some respects, be considered in the same point of view as a pension? And would not the apprehension of this make me less a free agent in other matters, and be productive of greater unwillingness to suggest for consideration such things as my experience and opportunities may have brought me to the knowledge of? In a word, altho' custom may have given sanction to the measure, of rewards where there are no stipulations, should I not thenceforward be considered as a dependant? one moments thought of which would give me more pain, than I should receive pleasure from the product of *all* the tolls; altho' I view them as the most improving Estate in this Country.

I have written to you with frankness—I could have said more on the subject; but I have said enough to give you the state of my mind on this act of the Legislature. I wished to have seen, & conversed fully & freely with you on the subject of it. I wished to know whether the ideas I entertain of this matter occurred to, & were expressed by any member, in or out of the House— Upon the whole, I do assure you my mind is not a little agitated. I want the best information & advice to settle it. I have no inclination, as I have observed before, to avail myself of the generosity of the Country on the one hand—nor on the other, do I want to appear ostentatiously disinterested; which, more than probable would be the construction of my refusal; or to slight the favor, which is as valuable for the flattering expressions with which it is conveyed, as for the magnitude of the sum. My difficulties however shall not impede the progress of the undertaking—I will receive the frank & candid opinions of my friends with thankfulness, & shall have time enough to consider them between this & the next session of Assembly.[2]

Did you not my good Sir tell me when I had the pleasure of spending an evening with you at Dumfries, that you either had or could procure me some Scions of the Aspin tree? Are there any young shoots which could be had of the Yew tree, or Hemlock (for I do not now recollect which of these it is) that grows on the margin of Quantico Creek? Plantations of this kind are now become my amusement & I should be glad to know where I could obtain a supply of such sorts of trees as would diversify the scene.[3] With great esteem & regard I am Dr Sir Yr mo: Obt humble Servt

G: Washington

LB, DLC:GW.

1. Grayson's letter has not been found, but see GW to John Fitzgerald and William Hartshorne, 18 Jan. 1785, and notes. Monday was 17 January. The "Books" have not been identified, unless they were the books to be kept for the Potomac River Company by Fitzgerald and Hartshorne.

2. See note 1 in Benjamin Harrison to GW, 6 January.

3. See Grayson to GW, 10 March.

To Benjamin Harrison

My Dr Sir,   Mount Vernon 22d Jan. 1785.

It is not easy for me to decide by which my mind was most affected upon the receipt of your letter of the 6th inst.—surprize or gratitude: both were greater than I have words to express. The attention & good wishes which the Assembly have evidenced by their act for vesting in me 150 shares in the navigation of each of the rivers Potomac & James, is more than mere compliment—there is an unequivocal & substantial meaning annexed—But believe me sir, notwithstanding these, no circumstance has happened to me since I left the walks of public life, which has so much embarrassed me. On the one hand, I consider this act, as I have already observed, as a noble and unequivocal proof of the good opinion, the affection, & disposition of my Country to serve me; & I should be hurt, if by declining the acceptance of it, my refusal should be construed into disrespect, or the smallest slight put upon the generous intention of the Country: or, that an ostentatious display of disinterestedness or public virtue, was the source of the refusal.

On the other hand, it is really my wish to have my mind, & the actions which are the result of contemplation, as free & independent as the air, that I may be more at liberty (in things which my opportunities & experience have brought me to the knowledge of) to express my sentiments, & if necessary, to suggest what may occur to me, under the fullest conviction, that altho' my judgment may be arraigned, there will be no suspicion that sinister motives had the smallest influence in the suggestion. Not content then with the bare consciousness of my having, in all this navigation business, acted upon the clearest conviction of the political importance of the measure; I would wish that every individual who may hear that it was a favorite plan of mine, may know also that I had no other motive for promoting it than the advantage I conceived it would be productive of to the Union, & to this State in particular, by cementing the Eastern and Western Territory together, at the same time that it will give vigor & encrease to our Commerce, & be a convenience to our Citizens.

How would this matter be viewed then by the eye of the world; and what would be the opinion of it, when it comes to be related that G: W——n exerted himself to effect this work—and G.W. has received 20,000 Dollars, and £5,000 Sterling of the public money as an interest therein? Would not this in the estimation of it (if I am entitled to any merit for the part I have acted; & without it there is no foundation for the act) deprive me of the principal thing which is laudable in my conduct? Would it not, in some respects, be considered in the same light as a pension? And would not the apprehension of this make me more reluctantly offer my sentiments in future? In a word, under what ever pretence, & however customary these gratuitous gifts are made in other Countries, should I not thence forward be considered as a dependant? one moments thought of which would give me more pain, than I should receive pleasure from the product of all the tolls, was every farthing of them vested in me: altho' I consider it as one of the most certain & increasing Estates in the Country.

I have written to you with an openess becoming our friendship—I could have said more on the subject; but I have already said enough to let you into the State of my mind. I wish to know whether the ideas I entertain occurred to, & were expressed by any member in or out of the House. Upon the whole, you may be assured my Dr Sir, that my mind is not a litt[l]e agitated—I want the best information & advice to settle it. I have no inclination (as I have already observed) to avail myself of the generosity of the Country: nor do I want to appear ostentatiously disinterested, (for more than probable my refusal would be ascribed to this motive) or that the Country should harbour an idea that I am disposed to set little value on her favours—the manner of granting which is as flattering as the grant is important. My present difficulties however shall be no impediment to the progress of the undertaking. I will receive the full & frank opinions of my friends with thankfulness. I shall have time enough between this & the sitting of the next Assembly to consider the tendency of the act—& in this, as in all other matters, will endeavor to decide for the best.[1]

My respectful compliments & best wishes, in which Mrs Washington & Fanny Bassett (who is much recovered) join, are offered to Mrs Harrison & the rest of your family. It would give us great pleasure to hear that Mrs Harrison had her health restored to her. With every sentiment of esteem, regard & friendship, I am My Dr Sir &c. &c.

G: Washington

LB, DLC:GW.

1. See note 1 in Harrison's letter to GW, 6 January.

To Bushrod Washington

Dear Bushrod,   Mount Vernon Jany 22d 1785

The enclosed letter was brought here some days ago. I desire you will present Mr Ryan's note to him for payment; which, if not immediately made, or such assurances as you can rely on, that he will make in a very short time, return it to me or to Mr Rumsey, if he is in Richmond, as I do not incline to transfer the debt from him to Ryan. It was not my intention to receive an order upon any one, for the Sum contained in the note. It was sent about the time it became due to Mr Henderson (one of the Members for this Country) to receive for me, who not having an oppertunity of presenting it (on Acct of Mr Ryans indisposition at Petersburgh) returned it to me a few days since.[1]

As you are now at the fountain head of information, I should be glad if you would examine into, and send me a Copy of some Ordainance which must have passed (according to Colo.

Crawfords letter to me) at the Session next preceeding the 20th of Septr 1776 (which is the date of that letter).[2]

There are some other little matters which I wanted you to do for me in Richmond, but they have escaped my recollection at this moment—when they occur again, I will write—the Ordainance above, may be necessary in the prosecution of my Ejectments over the Mountains, as Colo. Crawford in his letter to me says, it passed with an eye to such cases as mine, upon his representation.[3] All here join in best wishes for you—and I am Dr Bushrod Yrs affectionately

Go: Washington

ALS, CtY: Franklin Papers. GW sent this letter to the care of Edmund Randolph. On learning that Bushrod Washington was not in Richmond, GW wrote Randolph on 19 Mar. asking him to open the letter and comply with his request to Bushrod with regard to Dennis Ryan. Having learned that Ryan had left Virginia, Randolph returned this letter and its enclosures to GW on 5 April.

1. It is not clear what the enclosed letter was. For James Rumsey's debt to GW and Dennis Ryan's note, see Alexander Henderson to GW, 20 Dec. 1784, n.1. See also GW to Bushrod Washington, 3 April.

2. No letter from William Crawford to GW dated 20 Sept. 1776 has been found. A Virginia convention met in Williamsburg beginning on 6 May 1776 and enacted fifteen ordinances. GW may be referring to "An Ordinance for making farther provisions for the defence and protection of this colony," one section of which provided "That an additional duty or tax of one shilling for every hundred acres of land in this colony . . . whether of patented land, or land in the county of Fincastle, and district of West Augusta, for which no patents have been obtained . . . shall be paid, on or before the tenth day of June, 1777 . . ." (9 Hening 143–49).

3. See editorial note in Thomas Smith to GW, 9 Feb. 1785.

From Jacob Gerhard Diriks

Sir,   New-York 24th Jany 1785

The honor of having served under your Excellency engages me, arrived in America lately, to take a view of the States made happy by a peace, after a war ended with glory under you—to testify my great respect for you, as the Officer, under whose auspices, I received my Military Education—How happy should I be, if I could in person renew the acknowledgements I so justly owe you—But the distance of your dwelling, the rude season of the year, wc. renders travelling difficult, the little time I have to stay, before my departure for Holland, my country; and my business with Congress assembled here all deprive me of this pleasure. Your Excellency will permit me I hope to sollicit a continuation of your former kindness—I was once honored with it, and this engages me the more, still to sollicit it—Yes Sir, I feel my bosom animated on this present occasion, with the same fire as formerly; and I desire nothing, but to be able to be useful to my Country; at present menaced by a neighbouring power—Your Excellency, as my General, is acquainted with my conduct in the American war—If then you will be pleased to favor me with a letter to the count de Maasdam, General of the army of the united Provinces; a soldier devoted to liberty & his Country; and who, tho' personally unknown to you, has the highest esteem for you, I am persuaded, it will place me in the service of my Country, agreeable to my rank, where following the lessons I learned from you, I hope to acquit myself with honor—I hope Your Excellency will not refuse me this gracious mark of your friendship wc. will be ever dear to me, & crown my highest wishes[1]—I have the honor to be with profound respect, your Excellency's Very Hble & Obent servant

J. G. Diriks

Translation, in the hand of David Stuart, DLC:GW; ALS, in French, DLC:GW. A transcript of the ALS is in CD-ROM:GW.

In November 1776 Jacob Gerhard Diriks of the Netherlands received a commission in one of the Pennsylvania regiments of the Continental line and subsequently served as an assistant quartermaster general under Gen. Thomas Mifflin, with the rank of lieutenant colonel. Diriks went back to Holland in 1779 and attempted to float a loan for the United States. Diriks asserted in his petition to Congress of 3 Feb. 1785 (DNA:PCC, item 41) that he had returned from Holland to America in 1779 and remained in the army until 1782. On 17 May 1781 Congress voted to give him lieutenant colonel's pay from the time that he received, by brevet, that rank in November 1778. On 14 Mar. 1785 Congress ruled that Diriks had "no remaining Claims against the U.S. Congress," but it agreed to give him a certificate attesting that both in the line in the army and as an assistant to the quartermaster general, the Dutchman had "been justly esteemed for his Bravery and Vigilance, and that in all Cases he has recommended himself by his Zeal, Industry, and Integrity" (*JCC*, 28:151–53).

1. On 15 Mar. GW offered to give Diriks "a certificate of service," but he declined to write to Count von Maasdam, being unwilling, as he usually was, to take "liberties with exalted characters to whom I am not personally known."

From Otho Holland Williams

Sir   Baltimore 24th Jany 1785.

Major Turner of Philadelphia to whom, and Captn Claypole, was committed the buisiness of having the Diploma of the Society of the Cincinnati engraved on Copperplate, has sent me a bundle containing eighty three Diplomas on Parchment, with a list of fourteen members who have advanced to him one dollar each for the expence.[1]

Major Turner has importuned me exceedingly to pay him the money he has advanced on account of the Society; But I cannot do so without the means of reimbursing myself.[2]

If you Sir, will please to sign the Diplomas most of the members will be glad to have them, and a regular and true account shall be rendered of all monies received and paid by me.[3] I have the honor to be Sir Your most Obedient and Most Humble Servant

O. H. Williams Ass⟨. Secy⟩ &c.

ALS, DLC:GW; ADfS, MdHi: Otho Holland Williams Papers.

1. At the general meeting of the Society of the Cincinnati in Philadelphia, George Turner and Abraham Claypole, on 17 May, were made "a Committee to Superintend & procure the Engraving on the Copper Plate brought by Major L'Enfant from France, the written Form of the Diploma" (Winthrop Sargent's Journal, doc. II in General Meeting of the Society of the Cincinnati, 4–18 May 1784, printed above).

2. See GW to Williams, 2 February.

3. GW signed and sent the diplomas back to Williams, but they were stolen en route. See GW to Williams, 2 Feb., and Williams to GW, 20 April.

From John Armstrong

Dear General.   Carlisle [Pa.] 25th January 1785

My last to your Excellency was of the congratulatory Sort, written on the joyfull & acceptable subject of our Peace[1]—and whatever time has elapsed since that period, you have had a Silent Share of the best wishes that either my leisure or reflexion, enabled me to bestow; and altho' they are founded in publick considerations never to be forgotten, they have comparatively left the lofty Scenes of various description, wherin for a Season you have happily & necessarily been employed, chusing rather to follow you to the peaceful, but still important retreat of domestick life—happy indeed in itself—happy in the concurrence of a thousand temporal blessings; and many, too many there are, whos wishes either for themselves or their friends, reach no farther—but sorry should I be that (for the man to whom my country is so much indebted) mine should terminate in any thing below that *felicity*, for which we look in the far more important world which is to come. for this felicity, you & I, by the sparing mercy of God are still candidates—but the heavenly road is to be fought inch by inch! Your Corporeal Armour is laid off, I hope never to be put on again, but our Spiritual Armour, my dear General, is if possible every day more & more necessary—the three grand enemies of our immortal life, yet keep the field, and display their force in various direction; they are potent, implacable, insatiable—not to be diverted by the things in which too many place safety or happiness—as in learning—streng[t]h of reason—external peace—affluence &c.—nay so far from it, that often, these are the avenues, or covert ways thro' which we are either assailed by double force, or ensnared by double Subtilty—The mode in which these adversaries generally make their attacks, is either tht of Violence, or Subtilty—and a great Similarity I make no doubt there is, in the first operations of the Devil by seduction—the workings & tendency to moral evil ariseing from the natural, or inbred corruptions of the human heart and flesh—and the allurements of the present World. the former is thougt to carry his approaches to the human mind, by gaining it's outworks Viz. the imagination, or fancy. and whatsoever, by our lapsed State is wrong in us, being his offspring, will probably imitate his Steps. With none of these adversaries, are we in our own Strength by any means able to cope—nor will their indefatigable & perfidious nature, safely admit of any negociation—parley or Truse, the moment we agree to a Ceasession of Arms, and have recourse to supposed reason, in looking out for appologies to the temptation, or evil in question, metigating it's nature or extent, covering or at least palliating a total or partial compliance, by peculiar circumstances & resolve of future resistance &c. all this is forbidden & unequal ground, on which we shall infallibly be overcome. A rigid resistance therefore, ought both to begin & end, this kind of debate; and blessed be God that altho' we must

be instruments in this necessary War, and employ the weapons prescribed by his word with fidelity & hope, the final event is not left to us, but secured by the Captain of our Salvation, to all who truly fight under his banner, in the use of such Spiritual means as he hath appointed & graciously proposed to bestow. Many dutys indeed are required of us far above our natural Strength to perform; and for this cause many appear to stumble and Charge God foolishly—not considering that the divine right, and power to demand is not mutual, was not losst & imbezled, as was our Strength and power to obey, in our voluntary violation of the first Covenent with Adam. Nor do such consider that in the Lord Christ, the Second Adam, the federal & Spiritual head of his Church, full provision is made, not only for the removal of guilt, but also the quallification of all believers for glory—or in other words, there is not a duty required of man, but for which we may find a correspondent promise, made in consequence of the Covenant of grace with Christ, enabling all believers in the performance thereof—'tis in him all the promises center, and in order to be entitled to them, we must by faith receive, or accept him both for *righteousness &*
Strength.

From the above considerations, I am led to wish yr Excellency three things—first, that *too much,* of yr present precious time, may not be engrossed by company & the ceremony of polite life—That your Library, be rather well chosen than large; particularly on theological Subjects, doctrinal, practical & Polemical. and that some Orthodox & pious divine may minister to the Church in reach of your House. On the Subject of Christianity, I think the Divines of the last Centuary rather deserve a preference—Deism of late begins to speak proudly on this, *Dr Leelands View of the Deistick writers* may be Satisfactory. Socinianism that has slept for many years, has for it's revival the patronage of that great philosoper, but wretched divine—Dr Priestley of London, who has lately wrote & published in favour of that antient heresy—but this I think any Sensible man who believes and understands his Bible may refute. but the Young generation is in danger from both these errors. For the hints thrown out above, I shall use no other appology, than that you know I am nearer the threescore & ten than you are—I think by the Space of fourteen years; and that we are bound to excite each others remembrance.[2] My health is Still tolerable, except in the extremities of the Season, both of which I find difficult. My Eldest Son Dr Armstrong has for upward of a year past laboured under a threatning disorder of the pulmonary kind— has for the benefit of the Sea Spent most of last summer in England, chiefly in London which he much dislikes, but is returned with no more apparent advantage than that his Cough only appears to have ceased. he is trying the utmost that a weak regimen may do—rideing as the weather will permit, intends to meet an early Spring on the Rappahannock and thence proceed to what is called the Sweet Springs in Agusta, of which his friends in Berkley, give in that complaint a very favourable account.[3] I am Dear General, with the highest esteem Your invariable friend And most Obedt & humble Servant

John Armstrong

We hear nothing favourable nor certain from the Western Treaty—only it's said it will be tedious, and that the Shawanese refuse to attend, but desire a Seperate treaty in the Spring.

ALS, DLC:GW.
    John Armstrong (1717–1795) was born in Ireland and settled in Pennsylvania in the 1740s. He and GW were senior officers in the colonial forces that participated in the Forbes expedition of 1758 against Fort Duquesne. Armstrong was made a brigadier general in the Continental army in 1776 but served only briefly.
    1. Armstrong's letter is dated 22 April 1783.
    2. GW seems not to have made any response to Armstrong's admonitions. Armstrong wrote in a similar vein on 2 Mar. 1787 and again on 5 June 1787, but as far as can be determined it was not until after Armstrong wrote GW on 20 Feb. 1788 strongly supporting the new Constitution that GW responded, when he wrote to Armstrong, cordially and at some length, on 25 April 1788.
    3. This may be Sweet Springs which until 1769 was in Augusta County and thereafter in Botetourt County. Armstrong's son, Dr. James Armstrong, found a cure; he lived long enough to father nine children. The mother of his children was Mary Stevenson Armstrong, daughter of George Stevenson.

To Thomas Clarke

Sir,			Mt Vernon 25th Jan: 1785
    In your name & behalf Mr Laurens, as he passed thro' this State last Month on his way from the seat of Congress to Charleston[1]—presented me a very handsome gold headed cane: & accompanied it with such favorable sentiments of your

good wishes towards the American revolution—& the flattering opinion you entertained of me, as to induce me, contrary to my usual custom, to accept of it. With this acknowledgment thereof, I beg you to receive my thanks for so evincive a mark of your esteem & approbation, & the assurances of my being— Sir, Yrs &c.

G: Washington

LB, DLC:GW.

1. Henry Laurens (1724–1792) was captured at sea by the British in 1782 when he was en route to Holland to negotiate a loan for Congress. He was taken to the Tower of London, and after his release he became in May 1782 one of the peace commissioners for the United States. Laurens remained in England until 1784, arriving in New York on 3 August.

To James Jay

Sir,   Mount Vernon Jany 25th 1785
By means of the frost, & the consequent interruption of the Post, your favor of the 20th of December did not come to my hands until the 17th instant—It is to be regretted that Lady Huntingtons communications were not earlier made to the several Legislatures to whom they were addressed; for if the circumstances of any will allow them to be adopted, it will be found that a year will have been lost by the delay.[1] In some States, they must have reached the Exe[cu]tive after the Assemblies were up; in others, would get there towards the close of them, when fresh matters are rarely attended to—& some Sessions (as in this State) holden but once a year.

I am clearly in sentiment with her Ladyship, that christianity will never make any progress among the Indians, or work any considerable reformation in their principles, until they are brought to a state of greater civilization; & the mode by which she means to attempt this, as far as I have been able to give it consideration, is as likely to succeed as any other that could have been devised, & may in time effect the great & benevolent object of her Ladyships wishes; but that love of ease, impatience under any sort of controul, & disinclination to every kind of pursuit but those of hunting & war, would discourage any person possessed of less piety, zeal & philanthropy than are characteristick of Lady Huntington.

Of all the States to which her Ladyships addresses are gone,

New York I believe is the only one that *now* possesses unlocated lands in such quantities, & so contiguous to any Indian settlement, as to subserve her Ladyships plan of emigration; & whether that State can accommodate them to her & their satisfaction, you can determine with more precision than I. No part of the Western Territory of Pennsylvania is very contiguous to the habitations of the Indians, & if I mistake not, is besides otherwise appropriated. Virginia is not more convenient to them than Pennsylvania, & in her cession to the United States she was obliged to reserve Lands No. West of the Ohio to fulfil her own engagements to the military of the State: nothing then, in my opinion can be expected from her. And North Carolina having also made a similar cession is I believe, equally incapacitated to grant any great quantity of land in a body, or much in parcels. It is my opinion therefore, that Lady Huntington's proposals would come more properly before the United States, than any one, or more of them individually; & it is my sentiment clearly, that besides the pious & humane purposes which are in view, & of which we should never lose sight, motives of a political nature, should have considerable influence; because such a migration as her ladyship proposes must be an acquisition to any Country. There are but two reasons which my imagination suggests that can be opposed to it: the first is, the pressing Debts of the United States which may call for all the revenue which can be drawn from the most advantageous sale of their lands, and the discontents which might flow from discrimination, if peculiar exemptions in the original purchase, or indulgencies thereafter, are expected in favor of the class of Settlers proposed by the plan. And secondly, (which may have more weight) the prejudices of Monarchical people when they are unmixed with republicans, against those who have separated from them, & against their forms of Government; & this too in the vicinity of a British one—viz: Canada—Whether these are to be placed in competition with the charitable design of the plan, considered in a religeous point of view; or the great good which may result from the civilization of numerous tribes of Savages when measured on the political scale, becomes the wisdom of that honorable body to weigh with attention.[2]

If they should decide in favor of the measure, valuable Lands with respect to fertility of soil, salubrity of climate & other natural advantages might, in one body, & in any quantity, be reserved for the purposes of such emigration, until the result of her Ladyships endeavors to obtain them could be known; & this too either in the vicinity of the Indians towns, or at such convenient distance from them as might be most agreeable to the emigrants, there being no settlements or appropriations (except the reservation in favor of the Virginia line of the Army) to my knowledge in all the Country No. West of the Ohio, that could interfere therewith.

As I am well acquainted with the President of Congress, I will in the course of a few days write him a private letter on this subject giving the substance of Lady Huntington's plan, & asking his opinion of the encouragement it might expect to receive from Congress if it should be brought before that honorable body. Were you to do the same with your brother Mr John Jay now in Congress, and than whom none can judge better of the propriety of the measure, or give greater support to it if it should ultimately come before that supreme Council of the Nation, it might lay the foundation which might be serviceable hereafter.[3]

Without reverberating the arguments in support of the humane & benevolent intention of Lady Huntington to christianize & reduce to a state of civilization the Savage tribes within the limits of the American States, or discanting upon the advantages which the Union may derive from the Emigration which is blended with, & becomes part of the plan, I highly approve of them, & having, tho' concisely, touched upon the material parts of your letter, it only remains for me to express my good wishes for the success of such a measure, and to assure you that wherein I can be instrumental to its execution, my best endeavours may be commanded. I have the honor to be &c.

G: Washington

LB, DLC:GW.

1. See Lady Huntingdon's Scheme to Aid the American Indians, 20 Dec. 1784, printed above. Jay's letter is doc. I in that entry.

2. See GW to Richard Henry Lee, 8 Feb., Lee to GW, 27 Feb., and GW to the Countess of Huntingdon, 27 Feb. 1785, and notes in these documents.

3. GW wrote Richard Henry Lee on 8 February. James Jay talked to Lee of the Huntingdon plan (see Lee to GW, 27 Feb.).

Letter not found: from Battaile Muse, 25 Jan. 1785. On 5 Feb. GW wrote to Muse: "I have lately received two letters from you, one of the 14th & the other of the 25th of last month."

To Elias Boudinot

Dear Sir,   Mount Vernon 26th Jan. 1785

Early in Novr[1] I had the pleasure, by Post, to congratulate you & Mrs Boudinot on the Marriage of your daughter; & on her restoration to health; both of which we (Mrs Washington & I) heard with much satisfaction.

I took the liberty, at the sametime, to request the favor of you, if it could be done without much inconvenience to yourself, to procure for me as much of the Orchard grass Seed as would Sow about ten Acres of Land—to be forwarded by any Vessel which might be coming from New York to Alexandria; or if none should offer for that Port—then, to the care of Colo. Biddle of Philadelphia, who would contrive it to me from thence by Land, or Water, as an opportunity might offer— Having heard nothing from you since, and as the season is fast approaching when it shd be sowed if to be had, I have taken the liberty of repeating the substance of my former letter—to which I prayed the direction of some good farmer respecting the quantity which ought to be Sowed on an Acre. The cost of the Seed I will cause to be paid the moment I am acquainted with the price.[2]

Mrs Washington joins me in every good wish for you and Mrs Boudinot—& in compliments to the Newly Married pair—with sentiments of great esteem & regard I am—Dr Sir Your Most Obt Hble Sert

Go: Washington

ALS, PPRF.

1. GW's letter is dated 3 Nov. 1784.

2. Boudinot had already sent seed to Biddle. See note 2 in GW to Clement Biddle, 3 Nov. 1784.

From Samuel Hanway

Sir   Old Town [Md.] January 26th 1785

In a Short time after you left my office I Examin'd the falls of Cheat river agreeable to your request and find that it will be Imposible to effect a navigation up it through the Laurell Hill, I have made the stri[c]test Enquiry whare the most advantagious and nearest Communication by Land can be had from the north branch to the Western Waters, and find it Will be to the falls of the Tyeger Valley fork of Monongalia River, it will not Exceed forty miles from Logstones ford on the North Branch to the Said falls and I have reason to believe and am Confident from my own knowledge of the greatest part of the way and the Information I have had of the other part that a good road may be made[.] the falls of the Tyger Valley fork is about nine miles from its Junction With the West fork, and upwards of thirty miles above the mouth of Cheat river and near the Center of the most settled as well as most fertile part of the Counties of Monongalia and Harrison thence a navigation may easyly be had up the West fork and Consequently by a Short Land Carriage Down the little Kenhawa. I am Sir your most obedient and Verry humble Servant

Saml Hanway

ALS, MnHi.
Samuel Hanway (1743–1834), a Pennsylvanian, moved to Virginia in 1768 and later became a merchant in Petersburg. He returned to Pennsylvania in 1783 as surveyor of Monongalia County, a post he held for many years. GW consulted with Hanway, Zackwell Morgan, and others on 24 and 25 Sept. 1784 in the surveyor's office at John Pierpont's house about eight miles from where the Cheat and Monongahela rivers join. See *Diaries*, 4:38–50.

From Henry Knox

My dear Sir   Boston [Mass.] 26 Jany 1785.
The bearer Mr Laurence is a gentleman from Denmark who has been here some time, and is largely concerned in commerce to this Continent He is extremely anxious to have the honor to see you before he leaves the Country and has requested me to introduce him to you.[1] I am my Dear Sir With the most perfect respect and attachment your affectionate humble Servant

H. Knox

ALS, DLC:GW.
1. GW does not indicate in his diary that anyone named Laurence visited Mount Vernon in 1785.

From Melancton Smith

Sir   New York Jany 26th 1785
I received your favor of the 20th Decr.
I am extremely mortified that you have been subjected to the

inconveniency and loss you mention by not receiving timely information of the arrival of the Plate. You may be assured, Sir, that my not giving you earlier advice was not owing to the want of a disposition to oblige you, but to casualties that could not be prevented. I was out of Town when the Box arrived. Docr Craige received it, and had no directions how to dispose of it, when I returned which was several Weeks after, he informed me that the plate was in his possession. In a few days after it was forwarded to Philadelphia by Water, and I sent a Letter by a private hand to Philadelphia to Messrs Cox & Fraser to forward to you as soon as possible.[1]

I have made out the Account as you request, giving a credit for the Sum you mention to have paid Mr Parker (his Books are not with me) and have requested Messrs Porter & Ingraham Merchts in Alexandria to receive the Ballance for which purpose I have transmitted them a copy of the Account with an Order at foot. The Original Invoice is inclosed.[2] I am with respect Sir Your Obed. serv.

Melancton Smith

The Invoice having a Letter on the same sheet, which it is probable may be wanted, I will thank you Sir to return after inspecting.[3] I am as before Yours respectfully, M. Smith

ALS, DLC:GW.

1. The merchants Tench Coxe of Philadelphia and Nalbro Frazier of New England formed a partnership in Philadelphia in 1783 which lasted until Coxe left the firm in 1791. Andrew Craigie, the apothecary general of the Continental army, set up his drug business in New York in 1784.

2. The enclosed invoice from Smith & Wyckoff shows charges of £56.18.4 sterling by the London firm of Joy & Hopkins "for 1 case plate" and other charges by Smith & Wyckoff for freight and storage, bringing the total cost to GW to £111.10.9 current money, of which he had paid Daniel Parker £65.5.4. This left GW owing Smith & Wyckoff £46.5.5. See GW to Smith, 20 Dec. 1784, and the references in note 1 of that document.

3. The letter is one from Joy & Hopkins in London to Daniel Parker, dated 24 May 1784. The letter begins: "Agreeable to the orders of your Benjamin Parker we have the pleasure to annex you Invoice of one Chest ⅌ the Henry Captn Rawson, for his Excellency Genl Washington amtg to £56.18.4 which we hope may meet with his and your approbation, we have spared no pains to have every article as compleat as possible" (DLC:GW). GW apparently did not comply with Smith's request that the letter and invoice be returned to him. The following entry appears in GW's cash accounts for 14 Mar. 1785: "By Lancton Smith's Orders for Bale due Danl Parker for Plate Pd Porter & Ingraham 34.14.2" (Ledger B, 202).

From Thomas Stone

Dear Sir   Annapolis [Md.] 28 Jan. 1785

It gives me much pleasure to know that our Act for opening the Navigation of Potomack arrived in time to be adopted by the Assembly of Virginia. If the scheme is properly executed I have the most sanguine expectation that it will fully succeed to the wishes of those who are anxious to promote the wellfare of these States and to form a strong chain of connection between the Western & atlantic governments. Mr Jenifer[,] Johnson[,] Chase & myself are appointed Commissioners to Settle the Jurisdiction and Navigation of the Bay & the Rivers Potomack & Pocomoke with·the Commissioners of Virginia. We have also instructions to make application to Pennsylva. for leave to clear a Road from Potomack to the Western Waters—Our Assembly propose the Meeting of the Commissioners to be on the 21st of March at Alexandria, if agreable to the Commissioners of Virginia.[1] I have no doubt but the Subjects of our Mission will be setled to mutual satisfaction & it will add much to the satisfaction I shall feel in discharging this trust that I shall have an Opportunity of paying my respects to You at Mount Vernon; which I have long wished to do, but in truth the necessary attention to professional and public business have kept Me so closely employed that I have never had a time when I could gratify my inclination without neglecting some duty which I was particularly bound to perform. I hope nevertheless that You will do Me the justice to beleive that I warmly participate in the high Regard and Esteem in which You are held by all the friends of this Country & that I am sir with Sentiments of very sincere Attachment Yr most Obt & most humb. Sert

T: Stone

ALS, PHi: Gratz Collection.

Thomas Stone (1743–1787) was the nephew of Daniel of St. Thomas Jenifer (1723–1790) and as a young man had studied law under Thomas Johnson (1732–1819). He at this time was a member of the Maryland senate.

1. See James Madison to GW, 1 Jan., n.3, and Enclosure I in Madison to GW, 9 January. On 20 Mar., Stone, Daniel of St. Thomas Jenifer, and Samuel Chase (1741–1811) arrived at Mount Vernon with Alexander Henderson to join George Mason and GW and bring to a conclusion their Potomac (or Mount Vernon) conference. Documents relating to the Mount Vernon conference of March 1785 are conveniently printed in The Mount Vernon Compact, in Rutland, *Mason Papers*, 2:812–23.

From Clement Biddle

Dear General   Philad[elphi]a Janry 29. 1785
I just met with a Sloop going immediately for Potowmack by which I have time to send the Two bags of Grass seed received from mr Boudinot which the Captain has promised to deliver if possible at Mount Vernon otherwise to mr Thompson at Colchester.[1]
The other kind of Grass seed I could not yet procure tho' I have applied to every person in Town who collects those Articles & to several farmers. I have the honor to be with great respect Your Excellencys Mo: Obedt & very humle servt
                                        Clement Biddle

ALS, DLC:GW. Addressed: "By the Sloop Dolphin Cap: ⟨Rice⟩."
1. For reference to the grass seed, see especially GW to Biddle, 3 Nov. 1784, n.2. William Thompson was a merchant in Colchester, Virginia. Later this year Lund Washington's niece became Thompson's wife.

From Abraham Hite, Jr.

My Dear Genl   Jefferson County [Va.] January 29th [17]85
I am sorry to inform you I was mistaken in my opinion of having seen an Entry on the Books of the Surveyor of this County, in your name; I have since my Coming to this Country had an opertunity of making enquiry in the Surveyor's Office of this and of Fayette Counties, and Cant Learn that there are any Entries in Your name, or Warrants of Yours lodged in Either of those Offices. The first opertunity I have of making enquiry at the Surveyors Office of Lincoln County it shall be done & if I should get any more favourable Inteligence will Acquaint you with it by the first opertunity. I have the Honour to be With Great Respect Your Very Humbe Servant
                                        Abra. Hite Junr

ALS, DLC:GW.
When GW was on the frontier in September 1784, Abraham Hite, Jr. (1755–1832), accompanied him on 29–30 Sept. on the leg of GW's journey from the house of Abraham Hite, Sr. (1729–1790), in Berkeley County, to John Fitzwater's house in Brocks Gap, Rockingham County, Virginia. Before the war, young Hite spent time in Kentucky and surveyed land there. Jefferson County from where he was writing was one of three Virginia counties cre-

ated in the Kentucky region between 1777 and 1780. Both he and his father settled in Kentucky in the 1780s.

To Joseph Wright

Sir,   Mount Vernon 30th Jany 1785.

It has so happened that your card of Septr 1st, with the Bust which accompanied it, did not get to my hands until some time in the course of last month: & that a letter from your good mother dated Decr 8th 1783, only reached me the 12th of last December.[1]

For the first you will please to receive the united acknowledgements & thanks of Mrs Washington & myself. The large one she prays may give you no uneasiness or hurry; your convenience in the execution will be most agreeable to her wishes.

In answer to the second, I give you the trouble of forwarding the enclosed letter when you may have occasion to write to England[2]—our best wishes attend you; & I am Sir, Yr Mo: Obedt Servant

G. Washington

LB, DLC:GW.

1. See note 1 in Wright to GW, 1 Sept. 1784. See also GW to Wright, 10 Jan. 1784, and notes.

2. See GW to Patience Wright, this date.

To Patience Wright

Madam,   Mount Vernon Jany 30th 1785.

By what means it came to pass, I shall not undertake to devise; but the fact is, that your letter of the 8th of December 1783, never got to my hands until the 12th of the Same Month in the year following. This will account for my not having acknowledged the receipt of it sooner—and for not thanking you as I now do, before, for the many flattering expressions contained in it.

If the Bust which your Son has modelled of me should reach your hands, and afford your celebrated Genii any employment that can amuse Mrs Wright, it must be an honor done me. and if your inclination to return to this Country should overcome other considerations, you will, no doubt, meet a welcome reception from your numerous friends: among whom, I should be proud to see a person so universally celebrated; & on whom, nature has bestowed such rare & uncommon gifts.[1] I am— Madam Yr Most Obedt & very Hble Servant

Go: Washington

ALS, British Museum: Add. MSS 12099; LB, DLC:GW.

1. See GW to Joseph Wright, this date, n.1. Patience Lovell Wright acted as a secret agent for the Americans in London during the war.

To Elias Boudinot

My dear Sir,   Mount Vernon Jany 31st 1785.
Under a full persuasion that my letter of Novr, to you, had miscarried, I wrote to you again by the last Post and recited the contents of it. After having done so, I was honored with your favor of the 14th of last Month.[1]

At the sametime that I thank you for your attention to my request respecting the Orchard grass Seeds, I have to lament that it should be the means of taking from you, what you had provided for your own use; and to pray, if it is not now too late, that you would not forward it to Colo. Biddle—or at most, not more than part of it.

I can only repeat the assurances of my last, in which Mrs Washington (who does not enjoy very good health) joind me, in good wishes, & in the sincere esteem & regard with which I am—Dear Sir Yr Most Obedt & Very Hble Servt

Go: Washington

ALS, ViHi; LB, DLC:GW.

1. See GW to Boudinot, 26 January.

To Udny Hay

Sir,   Mount Vernon 31st Jany 1785
The interruption of the Post, by the frost, will occasion a delay of this answer, which otherwise would have been avoided.[1]

Not being able to decypher the name of the Merchant in London, to whose care you desired my letter to your brother might be addressed, I send the enclosed certificate for him, under cover to you.[2]

I thank you for your kind and friendly wishes, & with Mrs Washington's compliments to Mrs Hay & yourself, & a return of friendly sentiments. I am Sir &c.

G: Washington

LB, DLC:GW.
   1. See Hay to GW, 16 Dec. 1784.
   2. The following is written below the letter in the letter book: "Certificate inclosed—Neither directly, nor indirectly to my knowledge or belief, did I ever obtain the least information of the state of the British forces, or other concerns of theirs in Canada, from Mr Charles Hay, a subject of Great Britain under that Government—Certified at Mt Vernon in Virginia this 1st day of Feby 1785. G: W——n."

From Henry Knox

Boston [Mass.] 31st January 1785

I have the satisfaction, my dear Sir, to acknowledge the receipt of your kind favors of the 5th of Decr and of the 5th instant for which I beg you to receive my warmest thanks. I regard these letters as fresh proofs of your unchanging friendship and kindness, which I shall ever esteem among the cheif blessings of my Life.

The Indians being in a bad temper when you went to the Westward I felt great solicitude for your safety, as I was apprehensive you would have procceded to the utmost distance you at first intended. I was glad to learn that you altered your determination. You must have been chagrined to have found your lands possessed by a lawless people who hold in contempt Equity, one of the first principles of society. This and other circumstances, my dear Sir, you will experience as excercises to your Philosophy. But it will be to you a consolation, full of peace, to reflect, that you have in all your actions, obeyed the dictates of a mind replete with patriotism, and universal benevolence. This is a happiness that few possess, and perhaps not one on Earth, has reason to possess it, in a more eminent degree than you.

Your remarks on the present situation of our Country, are indeed too just. The different states have not only different views of the same subject, but some of them have views that sooner or later must involve the Country in all the horrors of civil War. If there is any good policy which prevades generally our public measures it is too misterious to be comprehended by people out of the Cabinet—A Neglect, in every State, of those principles which lead to Union and National greatness—An adoption of local, in preference to general measures, appear to actuate the greater part of the State politicians—We are entirely destitute of those traits which should Stamp us *one Nation*, and the Constitution of Congress, does not promise any capital alteration for the better. Great Measures will not be carried in Congress so much by the propriety, utility and necessity of the thing, but as a matter of compromise for something else, which may be evil itself, or have a tendency to evil. This perhaps is not so much the fault of the members, as a defect of the Confederation—Every State considers its representative in Congress not so much the Legislator of the whole Union, as its own immediate Agent or Ambassador to negociate, & to endevour to create in Congress as great an influence as possible to favor particular views &c. With a Constitution, productive of such dispositions, is it possible that the American ⟨*mutilated*⟩ can ever rival the Roman Name? The operation of opening the navigation of the Rivers so as to communicate with the Western Waters, is truly noble, and if successful, of which I hope there is not a doubt, it must be followed by the most extensively beneficial consequences, which will encrease in exact proportion to the encrease of the population of the Country. I am pleased that you interest yourself so much in this great Work.

You are so good as to ask whether General Lincoln and myself had an agreable tour to the eastward? and whether the State societies arnt making moves towards obtaining charters? We Went to the eastern Line of this State, and found that the British had made excessive encroachments on our territories. There are three Rivers in the Bay of Passamaquoddy to which the british have within 20 years past with a view to confound the business given the name of St Croix. But the ancient St Croix is the eastern River. The British have settled, and built a considerable Town called St Andrews on the Middle River, which has always sustained among the people in that Country, the Indian name Scudar. The proper St Croix, and the Scudar are only nine miles distant at their mouths—They run into the County about Sixty miles, and they diverge from each other so much, that athough at their mouths they are only nine miles apart yet at their Sources they are one hundred miles distant from each other. and it is from the source the North Line to the Mountains is to begin. The mountains are distant from the source about 80 or 100 miles—so the difference to this State is one hundred *miles square* above the heads of the Rivers and the Land between the Rivers, which must be 60 by 50 mile Square. Our Legislature have transmitted the report we made on this business to Congress and the Governor of Nova Scotia—The matter has been involved designedly by the british in such a manner but it can now be settled only by commissioners mutually appointed for that purpose. I have seen a letter from Mr John Adams, dated last October, which mentions that the River meant by the treaty of peace was decidedly the River next to St Johns River westward—And there are plenty of proof that the ancient St Croix was the next to St Johns—I have been particular, in this narration that you may know the precise State of this affair which it is probable will sooner or later occasion much conversation.[1]

As to the Cincinnati, the objections against it are apparently removed—But I beleive none have yet applied for Charters. In this State it is pretty evident from communicating with the members of the Legislature that we should not succeed—Howevever we shall attempt it previous to our next meeting in July.

I pray you my dear Sir, that you carry into execution your determination, that no circumstances of Civility shall restrain you from taking a proper proportion of exercise. Unless you do this, you will soon languish, and every ill conseq[u]ence to your health may be expected to ensue. Your own happiness, and the happiness of your friends depend upon it.

Most of the Stone Lime used in this Town and the neig[h]boreing Seaport Towns, is made at St Georges about 150 miles eastward of this place—before the War it used to be sold here from 20/ to 25/ ℔ hogshead of an 100 gallons each, the hogshead included—It is always brought to Market in hogsheads and *unslacked*—This lime is of excellent quality—The lowest price last year was *five dollars* ℔ hogshead, and it is supposed that the same sum will be nearly the price the Year ensuing— The price of the frieght to your house, or Alexandria would be uncertain, as much would depend, upon the quantity of loading the Vessell had, which should take it—I have made enquiry of the most intelligent who say that it might be 2 dollars, or if the Vessell had but little frieght, perhaps one and an half ℔ hogshead, or perhaps even so low as one dollar—This price of one dollar is given for the frieght from St Georges to this Town.

As the Lime is never sold slaked, but when it gets slaked by accident, and then it is always sold at an inferior price as damaged—and the masons say that it would be unfit for service before it reached you—No Vessell will take the unslaked Lime in *Bulk* on account of the danger attending it—It must be transported in hogsheads.

I never have heard of the Stone being sold unburnt, but undoubtedly it would be the cheapest method by which you could obtain the Lime as you have hands, and Wood of your own—If it were possible to find a Vessell (which it is not) going from St Georges to Alexandria it would fix the Matter—If we had the stone in this place, we might probably find Vessels going to Alexandria which might take it as ballast free of frieght—But frieght must be paid for it from St Georges here, as all the Vessells come from thence fully loaded with Lumber, wood &c.—I cannot say what this frieght would be, as there are no vessells in during this severe season.

As the Lime Stone is upon an Estate which belonged to Mrs Knox's family, I should be able to prevail upon the persons who occupy it, to send me the Stone, although contrary to thier general Custom, and to charge it low—In either case whether you would have the Lime burnt or the Stone unburnt I would chearfully undertake to send you the quantity you should require—and embrace the earliest conveyances to forward it—If you should find that you could obtain the Lime or Stone, on better terms here than elsewhere, the sooner you forward your orders to me the better, as it will require some time, to negoiate the matter at St Georges the distance being so great, and passages precarious during the Winter.[2]

After what you have said about writing too much it may appear strange that I should request you to embarrass yourself still more, but I am so circumstanced as to be constrained to make the application, and rely upon your goodness to excuse it—An Intimate freind of mine Mr Swan, a member of our Legislature and a gentleman of large Fortune intends going to

France with his wife to pass a year or two there and in other parts of Europe. He has solicited me that I would request two or three letters from you to Count DEstaing, Count Rochambeau, or whoever you may think proper—I will be responsible, that he will not disgrace your credentials.[3]

Lieut. Seaver and Lieut. Henly two officers who served with perfect reputation in the Massachusetts Line intend going into Foreign Service, the one in the Dutch and the other in the Russian Service. As the basis of their future happiness they request honorary certificates from you. I beg you to grant these for their sakes, & Mr Swans for mine.[4]

Mrs Knox's ____was a daughter, and a fine one it is. Mrs K. joins me in the most affectionate respect to you and Mrs Washington. I am my dear Sir with the utmost sincerity Your obliged & affectionate humble Servant

H. Knox

ALS, DLC:GW.

1. Having received reports of British encroachment on the territory of the United States at its eastern boundary in Maine, Congress on 29 Jan. 1784 adopted a report of a committee chaired by Thomas Jefferson recommending that the governor of Massachusetts be asked to take the matter up with the governor of Nova Scotia (*JCC*, 26: 52–53). In conformity with the resolution of Congress, the Massachusetts legislature named Knox, Benjamin Lincoln, and George Partridge to meet with representatives of the governor of Nova Scotia, and, at "the latter end of August," the three men sailed up to Passamaquoddy Bay, an inlet off the Bay of Fundy. They made their report to Gov. John Hancock on 19 Oct. in the form of a letter. The report, most of which Knox repeats here, was only one of a number of related documents that the secretary for the department of foreign affairs, John Jay, secured copies of and attached to his report to Congress of 21 April 1785 on "the Eastern boundary Line." In his report, Jay called for the choosing of commissioners by Great Britain and the United States to settle the dispute, but, in fact, the eastern boundary of Maine was not fixed until the signing of the Webster-Ashburton treaty in 1842. Among the documents attached to Jay's report was an extract of John Adams's letter to Caleb Cushing, written from Paris on 25 Oct. 1784, reporting that "it was Mitchel's Map upon which was marked out the whole of the Boundary Lines of the United States" and affirming that the "River St Croix which we fixed on, was upon that Map the nearest River to St Johns," or the easternmost one. The copies of the documents cited and quoted are in DNA:PCC, item 124. For earlier references to this mission, see Knox to GW, 5 Dec. 1784.

2. See note 6 in GW to Knox, 5 January.

3. For the letters GW wrote on behalf of James Swan, see GW to Knox, 28 Feb., n.1.

4. For the certificate GW wrote for James Sever (Seaver), see GW to Knox, 28 Feb., n.2.

To William Paca

Sir,   Mount Vernon Jany 31st 1785.
    Altho' I have no doubt but that your Excelly has been, or will be, informed of the Act of the Virginia Assembly respecting the Potomack Navigation from the Governor of the State, yet, as the Act could not be printed at Richmond in time for the use of the Managers, and was brought to Alexandria for that purpose—and as a pressure of other public matters may, possibly, have delayed the official communication, I do myself the honor of inclosing one of the copies wch was struck at the above place; and which only came to my hands in time to be forwarded by this Post.[1]
    If it should be the first that reaches you, you will have it in your power to make such use thereof as you shall think proper. If it should follow the official one, I have but to pray that it may be considered as an evidence of my good wishes to the undertaking, and not as an officious interference in the business of the Executive. I have the honor to be Sir Yr most Obedt & Very Hble Servt

                                        Go: Washington

ALS (photocopy), sold by Sotheby Parke-Bernet, catalog 5031, 26 April 1983; LB, DLC:GW.
    William Paca (1740–1799), of Annapolis and Queen Anne's County, was governor of Maryland from 1782 to 1785.
    1. See GW to John Fitzgerald and William Hartshorne, 18 January.

To Clement Biddle

Dear Sir,   Mount Vernon 1st Feby 1785.
    In a letter of the 14th of Decr from Mr Boudinot (which only came to my hands by the last Post) he informs me that he should send Six bushls of the Orchard grass Seeds to your care, for my use. If this has been done, I pray you not to forego the first opportunity of forwarding it to me, as it ought to be sowed as soon as the ground can be prepared, which I am now getting in order for its reception.[1]

I do not know how to account for it, but so the fact is, that altho' I am a subscriber to Messrs Dunlaps & Claypoole's Packet & daily Advertiser, I do not get one paper in five of them—was I to say one in ten, I should be nearer the mark.[2] Once I wrote to Mr Claypoole on this subject, but he never vouchsafed to give me an answer, and since I have been worse served. If I recollect right, this letter was accompanied with one to you requesting payment of my subscription; lest a tardiness in this respect, on my part, might occasion the omissions on his.[3] I now ask the same favor of you, and pray also, that you would be so obligeing as to enquire into, and let me know the cause of my disappointments—which I have regretted the more, since their publication of Cooks voyages; having never been able to get a bound and lettered sett of them.[4]

Be it remembered that, if the fulfilment of these requests of mine, places you in advance for me, it is because I cannot get a Statement of the acct between us, that I may know how the Balle stands. You talked of coming to Virginia, and I assure you I should be very glad to see you—but it seems as if it would end in talk.

I have received a Cask of clover Seeds & a box with a cast (from Mr Wright)[5] unaccompanied by a letter or Invoice. I do not know therefore whether to expect the English grass seeds of which you gave me hopes, or not[6]—We have heard of Mrs Shaws Marriage, on which occasion please to offer her mine, and Mrs Washingtons compliments of congratulation: at the sametime present our best wishes for Mrs Biddle & your family. I am—Dear Sir Yr most obedt Hble Servt

Go: Washington

P.S. Be so good as to let the enclosed go safe to Messrs Lewis's. it is to request them to provide me a *good* Miller of which I am much in want—and in the doing of which, if you could contribute, it would render me an essential Service.[7] G.W.

Since writing the foregoing, I have recollected a matter of business which I intended when you came here to have asked the favor of you to negotiate for me. I now enclose it, & would thank you for getting it settled, if it can be done, at the proper office in Philadelphia. The endorsements upon the cover of the Papers (which was made at the time they were put into my hands) contain all the light I can throw upon the business. I pray you to take care of it with the rest of the Papers and let me have it again with whatever settlement is made, or decision is come to; as I have no copy or other Memm by which I can settle an Acct with Gilbert Simpson, or John Johns relative to this matter.[8] I am as above. G. Washington

ALS, PHi: Washington-Biddle Correspondence; LB, DLC:GW.

1. Biddle wrote GW on 29 Jan. about having sent the grass seed.

2. With the issue of 21 Sept. 1784, David C. Claypoole's triweekly, the *Pennsylvania Packet, and General Advertiser* (Philadelphia), became Claypoole's and John Dunlap's daily, the *Pennsylvania Packet, and Daily Advertiser.*

3. As early as 19 Sept. 1782, GW was chiding Claypoole for not forwarding the *Pennsylvania Packet* to Mount Vernon. On 30 June 1784 GW gave Biddle instructions to pay Claypoole what he owed and enclosed a letter to Claypoole, which has not been found.

4. On 7 Mar. Biddle wrote that John Dunlap had assured him, "the papers shall be sent & a set of those with Cooks voyage." Biddle confirmed on 19 April that the papers would be sent regularly, but on 16 May GW wrote Biddle that he had not "received a paper from Messrs Claypool & Dunlap since your mention of their intention to forward them regularly," and that he intended never "to tak another of their Gazettes." On 27 July 1785, however, GW wrote to Biddle: "Since your last conference with Messrs Dunlap & Claypool, their Advertiser has come to hand regularly. I am content therefore to have it continued."

5. For the bust of GW that Joseph Wright made and sent, see GW to Joseph Wright, 30 Jan. 1785.

6. See GW to Biddle, 3 Nov. 1784.

7. See GW to Robert Lewis & Sons, this date.

8. In September 1784 GW ended his partnership with Gilbert Simpson who since 1773 had managed GW's property on the Youghiogheny River in Pennsylvania. See, particularly, GW to Simpson, 13 Feb. and 10 July 1784, and *Diaries*, 4:1–25. At the dissolution of the partnership, an undefined sum was due GW for the operation of the mill that he had built on the Washington Bottom tract at great expense. Although the surviving accounts of the partnership and its final settlement are sketchy, GW's subsequent correspondence with Biddle makes it clear that the "Papers" that he is now sending to Biddle are public certificates issued in payment for cornmeal and flour that Gilbert Simpson supplied from GW's mill for the use of the public, probably the army. Biddle wrote GW on 7 Mar. 1785 that he would send the certificate to Benjamin Stelle, the commissioner empowered by Congress to settle such accounts. He then wrote on 12 April that Maj. John Story had been appointed "an additional Auditor to settle the Accounts in this state [Pennsylvania] against the United States" and that he would consult him about the certificates. On 19 April Story's office still had not opened (see Biddle to GW, that date; see also John Story to GW, 20 May 1789). It was not until 5 July that Biddle wrote GW further about the certificates, and this letter is missing. GW

wrote Biddle on 27 July 1785 to thank him for his "attention to the Certificates" and went on to say that he would "obtain an order from Gilbert Simpson, by which the Interest may be received," declaring that this was "all I am likely to get for a Mill which he ran me to the Expence of £1200 hard money to build." What the disposition of these certificates was has not been determined, but nearly a year later, on 18 May 1786, GW sent Biddle a single United States certificate given to Gilbert Simpson in final payment for flour and meal from GW's mill at Washington's Bottom. GW left it to Biddle to sell the certificate or not. In the end, Biddle decided to collect the interest due and then lend the certificate to the state of Pennsylvania in return for a state certificate. The state certificate, which paid interest, he sent to GW. In addition to GW's letter to Biddle of 18 May 1786, see GW to Biddle, 21 June and 31 July 1786, and Biddle to GW, 25 June and 13 Aug. 1786.

To Robert Morris

Dear Sir,   Mount Vernon 1st Feby 1785.

I have been favored with your letter of the first of last month, by Doctr Gilpin & Mr Scott—Mr Colby, they informed me remained indisposed at Baltimore—It will always give me pleasure to see any Gentleman of your introduction—No apology therefore need ever accompany it.

Having begun a letter to you, I will take the liberty of suggesting a matter for your consideration; which, if it strikes you, in the important light it does me, & it is likely to be realized, you may profit by: if it does not, I hope at the same time that you may arraign my foresight, or charge me with being too sanguine, you will do justice to my motives; these, let me assure you, are friendly & pure.

No doubt, before this letter can have reached you, you will have heard, that the States of Virginia & Maryland have enacted laws for the purposes of opening & extending the navigations of the rivers Potomac & James, as far as is practicable; and communicating them by good roads with the nearest navigable waters (for inland craft) to the Westward: the first, to be undertaken by corporate companies with public aid: the other at public expence.

The tolls which are granted to encourage the first of these, are in my judgment, fully adequate to the purpose—as a candid man, I think them too high, considering the harvest which the public is preparing for the adventurers in that undertaking, by opening a communication between the Atlantic & Western Territory: but the importance of the object, considered either in a commercial or political point of view is so great—the combination of favourable circumstances at this epocha so many—and the abilities of the two States under their present pressure of debts, so incompetent to a work of this sort (even if it had been judged the best mode)—that to commence it without delay it was thought best to offer a productive field to those who are disposed to labour therein. And if I live to see the issue, I will, if it does not prove so, acknowledge myself more mistaken than I ever was before, in any speculative point.

I do not advance this doctrine my good sir, with a view to stimulate you to become a subscriber. If I was disposed to do this at the hazard of deception, I see not the occasion for it in the case before us; for it is more the expectation at present, that a redundency than a deficiency, will take place upon the opening of subscriptions for this river: And because your own judgment & convenience can best determine to what amount, or whether to subscribe anything towards the execution of this plan. There are some things however, of which some men have better opportunities to form opinions than others; & of the intercourse which this work is likely to open between the tide water of this river & the greatest extent of back Country within the United States. I have as good means to judge from as most men, & every proof that nature, & reflection upon its bounteous gifts can adduce, to convince me that there is no field for commerce equal to it—if extent of Country, population, & produce with the conveniencies of transportation, are essential to the encouragment & support of it—But these want to be embraced. This however, will not much longer be the case, a Mercantile eye is penetrating, and the first capital House, that is established may form connexions, & lay a sure foundation of trade to the greatest possible extent from the upper sea ports of this river.

No man who has any knowledge of the river Potomac, harbours a doubt of the practicability of its navigation from the great Falls to Fort Cumberland, (about 200 miles) & for 40 miles higher; and it is but very few only who have any doubt of the practicability of opening it from the great Falls, (inclusive) to tide water, which is under 9 miles. The acts I have spoken of

are to encourage & authorise these; and, as I have observed before, sufficient priviledges & immunities are granted for the
purpose.

From Fort Cumberland, a good road may be had to the Turkey foot, or three branches of the Yohoghaney, which will not I
am told, exceed thirty miles—From thence the navigation to
Fort Pitt, about 75 miles further, altho' there is one fall in the
way, can be made good at a very moderate expence. By going
up the No. branch of the Potomac about 40 miles above Fort
Cumberland, a portage may be had with the Cheat river, which
will not exceed 20 miles of good road—from hence to the Monongahela by land or water may be about 25 miles more. We
are then, as in the case of the Yoho[ghen]y communication,
open to the diffusive navigation (more extensive perhaps than
is to be met with in any Country upon Earth) in its natural
state—of the whole western Territory. And if I am not misin-
formed with respect to the carrying places between Cayahoga
(a water of Lake Erie) & big beaver, & Muskingum, which dis-
embogue into the Ohio at different points; there is no rout so
short, so easy & attended with so little expence, as those I have
just mentioned, to bring all the Fur & Peltry of the Lakes—
even from that of the Wood—to tide water. One of them (by
the Yohoghaney) is shorter by more than 150 miles, than that to
either Albany or Montreal: and the way open at seasons, when
the others are block'd—& is besides more independent of the
interference of foreign powers.

That the greatest part, if not all the produce of the Ohio & its
waters as low as the Falls, if a better channel cannot be found
for part of it by way of the Gt Kanhawa & James river to Richmond; or as low as the little Kanhawa, admitting this, I have
very little doubt. It is true that there are some branches of the
Alleghaney above Fort Pit, which communicate pretty nearly
with the waters of the Susquehanna, which by great exertion &
expence, may be made use of at certain seasons of the year, but
droughts in Summer, & Ice in Winter will render them of little
value.

But to place things in a less favourable point of view, I will
grant that a communication between the Kiskeminetas
Moghulbughkitum, or Toby's Creek (waters most favourable
for it) & the Susquehanna shall be opened, & that all the

produce convenient thereto, shall be transported that way to the Markets below: that the Gt Kanhawa shall be found free from obstructions, and easy both in its navigation, & communication with James river—& that all the produce below the mouth of the former, & as far up the ohio as the Little Kanhawa, shall be transported that way: there yet remains the thick settlement of the Ohio, between Fort Pit & Weeling—all the Settlement of the Monongahela, & all that of Yohioghany, which constitute a very large majority of the Inhabitants west of the Laurel hill, to bring their produce to the Markets of this river.

In admitting this, I admit, in my opinion a good deal; but if the plan for opening the navigation of Potomac should succeed, of which I have not the smallest doubt, I will go further and venture an assertion which I think is founded in fact; that without any support from the Western Territory, there is no place within my knowledge to which so much produce will, from the nature of things, be brought, as to the highest shipping port on this river. That this may not appear as mere assertion, I will give you my reasons.

At present, Baltimore not only receives the greatest part of the produce of Frederick County (Maryland) & the Counties above it on the No. side of Potomac, but a great deal also of that which is raised on the south side; & this thro' a long land transportation: besides which, the produce of that rich & extensive Country, between the blue ridge & Alleghany mountains, for at least 200 miles So. West of the Potomac, is (or such part of it as will bear land transportation) carried partly to Alexandria, & the towns below it on this river—partly to Fredericksburgh & Falmouth on Rappahannock—partly to Richmond & Petersburgh—& some part also to Hanover town, the highest navigation upon York river. But let the benefits arising from water transportation, be once felt, & then see, if men possessed of the spirit of commerce & large capitals should settle at the shipping ports at the head of this river, whether an atom of it will cross the Potomack for Baltimore; whilst every thing within its vortex on the No. side will be sucked into, and be transported by water. In like manner the Shannondoah will intercept every article 200 miles from its mouth, & water bear it to the Markets at the head of this river.

In Septembr last I was on the Shannondoah, near or quite 150 miles from its mouth, and was told by well informed Gentlemen living thereon that the navigation of it might be improved, & rendered fit for inland craft at the smallest expence imaginable, the distance here mentioned. In a word, the Shannondoah which runs thro' the richest tract of country in this State—the South branch of Potomac, which may, with great ease be made navigable 100 miles, & the intermediate streams of lesser note which pour into Potomac, will not only bring the land transportation of every farmer & Planter in that country, within the short distance of fifteen or twenty miles, but in the upper & more remote parts of it, induce hundreds & thousands of them to cultivate articles from the growth of which they have been entirely discouraged by the length & expence of land transportation—except in the article of live stock which will carry itself to market—attempting to raise no more than will supply their own necessities. On the other side of the river, the Conogoge and Monocasy, tho' of less importance, will be improved to great advantage.

The mercantile interest of Baltimore affect to treat the extension of the navigation of Potomac as a chimerical plan; but you may be assured Sir, that from the Great Falls, which are within eight or nine miles of tide water, to Fort Cumberland, there is no more difficulty or uncertainty in the execution, comparatively speaking, than there is in bringing water to a Mill by a common race: if nothing more therefore is ever effected, the object notwithstanding is immense, when the field into which it leads is considered. But I have no doubt of the practicability of accomplishing the whole if properly undertaken.

In one or two places of this letter, I have observed that to make proper advantages of this navigation, and the extensive commerce it opens a door to; it requires a large capital as well as a Commercial spirit—I will explain myself.

Alexandria & Georgetown are the highest shipping Ports of this river (if the latter can be call'd one). the trade of Georgetown, I am but little acquainted with; but if I have formed a right idea of the former, it abounds in small dealers: Men who import, or purchase their goods in the country upon credit—consequently obtain them under very great disadvantages: the former class too for the most part, go to one Market—chiefly to

England, for every article they purchase; by which means, such manufactures as Holland, Germany, France &ca could supply upon much better terms, (being of their own production) come with accumulated charges. These added to House rent, which is high in Alexandria, & sinks deep into the profits of a small capital, occasion considerable advance of the price of Goods; the consequence of which is, that the retail dealers in the interior parts of the Country, are induced to go—indeed are in a manner driven, to Baltimore or Philadelphia for their goods. How otherwise is this fact, & the transportation of the staple & other produce of this country, to those markets, to be accounted for? The navigation of this river is equal, if not superior to any in the Union. Goods, I presume may be imported into it, & the produce of the Country exported from it, upon as advantageous terms, as they can from either Philadelphia, Baltimore or any other place, which evinces the truth of my observation— or that the traders of Alexandria are not content with the profits of their fellow labourers in the places I have named. But would either of these any longer exist if large whole-sale Stores, upon the most advantageous terms, were established in that place? And the produce of the back Country brought thither by water, for one fourth of what it is now by land—or a sixth, perhaps tenth, (according to the distance it is carried) of what it can be transported to Baltimore?

At present every farmer who lives on the West side of the blue ridge verging upon Shenandoah, gives I am told one third of his wheat for bringing the other two thirds to any shipping port. Tobacco costs at least 40/ a Hhd—& other things in proportion. A little higher up, & the expence of transportation to a prohibition of the culture of them; tho' the land is better adapted, than any other in the State for the cultivation of them—But if water transportation is effected, that wheat which now costs a 1/3 , may be delivered for 6d. or less a bushel, and where the expence of carriage has hitherto discouraged the growth of it altogether, it will be raised in great quantities—& so with respect to Tobo & other articles.

Having given you this statement of the matter which has fallen under my observation, & which is not exagerated in any instance intentionally, I leave you to compare it with other information & your own observations, if you have opportunities of making any & drawing your own conclusions. I have no other objects in view, but to promote a measure which I think is pregnant with great public utility, & which may at the same time, be made subservient to extensive private advantages. Were I disposed to encounter present inconvenience for a future income, I would hazard all the money I could raise upon the navigation of the river. Or had I inclination & talents to enter into the commercial line, I have no idea of a better opening than the one I have descanted upon to make a fortune. But the first has no charms for me, & the other I never shall engage in.[1] My best respects & good wishes, with which Mrs Washingtons are united, are offered to Mrs Morris & the rest of your family; & I am, Dr Sir Yrs &c. &c.

　　　　　　　　　　　　　　　　　G: Washington

P.S. I send you a copy of the Bill passed by the two States, for opening & extending the navigation of the river Potomac.

LB, DLC:GW. A letter-book copy of this letter, addressed to Thomas Willing of Philadelphia, was advertised in Robert F. Batchelder's catalog no. 78 (1990), item 61.

　　1. GW includes in his letter to Morris much of the information about and arguments for the Potomac River enterprise that he had earlier written to interested Marylanders and Virginians, but his tone and emphasis are quite different in addressing the Philadelphia financier.

From Edmund Richards

Honoured Sir　　　　　Plymo[uth]. Dock [England] Febry 1st/85
　　I most humbly presume to take on me the freedom of acquainting your Noble Excellency that Richard Richards of Guynepe parish in the County of Cornwall lately posses'd of Severall plantations in Virginia and died there about 37 years Agone and left a Will in the possesion of your Excellency's hands Concerning the plantations with fourteen thousand pounds in Cash And by proof the will being produced the whole was left to Edmund Richards being my father and I being call'd Edmund after my Father's own Name but Richard Richards the Younger Brother of my fathers, after My father's death posses'd the plantations for Severall Years and died about 18 or 19 Years ago and he being Very Intimately acquainted with your Excellency left the Will in Your Hands with all the

Cash and Lands belonging to Richard Richards As your Excellency offer'd to be a Trustee for the same and whereas your Excellency was pleas'd to appoint Lawyer Haines of Virginia to draw out a Copy of the will and to Send itt to Lawyer Britton of Collumpton To have the Copy advertiz'd in the public papers So as to find out the Nearest Relation and I Edmund Richards hearing of the Same Can with every circumstance of truth prove that Richard Richards Was my Only Uncle Brother to My father Edmund Richards as no Other person can with fidelity and truth prove any other and now With advice from my Lawyer and Severall Responsible Gentlemen As Every thing being Settled Amicably between Great Brittain and the United States of America took this opportunity of Sending to your Excellency To Enquire into every particular Circumstance So as I might have itt from Under Your hand Whatt is my true and lawfull right as Me and no other Can Claim a Just and proper right to it.

And now Sir your Excellency will I hope be Carefully pleas'd to peruse this and youll find that the Whole properly belongs to me And I hope your Excellency on receiving this or Some Short Time After will be so Kind and Obligeing as to Send me the Whole particulars and in So doing youll Ever oblige Sir Your Excellency's Most Obedient Humble Servt to Command.[1]

Edmund Richard's

LS, DLC:GW; copy, DLC:GW. Both copies of the letter are addressed to "His Excellency General Washington of the United States Congress in America." The LS sent to GW by Richards is written in what appears to be a clerk's hand; the copy, which is marked "copy" and was enclosed in a letter to GW from Richard Thomas of 13 Aug. 1785 (see note 1), is either the copy of the letter that Richards sent Thomas or a copy of that made by Thomas.

1. GW wrote Richards on 15 June 1785 that he had "never heard of the man, his Will, or the Estate." This did not put an end to the matter, however. In late fall 1785 GW received a letter written on 13 Aug. 1785 from Richard Thomas of Charleston, S.C., enclosing a letter from Richards making Thomas his attorney in America to recover for him the estate in Virginia that he claimed to have inherited. GW wrote Thomas on 5 Dec. 1785 with some irritation that Richards was "under a delusion which has not a single reality for support." Before receiving this letter, Thomas wrote again on 10 Dec. asking for the supposed will and then, on 25 July 1786, wrote GW a letter of apology.

To Robert Lewis & Sons

Gentlemen,   Mount Vernon 1st Feby 1785

You may think me very troublesome—and the reason I assign for being so (that I am of opinion you can serve me better than any other) no good apology for the liberty I take.

My Miller (William Roberts) is now become such an intolerable sot, and when drunk so great a madman, that however unwilling I am to part with an old Servant (for he has been with me 15 years) I cannot with propriety or common justice to myself bear with him any longer.

I pray you once more, therefore, to engage & forward for me, a Miller as· soon as you may have it in your power; and whatever engagement you shall enter into on my behalf I will religeously fulfil. I do not stipulate for the Wages altho my Mill (being on an indifferent stream & not constant at work) can illy afford high wages.[1]

My wish is to procure a person who understands the manufacturing business *perfectly*—and who is sober and honest, that I may even at the expence of paying for it, have as little trouble as possible with him. If he understood the business of a Millwright and was obliged by his articles to keep the Mill works in repair, so much the better—Whatever agreement you may enter into on my behalf, I pray you to have it reduced to writing, & specifically declared, that there may be no misconception or disputes thereafter.

The House in which such Miller will live, is a very comfortable one, and within 30 yards of the Mill (which works two pair of Stones, one pair of them french Burrs)—it has a small Kitchen convenient thereto and a good garden properly paled in—There is a Coopers shop within 50 yards of the Mill, with three Negro Coopers which will also be under the direction of the Miller. whose allowance of Meat, Flour, & priviledges of every kind, I would have ascertained, to prevent *after* claims. I do not object to the Mans having a family (a wife I could wish him to have) but if it was a small one, it would be preferable.[2]

At any rate be so good as to let me hear from you, that I may know on what to depend, as it is no longer safe for me to entrust my business to the care of Willm Roberts. It only remains now for me to ask your forgiveness for this trouble, & to assure you of the esteem with which I am Gentn Yr friend & very Hble Se⟨rvt⟩

Go: Washington

ALS (photocopy), ViMtV; LB, DLC:GW.

1. For a summary of William Roberts's tenure as GW's miller and for references to GW's correspondence with Lewis in 1783 regarding Roberts, see Roberts to GW, 25 Nov. 1784, n.1. GW first wrote Lewis about replacing Roberts on 6 Sept. 1783.

2. The reply from Robert Lewis & Sons of 6 Mar. 1785 has not been found, but on 5 April the company wrote GW recommending that he hire Joseph Davenport, which he did. See GW to Robert Lewis & Sons, 12 April 1785. In its letter of 6 Mar., Lewis & Sons probably enclosed a copy of the following advertisement, dated 10 Mar., which appeared in the *Pennsylvania Gazette* (Philadelphia) on 30 Mar.: "EMPLOYMENT for an honest, sober, industrious man, who understands manufacturing wheat in the best manner, and is capable in every respect of the management of a mill, consisting of two pair of stones, one of which are French burrs, situate near Potowmack River, in Virginia, a fine healthy country—also, to superintend the business of a cooper's shop, wherein three hands are employed, near the mill.

"If his knowledge extends to the mill-wright business, so as to keep the running geers in repair, it would add to the convenience; and his having a small family would be preferable to none. He will be furnished with a comfortable dwelling-house contiguous to the mill, a good garden properly pailed in, and perhaps some other conveniences, as may be stipulated and agreed on. He must produce unquestionable recommendations of his honesty, sobriety, and industry, to his Excellency General WASHINGTON, Mount Vernon, in Virginia, or to the subscribers in Philadelphia, who will contract with such person on generous terms."

To Clement Biddle

Dear Sir,   Mount Vernon 2d Feb. 85.

The Writer of the inclosed letter, in person & character, is entirely unknown to me.[1] I have been at a loss therefore to determine what notice to take of it—at length I concluded to write the answer which is also enclosed; and to request the favor of you to send it to him, or return it to me, as you should just[2] best from the result of your enquiries; or from your own knowledge of the author, or his Works.[3] If he is a man of decent deportment, & his productions deserving encouragement, I am very willing to lend him any aid he can derive from the proposed dedication, if he conceives a benefit. His letter & proposals you

will please to return me—& Seal the letter to him, if it is forwarded to the address. I am—Dr Sir Yr most obedt Servt

Go: Washington

ALS, PHi: Washington-Biddle Correspondence; LB, DLC:GW.

1. This was the letter to GW from Aeneas Lamont, 31 Dec. 1784, printed above.

2. The letter book has "judge" rather than "just."

3. Biddle wrote below GW's signature in this letter: "March 7 Answered—I could not obtain such Information respecting the Author of the Poems as to induce me to deliver your letter but will make further Enquirey on that subject." See Biddle's letter of 7 March. Biddle decided not to deliver the letter (see the note in Lamont to GW, 31 Dec. 1784). The text of the letter of 31 Jan. to Lamont that GW enclosed was: "Sir, The interruption of the Post by the frost, withheld your letter of the 31st Ulto from me until within a few days.

"The liberty you have taken in dedicating your Poetical Works to me, does me honor—The conditions upon which you offer them to the Public are generous—evincive of their purity—and conscious worth. I shall with pleasure therefore take a few copies of the bound & lettered Books, when they are ready for delivery.

"It behoves me to correct a mistake in your printed address 'To the patrons of the fine arts' I am no Marshall of France—nor do I hold any Commission, or fill any office under that Government—or any other whatever. I am—Sir Yr Most Obedt Hble Servt Go: Washington" (ALS, PHi: Washington-Biddle Correspondence). There is also a letter-book copy, DLC:GW.

To Otho Holland Williams

Dr Sir,   Mount Vernon 2d Feby 1785.

Your letter of the 24th ulto with eighty three Diplomas came to my hands on Monday last. I have signed and returned them to Colo. Fitzgerald to be forwarded to you.

It would be hard indeed upon Majr Turner & Captn Claypoole not only to give them the trouble of producing the Diplomas, but to saddle them with the expence of it also. Was there no provision made therefor at the General Meeting? Do not the minutes of that meeting devise some mode of payment? I well remember that the matter was agitated, but I forgot what, or whether any conclusion was come to: & I recollect also that I desired Genl Knox when difficulties arose with respect to the business which had been entrusted to Majr L'Enfant to suggest, that the sum which I had proposed to subscribe for the purposes of the Society might be applied to any uses the Meeting should direct; but what the result of it was, I know not. It was observed at that time, that there was money in the hands of the Treasurer General—but not having the proceedings to refer to, and a bad memory to depend upon—these things appear like dreams to me.[1] With great esteem & regard I am Dr Sir Yr ob: humble Servant

G: Washington

LB, DLC:GW.

1. GW wrote in his diary on this day: "Employed myself (as there could be no stirring without) in writing Letters by the Post and in Signing 83 Diplomas for the members of the Society of the Cincinnati and sent them to the care of Colo. [John] Fitzgerald in Alexandria—to be forwarded to General Williams of Baltimore the Assistant Secretary of the Society" (*Diaries*, 4:83). The diplomas were stolen before reaching Williams (see notes 1 and 3 in Williams to GW, 24 Jan.).

From John Sullivan

Sir   Exeter in New Hampshire Feby 3d 1785
    The state meeting of the Cincinnati in New Hampshire have received and considered the proceedings of the General Meeting held at Philadelphia in May Last[.] when we view the respectable Characters which attended that Meeting and call to mind the repeated proofs they have given of their great abilities and penetration Nothing But the clearest conviction could bring us to believe an Error or an inconsistencey in their proceedings—The Society was Instituted by officers who having Endured Every species of Toil & danger Distress were about to return [to] their respective families many of which were by the Long absence brought to a Degree of poverty and Even those which were before in the most affluent Circumstances considerably reduced—such was the state of our public funds That instead of receiving & carrying home with them the reward of their services or the wages which they had stipulated for to relieve those who had patiently Suffered a Tedious absence they could only present them with Scars & ruined Constitutions—The freedom of their Country being effectually secured They then devised a Method for perp[et]uating that friendship for Each other which had subsisted among them through the Course of a Long & Tedious war supported under the severest

trials & Cemented by their Blood—They considered the Emblems of the society as the most Endeuring tokens of that friendship and wishd that it might be Cherishd among their Children.

The funds were intended to relieve the widows and orphans of their Brethren who had fallen in Defense of their Country & Members of the Society who might become objects of their Charity—If these were the principles upon which the Society was founded what good Reason can be assigned for not Suffering the same marks of mutual friendship to be held in grateful remembrance by their Children[1] which are allowed of Such high Estimation among the parents.

You will pardon us for observing that by placing the funds in the hands of the respective Legislatures it seems to indicate that Instead of officers reduced in Circumstances by the[2] want of pay & the common misfortunes of war they had arrived to such a Degree of wealth & affluence That they had Even so great a plenty of Cash that a new & unheard of method must be contrived to take it from them & place in hands which could at pleasure deprive them of it without their having the Least possible controul over it—or voice in Disposing of it—And we flatter ourselves that we cannot be accused of indecencey when we observe that as the Existence of the society is to End with the Lives of the present members the funds must consequently be a gift to the Several Legislatures or if continued by the admission of new members under Charters obtaind as proposed in the Last Meeting the funds will be Lost to the Donors & their posterity & together with those Endeuring Marks of friendship will be Enjoyed by neither the persons who had a right to claim them or by their Desendants—we know the uneasiness which the Institution of this Society created among the people & are at no Loss to conjecture the Occasion but if it was thought necessary to Quiet the minds of people & to Silence the Tongue of Envy, would it not have been done more Effectually by removing the Cause of Complaint—& abolishing the Society at once we are not Tenacious of contending for the power of writing to Each other as Societies though it might be difficult to assign a Reason why Ever[y][3] member of the united states Every Convention Committee of Safety & the persons Composing a Town Meeting should have a priviledg of Corrisponding with Each other upon public affairs & the officers of the American Army alone be Deprived of it.

The Establishing a Common fund & reserving Liberty to Dispose of it for Charitable uses has been complained of as Dangerous to the Liberties of this Country. societies of various kinds have often done this without alarming the people & if Joint merchants free masons or the Members of any other society took the Liberty of Disposing of their own money for Charitable purposes the right has never before been called in Question or the Charitable Disposition been Deemed a Crime.

But if pretences Like these are to be regarded or fears so ill founded are to be Quieted we wish the Ax may be Laid to the Root of the Tree & the Society be intirely abolished & Every member take back & Enjoy what he has put in the funds or dispose of it—according to his pleasure.

We became Members of the Cincinnati upon the original plan & cannot conceive ourselves bound by Articles to which we never subscribed and in Case it should become necessary to Establish a new system we shall Individually claim a right to determine for ourselves whether we will become members or whether we will not.

ADf, MHi: John Sullivan Papers. Sullivan may not have completed or sent this letter. No copy of it, and no acknowledgment of its receipt, has been found. Sullivan headed the draft: "To his Excellency General Washington president of the Society of the Cincinnati."

Gen. John Sullivan (1740–1795) did not attend the meeting of the Cincinnati in Philadelphia in May when the alterations in the society's Institution to which he is objecting were made. See Sargent's journal, doc. II in General Meeting of the Society of the Cincinnati, 4–18 May 1784, printed above.

1. Sullivan wrote "Childred."
2. Sullivan wrote "they."
3. Sullivan wrote "Ever."

To John Beckley

Sir,   Mount Vernon 5th Feby 1785.
Here with you will receive the ingrossed Bill which was forwarded to me by Colo. Grayson for the purpose of getting printed copies taken.[1]

I hope it will get safe to your hands—that I may be satisfied of this, be so good as to inform me thereof.[2] I am Sir &c.

G: Washington

LB, DLC:GW.
1. See GW to William Grayson, 22 Jan. 1785, and note 1.
2. Beckley acknowledged receipt of GW's letter on 11 February.

Letter not found: from Patrick Henry, 5 Feb. 1785. On 27 Feb. GW wrote to Henry: "I have had the honor to receive your Excellency's letter of the 5th."

To Benjamin Lincoln

My Dr Sir,   Mount Vernon 5th Feby 1785.

Not until within these few days have I been favored with your letter of the 18th of Octr introductory of Mr Porter. I beg you to be assured that I shall have pleasure in shewing him every civility in my power while he makes this region the place of his residence—as I shall to any other, to whom you may give letters recommendatory.[1]

A few days ago I received from on board some vessel in the harbor of Alexana—two cheese's, & a barrel (wrote thereon Major rice) of Cranberries, unaccompanied by a letter, but said to be a present from you. If this be the fact I pray you to accept my thanks for this token of your recollection—or to offer them to Majr Rice, if the barrel came from him.[2]

We have nothing stirring in this quarter worthy of observation, except the passing of two acts by the Assemblies of Virginia & Maryland (exactly similar) for improving & extending the navigation of the river Potomac from tide water, as high up as it shall be found practicable, & communicating it by good roads with the nearest navigable waters to the Westward: which acts in their consequences, may be of great political, as well as commercial advantages: the first to the Confederation, as it may tie the Settlers of the Western Territory to the Atlantic States by interest, which is the only knot that will hold. Whilst those of Virginia & Maryland will be more immediately benefited by the large field it opens for the latter. Books for receiving subscriptions are to be opened at Alexandria & other places the 8th instant, & continue so until the 10th of May; as the navigable part of the business is to be undertaken by a company to be incorporated for the purpose. With great truth & sincerity I am My Dr Sir &c.

G: Washington

LB, DLC:GW.

1. Letter not found. In 1784 Thomas Porter (d. 1800) established the mercantile firm of Porter & Ingraham in Alexandria. He became a friend of George Augustine Washington and often visited Mount Vernon.

2. Maj. Nathan Rice served as General Lincoln's aide-de-camp from 1777 to 1781.

To Battaile Muse

Sir,   Mount Vernon 5th Feby 1785.

I have lately received two letters from you, one of the 14th & the other of the 25th of last month.[1]

The Bonds which you have taken from Mr Whiting had better remain in your hands until they are discharg'd. And by the time you propose to be at Belvoir, in April—I will endeavour to prepare a proper rental for you, if it shall be in my power, from the pressure of other matters.[2]

It was always my intention, & ever my expectation, that the Tenants should pay the tax of their own Lotts; but if the Leases neither express nor imply it, I do not suppose there is anything else to compel them—consequently Mr Whiting must be allowed what he has actually paid—look however at his lease, and judge yourself of the fact; as I speak more from my expectation than reallity perhaps, & do not want to enter into an improper litigation of the matter. I am Sir &c.

G: Washington

P.S.—Mrs Washington begs you would get from some of my Tenants, or others 10 or a dozen lbs. of good hackled Flax for her.

LB, DLC:GW; printed, Thomas Birch's Sons, catalog 683, item no. 2, 5–6 April 1892. The transcription of the ALS letter printed in the catalog differs from the letter-book copy printed here mostly in punctuation, but the catalog copy indicates that in the third paragraph GW wrote, "as I speak more from what ought to be perhaps than what really is," whereas the clerk renders this passage in the letter-book copy, "as I speak more from my expectation than reallity perhaps." The postscript does not appear in the letter-book copy and is taken from the catalog.

1. Muse's letters of 14 and 25 Jan. have not been found.

2. For Muse's dealings with GW's tenant, Henry Whiting, see GW to Muse, 3 Nov. 1784, and the references in note 3 of that document. For GW's "rental," see his List of Tenants, 18 Sept. 1785, printed below.

To Benjamin Vaughan

Sir,   Mount Vernon 5th Feby 1785

I pray you to accept my acknowledgement of your polite letter of 31st of October; & thanks for the flattering expressions of it.[1] These are also due in a very particular manner to Doctr Price, For the honorable mention he has made of the American General, in his excellent observations on the importance of the American revolution—"Addressed to the free and united States of America" which I have seen & read with much pleasure.[2]

Capt. Haskeill in the Ship May arrived at the port of Alexandria a few days since; but the frost which at present interrupts the navagation of the river, has prevented my sending for the Chimney piece; by the number of cases in which it is packed, I greatly fear it is too elegant & costly for my room & Republican stile of living—I regret, exceedingly, that the politeness of your good Father, should have overcome my resolution, & thereby occasion the trouble & difficulty which this business seems to have involved. Nothing could have been more remote from my intention than to give this; & I earnestly, but in vain, entreated Mr Vaughan to countermand the order for its shipment.[3] I have the honor to be Sr, Your most obedt humble Serv.

G: Washington

Copy, ViMtV; LB, DLC:GW. GW sent his letters of this date written to Samuel Vaughan and his son Benjamin under one cover addressed to "Saml Vaughan Esqr. Philadelphia." Samuel Vaughan made this copy of GW's letter to Benjamin Vaughan, printed here, on GW's cover to the two letters, and then presumably forwarded the original letter to his son. The differences between it and GW's letter-book copy are few and unimportant.

1. Letter not found.

2. For references to GW's receiving several copies of Richard Price's pamphlet on the American Revolution and to GW's reaction to the pamphlet, see Richard Henry Lee to GW, 16 Jan., n.1, and 8 Feb. 1785, n.4.

3. By April 1784 GW knew that Benjamin Vaughan's father, the London merchant Samuel Vaughan, was sending him a marble chimneypiece for his "New Room" at Mount Vernon. See GW to Samuel Vaughan, 6 April 1784, and 5 Feb. 1785. The boxes containing the pieces of the marble mantle were opened at Mount Vernon on 6 April, but they were not installed until work on the room was resumed in 1786 (see *Diaries*, 4:114, and GW to Tench Tilghman, 30 Nov. 1785).

To Samuel Vaughan

Dr Sir,   Mount Vernon 5th Feby 1785.
   I have the honor to inform you that the Chimney piece is arrived, & by the number of Cases (ten) too elegant & costly by far I fear for my own room, & republican stile of living—tho' it encreases the sense of my obligation to you for it. The Ship arrived at her Port just as this second frost set in, so that it has not been in my power to send up for these cases by water, & I would not hazard the transportation of them by land, nine miles.[1]
   They were accompanied by a very polite letter from your Son Benjamin Vaughan Esqr. of London[2]—to whom under cover with this, I have acknowledged the receipt, with thanks for the favorable expression of it. I hope Mrs Vaughan & your family enjoy good health, to whom with Mrs Washington's compliments, I pray to be presented in respectful terms. With great esteem & regard I am Dr Sir Yrs &c. &c.
                                                  G: Washington

LB, DLC:GW. See the source note in GW to Benjamin Vaughan, this date.
   1. See GW to Benjamin Vaughan, this date, n.3.
   2. Letter not found.

Letter not found: to Josiah Parker, 6 Feb. 1785. On 24–28 Feb. Parker wrote to GW: "I feel myself much honored with your very friendly polite letter of the 6th Ultimo."

From Christopher Chamney

Sir   Whitehaven [England] February 8th 1785
   I have been 26 Years from Virginia Septr last, and for the last 7 Years I have enjoy'd an uninterupted State of good Health owing to Temperance, Exercise, & early going to Rest without Supper.
   The Irish are aiming at Independance—they have had no less than 5 Lord Lieutenants in 3 Years vizt
   Earl of Carlisle
   Duke of Portland
   Earl Temple
   Lord Northington, & at present the Duke of Rutland a Son of the late Marquis of Granby

Our Sir James Lowther is lately advanc'd to the House of Lords with the pompous Titles of
1. Baron Lowther of Lowther in the County of Westmorland.
2. Baron of the Barony of Kendal in the said County.
3. Baron of d[itt]o Borough in the County of Cumberland.
4. Viscount Lonsdale.
5. Viscount Lowther, &
6. Earl of Lonsdale

Mr John Hudson told me he saw you, & your Son Lund at Alexandria, it gave me great Pleasure to hear ye were well My best Respects to all my surviving old Acquaintance. I should be glad to hear from you yearly by some of our Whitehaven Vessels that load at Alexandria, a Virginia Almanack, & a Gazette will be very acceptable. Wishing you & Your's many happy Years I am Your most obedt Servant

Christr Chamney

ALS, DLC:GW.
Christopher Chamney's name appears in the Fairfax County records in 1749, and a Christopher Chamney kept a store in Richmond in the early 1750s. John Carlyle was only the most prominent of the merchants in Alexandria who had close business and personal ties with Whitehaven. John Hudson has not been identified.

From John Filson

Sir   Wilmington [Del.] Feby 8th 1785
I herewith send you a book and a Map enfolded, requesting Your Excellency to receive them, and if upon perusal you think them worth Notice, I presume you will favour the following requests with a letter to the Author, Containing a permission to dedicate a Second edition of this Narrative to Your Excellency, to which will be added interresting accounts. About the first of March the printer will begin the work, I request you will honour the publication with Your sentiments respecting the Commercial Circumstances practicable to be effected between the waters of Potowmack and Cheat rivers: This Sir may be of public utility and Certainly more acceptable from you than any other. Your Concern for the public good so gloriously Manifested to the world, and so deeply impressed on the hearts of Your grateful Countrymen will by this favour render the publication more acceptable and beneficial to Mankind. In Novem-

ber last I Consigned a Number of these books & Maps to Mr John Page at Rosewel desiring him to forward one to you, and a letter importing the substance of this, but probably they are Miscarried.[1] If we are to expect your addition to this work, it is humbly wished for before March. at present Will subscribe Myself Your Excellencies Sincere friend and humble Servt

                                                            John Filson
P.S. perhaps a few of these would be acceptable in your part.

ALS, DLC:GW.

1. GW wrote Filson on 16 Jan. 1785, in response to Filson's letters of 30 Nov. and 4 Dec. 1784, declining Filson's invitation to write something on the West for a second edition of Filson's *History of Kentucky*. See the notes in Filson's letter of 4 December. On 15 Mar. 1785, GW writes Filson to thank him for the copy of the Kentucky map and of his history.

From Benjamin Harrison

                                        Berkley [Charles City County, Va.]
My Dear Sir   Feby 8th 1785
    Your esteem'd favor of the 22d of last month reached me but a few days ago. Letters by post are some time geting to me, owing to the distance I am from the post road.

    I was fully aware of the difficulties the compliment made you by the assembly would lay you under, and assure you that the love and friendship I entertain for you, my earnest wishes that you might still support that noble disinterestedness of character that has hitherto mark'd all your steps and actions, and a perfect knowlege of the delicacy of your feelings, gave me a full share of perplexities on the occasion. If you were without enemies, or the eye of melevolence was not intently fixed on all your actions, I should not see the least impropriety in your accepting a present from your greatful country, particularly as every care has been taken in the preamble to the grant, to guard against the most distant appearance of its being a gratuity for the important services you have render'd America, and to fix it to the true objects of the Acts, the great and real advantages that will derive to the country from the extention of its navigation, the parent of which you have been, and to whom alone they owe their existence, or will probably owe their completion. But on the other hand when I view mankind, their pronen[e]ss to put the worst construction on every action of those of exalted character, and the triumph it will give your enemies, to have an apparent th'o false opportunity to attempt the lessening your reputation, I am at a loss what advice to give, and shall therefore leave the determination to your own far better judgment.

As to your fears of appearing ostentatious by a refusal, I think they are altogether groundless, your countrymen have too high an opinion of your discernment not to acquiesce in your determination but more especially in points where reputation is the stake. Their motives for what they have done were of the purest kind, they saw with concern the sacrafises you had made for their benefit, by a total neglect of your domestic affairs, and they have been earnestly seeking an opportunity to show their gratitude and love for you; they thought one presented itself that was out of the reach of detraction, and therefore embraced it with one voice, and as far as I could see with one mind, and I am certain would sensibly feel any slur cast on your reputation, with these sentiments th'o they will feel unhappy that they cannot be gratified in their wishes, yet they will not take amiss a refusal dictated by motives that have hitherto done you so much honor.

I am happy to find that th'o you have not taken your final resolution with respect to the compliment, that you will still forward the schemes, as the works under your patronage and protection will advance more rapidly than they would otherwise do, and the subscription probably be fill'd, as I fear would not be the case, if advantage is not taken of the ardour of the present moment.[1]

I am extremely oblig'd to my good friends at mount Vernon for their kind inquirey after the health of Mrs Harrison, who is geting better th'o slowly. I have hopes and indeed expect she will mend faster when the weather will permit her to use excercise, which seems to be her only remedy She and the girls join me in the most friendly and affect. compliments to you and the Ladies. I am my dear Sir with sentiments of the most perfect esteem and regard, your most obidient Humble Servant

Benj. Harrison

ALS, DLC:GW.

1. For a description of GW's perturbation over the gift of shares in the Po-

tomac and James River companies by the Virginia legislature, see note 1 in Harrison to GW, 6 Jan. 1785.

To Richard Henry Lee

Dear Sir,   Mount Vernon Feby 8th 1785

Since my last I have had the honor to receive your favors of the 26th of December, & 16th of January.

I have now the pleasure to inform you, that, the Assemblies of Virginia & Maryland have enacted Laws for improving & extending the Navigation of Potomk of which the inclosed is a copy—They are exactly similar in both States. at the sametime, and at the joint & equal expence of the two Governments, the sum of 6666⅔ dollars are voted for opening, & keeping in repair, a road from the highest practicable navigation of this River, to that of the river Cheat, or Monongahela as Commissioners (who are appointed to Survey & lay out the same) shall judge most convenient, & benificial to the Western Settlers; and have concurred in an application to the State of Pensylvania for permission to open another road from Fort Cumberland to the Yohiogany; at the three forks or Turkey foot. A similar Bill to the one inclosed, is passed by our Assembly, respecting the Navigation of James River; & the Communication between it & the Waters of the Great Kanhawa. And the Executive is Authorized, by a resolve, to appoint Commissioners to examine, & report the most convenient course for a Canal between Elizabeth River & the Waters of Roanoke; with an estimate of the expence; and if the best communication should be f[oun]d to require the concurrence of the State of North Carolina thereto, to make application to the Legislature thereof, accordingly.[1]

Towards the latter part of the year 1783, I was honored with a letter from the Countess of Huntingdon, briefly reciting her benevolent intention of spreading Christianity among the tribes of Indians, inhabiting our Western Territory; & expressing a desire that my advice & assistance might be afforded her, to carry this charitable design into execution. I wrote her Ladyship for answer that, it would by no means comport with the plan of retirement I had promised myself, to take an active or responsible part in this business; and that it was my belief, there would be no other way to effect her pious & benevolent design, but by first reducing these people to a state of greater civilization; but that I would give every aid in my power consistent with that ease, & tranquillity² I meant to devote the remainder of my life [to,] to facilitate her views—Since this—I have been favored with other letters from her, & a few days ago, under cover from Sir James Jay I received the Papers herewith inclosed.³

As the Plan contemplated by Lady Huntingdon, according to the outlines exhibited, is not only unexceptionable in its design and tendency, but has humanity & charity for its object—and may, as I conceive, be made subservient to valuable political purposes, I take the liberty of laying the matter before you, for your free & candid sentiments thereon. The communication I make of this matter to you, Sir, is in a private way; but you are at full liberty to communicate the Plan of Lady Huntingdon to the members individually, or officially to Congress, as the importance, & propriety of the measure may strike you.

My reasons for it are these, 1st I do not believe that any of the States to whom she has written (unless it may be New York) are in circumstances since their cession of territory, to comply with the requisition respecting emigration; for it has been privately hinted to me (& ought not to become a matter of public notariety) that notwithstanding the indefinite expressions of the address, respecting the numbers, or occupations of the emigrants (which was purposely omitted, to avoid giving alarms in England)—the former will be great, & the useful artizans among them, many. 2d because such emigration, if it should accomplish the object in view, besides the humane & charitable purposes which would thereby be answered, would be of immense political consequence: & even if this should not succeed to her Ladyships wishes, it must nevertheless be of considerable importance; from the increase of population by orderly & well disposed characters, who wd at once, form a barrier; & attempt the conversion of the Savages without any expence to the Union.

I see but one objection to a compact, unmixed, & powerful Settlement of this kind (if it should ever become so)—the weight of which you will judge of—it is (and her Ladyship seems to have been aware of it, and endeavors to guard against it) placing a people, in a body, upon our exterior, (contiguous to Canada) who may bring with them strong prejudices against us, and our forms of Government; and equally strong attachments to the Country & constitution they leave; without the means, being detached & unmixed with Citizens of different sentiments, of having them eradicated.

Her Ladyship has spoken so sensibly, & feelingly on the religeous, & benevolent purposes of the plan, that no language of which I am possessed, can add ought, to enforce her observations: and no place, in my opinion, bids so fair to answer her views, as that spot in Hutchins's Map Marked Miami Village, & Fort. From hence their is a communication to all parts by water; and at which, in my judgemt, there ought to be a Post.

Do not think it strange, my good Sir, that I send you the original papers from Lady Huntington.[4] Many, mistakingly, think I am retired to ease, & that kind of tranquillity which would grow tiresome, for want of employment. but at no period of my life—not in the eight years I served the public, have I been *obliged* to write so much *myself* as I have done since my retirement. was this confined to friendly communications, & to my own business, it would be equally pleasing & trifling; but I have a thousand references of old matters with which I ought not to be troubled, but which nevertheless must receive some answer. These, with applications for certificates, copies of Papers, &ca &ca &ca deprive me of my usual, & necessary exercise—I have tried to get a Secretary, or Clerk to take the drudgery of this business off my hands, but hitherto in vain. That you might not wonder at my parting with original papers, upon an interesting subject, I thought it incumbent on me to assign the reason—but I pray *you* to be *assured* that I have no other motive for it.

Please to accept my thanks for the Pamphlet you sent me—and the resolutions respecting the temporary & permanent residence of Congress[5]—If I might be permitted to hazard an opinion of the latter, I would say that, by the time your fœderal buildings on the banks of the Delaware; als in[6] the point of a triangle (when compared to the Shape, & extent of the Confed-[erate]d States) are fit for the reception of Congress it will be found that they are very inconveniently placed, for the Seat of the Empire &c. will have to undergo a *Second* edition, in one more convenient. If the Union continues and this is not the case

I will agree to be placed amongst the false prophets, & suffer for evil predictions.

The letter which went undr cover of my former, & which arrived too late for the Marqs de la Fayette, I pray you to forward to him by the Packet.[7] With great esteem & regard I have the honr to be Dr Sir Yr Most Hble & Obedt Servt

Go: Washington

ALS, PPAmP: Correspondence of Richard Henry Lee and Arthur Lee; LB, DLC:GW.

1. A summary of GW's activities in the founding of the Potomac River Company appears in the editorial note of his letter to Benjamin Harrison, 10 Oct. 1784. For the references to the James River Company and the Elizabeth River canal, see James Madison to GW, 9 Jan. 1785, Enclosure III.

2. In the letter book the word "Tranquillity" is followed by "to which."

3. See Lady Huntingdon's Scheme for Aiding the American Indians, 20 Dec. 1784, particularly doc. I: James Jay to GW, 20 Dec., and notes.

4. Lee returned the packet of paper on 27 Feb. with his letter giving the reasons why Congress had rejected Lady Huntingdon's schemes, which were the same objections that GW alluded to in this letter.

5. For Richard Price's pamphlet, see Lee to GW, 16 Jan. 1785, n.1; for Lee's news of Congress's decision to place the capital near Trenton, see Lee to GW, 26 Dec. 1784.

6. Instead of "also inn," the letter book has "along," but GW may have been using "als" as an old form of "as."

7. For the identification of the letter to Lafayette, see Lee to GW, 26 Dec. 1784, n.2.

From Elias Boudinot

My dear Sir   Elizabeth Town [N.J.] Febry 9th 1785

This Moment I am honored with your favour of the 26th Janry and am greatly mortified to find, that mine of the latter End of December had not then reached you, altho I delivered it to the post-Master myself.[1]

It ever gave me a peculiar Pleasure to obey your Commands, and to Oblige you in any thing this Country can afford, or to comply with your wishes, in any other way, will add greatly to the felicity, I enjoy from those domestic Blessings you with Mrs Washington so kindly participate in.

As soon as I recieved your favour of Novr I tryed to obtain the quantity of seed you requested, but the Season being past, could get only Six or Seven Bushells, which was immediately forwarded by the Stage to Coll Biddle, under the Care of our old Friend Coll Gibbs, who happened to be a Passenger, and by the next Post, I advised you of it.[2]

Since which, I have accidentally met with three Bushells and an half more, which I shall also immediately forward by the same Conveyance to Coll Biddle[3]—The reason of my preferring the Stage, arises from the incertainty of a Passage from New York, the danger of its being lost in the City, and the importance of your not being disappointed in having it early in the Season.

I have had another Conversation with a very experienced Farmer, on the manner of sowing it—He informs me that the Soil should be good, moderately dry and in good tilth—The Quantity of Seed, must be proportioned to the goodness of the Soil—the better the Ground, the greater the quantity of Seed—He has known in very high cultured Grounds, two Bushells used for one Acre, and he thinks it, the cheapest in the End—In good Land, he has generally used from one, to one & an half Bushell ℔ Acre—The more seed the finer the Grass. The earlier it is sown the better; provided you can harrow it, with some light Body, as a Thorn Bush or some other thick Bush, as it then covers the Ground well, before the Heats of Summer—To make Hay of it, you must cut it young when in full bloom.

It will give me great Satisfaction to hear, that both Parcells have got safe to hand, and answer your Expectation.

Mrs Boudinot enjoys a very good state of Health, as does Mrs Bradford in the City[4]—Mrs B. feels herself greatly indebted to Mrs Washington for her kind remembrance—She joins me in the most cordial wishes, for every Blessing of the Season to attend you both. I have the honor to be with the greatest respect My dear Sir Your most obedt & very Hble Servt

                                        Elias Boudinot

ALS, DLC:GW; LB, NjP: Thorne-Boudinot Collection.

1. No letter to GW from Boudinot dated in December 1784 has been found.

2. See GW to Clement Biddle, 3 Nov. 1784, n.2.

3. See Clement Biddle to GW, 7 March.

4. Mrs. Bradford was Boudinot's daughter Susan, wife of William Bradford.

From John Fitzgerald

Dear Sir   Alexandria [Va.] Feby 9th 1785

I am honor'd with your letter of this day & forward you by the Bearer 6 Copies of the Printed Bill should you think more necessary at any time please apply for them.[1]

Our Subscriptions I doubt not will be fill'd in the limited time[.] I keep my Book in order to have the pleasure of your name at the head of it. I have the honor to be Dear Sir your mo. Obed. Servant

John Fitzgerald

If you can conveniently come up to morrow please favor me with your Company at Dinner.[2]

ALS, DLC:GW.

1. Letter not found. The "printed Bill" is the act creating the Potomac River Company. See GW to John Beckley, 5 February.

2. GW wrote in his diary on 10 Feb., "Road up to Alexandria today and dined with Colo. Fitzgerald" (*Diaries*, 4:88).

From Lafayette

My dear General   Versailles february the 9th 1785

After a pretty tedious passage of thirty days we Have Safely Arrived at Brest, from whence I Came to paris through Rennes, where the States of Britanny were Assembled, and where their kindness to me Made it Necessary for me to Stop one day—My family, wife, children, and friends I found in perfect Health—the politics of Europe are not in a tranquil Condition, and from their situation a dreadfull war may Break out—What I Could Collect I Have writen to Mr jay, and inclose a Copy of my letter[1]—prince de Condi, and Marechal de Broglio are spoken of to Command the two Armies—Where I would Serve, I Had not yet time to Arrange—But it will not Be with my dear General, and Every thing is so short of that Happiness, that Nothing, when Compared to it, Can possibly please me—However, notwistanding all preparations, I still am of opinion matters will Be Compromised and, at least for this Year, I Hope no war will Be Necessary—the propriety of my not Arriving later than Now is very obvious—irish disputes are But little Spoken of, But may Revive with their Congress and their Reviews—England will take no part in the war, at least in the Begining—I Have obeyed your orders, my dear General, and Besides those you told me, I Have presented your Compliments to every Acquaintance of yours—in a few days I Hope for a letter from you—now, my dear General, that I Had once more Got Used to the Happiness of Being with, or at Least Near You, A punctual Correspondance, at least, is more than ever Necessary to my Heart—should a packet Come without a letter from you, I would indeed feel very unHappy—this letter will Be But short, not so much on Account of my late Arrival than Because I did not think the third tuesday was on the 15th—for the Same Reason my little girl will Be deprived of the Honour of Answering Her Sweet Correspondant untill next packet—those two letters Have almost turned Her Head[2]—Mde de Lafayette Requests Her most affectionate Compliments to you, and Mrs Washington. The Chevalier joins with me in Assurances of Respect to Her, to your Excellency, and we Beg to Be Remembered to the Young ones, and Mrs Stuard—My Compliments to the doctor and Mr lund W. Give me leave once more to Recommend two things to you—Riding now and then—and getting a Secretary—Adieu, Adieu, My dear General, Every Sentiment that love, Gratitude, Regard Can inspire, Every filial, friendly feelings, shall for ever Combine to put me at the Head of all those who ever loved a father and friend as Your affectionate and Humble Servant

Lafayette

ALS, PEL.

1. See Lafayette to John Jay, 8 Feb. 1785, in Idzerda, *Lafayette Papers*, 5:293–95.

2. Only one letter from GW to Anastasie de Lafayette in 1784, that of 25 Nov., has been found.

From John Rumney, Jr.

Sir   W[hi]t[e]haven [England] 9th Feby 1785

In Compliance with your request to me when in America I have made every Enquiry relating to the Flags that I could, I have sent you three Patterns in a Box, viz. one of black Stone or Marble from the Isle of Man which comes at 13d. ℔ Flag deliv'd in Douglass, the Freight from thence to this Place will be but trifeling, & whatever you pitch upon to have sent out, we shall be as reasonable as possible in the freight out from here.[1] The next is a white Flag from this Neighbourhood, with Veins in it, the Person which furnishes that will not do it under 9d. ℔ Flag, the other is a white Flag pretty hard & I think of a better Quality than the other, got in this Neighbourhood, which may be got for 7½ or 8d. I have been disappointed in getting some from Ireland, which I expect every Tide, I shall send them by a Vessel we have going to Alexa. in abt 6 Weeks.[2] I have inclos'd you a Plan I got from Ireland with Directions for laying the Flags for your Perusal, also one from the Person that furnishes the Vein'd Flag.[3] I have made every Enquiry I could for a Joiner & Bricklayer, but have only succeeded in the former who I now send out in the Cæsar Ct. Atkinson, he is a very sober industrious Young Man & a complat Worker. I got him on the best Terms I could as you will see by the inclos'd Indenture.[4] We have advanc'd him as under, which you will please stop out of his first Years Wages by Agreement, & at any Convenient Opportunity may pay said Sum into our Store in Alexandria to Mr Sanderson.[5] On your writing to me upon fixing which Flag you will have, I shall give the Orders to have them provided. I am with Compts to Mrs Washington, with the greatest Esteem, Sr Yr mo. obt Servt

                                                John Rumney

Advanced Mathew Baldridge	£ 6.	6.0
his passage to Alexandria	5.	5.
two Agreements on Stamps	1.	8.3
pd Mr Younger[6]	£12.	19.3

ALS, DLC:GW.

1. Douglas is a port on the Isle of Man.

2. Rumney was not able to send the samples of Irish flagstones until July 1785; in the meantime GW had decided to use the cheaper white ones from Rumney's "Neighbourhood." See Rumney to GW, 3 July 1785, and GW to Rumney, 22 June 1785.

3. One of these enclosures (DLC:GW) is a "Ruff Sketch of hand" of a floor paved with alternating black and white flagstones in a diamond pattern, followed by instructions for laying the flags to achieve the desired effect. The other one may be George Darley's plans for the Mount Vernon piazza, dated at North Strand, Dublin, 2 Nov. 1784. A photocopy of this is at Mount Vernon and a transcription of it is in CD-ROM:GW.

4. The joiner Matthew Baldridge arrived at Mount Vernon on 8 May. See

Diaries, 4:136. The indenture, which has not been found, provided that Baldridge would remain in GW's employ for three years (see note 6). Baldridge's salary was £25 per annum for the first two years (see Ledger B, 249).

5. By "as under," Rumney was referring to the notations at the end of his letter.

6. Another enclosure in Rumney's letter is a statement, dated 8 Jan. 1785, of payment of £1.8.3 by Rumney, "on Behalf of his Excellency General Washington," to Peter How Younger for drawing up for GW a three-year agreement with Matthew Baldridge and for paying the fees for the indenture (DLC:GW).

From Thomas Smith

[Carlisle, Pa., 9 Feb. 1785]

EDITORIAL NOTE

In the years immediately preceding the American Revolution, GW devoted considerable time and effort to the acquisition of large tracts of land in western Virginia and in the Ohio Valley. By 1775 he laid claim to over 37,000 acres in the West, acquired under the proclamations of 1754 and 1763 for his military services during the French and Indian War or through purchases from other veterans. In 1770, in payment for a debt of £2,000 owed him by his neighbor John Posey, GW received a warrant from Posey for 3,000 acres, the amount of bounty land that Posey was entitled to under the Proclamation of 1763. GW used the major part of the warrant to claim 2,813 acres on Millers Run, a tributary of Chartiers Creek, in an area that was then considered a part of Augusta County, Va., but by 1784 lay across the boundary in Washington County, Pennsylvania. William Crawford surveyed the tract for GW in 1771, but GW was not able to patent it until July 1774.[1] The remainder of Posey's warrant was applied to the 587-acre tract at Round Bottom on the Ohio River.

GW began to have difficulties with squatters on his Millers Run land in the early 1770s. Crawford reported in May 1772 that he had turned off several men who had built cabins on the land, paying them a small consideration for their improvements. Crawford then built houses on the land to establish GW's claim.[2] In October 1773, however, another, and more determined, group of settlers moved onto GW's land. Crawford wrote GW in December: "Som people, about 10 or 12 in number, has gon on your Cherter land within this few days and there is no geting them of without by Force of Arms They are in Couraged by Majr [Edward] ward Brother to Colo. Croghan, ho Claims the Land, and says he has grant . . . from Crown for that Land

and he will undemnifie them, if they will set in any house whare no Person is Living. . . . he farther ads that Colo. Croghan says you and my self has used his Brother Colo. Croghan very ill in pretending to bey his Land and did not, but want and took the best of it, and would not agree to pay him. . . . I think such Proceeding as those if not Stopd will soon set the Hole County in ruin those men have not bought of him, but took your Land and say the[y] will Keep it, I cold Drive them a way but they will com back Emedetly as soon as my back is turnd, They man I put on the Land they have drove away and Built a house so Colse to his dore he cannot get into the house at the dore."[3] George Croghan may indeed have urged the squatters to settle on GW's land. Croghan, one of Pennsylvania's largest land speculators, was undoubtedly piqued that he had failed in his attempts to enmesh GW in his land schemes.[4] In 1770, besieged by creditors on every side, Croghan had tried to retrieve his fortunes by an ambitious scheme to reactivate an earlier grant he had received from the Indians, setting up a land office at Pittsburgh to deal with sales of his claims. After GW visited Pittsburgh in October 1770 on his land-seeking western tour, he noted in his diary on 21 Oct. that all of the land between Raccoon Creek and Chartiers Creek was owned by Croghan and that by Croghan's account it was "a body of fine Rich level Land," which "he wants to sell, & offers it at £5 sterg. pr. hundd. . . . provided he can sell it in 10,000 Acre Lots."[5] Croghan, assuming that his bait had been taken, wrote a colleague jubilantly that he was "likely to sell another tract to Coll. Washington and his friends. If I do *that,* I expect to have one good nights rest before Christmas, which is more than I have had for eight months past I assure you."[6] As GW continued his trip down the Ohio, however, he began to have second thoughts about Croghan's proposals. "The unsettled state of this Country," he noted in his diary on 21 Oct., "renders any purchase dangerous." His suspicions of Croghan increased after William Crawford wrote that he feared Croghan "has not a proper title to what he now is Claiming."[7] GW's skepticism was well founded. After the final boundary settlement between Virginia and Pennsylvania, Croghan was able to obtain legal title to none of the lands he claimed.

During the next few years Crawford continued his attempts to keep squatters off the Millers Run land. As late as September 1776 he wrote GW that "your Land on Shurtees Creek is well Cultivated Redy to your hand; the men on it thinking you have no patent for the Land or that if you have that youl will Lease them the Land on Reasonable tearms."[8] In their conflict with the squatters, GW and Crawford were confronting a long-established if extralegal Pennsylvania land policy. Under the Penns a relatively lenient view of illegal settlers had evolved, the proprietors believing that any occupation of the land was preferable to leaving it vacant and unimproved. Original settlement and improvement had come to represent a more valid claim to unoccupied land than the mere possession of a patent. Boundary disputes often were referred to local tribunals where sentiment was strongly in support of illegal settlers and opposed to absentee land speculators.[9]

After his return to Mount Vernon in 1784, GW began to take stock of his western landholdings.[10] The Pennsylvania-Virginia boundary dispute finally had been settled in 1780, and when the line was run in 1784–85 it left GW's Chartiers Creek land on the Pennsylvania side of the boundary. Aware that squatters had long established themselves on his Millers Run land and made relatively extensive improvements, GW in the spring of 1784 instructed his nephew John Lewis to inform the settlers that he had a legal patent to the property and that he would "most assuredly assert his right to it." He was, however, willing that they should remain as tenants on the land "upon a just & moderate Rent." Lewis did not deal with the tenants directly but published advertisements informing them of GW's intention to repossess his land.[11]

In September 1784 GW decided to make a tour in which he would inspect his landholdings in the West, oversee the sale of the land at Washington's Bottom, Pa., held jointly with Gilbert Simpson, Jr., and investigate the possibilities of river navigation up the Potomac into the Ohio Valley. In addition, he contemplated at last a face-to-face meeting with the recalcitrant settlers on his Washington County land. Arriving in the area of Chartiers Creek on 18 Sept., GW met the assembled tenants on 20 September. The squatters were members of the Associate Presbyterian Church (Seceders' Church), a Presbyterian sect that had broken with the main church in 1733. All were men of some consequence in the community.[12] They did not come to the meeting in the role of supplicants. James Scott and Squire John Reed, spokesmen for the group, contended that while they had no doubts concerning the successful outcome of any legal action, they were willing to purchase the land if GW offered moderate terms. GW replied that even though he was not eager to sell he would make the group a final offer to sell the entire tract, which he did. After some discussion the settlers decided to take their chances in court.[13]

Determined now to submit the matter to litigation, GW met with attorney Thomas Smith in what is now Uniontown, Pa., on 21 September. The uncertainties surrounding GW's case are evident from notes on the case in Smith's hand:

Brief of General Washington's Land on Millers Run
23 March 1771 Col. Wm Crawford Surveyed 2813a. on Miller's Run for George Washington—the right not mentioned.

14 October 1770 John Posey entered into a Bond to Genl Washington Conditiond to Convey his Right to 3000a. under the Proclamation of 1763.

5th 1774 A Patent for 2813a. the above Survey granted to G. Washington but as the Copy of the Survey Returned to the Office by Lewis the County Surveyor, & on which the Patent Issued, is not obtained, the Date of it does not yet appear.

Col. Crawford made Improvements on the Land for General Washington before the adverse Parties claimed (but what those Improvements were does not appear)—1 May 1772. Col. Crawford found six Men on the Land who had built a House & cleared 2 or 3a.—he paid them £5 for their Improvement, & built 4 Cabbins viz. one on each Corner of the Land.[14]

While GW was gathering the papers pertinent to his case in Virginia, Smith made a preliminary entry for the case in the Washington County court for the December term.[15] Following GW's wishes, Smith had the case entered into the Pennsylvania Supreme Court docket and requested that Bushrod Washington help collect the necessary papers. In the meantime Smith also had ejection notices served on the squatters by the Washington County sheriff. The case was formally removed from the lower court in March 1785 and the papers delivered to the Supreme Court.[16] Determined to establish that his claim to the land on Chartiers Creek antedated the settlement of his opponents, GW devoted much time during the next year to marshaling his evidence. He consulted John Harvie, Virginia's land officer in Richmond, for assistance in retrieving documents from the land office, asked Edmund Randolph for advice, instructed his western Pennsylvania land agent Thomas Freeman to aid Smith "in hunting up the evidence necessary for the prosecution of my ejectments in the Court of Washington," and sought the testimony of prominent residents in Pennsylvania to support his claims. GW believed that a clear title to the tract "*may* make a difference of between £3500 and £4000 to me for which I can sell the Land in dispute if I establish my right to it."[17] Much of his correspondence on the case over the next year dealt with what he anticipated his opponents' arguments would be. It was essential to his case to establish not only that his claim antedated the settlement of the squatters but also that he had fulfilled the obligation of making improvements on the land before they occupied it, a major factor in previous ejectment cases in Pennsylvania courts.[18] GW himself was convinced that his opponents would base their case on the fact that they had occupied the land by October 1773. His position was further jeopardized by doubts about whether William Crawford was legally qualified to make the surveys on Millers Run. Crawford apparently had not taken the oaths required by his office. On the other hand, all grants for bounty lands had been confirmed in 1779 by an act of the Virginia assembly.[19] In July 1785 GW sent the documents he had collected to Smith with a spirited defense of his legal position in regard to the Millers Run land.[20] In addition he drew up a brief of the case giving both his position and that of his opponents:

> The ground on which it is presumed the Defendants will place their Defence;

Pleas

1st—That Captn Crawford was a great Land jobber, and to effect his monopolies had recourse to many expedients—amongst which, that of using the names of people of influence was one, to cover his claims until he could dispose of the Lands;—by which means it became difficult for strangers, and those who had lately come into the Country, to obtain settlements otherwise than by purchase from him.— That the Country was thereby injured, and emigrts imposed upon.—That as this was known to be the case, no credit could, or ought to have been given to his Notification that the Land belonged to me.

2d.—But, admitting the fact to be as it has since proved,—yet, my Survey they have said, and it is supposed will contend, was a private one, unauthorized, and consequently of no validity.

Answers

1st—The character, & general conduct of Captn Crawford must speak for themselves,—and these, I conceive, will bear the test of examination.—If he was a forestaller or monopolizer of Land, it is unknown to me.—I had no hand in the speculation.—nor have I a foot of Land in the Western Country that I do not hold under Military rights, except the tract on Yohiogany whereon Gilbert Simpson lives, and a small tract of between two & 300 acres at the Great Meadows; both of which I purchased.—Indeed, comparatively speaking I possess very little land on the Western Waters.—to attempt therefore to deprive me of the little I have, is, considering the circumstances under which I have been, and the inability of attending to my own affairs, not only unjust, but pitifully mean.

2d—This Survey was regularly made by a Person legally appointed for a special purpose— and, as far as his Surveys were covered by Military Warrants and rendered valid by the Surveyor of the County in which they lay, Patents were directed to issue on them, if no Caveats were offered in bar.

3d.—That their Occupancy pre-ceeded the date of Captn. Craw-fords Deputation, and legal return of the Survey upon which my Pa-tent issues; and consequently not be affected by transactions subse-quent thereto.

3d—If this is a fact, & it is essen-tial for them; it rests upon them to prove it.—but it must certainly be unimportant if I can prove my Survey—my possession—my pur-chase of the *first* claim to it.—the relinquishment of Col Cannon—the Warnings given them of my Right &ca.—all of which were pre-vious to any claim they can, or do pretend to have.

4th.—Supposing (they may say, because they have said it) that my Patent was originally good, yet, my right is forfeited for want of that cultivation and improvement which was required by Law, and which is conditional of the Grant.

4th.—It may be asked how I could improve or cultivate the Land when they had taken posses-sion of it & violently detained it from me?—But the fact is, and it is well known to Colo. [John] Ste-phenson, Gilbert Simpson, & many others, that I had a number of hands under a manager to whom I paid £100 pr ann, for the express, & only purpose of saving my Lands according to Law—That these people began on the Great Kanhawa where the Lands were first Patented—That they were working upwards therefrom to this very Tract, and would have saved this tract also if the disturbances with the Indians, which forced them to abandon the work (to my great disappointment & loss)— and the unjustifiable conduct of them-selves, would have permited it; as I had until June, or July 1777, to comply with the Law.

5th.—That one of the Defen-dants, in behalf of the rest had been sent to the Land Office of this State to ascertn the truth of the Report of my having a Grant of the Land;—but finding no Record of the Patent or Survey, the pre-

5th.—Whether this search was really made, or not, is not for me to determine; but admitting it, it can be no reason why I should loose my right, because they did not, or even could not, discover a record of it. if the fact existed &

sumption was, that none had ever been made; and was considered by *them* as an evidence that my name had only been used by Captn. Crawford to secure it for his own purposes.

unequivocal proof thereof can be adduced—of which the Patent is an incontestible one.

6th—That they never had any *legal* notice of its being my Land— nor legal warning to quit it—without which, under the conviction above, they were not bound to regard either.

6th—What *really* is, or *may* be construed, legal notice in such a case, is not for me to decide.—The fact is (& I believe it was pretty well known) that Captn. Crawford did business for me in that Country.— that as soon as they had taken possession of the Land, he either in person, or otherwise informed them that it belonged to me; and this without waiting for my orders.—That as soon as I was advertized of the matter, and frequently afterwards, it was impressed upon them; accompanied with assurances, that I should, as soon as it was in my power, assert my Right to it.

7th.—That no person was living on the Land when they took possession of it—and that the only House thereon was deserted.

7th—The matter as it has been represented to me, is, that the man whom Captn. Crawford placed on the Land to keep possession, being from home, they took advantage of his absence and built a House so close to the one in wch. he lived, as to exclude the entrance of it.— This is mentioned by Captn. Crawford in a Letter, & probably can be proved by Mr. Mar Stephenson, Morgan and others.

8th—That (provided they discover that their *possession* not prior to the *date* of the Warrt. to Captn. Posey) if my title is derived from a Military claim and the Warrt. which gives that claim is of subse-

8th.—The Act of 1779, with the measures, which had been previously taken by me,—and my claim before the Defendts had any knowledge of the Land, must obviate every plea of this kind.

quent date to their settlement, it can have no operation to their prejudice.

9th.—Under these circumstances, and this conviction, they took possession; and at great expense have improved the Land; and ought not in Law or equity to be deprived of it.

9th—This argument is pointedly against them because the fact is, & no doubt if proper pains is taken to obtain the evidence, the proof will be, that they knew this Land was reputed to be mine.— That as soon as they set down upon it, they were so informed, and repeatedly warned off, and admonished of the consequences of continuing thereon.—If notwithstanding, from disbelief of the report, or disregard of the several notices given them, they would persist, it, certainly, must be in their own wrong, and not to the loss of my property.—for was the case otherwise, no one could be secure in Lands at a distance—as possession & occupancy wd. set aside the best title, and put legal Right at defiance[21]

GW also prepared for Smith a statement of the "ground on which the title of G: Washington to the 2813 acres of Land in Washington County, State of Pensylvania, is founded; with the evidence in support thereof":

Ground

1st Colo. Crawford as an acquaintance and friend—and one who had a Military claim under the Proclamation of 1763, which he was desirous of securing—proposed to be at the trouble of looking out the Lands whilst GW was to use his endeavours to obtain the Warrants. accordingly the tract of 2813 acres which is now the subject of dispute, was explored, and allotted for the use of GW; and every

Evidence

1st—The Letters now sent, and those already in the hands of Mr Smith are declaratory of this.

measure which could be taken at that early period, was adopted to secure it.

2d—At the request of GW, and subsequent to the appointment of Captn Crawford by the Masters of William & Mary College (by whom all Surveyors were appointed), for the purpose of Surveying 200,000 acres of Land granted to the first Virginia Regiment as a bounty under the Proclamation of 1754, and previous to the Occupancy of the defendts he (Crawford) made an *actual* survey[22] of this tract, and returned a certificate thereof to G.W.

2d.—This Survey was left among other Papers in the hands of Mr Smith—or with Majr Thos Freeman of the County of Fayette; who does business for GW; the latter not having it, tho' he well recollects to have been possessed of it when he was last in the Western Country.

3d—Occupancy of the Western Lands before, at, long after this period, was expressly forbid by the Kings Proclamation:—His Governors instructed not to grant Patents;—and the Surveyors restrained from receiving Entries & locations; except to such as were entitled under the Proclamation of Octr. 1763 for Military Services which was permitted by a subsequent act of the Governor and Council and Warrants granted consequent thereof[.] Every step therefore which the defendants took was in open violation of the Acts of the then existing Government; even supposing there had been no prior claim to the Land in dispute;—but so far as was the case from this, that the Survey of it for GW which was long before they had come into the Country, and consequent of a Military claim which I had purchased from Captn. Posey, as will appear by

3d.—The Bond from Captain Posey is herewith sent, and sufficiently authenticated it is believed—The Warrent from some Papers GW has lately met with, and as he presumes it will appear by the Patent, which is in the hands of Mr. Smith, is not dated until the 25th. of Novr. 1773—How such a lapse of time should have happened betwn the purchase of the Right, and the obtainment of the Warrant, GW is utterly at a loss to acct. for.—If the discovery of this should be made by the defendants it is supposed they will lay much stress on it, as they pretend they came to the Land in Octobr. 1773, which being a month before the *date* of the Warr, they will say G.W. can derive no benefit therefrom— This should be guarded against.

Bond of the 14th. of Octr. 1770, with wch. the Land was covered as soon as a Warrant could be obtained, must do away every shadow of legal, or equitable claim from them.

4th.—Some person, or persons, setting up a calim to the Land, or part thereof, within the limits, wch. had been marked; rather than dispute with them, Captn. Crawford purchased for the use & benefit of GW this claim—This was previous to the coming of the Defendants into the Country; or to any knowledge they could have had of the land.

4th.—A Letter which it is *supposed* was left in the hands of Mr. Smith, from Captn. Crawford to GW, declares this; it not being in the possession of GW. tho well remembered having such as induces this supposition.

5th.—Colo. Cannon, a Gentleman of Reputation, who lives in the Country, and in the vicinity of the disputed Land—took possession of it, and made some improvements thereon; but upon discovering marked trees—and upon tracing them, finding a regular Survey, well bounded; and understanding upon enquiry, that the Survey was made by Colo. Crawford for the use & benefit of GW he quit it.—This also was antecedent to any view, or knowledge the Defendants had of the Land.

5th.—GW having received this information from Colo. Cannon himself, there can be doubt of his giving testimony thereto.—as also, that it was well known in those parts at the time the Defendants took possession of the Land, that it belonged to GW.

6th.—They were informed of this first instance—repeatedly & admonished afterwds.—& ordered to leave the Land, acknowledge themselves Tenants, or abide the consequences; as GW. was determined to prosecute his Right thereto as soon as circumstances would permit him to do it.

6th.—The Defendants could not indeed did not deny to GW having knowledge of these things.—they confessed that they had seen advertisements. posted on the Land giving this information; but may deny *it all* or be *silent thereafter* at the tryal.—Colo. Crawfords letters are expressive of it, and he, and his Brother Vale. were well knowing to it.—however, as they are both dead—the most likely persons to prove it now are Colo. John Stephenson, Marcus Stephenson, Colo. Cannon, Mr. Morgan (who Surveyed under Captn. Crawford) Mr Leet, Geo. McCormick— Gilbert Simpson Captn. [Van] Swearingin Cap: [Matthew] Ritchie & others, some of whom were connected with & aiding & assisting Crawford at those times.

7th.—It was currently reported, and as generally believed to be Land belonging to GW as the nature of the thing would admit of before, at the time, and after the Defendants had taken possession of it (which by their own accts was not until Octr 1773) no plea of ignorance therefore can possibly be offered in justification of their proceedings.

8th.—This Land was not only surveyed in the manner, and under the circumstances before mentioned; but improvements thereon were made for the use & benefit of GW & an expence incurred before the Defendants ever saw it. on his acct.

8th.—Colo. Crawfords letters declares this expressly, and it is believed that some one, or more of the persons named above will be able to prove it.—With respect to one Cabbin, there can be no doubt because it remains there to this day unless it has been removed, or destroyed since the 20th of September last; when, in Company with Col Cannon, Captn. Swearingen Captn. Richie Mr. Geo: McCormick & others GW was on the Land, saw another House built so close to it as, in a manner, to exclude the entrance into it; and heard them acknowledge that it was on the land before they cam to it.

9th.—In the Spring of 1774 (If memory serves) Captn. Crawford received a further appointment from the Masters of Willm. & Mary College to be Deputy Surveyor of Augusta County under Thos. Lewis Esq (in which County the Land *then* lay); immediately after which, a certificate was returned in due form to the Secretarys Office, reciting the Military right under which it was claimed—where upon a Patent, with the Seal of the Colony & the Governors issued without any opposition, in June, or July of the same year; which was as early as any legal Surveys were made, or could be made, in that Country.—but this Survey, with the proceedings antecedent thereto which were of record, being lost, nothing but presumptive proof can be drawn from thence.—this however must be as strong as any presumptive proof whatever can be, because we must suppose that public offices act agreeably to the Laws and Constitution of the Country in which they are instituted, or by established Rules & regulations of their own when these are silent—The Patent then (which. is yet in existance) being the last act for transfering the right of the Crown, to doubt the regularity of the proceedings in which it was founded, is to cha: the Land Office, and Executive for the time being of this state, with maladministration.

10th.—These proceedings being recognized by an Act of the Virga. Assembly entitled "An Act for adjusting & settling the titles of Claimers to unpatented Lands

9th.—Captn. Crawfords Commission to be Deputy Surveyor of Augusta, is to be found either in the Hands of Mrs. Crawford, his widow—or Mr Bradford's who has charge of his Papers—

The certificate from the Register of the Land Office, declares that the Survey with many other Papers fell into the hands of the enemy and were destroyed: no recourse therefore can be had to any records herein antecedant to the Patent; which by being in the possession of GW was saved, and has been put into the hands of Mr. Smith.

10th. The authenticated act (by the Seal of the Commonwealth of Virginia, and signature of the Governor) herewith sent, is very expressive of the case of G.W.

under the present & former Government previous to the establishment of the Commonwealths
Land Office" the first claim
therein declares expressly, that all
Surveys made before the *1st day
of Jany 1778* by the Surveyor of a
County under either of the rights
which are therein recited, and
against which no Caveat had been
entered, should be good & valid—
and moreover, that *Military* locations by *actual* Surveys made under
speical commission, should *become*
valid upon taling out Warrants and
resurveying according to Law.

All of which should have been
done; but in the case of GW. it was
altogether unnecessary; inasmuch
as the legal forms had all been
complied with four years before
the passing of the Act.

11th.—No Caveat was evr. entered by the Defendants in bar to
the right of GW, with a view to
prevent the issuing of a Patent;—
nor has any steps ever been taken
by them (known to GW) to obtain
the Land themselves,—either in
the State of Virginia or Pensylvania—Putting their whole dependance upon a violent obtrusion,
made under as unfavorable circumstances as can well be conceived.

11th.—The Register of the
Land Office has declared that no
Caveat was ever entered in the Ld.
Office of this State by the Defendants—That no application appears from the records, to have
been made to the Commissioners
who were appointed by the Act of
Assembly to hear & determine disputed titles—And that no location
thereof has ever been made in this
State by them, or any body in their
behalf.

12.—The letter from Mr. [John]
Harvie, Register of the Land
Office deserves particular consideration, as it points to the Rules
and Regulations of that Office, &
gives much useful information.

12th—This letter is sent and
may be used as occasion shall
require.

13th.—The agreement between
the States of Virginia & Pensyl-

13th.—An authenticated record
of this agreemt, is sent.

vania respecting territorial boundary—saves the private property,
and rights of all persons who may
have acquired titles under either
Country respectively, previous to
the ascertaining and running such
boundary, altho' they should be
found to fall within the other.

During the summer of 1785, GW continued to prepare his defense
in anticipation of the Pennsylvania circuit court hearing. Even without
complete documentary proof, he wrote Edmund Randolph in August, "the matter is so clear, in my judgment, as not to admit of dispute before an *impartial* Jury; but an *impartial* Jury I do not expect—
& much less since I have heard that the high Sheriff of the County
(lately chosen) is of the fraternity of my competitors."[23] By early September GW's annoyance with the settlers had increased to the point
that when he heard what proved to be an unfounded rumor of their
planning to move off his land, he instructed Smith to seek punishment for these "defendants as willful & obstinate Sinners." Because
"they have withheld the Land from me ten or twelve years after all the
admonition I could give, & the favorable offers which have been made
them—& finally have put me to the expence & trouble of bringing &
supporting Ejectments," he wrote Smith, "it is my wish & desire,
whether they leave the land voluntarily, or are compelled to do so by a
course of Law, that you will sue them respectively for Trespasses,
rents or otherwise as you shall judge best."[24]

In the summer of 1786, still in pursuit of evidence for the upcom-
ing hearing before the Pennsylvania circuit court, GW made the dis-
maying discovery that Posey's warrant was dated 25 Nov. 1773, "pos-
terior, according to my opponants acct to their settlement." Even so,
and in spite of the disappearance during the war of a number of legal
documents supporting his claim, GW remained confident enough of
the outcome to request Smith to offer the lands for sale subject to the
success of the ejectment proceedings. The lands "have been so unproductive of every thing but vexation and trouble," he wrote Charles
Simms in September 1786, "that I am resolved to sell them at long or
short credit, as may best suit the purchaser, provided I can get near
the value of them." Noting that the tenants at their meeting with GW
in September 1784 had chosen litigation instead of accepting his offer
of twenty-five shillings per acre, "they must give more now if I oust

them."[25] The *nisi prius* court, presided over by Pennsylvania Supreme Court justice Thomas McKean who was riding circuit, was set to try the case of *Washington v. James Scott et al.* at its September 1786 session in Washington County, with Hugh Henry Brackenridge appearing for the settlers. GW had hoped to attend but a brief illness prevented it.

The ejectment cases were heard on 24, 25, and 26 October 1786, after which Smith wrote: "I have the very great pleasure to inform you that Verdicts have been given in your favour in every one of them." Smith, having decided that James Scott was the leader of the settlers, had arranged for Scott's case to come up first. Each of the plaintiffs insisted on having his turn in court. Indeed, Smith wrote, "each would have demanded a separate trial; but as I had consolidated the Ejectments against these Dependants, they were obliged to try them all together, & the trial did not last long." Many of the jurors, he was convinced, would have preferred to find for the defendants. Smith's astute maneuvers in jury selection had aided GW's cause, which was also immeasurably strengthened by Thomas McKean's refusal to allow the question of improvements on the land to be entered as evidence in the proceedings. Though elated at his victory, Smith retained a certain sympathy for the settlers: "I believe that the Defendants in the Ejectments will be with you soon ⟨to⟩ endeavour to do what they ought to have done when you made them the Offer—I verily believe that it was more their misfortune than their fault that they then rejected it. You have now *thirteen* Plantations—some of them well improved—I take it for granted that the improvements increase the value of the Land much more than all the expences of the Ejectments—those who mad[e] them are now reduced to indigence—they have put in Crops this season, which are now in the ground—they wish to be permitted to take the grain away—to give this hint may be improper in me—to say more would be presumptuous."[26]

GW could now afford to be magnanimous. He wrote George McCarmick in November: "Altho' those people have little right to look to me for favor or indulgences, & were told, if they run me to the expence of a Law suit, that they were not to expect any; yet as they are now in my power, it is not my wish to intention to distress them more than the recovery of my property obliges. They may therefore continue on their respective places either as Tenants at an equitable rent which shall be deemed reasonable between man & man, or as purchasers, if the terms can be agreed on between us." In the end GW also allowed the tenants credit for part of their crops but not for the improvements they had made.[27]

During the 1790s GW continued to lease his Millers Run lands to new tenants, but difficulties in securing dependable agents and his growing conviction that distant land was "attended more with plague than profit" led him by 1794 to offer his Millers Run land for sale at four dollars an acre. In 1795 he sold the land to Col. Matthew Ritchie. Unlike some of the purchasers of GW's other land, Ritchie made prompt payments. After Ritchie's death in February 1798, considerable contention arose between GW and Ritchie's executors relating to payments and other matters concerning the land, and at the time of GW's death in December 1799 there were still payments due on the Millers Run land.[28]

1. See Bond of John Posey, 14 Oct. 1770, printed above; and Vi: Va. Colonial Land Patents (Grants), 1623–1774, Book 42, pp. 516–18. See also GW's letter of 17 Feb. 1774 to Thomas Lewis, surveyor for Augusta County, requesting Lewis to patent the tract. A resurvey of the Millers Run land during the 1790s indicated the area to be slightly more than 3,000 acres (Land Memorandum, 25 May 1794, and GW to Presley Neville, 16 April 1796). For GW's acquisition of bounty lands both for his own services and through purchase from other veterans, see the source note in GW to Samuel Lewis, 1 Feb. 1784.

2. See Crawford to GW, 2 Aug. 1771, 1 May 1772, 29 Dec. 1773, and Thomas Smith's notes for a brief in GW's ejectment case, 1784 (NhD). One of the men who moved onto the Millers Run land was John Cannon of Washington County who owned additional land on Chartiers Creek. See GW's brief, printed here.

3. Crawford to GW, 29 Dec. 1773.

4. See Crawford to GW, 12 Nov. 1773, reporting George Croghan's role in encouraging squatters on GW's property. See also Bothwell, "The Astonishing Croghans," 138. Local tradition holds that at least some of the squatters had originally purchased their land from Croghan. See William M. Farrar to Boyd Crumrine, 13 Sept. 1882 (PWW: Crumrine Papers).

5. *Diaries*, 2:295. For GW's account of his meeting with Croghan, see ibid., 292–94.

6. Croghan to Joseph Wharton, Jr., 25 Oct. 1770, in Wainright, *Croghan*, 277.

7. Crawford to GW, 20 April 1771. See also GW to Crawford, 6 Dec. 1771, and Crawford to GW, 15 Mar. 1772.

8. Crawford to GW, 20 Sept. 1776. See also Crawford to GW, 29 Dec. 1773.

9. See Schoepf, *Travels in the Confederation*, 1:221, and Wilkinson, "Land Policy and Speculation in Pennsylvania," 62–75.

10. See GW's detailed letters to Thomas Lewis, 1 Feb. 1784, and GW to John Harvie, 10 Feb. 1784.

11. GW to John Lewis, 14 Feb. 1784. See also Lewis to GW, 27 April 1784. GW states his position on the land most clearly in his letter to George McCarmick of 12 July 1784.

12. Washington County Supply Tax—1781, 715–17, 729, 758, 761–62, 768, 774. Among the tenants attending the meeting were James Scott, John Reed, William Stewart, Thomas Lapsley, Samuel McBride, Brice McGeehon (McGeehan), Thomas Biggert, David Reed, William Hillis, James McBride, Duncan McGeehon, Matthew Johnson, and John Glenn (*Diaries*, 4:28–30).

13. GW offered the settlers "the whole tract at 25/. pr. Acre, the money to be paid at 3 annual payments with Interest; or to become Tenants upon leases of 999 years, at the annual Rent of Ten pounds pr. ct. pr. Ann. The former they had a long consultation upon, & asked if I wd. take that price at a longer credit, without Interest, and being answered in the negative they then determined to stand suit for the Land" (ibid., 28). Local tradition holds that GW replied with some temper, "asserting that they had been forewarned by his agent, and the nature of his claim fully made known; that there could be no doubt of its validity, and rising from his seat and holding a red silk handkerchief by one corner, he said, 'Gentlemen, I will have this land just as surely as I now have this handkerchief'" (Crumrine, *Washington County*, 858–59).

14. Dartmouth College, Hanover, New Hampshire. A note attached to Smith's draft states: "Charles Morgan (came to me) can prove that he was with Crawford when he surveyed the Land—began a Cabbin in April 1771 and saw Crawford give his Note for £5 to Thomas Crooke Esqr for his Improvements—James Scott Brother to Thomas lives on the Plan[tation] on which a Cabbin was built by Crawford and Covered 14 feet Square—can prove Notice to settlers."

15. See Washington County Court, Appearance Docket, January 1782–June 1792, cause no. 110, p. 195; and Smith to GW, 9 Feb. 1785. The words "H.B. appears" on the appearance docket probably indicate that Hugh Henry Brackenridge (1748–1816), the prominent Pennsylvania lawyer who defended the squatters when the case appeared before the Pennsylvania Supreme Court, also acted for the settlers in the county court. Brackenridge was already well known as the author of a number of plays extolling the American military character. After studying law with Samuel Chase in Annapolis, he moved to Pittsburgh in 1781 where he opened a law practice and established a newspaper. A copy of the ejectment notice and a record of the case, both in Smith's handwriting, are in NhD. According to Smith's notes, witnesses for GW were "Charles Morgan, Chartiers[,] Thomas Bond Surveyor, Catfish[,] Mark Stevenson-Stewarts Crossings[,] Zachariah Stedham, Montains run[,] James McCormick, Berkeley County V.[,] James Bauercraft Raccoon[,] John Cannon Esqr.[,] [and] Col. David Shephard." For GW's attempts to marshal witnesses in his behalf, see his letter to Charles Simms, 22 Sept. 1786.

16. See Smith to GW, 9 Feb. 1785; and Appearance Docket, Washington County Court, January 1782–June 1792, cause no. 110.

17. GW to Freeman, 11 April, and GW to John Fitzgerald, 23 July 1785. See also GW to Harvie, 19 Mar. 1785, to Freeman, 16 Oct. 1785, from Harvie, 22 April 1785, to Smith, 28 July 1786, and to Charles Simms, 22 Sept. 1786. For the difficulty of securing supporting documents, see Edmund Randolph to GW, 29 July 1785.

18. For Smith's observations on the disposition of several early cases in which improvements had been offered as a defense, see his letter to GW, 17–26 Nov. 1785. GW's best information regarding the legal status of the land came from John Harvie (see Harvie to GW, 22 April 1785).

19. See GW to Edmund Randolph, 13 Aug. 1785. In the spring of 1775 rumors had circulated in Virginia that Crawford, who ran the bounty land surveys for the Virginia Regiment, had not qualified as a surveyor. GW wrote Lord Dunmore, governor of Virginia, to ask about the rumor, and Dunmore replied that there was indeed some evidence that Crawford had failed to qualify: "if this is the Case the Patents will of Consequence be declared Null and void" (GW to Dunmore, 3 April 1775, and Dunmore to GW, 18 April 1775). For the assembly's legislation on the bounty lands, see "An Act for adjusting and settling the titles of claimers to unpatented lands under the present and former government, previous to the establishment of the commonwealth's land office" (10 Hening 35–50).

20. See GW to Smith, 14 July 1785.

21. Typescript, PWW: Crumrine Papers.

22. The text of this brief is taken primarily from a typescript in PWW: Crumrine Papers. However, the material from the beginning of the brief to the words "actual Survey" is taken from a facsimile in GW's hand printed in Konkle, *Thomas Smith*, facing page 176.

23. GW to Randolph, 13 Aug. 1785.

24. GW to Smith, 10 Sept., 7 Dec. 1785. For Smith's attempt to dissuade GW from this course on the ground that it would elicit an adverse reaction from the jury who might well believe the defendants "rather unfortunate, than blameable," see Smith's letter to GW, 17–26 Nov. 1785. For GW's somewhat grudging agreement, see his reply to Smith, 7 Dec. 1785.

25. GW to Smith, 28 July, and to Charles Simms, 22 Sept. 1786. See also GW to Smith, 22 Sept. 1786, and George McCarmick to GW, c.31 Oct. 1786. A draft of the advertisement for the land is in DLC:GW.

26. Smith to GW, 7 Nov. 1786. See also Smith to GW, 17 Feb. 1787, and Rowe, *Thomas McKean*, 193–94. James Ross assisted Smith at the trial, and on 4 Mar. 1788 GW authorized from funds in Smith's hands a payment of £50 to each man "as a Compensation for yourself & Mr Ross for your trouble &c in prosecuting my Land suit in Washington Cty Pensylvania" (Ledger B, 259).

27. GW to George McCarmick, 27 Nov. 1786. See also GW to Presley Neville, 27 Nov. 1786, and GW to John Cannon, 16 Sept. 1787. Writing in 1814, Hugh Henry Brackenridge commented on this aspect of the case: "General Washington after the peace of 1783, instituted ejectments, and succeeded in recovering under a prior Virginia claim, a large tract of country containing a number of settled plantations which had been defended and cultivated during the Indian depredations upon that quarter, at the expence of life in many instances. It was sufficiently distressing to be obliged to leave their cultivated fields, meadows, orchards, and buildings. The general did not offer to make compensation for these. Nor in strict law, was he bound to do so. He could not be considered as under more than an imperfect obligation. It is possible he

might have thought of this, had he not taken it for granted, as he had a right to do, that the state of Pennsylvania who had taken away the property from the settlers, by ceding to Virginia, would have provided a compensation. This by strict law the state was bound to do. For though the ceding the jurisdiction is at all times a right of the society; yet the exercise of the *dominium eminens*, could not, under the constitution of 1776, or under the present, be justifable without providing a compensation. . . . But nothing of this was heard of with regard to land taken away by the Virginia claims in this disputed territory. And at this late period, it is not probable that we shall hear more of it. It remains now, not a matter of legal discussion, but of history" (Brackenridge, *Law Miscellanies*, 257–58).

28. GW to James Ross, 16 June 1794. See also James Ross to GW, 20 Aug. 1795, GW to Ross, 29 Aug. 1795, Alexander Addison to GW, 17 May 1798, GW to Addison, 3 June, 29 July 1798, 4 Mar., 24 Nov. 1799, and *Pittsburgh Gazette*, 3 Mar. 1798. The deed of 1 June 1796, signed by GW and Martha Washington and conveying the property to Ritchie for $12,000, is in the Washington County Court Deed Book 1, V, p. 324. GW's executors secured judgment against the mortgage in 1801 in the Washington County court and the land was sold in 1802 by the county sheriff to Alexander Addison, one of Ritchie's executors (statement in PWW: Crumrine Papers; see also Crumrine, *Washington County*, 859).

Sir   Carlisle [Pa.] Feby 9th 1785

Agreeably to the orders which I had the honour of receiving from you at the Court of Fayette County, I beg leave to inform you, that before I left the Court at Washington County, I prepared Ejectments against each of the People in Possession of your Land; I delivered those Ejectments to the Sheriff who served them all with a degree of regularity not very usual in that Country; as soon as the Returns were made, I consolidated the whole, except that of James Scott, the Brother to the Prothonotary,[1] having some reason to believe that it was in part, owing to his perswasions that most of the rest did not give up their claims; and finding, after the strictest enquiry which I could make, that the claims of the others are equally strong, or rather equally weak, and that if the claim of any of them be good, it is that of Mr Scott.

Having your orders to remove them without loss of Time into the Supreme Court, I took up Writs for that purpose with me to the last Court, and gave Mr Scott, the Prothonotary, the most pointed orders to Certify the Records, and to transmit them as soon as possible to Philadelphia, if a safe conveyance could be had; otherwise to send them to me at Carlisle & I would forward them, as I wish to have them entered in the Supreme Court before the next Term, which begins on the tenth Day of April, in order that they may be ready for Trial, as soon as it may be thought most proper. Mr Scott assured me he would send them down by the first Conveyance—I have not yet received them, nor have I heard of any Person from Washington County going down to Philadelphia, but I take it for granted Mr Scott will not affect any delay.

When you have a convenient opportunity of sending to Baltimore, or rather to Philadelphia, please to send the Title Bond, duly proved according to the Laws of Virginia so that it can be given in Evidence. The Entry of the Warrant by the Surveyor of the County, authenticated in like manner, will be necessary on the Trial: I am intirely unacquainted with the manner in which Titles to Lands are acquired by Improvement or Occupancy, by the Laws & Customs of Virginia, I suppose, it must be under certain conditions & restrictions—I presume Mr Washington, who was up with you, can give me full information on this head,[2] & can point out the Laws, if any; does the occupier forfeit his right of Pre-emption if he does not apply for an office-right, in a given Time? If so when? by what Law? or is it by the regulations established in the Land office? A Certified Copy of such regulations, if any. I entertain a high opinion of that young gentlemans knowledge of the Law, from the information of a Gentleman in whose Judgment I can confide, and would be much obliged to him if he would write to me on this subject—It is no doubt familiar to Mr Washington, and I wish to avoid the necessity of taking up a moment of your Time in making the investigation.

I have seen Mr Wilson since I had the honour of being employed by you, & mentioning that you had expressed a willingness that another Gentleman should be employed & had mentioned his Name: he assured me that he would go up, if you desired him; this declaration gave me great pleasure, as I don't know a Gentleman whom I would as soon have for a Colleague on this occasion—I was afraid that he could not attend the Trial, & I take it for granted, that he would not be willing to undertake the journey, for any other Person in the world. It was this which put it out of my power of being so explicit about a Colleague, as it was my wish to have been, not knowing which of the Gentlemen, who attend the Western Courts, to make choice of. But after the most deliberate consideration, I am of opinion it is a matter of too much importance for me to carry on without assistance, especially as I would have the strong & fomented prejudices of Party to contend with, and I have some reason to believe that a good deal of art & management were used, before the People were prevailed with to stand the Ejectments. If you should think proper to write to Mr Wilson[3] & should any accident prevent him from attending the Trial, I am perswaded that I could prevail on Mr Yeates of Lancaster to attend.[4] Mr Yeates is a Gentleman of the first eminence as a Lawyer. Either Mr Wilson or Mr Hilligas will transmit your orders to me carefully. I have the Honour to be, with that profound respect and veneration which fill the breast of every Citizen of America, your most obedient & very humble Servant

Thomas Smith

ALS, DLC:GW.

1. The prothonotary of Washington County was Thomas Scott (1739–1796), a native of Chester County, Pennsylvania. Scott lived in Lancaster until he moved with his family to an area near Monongahela about 1770. When Westmoreland County was formed in 1773, he was appointed justice of the peace. Heavily involved in Pennsylvania's border disputes with Virginia before the Revolution, he was briefly imprisoned for acting as a Pennsylvania official in territory claimed by Virginia. During the war Scott served in the Pennsylvania assembly and on the supreme council. In 1781 he was appointed prothonotary and clerk of the court for the newly formed Washington County. Scott served as a member of the Pennsylvania Ratifying Convention and was elected to the first Congress in 1789.

2. Bushrod Washington had accompanied GW on his trip to western Pennsylvania in 1784.

3. James Wilson (1742–1798) was one of Pennsylvania's most prominent lawyers. From 1785 to 1787 he served in the Confederation Congress and at this time was heavily involved in the development of the Somerset rolling and slitting mill on the Delaware.

4. Jasper Yeates (1745–1817), a prominent Pennsylvania lawyer, studied law under Edward Shippen, was admitted to the bar in 1765, and began practice in Lancaster. He had several local offices during the Revolution and acted as a commissioner to negotiate an Indian treaty at Fort Pitt. A leading opponent of the Pennsylvania constitution of 1776, he became a strong advocate of a new constitution for the state and a supporter of the federal Constitution in the struggle for ratification. In 1791 Gov. Thomas Mifflin appointed him an associate justice of the Pennsylvania Supreme Court, a post he held until his death.

From James Keith

Sir   New York 10th Feby 1785

Your Excellency will remember in Octr 1782 I was tried upon the following charges (Viz.) 1st for presuming "to detach a party of armed Men from the Garrison of West Point, without the consent or knowledge of the Commandant, and putting them under the direction of a person who was not an Officer; to the prejudice of good Order and Military discipline. 2d For a palpable contempt and disobedience of General Orders; having connived at, and assisted in the pernicious and illicit intercourse of traffic with the Enemy, by furnishing Joseph Brown with a Military Guard, which he made use of for the protection of Stores and merchandize brought from within the Enemy's lines;" *Putting the Guard under the direction of a person who was not an Officer* was the only part of the Charge of which I was found guilty; but such were the Clammours of the People, at that time, against the injurious practice of bringing goods from New York, that policy made it necessary to mark for a Victim the man, who first should be found in any degree, to have encouraged it. Appearances being suspicious, the censure of the Court Martial fell heavily upon me.

Although from the complexion of the whole case, one would naturally be induced to draw the most unfavorable conclusions respecting my intentions; yet with the utmost sincerity, I now Assure your Excellency (and appeal to that great being who knows the heart, as a Witness to the truth of the Assertion) that I had not, at the time, the most distant Idea, that the Stores and Merchandize, mentioned above, were of the contraband kind— they were reported to me to consist of boots, Shoes, and other Articles, of which I knew both officers & men stood in the greatest need; and considering the pressing wants of the Army, I conceived myself not only authorised, but in duty bound, to give them every protection in my power. under these impressions, I was incausiously led, for the greater security of the goods, to leave the Guard to the direction of the Owner of them. and however unwarrantable, or even Criminal, this measure might, at that time, appear; or with what degree of severity soever a military tribunal might have animadverted upon it, I am persuaded, from the tenderness shown by your Excellency to Officers who have been rather unfortunate than base, that I should have been treated as a Subject of pardon, had not policy dictated the impropriety of the Grant.[1]

I have therefore to solicit (as no evils can now result from the indulgence) that, should your Excellency be convinced that my Misfortune arose rather from inadvertence than foul design, and that the Claims of Justice are satisfied, you would condescend so far as to signify it by a line—this will wipe the reproach from my name—cheer the hearts of an indigent tho' innocent family—replace me in the Esteem of my Countrymen, and, by recommending me to the Compassion of Congress, may, possibly prove a means of procuring those emoluments, to which, after more than seven Years hard Service, I conceive myself justly Entitled.[2]

The papers accompanying this Address, as they speak the sentiments of a number of Gentlemen who from a long and intimate Acquaintance are best able to decide the motives of my Conduct, I beg leave to submit to your Excellency's perusal.[3]

Conscious I am that the freedom with which I have intruded upon your Excellency's retirement needs more than an appology—If a regard for my own quiet and a future wellfare of those with whom I am Connected by the dearest & most tender Affections have tempted me to the Commission of a second Offence, I have only to rely on your Excellency's goodness to pardon, what your nobility of Mind must forbid you to censure as a fault. I have the Honour to be With the most perfect Respect Your Excellency's most Obedient and Most Humbe Servt

James Keith

ALS, DLC:GW.

1. GW's general orders, dated 1 Oct. 1782, containing the charges against Maj. James Keith of the 8th Massachusetts Regiment and the findings of the court-martial, are printed in Fitzpatrick, *Writings of Washington*, 25:224–25. GW approved the sentence of the court discharging Keith from the service.

2. GW wrote Keith on 1 Mar. declining to comply with his request.

3. GW returned the enclosures to Keith. See GW to Knox, 28 February.

From John Beckley

Sir,   Richmond 11th feby 1785

Your favor of the 5th Instant, covering the Ingrossed Potowmac Bill, came to hand this day.

At the desire of Mr Ambler, I have now the honor to enclose

you, Six Copies of the Publication, which, as Managers at this place, we have deemed necessary on the same Business; we have also forwarded 100 Copies to the Managers at Alexandria and Winchester, respectively; others are distributed in the Southern Country, Petersburg Norfolk &c.[1]—We are apprehensive that the interference of another object, the opening and extending the Navigation of James River, may occasion little success to the present scheme in this Quarter; Our endeavors, however, will not be spared, and I trust, Sir, that under your auspicious patronage, and, the more succesful endeavors of the Managers, at the other places, complete success will attend a measure productive of consequences, so deeply interesting to the future prosperity of Virginia. With the highest regard and esteem, I have the honor to be, Sir, Your most obedient, humble servant,

John Beckley.

ALS, DLC:GW.

1. In a broadside dated 22 Jan. 1785, Jacquelin Ambler (1742–1798), treasurer of the state of Virginia, and John Beckley, as the two managers in Richmond for the Potomac River Company, announce that "a subscription book will be opened at the treasury office in the city of Richmond, on Tuesday the 8th of next month, and remain open until the 10th day of May" to receive subscriptions to the new company. The broadside describes the terms for subscription, or investment, lists the tolls that were to be charged, and includes the text of the report of the commissioners at Annapolis of 28 Dec. 1784, printed above in this volume as Enclosure I in George Washington and Horatio Gates to the Virginia Legislature, 28 Dec. 1784. A copy of the broadside is in DLC:GW.

From Richard Henry Lee

Dear Sir, New York feby 14th 1785

In reply to your favor of december the 14th I had the honor to write to you from Trenton, and I mentioned an enclosed letter from you for the Marquis Fayette, which coming to hand after the Marquis had sailed, I wished to know your pleasure, whether I should forward it to France or return it to you—I have not been honored with your commands upon that point.[1] Soon after my arrival in this city, I sent you one of the few pamphlets addressed to the President of Congress by Doctor Price—it will give me pleasure to know that you have received it.[2] The commissioners for treating with the western Indians did yesterday present to Congress the Treaty that they have made with the Wyandots, Delawares &c. A copy of the Treaty I have now the honor to enclose you. The Shawanese, you observe, are not there—it seems that persons, disaffected to us, prevented them from meeting the Commissioners.[3]

The Wyandots being stated as their superiors, may perhaps prevent any mischief from the Shawanese not being included in this Treaty—Another Treaty will be held with the more Southern Indians in the spring or first of the Summer—The policy, seems to be a good one, of enclosing as it were, the Indian nations within our acknowledged territory—It will probably tend to civilize them sooner, and by preventing intrigues with them, render them more certainly our friends.

The Court of Spain has appointed Mr Gardoque their Chargé des affairs to the United States, and we have reason soon to expect his arrival—We are to apprehend a very firm *ostensible* demand from him, of the exclusive navigation of the Mississippi. His secret orders touching an Ulterior agreement may be another thing.[4]

Time and wise negotiation will unfold this very important matter, and I hope may secure to the U.S. and those Individual States concerned, the great advantages that will be derived from a free navigation of that river.

My respects, if you please, to your Lady, whose health I hope is perfectly reestablished. I have the honor to be, with the truest respect and esteem, Sir your most obedient and very humble servant

Richard Henry Lee

P.S. I was honored with your favor of the 8th of feby with its enclosures after the above letter was written—I will shortly reply to its contents, and your letter for the Marquis shall be forwarded to France. R.H. Lee

ALS, DLC:GW.

1. For a discussion of the letter to Lafayette, see Lee to GW, 26 Dec. 1784, n.2. See also GW's letter to Lee of 8 February.

2. See Lee to GW, 16 Jan. 1785, n.1.

3. See Arthur Lee to GW, 19 Nov. 1784, and note.

4. Diego Maria de Gardoqui (1735–1798), who had been the Spanish consul in London, was made chargé d'affaires in the United States in the fall of 1784 and arrived in Philadelphia in June 1785.

To Lafayette

My Dr Marqs   Mt Vernon 15th Feby 1785.

I have had the pleasure to receive your affectionate letter of the 21st of December—dated on board the Nymph Frigate in the harbour of New York; & felt all that man could feel from the flattering expression of it.

My last to you, if I recollect right, was dispatched from Annapolis; whither I went at the request of this State to settle a plan (to be mutually adopted by the Legislatures of both States) for improving and extending the navigation of the river Potomac as far as it should be found practicable, & for opening a road of communication therefrom, to the nearest navigable water to the westward.[1] In both, I happily succeeded. The Bill, of which I send you a copy, was prepared at that time, & has since passed both Assemblies in the usual forms, & must speak for itself. The roads of communication is to be undertaken on public account, at the joint & equal expence of the two States. Virginia has passed a similar Act to the one enclos'd, respecting James river, & its communication with the waters of the Great Kanhawa, & have authorized the Executive to appoint Commissioners to examine, & fix on the most convenient course for a canal from the waters of Elizabeth river, in this State, to those passing thro' the State of No. Carolina; & report their proceedings therein, with an estimate of the expence necessary for opening such Canal, to the next General Assembly.

Hence my dear Marquis you will perceive that the exertions which you found, & left me engag'd in, to impress my Country men with the advantages of extending the inland navigation of our rivers, & opening free & easy communications with the Western Territory (thereby binding them to us by interest, the only knot which will hold) has not been employ'd in vain. The Assembly of this State have accompanied these Acts with another—very flattering one for me—but which has been productive of infinitely more embarrassment than pleasure. This Act directs the Treasurer of the State to subscribe fifty shares in each of the navigations, Potomac & James, for my use & benefit, which it declares is to be vested in me & my heirs forever: generous as this Act is, the reasons assigned for it, with the flattering, yet delicate expression thereof, renders it more valuable than the grant itself—& this it is which perplexes me. It is not my wish, nor is it my intention, to accept this gratuitous gift; but how to decline it without appearing to slight the favors of my Country—committing an act of disrespect to the Legislature—or having motives of pride, or an ostentatious display of disinterestedness ascribed to me, I am at a loss: but will endeavour to hit upon some expedient before the next session, to avoid these imputations. This was the closing Act of the last, without my having the most distant suspicion that such a matter was in contemplation; nor did I ever hear of it until it had passed, & the Assembly had adjourned.[2]

With what readiness the subscription Books will fill, is not in my power at this early stage of the business, to inform you; in general, the friends to the measure are sanguine; but among those good wishes are more at command, than money—consequently it is not only uncertain of whom the company may consist, but (as its existence depends upon contingencies) whether there will be one or not. therefore at this moment we are all in the dark respecting this & other matters—one thing however is certain, namely, if a company should be established & the work is undertaken, a skilful Engineer, or rather a person of practical knowledge, will be wanted to direct & superintend it. I should be glad therefore my Dr Sir if you would bear this matter in your mind—that if the company when formed should be disposed to obtain one from Europe, & should prefer France, proper characters may be applied to, without loss of time. You will readily perceive My Dr Marqs that this is more a private intimation of mine, than an authorised request, consequently how improper it would be to raise the expectation of any Gentleman to the employment, without being able to give him the appointment. If a company should be formed, it will be composed, no dout of many men, & these of many minds; & whilst myself & others may be disposed to go to France for an Engineer, the majority may incline to send to England for one, on account of the langu[a]ge, & from an opinion that there is greater similarity between the inland navigation of that Kingdom & the improvments which are intended here, than prevails between any in France & them; whilst others again may turn their Eyes towards Holland. The nature of our work, as far as I have been able to form an opinion of it, will be first, at the principal falls of the river to let Vessels down by means of Locks—or, if Rumsey's plan should succeed, by regular or gradual slopes—in either case, the bad effect of Ice & drift wood in floods, are to be guarded against—2d As the Canals at these places will pass thro' rocky ground, to be able to remove these with skill & facility, & to secure the Canals when made. 3dly—in other parts of the river, the water will require to be deepened, & in these places the bottom generally is either rock under water, or loose stone of different sizes; for it rarely happens that Sand or Mud is to be found in any of the shallow parts of the river. I mention these things because it is not the Man who may be best skilled in Dikes: who knows best how to conduct water upon a level—or who can carry it thro' hills or over Mountains, that would be most useful to us.[3]

We have had a mild winter hitherto, & nothing new that I recollect, in the course of it; for I believe Congress had determined before you left the country, to fix their permanent seat in the vicinity of Trenton; & their temporary one at New York. The little Sprig at Annapolis, to whose nod so many lofty trees of the forest had bowed, has yielded the Sceptre: thursday last placed it at the feet of Mr M: who perhaps may wield it with as much despotism as she did.[4]

If I recollect right, I told you when here, that I had made one or two attempts to procure a good Jack Ass from Spain, to breed from. Colo. Hooe, or rather Mr Harrison, was one of the Channels thro' which I expected to be supplied; but a day or two ago the former furnished me with the enclosed extract from the latter. As it is not convenient for me to pay such a price, I have desired Colo. Hooe to countermand the order— & the same causes induce me to pray, that if these are the prices of a good Jack (& no other I would have)—that you would decline executing the commission I gave you of a similar kind.[5]

I will use my best endeavours to procure the seeds (from Kentuckey) which are contained in your list; but as the distance at which I live from that country is great, & frequent miscarriages of them may happen, you must prepare yourself for delay.[6]

I will write as you desire, to Cary the late printer of the Volunteer Journal in Ireland. Bushrod Washington, sensible of your polite invitation, but unable to avail himself of it, wrote you a letter of grateful acknowledgments & thanks; which letter

I sent under cover to the President of Congress with a request to deliver it to you, but you had sailed: I presume he has since forwarded it to you.[7]

I am possessed of the Cypher which was used by Mr Livingston whilst he was Secretary of foreign affairs; if therefore he had not different ones, I can when necessary, correspond with you in his. Every body of this family, & those who are connected with it, join in the most sincere & affectionate wishes for you & yours, with the most affectionate of your friends

G: Washington

P.S. If it should so happen that the subscriptions for opening the navigations of the rivers Potomac & James should not (from the want of money here) fill in the time required by the Acts, do you think that there are persons of your acquaintance in France who might incline to become adventurers in it? I give it as my *decided* opinion to you that *both* are practicable beyond all manner of doubt; & that men who can afford to lay a little while out of their money, are laying the foundation of the greatest returns of any speculation I know of in the world.

LB, DLC:GW.

1. GW's letter to Lafayette from Annapolis is dated 23 Dec. 1784.

2. Lafayette does not write GW about the Virginia legislature's gift of shares in the Potomac and James River companies until 13 May. Lafayette makes clear his hope that GW will refuse to accept the gift and suggests to GW that perhaps "it Can Be gently turned towards some public popular establishement."

3. For GW's hiring of James Rumsey as engineer for the Potomac River Company, see GW to Rumsey, 5 June, 2 July, and Rumsey to GW, 24 June 1785.

4. John Francis Mercer married the heiress Sophia Sprigg (1766–1812) of Annapolis on 3 February. Arthur Lee was reported to be one of the disappointed suitors (see Jacob Read to GW, 30 July 1784, n.3). On 23 Feb., GW wrote Mercer: " . . . You will please to accept my congratulations, in which Mrs. Washington joins, on your marriage, & our best wishes for every felicity attending that state . . . If you should determine on a Southern Boat for your first visit, Mrs. Washington and I should be very happy to see you, if you steer northardly we wish you a pleasant journey and all the pleasures the gaiety of New York can afford" (fragment printed in Sotheby, Parke-Bernet catalog, 25 Jan. 1977). The ellipses are in the printed copy.

5. For correspondence regarding the jackass given to GW by the king of Spain, see William Carmichael to GW, 3 Dec. 1784, n.1. For Lafayette's gift of a jack, see Lafayette to GW, 16 April 1785, n.4.

6. See Lafayette to GW, 17 Dec. 1784.

7. See GW's letter to Matthew Carey, 15 March. For GW's letter to Lafayette, see Richard Henry Lee to GW, 26 Dec. 1784, n.2.

From La Luzerne

Sir. Paris February 15th 1785.

The Marquis de la Fayette has delivered to me the letters of your Excellency and I am extreemely flattered by this mark of your attention and of your remembrance.[1] I have executed your commissions near his Majesty and the Royal family, and the King is concerned that your domestic affairs deprive him of the satisfaction to see a man, whose talents and virtues have procured the hapiness of his Country and excited the admiration of all others.

I thank You heartily for the news, your Excellency has been pleased to give me of America. The present excellent formation of Congress gives me great hopes that the public debt will be secured and that all the other branches of administration will take a more regular form. A nation, which has done so great things, as Yours, during ten years, is expected to crown their atchievements by acts of justice. This qualification is so common in America that I am persuaded it's voice will be heared in all your assemblies and America will be at last as just in time of peace as it has been patient and brave during the War.

Since my arrival in Europe the different cabinets have been much agitated; the Emperor has produced some pretentions against holland which are not yet adjusted. He has likewise manifested a desire to annex the Dutchy of Bavaria to his Dominions and to cede by way of Exchange to the Elector the Austrian possessions in the Netherlands. This arrangement seems to displease very much to the different military powers in Europe. Preparations of War are going on at Vienna, at Berlin, in holland and in France. It is however very probable that the War will not take place in the course of this year; but a general flame is certainly very near to break out & tho' France and England be very far from wishing for War it will be very difficult to prevent the troubles of Germany if the Emperor does not of his own accord give up his pretentions. The Imperial Court seems to be intimately united with that of Russia; two powers rich in ressources and full of ambition; and as they are not happy enough to have, like America, at their head a man, who prefers the welfare of Mankind to his private advantage, there are great aprehensions of a general War in Europe. The events of it will be read by your Excellency in your retreat with a small degree of satisfaction, for you will observe that far from giving liberty to some nation this War will only serve to encrease the miseries of several countries during many years.

I am very thankful for the interest you are pleased to take in my fate, which is not yet decided. If I was allowed to follow my own inclination I should wish to return to America and to be happy with my old friends; but a consequence of my profession is: to accept of the destination which is prescribed to me. Whatever it may be I shall never forget the attention and friendship of your Excellency. I beg you to continue in those sentiments and to honor me sometimes with your letters. With the most sincere and respectful attachment and acknowledgement I have the honor to be Sir your Excellency's Most obedient and very humble Servant,

le che. de la luzerne

LS, DLC:GW.
 1. GW wrote La Luzerne on 20 Aug. and 5 Dec. 1784.

From Samuel Love

Sir   15th February 1785
 My Brother Colo. Philip Love of botitourt Coty (formerly a Subaltern officer in the Maryland Troops in the time of the Last French and Indian war) on his way down this winter to visit us,[1] Lodged with Colo. Thomas Lewis of Augusta County—who inform'd him you was anxious to See or hear from Some person that Could give any acct of the distance navigation, and Situation of the Several water Courses and hights of Land from fort-Pitt to Lake arie—at his Request inclos'd is a Rough Ideal map of the water Courses &c. from fort-pitt to Lake arie[2]—by which you will the better understand the description he gives of that part of the Country &c.—he Says that the alliganey River Continues nearly the Same width and depth as at pittsburg to the Mouth of French Creek—the distance 130 measured miles—to

Vinago a french fort thereon, from thence as the Road goes Sundry times Crossing French-Creek to Fort Lebeuff near a small Lake of the Same name, from which french Creek has its Source, is about 40 miles—from thence to the French fort on Lake Arie 15 Miles—that, there is a very wide Swamp or Reather Morass with a Small Stream of water Runing through the middle Cover'd all over with what they Call White Pine of an amazing Size and So very thick Set, that the Sun is hid at noon day—the Rise and Extent of this morass is unknown to him but is Some where beyond Lake arie and has its direction by that Lake (on the westward) at the distance of about a mile, and from thence Runs in a pretty Straight direction and falls into French Creek about 5 or 6 miles below fort-Lebeuff—the banks of the Lake my brother Say's are on that Quarter appearantly very high Except at the French fort and there he thinks they are not more than 8 or 10 feet from the Surface of the water to the top of the bank—from which the ground gradually descends to the morass above mention'd the distance about a mile or at the most not more than 1-[1]/2 miles—in his opinion the Surface of the Swamp Lays Several feet below the Level Surface of the water in the Lake—and thinks that if it was not for the Large and thick groth of pine in the Swamp—that if the water was let out of the Lakes it would of it Self Shortly make a passage for battows to French Creek. the ground all the way is very boggey and deep, So Soft that the French were obliged to Cossway the Road—from the enterance of the morass near Lake arie to fort Lebeuff for the Conveniance of Carriages and indeed Could no[t] now travel without, from fort to fort—but to Return to French Creek—my Brother Says he was Station'd at fort Lebeuff in fall 1760—and Continued till the Spring 1761—that he frequently visited the garrison wc. Likewise kept at the french fort on the Lake—by which he Came acquainted with the Situation of both places that at the time he took possession of fort Lebeuff there was a number of Large battows there nearly finished by the French (as they Supposed with which to Retake fort-pitt[)]—he Says, the French Creek is from Sixty to Eighty yards wide and a great part of the way deep water, yet there is Such a number of very Sharp turns and Shoales in it that it [is] not possible to Carry a vessel of burden down but in a high fresh and then very dificult on Some of the Shoales and points—the Creek is Remarkably Crooked and formes a number of horse Shoes which in Circumferance are five or Six miles and not more in many places then half a mile aCross from point to point—the french Left Likewise Several thousand feet of plank at Lebeuff which our people floated down with Some deficultly to Vinango—thus Sir, I have given you the best description of that part of the Country I Could from the notes my Brother Left with me. he Express'd a great desire to wait on you himself for the purpose: but time would not permit—he will be down again next fall if nothing prevents—and if you think to Converse with him will be more Satisfactory. he will then wait on you—in the mean time, if this Imperfect information will be of any Service to you it will give pleasure both to him and me—am with high Esteem and all due Respect Sir Your Most Hble Servt

Saml Love

ALS, DLC:GW.
    Samuel Love (born 1745–46) was a planter in Pickawaxon Parish, Charles County, Maryland.
    1. Philip Love was a private in the Maryland forces when in February 1758 he became a cadet in Alexander Beall's Maryland company. In November 1758 and until 1759, he was an ensign in Capt. John Dagworthy's Maryland company.
    2. Love drew his map on the last page of this letter.

From Charles Washington

Dear Brother   Ber[k]eley [Va.] Feby 19th 1785
    The Bearer Robt Carter (Overseer & Maneger for the two little Boys George & Laurence) is sent to you with £55.12.0 which you will please to Recieve and apply it to there use, and if this shou'd not be Sufficient a further supply shall be sent as soon as Possable.[1]
    I have never had an Oppertunity of seeing Mr Booth since I wrote you last and therefore am not Certain how it may sute him to take them, but if it is your Openion they are doing well where they are, I think they had as well Continue[2]—I am much Oblige to you for the Inteligence Inclos'd in your last Letter, Respecting my Son George, but have since been told Colo. Ball has Recd a Letter from him Dated at Chas Town, and that his health is much Improov'd. if you should of here'd any thing

from him lately, will thank you kindly to let me know,[3] any Letters for me which come by Post could wish them to be lodg'd at Kees's Ferry, my Wife & Dauther join in best Wishes for Mrs Washington and your self, and am Dr Sir with Great Regard your Loving Brother

Chas Washington

ALS, PHi: Dreer Collection.

1. Robert Carter arrived at Mount Vernon with the £55.12 on 21 February. Charles Washington made this notation at the bottom of his letter:

26 Guineas	£36. 8.0
8 half Joes	19. 4.0
	£55.12.0

GW wrote Charles Washington on 12 April that this amount probably would not be enough to pay the charges for the eight months that their nephews, George Steptoe Washington and Lawrence Augustine Washington, had spent in the Rev. Stephen Bloomer Balch's academy at Georgetown.

2. See Charles Washington to GW, 16 Nov. 1784, n.2.

3. He may be referring to GW's letter of 2 Aug. 1784, but it is more likely that there was a later letter that has not been found. Burgess Ball (1749–1800), of Spotsylvania County, was married to Charles Washington's daughter, Frances. Her brother, George Augustine Washington, wrote GW from South Carolina on 25 February.

From Hugh Williamson

Sir   New York 19th Feby 1785

Application has been made to Congress lately by James McMechen who is connected with James Rumsey of Virga in the newly invented Machinery for pressing Boats through the Water. Mr McMechen has laid before the Committee, to whom his Memorial was refer'd, a Certificate that you was pleas'd to give him respecting the Invention. We observe your Opinion that "He has discovered the Art of working Boats by Mechanism *and small manual Assistance* against rapid Currents."[1]

Though this Opinion is clearly in favour of the Invention the Committee have great Doubts whether Mr McMechen has interpreted it fairly. He says that his Boat will by means of the Machinery and *without any manual assistance* ascend a *rapid Stream* and that the small manual assistance which you mention refers only to working the Boat *in dead Water*. If this is true the motion of the Boat depends on the adverse motion of the Stream and it's Speed must be as the Resistance. The Committee would have presumed that the Progress of the Boat depended on the Mechanism, which being well contrived; the Boat with few Hands or with little force would go much faster either in a Current or in dead water than by help of any former Invention. But if it is true, as Mr McMechen alledges, that the Boat is forwarded by the Opposition of the Stream & that against swift Streams it does not even require the aid of manual Assistance the Case is essentially different and the Discovery extremely important.

Mr McMechen we find expects a Patent for the Invention from the Legislatures of the several States, but he further requests that Congress would give him a large Tract of Land in consideration of the Benefit which the western Country must receive from his Boat. Certainly an Improvement so well calculated to promote Commerce and Agriculture as Mr McMechen supposes his Boat, ought to be liberally encouraged but we fear that he colours too high, mistakes the Facts or miss-represents them.

It is with much Reluctance I give you any Trouble on this subject but being very desirous to know in what Rank this Improvement should be placed I am to request your Opinion on this Position *that the Boat stems the Current and requires least manual help where the opposite Stream is most swift,* for such Powers does he ascribe to his Boat.

You have probably heard some Time since that the Indian Commissioners have finished the second Treaty. The last was held with the Wiandot Delaware, Chippawa and Ottawa Nations. The Shawnees did not attend.

It is difficult even at this Hour to say how much Land is purchased for the Use of the United States. By the first Treaty the six Nations ceded all to the Westward of a certain Line, say to the west of Pensylvania. By the second Treaty the Indians first mentionned have reserved a Quadrangular Piece of Land viz.

Beginning at the Mouth of Cayahoga thence up the River to the Portage to the Tuscarawas Branch of Muskingum, then down that Branch to the Forks above Fort Lawrence, then West to the Portage of big Miami which runs into the Ohio, then along the Portage to the great Miami or Omai, thence down to its Mouth, thence along the south Shore of L. Erie to the Mouth of Cayahoga. Those Indians cede all to the East, South & West of the reserved Tract. Probably there may be 12 or 14 millions of Acres clear of any interfering Claims of Indians to the West or North. I presume Congress will soon try whether they can agree on the best mode of sinking Part of their Debt by this Land. I have the Honor to be with the utmost Regard Sir Your obedt hble Servt

Hu. Williamson

ALS, NIC.

1. For GW's certification that the model of James Rumsey's mechanical boat functioned in water in the way Rumsey claimed, see GW's Certificate for James Rumsey, 7 Sept. 1784, printed above. On 8 Dec. 1784 James McMechen, who had a long-standing interest in improving boats (see his petition of 11 July 1783, *JCC*, 24:433), presented James Rumsey's petition for a large grant of land west of the Ohio, if he should "construct a Boat of the Burthen of Ten Tons which by the influence of certain mechanical Powers shall be propelled from 50 to 80 Miles a day against the Current of the Ohio or Mississippi" by no more than three men (ibid., 28:349). Williamson was chairman of the committee to which the McMechen-Rumsey petition was referred, and on 11 May 1785 the committee recommended that 30,000 acres of land be given to Rumsey provided that he could make good his claims for his proposed boat.

To Charles Lee

Dear Sir, Mount Vernon 20th Feb. 1785

My Servant did not return with your letter, and the Papers therewith, until Nine o'clock last Night; so that I have scarcely had time to read the several Conveyances—In that from Mr & Mrs Dulany to me there is a capitol error. the Land held by the deceased Mr French, under the Proprietors Deed to Stephens and Violet, is no part of the Land exchanged. The original grant to Spencer & Washington, comprehends all the Land Mr & Mrs Dulany is to give for mine; and these are held by purchases from Richd Osborne (the quantity I know not) Arbuthnot for 150 Acres; Manley for 68 acres; and John Posey for 136 Acres.

If it is not essential to recite the quantities of Land had from each of the persons, with the dates of the several transfers of them, in order to give valuation to the Deed of Conveyance from Mr & Mrs Dulany; I see not the least occasion for it, on any other Acct; because, if they convey all their right to the Land within Spencer & Washingtons Patent, it gives all I want,

& cannot in the remotest degree affect any other Land they have, because they hold none other, within several Miles of it. and because it would be sufficiently descriptive, as the Patent of Spencer & Washington is well known, and the boundaries of it will admit of no alteration, having the River, Hunting Creek & Ipsawassan (or Dogues Creek) and a strait line between the two last, for its limits.

For these reasons I should think, if at the end of the Mark No. 1 line 29, you were to add "by means of sundry purchases by him made from Richard Osborne, the Executrix of Thos Arbuthnot, John Manley, John Posey &ca containing in Spencers moiety of the said Patent" (if it is necessary to specify the quantity) "by estimation about 500 Acres of Land, be the same more or less." it wd make the matter sufficiently clear for the precise quantity can only be ascertained by a strict investigation of lines & actual measurement; as part of Mr Frenchs purchases run into Washingtons moiety of the Patent, which can not be affected, tho' to ascertain the different lines, & rights, would give trouble, and was one inducement for me to make the exchange.[1]

In whatever manner you judge best, draw the Deed accordingly, all I pray is, that it may be ready for the Court, this day. Nothing else brings me up, and it is inconvenient to leave home—Besides, Mrs Washington, tho' not very well, will attend, in order to make a finish of the business[2]—With much esteem &ca I am Yrs

Go: Washington

P.S. As the Land I get, comes by Mrs Dulany, would it not have been right to have given her the same interest in the Tract I convey? this by the by, only. And should not there have been a note of the interleneation respecting the amt of the rent, in that Deed? or do you mean that it is not to be considered as an interleneation? My taking a Lease from Mrs French, of her life Estate, if she should be disposed to give me one, upon the paymt of an annual rent, cannot be considered as a compliance on the part of Mr Dulany & discharge of that proviso which is to extinguish his Rent?

ALS, PHi: Dreer Collection.

Charles Lee (1758–1815), Col. Henry Lee's brother, practiced law in Alexandria. GW often called on him to handle legal matters.

1. GW for long had been negotiating to obtain a 543-acre tract on Dogue Creek held by Mrs. Penelope French for her lifetime, the possession of which would allow him to fulfill his dream of controlling all the land on the neck at Mount Vernon between Dogue and Little Hunting creeks. On 3 Feb. GW agreed with Benjamin Dulany, Mrs. French's son-in-law, to give Dulany "the tract I bought of Messrs. Adam[,] Dow & McIver on Hunting Creek" (*Diaries*, 4:84) in exchange for the reversionary right of Dulany and his wife to Mrs. French's land. Until Mrs. French agreed to make the exchange, or until upon her death Mr. and Mrs. Dulany did so, Dulany would pay GW £120 a year in rent for the Dow tract. For a description of this transaction, see the editors' note in *Diaries*, 4:84–85. A transcription of GW's draft of his agreement with Dulany, dated 4 Feb. 1785, is in CD-ROM:GW.

2. GW has this entry in his diary on 21 Feb.: "Went to Alexandria with Mrs. Washington. Dined at Mr. Dulany's and exchanged Deeds for conveyance of Land with him & Mrs. Dulany—giving mine, which I bought of Messrs. Robt. Adam, Dow & McIvor for the reversion of what Mrs. Dulany is entitled to at the death of her Mother within the bounds of Spencer & Washington's Patent" (*Diaries*, 4:93).

From Frederick Weissenfels

Sir: New York Febr: 21st 1785.

When I had the honor to be under your Comand, my Sufferings, were alleviated in your presence, I underwent the Fatigues of the different Campaingns with Pleasure, and when finished I returned with my Numerous Family to the Cottage, not without Some hopes, of being rewarded by my Country but my reward proved paper Notes Which from necessity of my Family I am obliged to Sell at 2/6 for Every 20/. What litle I had before I entered in the Service, I Spent during the Contest; I have been an inhabitant of this State for upwards of 20 Years, no notice is taken of me, and I have reason to believe by Cause I am a foringner, with patience I have borne this neglect. I now take Shelter under your Exellencys Pattronage and take the liberty to ask for no more then a Letter of recomendation, Such as your Exellency thinks propre to bestow on my Military Character, and perhaps abilietys, in ordre that I may awaile mySelf of the Bounty Congress has been pleased to grant to foringn Officers, Which will Ennable me, to offer my Services Elsewhere, I wass bred to a Militairy life from my infancy, in that Employ I probable muss End my Days, and Which is infinitely more desirable then to linger out a life of Neglect and disappointment.

I flatter my Self, Sir, you will pardon the liberty I have taken, and permit me with the Sincerest Esteem and respect to be Your Exellencys Most obiedient Humble Servant

                                        Fredr. Weissenfels

I have to produce ample testimonials that I have Served in my Early days in the Prussian army and the States of Holland, from the latter, I Entered the last French Warr in the Brittish army and Came to this Country as a Comissiond officer. F:W:

ALS, DLC:GW.
   Frederick Weissenfels, who began his military service in 1775 as captain of a company in the 1st New York Regiment, rose to the rank of lieutenant colonel and commanded the 4th New York Regiment in 1779. GW wrote Weissenfels on 15 Mar. 1785 asking for more information. Weissenfels responded on 27 Mar. with a testament of his services from Gov. George Clinton, and on 10 April GW sent Weissenfels the certificate he wished for. Weissenfels approached GW in 1787 for a recommendation, which GW refused to give, and in 1789 he again wrote to GW in the vain hope this time that GW would give him a job in the new federal government (see GW to Weissenfels, 10 Jan. 1788, and Weissenfels to GW, 2 May 1789).

Letter not found: to James Rumsey, 22 Feb. 1785. On 10 Mar. Rumsey wrote to GW: "Your favour of the 22d Ultimo has Just Came to hand."

From Josiah Parker

                              Portsmouth [Va.] February 24[–28]th 1785.
   I feel myself much honored with your very friendly polite letter of the 6th Ultimo, which by some means or other did not reach me untill the 10th Instant.[1] About the 1st I sent to Richmond by my deputy a letter to my care from your Nephew to you. this letter was put into the post office at Richmond, but least it should miscarry I have the pleasure to inform you that about the middle of December he was at Turks Island on his way to Charles Town and much on the recovery.[2] next saturday I am to have your acorns from Princess Anne and some of the honey Suckles if to be found, but as it is not an evergreen it may be difficult now to procure, but as the Mistake if any will be of so little consequence I have requested my friends Colo. Thorowgood & Willoughby to send those supposed to be the Honey Suckle which probably may be the wild Jessamine, both of which I think beautifull;[3] some of my friends indeed I myself have some very good grape vines. It is not known by me if you have those things in abundance with you or not. The Live oak if

it will live with you at all must be in your most sandy soil. & the Jessamines & Honey Suckles in the most swampy.

The mode you have adopted for the remainder of your days are I think the most agreable you could fix on. nothing can be so delightfull to a great mind, as mixing in the most agreable walks of Nature richly cultivated by art; and so deranged as to have the most chosen of our heavenly beauties all arranged & mixed in pleaseing variety in one field, it is indeed my dear sir a paradise, and my ardent wish is that you may live to make one of your own in this world and that you will meet an everlasting one hereafter I doubt not. should it so happen that I could add any thing to the field it will add to my pleasure on every reflection; was our old friend Colo. Tayloe alive he would feel himself happy in your retirement and would add every thing to your happiness in his power.[4]

The vessell that carries this was ordered of very suddenly or the acorns &c. would have accompanied this. the next opportunity to Alexandria will certainly carry them if any time in March, but Should it so happen that no other goes, the vines as well as the Shrubs shall be conveyed in the fall, and in the course of the summer I shall make every enquiry into the vegetable fields that can be procured.

Every body here expresses there great desire to see you at this place and I flatter them it is probable you will feel an inclination in the spring to visit this part of the state. I can assure you there is no people more gratefull for your Services, or who would be more happy in convincing you of it than the citizens of the lower Counties. with every wish sir for your happiness, I do myself the honor and pleasure of writing myself your obliged very humble servant

J: Parker

Since writeing Colo. Willoughby has sent me up a box which accompanies this and is forwarded by Dear Sir your obliged friend & humble servt J: Parker
Portsmouth Feby 28th 1785

ALS, DLC:GW.

1. Letter not found, but the contents of this letter from Parker make clear that GW had asked the Norfolk merchant for seed and plants to be used in his landscaping at Mount Vernon. For GW's receiving of the plants and seed, see Parker to GW, 29 Mar., n.1.

2. In his letter of 6 Jan. to George Augustine Washington, GW wrote that

the day before he had received a letter from Parker informing him that George Augustine had left Bermuda. George Augustine Washington's letter of December 1784 has not been found.

3. These were Col. John Thoroughgood of Princess Anne County and Col. John Willoughby of Norfolk, Virginia. GW wrote in his diary for 6 April that he had planted in his nursery "13 of one, and 7 of another kind of what I suppose to be the wild Honeysuckle, they being in different Bundles, and he having been written to for the wild Honey Suckle" (*Diaries*, 4:114). These probably were the low bushes that have pink blossoms in the spring (*Rhododendron nudiflorum*) rather than the vine (*Lonicera peridymenum*).

4. GW's old friend John Tayloe of Mount Airy in Richmond County, Va., died in 1779.

From Rochambeau

My Dear Général   Paris february the 24th 1785.

I have Received by the Marquis de la fayette's hands the two letters wherewith you have honoured me on August the 20th and November the 25th ultimate. you may believe that Since his coming-back you are the main subject of our conversations. I have been ravished to Learn that you Was Philosophically Enjoying of the glory and of the Général consideration that the part which you had in the most memorable revolution during Eight years, has So rightfully deserved to you from all your countrymen and from all the universe.

We have here Some Storms which rumble about our heads, and yet, I do not believe that the navigation of the Escaut's river will bring us to war, and I believe that this navigation's quarral Will be sooner Settled than your pretentions against the Spanish on that of Mississipius.

as Soon as the Shores of the oyo will be peopled, that the Lands will be covered with harvest, the opening of this Wares will Engage your countrymen to force the barriers that the Spanishs lay on their territory to all Strange nations—I am Very Sorry that Mr Le Jay has not Settled this affair before his disparture. there were Some Conferences about it, and I was told, may be wrongfully, that the americans had been too Stiff. this affair cannot be conciliated but by a Convention of trade to the advantage of the two Neighbouring nations, which prevents every wrong use.

a Gread affair which threatens us here of War more than any other, it is the Succession of Bavaria circle, that the Emperor has an unmeasurable mind of joining to his other States, whether by Exchange or by any other Way, it is believed that the King of Prussia, and the other Sovereign States thire, will not Suffer that the Emperor increase So considerably his territorialy Dominion. The Elector of Bavaria is devoted to him and hates the Duc des Deux Ponts his natural inheriter. but the King of Prussia, but the Empire, but the Greatest part of Europe do not thing the Same.

my respects I beseech you, my Dear Général, to M[adam]e Washington and to all your familly, M[adam]e de Rochambeau and the mine give thousand Compliments, the most Sincere, to you, and take part as much as me to your happiness and to all What can Satisfy you. I am with respect and the most inviolable attachment my Dear Général Your most obediént and very humble servant.

le cte de rochambeau

ALS, DLC:GW.

To Thomas Jefferson

Dear Sir,   Mount Vernon 25th Feb. 1785

I had the pleasure to find by the public Gazettes that your passage to France had been short, and pleasant. I have no doubt but that your reception at the Court has been equally polite, & agreeable.

I have the honor to inclose you the copy of an Act which passed the Assemblies of Virginia and Maryland at the close of their respective Sessions; about the first of last month. The circumstances of these States, it is said, would not enable them to take the matter up, altogether, on public ground; but they have granted at the joint and equal expence of the two, 6666⅔ dollars for the purpose of opening a road of communication between the highest navigation of the Potomac, & the river Cheat; and have concurred in an application to the State of Pensylvania for leave to open another road from Fort Cumberland or Wills Creek, to the Yohiogany, at the three forks, or Turkey foot.

Besides these Joint Acts of the States of Virginia & Maryland the former has passed a similar law respecting the navigation of James River, and its communication with the Greenbrier; and have authorized the Executive to appoint Commissioners, who shall carefully examine & fix on the most convenient course for a Canal from the Waters of Elizabeth River in this State, to those passing through the State of North Carolina; and report their proceedings therein, with an estimate of the expence necessary for opening the Same, to the next General Assembly; and in case they shall find that, the best course for such canal, will require the concurrence of the s[t]ate of North Carolina in the opening thereof, they are further authorized & instructed to signify the same to the said State, and to concert with any person or persons who may be appointed on the part thereof, the most convenient and equitable plan for the execution of such work; & to report the result to the General Assembly.

With what Success the Books will be opened, I cannot, at this early stage of the business, inform you; in general the friends of the measure are better stocked with good wishes than money; the former of which unfortunately, goes but a little way in works where the latter is necessary, and is not to be had. and yet, if this matter could be well understood, it should seem that, there would be no deficiency of the latter, any more than of the former; for certain I am, there is no speculation of which I have an idea, that will ensure such *certain* & *ample* returns of the money advanced, with a great, and encreasing interest, as the tolls arising from these navigations; the accomplishment of which, if funds can be obtained, admits of no more doubt in my mind, under proper direction, than that a ship with skilful Mariners can be carried from hence to Europe. What a misfortune therefore would it be, if a project which is big with such great political consequences—commercial advantages—and which might be made so productive to private adventurers should miscarry; either from the inability of the two States to execute it, at the public expence, or for want of means, or the want of spirit or foresight to use them, in their citizens.[1]

Supposing a danger of this, do you think, Sir, the monied men of France, Holland, England or any other Country with which you may have intercourse, might be induced to become adventurers in the Scheme? Or if from the remoteness of the object, this should appear ineligable to them, would they incline to lend money to one, or both of these States, if their should be a disposition in them to borrow, for this purpose? Or, to one or more individuals in them, who are able, & would give sufficient security for the repayment? At what interest, and on what conditions respecting time, payment of interest, &ca could it be obtained?

I foresee such extensive political consequences depending on the navigation of these two rivers, & communicating them by short & easy roads with the waters of the western territory, that I am pained by every doubt of obtaining the means for their accomplishment: for this reason, I also wish you would be so obliging as to direct your enquiries after one or more characters who have skill in this kind of work; that if Companies should be incorporated under the present Acts, and should incline to send to France, or England for an Engineer, or Man of practical knowledge in these kind of works, there may be a clue to the application. You will perceive tho', my dear Sir, that no engagement, obligatory or honorary can be entered into at this time, because no person can answer for the determination of the Companies, admitting their formation.[2]

As I have accustomed myself to communicate matters of difficulty to you, & have met forgiveness for it, I will take the liberty, my good Sir, of troubling you with the rehearsal of one more, which has lately occurred to me.

Among the Laws of the last Session of our Assembly, there is an Act which particularly respects myself; and tho' very flattering, is also very embarrassing to me. This Act, after honorable, flattering and delicate recitals, directs the treasurer of the State to Subscribe towards each of the Navigations fifty Shares for my use & benefit; which it declares, is to be vested in me & my heirs forever. It has ever been my wish, & it is yet my intention, never to receive any thing from the United States, or any individual State for any Services I have hitherto rendered, or which in the course of events, I may have it in my power to render them hereafter as it is not my design to accept of any appointment from the public, which might make emoluments necessary: but how to decline this act of generosity without incurring the imputation of disrespect to my Country, & a slight of her favors on the one hand, or that of pride, & an ostentatious display of disinterestedness on the other, is the difficulty. As none of these have an existence in my breast, I should be sorry, if any of them should be imputed to me. The Assembly, as if determined that

I should not act from the first impulse, made this the last act of their Session; without my having the smallest intimation or suspicion of their generous intention. As our Assembly is now to be holden once a year only, I shall have time to hit upon some expedient that will enable me to endulge the bent of my own inclination, without incurring any of the imputations before mentioned; and of hearing the sentiments of my friends upon the subject; than whose, none would be more acceptable than yours.[3]

Your friends in our Assembly have been able to give you so much better information of what has passed there, & of the general state of matters in this Commonwealth, that a repetition from me is altogether unnecessary, & might be imperfect.

If we are to credit Newspaper Accts the flames of War are again kindled, or are about to be so, in Europe—None of the sparks, it is to be hoped will cross the Atlantic and touch the inflameable matter in these States—I pray you to believe that with sentiments of sincere esteem & regard I have the honor to be Dr Sir—Yr Most Obedt Hble Servt

                                              Go: Washington

ALS, DLC: Jefferson Papers; LB, DLC:GW.

1. The story of GW's leading role in the forming of the Potomac River Company is summarized in the editorial note, Benjamin Harrison to GW, 10 Oct. 1784.

2. GW made the same inquiry regarding an engineer for the Potomac River Company to Lafayette, 15 February.

3. See note 1 in Harrison to GW, 6 Jan. 1785.

From George Augustine Washington

Honord Uncle   Sandy Hill [S.C.] Feby 25th 1785

After so long an interval, I received with inexpressible pleasure Your two friendly Letters, of the 26th of Novr, and 8th of Decr—the former I acknowledged, but the latter by Mr Laurens (with a bundle) I was prevented as it came to hand at the time of my leaving the City[1]—Your Letters have communicated to me the only information of my friends since my absence, which so fully evinces Your goodness to me (by restoring my anxious mind to a state of tranquility) that words are wanting to express the sensations of a grateful heart—Colo. Washington brought me from Char[l]eston the painful information of Your indisposition; I felt as I ought, the keenest sensations, that gratitude, & affection are capable of producing, I have long anxiously feard that incessant attention to business would produce pernitious consequences; from the nature of Your complaint I presume that to be the cause, if so I hope that a little relaxation may prove an effectual remedy—General Greene wrote me from Charleston whose information gives me hopes that You have recoverd[2]—On my arrival I was much indisposed from the fatigues of a long and disagreeable passage, which I flatter'd myself I was rapidly recovering from, after I retired from the interuptions I met with in the City, with Colo. and Mrs Washington (to their Seat) who have done every thing in their power to contribute to my health & happiness which with the extreme pleasantness of the winter I hoped to have been perfectly restored, but my progress has been less fruitful than I flatterd myself, for eight, or ten days past I have experiencd a disagreeable increase of the pain in my breast attended with a giddiness and pain in my head—I have wrote to a very skillful Phisician in Charleston for His advise and hope that it will not be of a long duration as I expect He will direct the loss of blood which I hope will relieve my head—I shall continue here the ensueing Month, and should I find it advisable untill the latter end of April, and shall then take the first conveyance that offers for Virginia, where I must patiently wait, and with Christian fortitude acquiesce, to the decree of Providence, whose benevolence heretofore gives me hopes of happiness, here, & hereafter—I hope never to deviate from the paths of virtue which I have ever been desirous of inviolably preserving the happiness which must result from it will ever be a motive suffitiently powerful to urge me to a strict observance of it and hope never to be so unguarded as to be betrayed into a dishonorable action.

Your request to Colo. Washington He has kindly offer'd to comply with.[3] I consider it as such a mark of Your friendship, circumstanced as I know You must be for money, that You may rest assured that I shall not abuse it, the price of Horses, and the expence, that may attend my going by land, has determin'd me to decline it, shall theirfore I hope have a suffitiency—as I shall return by water, should their be any thing in this part of the world that You may wish, and that it may be in my power to

procure, You will make me happy by intrusting me with Your commands. the sincere affection I shall ever have for Mrs Washington and Yourself, will always interest me in Your happiness and shall ever rejoice in an opportunity of serving You— the prayers of a sincere heart is constantly offer'd for Your healths & happiness. I beg to be rememberd most affectionately to Mrs Washington, and the dear little Children, and respectfully to all enquiring friends—with the most unfeignd esteem & regard I am—Hond Uncle Your affectionate Nephew
Geo: A. Washington

P.S. After concluding, and about, dispatching this, Your favor of the 6th of Janry came to hand, replete with that friendship which has fully evinced Your goodness heretofore, I will not repeat my professions of gratitude, but time I hope will prove my sincerity, from Your not mentioning Your indisposition I please myself with the hope that You have recoverd—I lament that it will not be in my power to procure for You at this time the Acorns & Seeds You desire, the magnificent appearance of the Trees could not escape the Eye, I theirfore made early enquiries after my arrival to indeavour to procure the Seeds supposing they might be acceptable to You but found it too late as they fall from the Trees early in November, I have however taken a method of supplying You which I hope may prove more successful, I have transplanted (in two Boxes) very small about 50 or 60 of the Magnolia and a number of the live Oak in the earth to which they are naturallized as the most effectual method of preserving them; I concieve they will have an advantage over those rear'd from the Seeds as they will have acquired a degree of maturity which will render the change of climate less obnoctious, than those from the Seed which can only have the growth of a Summer, should I go by the way of Philadelphia shall from thence return by water therefore hope to get them safe as I shall take the greatest care of them—Millers discription of the Magnolia cannot be too highly embellished. their is a Species of them called the bay Lure'l but none that I have yet heard of under the denomination of the Umbrella, from the discription I have had of it, it will not answer Your purpose I presume, as it is said not to exceed the height of 6 or 7 feet.[1] it may rather be consider'd a shrub—the Magnolia are produced from Seed which are containd in Cones and the Oak from Acorns—those and every other evergreen natives of this Country my friend Colo. Washington promises me shall be carefully preserved and forwarded—I purpose visiting a Gentleman (as soon as I get a little better of the pain in my head) about 15 miles from this who is said to have one of the finest Gardens, and to be one of the best Botanists in this Country from whom I shall be able to get every information, and perhaps procure some Seeds that may be acceptable—my Letters since I left Bermuda I hope have got to hand—You speak of having heard of me from Colo. Parker but nothing of a letter I wrote You to His care from Turks Island—as a security to the inclosed I have taken the liberty of troubling You with them[5]—Colo. & Mrs Washington desire their Compliments to You & Mrs Washington, and to You both I beg leave to repeat my affection—the incorrectness of this needs an apology but from an assurance of Your goodness shall subscribe myself—Your affectionate Nephew

Geo: A. Washington

ALS, ViMtV.

1. GW's letter of 8 Dec. 1784 has not been found, but see note 1 in GW to George Augustine Washington, 6 Jan. 1785.

2. Except for his complaint that the press of business and the lack of a personal secretary were keeping him from taking needed exercise, GW makes no reference to ill health during the fall and winter of 1784–85 in his diary or in his correspondence.

3. In a letter of 25 Nov. 1784, GW requested William Washington to advance his nephew whatever money he might need when he arrived in South Carolina from Bermuda.

4. The sweet bay or swamp laurel is *Magnolia glavea*, and the umbrella tree is *Magnolia acuminata*.

5. George Augustine Washington wrote GW on 9 Oct. 1784 of his intention to leave Bermuda. Neither that letter nor any other letters he may have written after that and before this one of 25 Feb., has been found.

From Joseph Dashiell

Sir   Worcester County Maryland Feby 26th 178⟨5⟩

In consequence of my promise when at Annapolis[1] I have the Honour to inform you that the price of Lumber is much Higher with us this winter than usual, On acct its being remarkably dry, Many of our Mills not having water to cut more than half their usual quantity: shingles appear to be (from reasons I cannot account for) kept up in Proportion with plank.

I have thought proper to Insert the prices current at this time, for the articles inserted below.

If you should stand in need of any of the Articles here Mentioned, and cannot furnish them on better terms shall be glad to serve you, in forwarding a complyance with Any Bill you may send over.[2] I am Dear Sir with much Esteem your Very Hubl. Servt

Joseph Dashiell

ALS, DLC:GW.

Joseph Dashiell (1736–c.1787) was a planter and millowner at Wicomoco Hundred, Worcester County, Maryland.

1. Dashiell was a member of the lower house of the Maryland legislature, which was in session in Annapolis when GW met with the Maryland commissioners at Annapolis in December 1784 to facilitate the passage of the Potomac River bill.

2. Dashiell made the following notations at the bottom of his letter:

"18 Inch Shingles ¾ thick at 27/6 ℔   M

Inch Boards from   90/ to 100/ ℔   do.

1¼ Inch do   130/ to 150/ ℔   do.

1½ do do   150/ to 160/ ℔   [do]

Scantling of all kinds at superficial Measure at the prices of Inch boards the freight to your quarter is Generally one fourth and one dollar ℔ thousand for Shingles. J. D."

It has not been determined whether GW bought lumber at this time from Dashiell, but on 21 June 1786 GW wrote him to inquire about the price of lumber.

To George William Fairfax

My Dr Sir,   Mount Vernon 27th Feby 1785.

In a letter of old date, but lately received, from the Countess of Huntington, she refers me to a letter which her Ladyship says you obligingly undertook to forward to me:[1] never having received one from her to the purport she mentions, there can be no doubt but that this letter with your cover to it, have met the fate of some of mine to you; as I have wrote several within the last twelve or eighteen months, without any acknowledgement of them from you.

The only letters I recollect to have received from you since my retirement are dated the 9th of Decr 1783, and 10th of June 1784.[2] the first, relates to the heir of Mr Bristow—the second, to a case with pictures, which you were so obliging as to commit to the care of the revd Mr Bracken; & which has not yet got to hand. In Novr last at richmond, I happened in company with this gentleman who told me it was then in his possession at Wmsburgh, and that it should be forwarded by the first safe conveyance to this place—for your kind & polite attention in this matter, I pray you to receive my sincere thanks.

As soon as your letter of the 9th of Decr, abovementioned (accompanied by one from Mrs Bristow, & the memorial from the Executors of the Will of her deceased husband) came to my hands, I transmitted them to the Govr, who laid them before the Assembly which was then sitting; but what the result of it was, I have never yet heard, precisely. The case was involved in the general confiscation of British property, which makes discrimination difficult[3]—How far the Law on national ground is just—or the expediency of it in the political scale, Wise & proper, I will not undertake to determine; but of this I am well convinced, that the most wretched management of the sales has pervaded every State; without, I believe a single exception in favor of any one of them.

I cannot at this moment recur to the contents of those letters of mine to you which I suspect have miscarried; further than that they were all expressive of an earnest wish to see you & Mrs Fairfax once more fixed in this country; & to beg that you would consider Mt Vernon as your home until you could build with convenience—in which request Mrs Washington joins very sincerely.[4] I never look towards Belvoir, without having this uppermost in my mind. But alas! Belvoir is no more! I took a ride there the other day to visit the ruins—& ruins indeed they are. The dwelling house & the two brick buildings in front, underwent the ravages of the fire; the walls of which are very much injured: the other Houses are sinking under the depredation of time & inattention, & I believe are now scarcely worth repairing. In a word, the whole are, or very soon will be a heap of ruin. When I viewed them—when I considered that the happiest moments of my life had been spent there—when I could not trace a room in the house (now all rubbish) that did not bring to my mind the recollection of pleasing scenes; I was obliged to fly from them; & came home with painful sensations, & sorrowing for the contrast—Mrs Morton still lives at your Barn quarters—The management of your business is entrusted to one Muse (son to a Colonel of that name, whom you cannot have forgotten)—he is, I am told, a very active & industrious man; but in what sort of order he has your Estate, I am unable to inform you, never having seen him since my return to Virginia.[5]

It may be & I dare say is presumed that if I am not returned to my former habits of life, the change is to be ascribed to a preference of ease & indolence, to exercise & my wonted activity: But be assured my dear sir, that at no period of the War have I been obliged *myself* to go thro' more drudgery in writing, or have suffered so much confinement to effect it, as since what is called my retirement to domestic ease & tranquillity. Strange as it may seem, it is nevertheless true—that I have been able since I came home, to give very little attention to my own concerns, or to those of others, with which I was entrusted—My accounts stand as I left them near ten years ago; those who owed me money, a very few instances excepted, availed themselves of what are called the tender Laws, & paid me off with a shilling & sixpence in the pound—Those to whom I owed I have now to pay under heavy taxes with specie, or its equivalent value. I do not mention these matters by way of complaint, but as an apology for not having rendered you a full & perfect statement of the Accot as it may stand between us, 'ere this. I allotted this Winter, supposing the drearyness of the season would afford me leisure to overhaul & adjust all my papers (which are in sad disorder, from the frequent hasty removals of them, from the reach of our transatlantic foes, when their Ships appeared): but I reckoned without my host; company, & a continual reference of old military matters, with which I ought to have no concerns; applications for certificates of service &c.— copies of orders & the Lord knows what besides—to which whether they are complied with or not, some response must be made, engross nearly my whole time. I am now endeavoring to get some person as a Secretary or Clerk to take the fatigueing part of this business off my hands—I have not yet succeeded, but shall continue my enquiries 'till one shall offer, properly recommended.[6]

Nothing has occurred of late worth noticing, except the renewed attempts of the Assemblies of Virginia & Maryland to improve & extend the navigation of the river Potomac as far as it is practicable—& communicating it by good roads (at the joint & equal expence of the two States) with the waters of the amazing territory behind us—A copy of this Act (exactly similar in both States) I do myself the honor to enclose you. One similar to it passed the Legislature of this State for improving & extending the navigation of James river, & opening a good road between it & Green-briar. These acts were accompanied by another of the Virginia Assembly very flattering & honorable for me—not more so for the magnitude of the gift, than the avowed gratitude, & delicacy of its expression, in the recital to it—The purport of it is, to vest 100 shares (50 in each navigation) in me & my heirs forever. But it is not my intention to accept of it; altho', were I otherwise disposed, I should consider it as the foundation of the *greatest* & most *certain* income that the like sum can produce in any speculation whatever. So certain is the accomplishment of the work, if the sum proposed should be raised to carry it on—& so inconceivably will the tolls increase by the accumulating produce which will be water borne on the navigation of these two rivers; which penetrate so far & communicate so nearly, with the navigable waters to the Westward.

At the same time that I determine not to accept the generous & gratuitous offer of my Country, I am at a loss in what manner to decline it, without an apparent slight or disrespect to the Assembly on the one hand, or exposing myself to the imputation of pride, or an ostentatious display of disinterestedness on the other—neither have an existence in my breast, & neither would I wish to have ascribed to me. I shall have time however to think of the matter, before the next session; for as if it was meant that I should have no opportunity to decline the offer at the *last*, it was the closing act thereof, without any previous intimation, or suspicion in my mind, of the intention. Admitting that Companies should be incorporated for the purposes mentioned in the Act, do you conceive my good Sir, that a person perfectly skilled in works of this sort, could be readily obtained from England? and upon what terms?[7]

It is unnecessary I persuade myself, to use arguments to convince Mrs Fairfax & yourself, of the sincere regard & attachment & affection Mrs Washington and I have for you both, or to assure you how much, I am, My Dr Sir &c. &c.

G: Washington

P.S. Do you think it would be in your power, with ease & convenience, to procure for me, a male & female Deer or two. the cost of transportation I would gladly be at. If I should ever get relieved from the drudgery of the pen, it would be my wish to engage in these kind of rural amusements—raising of shrubberies &c. After what I have said in the body of this letter, I will not trouble you with an apology for such a scrawl as it now exhibits—You must receive it, my good Sir, as we have done better things—better for worse. G.Wn

LB, DLC:GW.

1. GW is referring to Lady Huntingdon's letter of 20 Mar. 1784. See doc. III in Lady Huntingdon's Scheme for Aiding the American Indians, 20 Dec. 1784, printed above.

2. On 10 July 1783 GW acknowledged the receipt of Fairfax's letter of 26 Mar. 1783 and wrote warmly and at length to his friend. In the letter, Fairfax congratulated GW on the role he had played in the winning of American independence. Fairfax also spoke of the numerous letters that he had written to GW which apparently had not reached him and told GW of how he narrowly escaped prosecution for his correspondence with the rebel general.

3. For a description of the Bristow affair, see GW to Benjamin Harrison, 14 June 1784, n.1.

4. The only letters known to have been written by GW to Fairfax after 1775 are those of 11 Mar. 1778 and 10 July 1783.

5. The Fairfaxes left Belvoir in 1773, and the contents of the house were sold in 1774 not long before it was destroyed by fire. GW had general supervision of Fairfax's affairs in America until he went to Boston in 1775, at which time Robert Carter Nicholas assumed responsibility. After Nicholas's death in 1780, his son George Nicholas acted for Fairfax. Battaile Muse since the fall of 1784 had in fact also been serving as GW's rent collector in Loudoun, Fauquier, and Frederick counties (see Muse to GW, 12 Sept. 1784, n.1). Andrew Morton lived at Belvoir for about a year before his death circa 1776.

6. William Shaw began work in late July.

7. For GW's response to the gift of shares in the Potomac and James River companies, see Benjamin Harrison to GW, 6 Jan. 1785, n.1.

To Patrick Henry

Dear Sir, Mt Vernon 27th Feby 1785.

I have had the honor to receive your Excellency's letter of the 5th, enclosing the Act of the Legislature for vesting in me & my heirs, fifty shares in the navigation of each of the rivers Potomac & James. For your trouble & attention in forwarding the Act, you will please to accept my thanks; whilst to the Assembly for passing it, these with all my gratitude, are due. I shall ever consider this Act as an unequivocal, & substantial testimony of the approving voice of my Country for the part I have acted on the Am[erica]n theatre, & shall feast upon the recollection of it as often as it occurs to me: but this is all I can, or mean to do. It was my first declaration in Congress after accepting my military appointment, that I would not receive any thing for such services as I might be able to render the cause in which I had embarked. It was my fixed determination when I surrendered that appointment, never to hold any other office under Government, by which emolument might become a necessary appendage: or, in other words, which should withdraw me from the necessary attention which my own private concerns indispensably required: nor to accept of any pecuniary acknowledgment, for what had passed—from this resolution, my mind has never yet swerved. The Act therefore, which your Excellency enclosed, is embarrassing to me. On the one hand I should be unhappy if my non-acceptance of the shares should be considered as a slight of the favors the magnitude of which, I think very highly of, or disrespectful to the generous intention of my Country. On the other I should be equally hurt if motives of pride, or an ostentatious display of disinterestedness should be ascribed to the action. None of these have existence in my breast; & none of them would I have imputed to me, whilst I am endulging the bent of my inclination by acting independant of rewards for occasional & accidental services. Besides, may not the plans be affected; unless some expedient can be hit upon to avoid the shock which may be sustained by withdrawing so many shares from them?

Under these circumstances, & with this knowledge of my wishes & intention—I would thank your Excellency for your frank & full opinion of this matter, in a friendly way, as this letter to you is written, & I hope will be considered. I am &c. &c.

G: Washington

LB, DLC:GW.

To the Countess of Huntingdon

My Lady,   Mount Vernon 27th Feby 1785.

The very polite & obliging letter which you did me the honor to write to me on the 8th of April by Sir James Jay, never came to my hands until the 17th of last month; & is the best apology I can make for a silence, which might otherwise appear inattentive, if not disrespectful, to a correspondence which does me much honor.

The other letter which your Ladyship refers to, as having passed thro' the medium of our good friend Mr Fairfax—has never yet appeared; & it is matter of great regret, that letters are so often intercepted by negligence, curiosity or motives still more unworthy. I am persuaded that some of my letters to Mr Fairfax, as well as his (covering your Ladyships) to me, have miscarried, as I have never received an acknowledgment of some of mine to him, tho' long since written.

With respect to your humane & benevolent intentions towards the Indians; & the plan which your Ladyship has adopted to carry them into effect, they meet my highest approbation; & I should be very happy to find every possible encouragement given to them. It has ever been my opinion, since I have had opportunities to observe, & to reflect upon the ignorance, indolence & general pursuits of the Indians, that all attempts to reclaim, & introduce any system of religeon or morallity among them, would prove fruitless, until they could be first brought into a state of greater civilization; at least that this attempt should accompany the other—& be enforced by example: & I am happy to find that it is made the ground work of your Ladyships plan.

With respect to the other parts of the plan, & the prospect of obtaining Lands for the Emigrants who are to be the instruments employed in the execution of it; my letter to Sir James Jay in answer to his to me on this subject, will convey every information, which is in my power, at this time to give your Ladyship; & therefore I take the liberty of enclosing a transcript of it. Agreeably to the assurance given in it, I have written fully to the President of Congress, with whom I have a particular intimacy, and transmitted copies of your Ladyships plan, addresses & letter to the several States therein mentioned, with my approving sentiments thereon. I have informed him, that tho' it comes to him as a private letter from me; it is nevertheless optional in him to make it a matter of private communication to the members individually, or officially to Congress, as his judgment shall dictate; giving it as my opinion, among other reasons, that I did not belive since the cession of Lands by individual States to the United States, any one of them (except New York) was in circumstances, however well inclined it might be, to carry your Ladyships plan into effect.[1]

What may be the result of your Ladyships Addresses to the States of North Carolina, Virginia, Pennsylvania and New York, individually; or of my statemt of the matter in a friendly way to the President of Congress for the united deliberaion of the whole—is not for me to anticipate, even were I acquainted with their sentiments. I have already observed, that neither of the States (unless Nw York may be in circumstances to do it) can in my opinion furnish good Lands in a body for such emigrants as your Ladyship sccms inclin'd to provide for. That Congress can, if the treaty which is now depending with the Western Indians should terminate favourably & a cession of Lands be obtained from them, which I presume is one object for holding it, is certain; & unless the reasons which I have mentioned in my letter to Sir James Jay should be a let or bar, I have not a doubt but that they would do it; in which case, any quantity of Land (within such cession or purchase) might be obtained. If, ultimately, success should not attend any of these applications, I submit as a dernier resort, for your Ladyships information & consideration, a Gazette containing the terms upon which I have offered several tracts of Land (the quantity of which is since encreased) of my own in that country, & which lie as convenient to the Western Tribes of Indians, as any in that territory (appertaining to an individual State)[2]—as your Ladyship may perceive by having recourse to Hutchens's[,] Evans's, or any other map of that Country, and comparing the descriptive

Lands therewith; & being informed that Virginia has ceded all her claim to lands No. West of the Ohio, to the United States— & that the Western boundary of Pennsylvania is terminated by a meredian which crosses the river but a little distance from Fort Pitt.

It will appear evident, from the date of my publication, that I could not at the time it was promulgated, have had an eye to your Ladyships plan of emigration; and I earnestly pray that my communication of the matter at this time, may receive no other interpretation than what is really meant—that is, a last (if it should be thought an eligible) resort.

I have no doubt but that Lands, if to be had at all, may be obtained from the United States, or an individual State, upon easier terms than those upon which I have offered mine; but being equally persuaded that these of mine, from their situation & other local advantages, are worth what I ask, I should not incline to take less for them, unless the *whole* by good & responsible characters (after an agent in their behalf had previously examined into the quality & conveniency of the land) should be engaged upon either of the tenures that are published; especially as these Lands, from their particular situation, must become exceedingly valuable, by the Laws which have just passed the Assemblies of Virginia & Maryland for improving and extending the navigation of Potomac, as high as is practicable, & communicating it with the nearest western waters by good roads: & by the former assembly to do the same thing with James river, & the communication between it & the Great Kanhawa—by means of which the produce of the settlers on these Lands of mine, will come easily & cheaply to market. I am &c. &c. &c.

                                        G: Washington

LB, DLC:GW.

1. For copies of, or extensive references to, all of the letters or documents to which GW refers to here, see Lady Huntingdon's Scheme for Aiding the American Indians, 20 Dec. 1784, printed above.

2. GW's advertisement of his lands on the Ohio and Kanawha are printed above, as an enclosure in GW to John Witherspoon, 10 Mar. 1784.

From Richard Henry Lee

Dear Sir,   New York feby 27th 1785

I am now to thank you for the letter that you did me the honor to write to me on the 8th of this month, and which I received on the 17th with the enclosures.

Sir James Jay had mentioned the plan of Lady Huntingdon to me, previous to the receipt of your letter, and at the same time that your packet reached me, there came one to Congress from Governor Henry with her Ladyships letter and plan enclosed, which the Governor strongly recommended. It was presently observed that the terms upon which lands had been ceded to the United States did not leave it in the power of Congress to dispose of them for any purpose but for paying the debts of the public by a full and fair sale of all the ceded lands— It was indeed remarked, that those religious people whom her Ladyship had in prospect to transplant & fix on our frontier were remarkable in the late war for an unanimous and bitter enmity to the American cause, and as such might form a dangerous settlement at so great a distance, contiguous to the Indians, & easily accessible to Canada. Especially in the present very unfriendly temper of mind that we now suppose the British nation possesses with respect to us. It was therefore ordered that Governor Henry's letter with the enclosures should be filed, but nothing more done in the affair [1]—Finding this, I concluded it not necessary to shew your letter, either publickly or privately—I have therefore returned to you, Lady Huntingdons packet. [2] It appears to me, that Georgia is the most likely State in the Union to close with her Ladyship, if the latter argument mentioned in Congress should not prevent it. I am sorry to hear that you are so interrupted by applications that ought not to be made—I hope however that you will not suffer them so to prevent your necessary exercise, as to injure your health.

The investigating and opening our western navigation is an object of great importance and well worthy of your patronage—I believe, as I hope, that it will be found by experience to be of great utility both to the public and to the private adventurers. Very little has yet been done in Congress respecting the Western Country—but a very full discussion of that business will soon come on, when it is to be expected that our affairs in that quarter will be put under better regulations than hitherto they have been. The mischiefs that experience & reason both join in proving to flow from the Sessions of Congress being held in our large Citys, produced the necessity of determining on some place of easy retirement for the federal government, and the unhappy neglect of attendance on the part of the Southern States has furnished an opportunity for a Majority in Congress to fix on a spot too excentric—My wishes would have been to have gone further south, but of two evils it was best to choose the least, and therefore we thought it better to fix somewhere in retirement than to continue wandering, or to fix in the midst of dissipation.

We had but just determined upon sending a Minister to the Court of London (Mr John Adams) when this day 28th feby, we receive a letter from our Commissioners for making treaties &c. at Paris, the copy of a letter from the Duke of Dorset, Minister from London to Versailles, to our Ministers, in answer to a proposition from them for making a treaty of Commerce with G. Britain for settling other points of difficulty arising from the late peace—for which his Grace declares the determination of his Court to be ready to settle all these affairs upon terms of equal & lasting good to both countries whensoever the U. States shall send to their Court a Minister properly authorised for the business—This *looks* well at least—and we shall shortly make the experiment of their sincerity—The King of Prussia thinks that there will be no war between the Emperor & Holland, and indeed it does now seem probable that his judgement will prove right—I have sent the letter you committed to my care for the Marquis on to France by the packet.[3] I have the honor to be, with the highest esteem and regard dear Sir Your most obedient & very humble servant

Richard Henry Lee

ALS, DLC:GW.

1. Patrick Henry's letter to Congress of 3 Feb., enclosing copies of James Jay's letter of 20 Dec. 1784 and Lady Huntingdon's plan (see Lady Huntingdon's Scheme for Aiding the American Indians, 20 Dec. 1784, printed above), was received on 7 February. In his letter, Governor Henry declared: "If it depended on the Executive here, to give the necessary assistance to the views of this worthy Lady, a moment would not be lost. . . . [But] I fear even

the Legislature will be embarrassed in this affair, because all the lands bordering on the Indians in this State, are ceded to Congress" (DNA:PCC, item 71).

2. See GW's letter to Lee of 8 February.

3. The lapse of only thirty days between the time (17 Feb.) of Lee's receiving GW's instructions to forward a letter written to Lafayette in December and the time (19 Mar.) of Lafayette's acknowledgment of the receipt in Paris of GW's letter of 23 Dec. gives added weight to the supposition set forth in note 2 of Lee's letter of 26 Dec. 1784 that it was not the letter of 23 Dec. which Lee forwarded but rather another December letter which has not been found.

From Daniel of St. Thomas Jenifer

Dear Sir, Annap[oli]s [Md.] Feby 28. 1785

It will not be the smallest inconvenience to me, to keep your Trees til the Fall, which I believe to be the best time for Transplanting, provided they be tied to Stakes with Straw to prevent the Hard Winds incident to our Winters from shaking them too much. It will also be necessary to put a little litter of some kind or other, no matter what, about the bottoms of the Stocks to guard the Roots against our severe Frosts, which I have found from experience to be very injurious where this precaution has not be taken. The Certificates you mentiond signed by Mr Hiligas & Mr Hopkinson & countersigned by Mr Harwood This State cannot without a special direction from Congress I believe pay. Perhaps Mr Lund Washington intended to have lent the Money to Maryland Mr Harwood having then Acted in a double capacity. if there should have been any mistake in this business it may be rectified.[1]

I hope to have the pleasure of being at Mount Vernon on the 19th of March when this transaction may be further explained, for be assured My dear Sir that it will ever afford me the greatest pleasure to serve you or any of your Connexions to the utmost of my power being with the most perfect Attachment Dear Sir Your Excellencys most obedient Servt

Dan. of St Thos Jenifer

Be pleased to present my most respectful Compliments to your Lady & family.

ALS, DLC:GW.

1. At some short time before this, GW had, either by mail or in person, consulted Jenifer in his capacity of intendant of the revenue for the state of

Maryland about fifty-four Continental loan office certificates that Lund Washington had bought for GW from the Maryland Continental loan office in February and March 1779. At the time Lund Washington bought the certificates, Thomas Harwood (1743–1804) was both the treasurer of Maryland's Western Shore and the United States commissioner of the Continental loan office in Maryland. The Maryland legislature enacted a law in 1782 providing that those who had bought Continental certificates in Maryland and were citizens of Maryland could exchange the Continental certificates for Maryland certificates. GW may have had this in mind when he approached Jenifer. In any case, GW and Jenifer had an opportunity to talk further when Jenifer was at Mount Vernon on 20 and 21 Mar. as one of the Maryland commissioners meeting with the Virginia commissioners about Potomac River matters. It was at this time that GW turned over to Jenifer his certificates, along with the descriptive list that GW had made. Jenifer returned GW's list, and GW endorsed it: "Received April 4th 1785. From Danl of St Thos Jenifer Esqr. One thousand and sixty nine pounds one shilling and seven pence specie; ⟨*illegible*⟩" (CSmH), before returning it to Jenifer on 12 April. The total face value of the loan certificates was 19,400 dollars. See Jenifer to GW, 31 Mar., n.2. On 31 Mar. Jenifer wrote a letter to GW enclosing the Maryland auditor general's computation of the depreciation of GW's certificates and the value in specie of Maryland currency on 31 Mar. 1785. He also enclosed an order on the Alexandria firm of Robert Hooe & Co. for £1,069.1.7, the computed present value of the certificates. Michael Hillegas (1729–1804) signed the certificates in 1779 as United States treasurer, and Francis Hopkinson (1737–1791) signed them as United States treasurer of loans.

To Henry Knox

My Dear Sir,   Mount Vernon 28th Feby 1785
    Your favor of the 31st Ulto came to my hands by the last Post. enclosed are letters under flying Seals to Count de Rochambeau & the Marqs de Chastellux (late Chevr) introductory of Mr Swan.[1] also certificates for Lieutts Seaver & Henley.[2] if these will answer the purposes designed, I shall think nothing of the trouble, but be happy in having given them.
    Upon summing up the cost of my projected building in Alexandria, I found my finances not equal to the undertaking; & have thereupon suspended, if not altogether declined it. Notwithstanding, if any Vessel should be coming hither from that part of your state where the Limestone abounds, & where it is to be obtained at a low price, & would bring it at a low frieght, unburn'd: or if in this State it could be brought hither from Boston as Ballast, or at a low freight, I should be glad to get some; in either of these ways. I use a great deal of lime every

year, made of the Oyster shells, which, before they are burnt, cost me 25 a 30/ pr hundred Bushels; but it is of mean quality, which makes me desirous of trying Stone lime.[3]

The Assemblies of Virginia & Maryland passed laws before their adjournment, for improving and extending the Navigation of this River as far as it shall be found practicable; a copy of which (for they are exactly the same in both States) I send you—they also gave a sum of money for the purpose of opening, & keeping in repair, a good road of communication between the Eastern & Western Waters. And this State passed a Similar Act respecting James River, & the Communication with Green Brier (a branch of the Great Kanhawa) which opens equally advantageously to another part of the Western territory; Shares in either or both of which, in my opinion, presents to monied men the most certain, & lucrative Speculation of any of wch I can have any idea.

The State of Virginia accompanied these proceedings with another Act, which particularly respected myself; & tho' generous in the extreme, is rendered more valuable by the flattering, yet delicate expression of its recitals. It directs their Treasurer to subscribe for my use & benefit, one hundred Shares (50 in each Navigation); which it declares vested in me & my heirs for ever. But I can truly aver to you, my dear Sir, that this Act has given me more pain than pleasure—It never was my inclination—nor is it now my intention, to accept any thing pecuniary from the public: but how to decline this gift without appearing to slight the favors (which the assembly ascribe to a sense of gratitude) of my Country, and exhibiting ⟨an⟩ act of seeming disrespect to the Legislature on the one hand—or incurring ⟨the⟩ imputation of pride, or an ostentatious display of disinterestedness on the other, is my embarrassment: but I must endeavor to hit upon some expedient before the next Session (for I had not the smallest intimation of the matter before the rising of the last) to avoid any of these charges, and yet follow the bent of my wishes; which are to be as independent as the Air—I have no body to provide for, & I have enough to support me through life in the plain, & easy style in which I mean to spend the remainder of my days.

I thank you for the particular acct which you have given me of the different Rivers to which the British have given the names of St Croix—I shall be much mistaken if they do not in other matters, as well as this, give us a good deal of trouble before we are done with them. and yet, it does not appear to me, that we have wisdom, or national policy enough to avert the evils which are impending—How should we, when contracted ideas, local pursuits, and absurd jealousy are continually leading us from those great & fundamental principles which are characteristic of wise and powerful Nations; & without which, we are no more than a rope of Sand, and shall as easily be broken.

In the course of your literary disputes at Boston (on the one side to drink Tea in Company, & to be social & gay—on the [other] to impose restraints which at no time ever were agreeable, & in these days of more liberty & endulgence, never will be submitted to) I perceive, & was most interested by something which was said respecting the composition for a public walk; which also appeared to be one of the exceptionable things. Now, as I am engaged in works of this kind, I would thank you, if there is any art in the preparation, to communicate it to me—whether designed for Carriages, or walking. My Gardens have gravel walks (as you possibly may recollect) in the usual Style, but if a better composition has been discovered for these, I should gladly adopt it. the matter however which I wish principally to be informed in, is, whether your walks are designed for Carriages, and if so, how they are prepared, to resist the impression of the wheels. I am making a Serpentine road to my door, & have doubts (which it may be in your power to remove) whether any thing short of solid pavement will answer.

Having received a letter from Majr Keith (dated at New York) and not knowing where to direct my answer, I take the liberty of putting it & the Papers wch it enclo[sed] under cover to you, as he was of the Massachusetts State, & I presume only came to New York on business. He is one, among numberless others, who want me to do inconsistent things. namely to annul—or rather do away, the effect of his Court Martial. The other letter for a Mr Palmer, be so good as to put into a channel for delivery.[4]

Mrs Washington joins me in affectionate regards for Mrs Knox, and the rest of the Family, & I am My dear Sir, With great truth and sincerity—Yrs

Go: Washington

ALS, MHi: Knox Papers.

1. Maj. James Swan (1754–1831) came to Boston when very young, learned the mercantile business, became an active speculator, and married well. He went to France early in 1788 and during the years of the French Revolution enjoyed a career as a promoter, publicist, and man of commerce. Swan returned to America in 1794 as the agent of the French government to secure in the United States desperately needed supplies for France. He later went back to France and in 1808 was imprisoned for debt. He remained in debtors prison in Sainte-Pélagie until 1830, shortly before his death. See Howard C. Rice, "James Swan: Agent of the French Republic, 1794–1796," *New England Quarterly*, 10 (1937), 464–86. Unless Swan visited France before moving there in 1788, he probably did not present GW's letters of introduction to Chastellux and Rochambeau, both of which are dated 28 Feb. 1785.

The text of GW's letter to Chastellux reads: "I take the liberty of introducing Mr Swan, a member of the Massachusetts Assembly, to your usual polite attention to strangers. He proposes, with his Lady, to spend some time in France, & would be happy in the honor of your acquaintance. He is a Gentleman of character & fortune, & well recommended to me by Genl Knox & others, which must plead my excuse for this trouble" (LB, DLC:GW). And the letter to Rochambeau reads: "Permit me to introduce Mr Swan, a member of the Massachusetts Assembly who, with his Lady intends to spend some time in France, to your civilities. I have not the honor of a personal acquaintance with Mr Swan, but from the character given of him by Genl Knox & others, I can venture to assure you that he is a man of fortune & character, & would be happy in the honor of your acquaintance; & this must be my apology for the liberty of introducing him & his Lady to it" (LB, DLC:GW).

2. The certificate for Lt. Samuel Henly of the Massachusetts forces has not been found, but GW sent this, dated 28 Feb., for James Sever: "I certifye that [   ] Seaver was a Lieutenant of the Massachusetts Line in the Service of the United States of America. And from the testimony of the General Officers under whose orders he acted that he is brave & intelligent—and in all respects has supported the character of a Gentleman and man of honor. Given under my hand this 28th day of Februy 1785. Go: Washington late Comr in Chief of the Armies of the U.S." (ADS [photocopy], Paul C. Richards catalog no. 209, June 1986).

3. See GW to Knox, 5 Jan., n.6.

4. James Keith's letter is dated 10 Feb., and GW's response, 1 March.

To Hanna Moore

Madam,   Mount Vernon 28th Feby 1785.

I received your favor of the 20th of January, some considerable time after the date of it. I have never received, nor have I ever heard any thing of Mrs Savages Will, since your deceased husband put it in to my hands, & then reclaimed it in December

1783 as I passed through Baltimore on my way to Virginia, to be sent (for I could see no propriety in any thing else) to the Executors named therein, to act under. I am Madam Yr Mot Obt servant

G: Washington

LB, DLC:GW.

From Charles MacIver

At the Printing-office in Alexandria [Va.]

May it please your Excellency   [February 1785]

I presumed to do myself the Honour of writing you last November, on the first Prospect of Convalescence, after a lingering Illness. A few Weeks afterwards my Health was perfectly reestablished; in so much that I might have resumed my Business, or accepted more eligible Offers. But the Affair on which I wrote your Excellency lay so much at my Heart that I was unwilling to come under any permanent Engagements till I should hear from your Excellency. In such Circumstances, may I therefor hope that your Excellency will condescend to drop me a Line expressing your Opinion of the Practicability or Expedience of my Proposals.[1] I am, very respectfully, Sir Your most devoted & humble Sert

Chas MacIver

ALS, DLC:GW.
    1. See MacIver to GW, November 1784, and note.

To Matthew Campbell

Sir,   Mount Vernon [c.1] March 1785
    You cannot be more concerned than I am at the misunderstanding respecting the plaister of Paris, but as I conceive you have been much imposed upon in the cost at New York, & in the freight of it to Virginia (for it certainly might have come as ballast)—and as your reduced price is far above what I ever had the smallest idea of giving by the quantity, it must await your order at my landing: or, as it was landed there from a want of that previous advice of the price which I expected, & which was to have determined me as to quantity—I will, if it is more

agreeable to you, send it to Alexa. to whomsoever you may direct. This is all Mr Graham's letter (which I enclose for your satisfaction) required of me, if I did not like the price.

If Mr Graham did not tell me that you believed you could afford to take about ten Dollars per ton for it; I am more mistaken than I generally am in transactions of this sort. But as it was not my intention to give even this price by the quantity, I requested—& Mr G____m promised to let me know your lowest price & inform me thereof: this advice I expected by the Post, for I do not recollect to have heard that any was to be sent to Alexandria. I told Mr Gra[ha]m then, & I repeat it now, that for a small quantity merely for the purpose of experiment I should not regard the price: but to pay thirty odd pounds, & to be at the expence of preparing it by pulverization afterwards, is too costly an essay to satisfy my curiosity to discover whether it be a good manure or not.[1]

You have been deceived too Sir by the person or persons, to whom you entrusted the measuring or weighing; for as soon as I return'd from Annapolis, I made my overseer, John Fairfax, weigh the whole very carefully, and it amounted to no more than 17,550 pounds, which he is ready to swear to—& this after a good deal of wet had fallen on it, part of which it must have imbibed; especially that part which was in powder in two large casks, & which I conceive must have lost all its virtue

If you incline to let me have a small part of what was landed here, I should be glad to know it by return of the Post; as it must either be run thro' a Mill (which I believe millers will hardly agree to) or be pounded by hand (which will be a tedious operation) before it can be used, & the season is at hand for spreading it on the ground. I will render an exact accot of every ounce I use, & you may charge what you think proper for it.[2] I am &c.

G: Washington

LB, DLC:GW.
　　1. See GW to Campbell, 22 Jan. 1785.
　　2. No reply to either of Campbell's letters has been found. John Fairfax (c.1764–1843) of Charles County, Md., began working for GW in the fall of 1784 as overseer of the Mansion House farm at Mount Vernon.

To James Keith

Sir,   Mount Vernon 1st March 1785.

However much I may wish to see every slur wiped from the character of an officer who early embarked in the service of his Country; & however desireous I may be to alleviate his misfortunes—it is nevertheless incumbent on me to have regard to consistency of conduct in myself. With what propriety then could I, a private citizen, attempt to undo things which received my approbation as a public officer, & this too without the means of information, as the proceedings of Courts Martial are not with me: but if the case was otherwise, I could neither answer it to myself or country, to retread the ground I have laboriously passed over—was a door of this kind once opened, I should be overwhelmed with applications of a similar nature; for I cannot agree that either the judgment of the Court martial, or the approbation of it proceeded, as you suppose, from the policy of offering a victim to appease the clamors of the populace—It is unnecessary however to go into argument upon the subject when, admitting there was error, redress can only be had from the supreme Council of the nation, or to the State to which you belong. I am sorry it has been your lott to be brought before a court—much more so for the issue, & if I could with propriety place you in the full enjoyment of every thing you wish, I shou'd have pleasure in doing it—but it is not in my power in the present instance.[1] I am Sir &c.

                                              G: Washington

LB, DLC:GW.
   1. GW enclosed his letter to Keith in his letter to Henry Knox of 28 February. See Keith to GW, 10 February.

To Charles MacIver

Sir,   Mount Vernon 1st March 1785.

Whilst I was at Richmond in November last, I received a letter & extracts from you on the subject of emigration—It was put into my hands at a time when I was much engaged, accompanied by many other papers, which with them were put by & forgotten, until your second letter reminded me of them. As I do not clearly comprehend your plan, & if I did, as a discussion of it by letter would be tedious & less satisfactory; if you will be at the trouble of calling upon me at any time when I am in Alexandria, or of riding down here; I will give you my sentiments with freedom & candour, when I more fully understand it.[1] I am &c.

G: Washington

LB, DLC:GW.
    1. See MacIver to GW, November 1784, and note.

Letter not found: from Joseph Mandrillon, 1 Mar. 1785. On 22 Aug. GW wrote Mandrillon: "I had the honor to receive your letter of the first of March."

Letter not found: from Edward Newenham, 3 Mar. 1785. GW wrote Newenham on 25 Nov.: "I have been favored with your letter of the 3d of March. . . ."

From John Boyle, Jr.

Sir   Richmond [Va.] 4th March 1785.
    I have now the honour to forward your Excellency a Letter from my good friend Sir Edwd Newhenham, as also four small Packages for you, which were entrusted to my care by the same Gentleman—Upon my Arrival here I was inform'd you was gone with Le Marquis de Fayette to Annapolis, & I could not learn with any certainty how soon you might return to Mount Vernon, as it was my intention immediately upon my Arrival, to have done myself the honor of waiting upon your Excellency with the said Packages &c. I was at a loss what to do, the Ice blocked my Vessell up a considerable time in the river, & the danger of the Thaw's made my Attendance there, absolutely necessary. So that 'tis only within these few days that I was inform'd of your Excellency's return to Mount Vernon. I still intended to have done myself the pleasure of waiting upon you, but that the hurry of Business & having just parted with my Chief Mate, to go Master of another Vessell, made my stay here indispensably requisite. So that I hope your Excellency, will excuse this seeming inattention in me, & attribute it solely to the true cause which sprung from my desire of delivering them in person—His Excellency Govr Henry, having intimated that he

would forward them, I have accordingly given them into his hands for that purpose. Should your Excellency have any thing to forward to Sir Edwd Newenham or any other Gentleman in Ireland, shall be happy in being favor'd with your Commands, As I shall be ready to Sail about the 30th Inst. for Dublin,[1] and have the honor to be with much respect, Your Excellency's Most obedt hble servt

John Boyle Junr

P.S. You have also inclosed a Letter for Lady Washington, but I don't know who it is from as it was put on board the Ship in my Absence.[2]

ALS, DLC:GW.

1. Patrick Henry apparently sent Sir Edward Newenham's letter or letters and two of the packages with his own letter of 12 Mar. and sent the other two packages with his letter to GW of 19 March. GW wrote Newenham on 20 Mar., thanking him for his letters of 2 and 13 Oct. and for "packages." GW sent this letter written to Newenham to Governor Henry to be forwarded to Captain Boyle "of the Ship Jane & Diana" for conveyance to Dublin.

2. The letter to Martha Washington has not been identified.

From Lebarbier

Paris 4th March—1785
Sir,   rue de Choiseul &c.

Vouchsafe to honor me with the acceptance of two copies of a work, in which, you will find the most unequivocal proofs, of the high opinion which its Author has so justly concieved of the virtues, and rare humanity of the American Heroe—Let not your modesty Sir, be alarmed at a truth, which I have so much pleasure in pronouncing; and for which, you have long since recieved the plaudits of the Universe—If you find Sir, the manner in which I have attempted to paint in my drama of Asgill, your character and love of your Country, to fall short of the sentiment which animated you in her defence; it is, because it belongs only to you, to express with unaffected warmth, a sentiment, which united with your great virtues, has secured you the most lasting fame—If I had the honor Sir, of being acquainted with you, you would not need to be assured, that I never felt a disposition to admire or love any, but beings, who like you have a real right to the homage of honest men—I hope Sir, you will not disapprove of my zeal, in publishing your sublime virtues in my performance; and be persuaded that nothing in the world will give me more pleasure, than to recieve an answer from you—I beg you to believe this, and that I am with every sentiment of respect Sir, Your very Hble & Obnt Servt

Le Barbier the younger— [1]

P:S: I have besought Mr Lee President of Congress, (to whom I have sent copies of my Drama, to be presented to the members of Congress) to send you the two I have addressed to you,[2] I have not dissembled to him, the noble desire I had of tracing over again, by the assistance of painting, my profession; the brilliant exploits of the Americans, and the chieftains who took you for their model.

Translation, in David Stuart's hand, DLC:GW; ALS, DLC:GW. A transcript of the ALS is in CD-ROM:GW. The author signs the letter "Le Barbier Le jeune," or perhaps "Lebarbier."

Even though GW could not, and did not, read the play that Lebarbier sent him, the title page alone must have had an unhappy effect on him: "Asgill, Drame, en Cinq Actes, en Prose; Dédié à Madame Asgill, par J. L. Le Barbier le jeune," published in London and Paris in 1785. The death sentence that GW imposed in 1782 upon the young guardsman, Charles Asgill, became a cause célèbre which at the time brought GW much pain and criticism. In May 1782 Charles Asgill, a captain of the First Foot Guards and a prisoner of war, not yet 20 years old, was chosen by lot and ordered, by GW, to be executed in retaliation for the hanging of a New Jersey militia captain by Loyalists. Asgill was the son of Sir Charles Asgill, former lord mayor of London, and of Theresa Pratviel Asgill, the daughter of a wealthy French Huguenot émigré. At the time that word arrived in England of Asgill's plight, his father lay seriously ill and his mother led the fight to save their son's life. It was a letter from her to Vergennes that prompted the French foreign minister to intervene with GW on Asgill's behalf, leading to Asgill's release in November and his return to London (see particularly Vergennes to GW, 29 July 1782, and GW to Asgill, 13 Nov. 1782). The action of the play takes place at GW's headquarters. Asgill and his faithful friend, Maj. James Gordon, are the heroes of the piece. GW is portrayed sympathetically, as one who is trapped by circumstances but in the end is magnanimous. Most of the important documents relating to GW's involvement in the Asgill affair are quoted in Katherine Mayo's book-length account, called *General Washington's Dilemma*, published in New York in 1938. For GW's guarded words of thanks for copies of the play, see GW to Lebarbier, 25 Sept. 1785. For GW's angry reaction to reports in 1786 that Asgill was making charges of cruel treatment at the hands of the Americans, see GW to James Tilghman, 5 June 1786.

1. Lebarbier, "Le jeune," may be the son or brother of the court painter Jean-Jacques-François Lebarbier, "l'aîné" (1738–1826).

2. Richard Henry Lee sent the copies of the play to GW in July. See Lee to GW, 23–31 July 1785. In his response of 22 Aug., GW wrote Lee: "for want of knowledge of the language, I can form no opinion of my own of the Dramatic performance Monsr Servitieur [*sic*] la Barbier."

From George Clinton

Dear Sir   New York 5th March 1785

I wrote you on the 26th December inclosing a Deed &c. which I hope came safe to Hand. In that Letter I also mentioned my having shipped on Board of a Vessel bound to Suffolk several small Articles for your Excellency, the Gentleman to whom they were addressed has since advised Colo. Walker of their safe arrival at that place, and promised to forward them by the first safe Conveyance, so that before this I flatter myself you must have recevd them. It was not a Little unfortunate that having been disapointed by the Change of Voyage in the first Vessel on Board of which they were to have gone, that we shipped them for Suffolk, but a very few days before a Vessel of Colo. Sears's was advertised for Alexandria and which I have since been Informed Landed some Articles for your Excellency at your own House.[1]

I now send by the Ship Gustavis Capt. [   ] which is to sail on Monday next for Alexandria, one Barrel of small white Indian Corn and a Box both marked GW the latter contains a Glass Case with Wax or Grotto Work, presented by Mr Francis to Mrs Washington and by him left with Mrs Clinton to forward. I have put it up with all possible Care and earnestly hope it may arrive safe, tho' I confess I would not be willing to Insure it as it appears to me to be a very Ginger Bread piece of work— If any of the parts should get loose they must be fastened with a little Rosen and white Wax—this is the makers direction which he desired might be communicated.[2]

In Consequence of your Excellency's last Letter I applied to Mr Beekman for the Grape Vines in order to forward them by the present Conveyance, It being about the proper Season, but to my great disappointment I find there is no such Thing— They were put in his Garden after a very tedious passage from Europe and not a single Cion lived nor did one of the seeds which accompanied them ever come up. Mr Beekman informs me that Mr Williamous was apprized of this in July last, and that from their bad Condition when put in the Ground he had little hopes of their growing and when he found they did not, he said he would bring over a new Assortment from France for which place he Sailed last Fall.[3]

The River yet remains shut up with Ice so that it is not possible at present to procure the other Plants as soon as it is they shall be forwarded.

Should the Indian Corn succeed, and I presume the present will be sufficient to make the Experiment it will be best to procure at least every three years new Seed from this Quarter.

Mrs Clinton begs you to present her Affectionate respects to Mrs Washington and joins in sincerest wishes for your Felicity with Dear Sir your most Affectionate Humble Servant

Geo. Clinton

P.S. Colo. Walker will transmit your Excellency the Capt. Receipt for the Articles now Shipped with advice where to find them at Alexandria—The Box should be brought from thence by Water as it will not bear Land Carriage.[4]

ALS, DLC:GW.

1. On 5 April GW acknowledges receipt of Clinton's letter of 26 Dec. 1784, which has not been found. The "Deed" was a copy of the deed to the land in upstate New York that Clinton had bought jointly for himself and GW (see GW to Clinton, 25 Nov. 1784, n.2). For the "small Articles" sent to Norfolk, Va., not Suffolk, see Benjamin Walker to GW, 20 Dec. 1784, and notes. Isaac Sears (1730–1786), leader of the New York Sons of Liberty before the war, returned from Boston to New York City in late 1783 when the British evacuated the city and resumed his mercantile business there.

2. Benjamin Walker wrote on 11 Mar. that Clinton's parcels were sent to Alexandria on 10 Mar. aboard the *Hope.* GW wrote on 20 April thanking him for the various things Clinton had sent him in November, December, and March (see the references in note 1). The grotto work in the glass case, probably made of shells attached to a wax mold, "came very safe" (GW to Clinton, 20 April).

3. See GW to Clinton, 25 Nov. 1784, n.5.

4. See note 2.

From Patrick Henry

Dear sir   Richmond [Va.] March 5th 1785

The Bearer hereof Mr Alexander Donald wishes to have the Honor of presenting himself to you, & has entreated of me to sollicit for him permission to do so.

I take the Liberty therefore to introduce him to you, not doubting but you will find him agreable. With the highest Esteem & Regard I am Dear sir, your most obedient Servant

P. Henry

ALS, ViMtV.

Alexander Donald, a close friend of Thomas Jefferson, was a merchant in Richmond and was associated in business with Robert Morris of Philadelphia. He arrived at Mount Vernon on 16 Mar. with Governor Henry's letter.

From Clement Biddle

Dear General   Philadelphia 7 March 1785

I must appologise for not answering your esteemed favours of 1st & 2d Ulto (which reached me about a fourtnight ago) before this Time but hope you will excuse me when I enform you of the Occasion.

A number of losses in Trade during & since the war had so much involved my Affairs that altho' I had property in value equal to what I owed it was so much scatterd that I found myself under a necessity of suspending payment & give up my Estate in trust for the use of my Creditors, but I have experiencd much Kindness & hope not only to do well yet but to have it in my power to make up any deficiency in my present Affairs which will be my greatest happiness[1]—I shall now very soon transmit your account wch I would have done before but my mind was too much oppressed to Attend to it—I am now more at liberty & can execute any Orders you may be pleased to favour me with and which I shall esteem as a great Obligation to have your Continuance of as I hope I shall not forfeit your Friendship & tho' I may not engage in the Commercial Line shall pay the greatest Attention in future to your Commands— I have deliverd the Letter to Mr Lewis respecting the Miller[2]— I hope the Grass seed which I sent by Capt. Rice has reachd you as I have advise of its safe Arrival to Mr W: Thompson at Colchester—Within a few days another parcel (a barrel) of Grass Seed arrived from Mr Boudinot but no Conveyance has since Offerd for Potowmack, but I expect one daily when it shall be sent. I have not been able to get any of the Green or spier Grass seed tho' I have constantly kept up my Enquiry for it.[3]

I have the accounts respecting the Indian Meal & flour in my hands—they must be passed by Mr Benjn Stelle the Commissioner appointed by Congress for settling those Accounts—he is now at Carlile in Cumberland County & I shall write to him and inclose them by the Members of our Assembly who expect to return home in a fourtnight & are the first Conveyance I could depend on.[4]

I could not Obtain such Information respecting the Author of the Poems as to induce me to deliver your Letter but will make further Enquirey on that subject.[5]

Mr Dunlap has assured me the papers shall be sent & a set of those with Cooks voyage.[6]

Mrs Biddle begs leave to join in most respectful Complements to Mrs Washington with your Excellencys most Obedt & very humle servt

Clement Biddle

ALS, DLC:GW.

1. On 28 Feb. Biddle put both his real and personal property in the hands of trustees empowered to satisfy his creditors. See Biddle to William Thompson, 3 Mar. 1785 (Biddle Letter Book, ViMtV).

2. GW's letter to Robert Lewis & Sons is dated 1 February.

3. For Boudinot's grass seed, see GW to Biddle, 3 Nov. 1784, and note 2 of that document. Biddle wrote to William Thompson at Colchester on 8 Feb.: "I had put the soap & Candles & some grass seeds for General Washington—on board the Sloop Dolphin Cap. Rice who was clear'd to sail but was stopp'd by the Sea last Sunday" (Biddle Letter Book, ViMtV). For the second shipment of Boudinot's grass seed, see Biddle to GW, 12 April.

4. See GW to Biddle, 1 Feb., n.8.

5. See GW to Biddle, 2 Feb., and notes.

6. See GW to Biddle, 1 Feb., n.4.

To William Gordon

Dr Sir,   Mt Vernon 8th March 1785.

Since my last to you, I have been favored with several of your letters, which should not have remained so long unacknowledged, had I not been a good deal pressed by matters which could not well be delayed, & because I found a difficulty in complying with your request respecting the profiles—the latter is not in my power to do now, satisfactorily. Some imperfect miniature cuts I send you under cover with this letter—they were designed for me by Miss D'Hart of Elizabethtown—

& given to Mrs Washington; who in sparing them, only wishes they may answer your purpose. For her I can get none cut yet. If Mr Du'Simitere is living, & at Philada, it is possible he may have miniature engravings of most, if not all the military characters you want, & in their proper dresses: he drew many good likenesses from the life, and got them engraved at Paris for sale; among these I have seen Genl Gates, Baron de Steuben, &c.—as also that of your humble servt.[1] The Marqs de la Fayette had left this before your request of his profile came to hand.

You ask if the character of Colo. John Lawrens, as drawn in the Independant Chronicle of the 2d of Decr last, is just. I answer, that such parts of the drawing as have fallen under my own observation is literally so; & that it is my firm belief his merits & worth richly entitle him to the whole picture: no man possessed more of the amor patria—in a word, he had not a fault that I ever could discover, unless intripidity bordering upon rashness, could come under that denomination; & to this he was excited by the purest motives.[2]

The order alluded to in my private letter, a copy of which you requested, I now send. You might have observed, for I believe the same private letter takes notice thereof, that it was consequent of a resolve of Congress, that Fort Washington was so pertinaceously held, before the Ships passed that Post. Without unpacking chests, unbundling papers &ca, I cannot come at to give you a copy of that resolve; but I well remember that after reciting the importance of securing the upper navigation of the Hudson, I am directed to obtain hulks, to sink them for the purpose of obstructing the navigation, & to spare no other cost to effect it. Owing to this the Posts of Forts Washington & Lee, on account of the narrowness of the river—some peculiarity of the channel, & strength of the ground at these places, were laboriously fortified—owing to this we left Fort Washington strongly garrisoned, in our rear, when we were obliged to retreat to the White plains; & owing to this also, Colo. Magaw, who commanded at it, was ordered to defend it to the last extremity. But when, maugre all the obstructions which had been thrown into the channel—all the labour & expence wch had been bestowed on the works—& the risks we had run of the Garrison theretofore, the British Ships of War had, & could pass those Posts, it was clear to me from that moment, that they were no longer eligable, & that that on the East side of the river ought to be withdrawn whilst it was in our power: in consequence thereof the letter of the 8th of Novr 1776 was written to Genl Greene from the White plains; that Post & all the troops in the vicinity of it being under his orders.[3]

I give this information, and I furnish you with a copy of the order for the evacuation of Fort Washington, because you desire it, not that I want to exculpate myself from any censure which may have fallen on me, by charging another.

I have sent your recipe for the preservation of young plants, to the Alexandria printer; & wish the salutary effect which the author of the discovery in the annual register has pointed to, may be realized: the process is simple, & not expensive, which renders it more valuable.[4]

Some accots say, that matters are in train for an accommodation between the Austrians & Dutch; if so the flames of war may be arrested before they blaze out & become very extensive; but admitting the contrary I hope none of the sparks will light on American ground—which I fear is made up of too much combustible matter for its well being.

Your young friend is in high health, & as full of spirits as an egg shell is of meat[5]—I informed him I was going to write to you, & desired to know if he had any commands—his spontanious answer—I beg he will make haste & come here again. All the rest of the family are well, except Mrs Washington who is too often troubled with bilious and cholicky complaints, to enjoy perfect health; all join in best wishes for you & yours with, Dr Sir Yo[ur]s &c. &c.

G: Washington

LB, DLC:GW.

1. The only letter of Gordon's written before this time and after GW's letter to him of 20 Dec. 1784 which has been found is that of 10 January. The letter making the "request respecting the profiles" is among those missing. Pierre Eugène Du Simitière (c.1736–1784), a native of Switzerland, was an artist and naturalist who from 1766 until his death lived in Philadelphia. His engravings of portraits of thirteen of the leaders of the American Revolution were published in London in 1783. Sarah De Hart made the silhouettes of GW in 1783.

2. John Laurens (1754–1782), the son of Henry Laurens, returned from England in 1777 and joined GW's staff as a volunteer aide-de-camp. He had a brilliant career in the army before being killed in a local action in South Caro-

lina in 1782. The *Independent Chronicle* (Boston), 2 Dec. 1784, printed as a footnote to a letter on slavery an appreciation of John Laurens's career and character. After recounting instances of Laurens's extraordinary courage, the writer of the note asserted: "Those who were intimately acquainted with this young man, will rank his martial qualities, by which he was chiefly known, as lowest in the catalogue of his virtues." The writer then goes on to speak of Laurens's "clear discerning mind, that united the solid powers of the understanding with inflexible integrity" and to refer to him as a "noblest and most useful citizen . . . kindest and most affectionate friend . . . a generous and disinterested patriot."

3. See Gordon to GW, 10 Jan. 1785, nn.1 and 2. Robert Magaw was the commander of Fort Washington who surrendered it to the British on 16 Nov. 1776.

4. The following item appeared in the 17 Mar. issue of the *Virginia Journal and Alexandria Advertiser*: "A Gentleman reading in the *Annual Register* for 1781, ingenious 'Thoughts on the Rot in Sheep, by Benjamin Price;' and therein meeting with the following Assertions, viz. 'Salt is pernicious to most Insects; they never infect Gardens where Sea-Weed is laid:' It immediately occured to him, that, if so, the loss of various excellent young Plants, destroyed by Insects in the Beginning of Spring might be prevented, by laying fresh Sea-Weed near the Plants, or, when Distance hinders the obtaining of Sea-Weed, Hay well sopped in a strong Brine. It is supposed, that the salted Hay, if not fouled with Dirt, will afterword be an acceptable Food to Cattle."

5. George Washington Parke Custis.

Letter not found: from Robert Lewis & Sons, 8 Mar. 1785. On 5 April they again wrote to GW: "We had the pleasure of writing to your Excellency the 8th Ulto by Post."

To John Witherspoon

revd Sir,   Mount Vernon 8th March 1785.

From the cursory manner in wch you expressed the wish of Mr Bowie, to write the Memoirs of my life—I was not, at the moment of your application & my assent to it, struck with the consequences to which it tended:[1] but when I came to reflect upon the matter afterwards, & had had some conversation with Mr Bowie on the subject; I found that this must be a very futile work (if under *any* circumstances it could be made interesting) unless, he could be furnished with the incidents of my life, either from my papers, or my recollection, and digesting of past transactions into some sort of form & order with respect to times & circumstances: I knew also that many of the former relative to the part I had acted in the war between France & G:

Britain from the year 1754, until the peace of Paris; & which contained some of the most interesting occurrences of my life, were lost; that my memory is too treacherous to be relied on to supply this defect; and, admitting both were more perfect, that submitting such a publication to the world whilst I continue on the theatre, might be ascribed (however involuntarily I was led into it) to vain motives.

These considerations prompted me to tell Mr Bowie, when I saw him at Philada in May last,[2] that I could have no agency towards the publication of any memoirs respecting myself whilst living: but as I had given my assent to you (when asked) to have them written, & as he had been the first to propose it, he was welcome if he thought his time would not be unprofitably spent, to take extracts from such documents as yet remained in my possession, & to avail himself of any other information I could give; provided the publication should be suspended until I had quitted the stage of human action. I then intended, as I informed him, to have devoted the present expiring winter in arranging all my papers which I had left at home, & which I found a mere mass of confusion (occasioned by frequently shifting them into trunks, & suddenly removing them from the reach of the enemy)—but however strange it may seem it is nevertheless true, that what with company; referrences of old matters with which I ought not to be troubled—applications for certificates, and copies of orders, in addition to the rotine of letters which have multiplied greatly upon me; I have not been able to touch a single paper, or transact any business of my own, in the way of accots &[c]. during the whole course of the winter; or in a word, since my retirement from public life.[3]

I have two reasons, my good sir, for making these communications to you—the first is, by way of apology for not complying with my promise in the full extent you might expect in favor of Mr Bowie. The second is, not knowing where that Gentleman resides I am at a loss without your assistance, to give him the information respecting the disordered state of my papers, which he was told should be arranged, & a proper selection of them made for his inspection, by the Spring. Upon your kindness therefore I must rely to convey this information to him;[4] for tho' I shou'd be glad at all times, to see Mr Bowie here, I should be unhappy if expectations which can not be realized (in the present moment) shou'd withdraw him from, or cause him to forego some other pursuits which may be more advantageous to him. My respects if you please to Mrs Witherspoon. I have the honor to be &c.

G: Washington

LB, DLC:GW.
    1. See GW to James Craik, 25 Mar. 1784, and note 1 of that document.
    2. GW attended the general meeting of the Society of the Cincinnati in Philadelphia in May 1784.
    3. For references to GW's concern for his papers, see the notes in GW to Varick, 1 Jan. 1784. GW succeeded in hiring a clerk in July (see GW to William Shaw, 8 July 1785).
    4. See Witherspoon to GW, 14 April 1785.

From Jacob Read

Sir   New York 9th March 1785
    When I had the pleasure to See you last Summer at Mount Vernon I believe I informed you in answer to a question on the Subject that Congress had received a Copy of the Roll of Negroes &Ca taken by the Commissioners for Superintending the Embarkations at New York at the time of the removal of the Refugees and British Garrison from this City—I now find I was mistaken and that the one I had Seen in the office of the Secretary of Congress was only of 168 Negroes being the last Inspection of the Whole and made on board some Transports at that time at Anchor at Staten Island—The General roll never has been seen by Congress and is at this time wanted to enable our Ministers in Europe to proceed to execute the Instructions of Congress of 1783 on the Subject of Negroes Carried off in Contravention of the Treaty of peace.[1]
    I request Your Excellency to forward the Document alluded to as early as possible.[2]
    As I embark in a day or two for So. Carolina to be absent for 2 or 3 Months I cannot flatter myself with the pleasure of any Correspondence with you till my return unless I can tender you any Service in Charles Town—I beg you'l Command me in such Case Without reserve and assure yourself I Shall feel the greatest pleasure in obeying your Commands.
    The Public Prints will ere this have informed you that Mr Jno. Adams is elected Minister to the Court of London. I had

the happiness to Succeed in my endeavours to Send Col. Wm Smith as Secretary to the Legation. Mr McHenry of Maryland now in Congress offerrd himself & there were sevl other Candidates but finding himself not likely to be elected, Mr McHenry with a wonderful dexterity rose & nominated the very man whom he in a conversation with me had offered a great many arguments to defeat, it was the Coll's wish to Stand on the Nomination of So. Carolina. but we were Supplanted by this little Son of Esculapius, however Smith was at once Elected.[3]

Congress Yesterday Elected Genl Knox Secretary at War. I put Coll Walker of your late Family in Nomination & he had an Honourable Support. The Sallary is Cut down to Twenty four hundred & fifty Dollars, not I am Sure Sufft to render it worth Genl Knox's acceptance. With this Idea I brought forward Col. Walkers Name—he woud have been Elected but the New Englanders thought Genl Knox wou'd accept & rely on the future generosity of Congress to make him Some Allowances of Hou. rent travelling expences &Ca.[4]

From the want of a full Congress the great national questions Still remain untouched & will not be attempted till late in the Spring When tis hoped we may assemble the Whole force of the Union & try if we can Act as a Nation, which by the bye I very much doubt now the Common tye of danger is removed.

Do me the favour to present my most respectful Complements to Mrs Washington.

I thank your Excellency for you[r] full Communications in answer to my Enquiries. They afforded me great Satisfaction & have confirmed sevl Opinions I had early adopted.[5] I am with the greatest respect & regard Sir Your most obedt and most Humle Servt

Jacob Read

ALS, DLC:GW.

1. For the rolls listing the slaves who sailed from New York in 1783, see the Commissioners of Embarkation at New York to GW, 18 Jan. 1784, and, particularly, the source note and nn.3 and 6. Congress on 22 Dec. 1783 instructed its ministers to demand "full satisfaction for all slaves and other property belonging to citizens of these States taken and carried away in violation of the preliminary and definitive articles of peace," and it promised to provide the ministers "with necessary facts and documents" to accomplish this (*JCC*, 25:825).

2. GW wrote Charles Thomson, secretary of Congress, on 5 April offering, with considerable reluctance, to send his copy of the rolls. On 22 April,

Thomson replied that he was suggesting to John Jay that he send someone to Mount Vernon to make a copy of the lists. Jay and the Congress accepted Thomson's suggestion, and in September Jay sent down to Mount Vernon his clerk George Taylor, Jr., to do the copying. See Jay to GW, 25 Aug., and enclosures, and GW to Jay, 27 September.

3. James McHenry (1753–1816) studied medicine under Benjamin Rush and during the war served as a military surgeon before becoming GW's secretary in May 1778. He was a delegate to Congress from Maryland from 1783 to 1786. He also served in the Constitutional Convention in 1787. In 1796 GW made him secretary of war, a post he held until 1800 when President John Adams forced his resignation. William Stephens Smith served as secretary of John Adams's legation in London and also married Adams's daughter.

4. See Henry Knox to GW, 24 Mar. 1785.

5. Read is referring both to his own letter of 22 Oct. 1784, in which he expressed the wish "to be favoured with Any observations that may be Essential towards my forming a proper Judgment on Any Measures Congress may have in View respecting the Western Territory," and to GW's lengthy response of 3 Nov. 1784.

From James Duane

Dear Sir   New York 10th March 1785

An Opportunity at length presents itself of forwarding to your Excellency a packet which has been detained ever since I left Trenton, as I did not wish to hazard it by the Post.[1]

Congress are fixed here for the present apparently to their Satisfaction. They are busily employed in arranging the national Affairs. Mr Adams is appointed Minister for the Court of London Mr Jefferson for Versailles: who will be sent to the Hague is undecided. The five per Cent Requisition goes on heavily and I am very apprehensive of it's Fate even in this State which once took the Lead in every federal Measure. The Rhode Island and other Eastern publications against this Grant have made a deep Impression in the Counties most exposed to their Influence—A bill on this interesting Subject is under Commitment in the Senate and will be brought forward in a few days. It is to be lamented that even there it will meet with warm Opposition.[2]

Our legislature I take it for granted will in the Course of this Month pay into the Continental Treasury 110,000 Dollars in Specie and 37000 in Certificates in full of their Arrears which will be a present supply. A bill for this purpose has passed the Senate.

It seems still to be doubtful whether the Emperor will persist in his Hostilities or retract or suspend his Claims. Whatever may be the Event I feel for the Dutch. Their Conduct to us is a proof of their magnanimity and their Sense of the Value of Liberty—and yet it is their Fate to be in the neighbourhood of three mighty Monarchs who in turn assume authority to direct and controul them—to say nothing of Great Brittain which does not regard them in a friendly Light. If the Dutch consulted their Happiness they woud transport themselves their arts And their wealth and partake with us in the Blessings which we enjoy in a Land of Liberty and plenty out of the Reach of Kings. I ventured in a social Hour to drop a hint of this kind to Mr Van Berckel; it cannot be supposed that it admitted of Discussion: but I was not only in earnest, but am fully perswaded that if any considerable Misfortune shoud befall the Dutch from the Rapacity of their Neighbours this in a great Degree will be the Event: nor when I consider how little of Principle is to be found in most of the Cabinets of Europe, and how shamefully Poland was plundered and divided without a pretence of Right, do I beleive such an Event at any great Distance.

Mrs Duane and our Daughter Join me in our most respectful Compliments to yourself and Mrs Washington; and I beg you will believe that among your numerous Friends there is none more firmly attached to you by Sentiments of Affection Respect and Esteem than him who has the Honor to be Dear Sir—your most obedient & very humble Servant

Jas Duane

ALS, DLC:GW.

1. The packet included Duane's letter of 16 Dec. 1784, an address from the City of New York, and the extension to GW of the freedom of that city, all printed above. For GW's responses to the city, see his letter to Duane of 10 April.

2. A bill to empower the Congress of the Confederation to levy a duty of 5 percent on foreign imports was kept alive until its final defeat in 1786.

From William Grayson

Dear Sir   New York March 10th 1785.

I had the honor of your favor of the 22nd of Jany just as I was setting of from Dumfries, and I should have answered it from Mr Orr's in Loudoun, where I was detained some time on account of Mrs Grayson's illness, if I had not wish'd for more time to reflect on the subject matter of it: It would have giv'n me great pleasure (if my particular situation would have permitted) to have waited on you at Mount Vernon and to have convers'd with you on the occasion as I could in that case have entered more fully into the different circumstances than it is practicable to do by any communication on paper; I shall now however give you the best information in my power, as also my own sentiments with the utmost candor & sincerity;[1] It was talk'd of by gentlemen of the House that some mark of attention and respect (not barely complimentary) should be paid you by your native Country; that the other States in the Union knew you only as an American, but that your own knew you as an American and a Virginian; the only difficulty was, how to fall on any expedient that might not wound your feelings on the one hand or be unworthy of the Legislature on the other; While matters remain'd in a situation altogether inconclusive, a gentleman of the Ass[embl]y made a motion respecting you, which it was thought adviseable to oppose on the principle of particular impropriety; however it was soon discovered from the temper of the House that if the question had been put it would have been carried without a dissentient as those in the opposition would also have voted for the measure; recourse was therefore had to intreaty & he was prevail'd on to withdraw it, on being promis'd a plan should be brought forward which should in some degree imbrace his views as well as the wishes of the House; accordingly the act which took effect was presented the next day, & immediately pass'd both Houses.

Some of the reasons which suggested it were these; It had appeared by conversations out of doors, on the passage of the river bills, that the House were anxious (as you had patronized them and opened their importance to public view) that the credit of the undertaking should be ascrib'd to yourself & it was wish'd that this might appear by some public act of the legislature; In pursuing this idea, it was thought that such an act might with propriety contain a grant of a certain number of shares to yourself which at the same time that it would be an instance of the attention of the House might also serve in part as a reason for taking up the subject and introducing the other matter; It was reasoned by those who countenanc'd this particular plan, that the grant when measured by the European scale (the only criterion by which it could be judged) was so relatively inconsiderable, as to exclude every idea of it's being looked upon as a reward for services; that the value of the subject was so precarious, & depended on such a variety of circumstances as almost to prevent the sensation of property in the mind; That the act would carry to Posterity an evidence of the part you had acted in this great undertaking, the remembrance of which would be kept up by the possessions which were granted by the Assembly and retained by your family; That under every view of the subject it could be considered in no other light than the Act itself set forth, an honorable testimonial of the gratitude & affection of your native Country; The gentlemen who favored this particular mode, designedly contracted the number of shares in order to guard it against the objections which you now suppose it to be liable to, as the blank with equal facility might have fill'd up in such a manner as to have comprehended objects of much greater magnitude; The idea of your being subjected to the performance of any particular service never once occurred and so far from it's being suppos'd that you are in any degree circumscribed by the act I am perfectly satisfyed you will yourself confer the obligation by the acceptance; I will not pretend to say that the House do not wish you to devote some portion of your leisure reflections to the furtherance of this great national object; this is also I verily believe the case with every man in the State who has reflected on the matter; indeed numbers rest the success of the measure in a great degree on such an event; But then Sir this is hop'd for, not as the effect or condition of the act but merely as the result of your own inclinations; they suppose such a line of conduct will at the same time be highly honorable to yourself & that this is one of those few great objects on which you can now with propriety fix your attention; The House I am convinc'd would feel very sensibly if they suppos'd you concieved yourself to be less independant on this account, or that any act of theirs should have a tendency to prevent you from offering your advice to your Country whenever you concieved it to be necessary.

These were the ideas which prevaild in general on the occasion; there was a great variety of sentiments, and a great deal said about the matter particularly with[ou]t doors where every

man spoke his mind freely; indeed candor obliges me to inform
you that there were not wanting some who thought you were
plac'd in a situation which call'd for assistance of a very different nature from the present; With respect to what you hint as to
it's being considered in the light of a pension, I am satisfyed it
can never be the case under any view of the subject; indeed I
cannot concieve there can be any such thing in our goverments
according to the ideas generally annex'd to it, and if instead of a
precarious unproductive property it had been the grant of an
annuity from the United States, I think it would not have been
liable to this appellation, for I look upon the uninfluenced
grant of a free people in a very different light from a gift which
proceeds from the caprice of Princes or Ministers and which is
always supposed whether true or false to be founded on the
principle of favoritism; this distinction is preserved in the Brittish constitution & is productive of sensations essentially different, the one conveying the idea of personal favor and the other
that of acknowledg'd merit; if then the grants of parliament in
a Monarchy are looked upon as highly honorable to the person
who recieves them, how much stronger ought the impression to
be in a republican government, where the principle of action is
always suppos'd to be Virtue. Upon the whole however as you
have plac'd so much confidence in me as to consult me on
the occasion, and as the subject is a very delicate one, I would
rather advise that you should not accept the grant at present in
any other manner than that of acting under it, leaving your ultimate decision to time & future reflection. There are persons
in the world interested in defeating the whole undertaking, and
from motives of resentment alone might be induc'd to mis-
represent the purity of your intentions; & though I have not
the least doubt myself of the propriety of your accepting the
grant yet it would be a painful reflection in me to think I had
recommended a measure which had the most distant tendency
in lessening you in the estimation of the world; it is certain if I
had thought it not[2] decidedly right, I never would have voted
for it as a representative of the people; and I have every reason
to believe that this was the case with every member of the
House, who never would have offered a thing which they con-
ciev'd it was improper in you to recieve; If you should at a future period and after the maturest consideration find yourself

unalterably determined against converting it to your own use, you will always have it in your power to appropriate either the principal or profits to public purposes of essential utility; though this will contradict the desires and wishes of your fellow Citizens, and counteract the purposes which gave rise to the measure, I think it will be less objectionable than an absolute rejection in the first instance It will shew a willingless on your part to comply with their request as far as your own sensations would permit you; I hope however that at some future period, and after you have thoroughly weighed all the circumstances, you will find yourself disposed as well from the propriety of the thing itself, as the impulse of your own feelings towards your parent State, to accept of the grant in the manner originally designed by the legislature, and that the same may go and descend to your representative agreable to their intentions; The Assembly of Virginia have no doubt a reguard for your interest, but I am satisfyed they have a much higher one for your personal fame & honor. I shall now leave this subject with observing that there are strong reasons to be urged against your parting with the favor[3] giv'n you by the act, and which in my opinion essentially reguards the success of the undertaking, but as your own feelings are connected with the subject I find a repugnance in pressing them in point of delicacy, I shall therefore leave them & their operations to the suggestions of your own mind making no doubt they will have such an effect as the magnitude of the object and your attachment to it's success may with propriety point out. With respect to the Aspen & Yew trees, I beg leave to acquaint you, that I sent to Sprigg's ford to see if the tree which the Doctr had giv'n me had produc'd any scions, and was inform'd there were none; I then applied to Mr Landon Carter who had several at his plantation on Bull run; Mrs Grayson whom I left at Mr Orr's promis'd me to carry them behind her carriage to Dumfries & to send them from thence to Mount Vernon together with any scions of the yew tree which she with the assistance of Doctr Graham & Mr R. Graham, might be able to procure.[4] We have very little news here, Mr Marbois has inform'd us there will be no war between the Emperor and the Dutch, & the Minister of the latter expresses himself to the same purpose, but neither have communicated the terms of the pacification.

Congress are engaged in a plan for opening their Land Office on the Western waters.

In recommending a plan for extending their powers in forming Commercial treaties.

In regulating the Post Office and in making a Peace establishment. They have directed a treaty to be form'd if practicable with the Piratical States on the Coasts of Africa; I expect a Minister will be appointed to the Court of Spain after the arrival here of Don Diego Gardoqui; & one I presume will be appointed to Holland in the room of Mr Adams who goes to the Court of St James. I have the honor to be with the highest respect Yr Affecte friend & Most Obedt Servt

Willm Grayson

ALS, DLC:GW.

1. For references to GW's anguished appeals for advice regarding the gift to him by the Virginia general assembly of stock in the Potomac and James River companies, see Benjamin Harrison to GW, 6 Jan. 1785, n.1. John Orr (b. 1726) was Grayson's brother-in-law.

2. Grayson inserted "not" before rather than after "it."

3. Grayson wrote "savor."

4. Dr. Graham is William Graham (1751–1821) of Dumfries, Va., who was a surgeon's mate in the 2d Virginia Regiment during the Revolution; R. Graham is the Dumfries merchant Richard Grayson. Grayson's wife, Eleanor Smallwood Grayson, sent GW "8 Yew & 4 Aspan trees" (entry of 22 Mar. in *Diaries*, 4:107). Spriggs Ford has not been located, but before the Revolution Edward Sprigg was an agent in nearby Colchester for the Maryland firm of Barnes & Ridgate.

From Alexander Hamilton

Dr Sir   New York March 10: 1785

I am requested by Mr Oudinarde to transmit you the Inclosed Account[1]—I observed to him that it was a little extraordinary the account had not been presented before; and that it was probable your accounts with the public had been long since closed, and that, by the delay, you may have lost the oppurtunity of making it a public charge, as it ought to have been. But as the person was very importunate I told him I should have no objection to be the vehicle of conveyance to you. In this view I transmit the account; and remain with much respect D. Sr Yr Obed. & humb.

Alex. Hamilton

⟨Mrs⟩ Hamilton joins in compliments to ⟨Mr⟩s Washington.

ALS, DLC: Hamilton Papers.
    1. The enclosed account, probably of the firm M. and H. Oudenarde, 18 Hanover Square, New York City, has not been found.

Letter not found: from John de Neufville, 10 Mar. 1785. On 8 Sept. GW wrote de Neufville: "I have lately been honored with your favors of the 10th & 15th of March."

From James Rumsey

Dear Sir   Bath [Va.] March the 10th 1785
    Your favour of the 22d Ultimo has Just Came to hand[1] And it gives me much Uneasyness that I Should though unintentionly, have gave you So much trouble abought Ryans note, as well as not Comeing up to my promis in the Repayment of the money you Lett mr Herbert have on my acount, I am also hurt that from the present apearance of things you have Reason to think me a person not posessed of the Least honor Or Delicacy, to be Capable, as you have Very Justly Observed, of Sending you the note of a Shufling player, for Shufling he Certainly is, But your goodness Sir, is Conspecuous in your Letter to me (as well as on all Other ocations,) to give me Such Indulgences as you have proposed at a time when you have Reason to think I Do not Deserve it. But although I am Senceable that nothing I Can offer as Excuse Should be Receivd as full Satisfaction as the money was not paid yet I trust that you may not think So hard of me when I give you a Detail of my proceedings after I had the honour of Seeing you Last. I Stayed at Richmond near two weeks after my buisness was Done Endeavouring to get Sum money of Ryan But To Little purpose Except Sufisiant to pay my Expences I then Toald Him the Solemn Ingagement I was under to you For the payment of fifty pounds in a few weeks and as I thought It might tend to make him punktial I took the Liberty to have the note drawn in your name But never Intended you Should See it much more to have So much troubl with it. When I was On my way home I met with a Mr Klinehoof of Alexandria knowing him to be a Safe hand, and thinking my acquantance with Mr Herbert, would Intitle me to ask him a Small favour, as I Conceivd it, I Enclosed the note in a Letter to

him and beged him In the most Serious and pressing terms to Send the note to his freind in Richmond for payment against the Day it was Due and if the money was Obtained to give it to you Immediately But by no means to present the note to you that it was only Drew in your name to urge the other to payment. my hearing no more of the matter for Sumtime gave me hopes that the money was Receivd by Mr Herbert, A bought the first of Febuary I had an Opertunity of writeing to Mr Herbert abought the matter and Sum other Buisness But to my great Surprize his answer Respecting the note was—"The note being Drawn In the Generals name I Delivered it to him,["] This answer gave me great uneaseyness Least it Should turn out as it Realy has. I had one Chance that I thought good in Berkeley to get the money where it was Due me, But all my Indavours proved Inefectual or I Should have Immediately Came Down, I therefore waited the Event of Ryans note with great anxiety, your Letter Announced it and your Indulgence Exceeded my most Sanguine Expectations. I had an Opertunity to Richmond and pressed Ryan hard to pay the note had no answer but heard of his Sickness and his Since Removeing to Norfolk if you will be kind enough to Leave the note with Mr Herbert when I Come or Send to alexandria perhaps I may yet get in his favour to forward it to Ryan if not I Can have it home.[2]

Respecting your houses Sir, they will Shorely be built agreeable to your Directions, and would have been had I not have heard from you at all as I had Spoke to a man before I went to Richmond that kept two or three workmen to build me the kitchens and Stables of all the houses I had to build, my Stay was So Long that before I got home the Loggs were all hewed the Shingles got and are all on the Spott Readey for Raising. I hope Sir you Will not Disaprove when I tell you of my proceedings Respecting your Big house, nor Constru it Into a Desire of me to Revive our old agreement, But I have it under way the window Shutters Doors and Sash are All made and the most of the moaldings Every Inch of the Stuff is Sawed and I have agreed with a man to frame and Raise it against the first Day of may, I Shall not Call upon you nor Draw any Orders more for money nor Do I Desire that you Should Send me any Except you Can Spare it with the greatest Convenance, and I now give you my word that I Will not Distress myself to finish it if I find I Cannot Do it without, I will Quit when I have it Inclosed which

I Can Do with But Little more Expence, and it will then Be as Secure against the weather as if it Was Done.[3]

Respecting my Boats[,] Georgia & South Cariline I have petioned, North Carolina I have But have not heard what they have Done, maryland, I hear has gave me an Exclusive Right under a redemtion by the Legeslature, pensylvania has Done the Same, the Jerseys threw it out of the house by a majority of four, new york asembly was not Siting which was the farthest that I made applycations to northward—I have made many neat and accurate Experiments with my Boats Since I Saw you, and find She far Exceeds my Expectations on the first Experiments made Last fall I find She will go a greater proportion of the Velocity of the water in Rapid Currents than Slow ones. the Reason is, the friction is nearly the Same In Boath Cases, it therefore takes a greater part of the force of a Small Current to over Come it, when a Very Small proportion will Do it with Ease in Rapid water, I have Deduced a Rule from Experiments By which I can tell what Quantity of paddle Boards a head, to Each tun, the Boat Caryes, is nesasary to go up with any proportion you think proper to the Stream that Comes Down, by which I find that the Resistance of water against Boats Increases Exactly as the Squares of the Velocity of the Boats against it, Nether Can their be a general Rule to give the Resistance that Boats of the Same Burthen and Velocity meets with If their formes is Different for I find that Bad Shaped Boats meets with nearly three times the Resistance that good ones Do of the Same Burthen, a well Shaped Boat will move a head be her Burthen what it may, as fast as the water Comes Down with three Square feet of paddle Board ahead for Each tun weight taken Up, the Boats weight Included, the fourth part of that much paddle Board will move her up half as fast as the Current Comes Down and four times that much paddle Board will Move her up twice as fast as the Current Comes Down, it then follows that if a Boat and her Load weighing Eight tun, with twenty four Square feet of paddle Boards, a head was to move up a River as fast as the Current Came Down, that if Six tuns was taken out of Said boat which would Leave But Little more than an Emty Boat that She would then go up the River with twice the Velocity that the Current Came Down So much for the kind of Boats, the Modle of which you Saw.[4]

I have taken the greatest pains to afect another kind of Boats upon the princeples I was mentioning to you at Richmond I have the pleasure to Inform you that I have Brought it to the greatest perfection It is true it will Cost Sum more than the other way But when Done is more mannagable and Can be worked by as few hands the power is amence and I am Quite Convinced that Boats of pasage may be made to go against the Current of the Mesisipia or ohio River, or in the gulf Stream from the Lewerd to the Windward Islands from Sixty to one hundred miles per Day I know it will apear Strange and Improbeble and was I to Say thus much to most people in this neghbourhood they would Laugh at me and think me mad But I Can ashore you Sir that I have Ever Been Very Cautious how I aserted any thing that I was not Very Certain I Could perform Besides it is no phenomena when known, But Strictly agreeble To philosiphy, The princeples of this Last kind of Boat I am Very Cautious not to Explain, to any person, as it is Easey performed and the method would Come Very nateral to a Rittenhouse, or an Elicott.[5] The plann I mean to persue is to Build the Boats with Boath the powers on Board on a Large Scale and then Sir if you would Be good enough Once more to See it make actual performances I make no Doubt but the asembleys will alow me Sumthing Clever which will be better for the public as well as my Self, than to have the Exclusive Rights. I am astonished that it is So hard to force an Advantage on the public. admit ⟨it⟩ Did make the fortune of one man. I Cannot help But Stare when I Look back at the Lenth of my Letter. it is a very Strikeng Representation of the propensity a man has to Say a great deal when he gets upon his favorite Theme, Least the Lenth of my Scrawl Should become tiresom to Read. I shall threfore Conclude by Returning you my most Sincere thanks for the many favours you have Done me, & am with Every Sentiment of Regard your Sincere freind and Very hble Servt

James Rumsey

ALS, DLC:GW. GW docketed the letter: "Recd May 7th—85."

1. Letter not found.

2. For references to GW's dealings with Rumsey regarding Dennis Ryan's note, see GW to Alexander Henderson, 20 Dec. 1784, n.1. See also GW's response to this letter on 5 June.

3. On 6 Sept. 1784 GW contracted with Rumsey to build for him at Bath, or Berkeley Springs, in Berkeley County, a two-story house with outbuildings to be completed by 10 July 1785. For GW's description of the proposed buildings, see *Diaries*, 4:9–12.

4. On the same day that Rumsey agreed to build GW's house, he demonstrated for GW at Bath how his model of a boat would go upstream on its own. See *Diaries*, 4:9, 12–13, and GW's certificate to Rumsey, 7 Sept. 1784.

5. David Rittenhouse (1732–1796), of Philadelphia, was an astronomer and mathematician. Andrew Ellicott (1754–1820), mathematician and surveyor who in 1784 was one of the Virginia commissioners to complete the Mason and Dixon Line, was in 1785 teaching at the academy in Baltimore. It was he who surveyed the Federal City in 1791–93.

From Benjamin Walker

Dr Sir   New York March 11th 1785
I had the pleasure to write to your Excellency in Decr last and at the same time to send you (Via Norfolk) some Trees and other things which must I think have got to hand as I heard of their safe arrival at Norfolk from whence they were to be immediately forwarded.[1]

Mr John Blaggs who went supercargo of the Ship Hope for Alexandria which Sailed yesterday was so good as to take Charge of a Case and a barrell—the former containing some Wax Work and the latter some Pease delivered me by the Governor to ship to you[.] the Vessell sailed rather sooner than I expected & thereby prevented my giving the Letter to Mr Blaggs—I do not know whether Gov. Clinton informd you that the Grape Cuttings left by Mr Williamos—with Mr Beekman— all Died it seems they were so far gone on their arrival that they could not be recovered tho' great pains were taken, by Mr Beekmans Gardiner, for the purpose.[2]

Your Excellency I doubt not has such frequent & better information than I could give—of the State of public matters, that it [is] not worth while for me to enter on them—You will have heard that Genl Knox is put at the head of the War Office—my old Friend the Baron is here and I believe is making a final Settlement with Congress—I sincerely wish they had the power and disposition to do something that would enable him to pass the remainder of his days easy but your Excellency knows as well as myself—that it is not a small matter would suffice for this—I believe he means to go to Europe if a War should break out there & he cannot get a provision here.[3]

Colo. Smith has obtained the Post of Secy to the Embassy to the Court of London with an appointment of 3000 Dollars— without any profession but the Military and accustomed to move in a certain Stile he really wanted something of the kind and I am heartily glad he has got it—Humphreys it seems has not lost his Military views but has written to Congress for a Regiment on any Establishment that may take place.[4]

Permit me to present my most respectfull Compliments to Mrs Washington and to the rest of the family and be assured of the inviolable attachment with which I have the honor to Dr Sir Your Excellys obliged & Obedient Servant

Ben Walker

ALS, DLC:GW.

1. Walker wrote to GW on 20 Dec. 1784. See note 1 of that document.

2. See George Clinton to GW, 5 March.

3. For the attempt to settle General von Steuben's accounts, see GW to Thomas Jefferson, 15 Mar. 1784, and notes.

4. On 9 Nov. 1784 David Humphreys wrote the president of Congress from Paris, where he was secretary to Thomas Jefferson's trade commission, and asked to be permitted "to continue to hold the rank & commission of Colonel," which, as he pointed out, "would tend perhaps to make a public character more respectable in some of the countries, where my present office may oblige me to travel or reside" (DNA:PCC, item 59).

From Patrick Henry

Dear Sir   Richmond [Va.] March 12th 1785

The Honor you are pleased to do me in your Favor of the 27th ulto in which you desire my Opinion in a friendly way concerning the Act I inclosed you lately, is very flattering to me. I did not recieve the Letter 'til Thursday, & since that my Family has been very sickly. My oldest Grandson a fine Boy indeed about 9 years old lays at the Point of Death. Under this State of Uneasiness & perturbation, I feel some unfitness to consider a Subject of so delicate a Nature as that you have desired my Thoughts on. Besides, I havé some Expectation of a Conveyance more proper, it may be, than the present, when I would wish to send you some packets received from Ireland, which I fear the post cannot carry at once. If he does not take them free, I shan't send them, for they are heavy. Capt. Boyle who had them from Sir Edwd Newenham, wishes for the Honor of a Line from you, which I have promised to forward to him.[1]

I will give you the Trouble of hearing from me next post if no

Oppertunity presents sooner & in the mean Time I beg you to be perswaded that with the most sincere attachment I am dear sir your most obedient Servant

P. Henry

ALS, DLC:GW.
1. See Henry to GW, 19 March. See also John Boyle, Jr., to GW, 4 March.

From Henry Lee, Jr.

My dear Genl   Stratford [Va.] 12h March 1785
    Apprehending the escape of the season before your vessel may arrive, I have got the favor of Mr Hall to permit his servant to call at Mount-Vernon.
    He has twelve horse chesnut, twelve box-cuttings & twelve dwarf box-cuttings—you may have any supply of either box, you please to order—I can supply you also with cypress & holly which can be ready at the shortest notice—Perhaps we may have some fruit trees you may want—In any thing please to command me, as I feel singularly happy in administering to the wishes of a character I so much love and respect.[1]
    Mrs Lee joins in compliments to your lady. I am dear Genl unalterably your friend & servt

Henry Lee Junr

ALS, DLC:GW. Lee wrote on the cover: "Sickness stopped the messenger. Mr Read is taking up the trees &c."
1. GW records in his diary on 13 April having received from "Colo. Henry Lee of Westmoreland" (Light-Horse Harry Lee of Stratford Hall) these plants and cuttings, which he had planted (*Diaries*, 4:118). Mr. Hall has not been identified.

To Sarah Bomford

Madam,   Mount Vernon 15th March 1785.
    I have had the honor to receive your favor, & duplicate, of the 8th of Octor from Lisle in Flanders. I have also seen the Will of the deceased Mrs Savage.[1]
    In December 1783 on my quitting public life; & as I was returning to my own home, I met at Baltimore in Maryland a Mr Moore, who shewed me this Will; & as it appeared to be the original (for I perfectly recollected the writing of Mrs Savage), I

told him it ought to have been placed in the hands of the Executors therein named, that it might be recorded & acted upon, instead of bringing it to this Country—& proposed to transmit it to them myself for this purpose: he placed it [in] my hands accordingly, but in less than half an hour reclaimed it; adding that as he was about to sail for Ireland, he would take it there himself. As I knew not by what means he became possessed of this testament, I knew no right by which I could withhold it from him, & therefore returned it; with a request that he would furnish me with a copy thereof—which was done some considerable time thereafter. From that period I heard nothing further of Mr Moore, the Will or anything respecting it, until last month; when I received a letter dated Jan. 20th 1785, from a person at Baltimore, subscribing herself—"Hannah Moore"— of which the enclosed is a copy—upon the receipt whereof I informed the writer, that neither the Will, or any accot of it, had reached my hands; nor had I heard a tittle of it since.

I confess there is something in this transaction which carries with it the face of mistery. How it should have happened that Mr Moore, whose name is not once mentioned in the will should become possessed of it: that his widow should be enquiring after it, with the eagerness of a person deeply interested therein—and that the Executors, who *really* are so, first as *principal* legatees, & 2dly as *residuary* Legatees, should never have written a line on the subject, or made the most distant enquiry after the only property from whence they could derive benefit themselves, or administer it to others agreeably to the testators directions, is unaccountable to me upon any other principle, than that of the Will's never having yet got into their hands.

After assuring you Madam, that I should be happy to render you any services my situation will admit of; I must beg leave to inform you, that you mistake the case entirely, when you suppose that it is in my power to dispose of any part of the deceased Mrs Savage's property. All that her Trustees could have done, even in her lifetime, was to *recover* the annuity, which was as unjustly, as ungenerously withheld from her by Doctr Savage her husband:[2] but with respect to the disposal of it afterwards, we had no more authority than you: now she has made an absolute distribution of it herself by Will, which her Executors therein named, are to see duly executed. Every lawful & equitable claim therefore, which you may have had against Mrs Savage in her lifetime, must now be presented to her Executors; for it is they, & they only, (or the Laws if they refuse) who can now do you justice. From the words of the Will it would seem to me that the legacy which Mrs Savage has left you, does not preclude any just charge you may have had against her for board &c., if it was known to be your intention to make it: but this is a matter of which I have not the smallest cognizance—it must be settled between you & the Executors of her Will, when the money can be recover'd from the Estate of Doctr Savage, who is also dead.

In what state the Suit is, I am unable to inform you. My situation before Peace was established, & engagements since have obliged me to depend wholly upon Mr Fairfax (the other Trustee) to prosecute it; who, besides the shutting of the Courts at one time, & the litigiousness of them at all times, has had all the villainy of Dr Savage, & the chicanery of his lawyers to combat. The Doctr, rather than fulfill an engagement, which generosity, justice, humanity & every other motive which should have influenced an honest mind—had recourse to stratagem, & every delay, to procrastinate payment; altho', from report, he has made an immense fortune. I have the honor to be &c.

G: Washington

LB, DLC:GW.

Sarah Bomford of Dublin took in Margaret Savage in 1772 when her husband, Dr. William Savage, abandoned her. She then took care of her for four years, until 1776, according to Mrs. Bomford. Mrs. Bomford continued to press for the legacy provided for in Mrs. Savage's will. See note 3 in GW to Bryan Fairfax, 6 April 1789.

1. Letter not found. See Hanna Moore to GW, 20 Jan. 1785, and GW's response of 28 February.

2. For a general discussion of GW's involvement with the Savages, see Henry Lee and Daniel Payne to GW, 24 April 1767, n.1.

To Mathew Carey

Sir,   Mount Vernon 15th Mar: 1785

I purposed, so soon as I understood you intended to become the Publisher of a News Paper in Philadelphia to request that a copy of your weekly production might be sent to me. I was the more pleased with this determination, when, by a letter from my friend the Marquis de la Fayette, I found he had interested himself in your behalf.[1]

It has so happened, that my Gazettes from Philadelphia, whether from inattention at the Printing or Post offices, or other causes; come very irregularly to my hands: Let me pray you therefore, to address those you send me, in the appearance of a letter. The common paper, usually applied, will do equally well for the cover—It has sometimes occurred to me, that there are persons who wishing to read News Papers without being of the expence of paying for them, make free with those which are addressed to others. under the garb of a letter, it is not presumable this liberty would be taken.[2] I am—Sir Yr most obedt Servt

                                        Go: Washington

ALS, DLC: Papers of William C. Rives; LB, DLC:GW. Facsimiles of the letter may be found in a number of depositories.

1. See Lafayette to GW, 21 Dec. 1784, and particularly note 4.

2. The second paragraph is one of those relatively rare instances where the changes the copyist makes in GW's language serve to clarify and make it more direct: "It has so happened that my Gazettes from Philada whether from inattention at the printing or post offices, or other causes, come very irregularly to my hands; I pray you therefore to fold it like, & give it the appearance of a letter—the usual covering of your Newspaper will do. I have sometimes suspected that there are persons who having stronger desires to read Newspapers than to pay for them, borrow with a pretty heavy hand: this may be avoided by deception, & I know of no other way." GW wrote Clement Biddle on 1 Feb. 1785 to complain about not receiving copies of the *Pennsylvania Packet*. See note 4 of that document.

From James Cross

Sir   Manchester [Va.] 15th March 1785

I beg leave to hand you inclosed copy of a Letter I received from Dr Patrick Wright of Glasgow respecting a tract of Land which fell to a Brother of his Leut. William Wright who was killed in Genl Braddock's defeat and now belong's to him or some of his other Brothers, and requests I will inform how it may be recovered and what it may be worth—as I am utterly at a loss to whom to apply for this information but to You, I have therefore taken the liberty to request the favour that You will take the trouble to advise me what mode should be adopted for the recovery of it, what it may be worth.

I applyed at the Land office and was informed by Mr Harvey that he expected, that the right of that whole Grant Still lay in You and it was only in your power to make a Deed for it. Altho I have no power to transact the Business further then gett information respecting—Yett if a Deed could be gott for it I woud pay any expence attending it, and write for a Power of Attorney if You thought proper. I am with Esteem most respectfully— Sir Your Most Humble and Obedient Servant

James Cross

ALS, DLC:GW.

James Cross, a native of Scotland, died in Norfolk, Va., in January 1787. He was a merchant in Manchester, across the James River from Richmond.

William Wright, a protégé of the prominent Scottish merchant in Dumfries, Va., Allan Macrae, served as a cadet in GW's Fort Necessity campaign in 1754. On GW's strong recommendation, Gov. Robert Dinwiddie made him an ensign in the Virginia Regiment, and on 28 Oct. 1754 Wright became a lieutenant in the regiment. He did not take part in the Braddock expedition; but he was killed in the summer of the expedition, by Indians in July 1755 on the southwestern frontier of Virginia at Reed Creek. GW's response to this letter has not been found.

To Jacob Gerhard Diriks

Sir, Mount Vernon 15th March 1785.

Your letter of the 24th of January came duly to hand; but being written in French (a language I do not understand) some time elapsed before an opportunity presented to get it translated—This I hope will be received as an apology for the delay of my answer.

However much your merits deserve recommendation—& however pleasing it might be to me to offer my testimony to such facts as have come to my knowledge, respecting the services you have rendered to these States, yet to comply with your request of a letter to the Count de Maasdam, would be inconsistent with the line of conduct I have prescribed for my Government.

It is a maxim with me Sir, to take no liberties with exalted characters to whom I am not personally known, or with whom I have had no occasion to correspond by letter: but if you shou'd think a certificate of service from me can avail you in any degree, & you would please to furnish me with your appointmts & places of service (as they have not been much under my immediate command) I shall have pleasure in furnishing one.

If circumstances had permitted, I should have been happy in the honor of a visit from you. I have a grateful sense of the polite & flattering expression of your letter; & with best wishes for you in your future pursuits, I have the honor to be Sir, &c.

G: Washington

LB, DLC:GW.

To John Filson

Sir,   Mt Vernon 15th March 1785.

It was but a few days ago that I was favor'd with your letter of the 8th of Feby accompanied by your Map & history of Kentucke, for which you will please to accept my thanks. Those which you expect were handed to me by Mr Page of Rosewell, are not yet arrived; nor have I heard anything from that gentleman respecting them.

Previous to the receipt of the above letter, I had written to you & addressed my letter to the care of Mr Dunlap printer in Phila.—taking it for granted you must have received it 'ere this, I beg leave to refer to its contents, as aught I could say on this subject would be only repetition. I am Sir &c.

G: Washington

LB, DLC:GW.

To Arthur Lee

Dr Sir,   Mo[un]t Vernon 15th March 1785.

I had the honor to receive a letter from you dated at Carlisle the 19th of Novr last, which should not have remained unacknowledged until this time, if I had known of any opportunity of addressing a letter to you in the Western Territory.

I have now heard of your passing thro' Philada on your way to Congress, & have been honor'd with a copy of your second treaty with the Western tribes of Indians, from the President. I am pleased to find that the Indians have yielded so much: from the temper I heard they were in, I apprehended less compliance on their part. This business being accomplished, it would give me pleasure to hear that Congress has proceeded to the disposal of the ceded Lands at a happy medium price, in a District sufficient & proper for a compact State. Progressive seating will be attended with many advantages; sparse settlements with many evils.

I congratulate you on your safe return: the season was inclement, and very unfit for the place & business you were engaged in. Mrs Washington presents her compliments to you, and I have the honor to be Yrs &c.

G: Washington

LB, DLC:GW.

To Richard Henry Lee

Dear Sir, Mount Vernon 15th March 1785
I have had the honor to receive your Excellencys favor of the 14th of Feby; and pray you to accept my thanks for the copy of the treaty with the Western Indians, with which you were so obliging as to furnish me.

From the accts given me last Fall (whilst I was on the Ohio) I did not expect such a cession of territory from the tribes that met. The Shawneese are pretty numerous; and among the most warlike of the Ohio Indians; but if the Subscribing Indians mean to keep good faith; and a treaty should be favorably negotiated with the more Southerly Indians; their spirit must yield, or, they might easily be extirpated.

The wisdom of Congress will now be called upon to fix a happy medium price on these Lands—and to point out the most advantageous mode of Seating them, so as that Law & good government may be administered—and the Union strengthened, & supported thereby. Progressive Seating, I conceive, is the only means by which this can be effected; and unless, in the scale of politic's more than one new state is found necessary, at this time, the unit, I believe, would be found more pregnant with advantages than the decies. The latter if I mistake not will be more advancive of individual interest, than the public welfare.[1]

As you will have the untowardness, jealousy & pride which are characteristic of the Spanish Nation to contend with, it is more than probable that Mr Gardoque will give Congress a good deal of trouble, respecting the Navigation of the river Mississipi. To me, it should seem that, the true policy of that Goverment would be to make New Orleans a free mart, instead of shutting its ports. but their ideas of trade are very confined I believe.

I take the liberty of putting a letter under cover of this to Mr Lee[2]—Mrs Washington offers her respectful compliments to you. I have the honor to be with great esteem & regard, Dr Sir Yr most obedt Hble Servt

Go: Washington

ALS, PPAmP: Correspondence of Richard Henry Lee and Arthur Lee; LB, DLC:GW.

1. In his letter of this date to another member of Congress, Hugh Williamson of North Carolina, GW expands on his ideas regarding the organization and disposition of the lands beyond the Ohio. Lee referred this letter from GW to the congressional committee that was drawing up the Land Ordinance of 1785 (see William Grayson to GW, 15 April 1785, and GW's response of 25 April).

2. GW wrote to Arthur Lee on this date.

Letter not found: from John de Neufville, 15 Mar. 1785. GW wrote de Neufville on 8 Sept.: "I have lately been honored with your favors of the 10th & 15th of March."

To Frederick Weissenfels

Sir,   Mount Vernon 15th Mar. 1785

I was favored with your letter of the 21st of Feby by the last Post. It never fails to give me pain, when I receive an acct of the sufferings of a deserving Officer—in which light I always considered you. It ever has been amongst my first wishes, that the circumstances of the Public had been such, as to have prevented the great loss which both Officers & Soldiers have sustained by the depreciation of their Certificates. and, that each State might have it in its power to do something for those of its own line in the civil department. But having many to provide

for, & few places, or things to bestow, it is matter of little wonder that many—very many—should go unnoticed, or to speak
more properly, unprovided for.

It has ever been a maxim with me, & it gives regularity &
weight to my Certificates, to found them upon the testimony of
the General Officers under whom the Applicant had served.
This brings with it, dates & circumstances, with which, I am oftentimes unacquainted. In your case it is essentially necessary,
because from your having been long out of the Continental line
of the Army I cannot, with precision, speak to facts—If therefore, as you have been in the Service of the State of New York,
you will forward to me the testimonial of His Excelly Govr Clinton, I will gladly accompany it with a Certificate of mine, if you
think it will be of any Service. To do wch can only be attended
with a little delay, as letters will come & go free from Postage.[1]
with esteem and regard I am—Sir Yr Most Obt Servt

Go: Washington

ALS (photocopy), Sotheby catalog 5504, item 141, 29 Oct. 1986; LB,
DLC:GW.

1. See note in Weissenfels to GW, 21 Feb., and Weissenfels to GW, 27
March.

To Hugh Williamson

Sir,   Mount Vernon 15th March 1785

It has so happened, that your favor of the 19th Ulto did not
come to my hands until the last mail arrived at Alexandria. By
the return of which, I have the honor to address this letter
to you.

Mr McMeikenss explanation of the movements of Rumsey's
newly invented Boat, is consonant to my ideas; and warranted
by the principles upon which it acts. The small manual assistance to which I alluded, was to be applied in still water; & to
the purpose of steering the vessel. The counteraction being
proportioned to the action, it must ascend a swift currt faster
than a gentle stream; and both, with more ease than it can move
on dead water. But in the first there may be, & no doubt is, a
point beyond wch it cannot proceed without involving consequences which may be found insurmountable.[1]

Further than this I am not at liberty to explain myself; but if a model, or thing in miniature can justly represent a greater object in its operation, there is no doubt of the utility of the invention. A view of this model with an explanation, removed the principal doubt I ever had in my mind, of the practicability of its progressing against stream, by the aid of mechanical Powers; but as he wanted to avail himself of my introduction of it to the public attention, I chose, previously, to see the actual performance of the model in a descending stream, before I passed my certificate, & having done so, *all* my doubts were done away.

I thank you, Sir, for your acct of the last Indian treaty. I had received a similar one before, but do not comprehend by what line it is, our northern limits are to be fixed.

Two things seem naturally to result from this Treaty. The terms on which the ceded lands are to be disposed of; & the mode of settling them. The first, in my opinion, ought not to be delayed. The second, ought not to be too diffusive. Compact and progressive Seating will give strength to the Union; admit law & good government; & fœderal aids at an early period. Sparse settlements in *several* new States; or in a large territory for one State, will have the direct contrary effects. & whilst it opens a large field to Land jobbers and speculators, who are prouling about like Wolves in every shape, will injure the real occupants & useful citizens; & consequently, the public interest. If a tract of Country, of convenient Size for a new State, contiguous to the present Settlements on the Ohio, is laid off, and a certain proportion of the land therein actually seated; or at least granted; before any other State is marked out & no land suffered to be had beyond the limits of it; we shall, I conceive, derive great political advantages from such a line of conduct, & without it, may be involved in much trouble & perplexity, before any New state will be well organized, or can contribute any thing to the support of the Union.[2] I have the honor to be Sir Yr Most Obt Hble Sert

Go: Washington

ALS, NHi; LB, DLC:GW.

    1. See note 1 in GW's Certificate for James Rumsey, 7 Sept. 1784.

    2. See GW to Richard Henry Lee, this date.

From George William Fairfax

My dear General   Bath [England] 19th March 1785
    Mr Thomas Corbin, now in my House, proposing to Embark
in a few days for Virginia, has earnestly Sollicited, that I would
give him a line to you, respecting his Conduct since his return
to England. The unfortunate youth, has been most cruelly
used, and barbarously aspersed by his Brother Dick, and his ad-
herents, insomuch that Tom had a property of five thousand
Pounds in the Funds, he must have rotted in a Jail, but for the
interposition of his Fathers friend Mr Athawes, who stept in to
save him from impending destruction. All this is not yours or
my affair, I hear you say, and my good Sir it is true, but as there
has been a Combination to destroy the reputation of a young
Man, just setting out in Life, I cannot refuse when called upon,
to give my Testimony, that from the information of a Gentn of
great Probity, intimately acquainted with all the horrid transactions of Dick Corbin, Tom has acquitted himself through the
whole business, as a Man of honor, honesty, and great humanity, as will appear by his paying about 1400£ for his Brother
Dick and also the debts of Frank, who could not have left England but by his assistance.[1]
    I beg your forgiveness for troubling You with the above te-
dious detail, be assured, I have done it with the greatest reluctance, but a particular friend of mine coming from London
with Mr Corbin, to ask this address of me, it was not to be par-
ried. Since the Peace I have availd myself of several opportunities of enquiring after your, and Mrs Washingtons hea[l]th, but
have received only one from you, And some time ago, I took
the liberty of sending a beautiful Print of the great Revolution,
in which you had so principal a part, it would give me pleasure
to hear it got safe and was acceptable. Mrs Fairfax and myself
has been better this severe Winter, than any one of those we
have spent in England.[2]
    It would give us pleasure to hear, when your leisure will per-
mit, that you and your good Lady enjoy health. That you may
be long blessed with it, and every other felicity is the earnest
wish of my Dear Sir Your Affecte and much Obliged Friend
and humble Servt
                                        Go: Wm Fairfax

Mr David Hartley (whos character you must know) has often requested, that I would present his best respects to you. he added that it would give him infinite pleasure to take by ⟨*mutilated*⟩ Person whoes health he has so often drunk.[3]

ALS, DLC:GW. The letter was brought to Mount Vernon on 7 July by Richard Corbin's steward, with a missing letter from Corbin dated 24 June (*Diaries*, 4 : 161).

1. The three young Corbins in England, Richard (b. 1751), Thomas (b. 1755), and Francis (1759–1821), were the three younger sons of Richard Corbin (c.1714–1790), who in 1754 used his influence to promote GW's military career (see GW to Richard Corbin, February–March 1754, and notes). At the outbreak of the Revolution Corbin was a member of the royal council in Virginia and receiver general, and though choosing to remain loyal to the crown, he lived quietly through the war at his home in King and Queen County. Before their return to Virginia in 1785, Thomas Corbin had been in the British army and Francis Corbin had been studying at Cambridge and at the Middle Temple. On receiving their letters on 7 July, GW promptly wrote both Fairfax and Corbin, saying to Fairfax that some of young Richard Corbin's Virginia friends were saying he, not Thomas, was the aggrieved brother. GW's letter to Thomas Corbin is dated 8 July and the one to Fairfax is dated 30 June. Fairfax wrote GW on 23 Jan. 1786, apologizing for having drawn him into the Corbin squabble and explaining that Thomas Corbin and Edward Athawes, one of the leading merchants among those who had been engaged in the Virginia trade before the Revolution, came "from London to my House to obtain that Letter. nor would they take a denial, or quit me without it."

2. For a discussion of the wartime correspondence between GW and Fairfax, see the source note in Fairfax to GW, 10 June 1784. See also note 1 in GW to Battaile Muse, 3 Nov. 1784.

3. David Hartley (1732–1813) actively opposed both Britain's war in America and the African slave trade. He was a particular friend of Benjamin Franklin and with him drew up and signed the definitive treaty of peace in Paris on 3 Sept. 1783.

To John Harvie

Sir,   Mt Vernon 19th March 1785.

If I recollect right, I mentioned when I had the pleasure of seeing you at Mr Jones's the first of last October, that I was reduced to the necessity of bringing ejectments against sundry persons who had taken possession of a tract of Land which I hold, not far from Fort Pitt in the State of Pennsylvania, by Patent under this Governmt for 2813 acres.[1]

I have lately received a letter from my Lawyer, Mr Thos

Smith, of Carlisle requesting information on several points; the following are his own words—"I am entirely unacquainted with the manner in which titles to Lands are acquired by improvement or occupancy, by the Laws & customs of Virginia—I suppose it must be under certain conditions & restrictions. I should be glad to have the Laws, if any, pointed out—Does the occupier forfeit his right of pre-emption, if he does not apply for an Office right in a given time? If so, when? By what Laws? Or is it by the regulations established in the Land office? A certified copy of such regulations, if any, may be necessary."[2]

At the interview I had with that Gentleman in September,[3] he told me it would be necessary to obtain a certified copy of the Surveyors return to the Land Office, & of the date of the Warr[an]t upon which it was made. The latter I presume is in the hands of the Surveyor, but the date no doubt, is recited in the return. Having (in the lifetime of Colo. Crawford, & by letter from him) received information that at the convention next before the 20th of Septr 1776, (the date of his letter) an ordinance passed for the purpose of saving equitable claims to the Western Lands—Mr Smith requested some precise information respecting this Ordinance—that is, how far it will apply in my case.

After the many obliging acts of kindness I have received from you, & the generous terms upon which they have been rendered, I am really ashamed to give you more trouble; but as the dispute in which I am engaged is of importance, & a very ungenerous advantage has been taken of a situation in which I could not attend to my private concerns, or seek justice in due season, and as I believe no person can solve the queries of Mr Smith, & give such accurate information on such points as can be made to subserve my cause as you—I am, however reluctantly, compelled to this application.

Mr Smith's own words, which I have quoted, & his verbal application to me, wch I have just now recited, will sufficiently apprize you of what has occurred to him; but I will go further, & take the liberty my good Sir, of giving you a state of the whole matter; from whence you will discover the points on which my opponents mean to hinge the success of their cause.

Colo. Crawford a liver on Yohioghaney, an old and intimate acquaintance of mine, undertook to procure for me a tract of land in that Country; & accordingly made choice of the one, now in dispute, on the waters of Racoon & Millers runs, branches of Shurtees Creek, surveyed the same, amounting to 2813 acres, & purchased in my behalf the claim of some person to a part of the land, who pretended to have a right thereto. After this he built, or intended to build according to his own accot, & to the best of my recollection, (for the papers being in the hands of my Lawyer, I have memory only, & that a bad one, to resort to) three or four cabbins on different parts of the tract, & placed one or more persons thereon to hold possession of it for my benefit. All this preceeded the first view the present occupiers (my opponents) ever had of the Land, as they themselves have acknowledged to *me*, & which I believe can be proved. So far as it respects one cabbin there can be *no* doubt, because it remains to this day; & is acknowledged by them to have been on the land when they first came to it. They built another cabbin so close to the door of it, as to preclude the entrance of it: Crawford in his accot of it to me, says, with a view to prevent occupation: they, on the other hand, say there was no inhabitant in the house at the time. Both may be right, for the fact is, as I have been informed, the owner being from home, this transaction took place in his absence.

It may be well to observe here that Colo. Crawford was only acting the part of a friend to me: for at that time, tho' he was a Surveyor by regular appointment from the College of Wm & Mary, it was for the local purpose of surveying the 200,000 acres granted by Dinwiddie's Proclamation of 1754 to the Troops of this State, who were entitled to it as a bounty: but as I proposed to cover this survey with a military warrant as soon as circumstances would permit, these steps were preliminary to obtain the Land. Accordingly, a Warrant which I obtained in consequence of a purchase from one Captain Posey (who under the British Kings proclamation of 1763 was entitled to 3000 acres) whose Bond I now have bearing date the 14th of Octr 1770, assigning to me all his right to land under it, was located there on; and Colo. Crawford, after receiving a commission to act as Deputy to Thos Lewis, made a return of this survey to his principal, who returned it to the Secretary's Office, from whence a Patent issued, signed by Lord Dunmore in June or July 1774, for 2813 acres, reciting under what right I became entitled to the Land. Hence, & from the repeated warnings, which it is said can be proved were given at the time my opponents were about to take possession of the Land, & afterwards, comes my title.

The title of my opponents I know will be—1st That Crawfords survey was illegal; at least, was unauthorised—2d That being a great land-jobber, he held, or endeavored to monopolise under one pretence or other much land: and tho' (for they do not deny the fact *to me* in private discussion, altho' considering the lapse of time[,] deaths, & dispersion of people, I may find some difficulty to prove it) they were told this was my land; yet conceiving my name was only made use of as a cover, & in this they say they were confirmed, having (after some of the warnings given them) searched the Land Office of this State without discovering any such Grant to me—3d That their possession of the Land, preceded my Patent or date of the Surveyors return to the Secretary's Office; or even the date of Crawfords deputation under Lewis—before which, every transaction they will add, was invalid.

But to recapitulate, the Dispute, if my memory for want of papers does not deceive me, may be summed up in these words.

1st In the year 1771, Crawford at my request looked out this Land for me, & made an actual survey thereof on my account.

2d Some person (not of the opponents) setting up a claim to part included by the survey, he purchased them out—built one cabbin, if not more, & placed a man therein to keep possession of the Land.

3d It was called my land, & generally believed to be so by every body, & under that persuasion was left by some, who uninformed of my right, had begun to build, before the present occupants took possession to the exclusion as I have related before of the person placed thereon by Crawford.

4th That sometime in Octr 1773 according to their own accot, these occupants took possession.

5th That upon their doing so, & at several times thereafter, they were notified of my claim and intention to assert my right.

6th That no survey was ever made of this Land, but the first one by Crawford.

7th That it is declared in the Surveyors return, to be consequent of a warrant granted by Lord Dunmore to Jno. Posey assigned to me. But whether this warrt is dated before or after possession was taken by my opponents, I know not—but the Survey will shew this.

8th That after he received his deputation (which I believe was subsequent to their occupancy) he made a return of the survey to Mr Lewis, who returned it to the Secretary's Office in the early part, I believe, of the year 1774—& a Patent issued without any caveat or opposition from these people.

9th I believe, because I never heard otherwise, that no Office rights either in this State or that of Pennsylvania, were ever obtained by my opponents—resting their title upon possession.

Under this statement of the matter, in which I have conceded every thing I know, or which I think can be urged against my claim, I would thank you, as the matter will be determined in another State, for such advice & information of Acts of Assembly, Acts of Convention, or rules of office which make to the point, as my long absence renders me quite an ignoramus in these matters—& as unfit for, as I am disinclined to controversies of this kind.

If pre-occupancy will take place of legal right, under the circumstances here mentioned; it remains still a question how far the possession and improvements which were made in my behalf, previous to those of my opponents, will avail me—that is, under what title I should then claim the Land—& under that title how much of it I should hold, supposing one cabbin *only* to have been built and occupied, by any rule of Office, or act of Government.

When I look back at the length of this letter, & consider how much trouble I am giving you, I must throw myself upon your goodness for an apology, whilst I assure you of the esteem & regard with which I am Dr Sir, &c. &c.

G: Washington

LB, DLC:GW.

1. John Harvie (1743–1807), register of the Virginia land office, was visiting his father-in-law, Gabriel Jones, when GW had dinner in October at Jones's house on the South Fork of the Shenandoah, near present-day Port Republic.

2. See Thomas Smith to GW, 9 February.

3. See GW's diary entry for 22 Sept. 1784 and the editors' notes (*Diaries,* 4:32–38). GW wrote: "I set out for Beason Town, in order to meet with &

engage Mr. Thos. Smith to bring Ejectments, & to prosecute my Suit for the Land in Washington County, on which those, whose names are herein inserted, are settled" (p. 32).

From Patrick Henry

Dear Sir   Richmond [Va.] March 19th 1785

The Honor you are pleased to do me in your Favor of the 27th ulto, desiring my Opinion in a friendly Way on the Subject of the Act for vesting the Shares in the Patowmack & James River Navigation, is very flattering to me. And I should ill deserve the Confidence you are pleased to place in me if I should forbear to give you my unreserved Sentiments on it.

I will freely own to you that I am embarrassed to reconcile the Law taken in its full Extent, with the Declarations you mention, & a fixed purpose of refusing pecuniary Rewards. If this was the sole Object of the Act, I should not hesitate to dissent to its propriety. The united States seem most properly constituted to take into Consideration a Matter of that Nature, for a Variety of Reasons, which I need not enumerate. But the Preamble of the Law, compared with a few Facts that preceded the enacting of it, will present it in a View different from that of rewarding past military Services. The Facts I allude to are these.

The great Business of opening the Navigation of Patowmack & James River, & connecting it with that of the western Waters, was taken up by you, & pressed with that Earnestness so interesting a Matter deserved. The Difficultys which Nature had interposed, were encreased by a Combination of Interests, hard to develope & explain, & stil harder to reconcile. To all these was added another Impediment arising from the Scarcity of Money & the exhausted condition of the Country. The Time however was critical; & your Observations sent to the Assembly, proved that it was good policy to encounter every Obstacle & begin the Work.[1] The patronage of it seemed naturally to devolve on you Sir; & the Assembly desiring to give Efficacy to that patronage vested the Shares in you.

This Navigation depends upon private Subscription for Success: So that unless you had subscribed, you could not have been concerned. You will forgive me for supposing that your Finances could not have made it desirable, to risque a Sum of

Money on the Success of an Enterprize like this. For your Estate could not have been exempted from that Loss in its produce experienced by other Gentlemens Estates throughout the Country during the War—Considering then, that your promoting this great Affair necessarily obliged you to subscribe to it, & besides to encounter all the Difficultys arising from the Nature of it, the Variety of Interests, Veiws, & Circumstances which attended it, and that in arranging & conducting all these, not only great Labor & Attention as well as Abilitys are requisite, but also Expence of Money & Loss of Time, it would seem at Least, that you ought to be secured against the Chance of loosing by subscribing. And this is all the Law can be said to do, inasmuch as it must remain uncertain whether the Shares are worth any thing 'til the Business is compleated. If this never happens to be accomplished, your Labor Time, &c. &c., are lost, & the Donation proves an empty Sound.

Your Acceptance of it, will prevent that Shock which you justly observe will be given by a Refusal—And I submit to your Reflection how far your Resignation of the Shares may throw a Damp on that Ardor, which I have the pleasure to hear prevails at present, to promote the Undertaking. I must beleive, that at least a temporary Check would be given to its progress 'til the Means of replacing so many Shares could be found, & I am really not able to find out the Way to do it.

Your Acceptance will avoid this embarrassing Circumstance. And if after reviewing the whole Matter you shall think it inadmissable to hold the Shares in the Manner the Law gives them, You will be at Liberty to make such alteration in the Interest, or Disposition of the Use, as shall be most agreable to your self.

If I have exceeded in the Freedom with which I have treated this Subject, I must entreat your Forgiveness; For I have no Motive but to evince on every Occasion that I am with unalterable Affection & the most sincere Attachment dear sir your very obedient Servant

P. Henry

P.S. Two other large packets from Ireland accompany this. The post could not carry them all at once. No other Conveyance seems to present soon, & the Capt (Boyle) begs to receive your Commands soon as convenient.[2]

ALS, DLC:GW.

1. See GW to Benjamin Harrison, 10 Oct. 1784.
2. See John Boyle, Jr., to GW, 4 Mar., and GW to Edward Newenham, 20 March.

From Lafayette

My dear General   Paris March the 19th 1785

Your letter december the 23d Has Safely Come to Hand, and Nothing short of the pottowmack plan Could Have Accounted with me for Your leaving Mount Vernon. I am glad to Hear You are likely to succeed, as it seems to me a Matter of Great Moment—and the part You Have taken in the Business Cannot fail, still more particularly to interest me in its success—I thank you, my dear General, for your information Respecting the Act of Maryland—it is an Honour Equally flattering to my pride, and pleasing to My Heart.

European politics are not Yet settled—but there is much Reason to Hope this will end without Bloodshed—inclosed you will find a declaration from the king of France to the Emperor Respecting the dutch war—Count de Maïllebois is gone to Holland where they are Raising troops, and where parties Run very High—a plan of the Emperor for the Exchange of Baviera, of which I spoke to you in my last, Has Been opposed By the duke of deux ponts Nephew and Heir to the elector—So that Upon the whole I don't think we shall Have a war—in Case the dutch make Some sacrifices, they will Be small—the intervention of France has saved them—and Count de Vergennes deserves great Credit.[1]

Great Britain Continues to Be very Backward in treating with America—our friend john temple is appointed British Consul to the United States—Notwistanding the ill will and Narrow policy of England they Run a way with all the Commerce of America—that total interruption of trade gives a new force to the Clamours of the French Merchants Against the late Admission of foreigners in the West indias, and Makes it impossible to obtain the addition of flour and sugars—at least in the present period—I am Very Busy about introducing the Whale oils in France, and notwistanding Every obstacle, Hope at least partially to succeed.[2]

on my Arrival, I Have Repeated what I Had writen Respecting the Mississipy—viz.—the idea, either to get New orleans, or to advise the spaniards to make it a free port—the former is impossible—as to the second I Had no positive Answer—But I am sure my opinion Was not thrown a Way—I Have Requested a Conference with the duke de La Vauguion who is going to spain as an Ambassador—it will Be very difficult to get that point, and altho I would not advise America to deviate from firmness, I think they must act with Moderation in this affair.

Inclosed is the extract from a Book of Mr Necker which I thought Might give Agreable information—I send it in French, Because You will find translators enough—that Book is a Very Good one, But Has Raised Both a jealousy against, and an adoration for the Author which Runs into an Excess—He is However one of the ablest men in Europe, and certainly one of the first financeers.[3]

The irish affairs seem to subside—in the Course of the summer, I will, I think, Visit the prussian and austrian armies, provided there is no war—my ideas about 29 are not very Unlikely to succeed—102 in this Kingdom are My present object[4]—and I am not without Hopes, with Respect to a part of what a Rational Man Might Expect *at this period*. My little family Have Been writing to Yours By Mr Williams an American Gentleman[5]—they join with Mde de lafayette and me in Most affectionate Respects to Mrs Washington and You—Remember me to all our friends—Adieu, Adieu, My Beloved General, think often of Your absent, tender friend—Never Could any Being in Creation love you more, Respect you more than I do—Be so Kind as to let me Hear from You By every packet—Adieu, My dear General, Your Respectfull and affectionate friend

Lafayette

Chevalier de Caraman presents His Best Respects to Mrs Washington and to You—I kiss Squire tub, and the young ladies.

ALS, PEL.

1. Lafayette reported in detail on the Dutch war to John Jay on 8 Feb. 1785. See Idzerda, *Lafayette Papers*, 5 : 293–95.

2. See Lafayette to GW, 13 May 1785, n.5.

3. Lafayette also sent on this date extracts of *De l'administration des finances de la France* (Paris, 1784) to Nathanael Greene and John Jay.

4. The number 29 is the code for Parliament (parlement de Paris) and 102 is for Protestants.

5. Jonathan Williams (1750–1815) was Benjamin Franklin's nephew and secretary.

To Edmund Randolph

Dr Sir,   M[oun]t Vernon 19th March 1785.

Some considerable time ago I wrote a letter to my Nephew, Bushrod Washington, and used the freedom of addressing it to your care—At that time I conceived he was living at richmond, but the establishment of circuit Courts it seems has changed his plan: he now intends to fix at Fredericksburg. Will you allow me the liberty my dear sir, to request the favor of you to open my letter to him, if it is yet in yr possession, & comply with a request therein, respecting a promisary note of Mr Rian's, if he is in Richmond; or cause it to be complied with if he is at Petersburgh.[1] If my memory serves me, I have gone into the detail of the matter to my Nephew—I will not trouble you therefore, with a repetition of it—nor will I take up your time with an apology for the trouble this must give you. Mrs Washington unites in best wishes for yourself & Mrs Randolph with, Dr Sir &c. &c.

G: Washington

LB, DLC:GW.

1. See GW to Bushrod Washington, 22 Jan. 1785, and note 1 of that document. See also GW to Bushrod Washington, 3 April.

From William Blake

Dear Sir   Charleston [S.C.] March 20th [1785]

The want of an Opportunity has prevented me from hitherto forwarding you the Seeds and Plants I promised when I had the Honor of paying you my Respects at Mount Vernon; I wish they may answer your Expectations, such a Hedge will be an acquisition.[1]

Our State is anxious for the Honor of a Visit from you, I need not repeat, it woud gratify the summit of our Desires. Permit me, Sir, without intruding more on your Time to make a

Tendre of my best Respects to Mrs Washington, and to assure you with greatest Regard & Esteem I remain Dear Sir Your most Obedient Humble Sert

William Blake

ALS, DLC:GW.
William Blake of Charleston (died c.1803) was a wealthy planter with extensive landholdings in South Carolina.
1. It is not known when William Blake was at Mount Vernon. On 21 May GW's barge brought back from Pope's Creek an assortment of trees and plants sent from South Carolina, including magnolia, live oak, sour orange, and "the Palmeto royal which Mr Blake of So. Carolina had sent me accompanied by some of the Plants" (*Diaries*, 4:143–44).

To Patrick Henry

Dear Sir,	Mount Vernon 20th Mar. 1785
Your favor of the 12th together with the letters and parcels from Sir Edward Newenham, came safe to hand. For the trouble you have had with the latter I offer you my thanks, at the sametime I beg your excuse for adding to it by causing the letter herewith enclosed to be forwarded to Captn Boyle of the ship Jane & Diana when a safe conveyance offers.[1]
I hope this letter will find your family in better health than when you last wrote, and your Grandson perfectly restored.[2] With very great esteem regard & respect I am—Dear Sir Yr Most Obt Hble Ser⟨vt⟩

Go: Washington

ALS (photocopy), Sotheby, Parke-Bernet catalog, item 24, 20 Mar. 1973; LB, DLC:GW.
1. See GW's letter of this date to Sir Edward Newenham.
2. It was on this day that the men who were participating in what came to be known as the Mount Vernon conference left Alexandria and came to Mount Vernon to conclude their deliberations. See Thomas Stone to GW, 28 Jan. 1785, n.2.

Letter not found: from John Francis Mercer, 20 Mar. 1785. On 27 Mar., GW wrote Mercer: "Mr Stone gave me your favor of the 20th."

To Edward Newenham

Dear Sir, Mount Vernon 20th March 1785.

I regret very much that your letters of the 2d & 13th of October should have been detained from me until this time. The last Post *only*, from Richmond, brought them to me.[1]

If you should have fulfilled your intention of embarking at the early period proposed in the first of the above letters—and I hope no untoward accident will have happened to prevent it—this answer will come too late, and my silence will leave you in doubt respecting Horses; besides carrying with it the appearance of inattention. As, however, there is a possibility that this letter may yet find you in Ireland, I will relate the mode of travelling in this Country, and submit to your own Judgment the propriety of depending on it, or bringing Saddle or Carriage Horses of your own.

From the Southern parts of this State, say from Norfolk, through Hampton, Richmond, Fredericksburgh, and Alexandria (which is within a few miles of this Seat) there is regular Stages which passes thrice every week. They are not of the best, nor worst kind—From Alexandria, through the Metropolis of every State, Annapolis in Maryland excepted (which lyes a little to the right of the Post road to Baltimore) there are also regular Stages to Portsmouth in New Hampshire. These are of a similar kind, & pass as often as those last mentioned. So that not more than three days can intervene betwn one Stage day & another. A person may therefore, at any time between the first of April, & middle of November, travel from Richmond (the Metropolis of this State) to Boston in ten or twelve days, and return in the sametime. Between this State & Charleston (South Carolina) no Stages are, as yet, established; and the Country for the most part being poor, and thinly inhabited, accomodations of every kind, I am told, are bad.

So much for public convenience. I do not think I should decieve you much, were I to add that Sir Edward Newenham would find no difficulty to get accomodated in this, and some other States, with the Horses and Carriages of private Gentlemen from place to place, where inclination, or business, might induce him to go.

What the expence of transporting Horses to this Country would be, I am unable to decide; but I conceive they would not be fit for immediate use if they were brought, if the passage should be long; but at the sametime I deliver this opinion, I must accompany it with another, viz.—that if you *should* bring Horses, and might not incline to take them back again, you could if they are young, likely and well bought, sell them for their original cost & the charges of transportation at least, especially if they should happen to be of the female kind.

I have not had the pleasure of seeing either Mr Rutherford or Captn Boyle; but the latter accompanying your Letters & packages—for which I pray you to accept my thanks—with a few lines giving reasons for their detention, and information of his Sailing in the course of a few days;[2] I have, in haste, wrote you this letter by return of the Post, hoping it may get to Richmond in time to receive a conveyance by the Jane and Diana, that it may repeat to you (if it should arrive in time) the pleasure I shall have in seeing you, and your fellow travellers under my roof, and in paying you & them, every attention in my power.

The chances being against this letter's finding you in Ireland, I will not, at this time, touch upon the other parts of your several favors; but leaving them as matters for personal converse beg that my respectful compliments, in which Mrs Washington joins, may be presented to Lady Newenham: With very great esteem and regard I am—Dr Sir Yr most Obedt Hble Servt

Go: Washington

ALS, PWacD: Sol Feinstone Collection, on deposit PPAmP; LB, DLC:GW.

1. Neither of these letters has been found, but see Newenham's letter of 10 June 1784.

2. See John Boyle, Jr., to GW, 4 March. "Mr Rutherford" was probably Thomas Rutherford, an Irish merchant who arrived with goods at Hampton, Va., in January 1784 as a representative of the Dublin firm of Hanksley & Rutherfoord. Rutherfoord opened a store in Richmond and did not return to Ireland until the summer of 1786.

Letter not found: from Bushrod Washington, 20 Mar. 1785. On 3 April GW wrote to his nephew Bushrod: "Your letter of the 20th Ulto did not come to my hands until the 31st."

From St. John de Crèvecoeur

New York 21st March 1785
I have duely Received Your Excellency's Letters for France, & have put them in the Mail which is To Sail on Wednesday[1]—I beg that whenever Your Excellency may have any Letters or Papers to be Sent to Europe—that they may be addressed To me who will with Great Pleasure & Punctuality Forward Them To their destinaton. I have the Honor To be with the Most Sincere Respect Your Excellency's Most obedient & Very Humble Servt

St John

ALS, PHi: Gratz Collection; Sprague transcript, DLC:GW.
 1. No letters to persons in France written by GW in March 1785 have been found.

From John Craig

Sir   Philad[elphi]a March 22nd 1785
    The Knowledge I have of your Benevolence & Condescencion Encourages me to Take a Liberty, which by any other than your Excellency might be deemed unpardonable—The Request of a Self Interested Individual who has not the honor to be much Known to your Excellency requires both Preface & Apology, but Rather than Trespass on your Time, I take the Liberty to begin Rather Abruptly & doubt not but your Excellency will Dispense with the Form—The Discouraging Prospect of Trade in General here & the little Probability that it will Soon take a favourable turn has induced me to turn my thoughts towards a Country Life—I wish to Settle myself in a place of Retirement in Such a Situation as woud Soon Afford the Conveniencies of Life & ultimately promise Essential Advantages—I have heard there are Situations on the Susquehanna & Monogahela Rivers which Promise in Time to be very Valuable, but it is So Difficult to Procure Information on which one may Depend, that I have at last determined to apply to the Fountain head & Request your Excelency to favour me with a few Lines of Advice upon the Execution of my Plan[1]—My Father has Some Lands on Cheat River which I mean to Explore this

Spring, but I think the Susquehanna which will Communicate with the Potomack promises to yield the most Profitable Settlements & Could I Procure (on tollerable easy Terms) a healthy fruitfull Place with the Advantages of Navigation & one or two Mill seats, I would Gladly Employ what little Capital I have in the purchase & Cultivation of it.

I have not yet mentioned my Plan to any Person, nor shall I till I am determined by your Excellencys Advice on what part of the Country you would think it most advantageous to Settle— Once more I beg your Excellencys forgiveness for the Liberty I take—the Wellfare of my family Depending on yr Information will I am sure be a sufficient Apology to a heart so Benevolent as yours, I have the honor to be with the Greatest Respect & Esteem yr Excellencies very hble Servt

John Craig

ALS, DLC:GW.

John Craig (c.1754–1807) was a merchant in business with his father, a Scot named James Craig, at 12 Dock and 161 South Second streets, Philadelphia. He did not pursue the plans expressed here of moving westward but remained in the city.

1. See GW to Craig, 29 March.

From Elkanah Watson

Sir   Providence [R.I.] 22d March 1785

I have bore steadily in mind the circumstance of the dutch gardener, but Mr Brown cannot recommend him so fully as he could wish.[1]

This will be handed by Mr Howel a gentleman who is connected with Mr Brown & who intends doing himself the honour to pay his respects to your Excellency.[2] The information you was so polite as to communicate to me, relative the plan of opening the Potowmack, the interior country &c.—I trust will not be fruitless as I took my notes, & have uniformly made it my standard of conversation along the Continent, & I cannot but hope with some success, as I find the Potowmack has now become an object of such magnitude as to draw the attention of our enterprizing genius'es to Alexandria which I am persuaded will shortly feel the effects.[3]

Mr Brown has it seriously in contemplation to lay the foundation of a new City between the first falls & Alexandria upon the Virginia side I am not authoriz'd by him to write your Excellency upon the subject, but I am so intimately connected with him that I am well persuaded If you thought the plan eligible, & he could obtain information respecting the debth of water near the falls that he would bend his Interest & efforts to this point which you are sensible would be an important acquisition in the infant state of your noble river.[4]

Permit me to tender my respectfull compliments to Lady Washington & to assure your Excellency of my profound veneration & hommage.

E. Watson

I should be highly flatter'd to receive your Excellencys commands in this quarter.

ALS, DLC:GW.

1. Watson, who had returned only in October to Providence from abroad, visited Mount Vernon on 19 and 20 Jan. 1785. In his memoirs written many years later, Watson devoted four printed pages to an account of his stay. Upon his arrival, Watson remembers that he found GW, "at table with Mrs. Washington and his private family, and was received in the native dignity and with that urbanity so peculiarly combined in the character of a soldier and eminent private gentleman. He soon put me at ease, by unbending, in a free and affable conversation." That first evening the two men "sat a full hour at table by ourselves, without the least interruption, after the family had retired." Watson had a bad cold and upon going to bed was wracked with coughing. "When some time had elapsed," Watson recalled, "the door of my room was gently opened, and on drawing my bed-curtains, to my utter astonishment, I beheld Washington himself, standing at my bed-side, with a bowl of hot tea in his hand" (Watson, *Men and Times of the Revolution*, 243–44). Watson's description of GW is more specific than most of the other and relatively rare ones of this period: "I found him kind and benignant in the domestic circle, revered and beloved by all around him; agreeably social, without ostentation; delighting in anecdote and adventures, without assumption; his domestic arrangements harmonious and systematic. His servants seemed to watch his eye, and to anticipate his every wish; hence a look was equivalent to a command. His servant Billy, the faithful companion of his military career, was always at his side. Smiling content animated and beamed on every countenance in his presence" (ibid., 244). See also Nathanael Greene to GW, 2 Dec. 1784, n.1, and *Diaries*, 4:78–79. The gardener that Watson's former patron, the Providence merchant John Brown, could not recommend has not been identified.

2. GW does not record in his diary a visit from a Mr. Howel. Watson may be referring to David Howell (1747–1824), who had been a teacher in Rhode Island College before becoming a lawyer in Providence.

3. Watson wrote in his memoirs: "Much of his [GW's] conversation had reference to the interior country, and to the opening of the navigation of the Potomac, by canals and locks, at the Seneca, the Great and Little Falls. His mind appeared to be deeply absorbed by that object, then in earnest contemplation." Watson took "minutes" from GW's "former journals on this subject" and found the scheme "worthy the comprehensive mind of Washington" (Watson, *Men and Times of the Revolution*, 244–45).

4. According to Watson, GW pressed him "earnestly to settle on the banks of the Potomac," and, "At his suggestion," Watson "proceeded up the southern shore of the river" to the Great Falls (ibid., 246).

To William Hunter

Mount Vernon 24th March 1785.
G. Washingtons Compliments to Mr Hunter—would thank him for forwarding the enclosed letter by a *good* oppertunity when any such offers.[1]

He would thank Mr Hunter for the Currt *Cash* prices of good Plank in Alexandria—Inch—Inch & Quarter—and Inch and half. this by the bearer.

If there is any Vessel in the harbor with these, & do not meet a ready Sale, he would take some, *if good*, of each, if the Master would call in his way down.

AL, ViMtV.
1. None of the letters dated after 15 Mar. printed in this volume are likely to have been the one that GW was asking the merchant in Alexandria to forward for him.

From Henry Knox

My dear Sir. Boston [Mass.] 24 March 1785
I thank you for your kind favor of the 28th ultimo, which I received last evening with its enclosures & I sincerely hope I shall not be under the necessity of troubling you *so much* again. But in the present instance I am under the necessity of mentioning that Major Winthrop Sargent has repeatedly informed me, that a certificate from you would be one of the most desirable and acceptable things to him. I at length promised him that I would request it of you. He is really clever, and was an excellent Artillery officer.[1]

I will endevor to make an arrangement of the lime stone in

the manner that shall be the least expensive; but our spring is so backward that we have but little prospect of getting the Stone from the eastward before the month of June, It shall be forwarded by the earliest opportunity to your house, or Alexandria. The weather is now as severe as at any time during the Winter, and the Snow & Ice are nearly three feet upon a level.[2]

I am highly delighted with the delicate gratitude of Virginia, and am at the same time charmed with your sentiments, and reasoning upon it. I sincerely hope circumstanced as you are that you may find a mode of declining the intended appropriation so as to enhance the respect and affection of your fellow citizens. My jealousy for your fame is so high, that I should prefer seeing you Cincinnatus-like following your plow, rather than accept the least pecuniary reward whatever. Your services are of that nature as to demand the approbation and admiration of succeeding generations, but cannot be rewarded by money. Thank the supreme God you are happily placed above the necessity of receiving any assistance.

Perhaps my dear Sir you could intimate to the Legislature in a manner which would be clear of every indelicate imputation that should they think proper to apply the produce of this fund to the maintainance of the Widows, and the support, and education of the children of those men of their own line, who sacrificed their lives in defence of their Country, and of the maimed soldiers, that the measure would rear an eternal monument to the virtue of the Commonwealth of Virginia. An event of this kind, which I am persuaded has been among the number of expedients conceived by you, would rank Virginia higher in the annals of America than any other State, and the idea coming from you, would place your warm and disinterested attachment to suffering in a durable and glorious point of view—let my affection plead my excuse for this freedom.

The Mall in this Town has been repaird and the trees replaced. But I beleive the gravel walk is only upon the common principle without any cement whatever. I will however enquire and if there should be any improvement, I will with pleasure communicate it—You may probably have heard that Congress have been pleased to appoint me secretary at War. I have accepted of the office and expect to be in New York about the 15th of next month. From the habits imbibed during the War, and from the opinion of my friends that I should make but an indifferent trader, I thought upon mature consideration that it was well to accept it although the salary (2450 dollars) would be but a slender support. I have dependence upon an unweildy Estate belonging to Mrs K.s family, and upon the public certificates given for my services, but neither of these are productive, and require a course of years to make them so. In the mean time my expences are considerable, and require some funds for their supply—Congress have rendered the powers, and duties of the Office respectable, and the circumstances of my appointment were flattering, being without solicitation on my part, and nine states out of eleven voting for me—for this favorable opinion of Congress I conceive myself indebted to your friendship—I do not intend to move my family to New York Untill next June—Mrs Knox who with her little ones, are well Unites with me in presenting our affectionate respects to Mrs Washington. I am my dear Sir Your truly affectionate humble Servant

H. Knox

ALS, DLC:GW; ADf, MHi: Knox Papers.

1. Winthrop Sargent's journal of the meeting of the Cincinnati is printed above as doc. II in General Meeting of the Society of the Cincinnati, 4–18 May 1784.

2. See GW to Knox, 5 Jan. 1785, n.6.

From William Carmichael

Madrid 25 March 1785

P.S. As I have lately recd Letters from the Marquis & Marchioness de la Fayette which announce his arrival in Europe,[1] I take the Liberty of sending you a Triplicate of a Letter which I had the honor to write you under cover to the Marquis the 3d of Decr 1784. His return to Europe may otherwise occasion surmises which would hurt me as a delay of this communication might appear Singular on my part. I shall have the honor to send you with the Jack Asses an acct of the mode of treating them & of rendering them useful to the propagation of Mules.[2] Mr Gardoqui I hope will be in America & treating with Congress before this can reach you. I beg your Countenance to this Gentleman, who Mr Jay will inform you, has had ever the most Liberal Sentiments with respect to America. I am informed the English wish to blow the flame of Discord between us & Spain in America on acct of the Navigation of the Missisippi. I can assure you that the Same Endeavours are imployed here—The Minister of G.B. has just left me, holding the Same Language, while I know he holds the Contrary to the Ministers of this Country.[3] Union & Energy in the Representants of the States & activity in each State respectively to support the Confederation will soon show the futility of these little political maneuvres & place America on that firm basis of Political consistance which must make the United States Usefull friends or dangerous Enemies. Their Consequence in the political & Commercial scale may be accelerated by the Turn affairs are like to take in Europe. In the meantime I cannot but counsel from what I see & what I know, but firmness, a proper sense of National honor & vigor & unanimity the Most Cordial in every State.

I am not afraid of hazarding these Sentiments to you. They are your own. With the highest respect & affection I have the honor to repeat Myself your Most Obedt & Most Humble Sert

Wm Carmichael

ALS, DLC:GW. This was written as a postscript to a copy of a letter Carmichael initially wrote to GW on 3 Dec. 1784, which GW did not receive. See the source note, Carmichael to GW, 3 Dec. 1784. The postscript, written nearly three months after the letter to which it was attached, is printed here as a separate document.

1. Neither Lafayette's letter to Carmichael nor Lafayette's wife's letter has been found, but on 10 Mar. 1785 Lafayette wrote Carmichael: "A few days Ago I Had the pleasure to write You a line, inclosing Mde. de Lafayette's letter" (Idzerda, *Lafayette Papers*, 5:300–302).

2. For the jackasses presented to GW by the king of Spain, see Carmichael to GW, 3 Dec. 1784, nn.1 and 2.

3. Philip Stanhope, earl of Chesterfield, was the British ambassador to Spain.

From La Luzerne

Sir.   Paris March 25th 1785.

I have received by the Marquis de la Lafayette, on his arrival in France, the letters your Excellency has honoured me with.[1] I can not express how much I am sensible of these marks of your Kindness and Friendship; I am likewise extreemely flattered by the interest you take in my future employments. Permit me to assure you that wherever the King may send me, he can not entrust me a commission as flattering as that which has rendered me a Wittness of the glory and hapiness of a people which owes it's liberty to the superior talents and Wisdom of Your Excellency.

The King, his Court and the whole nation, Sir, had been pleased in the expectation to see you at Paris and it is with the greatest regret that I saw by your last letters that we must give up our hopes. I can assure you that you would have found amongst my Countrymen as many Friends and Admirers as amongst your own fellow citizens.

We have heared with pleasure the happy turn of the American negociations with the Indians and I hope that Your Country will enjoy at last a perfect tranquillity. However I do not see without concern the delays of England with respect to the restitution of the forts of Detroit and Niagara. I hope that the new Congress, who, I am informed, are very well chosen, will take the proper measures to terminate this business. Another very interesting object for your Nation will be to raise a fund for paying the interest of and sinking the national debt. You can not imagine how much so just an operation would encrease the credit and consideration of your Country.

They intended in England to propose in Parliament a Bill for the regulation of Commerce between great Britain and the united States; but I believe the Bill will not even be debated this Year. Ireland, the East India affairs and above all the altercations between Mr Fox and Pitt engrosse the whole attention of Parliament. Mr Pitt has had great advantages in the beginning of the Sessions but his Antagonist seems to have since gained a superiority and the King of England will perhaps be once more obliged to take him into the Ministry.

The other European affairs are not yet arranged. The Emperor requests from the States General a Step, which these think to be injurious to their dignity. However it is not likely that we shall have a War this Summer; and the preparations that had been made every where are considerably abated. Some days ago matters appeared even entirely adjusted and the difficulty to satisfy the honor and dignity of the two powers has more retarded the business than the principal object.

I have not failed to present to the King and the Royal Family the regrets of your Excellency not to be able to offer them your respect and your acknowledgements. They participate with the whole nation the esteem and Veneration, which Your eminent qualities have inspired them, and are very sorry not to have it in their power to give you any direct proof of their sentiments.

I hope that in some moments of leisure you will remember me; you may rely upon an European Correspondent who is very devoutly attached to you and who most sincerely wishes to convince you of his veneration and of the sentiments of respect with which he has the honor to be Sir, your Excellency's Most obedient and very humble servant

le che. de la luzerne

P.S. Will you be so obliging as to present my respectful Compliments to Mrs Washington.

LS, DLC:GW.

1. La Luzerne is referring to GW's letters of 20 Aug. and 5 Dec. 1784.

To John Francis Mercer

Dear Sir,   Mount Vernon 27th March 1785.

Mr Stone gave me your favor of the 20th.[1]

When I had the pleasure of seeing you at this place, I informed you fully, & truly, of my want of money—I am at this moment paying 7 prC. interest for a pretty considerable Sum which I borrowed in the State of New York (through the means of the Governor)[2]—& not being able to obtain a surety of holding it for more than one year from the establishment of Peace, I am in continual fear, notwithstanding the high interest, of having it recalled.

After this declaration, it is unnecessary to add, how acceptable it would be to me to receive payment of the money due to me from your Father's Estate[3]—or part of it; but to take it in small driblets from the hands of your Lawyers would not answer my purposes; as it is more than *one* considerable payment, I have to make from this fund.

If you should go to Congress, I should be glad if the money

arising from the arrangement you have made, was ordered into the hands of your Brother—or your Attorney here; and he directed to pay it to me in such sums as I could apply in discharge of my own debts[4]—for the fact is, I shall receive with one hand, & pay with the other (if I may be permitted to use the phraze) and, but for which, it would not be required from you. If you do not go to Congress, I shall expect the same from yourself. My Compliments, in which Mrs Washington joins, are offered to your Lady & Mr Sprigs family; with esteem, I am Dr Sir Yr most Obedt Hble Servt

Go: Washington

ALS, MAnP; LB, DLC:GW. GW wrote on the cover: "Favored by Majr Jenifer."

1. Letter not found. Michael Stone, probably Michael Jenifer Stone (1747–1812) of Charles County, Md., called briefly at Mount Vernon on 25 February.

2. GW is probably referring to the money he borrowed in December 1782 from Gov. George Clinton, which he repaid in April 1785. See Clinton to GW, 27 Feb. 1784, n.1, and GW to Clinton, 25 Nov. 1784, and 5, 20 April 1785. But he may be referring to what he owed for the land in New York which he and Clinton had bought jointly (see GW to Clinton, 25 Nov. 1784, n.2).

3. For the indebtedness of the heirs of John Mercer (d. 1768) to GW arising out of loans made to Mercer by Martha Custis before her marriage to GW, see especially GW to John Francis Mercer, 8 July 1784, n.1.

4. If Mercer responded, the letter has not been found, but see GW's even more pressing letter to Mercer of 20 Dec. 1785.

From Frederick Weissenfels

Sir.   New York March 27th 1785.

Your Exellencys favour of the 15th instant, With which I was honored, leaves my Mind in the most perfect tranquility, that I may Expect the honor to recieve your Certificate, when your Exellency is furnished with one from his Exellency Governor Clinton, Which I here inclose.[1]

The Governor has mentioned my derangement, from the Continental Line, and although no Date by him Citet, I beg leave to Say, that it wass in the year 1780, after I had without intermission Served from the year 1775, (When in Canada with the late General montgomorie,) to that Periode. as upon the Journals of Congress will appear, that I wass promoted by their authority to a Lt Colo. in the year 1776.

I have with Chearfulness So Early Complied with your Exel'cys request, and mentain a pleasing prospect on its return. I am with Sentiments of great respect Your Exellencys most obiedent most humble Servant

Fredk Weissenfels

ALS, DLC:GW.

1. The certificate that George Clinton gave Weissenfels has not been found, but GW wrote Weissenfels from Mount Vernon on 10 April: "Inclosed I give the certificate requested of me. If it shou'd conduce to your satisfaction, or be productive of any advantage to you—it will give me pleasure" (LB, DLC:GW). The text of the enclosed certificate was: "This certifies that Fred: Weissenfels Esqr. has served in the Foederal army of the United States of America from the year 1775 until the reduction which took place in the year 1780: that in the year 1776. he was promoted to the rank of Lieut: Colonel, & continued therein until the reduction above mentioned; after which (as a testimony of the good opinion entertained of him) he was appointed by the State of Nw York (in which he is a citizen) to command a regiment of State troops. That during the whole of this period, as far as his conduct came under my observation—& from the information of the General Officer under whose immediate command he served, he displayed a zeal, bravery & intelligence, which did honor to the military character—& in every respect has conducted himself as a Gentn & good Citizen. Given at Mount Vernon this 10th day of April 1785. G: Wn—late comr of the armies of the U.S." (LB, DLC:GW).

From William Gordon

My Dear Sir   Jamaica Plain [Mass.] March 28. 1785

Your obliging favours of the 8th inst. were recd on the Saturday. From them I infer not only the continuance of your friendly assistance, but that the papers are regularly received; as yet I have not missed sending, tho' the post has at times been delayed thro' the snows: The face of the earth is still covered with them, in these parts, a few trifling spots excepted; & should a thaw come on rapidly, the floods that must follow will probably do great damage. We have no prospect of gardening for some weeks.

The present of your miniature cuts is highly acceptable, as they are a token of affection; but they are indeed too imperfect to admit of my copying from them. I shall endeavour to procure a more expressive likeness, in one way or other, by which all who know the original may be at once reminded of him, & those who know him not may obtain such an idea of him, that should they meet him in the street they may know him, as happened many years back in reference to Mrs Gordon, who when going thro' the streets of London to her Brothers, was known by a maid servant in the family, from her having frequently seen a miniature picture in the Brother's possession. In some cases profiles will not answer, & where I find it to be so, must have a recourse to pictures. Your mention of Mr Semitere was kind. I shall make application to some friend at Philadelphia to inquire concerning his engravings, & when the likeness is good will endeavour to procure them or the prints.

I do not recollect that the private letter alluded to takes notice that it was consequent of a resolve of Congress, that Fort Washington was so pertinaciously held, previously to the ships passing that Post. The re-capitulation of it, & other matters relating to it, is therefore serviceable.[1] Your private letters, & the silence you observed upon the subject at the time, shew that you want not to exculpate yourself from any censure which may have fallen upon you (when justly) by charging another. Lee had a peculiar mode of writing, which was not always pleasing even when he confined himself to truth: but I believe he was right, when he imputed the loss of the Fort to your depending upon another persons judgment, instead of relying upon your own: & have been ready to think, that, had not Genls Putnam & Greene told you what they did when you met them recrossing from the Fort, & thereby encouraged you to risk it, you would have withdrawn the garrison the night before the attack. But that our military officers, tho' not wanting in personal courage, should be deficient in experience, & thereby be led into errors, in that early stage of the war, is not to be wondered at. Scarce any had seen service upon so large a scale; & mere instructions & knowledge gained by reading will not make an adept in practice, there must also be experience. I was pleased with your wish—& the reason for it—"I hope none of the sparks will light on American ground—which I fear is made up of too much combustible matter, for its well being"—for I had the same hope, & the same fear. By what Mr Jefferson writes about the 16th of last Decr to Mr Lowell I am apprehensive that the flames of war have burst out in Europe. The purport of his letter as related to me by Mr Lowell is, that tho' the people at large talked of an accommodation, there were no whispers of that kind from the cabinets; ⟨th⟩at the measures taken indicated the contrary; so that he expected Holland & France would engage the Emperor for a while, that Russia would then join the latter, on which Prussia & the Turks would become the ⟨enem⟩ies of the former, while Britain from her present weakness or good policy would not take part in the quarrel, but reap from it all the benefit that a neutrality would procure.[2] I learnt also from Mr Lowell, that the Duke of Dorset was appointed to negotiate a treaty of commerce with our Commissioners, that he had written to them, observing that while France & America were allies in war, there was a propriety in treating at Paris; but that the case being altered, it did not consist with the dignity of his Sovereign to treat now at Paris: that if the Americans chose it, an agent would be sent to America to transact the business, or that he should be ready to treat with them at London, upon which our Commissioners intended to repair to London.

My young Friend by his spontaneous answer has given me the *tone* of the family, for which I am much obliged to him; we know from the proverb that children speak *true*, not being versed in the arts of deceit. My love to him: but tho' I recollect with pleasure the entertainments afforded me at Mount Vernon, I have little or no expectation of being in the way of a repetition. Am sorry that your Lady is so often troubled with billious complaints. I am no M.D., or might give my opinion, but as I am a lover of porter may mention having heard of its being good in such cases. I frequently drink half a pint at night, & pronounce myself better for it. Billious complaints I am not subject to. The porter I drink, tho' bottled, is not windy; the utmost extent of its life serves only to varnish it out with a thin surface of white. Your Excellency will be pleased to present our best respects to the Family. With increasing esteem I remain Your Excellency's sincere Friend & very humble Servant

William Gordon

ALS, DLC:GW.

1. The private letter was that of GW to Joseph Reed, 22 Aug. 1779. See Gordon to GW, 10 Jan., especially nn.1 and 2, as well as GW to Gordon, 8 March.

2. Jefferson's letter to John Lowell, dated 18 Dec. 1784, is printed in Boyd, *Jefferson Papers*, 7:576–78.

From Reuben Harvey

Respected Friend   Cork [Ireland] 28th March 1785

I am to acknowledge the receipt of thy acceptable favour dated August 30th.[1] Our last Wheat Harvest proved good & caused the prices of Wheat to keep low for some Months past, Viz. from 26/ to 20/ ℔ bble weighing 20 Stones or 280 suttle pounds; We cannot import your Wheat &* Flour except the middle price of Wheat be 30/ ℔ bble or more, but liberty is given to share them in order for being reshipped to a Foreign Market, if the Mercht finds the home Market not likely to advance to 30/ ℔ bble in any reasonable time after they have been landd. English Wheat & Flour can be imported when our price is 27/ ℔ bble or more, so that there is 3/ difference made, which a virtuous or good Irish Parlt, that regards it's Country's real interest, ought not to make, seeing there is a valuable Export of Linnens & other Manufactures from Ireland to America. At present the English People seem great⟨ly⟩ displeased with a Commercial Bill brough⟨t⟩ into their House of Commons by Pitt, which they think will givè this Country some small advantages in Manufactures, And this their selfish grasping dispositions cannot bear; Whether the Minister will be able to effect his purposes, time only can determine, but be the event what it may, Ireland is smartly taxed by her own venal Parliamt, & the large Military Force kept up, together with a Militia Bill design'd to establish a Militia of Government's own making, will probably enable Parlt to tax the Country as they please, especially as the Volunteers in most Southern Countys are altogether languid; Such is the political state of Ireland! I hope America will avoid the corrupt examples of those Islands, & that also avoiding internal disputes she will long remain flourishing & happy. With sincere regard I am Thy respectful Friend

Reuben Harvey

*Foreign *Flou*r cant at any time be consumed, here, by a late Act of Parlt being prohibited.[2]

ALS, DLC:GW.

1. The ALS has not been found, but the letter-book copy, dated 25 Aug., not 30 Aug., 1784, is printed above.

2. Below this, Harvey lists: "Mess Beef 46/ ℔ bble; Do Pork 52/ ℔ do; Butter 52/ ℔ ct; Mold candles 6 d. ½ ℔ ct; Barrels staves £7 ℔ M."

To John Craig

Sir,   Mt Vernon 29th March 1785.

If I could give you any useful information on the subject of your letter to me, I would do it with pleasure; but, altho' I have a good general knowledge of the Western Country, I am very little acquainted with local situations—& less with those on the Susquehanna than any other.[1] Monongahela, of which Cheat river is a branch, is gentle in its current—easy of navigation—& besides, is supposed, either by the Cheat, or the Yohioganey (which is another branch of it) to approach nearest to, & to afford the best communication or portage with the Atlantic waters of any in all that extensive territory: consequently seats thereon, from this circumstance alone, must be valuable; but the quality of the Land is inferior to none, until you penetrate much further to the Westward, or much lower down the Ohio; and is besides much better settled than any part of the Country beyond the Alleghaney Mountains. Upon what terms you could buy (to rent I presume you are not inclined, or the difficulty might be less) a Seat having such conveniencies as you want, I am unable to inform you. The prices of Land there are rising every day, & if the plan which is now in contemplation for extending the navigation of Potomac & opening roads of communication short & easy, between it and the waters above mentioned, should be effected, of which I have no doubt—the price will encrease much faster. My complimts & best wishes to Mrs Craig[2]—I am Sir &c.

G: Washington

LB, DLC:GW.

1. See Craig to GW, 22 Mar. 1785.

2. Mrs. Craig was born Margaret Craig in Tobago. She spoke French and Italian and the Craig house at 181–83 Chestnut Street was a favorite of the European officers during the Revolution. The marriage of the Craig daughter to Nicholas Biddle was performed at Andalusia.

Letter not found: to Robert Townsend Hooe, 29 Mar. 1785. On the same day Hooe wrote to GW: "I had the honor of receiving Your Excellency's favor of this date."

From Robert Townsend Hooe

Sir,   Alexa[ndria, Va.] March 29. 1785.
I had the honor of receiving Your Excellency's favor of this date by your Man this day.[1]

Major Jenifer writes me he intended to draw in your favor for 1000—or 1200£ Md Currency—every attention shall be paid to his draft—& I wish immediately to know the exact sum you want in New York, as I can accommodate you there, I believe—The sooner I get your demand upon that place the sooner I can make provision for it.[2] I am sir, Yr Excellencys most Affe Servt

R. Td Hooe

ALS, DLC:GW. GW wrote on the cover: "favor of Doctr [David] Stewart."
1. Letter not found.
2. See Daniel of St. Thomas Jenifer to GW, 28 Feb. and 31 Mar., and Hooe to GW, 3 and 6 April.

From Robert Townsend Hooe

Sir,   Alexandria [Va.] March 29th 1785.
It is with pleasure I sit down to do myself the Honor of giving Your Excellency an extract of a Letter I received Yesterday from Cadiz. It is as follows—"We have the pleasure to inform you that on Licence being asked of the King to Ship a Jack Ass for Genl Washington, his Majesty not only granted it, but at the same time most Graciously insisted on making a present of two of them to the Genl—adding he was happy in an oppty of Testifying his esteem and regard for so great a Character—Orders are given for the Purchase of two of the best in the Kingdom to be put under the direction of Mr Carmichael, who will send them down here or to Bilboa to be Shipt by different Vessells. Mr Carmichael & ourselves are equally pleased with the exit of this little Negotiation, & of which you will be pleased to advise his Excellency."[1]

I hope both these valuable Annimals will before long arrive safe—And I beg Yr Excellency to believe me to be sir, Yr most Affe hble servt

R. Td Hooe

ALS, DLC:GW.

1. The letter being quoted was undoubtedly one from Hooe's business partner in Cadiz, Richard Harrison. See William Carmichael to GW, 3 Dec. 1784, and particularly note 1 of that document.

From Christopher Ludwick

Philad[elphi]a March 29. 1785.

As Your Excellency often expressed a friendship and Regard for your old Baker Master, and well know what Service he was to the Army—I now beg leave to acquaint you that, finding my private Property greatly injured and diminished by my Attention to, and Exertions in the Public Service, and by necessary Advances of my remaining Cash to some near Relations of my Wife who by the Event of the Revolution have been reduced to indigent Circumstances, I have been obliged to apply to Congress for Compensation—Inclosed is a Copy of my Memorial to Congress, which I transmit for your Excellency's Perusal.[1]

Several Gentlemen late Officers in the Army have chearfully granted me their Recommendation, but in Order to ensure my Success I wish to have a Recommendatory Letter from Your Excellency in my behalf to Congress on the Subject of my Memorial[2]—I flatter myself that You will not refuse me this favor, and am with great Respect & Esteem Your Excellency's Most obedt & very humbe servt

Christopher Ludwick

P.S. should your Excellency grant my Request, a Letter by the Post will be very acceptable to C. Ludwick who is now 65 Years of Age.

ALS, DLC:GW.

1. "The Memorial of Christopher Ludwick late Superintendent of the Baking Department in the Army of the United States" (DNA:PCC, item 41) is dated March 1785. Ludwick, who says he was out-of-pocket for large sums that he paid his bakers and that the thousand-dollar bounty he received was severely "reduced by Depreciation," asked for "a Compensation or Bounty in Land or otherwise equal with other Officers who have served in the American Army." On 13 June 1785 Congress voted to pay Ludwick 200 dollars.

2. Attached to the copy of Ludwick's petition that he sent to GW (see note 1) were copies of three certificates: one signed by Arthur St. Clair, William Irvine, and Anthony Wayne; another by Timothy Pickering; and a third by

Thomas Mifflin. A certificate, in GW's letter book, misdated 12 April 1787 instead of 1785, reads: "I have known Mr Christr Ludwick from an early period of the War; and have every reason to believe, as well from observation as information, that he has been a true and faithful Friend, and Servant to the public. That he has detected and exposed many impositions which were attempted to be practiced by others in the department over which he presided. That he has been the cause of much saving in many respects. And that his deportment in public life has afforded unquestionable proofs of his integrity & worth.

"With respect to the particular losses of which he complains, I have no personal knowledge of them, but have often heard that he has suffered from his zeal in the cause of his Country. G. Washington" (DLC:GW).

From Josiah Parker

Norfolk [Va.] March 29th 1785

Sometime since I did myself the pleasure of sending you some shrubs & vines which I hope got safe up; with this goes Some more but I am affraid this will be too late.[1] With pleasure Dear sir I do myself the honor of subscribeing your respectfull & Obedient servt

J: Parker

ALS, DLC:GW.

1. GW received the first of the plants and acorns from Parker on 18 March. He set out the plants on 6 April. On 13 April he sowed the acorns and also planted the live oaks that came in the second shipment from Parker. See *Diaries*, 4:104, 114, and 118.

Letter not found: from Mathew Carey, 30 Mar. 1785. On 20 April GW wrote to Carey: "I have received your letter of the 30th Ulto."

To Lucretia Wilhemina van Winter

Madame　　　　　　　　　　　　Mount Vernon 30th March 1785

The honor which your Pen has done me, so far exceeds my merits, that I am at a loss for words to express my sense of the compliment it conveys.

The Poem, in celebration of my exertions to establish the rights of my Country, was forwarded to me from Philadelphia by Mr Vogels, to whom I should have been happy to have offered civilities, but he did not give me the pleasure of seeing him.[1]

At best, I have only been an instrument in the hands of Providence to effect, with the aid of France, and many virtuous fellow Citizens of America, a revolution which is interesting to the liberties of Mankind—and to the emancipation of a Country which may afford an asylum (if we are wise enough to pursue the paths which lead to virtue & patriotism) to the oppressed and needy of the Earth.

Our region is extensive. Our plains are productive. and if they are cultivated with liberallity and good sense, we may be happy ourselves, and diffuse it to all those who incline to participate of it.

The lady of whom you have made Such honourable mention, is truly sensible of the obligation, and joins me in wishing you every happiness which is to be found here, and met with hereafter. I have the honor to be Madame Yr most Obedt and Most Hble Servant

Go: Washington

ALS, Collective Six: Amsterdam, Holland; LB, DLC:GW. Van Winter apparently did not receive GW's first copy of this letter. See GW's letter to her of 5 Oct. 1785, when GW sent her the letter printed here, marked "Duplicate."

1. See Gerard Vogels to GW, 10 Mar. 1784, and particularly the notes.

From Daniel of St. Thomas Jenifer

Intend[an]ts Office [Annapolis, Md.]
Dear Sir   March 31st 1785
Inclosed your Excellency will receive an Order on Col. Hooe & Co. for £1069.1.7 which I have not the smallest doubt will be duely honored[1] you have also the Account of your Certs. liquidated by the Auditor.[2]

I shall always be made happy by the execution of any business that you may have to transact on this side of Potomack, being with the most perfect respect & esteem for all at Mount Vernon. I am Dr Sir Your Excellencys most affectionate & obedient Servant

Dan. of St Thos Jenifer

ALS, DLC:GW.

1. This was the amount due GW for the Continental loan office certificates that Lund Washington had bought for him in 1779. See Jenifer to GW, 28 February. GW wished to have the money paid to Robert Townsend Hooe in Alexandria so that Hooe could buy a bill in New York for GW to pay George

Clinton what he had borrowed from him in 1782. See George Clinton to GW, 5 Mar. 1785, n.1. Hooe wrote GW on 29 Mar. and 3 April that he would get the bill in New York for him and, on 6 April, that he had done so (see GW to Jenifer, 12 April 1785).

2. Christopher Richmond, the Maryland state auditor general, "liquidated" GW's Continental loan office certificates by providing GW on 31 Mar. 1785 with a statement of their value, after depreciation, in Maryland currency: £1,069.1.7. Richmond's statement is in DLC:GW. See GW to Richmond, 6 April, and Richmond to GW, 8 April. See also Jenifer to GW, 28 Feb., n.1, GW to Jenifer, 12 April, and Jenifer to GW, 15 April.

Letter not found: to Robert Townsend Hooe, 3 April 1785. On the same day Hooe wrote to GW: "Your favor of this Date I have just rec'd."

From Robert Townsend Hooe

Sir,   Alexandria [Va.] April 3rd 1785.
    Your favor of this Date I have just rec'd and have only to inform that you may rely on me for the Amount of twenty five Hundred Dollars in New York.[1] I am, Sir, Yr most obdt Servant
                                                        R. Td Hooe

ALS, DLC:GW.
    1. Letter not found, but see Hooe's letters of 29 Mar. (first letter) and of 6 April. See also Daniel of St. Thomas Jenifer to GW, 28 Feb. and 31 Mar., and notes.

To Bushrod Washington

Dear Bushrod,   Mount Vernon 3d April 1785.
    Your letter of the 20th Ulto did not come to my hands until the 31st[1]—Whenever you have occasion to write to me from the line of the Post, always put your letter into the Mail. all other conveyances are uncertain; at best, irregular.
    Not expecting you were going to Richmond, I did, previously to the receipt of your letter, write to the Attorney General (to whose care my letter to you had been addressed) requesting him to open it; and so far as it respected the promisary Note of Ryan, ⟨to⟩ comply with my desire on that ⟨head.⟩ Being on the spot, you can be informed of the state of this matter, & govern yourself accordingly.[2]
    By the last Post I inclosed an Advertisement to Mr Hayes (the Printer) requesting a meeting of the Proprietors of the Great

dismal Swamp. The Servant by whom I sent it to Alexandria got there after the Mail was dispatched; but meeting with the Stage, he says he put it into the hands of *somebody* who promised to take care of it; as this may, or may not be the case, I beg you will make immediate enquiry, & in case of failure, desire him to insert the one herewith inclosed three weeks in his Gazette. And, as the Notice will be short, to have it also published in some other Paper of general Circulation. If nothing unforeseen should happen to prevent it, I expect to be in Richmond at the appointed time, & having no other business, should regret a disappointment.[3]

The Holly berries, Geese & Swan, are here, but no mention made of the Cotton[4]—All here join me in best wishes for you. I am, Yr Affecte Uncle

Go: Washington

P.S. Upon second thoughts I have sent the Advertisement to the Printer himself lest this letter should lye in the Post Office for want of your knowing it is there. The one inclosed for Doctr Walker endeavor to forward by some safe hand.[5]

ALS (photocopy), NjP: Armstrong Collection. The letter was sold in 1947 by Gimbel Brothers, item 202.

1. Letter not found.

2. See GW to Bushrod Washington, 22 Jan., and GW to Edmund Randolph, 19 Mar., and notes. See also Randolph to GW, 5 April. The two words in angle brackets are taken from the portion of the letter printed in Gimbel Brothers catalog, 1947, item 202.

3. GW's announcement, dated 25 Mar. 1785 at Mount Vernon, had already been printed on 2 April in the *Virginia Gazette, or, The American Advertiser* (Richmond): "THE PROPRIETORS *of the* Dismal Swamp, *are desired to meet at* Richmond, *on Monday the 2d day of May next.—Many unsuccessful attempts having been made to assemble the Members, and the business of the Company being in a deranged state; a full meeting is now become indispensably necessary, and is earnestly requested.*

"*It were to be wished that every Member would bring with him such papers as he is possessed of respecting this concern, that there may be proper adjustment of it, and some decisive measures adopted for the benefit of the Company.—Done at the request of several Members.* G. WASHINGTON."

The advertisement ran for four issues. GW records in his cash accounts having paid fifteen shillings at Richmond on 4 May to "[James] Hayes Printer Advertisg a Meeting Swamp Co." (Ledger B, 202). For the meeting of the Dismal Swamp Company on 2 May in Richmond, see GW to Thomas Walker, 10 April, n.1.

4. In his diary entry of 19 Mar., GW wrote: "Received a Swan, 4 Wild Geese, & two Barrels of Holly Berries (in Sand) from my Brother John" (*Di-*

aries, 4:104). Bushrod was the son of GW's brother John Augustine Washington.

5. See GW to Thomas Walker, 10 April.

From Patrick Henry

Dear Sir.   Richmond [Va.] April 4th 1785

I beg Leave to introduce to you the Bearer Mr Arnold Henry Dohrman. He is of Lisbon, but has spent a year or two in America, gratifying himself with the Sight of a Country to whose Interests he devoted himself & his Fortune in the very early Periods of the late War. Hundreds (I believe I am within bounds) of our captive Countrymen, bereft of Clothes Victuals Friends & Money, found all these in his Bounty; And this at a Time & place when the Fury & Rage of our Enemys against what they called Rebellion carry'd them to Acts of Cruelty & great Inhumanity. Congress sensible of his Merit, several years ago made him Agent for the united States in Portugal, & I beleive would have gladly given him more substantial proofs of the public Gratitude had oppertunity presented. Our Senate gave him their Thanks & I beleive the Delegates would have done so, had it not been that he arrived here just at the close of a tedious Session, in very bad Weather when every Member was anxious to get away & Business of great Extent & Magnitude was crouded into the Compass of one or two Days Discussion.

Mr Dohrman has liberal, extensive, & usefull Intentions respecting America. He has a good Deal of Business with Congress & intends to spend some time at New York. I feel myself much interested in the Reception he meets with there, sensible as I am of his great Merit & amiable Disposition. And I cannot but hope, our Country may be availed of his unbounded Zeal for her Service, joined to very respectable Abilitys, & Experience in European Business & Politics.[1]

In giving this worthy person your Countenance you will much oblige him who is with the sincerest Attachment Dear sir your most obedient Servant

P. Henry

ALS, DLC:GW.

1. Arnold Henry Dohrman (1749–1813), a Portuguese merchant, came to the aid of American seamen captured during the war by the British and put

ashore in Portugal. In 1780 he became the agent in Portugal for the United States. Dohrman at this time was in the United States to collect from Congress what was owed him. When he stopped at Mount Vernon on 9 July 1785, GW gave him supporting letters to four members of Congress. Congress settled with Dohrman in 1787, and twenty-two years later Dohrman and his family came to Ohio to live. See *Diaries*, 4 : 163.

To George Clinton

Dear Sir,   Mount Vernon 5th Apl 1785.

A few days ago I had the pleasure to receive your favor of the 5th Ulto—Your other letter of the 26th of December came duely to hand, and should not have remained so long unacknowledged had I not been in daily expectation of accompanying my answer with a remittance.[1]

Disappointment followed disappointment, but my expectation being kept up, I delayed writing from one Post day to another until now, that I am assured by a Merchant in Alexandria that I may depend upon a Bill, in a few days, upon a Mr Sylvanus Dickinson of the City of New York for Two thousand five hundred Dollars.[2]

As it is probable I shall receive it before the next Weeks Post, I will, on that occasion, write you more fully—At present I will only add the sincere good wishes, & best respects of Mrs Washington to Mrs Clinton, yourself & family, in wch I sincerely unite—and with great esteem & regard remain, Dr Sir—Yr most Obedt & Affecte Hble Servt

Go: Washington

P.S. Since writing the above I have received the inclosed Bill[3]— The Second shall be sent by next Post when I will be more particular. Go: W——n

ALS, DLC:GW; LB, DLC:GW. GW may have attempted to alter the date to the "6th" of April.

1. Clinton's letter of 26 Dec. 1784 has not been found, but see his letter of 5 Mar. 1785.

2. See Robert Townsend Hooe to GW, 6 April.

3. See note 1, and GW to Clinton, 20 April.

From Sidney Lee

Sr   Westminster [London] April 5th 1785
   Your very obliging Letter of October 20th I had not the pleasure of receiving before the last month was pretty far advanced,
when I was extremely ill, occasion'd by a cold I brought out of
the Country with me, that at first seemed very insignificant, but
afterwards brought on a severe indisposition, that prevented
my presenting my sincere thanks by the last packet for the
many acts of kindness you have honor'd me with and that I now
warmly beg your acceptance of.[1]
   Was brought here in consequence of the most satisfactory accounts from Mr White and Mr Morris of Philadelphia (of who's
integrity I have the highest Opinion) of the train they had put
the business in which I am interested. And powers sufficient to
give full security to Messieurs M: & W., that they could not possibly run any risque in paying the money to wch they deny not
my right. But Este⟨emed⟩ Sr these Contractors bear no resemblance to Mr Morris & Mr White; therefore have catched at a
slight Ommission in a matter of form to protract payment And
as we must now wait for further authority from my American
friends, intend to return into the country next Week.[2] But
could not bear the thoughts of removing without first assuring
you I must to the end of my days, remain with the truest gratitude & respect, Sr Your exceedingly obliged, faithful & obedient humble Servant

                                                        Sidney Lee

ALS, DLC:GW. The letter is addressed to GW at Mount Vernon in "the Prov-
ince of Virginia."
   1. For a discussion of the measures that Sidney Lee took to settle the
American estate of her brother, Gen. Charles Lee, see her letter to GW of 23
May 1784 and particularly note 3 of that document.
   2. For the explanation by Miss Lee's American attorney of this delay in the
settlement of the estate, see Alexander White to GW, 26 July 1785.

From George Mason

Dear Sir   Gunston-Hall April 5th 1785.
   I have broach'd four or five Hogsheads of Cyder, & filled
Your Bottles with what we thought the best; tho' the Difference

in any of it is hardly distinguishable, all I now have being made of the Maryland red streak, & managed in the same Manner. I hope it will prove good, tho' my Cyder this Year is not so clear & fine, as it generally has been; from what Cause I don't know, unless that I ground my Apples last Fall rather later than usual. As the Cyder in the Bottles will not ripen, fit for use, 'til late in May, I have also filled a Barrel, out of the same Hhd which I beg Your Acceptance of. If You use it out of the Barrel, You will find it (as all sweet Cyder is) much more grateful to the Stomach, by having a little Ginger grated upon it.

I beg pardon for having forgot the Water-Melon Seed; & now send it by the Bearer. I was a good deal alarm'd two or three Days ago, by the Gout in my Stomach; which after giving me a very uneasy Night, has gone off again, as it has done several times this Winter, without getting into my Feet; and until it does, I have little Hopes of recovering a tollerable State of Health; so that, notwithstanding the extream pain I know a regular Fit must bring with it, I most heartily wish for one.

Mrs Mason & the Family here[1] join in their Compliments to You, Your Lady, and Miss Bassett, with Dear Sir Your affecte & obdt Sert

G. Mason

ALS, DLC:GW.
1. Mason's second wife was Sarah Brent Mason (c.1730–1806), daughter of George Brent of Woodstock, whom Mason married in April 1780.

From Edmund Randolph

Dear sir   Richmond [Va.] april 5. 1785.
Your favor of the 19th Ulto was put into my hands this evening for the first time. I accordingly opened the inclosed letter to Mr Bushrod Washington, which has remained with me to the present moment. It would give me the sincerest satisfaction to execute, what you there confided to him. But I believe it is too notorious, that Mr Ryan has quitted Virginia, utterly incompetent to discharge his debts, and that an attempt to collect the note from him would have been too late, even at the date of your letter to your nephew. I therefore now inclose the letter and its inclosures.

Mrs Randolph and myself present our best respects to Mrs Washington and yourself: and I particularly request you to believe, that I am My dear sir yr obliged and affectionate friend

Edmund Randolph.

ALS, PHi: Gratz Collection.

From Robert Lewis & Sons

Philad[elphi]a April 5th 1785.
We had the pleasure of writing to your Excellency the 8th Ulto by Post, under cover from Coln. Biddle,[1] & have now to acquaint you, that we have partly engaged one Joseph Davenport to serve you as a Miller for one Year on trial, or longer as may hereafter be agreed on by both parties.

He served an Apprenticeship at one of our Mills, & we have known him from a Boy, to be of good Character, is about 25 Years of Age, has a Wife, two Children, & a bound Girl of about ten Years old, who compose his Family—He is a sober Man, not by any means addicted to Drink too excess, is a good Miller & Cooper, can fasten a Gudgion, put in a Cogg, & perform other Jobs of the kind about a Mill, but is not a MillWright—He writes a tolerable hand, is capable of making Entrys in a common Day Book of the transactions in a Mill, casting up the Measure or weight of Wheat & Flour, receiving & paying Money, but is not acquainted with the method of Posting Books—We have every reason to believe him strictly honest & inoffensive, being a plain Man of few words, & no great address, but on the whole we hope he will prove a suitable Person to transact your Business. But we are much at a loss to stipulate his Wages & privileges, not having such full directions from you as we could wish on that head, The terms he proposes are, to be furnish'd with a comfortable Dwelling-House & Garden (such as you mention) rent free, keeping of one Cow the year round, a sufficient quantity of Fire Wood, standing in the Woods, as convenient as possible to the Dwelling House, six hundred weight of good Pork, or equivalent in Beef & Pork, deliver'd to him in killing time, or this present Year when he may want it, & two hundred Dollars in Cash. Also, to be supply'd with Flour, Midlings, Corn &ca as much as will support his Family from time to time as they may have occasion, at the same rates & prices as those Articles are sold to others for Cash out of the Mill, charging himself therewith.

He will be ready to set out from hence in the course of three Weeks, & depends on your paying all reasonable Expences of removing his Family from this City to Virginia, & he will proceed in the cheapest manner, & with as few Articles of Houshold Goods as possible—We hope those terms will meet your approbation, but should you be of Opinion they are too high, we will endeavour to persuade him to lessen the sum payable in Cash if possible, but we think he cannot well do without the privileges proposed, to which we hope you will have no material objection, & should you judge the terms rather too low, he relys on your Excellency's generosity according to his industry & good conduct, in case you should think proper to continue him in the employment next Year, or for a number of Years to come—But we should be glad to receive a line of directions from you respecting Wages & privileges, before the contract is finally closed, so that we may endeavour to give satisfaction to both parties, & commit the Agreement to Writing, in Order to prevent any after claims, or uneasiness[2]—A number of applications have been made to us, in consequence of an Advertisement publish'd in several Papers,[3] & other enquirys, but none in our Opinion equal to Davenport. We have done every thing in our power to serve your Excellency in this matter, & wish our endeavours may give satisfaction, which will afford great pleasure to Your sincere Friends

Robt Lewis & Sons.

L, DLC:GW.

1. The Lewis letter of 8 Mar. has not been found, but on 12 April GW acknowledges having received it. In his letter to GW of 7 Mar., Clement Biddle mentions that he has delivered GW's letter "respecting the Miller," which is dated 1 Feb., but Biddle does not indicate that he is enclosing a letter to GW from Robert Lewis & Sons.

2. GW writes Robert Lewis & Sons on 12 April accepting their suggested terms for Joseph Davenport's employment, but he asks that the agreement be for two years rather than one. On 23 May Davenport signed an agreement drawn up by Lewis & Sons. It provided that Davenport should "immediately proceed with his Family to a Mill near Mount Vernon, the property of General Washington, where & by whom he is to be employ'd as a Miller & Cooper for the space of two whole Years, to commence the first day of June next"

(DLC:GW). GW complained on 25 May that Davenport had not shown up, but the new miller began work on about 1 June and remained at the mill for more than a decade. He died suddenly on 17 Jan. 1796, just "when we had a good head of water and was Giting on with grinding our wheat" (William Pearce to GW, 17 Jan. 1796).

3. The advertisement for GW's miller is printed in note 2, GW to Robert Lewis & Sons, 1 February.

To Charles Thomson

Dear Sir,   Mt Vernon 5th April 1785.

In the latter part of last Spring, the Commissioners appointed to attend the embarkations at New York, previous to the evacuation of the city, made a report of their proceedings to me, accompanied by a voluminous list of the Slaves which had left that place.[1] Soon after having the pleasure of Mr Reeds company here, he informed me in conversation, that the list I had received was a duplicate of what had been sent to Congress; upon which I filed it with my public papers.

By the last Post he says he had been under a mistake, & wished me to forward the papers which are in my hands, to Congress. This I most assuredly would have done, but they are too bulky for the mail, & liable to much injury from the nature of such a carriage. However I will wait your direction, after acquainting you that two of the Commrs, Egbert Benson Esqr. & Lieut: Colo. Smith, with the Secretary Mr Saml Inches (& undoubtedly the papers from which the report, & proceedings were founded) are in N: York. If notwithstanding it is necessary to resort to me, the originals (for it is not in my power to make copies) shall be sent; altho it will make a chasm in my files, & disappoint many who apply to them for information respecting their negroes.[2] With great esteem & regard I am Dr Sir &c.

G: Washington

LB, DLC:GW; LB, enclosed in Thomson to John Jay, 27 April, DNA: RG 59, Domestic Letters.

1. The commissioners report to GW is dated 18 Jan. 1784. See Commissioners of Embarkation at New York to GW, 18 Jan. 1784, printed above. For the rolls of slaves who embarked, see note 3 of that document.

2. Jacob Read wrote GW on 9 Mar. 1785 asking that he send the slave rolls to Congress. At Thomson's suggestion, John Jay instead sent a clerk to Mount Vernon in late summer to make copies of the rolls. See note 2 of the letter from Read and its references.

From Robert Townsend Hooe

sir,   Alexandria [Va.] April 6th 1785.

I am extremely sorry it was not my power to wait on Your Excellency the other day, and Yesterday I found my self so very unwell all day as to be unable to do any thing or would have sent down the Bill. I now enclose one for 2500 Dollars on Mr Sylvanus Dickenson of New York. The Ballance of Major Jenifers draft I will be Collecting together as fast as in my power.[1] I am, sir, Yr Excellencys Most Obt Serv't

                              R. Td Hooe

ALS, DLC:GW.

1. For GW's negotiations with Daniel of St. Thomas Jenifer and Hooe to obtain the New York bill of exchange, see the references in note 1 in Hooe to GW, 3 April. GW sent Hooe & Harrison's second bill on Sylvanus Dickinson (Dickenson) to George Clinton on 20 April.

To Christopher Richmond

Sir,   Mount Vernon April 6th 1785.

By the last Post Majr Jenifer transmitted me an Acct of my Continental Certificates as they had been Audited in your Office; by which there is a difference of £64.14.7⅛ short of my estimation of their value.[1]

This (for I did not go into the examination of figures) appears to have originated from the times of calculating the depreciation. I have always understood that depreciation was the same thro' the Month, and if I did not misapprehend the Intendant, his ideas of it, accorded therewith.

However, I only ask for information, and because I had calculated myself in this manner, for I want no other measure than what is given to others. I am—Sir Yr Most Obedt Servt

                              Go: Washington

P.S. How does yr Subscriptions to the Potomk Navigation go on?[2]

ALS, MdAA.

Christopher Richmond came to Maryland before the Revolution to become Thomas Howe Ridgate's storekeeper in Port Tobacco, Charles County, Maryland. During the war he was named auditor general for the state, an important post. Richmond also was one of the two managers for collecting at Annapolis subscriptions to the Potomac River Company.

1. See Daniel of St. Thomas Jenifer to GW, 31 March.
2. See Richmond to GW, 8 April, for Richmond's answer to this query.

Letter not found: from Chastellux, 8 April. On 5 Sept. GW wrote Chastellux: "I am your debtor for two letters—one of the 12th of Decemr—the other of the 8th of April."

From George Crocker Fox & Sons

Falmouth [England] April 8. 1785

George C. Fox & Sons, very respectfully, beg leave to inform General Washington that the inclosed letter from their Friends Rolland & Co. Amsterdam, was receiv'd a few days too late for the March Mail, but now goes forward ℔ the Halifax Packet for Newyork.

If they can be useful to Genl Washington in forwarding any letters he may have occasion to send to Europe thro' this Post, it will give them pleasure to obey his commands.

L, DLC:GW. Addressed to "General Washington, Mount Vernon Virginia Charlestown."

Tench Tilghman was in correspondence in 1784 and 1785 with Fox & Sons, one of the firms with whom Tilghman's present business associate, Robert Morris of Philadelphia, did business before the war.

From Christopher Richmond

Sir   Annapolis [Md.] 8th April 1785

I had the honour of receiving your Letter of the 6th Instant, this day. In answer to that part of it relating to the depreciation on Continental Loan Office Certificates—I have to inform you, that the value of them is calculated from, and by, a table published by order of Congress; which commences the First day of September 1777 at par, and from that day, daily varying to the Eighteenth day of March 1780; when the Value of One hundred Continental, was Two Dollars and forty five Ninetieths of a Dollar—or Forty, for one, to this Table the Act of Assembly of Maryland directing its officers to liquidate Loan Office Certificates; both Continental and State, refers—I hope, I have been accurate in taking the Rates off the table abovementioned, for those belonging to you—however in the Manner you calculated them by the monthly rates of Depreciation, it is very likely, there would be the difference mentioned in your Letter.

I most heartily wish, I could give an Account of a much larger Subscription for the opening Potowmack, than this District has afforded, or is likely to do. Enclosed is a Copy of the Subscription as it now stands, which I think would be considerably encreased, were not many persons detered from subscribing by their Fears of not being able to make good their Payments at the Times prescribed by the Acts of Assembly.[1]

I have been lame for Eight Weeks past, so that I could not waite upon several Persons who I believe will subscribe. I will not neglect them when able to walk about.[2] With the highest Respect I have the Honor to be Sir Your obedient hble servant

Chrisr Richmond

ALS, DLC:GW.

1. The enclosure lists only three subscribers to the Potomac River Company, who bought a total of "Sixteen Shares": "Governor [William] Paca—Four Shares; Charles Carroll of Carrollton—Six do; Wallace[,] Johnson & Muir—Five do."

2. On 10 May Richmond again reported little success in securing at Annapolis subscribers to the Potomac River Company, but by the time of the first meeting of the company at Alexandria on 17 May seventy-three shares at Annapolis had been subscribed to.

To James Duane

Dear Sir, Mount Vernon 10th Apl 1785.

Enclosed you have my answer to the Acts of your Corporation, which I pray you to present.[1]

I thank you for the Arguments & judgment of the Mayor's Court of the City of New York in the Cause betwn Elizabeth Rutgars & Joshua Waddington[2]—I have read them with all the attention I could give the subject, and though I pretend not to be a competent judge of the Law of Nations, or the principle & policy of the Statute upon which the Action was founded; yet, I must confess, that reason seems very much in favor of the opinion given by the Court, and my judgment yields a hearty assent to it.

It is painful, to hear that a state which used to be foremost in acts of liberality, and its exertion to establish our fœderal system upon a broad bottom & solid ground is contracting her ideas, & pointing them to local & independent measures; which, if persevered in, must sap the Constitution of these States (already too weak)—destroy our National character—& render us as contemptable in the eyes of Europe as we have it in our power to be respectable—It should seem as if the Impost of 5 pr Ct would never take place, for no sooner does an obstinate State begin to relent, and adopt the recommendation of Congress, but some other runs restive; as if there was a combination among them, to defeat the measure.

From the latest European Accts it is probable an accomodation will take place between the Emperor and the Dutch—but to reverberate News to a Man at the source of intelligence would be idle—therefore Mum—The Dutch I conceive are too much attached to their possessions & their wealth, if they could yield to the pangs of parting with their Country, to adopt the plan you hinted to Mr Van Berckel. The Nations of Europe are ripe for Slavery—a thirst after riches—a promptitude to luxury—and a sinking into venality with their concomitants, untune them for Manly exertions & virtuous Sacrafices.

I do not know from whence the report of my coming to Trenton could have originated—unless from the probability of my accompanying the Marquis de la Fayette as far as New York should have caus'd it—he pressed me to the measure, but the Season was too much opposed to it, to obtain my consent.[3]

Mrs Washington & myself, entertain a grateful sense of the kind recollection of us by you, Mrs & Miss Duane, & the other branches of your family, & beg leave to present our Compliments to, & best wishes for, them all. With very great esteem & regard I have the honor to be—Dear Sir Yr Most Obedt & Affecte Hble Servt

Go: Washington

P.S. If our Rocky-hill acquaintance—Mrs Vanhorne—has removed (as they talked of doing) to the City of New York I pray you to recall me, in respectful terms, to her remembrance.[4] Go: W——n.

ALS, NHi: Duane Papers; LB, DLC:GW.

1. On 16 Dec. 1784 Duane wrote to GW enclosing an address from the City of New York and a certificate making him a freeman of the city, but Duane

did not send the packet until 10 Mar. 1785 when he enclosed both the letter and its enclosures in a letter of that date. The certificate and address are printed above in note 1 of Duane's letter of 16 December. In this letter of 10 April to Duane, GW enclosed a formal letter of thanks to Duane and another to the city officials, both also dated 10 April.

The text of GW's formal letter to Duane as mayor of New York is: "A few days since by Doctr [Arthur] Lee, I had the honor to receive your favors of the 16th of December from Trenton, and 10th of March from the City of New York. The former enclosing an Address of the City, and the freedom thereof in a very handsome golden Box.

"For the flattering expression of the Address, & the honor which it conferred on me by the freedom of the City, I entertain a grateful sense. I wish my powers were equal to my feelings, that I might express the latter in more lively terms than are contained in the enclosed answer.

"Let me beseech you, Sir, at the moment you shall have laid it before your Worshipful Board, to add the strongest assurances of the respect and attachment with which I have the honor to be, their, and your Most Obedt & Very Hble Servant Go: Washington" (ALS, NHi: George and Martha Washington Papers). GW's draft and letter-book copy are in DLC:GW. Dr. Arthur Lee "came to Dinner" at Mount Vernon on 30 Mar. (*Diaries*, 4:109).

The text of GW's letter "To The Honble the Mayor, Recorder, Alderman & Commonalty of the City of New York," is: "Gentlemen, I receive your Address, and the freedom of the City with which you have been pleased to present me in a golden Box, with the sensibility and gratitude which such distinguished honors have a claim to. The flattering expression of both, stamps value on the Acts; & call for stronger language than I am master of, to convey my sense of the obligation in adequate terms

"To have had the good fortune amidst the viscissitudes of a long and arduous contest 'never to have known a moment when I did not possess the confidence and esteem of my Country.' And that my conduct should have met the approbation, and obtained the Affectionate regard of the State of New York (where difficulties were numerous & complicated) may be ascribed more to the effect of divine wisdom, which had disposed the minds of the people, harrassed on all sides, to make allowances for the embarrassments of my situation, whilst with fortitude & patience they sustained the loss of their Capitol, and a valuable part of their territory—and to the liberal sentiments, and great exertion of her virtuous Citizens, than to any merit of mine.

"The reflection of these things now, after the many hours of anxious sollicitude which all of us have had, is as pleasing, as our embarrassments at the moments we encountered them, were distressing—and must console us for past sufferings & perplexities.

"I pray that Heaven may bestow its choicest blessings on your City—That the devastations of War, in which you found it, may soon be without a trace—That a well regulated & benificial Commerce may enrichen your Citizens. And that, your State (at present the Seat of the Empire) may set such examples of Wisdom & liberality, as shall have a tendency to strengthen & give permanency to the Union at home—and credit & respectability to it abroad.

The accomplishment whereof is a remaining wish, & the primary object of all my desires" (ALS, NHi: George and Martha Washington Papers). GW's draft and letter-book copy are in DLC:GW.

2. See Duane to GW, 16 Dec. 1784, n.3.

3. For references to the widespread report that GW intended to visit Philadelphia, New York, and New England in the fall of 1784, see GW to Knox, 23 Nov. 1784, n.2.

4. "Mrs. Vanhorne" may be the wife of David Van Horne (d. 1807).

Letter not found: from Lucretia Wilhelmina van Winter, 10 April 1785. GW wrote van Winter on 5 Oct.: "I have now to acknowledge the receipt of your favor of the 10th of April."

To Thomas Walker

Dear Sir,   Mount Vernon 10th Apl 1785

At the request of the Gentlemen who met in Richmond the day you parted with us, I have requested a meeting of the Proprietors of the Dismal Swamp in Richmond on Monday the 2d day of May next—at which time & place I should be glad to see you as it is indispensably necessary to put the affairs of the Company under some better management—I hope every member will bring with him such papers as he is possessed of respecting this business.[1]

I wrote you a line similar to this, to go from Richmond, but Mr Carter informing me that he is about to send a Servant into your neighbourhood I embrace the oppertunity as more certain to give you this information.[2] I am—Dr Sir Yr most obedt Hble Servt

Go: Washington

ALS (photocopy), DLC:GW; LB (incomplete), DLC: William Cabell Rives Papers.

1. For a brief survey of the early history of the Dismal Swamp Company from its founding in 1763 by GW and his associates, see Walker to GW, 24 Jan. 1784, n.1. Some of the other members were in Richmond in October 1784 for a meeting of the company which did not materialize (see Thomas Walker to GW, 29 Aug. 1784, n.2), but as his diary and correspondence make clear, GW did not go to Richmond until mid-November 1784 and had not been there since. It is clear, therefore, that "the request of the Gentlemen who met in Richmond that day you parted with us" was made in November 1784. In any case, GW sent a notice to the printer in late March 1785 to be placed in the Richmond newspaper, calling for a meeting of the company in Richmond on 2 May (see GW to Bushrod Washington, 3 April). GW left Mount Vernon

on 29 April and arrived in Richmond on Sunday afternoon, 1 May. The members of the Dismal Swamp Company met in the senate chambers on 2 and 3 May. For the work of the meeting, see the Resolutions of the Dismal Swamp Company, 2 May, printed below.

2. The letter to Walker that GW sent to Bushrod Washington in Richmond on 3 April for forwarding has not been found.

To Thomas Freeman

Sir,   Mt Vernon April 11th 1785.

Not having heard a tittle from you since I left Mr Simpsons in Septr last, I wish for the detail of your proceedings in my business since that period, particularly with respect to applications, if any, for my Lands in your neighbourhood or elsewhere, & what has been done with the mill.[1] I have obtained, some time since, a Patent for the round bottom above Captenon, which may be rented upon the terms of my printed advertisements.[2]

Mr Smith (especially as he lives at a distance, & is only in the County at the assizes) should have every assistance in hunting up the evidence necessary for the prosecution of my ejectments in the Court of Washington, particularly as they respect the improvements in my behalf, antecedent to the possession of the Land by the present occupants; & the notices given them of its being mine, at, or immediately after the Settlements made by them. Colo. John Stephenson, Mr Marc[u]s Stephenson & Mr Danl Morgan are, I shou'd suppose, most likely to be acquainted with Colo. Crawfords proceedings in this business. It is of consequence to ascertain all the improvements which were made for my use & benefit previous to the settlements of the present possessors. Colo. Crawford in a letter to me says, he built four houses on different parts of the Land; or made four improvements of some kind: if this can be proved it would defeat my opponents upon their own ground.[3]

I should be glad to hear frequently from you—Letters lodged in the Post Office at Baltimore or Alex[andri]a, will not fail of getting safe to my hands. I am &c. &c.

G: Washington

LB, DLC:GW.

1. See GW to Freeman, 23 Sept. 1784.

2. GW secured his patent to the Round Bottom tract in October 1784. See GW to Thomas Lewis, 1 Feb. 1784, n.3. On 20 May 1785 John Harvie in-

formed GW that the heirs of Michael Cresap had revived Cresap's claims to the tract. See GW to Harvie, 31 May 1785, in which GW sets out the basis for his right to the tract and asks to have a caveat entered to prevent a patent being issued to the Cresap heirs. Captenon Creek is Captina or Fox Grape Vine Creek.

3. For GW's attempt to remove the settlers on his Millers Run (or Chartiers Creek) lands in Pennsylvania, see the editorial note in Thomas Smith to GW, 9 Feb. 1785.

From Clement Biddle

Dear General   Philadelphia April 12. 1785
By a Schooner Capt. McLean which saild last week for Alexandria I sent a barrel which I received from Mr Boudinot with Orchard Grass seed—it went to the Care of Colo. Hooe to whom I forwarded the Captains receipt—this was the first Conveyance I could hear of since it came to hand.[1]

I shall pay Mr Boudinots Account & send you the same with his receipt.[2]

Inclosed is your account Current previous to my failure ballance £2.3.0½ which you will please to examine if right especialy the sums paid to Mr Richardson which I have from his Books.[3]

Major Storey is appointed an additional Auditor to settle the Accounts in this state against the United States & is expected here to act in a few days therefore I thought it more prudent to keep the Accounts you inclosed me to lay before him than to trust them to Lancaster or Carlile where the other Auditor now attends.[4]

Mr Paine being in town I Shewd your Letter to Mr Lamont to him & he advised that I should not deliver it without your further Order, As the Author of the Poems might say it was dedicated by your Permission when the work might not merit it.[5] I have the honor to be with the greatest respect Your Excellencys Most Obedient & very humle servt

Clement Biddle

ALS, DLC:GW; LB, ViMtV.
    1. On this day, Biddle wrote Robert Townsend Hooe of Alexandria that he was sending "a Barrel Grass Seed" for GW, which Hooe was "please to receive & forward" (Biddle Letter Book, ViMtV). See Biddle to GW, 7 March.
    2. This is payment for grass seed. See GW to Biddle, 3 Nov. 1784, n.2.

3. Biddle wrote GW on 7 Mar. that his commercial business had failed. GW did not respond until 16 May when he informed Biddle that he had made arrangements to pay him the £2.3.0½ that he owed him.

4. See note 8 in GW to Biddle, 1 February.

5. See GW to Biddle, 2 February.

To Daniel of St. Thomas Jenifer

Dear Sir,   Mount Vernon 12th Apl 1785.

The Post preceeding the last, brought me your favor of the 31st Ulto—The next day I waited upon Colo. Hooe with your order, but he was confined to his bed & unable to do business. Two days after he sent me a Bill on New York for 2500 Dollars, payable at fifteen days sight; & gave me assurances that he wd pay the Balle shortly.[1]

In consequence, you have my receipt for £1069.1.7 specie at the foot of the enclosed list.[2] I have given it for specie because you desired it; in full confidence however, that if the Bill shd not be duely honored; or that I should meet with delays, or difficulty in receiving the Balle, that it will be null, or have proper attention paid to the circumstances; for, otherwise, the interest of this money which was intended to pay a debt at New York will cease, when a higher interest *there*, will be accumulating that debt & defeat my intention.[3]

I had taken up an idea, that, depreciation was the same thro' the Mo.; & had calculated my demand accordingly. Mr Richmond varies the depreciation every day; by which his acct & mine differ £64.14.7⅛. I suppose he is right, & that I must submit to the disappointment.[4]

I am exceedingly obliged to you for your ready, & pointed attention to this business. Mrs Washington & Fanny Bassett present their Compliments to you; & I pray you to be assured of the sincere esteem & regard with which I am, Dear Sir, Your Most Obedt and Affectionate Hble Servt

                              Go: Washington

ALS, CSmH; LB, DLC:GW.

1. See GW to Robert Townsend Hooe, 6 April.

2. See Jenifer to GW, 28 Feb., n.1.

3. See Jenifer to GW, 15 April.

4. See GW to Christopher Richmond, 6 April, and Richmond to GW, 8 April.

To Lafayette

My dear Marqs   Mount Vernon April 12th 17⟨85⟩

Your letter of the 15th of Septr last year, introductory of Mr Duchi, I had the honor to receive a few days since.[1]

However great that Gentleman's merits are, and however much I might be inclined to serve him, candor required me to tell him, as I now do you, that there is no opening (within my view) by which he could enter, & succeed in the line of his profession, in this Country.

Besides being a stranger, and unacquainted with the language of these States—perfectly—many of them, to prevent an inundation of British Attorneys of which they were apprehensive, & of whose political principles they entertained not the most favorable sentiments; have passed qualifying Acts, by which *residence* & *study* in *them* for a specific time, is made essential to entitle a Lawyer to become a practitioner in our Courts of justice.

Therefore, should Mr Duchi incline, notwithstanding, to settle, altogether, or spend any considerable portion of his time in this Country, his friends cannot serve him better than by obtaining for him some appointment in the Consular department; for the discharge of which, I presume he must be well qualified. With great attachment and the most Affectionate regard I am—My dear Marqs Yr sincere friend and Obedt Hble Servt

                                        Go: Washington

ALS, PWacD: Sol Feinstone Collection, on deposit PPAmP; LB, DLC:GW.

1. The text of Lafayette's letter to GW about Ducher (Duché), written in New York and dated 15 Sept. 1784, is: "This letter will be delivered By Mr duché, whose principles, character, and Misfortunes entitle Him to Your Excellency's patronage—He Has a great share in Chev. de chattelux's esteem, and is Most particularly Recommended By my friend Mr de MalesHerbes, who Had an opportunity to know Him when a lawyer in the City of paris—this Gentleman Came with a Good sum of Monney which He intended to Settle with in America—But the Greater part, Having Been lost in a shipwrek, He Still more Stands in Need of Advice and patronage—Both of those, my dear General, I earnestly request in His favour, and am Happy to Assure you that He Ever Has been a friend to the Rights of Mankind, and that His situation deserves particular Notice" (ALS, PEL). The letter is dated 14 Sept. in the Calender of Omitted Letters in Idzerda, *Lafayette Papers*, 5:438.

Gaspard-Joseph-Armand Ducher came to America to study the commercial laws of the various newly founded states. After his arrival in America, he spent the night of 11 April 1785 at Mount Vernon. Ducher wrote GW on Christmas day 1785, in passable English, to thank him for his hospitality and to tell GW of his being appointed, on 1 Sept., vice-consul at Portsmouth, New Hampshire. In 1787, he became French consul at Wilmington, North Carolina. During his years in America, Ducher wrote influential reports about commercial matters relating to the United States and France.

To Robert Lewis & Sons

Gentlemen,   Mount Vernon 12th Apl 1785.

I have received two letters from you—one of the 8th of March—the other the 5th instt—& thank you for both.[1]

I acquiesce readily to the conditional terms you have made on my behalf with Joseph Davenport.[2] His demand of Wages are as high as the best Mills in this Country afford; & the priviledges for wch he stipulates, shall be granted him with this addition, that his fire wood shall be Carted to his door, at my expence; and he may raise Poultry for his own eating at my cost; but under *no* pretence *whatever* to sell any.

I wish the charge of removing him could be stipulated, & made as reasonable as possible; otherwise the addition of it to his Wages & priviledges for a year only, will make him come high to me. for this reason, if you entirely approve of him as a Miller & man of character, I had rather the contract should be for two years than one, if he can be engaged for that term. At present my Mill has the reputation of turning out superfine flour of the first quality; it commands a higher price in this Country & the West Indies than any other, & I should be unwilling it should loose its character from ignorance, or bad management of the Miller.

William Roberts (my present Miller) for skill in grinding & keeping a Mill in order, is inferior to *No* Man—Owing to this— to the times—and to the aversion I have to frequent changing of people, I have submitted for more than Seven yrs to his impositions. He is an excellent Cooper & Millwright—He has lived with me near 15 years, during which period I have not paid a shilling for repairs[3]—He came to me with a full grown Apprentice—for both I only paid £80 Pensa Cy pr Ann: but during my absence he was continually encreasing his wages and previledges, in proportion as he faultered in his Services; so that I had determined, now that I could look a little into my own business, even if there had been an entire reformation in his conduct, to have reduced his wages & previledges (or parted with him) to the very standard of your letter; which I believe is as high as the best, & most extensive Manufacturing Mills in this State afford. Mine is but a poor stream, wanting water near half the year; for which reason, if Davenport (being a Cooper) is to work at this business (there being a very good shop within 50 yds of the dwelling Ho. & Mill) when he is not engaged in grinding, Packing &ca, I wish it to be specified. In short, whatever is expected of either, by the other party, I pray may be explicitly declared, to avoid all disputes, misconceptions, afterclaims, & uneasinesses. You know full well what I ought to expect from a Miller, and whatever you engage on my behalf, shall be religiously fulfilled.

As you must have incurred expence on my Acct, in this business, I am ready, & willing, to discharge it with many thanks for the trouble you have been at, to serve me—and if it should ever be in my power to render you any return, I should be happy in doing it. I am Gentn Yr Most Obedt & obliged Hble Servt

Go: Washington

ALS, owned (1976) by Dr. Robert Stein, Cincinnati; LB, DLC:GW.

1. The letter from Robert Lewis & Sons of 8 Mar. has not been found. See note 1 in the Lewis letter of 5 April.

2. See Robert Lewis & Sons to GW, 5 April, n.2.

3. Despite the pleas of Roberts, GW fired him well before Davenport arrived about 1 June. See William Roberts to GW, 14 April, and GW to Robert Lewis & Sons, 25 May.

To Charles Washington

Dear Brother,   Mount Vernon ⟨12⟩th April ⟨17⟩85.

The enclosed is the last letter I have had from your Son George—why it is so, I cannot r⟨eadil⟩y Acct, except ⟨for⟩ the irregularity of the Post Office ⟨which⟩ seems to be under very bad management. Another letter of his, of the ⟨*mutilated*⟩ to a young Lady of this family ⟨*mutilated*⟩ reason to look for him here the latter ⟨end⟩ of this, or beginning of next Month.[1]

I lend our Nephew Geo: Steptoe Washington a horse Saddle & Bridle to visit his ⟨moth⟩er's, of which he seems desirous—it would be well for you to have attention to his return in time. Mr

Balch, Master of the Academy at which he is, speaks of him in favorable terms.[2]

Immediately upon receipt of the ⟨mon⟩ey I informed Mr Balch that I was ready to discharge any Expences which had been incurred on Acct of the Boys—the enclosed letter from him is the only answer I have got to it.[3] As they have been there near Eight Months the Sum you sent me will not, I expect, discharge what may be due for Schooling, Board & Cloathing. I therefore wish to have more sent me as my own expenditures are too great to allow me to be in advance for them. I have desired Mr Balch to receive the Boys into his own family again as soon as his house is in order for it. Mrs Washington joins in love to my Sister & yr family. And I am Yr Affecte

Go: Washington

How does yr Subscriptions to the Potomk Navigation go on?

ALS, CSmH. The text of the letter is torn; words in angle brackets are taken from Fitzpatrick, *Writings of Washington*, 28:131–32.

1. The most recent letter that George Augustine Washington is known to have written to GW, printed above, is dated 25 Feb. 1785. The "young Lady of this family" was Fanny Bassett.

2. George Steptoe Washington was the son of Anne Steptoe Washington, the fourth wife of the late Samuel Washington. She lived at Harewood in Berkeley County not far from Charles Washington's residence. George Steptoe and his brother Lawrence Augustine Washington were at this time in the Rev. Stephen Bloomer Balch's school in Georgetown, Maryland. See GW to David Griffith, 29 Aug. 1784, n.1.

3. The letter from Balch has not been found.

From John Harvie

Sir   Richmond [Va.] April 13th 1785

I have to Regret that an Excursion into the Country for Eight or ten days past prevented my receiveing your Letter of March the 19th in time to Answer it by this Weeks post—I shall Sir with the highest Satisfaction look into the several Acts of Convention and Assembly that make any thing to the point and do myself the Honour of Communicating to you the Necessary References to them by the next post.[1] I am Sir With Every Sentiment of Esteem Yr Most Obt servt

Jno. Harvie

ALS, DLC:GW.

1. See Harvie to GW, 22 April.

From William M. Roberts

Sir   14th of April [1785]
   your Exsellency has Got in A Pasion with Me Which I am
Vary Sorry for, & Taking Me at anon plush in Many Respects I
always thought From the Bisoness I Call my Salf Master of I
aught To have the wages you have Genaresty paid Me, but As
your Stream is Light & I at this Time Know Not Whare to Go I
woud Take 70 pound a year if youd Agree to Imploy Me for 10
years if its pleas God To Continew you & Me So Long, And As
for my folley of Drinking I Shall Sollomly Decline As its hurtful
To Me in this Life As wall As that to Come[1]—Pray Consider my
Destress & how Unwelling I am To Leve you. From Sir your Exsellencys Most Obt Servt

                                                         Wm M. Roberts

ALS, DLC:GW.
   1. For the steps GW took to replace Roberts as his miller at Mount Vernon,
see the notes in Roberts to GW, 25 Nov. 1784, GW to Robert Lewis & Sons, 1
Feb. and 12 April 1785, and Robert Lewis & Sons to GW, 5 April 1785.

From John Witherspoon

Respected & Dear Sir   Tusculum [N.J.] April 14. 1785
   Your Favour of the 8th of March reached me towards the
End of that Month At that Time I was entirely ignorant where
Mr Bowie was but in general supposed him to be at a great Distance in the Back Countries. However when deliberating how
to get a Letter conveyed to him I receivd a few Days ago a Letter from himself dated at Chambers Town Feby 28 and though
there is nothing in the Letter from whence I can judge with certainty whether he has a fixed or temporary Residence theer I
have written to him to that Place & informed him of the Contents of your Letter respectng his Application to You. I can
truly say that I approve of your Resolution fully though it will
not be improper that some Person should be collecting Materials in the mean while. The application I made in Mr Bowies Behalf was sudden & unpremeditated. It arose in him from Zeal &
Attachment & perhaps he may live to have an Opportunity of
doing something that Way hereafter. Ever since I came to this
Country I have been more & more convinced that it is extremely difficult for any Person acquainted only with the Euro-

pean Countries to form just Sentiments or to Speak with Propriety upon american Persons and Affairs. There are certain general Classes of Ideas as well as Modes of Practice arising Naturally from the Newness of the Country which are incommunicable to those who have never been heer. I had the Honour to predict & the Happiness of seeing my Prediction accomplished that this Circumstance would greatly embarrass both the Councils & Army of great Britain in her Contest with America.

From your making no Mention of it at all I am apt to suspect that the Answer I wrote to the Letter I had the honour of receiving from you in London has never reached you. I sent that Letter by a Gentleman who seemed very ambitious of conveying it so that I thought it safer than almost any other Conveyance. The Substance of it was to inform you that it was unsafe for me or any American to have a visible Hand in bringing out Emigrants.[1] We were fully convinced that Mr Reed my self Col. Wadsworth Mr Bingham & many others were strictly watched.[2] A Friend of mine sent me as a Caution a Copy of an Act of Parliament laying a Fine of £500 Sterling on any that should engage Artificers to leave the Kingdom and though this was cheifly designed against transporting the finer Artists it would have been without Scruple applied to us if theer had been but a Weaver or Blacksmith in a Ships Company. For this Reason neither I nor any other took the least Step to promote Emigration although pester'd with Solicitations for that purpose. All I did therefore was by general very cautious Discourse in Scotland. I also observed in that Letter that I thought Your proposals might be altered & yet answer the same End by Selling in fee Simple a certain Number of Lots in every District reserving the rest to yourself to partake of the improved Value. This is the Way taken in the northern Parts where they understand making New Settlements very well. My Compliments to Mrs Washington to whom & you I wish all the Comforts of Your honourable Retirement & Am Sir your most obedt humble Servant

Jno. Witherspoon

ALS, DLC:GW.

1. On 10 Mar. 1784 GW wrote John Witherspoon (1723–1794), the noted president of the College of New Jersey at Princeton, a long letter about placing tenants from abroad on his Ohio lands. In his response from London on

7 June, Witherspoon reported that for reasons GW would understand, he would "make no Mention whatever of this Matter in England except to a few Confidential Friends."

2. Joseph Reed (1741–1785), at this time a lawyer in New Jersey, accompanied Witherspoon to Britain and died on 5 Mar. not long after his return. Jeremiah Wadsworth (1743–1804), of Connecticut, was in London at the time on business, and William Bingham (1742–1804), a Philadelphia businessman and banker, was in Europe with his wife, Anne Willing Bingham, from 1783 to 1786.

From William Grayson

Dear Sir   New York Apl 15th 1785

I did myself the honor of writing to you by Post the 10th of March last in answer to your favor of the 22nd of January, & I hope my letter has before this got safe to hand.

On my being appointed one of the Commee for draughting the Ordnance for ascertaining the mode of disposing of lands in the Western territory, the President was kind enough to furnish me with an extract of your letter to him on the subject of the back Country, which now induces me to conclude it will be agreable to you to be informed of the farther progress of this important business.[1]

The Ordnance was reported to Congress three days ago, & ordered to be printed, & I now take the earliest opportunity of sending you a copy;[2] The idea of a sale by public Vendue, in such large quantities, appears at first view eccentric, & objectionable; I shall therefore mention to you the reasons which those who are advocates for the measure offer in it's support; They say this cannot be avoided with[ou]t affording an undue advantage to those whose contiguity to the territory has given them an opportunity of investigating the qualities of the land; That there certainly must be a difference in the value of the land in different parts of the Country, and that this difference cannot be ascertained witht an actual survey in the first instance & a sale by competition in the next.

That with respect to the quantity of land offered for sale in a township, it will not have the effect of injuring the poorer class of people, or of establishing monopolies in speculators & ingrossers: That experience is directly agt the inference, for that the Eastern States, where lands are more equally divided than in any other part of the Continent were generally settled in that manner; That the idea of a township with the temptation of a support for religion & education holds forth an inducement for neighbourhoods of the same religious sentiments to confederate for the purpose of purchasing and settling together⟨,⟩ That the Southern mode would defeat this end by introducing the idea of indiscriminate locations & settlements, which would have a tendency to destroy all those inducemts to emigration which are derived from friendships religion and relative connections; That the same consequence would result from sales in small quantities under the present plan.

That the advantages of an equal representation the effect of laying off the country in this manner; The exemption from controversy on account of bounds to the latest ages; the fertility of the lands; the facilities of communication with the Atlantic through a variety of channels, as also with the Brittish & Spaniards; the fur & peltry trade: & the right of forming free governments for themselves, must solicit emigrants from all parts of the world, & insure a settlement of the country in the most rapid manner, That speculators & ingrossers if they purchase the lands in the first instance cannot long retain them on account of the high price they will be obliged to give & the consequent loss of interest while remaining in their hands uncultivated; That if they however should make money by ingrossing, the great design of the land office is answered which is revenue; and that this cannot affect any but European emigrants or those who were not at hand to purchase in the first instance; that if it is an evil, it will cure itself, which has been the case in Lincoln County Virginia, where the lands were first in the hands of Monopolists: but who were forced to part with them from a reguard to the general defense.

That the expence & delay would be too great to divide the territory into fractional parts by actual surveys, and if this is not done sales at public vendue can not be made, as witht a previous knowledge of the quality of the lands no comparative estimate can be form'd between different undivided moities.

That the offering a small number of townships for sale at a time is an answer to the objection on account of delay, and at the same time it prevents the price from being diminished on acct of the Markets being over stocked.

That the present plan excludes all the formalities of warrants entries locations returns & caveats, as the first & last process is a deed.

That it supersedes the necessity of Courts for the determination of disputes, as well as that of creating new officers for carrying the plan into execution; That the mode of laying out the same in squares is attended with the least possible expence; there being only two sides of the square to run in almost all cases. That the expence will be repaid to the Continent in a ten fold ratio, by preventing fraud in the Surveyors.

That the drawing for the townships and sending them on to the different States is conformable to the principles of the government, one State having an equal right to the best lands at it's market with the other: as also of disposing of it's public securities in that way.

That if the Country is to be settled out of the bowels of the Atlantic States it is but fair the idea of each State's contributing it's proportion of emigrants should be countenanced by measures operating for that purpose.

That if the plan should be found by experience to be wrong it can easily be altered by reducing the quantities & multiplying the surveys.

These were the principal reasonings on the Commee in favor of the measure and on which it would give me great satisfaction to have your sentiments, as it involves consequences of the most extensive nature, and is still liable to be rejected altogether by Congress, or to be so altered as to clear it of the exceptionable parts; perhaps the present draught might have been less objectionable, if we had all have had the same views; Some gentlemen looked upon it as a matter of revenue only & that it was true policy to get the money witht parting with inhabitants to populate the Country & thereby prevent the lands in the original states from depreciating: Others (I think) were afraid of an interference with the lands now at market in the individual States: part of the Eastern Gentlemen wish to have the lands sold in such a manner as to suit their own people who may chuse to emigrate, of which I believe there will be great numbers particularly from Connecticut: But others are apprehensive of the consequences which may result from the new States taking their position in the Confederacy: They perhaps wish that this event may be delayed as long as possible. Seven hundred men are agreed on, in Congress, to be raised for the purpose of protecting the settlers on the Western frontiers & preventing unwarrtable intrusions on the public lands; & for guarding the public stores.

I must now apologize to you for the length of this letter; the subject appeared to me of the greatest consequence & I was desirous you might have the fullest information thereon; As the communicating a report of a Commee while under the deliberation of Congress is agt rule, I shall thank you to retain the possession of it yourself. I have the honor to be with the highest respect Yr Affect. friend & Most Obed. servt

Willm Grayson

ALS, DLC:GW.

1. Grayson is referring to the letter of 15 Mar. to Richard Henry Lee in which GW gives the basic principles on which he believes the "Seating" of the Northwest should be based.

2. The text of the Land Ordinance of 1785 is printed in *JCC*, 28:375–81.

From Daniel of St. Thomas Jenifer

Dear Sir   Intendants Office [Annapolis, Md.] Apl 15. 1785

Should you meet with delay, or disappointments from Col. Hooe in payment of my Order; the Interest shall be allowed on any sum that he may be tardy in paying, but to prevent this being the case, I wish that Mr Lund Washington would put the Colo. in mind of the promise he made me, that you should not be disappointed.[1]

Mr Richmond has calculated the depreciation on your Certs. agreeably to the scale laid down by our Law. With my respectful Compliments to the Ladies I am my dear Sir Your most affectionate friend and Obedient Servant

Dan. of St Thos Jenifer

ALS, DLC:GW.

1. See GW to Jenifer, 12 April. Precisely what "promise" Robert Townsend Hooe made to Jenifer has not been determined.

From Adrienne, Marquise de Lafayette

sir,   paris ce 15 april 1785
   every mark of your kindness, is very precious to me, and
amidst all my feelings at the marquis's return, I received an additional joy, by the obliging Letter, he brought me from you.[1] I
hope that during this Late stay at mount vernon, where he was
so happy, he has found an opportunity, in some of your conversations, about domestic Life, to mention his wife and his children, and speak to you of the Sentimens, of attachment and
tender respect to you, that grows with them, and with which
their mother is so strongly impressed. how happy should I be,
to meet with mrs Washington, to recall together, all the circumstances of the war, every period of our anguish, and of your
glory, and to see our children playing together. wishing for so
happy a moment, anastasie and Georges beg Leave, to send to
the two youngest, miss Custis a toilett and a doll that is two play
things with which my daughter is more delighted since two
months, she is in possession of that she hopes, that her remembrance being some time mingled, with their entertainements,
she may obtain some part in their frienship, whose she is so desirous of.
   for the eldest miss Custis, we have so exalted an idea, of her
reason and gravity, that we have only dared send to her a neet-
ing bag, because she may with it, keep mrs Washington company, because I hear that she Likes this kind of work. we send
master Georges also, an optick with different wiews; but we
have been moved by a personal interest, making him this gift. I
hope that Looking at it, he will become fond of travelling that
his travels will conduct him, into france, and perhaps he may
bring you and mrs Washington here.[2] this idea is too delightful,
to fix my mind upon it, without a founded hope. permit me
only to Lament here that the marquis, could not obtain this
favour, from you. at Least I hope to go my Self to america, at
the marquis's first journey. he is returned Loaded with every
mark of kindness, and goodness, from all the united States. his
heart is full of gratitude, and the mine partak it. I should be
delighted to be a Witness of all this favours, but one of my
greatest pleasure, would be to present to General Washington
the hommage of the gratitude, and all the sentimens of the

great affection and regard with which I have the honour, to be sir your most humble and very most obedient servant

noailles de la fayette

Should I dare, beg you to pay my respects to your mother, I will certainly receive, an additional pleasure, in america, to present my self in person my respectful hommage.

ALS, NIC.
   1. GW's letter is dated 25 Nov. 1784.
   2. For further references to these gifts, see Lafayette to GW, 16 April; Thomas Ridout to GW, 1 May; GW to Lafayette, 25 July; GW to Ridout, 20 Aug.; Ridout to GW, 31 Aug., 7 Sept., and 4 Nov. 1785. GW wrote the marquise on 10 May 1786 that only the month before had he received her letter and the packages.

From Lafayette

St Germain Near Paris

My dear General   April the 16th 1785
   To My Great disappointement I Had no letter from You By this packet—it is However the only Regular Way to Get intelligences, and Mercantile Opportunities are not By far So much to Be depended on—I warmly Beg, my dear General, you will not let me Be Uneasy for want of a line from You—the distance is already so great in itself, and So much Greater for the feelings of the tenderest friendship, that the only means ought to Be Scrupulously observed that tend to Alleviate the Cruel Separation—Since my last letter, there is Very little News [1]—Warlike preparations Have not Been Given up—But the Negotiations are Come to this point Which leaves no probability of a War—the proposition to Exchange Baviera for the Austrian low Countries, With the title of Kingdom of Austrasia, Has not Been Accepted—a New object for disputes Might Be the Election of a King of the Romans, which you know is the title which marks the Successor to the Empire—the Emperor's interest will Be in favour of His Nephew the Young arch duke Francis of tuscany—England and ireland are negotiating with each other, and will Be puzzled to agree, unless the Volonteering flame once spent out Ceases to Support their Country—the British Governement Seems in no Hurry to make a treaty of Commerce—much less so, if possible, to give up the posts—I Have

Had a Conference With the duke de la vauguion who is gone to Madrid Respecting the Mississipy—But the Spaniards are still obstinate, and You Will Have full time to oppen Your Navigation, which I Consider as the first political, Mercantile, and National plan which Can now Employ the United States—there are Great Complaints of the Merchants Against the Arrêt du Conseil in favour of the West india trade—altho' flour and sugars are Excepted—But the Ministry will stick By it, and More Cannot Be Got for the present—Every thing in Europe More and More Convinces me of the Necessity there is for the States to give Congress power to Regulate trade.

By mr Ridout's Vessel my children Have Sent to yours at Mount Ve[r]non a few trifles which are very indifferent But may Amuse them two or three days[2]—English dogs are so much in fashion Here that the King who likes to Ride fast Has no french Hounds which, says He, are Very Slow—at last I Have discoverd a tolerable good Breed of them, which young M. Adams will take with Him in the Next packet[3]—a jack ass Has Been Sent to You from Cadix—I expect one from the isle of Maltha and will forward it.[4]

in the Course of the Summer I will Visit the prussian and Austrian troops—I will Have the pleasure to speack much of You—But Had Rather Speack with you—and instead of those German troops, I wish I could once more Give you a dinner with my light infantry friends.

Adieu, My dear General, Be So kind as to present My Most tender Respects to Mrs Washington—Mention me to the Young ones—mrs Stuard, the doctor, m. Lund W., Miss Basset if she is with you—I am Uneasy about George—My Respects wait Upon Your Respected Mother, and all the family—Remember me to our friends—mde de Lafayette Begs you and mrs Washington to accept Her most Affectionate Compliments—Adieu, My dear General, think often of your Bosom friend, your adoptive son, who loves you So tenderly, and who is with every Sentiment of Respect, Gratitude, and Affection Your devoted friend

Lafayette

The queen and Her second son are in perfect Health.

ALS, PEL.

1. Lafayette wrote on 19 March. GW's most recent letter to Lafayette is dated 15 February.

2. See Adrienne, marquise de Lafayette, to GW, 15 April.

3. John Quincy Adams resumed his studies at The Hague in 1783 but shortly became his father's secretary in Paris during the peace negotiations. John Adams had recently been appointed to the U.S. mission in London, and the son decided to return to Boston. GW asked Lafayette, when Lafayette was in America in the fall of 1784, about getting several French hounds for him (see Lafayette to GW, 13 May, and GW to Lafayette, 25 July 1785). GW noted in his diary on 24 Aug. 1785 that he had "Receiv'd Seven hounds sent me from France by the Marqs. de la Fayette, by way of New York viz. 3 dogs and four Bitches" (*Diaries*, 4:186). Thomas Ridout wrote GW on 1 May from Bordeaux that he was sending his brig back to Alexandria but that the packages Lafayette had asked him to forward had not arrived at Bordeaux.

4. In his letters to Lafayette of 25 July and 1 Sept. 1785, GW reveals that he misunderstood Lafayette's reference to jacks here and thought Lafayette was referring to the two jacks that the king of Spain was giving him through the agency of William Carmichael (see Carmichael to GW, 3 Dec. 1784, n.1). The jackass that Lafayette sent from Cadiz did not survive the voyage, and the one from Malta did not arrive until November 1786 (see James McHenry to GW, 5 Nov. 1786 [PHi: Gratz Collection]).

From Henry Lee

Dear Sir   Leesylvania [Va.] April 16th 1785
    I have Sent you by your Servant 2½ bushels of the Naked Italian Barley wch will be Enough for your ground as it branches much I never Sewed it very thick; it requires Strong Land, & never grows tall, has a thick Stem & large luxuriant heads, wch hangs near the Earth, and if Cut there is a great waste of the grain in harvesting; therefore I have it pulled up by the hand, and as it is a rear ripe grain to Prevent the birds (who are very fond of it) from distroying it I Sow it in the Neighbourhood of Oats—I have also Sent you a few of Madzays Italian Peas wch are fine for the table I think nearly equal to the Marrowfat—you will also receive 14 of the Cotton Scions wch require Low sunken ground,[1] Mrs Lee joins in best Wishes for Mrs Washington & yourself With the greatest Esteem & regard I am Dr Sir Your Most Obt hble Servt
                                        Henry Lee

ALS, DLC:GW.

1. In the spring of 1785 GW fills his diary with entries about receiving from friends plants, seed, and cuttings for the grounds at Mount Vernon or to be tried in his gardens or fields. Much of this GW either took from (or repeated in) his lengthy and elaborate "Notes & observations" on his planting operations and experiments for 1785 and 1786, both in the gardens, borders, and

lawns of the manor house and in the fields of the various farms at Mount Vernon. These notes and observations are in DLC:GW, and a transcription of the manuscript is in CD-ROM:GW. GW wrote in his Notes and Observations for 18 April 1785: "Sowed the point . . . from a dble Chesnut tree downwards with Barley had from Colo. Henry Lee—The East Side of this was sprinkled with 2 bushels of the Plaister of Paris (powdered) and harrowed in along with the Barley." On 26 April, "the Barley and Pease were perceived to be coming up, the first very generally—the latter just making their appearance"; on 7 May, "the Barley & Pease seem to have come in well"; and on 25 May, "Pease were brought to Table for the six time in the Season to day." It is not clear whether or not these were the Mazzei peas (see George Divers to Thomas Jefferson, 11 April 1814, quoted in Betts, *Jefferson's Garden Book*, 532). Marrofats were popular late peas.

From Robert Morris

Dear Sir   Philadelphia April 17th 1785.

I received in due time the Letter you were so obliging as to write me of the 1st February and am quite ashamed that I should have suffered so long a period to elapse, without acknowledging its Receipt, but this was owing to my having delivered it to some of my Friends for their Perusal who detained it longer than I expected, and have only now, returned it to me.

The Extent of inland Navigation therein pointed out is amazing indeed, and if brought to perfection cannot but be productive of the greatest advantage to the neighbouring Country, and indeed to all America. I think Alexandria must in that case, become a very flourishing City, where such an Establishment as you mention, I have no doubt would meet with very great Success, but for my own part I have no Intention at present to form other Connections in a Commercial Line than those I already hold. I shall make it a point to promote the undertaking by every means in my Power and particularly by recommending my Friends to become adventurers and shall subscribe some Shares for my Children, who, if the Plan succeeds will reap the Benefit thereof at a future day.

Be assured Sir, that I am sensible of the pure & disinterested motives which have induced you to take the trouble of giving me the very useful Information contained in your Letter—I know that none others can enter your mind, and I request you will accept my warmest acknowledgements.

Mrs Morris and the Family are well and join me in affe. Regards to Mrs Washington and yourself. With Sentiments of the most perfect Attachment I am Dear Sir Your most obedient & humble Servant

Robt Morris

P.S. I yesterday took the liberty to give Mr Pine, an Historical & portrait painter of some Eminence, a line of Introduction. He is drawing some interesting parts of our History and your Portrait is indispensably necessary to his Werks.[1]

LS, DLC:GW.
    1. Morris's letter of 15 April introducing Robert Pine is printed in part in note 1, Francis Hopkinson to GW, 19 April.

From Clement Biddle

Dear General   Philad[elphi]a April 19. 1785
    Since my last I paid Mr Claypoole your account for Advertisements for which the receipt is enclosed—he again assures me the papers have been Constantly sent & their miscarriage must be owing to the post Office.[1]
    I wrote to a Gentleman at New York to pay Mr Boudinots Account at Elizabeth Town.
    I hope the last Grass seed by Capt. McClean has come safe to hand. I could not procure any of the other Kind of seed tho' the different Collectors of seeds, here promised if any came in to let me have it—Major Storcy has not yet Opend his Office.[2] I am with the greatest respect Your Excellencys Mo: Obedt & very hume sert

Clement Biddle

Mr Claypoole could not make out the Account for the papers but will soon furnish it.

ALS, DLC:GW.
    1. See GW to Biddle, 1 Feb. 1785, nn.2–4.
    2. See GW to Biddle, 1 Feb., n.8.

From Francis Hopkinson

Dear sir   Philad[elphi]a 19th April 1785
    Encouraged by the friendly Notice with which you have upon every Occasion been pleased to honour me, I take the Liberty

of recommending to your kind Attention my Friend Mr Pine, an Artist of acknowledged Eminence, & who has given the World many pleasing & forcible Specimens of Genius. Zeal for the American Cause has brought him over from England, to secure, whilst it is yet possible, faithful Representations of some of the most interesting Events of the late War—not ideal Pictures, but real Portraits of the Persons and Places concerned— You will easily discover the Tendency of this Letter & of Mr Pine's Visit. Scenes, wherein you bore so conspicuous a Part, cannot be *faithfully* represented if you are omitted. I know you have already suffer'd much Persecution under the Painter's Pencil—& verily believe that you would rather fight a Battle, on a just Occasion, than sit for a Picture. because there is Life and Vigour in *Fortitude*, & *Patience* is but a dull Virtue. I would not insinuate that you have not much Patience, but am very sure that you have a great deal of Good-Nature—& on this we depend on the present Occasion.

It would be no Compliment to Mr Pine to say he is the most eminent Artist, in his Way, we have ever had in this Country. But his own Pencil will display his Abilities in much better Terms than my Pen, & I have no Doubt but you will find him worthy of your Notice in every Respect.[1]

Mrs Hopkinson joins me in most respectful Regards to your good Lady. With sincerest Wishes for your Health & Prosperity, I am, Dear sir, Your ever affectionate friend & faithful humble servant

Fras Hopkinson

ALS, NN: Emmet Papers.

1. Before the artist Robert Edge Pine arrived at Mount Vernon on 28 April with letters from Hopkinson and other prominent Philadelphians, GW heard from England about him and his intended visit to America (see George William Fairfax to GW, 10 June and 23 Aug. 1784). The letters of introduction varied only slightly in content. In his letter of 14 April, John Dickinson wrote: "Mr Pine has been engaged for several Months in painting one of the most distinguished scenes in the late Revolution. . . . His attachment [to] the American Cause, his Merit in his Profession, and his good Behaviour here, have acquired him . . . a general Esteem in this Place" (PCarlD). Robert Morris, writing on 15 April, called Pine "an Eminent Historical & Portrait Painter, who has come over from England for the purpose of perpetuating in his way some of the most Striking Scenes of the late Revolution." Morris assured GW that his own "Portrait will be the Capital Figure in most of these pieces" and informed him that "Mr Pine is also ambitious of taking the likeness of Mrs Washington" (DLC:GW). Charles Thomson wrote of Pine on 22 April: "Early

in our late contest he gave a display of his genius as well as of his attachment to our cause by a piece which he designed, executed & published under the title of 'An Appeal to Heaven.' Animated with a desire to give further proofs of his abilities he determined to select, for his subjects, some interesting scenes in our late revolution, & with this view is come to America that he may gain a personal knowledge of the principal actors" (DLC:GW). Thomas McKean wrote on 23 April that Pine "is by profession a History and Portrait Painter," whose "visit to Mount Vernon is with the sole view of . . . taking an original likeness, which he intends to copy into some of his pieces, particularly one, which he calls the Resignation" (MA). And Thomas Mifflin, in a perfunctory letter dated 24 April, indicated that Pine was going to Mount Vernon "to obtain the best Information respecting the most important Occurrences of the War" (DLC:GW). The complete texts of all these letters appear in CD-ROM:GW. During his visit to Mount Vernon from 28 April to 19 May, Pine painted not only GW's and Martha's portraits but also portraits of the four Custis grandchildren as well as one of Martha's niece Fanny Bassett (see GW to Hopkinson, 16 May).

To Mathew Carey

Sir, Mount Vernon Aprl 20th 1785.

I have received your letter of the 30th Ulto[1]—If it should ever be in my power to render you any Service, I shall be ready, & happy to do it. With the Gentlemen of my acquaintance in Philadelphia, I persuade myself you stand as well, as my introduction could place you. If there are any here, to whom the mention of your case would be of any avail, I should have pleasure in doing it.

I thank you for your kind offer of forwarding, with safety, the Gazettes of Philadelphia; but believe there will be no occasion for giving you the trouble at present. I am Sir Yr Most Obedt Servt

Go: Washington

ALS, PHi: Edward Carey Gardiner Collection; LB, DLC:GW. The letter is addressed to the "Printer of the Eveng Herald Philadelphia."

1. Letter not found. See GW to Carey, 15 Mar. 1785.

To George Clinton

Dear Sir, Mount Vernon 20th April 1785.

I promised you a letter by the last Post,[1] but it was not in my power to fulfill it, business not my own, & with which I really ought not to be troubled, engrosses so large a portion of my time (having no assistance) that that which is essential to me, is entirely neglected.

I now send you Hooe & Harrisons second Bill upon Mr Sylvanus Dickenson; altho' I hope, & expect the first will have been paid before it reaches. I also send you a statement of the payments, as they *ought* to have been made to you, & should be obliged to you for comparing them with your own receipts, & for informing me of their correspondence[2]—The money now remitted I wish to have placed to the credit of my Bond; & the balance, if any, carried to that of the accot sent me in December last—I should be glad also to have as early & long notice of the call for this last sum, as can knowingly and conveniently be given;[3] for I find it (under my present circumstances) very difficult to raise money equal to the pressure of my wants: those who owed me before the commencement of hostilities, having taken advantage of my absence & the tender laws, to discharge their debts with a shilling or six pence in the pound: & those to whom I owed money, I have now to pay in specie at the real value.

I have to thank you my dear Sir, for the duplicate Deed, & plan of our purchase in the Ochriskeney Patent; & pray you to take the trouble of doing with my moiety the same as you would do with your own at all times & in all respects.[4]

The lime trees which you were so obliging as to send me last November were unfortunate; they lay at Norfolk until the frosts were entirely over, & only came to my hands the 18th of Feby: I immediately planted, & have since been nursing them; they have yet the appearance of *feeble* life, but I have no expectation of their living. My thanks nevertheless are equally due for these—for the nutts, the corn & the pease; the last of which I sowed yesterday: if I am too late in doing it, the Spring (which has been the most unfavourable I ever knew)—& not me, is to blame; if too early, it is from ignorance & my neglect in not making the necessary enquiry for the proper season. The corn I shall begin to plant in a few days & will renew the seeds occasionally.

I will rely upon your Excely for the seeds of the Balm tree, White & Spruce Pine—I believe it is the most certain way of raising them: most of the trees evergreen, not sowed where they are to stand, or not raised in Nurseries & early transplanted, are unsuccessful; & tho' our impatience will not suffer us to adopt the practice, it is the opinion of Miller (in his Gardeners Dy)[5] who seems to understand the culture of Trees equal to any other writer I have met with, that it is the most expeditious method of rearing them. As a quantity of these seeds would be bulky in the cones, they would be equally good taken out & packed in dry sand; & is the method I would beg leave to recommend. To them I should be glad to have added some of the Hemlock—& indeed any other seeds of trees which are not common in this climate. I shall make no apology for the trouble I know this request must give you, because I persuade myself you will have pleasure in contributing to an innocent amusement. I have planted within these few days many of the hickory nuts which you sent me, not doubting their successful growth here. Mrs Washington desires me to present her compliments & thanks to you, for your care of the case of Grotto work—it came very safe—She also joins me very sincerely in congratulating Mrs Clinton & yourself on her restoration to health, & in wishing it may be of long continuance.

I am sorry for the loss of my Vines, they were of the first quality in France; & sent to me by one of the first characters in it, for abilities, respectability & his curious attention to these things. I was in hopes there had been an abundance, & that you would have participated in the fruit of them.[6]

As you are at the source of intelligence, it would be idle in me to reverberate what is brought by the packets, & we have little of a domestic nature worthy of attention. There are plans in ag itation for improving and extending the inland navigation of this country; & opening roads of communication between the heads of the rivers Potomac & James, & the western waters. They have received public countenance & support—but I cannot at this moment speak decisively to the issue—we flatter ourselves it will be favourable, but may be mistaken. Mrs Washington joins me in very best wishes for you & all your family. With regard & attachment I am Dr Sir, Yrs &c.

G: Washington

LB, DLC:GW.

1. See GW to Clinton, 5 April.

2. For the Hooe & Harrison bills on Sylvanus Dickinson, see the references in Robert Townsend Hooe to GW, 3 April, n.1. The bills were to discharge the

debt that GW incurred in 1782 when he borrowed £1,870 from Governor Clinton to purchase the Dow tract at Mount Vernon. For the details of this transaction, see the source note in Clinton to GW, 27 Feb. 1784.

3. The "accot sent me in December last," which, along with Clinton's letter of 26 Dec. 1784, is missing, relates to the joint purchase by Clinton and GW of a large tract of land in upstate New York, for which GW owed one half the cost. This transaction is described in GW to Clinton, 25 Nov. 1784, n.2. See also Clinton to GW, 5 Mar. 1785.

4. See note 3.

5. In the inventory of GW's books made after his death, there was a copy of Philip Miller's *Abridgement of the Gardener's Dictionary* (London, 1763).

6. For references to the various shipment of plants and other articles from Clinton to GW during the winter, as well as to the loss of the grapevines, see Benjamin Walker to GW, 20 Dec. 1784 and 11 Mar. 1785, and Clinton to GW, 5 Mar. 1785.

Letter not found: from La Serre, 20 April. On 12 May GW wrote La Serre: "The letter which you did me the honor to write to me the 20th of last month."

From Otho Holland Williams

Sir   Baltimore [Md.] 20th April 1785

I have not had the honor of a line, or message from you since I forwarded, to Mount Vernon, the Parchments which Major Turner sent to me from Philadelphia,[1] and I was uncertain of your intentions respecting the Diplomas 'till about ten days ago, a gentleman Mr Hamilton, ⟨⟨⟩of this town) desired me to look at two blanks to which your name was subscribed—they were Diplomas, and upon enquiry I found they had been taken from a fellow suspected of a theft—He was in prison and I used every means in my power to know how he came by them, but to no effect—He said he found them in a particular part of the Town. I went there, but to no purpose; it was the residence of Vice, and my researches were fruitless—I concluded that the packet of parchments had been sent by the Stage Waggon and [I] went to the Stage office to know if it had not been stolen from thence, but no bill or entry of it could be found there I am now in doubt about the cause of the miscarriage and think it incumbent on me to give you the trouble of this information. I am most respectfully Sir, your Most obedt & mo: Hble Servt

O.H. Williams

ADfS, PHi: Dreer Collection.

1. The original of this letter never reached GW. It was not until he got William Jackson's letter of 19 July that GW learned of the loss of the Society of Cincinnati diplomas that he had signed and sent back to Williams. The letter that GW then wrote to Williams, on 26 July, has not been found, but Williams responded on 15 Aug., giving GW further details of his investigation of the theft of the certificates. In the end, GW signed a new set of diplomas for the members of the Pennsylvania Society of the Cincinnati (see GW to Williams, 25 Sept., and William Jackson to GW, 24 Oct.).

From William Washington

Dear Sir   Sandy-Hill [S.C.] April 21st 1785

Major George Washington arriv'd at this place in January & has favor'd me with his company ever since his arrival. It wou'd give me great pleasure to inform your Excellency that our Southern Climate had accomplish'd the Object of his peregrination; but I am apprehensive that his disorder is too inflexible to be remov'd by mere Change of Climate. His agreeable Manner has much interested me in his welfare & I sincerely wish him a speedy recovery.[1] Mrs Washington joins me in best respects to yourself & Lady. I am dear Sir with much Respect & Esteem yr Obedt Servt

W. Washington

ALS, ViMtV.

1. After spending the winter at William Washington's place in South Carolina, George Augustine Washington arrived at Mount Vernon on 14 May.

From John Harvie

Sir   Richmond [Va.] April 22nd 1785

Upon my Researches into the Ordinances of Convention and Acts of Assembly to see if I could discover any General principle in either, Effective of your Title to the 2813 Acres of patented Land, that is the present Subject of your Ejectments,[1] I can find no Law or Ordinance, in my Opinion Materially applicable, except the Act of Assembly that pass'd in the year 1779, Intitled an Act for Adjusting and Settling the Title of Claimers to Unpatented Lands under the present and former Government previous to the Establishment of the Commonwealths

Land Office—in the first Section of which Act, Surveys upon all Military Rights are declar'd good and Valid, in a Subsequent clause indeed of the same Law it is provided that where Locations upon Military Warrants shall Interfere with the Rights of Settlers, in such Cases the latter shall be prefer'd, but this Rule is Specially confin'd to Locations—and cannot apply to Warrants Carry'd into Effect by actual Survey, and much less so to Patents which have been Regularly Obtain'd under our former Government; for it is well known to you Sir, that the King of Englands Instructions to his Governors in Virginia in and after the year 1763 restrain'd them from Granting or Signing patents for any Lands on the Western Waters—except upon Surveys for such Lands as was given as Bountys for Military Service, and from the date of the proclimation in 1763 untill the time of opening the Commonwealths Land Office in the year 1779 No County Surveyor could receive or admit an Entry on his Books for such Lands upon any other Right, and so farr from the Settlers on the Western Waters being Countenanced by Government they were by repeated proclimations Order'd off from those Lands—wherefore Titles by Occupancy was in no Instance whatever Recognized by the Laws of Virginia till the Convention of 1775—when Occupants were put on the footing of Freeholders as to Electing or being Elected Members of the Convention—in the years 1776 & 1777 other Resolutions pass'd still farther declaratory of their Rights and Subjecting them to the payment of Taxes for such Lands as they had Mark'd out as the Limmits of their respective claims in right of Settlement—in the year 1778 another Resolution pass'd forbidding any farther Settlement of the Western Lands untill a Land Office for the Commonwealth should be Establish'd—in the year 1779 the Commonwealths Land Office was Open'd and as a Variety of rights had taken rise upon the Western Waters from the time the Governors had refus'd to Sign patents, the Law under the Title I have first mention'd preceded the Land Law, by which all such Rights as appear'd to be just and Reasonable were Confirmed & Establish'd, & others declar'd Void & of no Effect—but where Lands had been Patented under the former Government, the Legislature most Carefully Avoided any Interference, not Conceiveing they had the Power to destroy a Title Convey'd by the Crown whose perogative it was to Grant

those Lands when & to whom the King should think proper—
and here it may not be amiss to observe that by the Laws of this
Country when a Legal Title is Vested by Patent, such Title cannot ever be call'd in Question in the Courts of Common Law,
but the party who Supposes himself Injur'd must Resort to the
Chancery Court for Relief, the previous Title Act, directs the
Appointment of Commissioners to adjust the claims to all Unpatented Lands lying on the Western Waters (patented Lands
not comeing under their Jurisdiction) which Commissioners
were also Impower'd to hear and determine all Disputes between Partys Contending, and upon a Right of Settlement
founded upon a Residence of twelve Months or raiseing a Crop
of Corn in the Country, being Establish'd, the Commissioners
were directed to Grant a Certificate of such Right to the person
Intitled—which Certificate was Sufficient authority for the Surveyor of the County where the Lands were to lay off and Survey
the Land therein Described, and upon a Survey therefor being
return'd to the Land Office, and lying Six Months open to the
Caveat of any person who should lay claim to the whole or any
part thereof—if no Caveat should be Enter'd in that time a
Grant was Ex Officio to issue to the person in whose Name the
Survey was made—such Settler was also Intitled to the preemption of 1000 Acres adjoining his Settlement upon his first paying the price that the State demanded for other Lands Sold by
them—and takeing from the Land Office a Warrant under the
Register(s) Hand and Seal for the same, which Warrant should
Intitle him to an Entry with the County Surveyor where the
Land lay—and upon a Survey being Return'd and lying in the
Office as above mention'd a Grant shall issue—As the Commis-
sioners for the District of Monongalia Yohogany and Ohio had
several meetings and Continued to sit till they went through all
Business that came before them under their Commission—putting your patent Intirely out of the Question—the Occupants
who are Contending with you could no otherways acquire
Titles to those Lands than by Submitting their Rights to the
Commissioners and Obtaining from them Certificates Agreable
to the directions of this Law, and if they could have made such
Submission, as your first Settlement and Improvement pre-
ceeded theirs your Right to 1400 Acres of the tract must have
been prefer'd—but no such Submission could have been by

them Legally made as the patent is Conclusive as to the Title—
and as your Opponents set up a Right to the Land the Law was
Open to them, for they had it in their Option to Enter a Caveat
against a patent issueing to you, till the Matter of right should
be determin'd between you, and as they fail'd to do this, I must
again observe that your Title under the Patent in a Court of
Common Law seems to me to be Unimpeachable—what I have
here Stated to you are the Laws, Rules & Regulations for Ac-
quireing Landed property upon the Western Waters in this
State, and by which I Conceive your Title must be determin'd,
as the Resolution I now Inclose you fixing a Temporary Boundary between the States of Virginia and Pensylvania—which was
Consented to and Adopted by the State of Pensylvania[,] Saves
the private property and Rights to all persons who may have
Acquir'd Titles under either Country Respectively previous to
the Asscertaining and Running such Boundary although they
should be found to fall within the Other—thus Sir have I endeavour'd to give you Information respecting the Land Rights
of Settlers or Occupants on our Western Waters and wish Sincerely that it may in any Measure Illustrate the permenancy of
your Title—the Law of 1779 that I have particularly Refer'd to,
if you have it not—may I immagine be Easily obtain'd from any
Gentleman of the Law in your Neighbourhood[.] however if
this should not be the Case, and either you, or Mr Smith who
Advocates your Title, should think it Necessary to be produced
on the Tryal, I will at any time forward it to you, I have to Lament that the Original Survey upon which your Patent issued
with a Number of other Publick papers fell into the Hands of
the Enemy and were destroy'd by them, wherefore the date of
Capt. Poseys Warrant assign'd to you cannot be asscertain'd in
the Land Office—if any farther Enquiry dureing the prosecution of this Business should Occur to you, I beg that you will at
all times Command my Attention to it without Reserve—for believe me Sir that it will ever afford me the highest Gratification
to be in any Respect whatever Useful or Convenient to you. I
have the Honour to be Sir Yr Most Obt & Very Humble Servt

John Harvie

ALS, NhD; copy, in George Augustine Washington's hand, DLC:GW.

1. For GW's ejectment suit against the squatters on his Millers Run (or
Chartiers Creek) land, see the editorial note in Thomas Smith to GW, 9 Feb.
1785.

From Charles Thomson

Dear Sir,   Philadelphia 22 April 1785

I received yesterday your letter of the 5. And as the subject therein referred to belongs to the department of foreign affairs, I have transmitted it to Mr Jay.

I have no doubt but the Minister who is to negotiate with the court of London will have occasion for the list; but as it would not be safe to trust a paper of such importance to the common conveyance by the post, and as it is proper that you should keep either the original or a copy to prevent a chasm in your files, I have taken the liberty of suggesting to Mr Jay the propriety of sending one of his clerks to take a copy & to bring up either it or the Original leaving the other with you.[1]

The last time I had the pleasure of seeing you I entertained, & I believe expressed a fond hope that measures would speedily be adopted to enable you, without much trouble & without putting you to any expence, to have your files arranged, copied & secured so as to be preserved from danger or accident. I consider them as invaluable documents from which future historians will derive light & knowledge. I consider it as a most fortunate circumstance that through all your dangers and difficulties you have happily preserved them entire. And although the adjournment which took place last Summer and the subsequent removals since the meeting in November have prevented Congress from adopting the measures I wished, yet I trust they will at a convenient time attend to the Subject, and take proper Steps for preserving so valuable a treasure.[2]

I am now busily employed in preparations for the removal of my family to New york. If there be any thing in which I can serve you I hope you will command me. Mrs Thomson joins in respects to Mrs Washington. with the most sincere Esteem I am Dear Sir Your affectionate Friend & humble Servt

Chas Thomson

ALS, DLC:GW.

1. On 25 Aug. 1785, John Jay wrote GW that he was sending his clerk to copy the lists of the slaves that embarked from New York in 1783 during the British evacuation of the city. Jay enclosed both an extract of the letter from Thomson, dated 22 April, suggesting he do this and a copy of the letter Jay wrote to the president of Congress on 27 April agreeing to Thomson's suggestions. For Jacob Read's request that GW send his lists of evacuated slaves to Congress, see Read to GW, 9 Mar. 1785, and notes 1 and 2 of that document.

2. For the steps that GW took to preserve his Revolutionary War papers, see GW to Richard Varick, 1 Jan. 1784, and notes.

From John Baylor

Dr Sir   Newmarket [Va.] Ap⟨ril the⟩ 25 1785—
    I am just returned from Richmond, where by appointment, I was to have met Mr Dandridge and to have fixed upon some Mode of settling the Debt due from my Father's Estate to Mr Custis's, as his Death prevents that settlement and the only Administrator[1]—as I am informed. I should now bee happy to have an interview with you, I should have waited upon you, but by your Advertisment, I find you are to be in Richmond in a few Days, therefore hope if not inconvenient, that I may either have the pleasure of your Company here or meet you at the Bowling Green the Day that you will be there[2]—This sum is to be raised by my Brother George's Estate,[3] I have given a replevy Bond for upward of thirty three hundred Pounds, and if the affair is rigorously enforced, it would greatly prejudice my Brother's Estate, he has directed by his Will that as much of his Land shall be sold as will pay his proportions of my Father's and his own Debts, I would also give up as many Negroes at present as would prevent Mr Custis's Estate from falling into any disagreeable Situation—Mr Dandridge in a late letter did observe that if I could raise about one fourth Part of the Sum this Month, that he could wait for the Ballance[4] I very much wish to see you—I have the Honor to be Dr Sir Yr
                                                        John Baylor

ALS, DLC:GW.
    John Baylor (1750–1808) of Newmarket, Caroline County, was the eldest son of John Baylor (1705–1772), from whom he inherited Newmarket.
    1. Bartholomew Dandridge was the sole administrator of the estate of his nephew, John Parke Custis, who died in 1781. Dandridge had died earlier this month, and so Baylor was turning to GW, as Custis's stepfather, to deal with the Baylor family's indebtedness to the Custis estate.
    2. For GW's "Advertisement" regarding the meeting of the Dismal Swamp Company on 2 May, see GW to Bushrod Washington, 3 April, n.3. GW spent the night of 30 April at Baylor's Newmarket en route to Richmond to attend the meeting. Bowling Green was an ordinary in Caroline County at the present site of the town by that name.
    3. John Baylor's younger brother George Baylor, GW's aide-de-camp during the Revolutionary War, had died in November 1784 in Barbados.

4. When the Daniel Parke Custis estate was settled in 1761, Martha Parke Custis received as a part of her share of her father's estate Bernard Moore's bond of £1,400 sterling. See doc. III-B, in Settlement of the Daniel Parke Custis Estate, 20 April 1759–5 Nov. 1761, printed in *Papers, Colonial Series*, 6:252–61. In June 1778 GW formally turned over to John Parke Custis half of his sister's estate. In Ledger B, 216, GW noted in one instance that Custis had received £1338.11 sterling, "Bernard Moore's & John Baylors Bonds allotted him." He also noted that Custis was entitled to £2,360.0.2, "Bernard Moore's & John Baylor's Bonds the Moiety of the Ballance due to his Sister Miss Custis at her Death as ⟨was⟩ Settled by the General Court." In 1786 a judgment was rendered against the John Baylor estate for £6,771.17.4 in favor of John Parke Custis's heirs, and on 28 Nov. 1786 GW secured an order of the Caroline County court for the sheriff to sell thirteen of the slaves belonging to the estate of George Baylor for partial payment of one half of the £6,771.17.4 that was owed to the Custis heirs by the estate of the elder Baylor, who had acted as security for his friend Bernard Moore (see Moore to GW, 11 May 1772).

To William Grayson

Dr Sir,   Mt Vernon 25th Apl 1785.

I will not let your favor of the fifteenth, for which I thank you, go unacknowledged, tho' it is not in my power to give it the consideration I wish, to comply with the request you have made; being upon the eve of a journey to Richmond to a meeting of the Dismal Swamp company, which by my own appointment is to take place on monday next; & into that part of the country I am hurried by an express which is just arrived with the accot of the deaths of the mother & Brother of Mrs Washington—in the last of whose hands (Mr B. Dandridge) the embarrassed affairs of Mr Custis had been placed, & call for immediate attention.[1]

To be candid, I have had scarce time to give the report of the Committee, which you did me the honor to send me, a reading—much less to consider the force & tendency of it. If experience has proven that the most advantageous way of disposing of Land, is by whole Townships, there is no arguing against facts; therefore, if I *had* had time I shou'd have said nothing on that head: but from the cursory reading I have given it, it strikes me that by suffering each State to dispose of a proportionate part of the whole in the State, that there may be State jobbing: in other words, that the Citizens of each State may be favored at the expence of the Union; whilst a reference of these matters to them has, in my opinion, a tendency to set up seperate interests; and to promote the independence of individual States upon the downfall of the fœderal government, which in my opinion is already too feeble, much too humiliated & tottering to be supported without props.

It is scarcely to be imagined that any man, or society of men, who may incline to possess a township, would make the purchase without viewing the Land in person or by an agent—wherein then lies the great advantage of having the sale in each State, & by State officers? for from the same parity of reasoning, there should be different places in each State for the accommodation of its citizens. Would not all the ostensible purposes be fully answered by sufficient promulgation in each State, of the time & place of Sale to be holden at the nearest convenient place to the Land, or at the seat of Congress. Is it not highly probable that those who may incline to emigrate, or their Agents would attend at such time & place? and (there being no fixed prices to the Land) would not the high or low sale of it depend upon the number of purchasers & the competition occasioned thereby; & are not these more likely to be greater at one time & place than at thirteen? One place might draw the world to it, if proper notice be given: but foreigners would scarcely know what to do with thirteen—to which, or when to go to them. These are first thoughts—perhaps incongruous ones, & such as I myself might reprobate upon more mature consideration: at present however, I am impressed with them—and (under the rose) a penetrating eye, & close observation, will discover thro' various disguises a disinclination to add new States, to the confederation, westward of us; which must be the inevitable consequence of emigration to, & the population of that territory: and as to restraining the citizens of the Atlantic States from transplanting themselves to that soil, when prompted thereto by interest or inclination—you might as well attempt (while our Governmts are free) to prevent the reflux of the tide, when you had got it into your rivers.

As the report of the Committee goes into minutiæ, it is not minute enough, if I read it aright; it provides for the irregular lines, and parts of townships, occasioned by the interference with the Indian boundaries, but not for its interference with

Lake Erie, the western boundary of Pennsylvania (if it is governed by the meanders of the Delaware) or the ohio river which separates the ceded Lands from Virginia—all of which involve the same consequences.[2]

I thank you for the sentiments & information, given me in your letter of the 10th of March, respecting the Potomac navigation. My present determination is, to hold the shares which this State has been pleased to present me, in trust for the use & benefit of it: this will subserve the plan—encrease the public revenue, & not interfere with that line of conduct I had prescribed myself. I am &c. &c.

G: Washington

LB, DLC:GW.

1. News was received on 24 April of the death of Frances Jones Dandridge and of her son Bartholomew Dandridge. GW did not leave for Richmond until 29 April, and Martha Washington did not accompany him.

2. On 15 April Grayson sent GW a printed copy of his committee's proposed Land Ordinance of 1785 and wrote him at length about its passage.

From Nathanael Greene

Dear Sir   Charleston [S.C.] April 25th 1785

Some little time ago Capt. Gunn formerly an officer in the horse sent me a challenge to fight him upon the footing of equality as Citizens.[1] His reasons for it are he says I injured him in a tryal while I was in command in this Country. He sold a public horse and was called to account for it. To avoid breaking him I refered the matter to a board of Officers in preference to a Court Martial. I was at the time charitably disposd to think he had done the thing partly through ignorance. His pretence was that the public owed him a horse and that he thought he had a right to sell their property to pay himself. Such a precedent in our service would have given a fatal stab to the very existence of the Army—for soldiers might with the same propriety sell their Arms as Officers their horses. But to my very great surprise the Board of Officers reported that Captain Gunn had a right to sell a public horse. I disapproved of the opinion of the board in General Orders and refered the matter to Congress. They also condemned the proceedings of the board, confirmed my sentiments on the subject, and pointedly censured Capt. Gunn and directed him to return the horse.[2] Capt. Gunn thought himself injured because I did not confirm the opinion of the board of officers and urged it very indecently both by letter and language for which I gave him a reprimand. It is for this he says he thinks himself entitled to satisfaction affecting to discriminate what was in the line of my duty as an officer and what was other wise. I refused to give him any satisfaction having done nothing more than my public duty imposed upon me in support of the dicipline of the Army. If a commanding Officer is bound to give satisfaction to every Officer who may pretend he is injured and the pretence would not be wanting to try to wipe off the disgrace of a public tryal and condemnation, it places him in a much more disagreeable situation than ever had occured to me before. But as I may have mistaken the line of responsibility of a commanding officer I wish for your sentiments on the subject. It is possible you may be placed by the ignorance of sum or the impudence of others in the same predicament tho I believe few will be hardy enough to try such an experiment. If I thought my honor or reputation might suffer in the opinion of the World and more especially with the Military Gentlemen I value life too little to hesitate a moment to answer the challenge. But when I consider the nature of the precedent and the extent of the mischief that it may produce I have felt a necessity to reject it. Thus far I have offered nothing but my public reasons; but the man is without reputation or principle. Indeed he is little better than a public nuisance being always engaged in riots and drunken fl⟨aunts⟩. I do not wish these circumstances to have any influence upon your Opinion. Because if they were the only objections I would fight him immediately.

I am still embarassed with Banks affairs and God knows when I shall be other wise.[3] Present me affectionately to Mrs Washington and the family. I am dear Sir with esteem & affection Your Most Obed. humble Sert

Nathl Green

ALS, DLC:GW.

1. In the Revolution, James Gunn (1753–1801) was a captain of the dragoons in the Virginia line. Settling in Savannah after the war, he entered politics and became one of the two men first elected to the United States Senate from Georgia. He is best known for the part he played in the notorious Yazoo fraud of 1795.

2. See Greene to the Court-martial Board of James Gunn, 1782; Proceedings of the Court-martial Board, 3 June 1782; Greene to Benjamin Lincoln, 22 June 1782; and the Report of the Secretary at War re Sale of Public Horses, 20 Aug. 1782, all DNA:PCC, item 149.

3. For Greene's financial difficulties, which related in large part to his wartime dealings with John Banks & Co., see Report on the Petition of Catharine Greene, 26 Dec. 1791, in Syrett, *Hamilton Papers*, 10:406–68. See also Greene to GW, 29 Aug. 1784, n.2.

From John Murray & Co.

Sir   Alexandria [Va.] April 25th 1785

Agreable to your request have sent you twelve yard of the Calicoe you pick'd out when up here, being the Amot of the money sent by your Servant.

The enclosed was left with us by a person from N. England. Very respectfully and Yr Excellency Most obedt Servts

John Murray & Co.

L, DLC:GW.

John Murray's store in Alexandria at this time was near the courthouse on Fairfax Street. On Thursday, 21 April, GW "Called at Alexandria & staid an hour or Two" (*Diaries*, 4:124).

From Charles-Louis de Montesquieu

General,   Paris 25th April—1785

I recieved at Paris, the letter Your Excellency did me the honor of addressing to me, in behalf of Mr Ridout[1]—I regret much, I was not at Bourdeaux, at the time he arrived there— But, if he passes any time there, I shall still have the pleasure of seeing him; and making him acquainted with my friends—I have written to my Father, to make amends for my absence from Boudeaux, by being as useful as possible to Mr Ridout— But I have to lament, from his great age, and unhappy loss of sight, he cannot be so serviceable to him, as I would wish him to be; and, as he will himself wish to be, on the reciept of my letter[2]—Your Excellency's remembrance of me, flatters me much—I shall never forget the kindnesses with which I have been loaded by you. It will ever be a new source of pleasure to me, to call to mind, the time I have spent, near the greatest, and, most virtuous man of his *Age*.[3] I beg you will not consider this as flattery—it is the real sentiment of my heart; and, I have not renounced the hope of again seeing America, and admiring the Author of her liberties.

I shall depart for Metz, about May, to my Regiment; where, I shall often with my Officers, drink to your Excellency's health— All who have been under your orders in America, would get drunk with pleasure to this toast. We all love, and respect you— Such is the effect of Virtue. She maintains her empire over all men, notwithstanding their profligacy, and corruption.

It will not be in my power to be at Bourdeaux, 'till October; when I shall have the pleasure of conversing with Mr Ridout about you—But, I percieve, my letter is already too long; and that I ought not to trespass so much, even on your leasure.[4] I beseech you to be persuaded of the respect, and unalterable attachment, with which, I am General, Your very Humble & Ob[edie]nt servant

Montesquieu.

Translation, in David Stuart's hand, DLC:GW; translation, DLC:GW; ALS, DLC:GW. A transcription of the French ALS is in CD-ROM:GW. The second translation is in the same hand as the translation of the letter of 2 May from Montesquieu père, both probably made in France.

1. The text of the letter that GW wrote from Annapolis on 23 Dec. 1784 to Montesquieu on behalf of Thomas Ridout is: "It has been requested of me, to introduce Mr Ridout who will present this letter to you, to your acquaintance, & to those civilities which I know you are happy whenever it is in your power, to bestow on any Gentlemen.

"Mr Ridout is a stranger to me, but is said to be a Merchant of good character. He is about to embark for France & has some thoughts I am informed of settling at Bourdeaux, which makes him desirous of the honor of being known to you, & will be my best apology for this liberty" (LB, DLC:GW). Thomas Ridout (1754–1829), formerly of Annapolis, was at this time a commission merchant in Bordeaux. For several years he regularly sent his brig to Alexandria. See his letter to GW, 1 May.

2. Montesquieu wrote to Ridout at Bordeaux on this day and presumably also to his own father at Rouen. See Ridout to GW, 1 May, and the letter of 2 May to GW from Montesquieu's father.

3. Montesquieu, who served as Chastellux's aide in America, wrote here: "je me rappelerai toujours avec un nouveau plaisir le tems que jai passé aupres de l'homme plus grand, et le plus vertueux de Son Siecle."

4. GW's letter-book copy of his acknowledgment of Montesquieu's letter, dated 20 Aug. 1785 from Mount Vernon, reads: "The receiving a letter from you is pleasing—the expression of it is flattering; & for the valuable testi-

mony of your recollection of me, I pray you to accept my warmest acknowledgements.

"The bare intimation of your once more making a visit to the Land, to the
liberties of which your sword has contributed, is flattering, & should you realize it, I hope you will consider my seat as your head quarters whilst you remain in the United States. I can assure you, you would no where meet with a
more cordial reception, or give more pleasure, as I have ever had a high esteem & regard for you: but whether in this tour, or any other to which
you may be called by duty or inclination—my warmest wishes shall always attend you."

From Samuel Powel

Dear Sir   Philadelphia 25 April 1785
    Tho' I am apprehensive that you may be fatigued with
Letters of Recommendation, yet I cannot suffer the Bearer
hereof, Dr Moyes, to leave this City on his intended Tour to the
southern States, without requesting Permission to introduce
him to your Notice. To General Greene I am indebted for an
Introduction to this Gentleman, & hold myself his Debtor for
remembering me on the Drs Subject, from whose interesting
Conversation I have derived both Amusement & Instruction.
His Lectures, on the Philosophy of chemistry & natural History,
in this City, have been much frequented & greatly approved; &
he is, I believe, universally esteemed to be both a rational &
agreeable Companion, by those who have had the Opportunities of knowing him best.[1]
    Mrs Powel begs Leave to join her best Wishes, for Mrs Wash-
ington & yourself, to those of Dear Sir Your most obedt humble
Servt

                                                Samuel Powel

ALS, DLC:GW.

1. On 20 Mar. 1785 Francis Hopkinson wrote Thomas Jefferson in Paris
about having recently had at his house in Philadelphia "Dr. Moyse the blind
philosopher." He went on to say: "I have mentioned Dr. Moyse. I will now tell
you who he is. He is a Scotchman by Birth and a Philosopher by Profession.
He came to America from England with the famous Mrs. Haley. He arrived I
believe about a Year ago at Boston and has come from thence to this City,
giving public Lectures in Natural philosophy all the way. He spent the beginning of this Winter at New York, where he became very popular and a great
favourite of the Ladies in particular who crowded to his Lectures, and happy
was she who [could] get him to dine or drink Tea at her House. Having gone

thro' his Course there and reaped no small Honour and Profit, he is now performing with us. But the Rage for philosophy at New York, is not to be compared with that of Philadelphia. He exhibits three Evenings in a Week in the College Hall, he has already given 10 or a Dozen Lectures to an Audience of not less than 10 and most commonly 1200 Persons. The Ladies are ready to break their Necks after him. They throng to the Hall at 5 o'Clock for places, altho' his Lecture does not begin till 7. He has been blind from his Infancy, has made Philosophy his Study and is well acquainted with the present admitted Systems, adding sometimes Theories of his own, which he does however, with rather too much Arrogance" (Boyd, *Jefferson Papers*, 8:50–52). Nancy Shippen in Philadelphia wrote in her diary on 9 March: "Heard Dr Moyse again this Eveng upon trade winds & he gave us an account of the formation of the earth" (*Nancy Shippen Journal*, 228). For further reference to Henry Moyes (Moyse) and his lectures, see Powel to GW, 24 June. The heat of the weather forced Dr. Moyes to beat a retreat before he reached Mount Vernon (Powel to GW, 5 July).

From Lyonel Bradstreet

Ship Potowmack Apl 26 1785

It is with Pleasure that I now forward your Excellency a Case which was delivered to my Care in London, & for which I paid 16/ Sterlg for Custom House Charges &C. it being foreign, I hope it will be delivered to you in Safety. I am with the utmost Respect Your Excellencys Mo: Obt Servt

Lyonel Bradstreet.

ALS, DLC:GW.

Letter not found: from Thomas Newton, 27 April. GW wrote Newton on 3 Sept.: "I have suffered your letter of the 27th April . . . to remain . . . unacknowledged."

From Henry Hollyday

Maryland, Talbot County,

Sir,   30th of April 17[8]5.

At the instance of my Neice Miss Harriot Rebecca Anderson, the youngest Daughter, and, now, only surviving Child of Mr William Anderson Merchant of London, deceas'd, I am induced to make this application to You, as one of the Executors of the late Colo. Thomas Colvill of Virginia, for payment to her of a Legacy devised her by that Gentleman.[1]

This Lady, who came into Maryland, from London, in October, 1775, & for several years past has been one of my family, is possess'd of a Letter on this subject dated Mount Vernon Septr 10th 1773, from You, Sir, to her brother Edward Anderson, who had from her Guardian a power of Attorney to receive this Legacy; but, as He died in the course of the following Spring, I conclude You never heard anything farther from him.[2] She is also in possession of a Letter from Mr John West junr, another of the Colonel's Executors, dated Alexandria Feb. 7th 1776, to her Uncle James Hollyday, of Queen Ann's County; in which Mr West, among other things, says: "The late Colo. Thos Colvill died Octer 10th 1766, he made his will a few days before, and among other Legacies left Sixty or Eighty Pounds Sterling (Eighty I believe) to the youngest Daughter of Capt Wm Anderson in London."—"The Money lies ready in London at any time, and we may expect the Genl* will return soon when this Affair shall be settled. I hope the young Lady will not be much injur'd by a few Month's delay."

Thus, Sir, has this matter rested till now, from a conviction of the impropriety of any measure which might have a tendency to divert your attention, from the great & important Affairs of the War, to the private concerns of an Individual.

I relie on the favor of Colo. Tench Tilghman to transmit this Letter under his own cover, & to inform you that the Lady in question, who is personally known to him, was received, and, ever since her arrival in this Country, has been acknowledged & treated, by her numerous Connexions & friends in these parts, as the person above described.

You will be pleas'd, Sir, to oblige me with an Answer through the hands of that Gentleman, and, if farther proof of Identity should be judged necessary, to point out the mode. I have the honour to be, Sir, Yr most obedt Servt

Henry Hollyday

*Mr West had previously observed that General Washington was then absent on public affairs.

ALS, DLC:GW. Hollyday mistakenly dated the letter 1775.

Henry Hollyday (Holliday; c.1725–1789), of Ratcliffe Manor, Talbot County, Md., was subjected to a treble tax during the Revolution for refusing to take the oath of fidelity to the new government and was, for a time, in desperate financial straits. Tench Tilghman forwarded this letter with a covering one of his own, dated 14 May.

1. Edward Anderson wrote GW from Annapolis on 13 Aug. 1773 that Rebecca Anderson had sent him her power of attorney to collect for her ward, Harriott Rebecca Anderson, the £80 sterling left to her by Thomas Colvill. For some of the difficulties GW encountered as an executor of Thomas Colvill's estate, see GW to John West, Jr., December 1767, and notes.

2. Tench Tilghman in his letter of 14 May confirmed what Hollyday wrote about Harriet Anderson, who, by the "imprudence of a Brother," had been reduced "from affluence to intire dependance." GW wrote Tilghman on 23 May, referring him to John West's executor, his brother the Rev. William West (c.1736–1791), in Baltimore, for information about Miss Anderson's legacy; but Tilghman reported that West had no papers relating to the Colvill estate. After Tench Tilghman's death in March 1786, his father James Tilghman wrote GW about Miss Anderson and her legacy. GW responded that he still could not give "any satisfaction regarding the affairs of Colo. Thos Colville's Estate; & of what can be done with the claim of Miss Anderson" (James Tilghman to GW, 7 July 1786, GW to James Tilghman, 20 July 1786; see also Thomas West to GW, 27 June 1786). For GW's summary of how things stood with the Colvill matter one and a half years later, see GW to John Rumney, 24 Jan. 1788.

From Thomas Ridout

Sir—   Bordeaux [France] 1 May 1785.

By return of my Brig to Alexandria I have taken the liberty of sending you a few Cases of wine &c. as ℔ the invoice inclosed, to the address of Colo. Fitzgerald. It will give me great pleasure if I hear of their being agreable to you.[1]

Some days ago I had the honor to recive a letter from the Marquis de la Fayette—dated at Paris the 8th of April in which he mentions to have sent a few packages for your Excellency to my Care, I have not been so fortunate as to receive any, of which I have informed the Marquis, but hav'nt heard from him since.[2]

I yesterday received a letter from the Baron de Montesquieu—Dated 25 April at Paris Covering the letter herewith inclosed—he has ordered to be shipped on board my Brig four Cases of white wine & a Case of Nuts as ℔ the Bill of Lading inclosed—& which I hope will be delivered in good order.

I cannot Sir Express how sensible I am for your obliging introduction of me to the Baron de Montesquieu,[3] he tells me he shall visit Bordeaux in October next when I shall enjoy in a more particular manner the favor you have conferred on me. I have the Honor to be with the greatest respect—Your Excellency's most Obedt & very Humble servant

Thos Ridout

ALS, DLC:GW.
1. These articles arrived "in good order." See GW to Ridout, 20 August.
2. See Adrienne, marquise de Lafayette, to GW, 15 April, n.2.
3. See Montesquieu to GW, 25 April, n.1.

From William Fitzhugh

Dear General   Maryland. Millmont May 2 1785

My delay to Address you on the the subject of Mr Bolton, & his to wait on you before the 25 ulto as you desir'd—Have proceeded from his being absent on an Excursion to Baltimore when I return'd from Virga—I have seen Him to day, and He promises to wait on you about the 20th of this Month the time I supposed you wou'd be return'd from Richmond—He will then carry a List of Materials which I have Imported from England, for a Larger Building than I now intend to Execute—such as Crown Glass 10 Inches by 12—white lead—Oil—paint, Nails, Sprigs Brads Hinges Gross window Lead—Line and pullies with Brass Boxes—Particularly Large Brass Spring Hinges which may suit your doors & I shall not want—such of these Articles as are wanting You may have at cost & charges.[1]

Bolton I believe is one of the first trademen in America[2] & particularly calculated for the work you want Executed—He has since my return from Virga lost His wife, so that he has now no Family Except a Negro Lad an apprentice.

Mrs Fitzhugh Joins in respectful Complts to you your Lady & Family. I have the Honor to be with Perfect Esteem & respect Dear General Your affect. & oblig'd Hle Sevt

Willm Fitzhugh

ALS, DLC:GW.
1. GW's old friend Col. William Fitzhugh visited Mount Vernon on 7 and 8 April. GW returned from his meeting of the Dismal Swamp Company on 6 May, and Richard Boulton, the skilled builder from Charles County, Md., came to Mount Vernon on 20 May. Boulton signed an agreement to complete the unfinished "New Room" at Mount Vernon, but GW was soon to learn that Boulton could not be persuaded to return to Mount Vernon and do the work that he had agreed to do. See Fitzhugh to GW, 13 May, 4, 16 July, GW to

Fitzhugh, 21 May, 14 July, Richard Boulton to GW, 4 June, and GW to Boulton, 24 June.

2. A tradesman is an artist or craftsman.

From Jean-Baptiste de Montesquieu

Bordeaux [France] 2d May 1785

My Son has Order'd me to Send to your Excellency One Hundered & Twenty Bottles of White Wine, made at Bordeaux.[1] he Told me that during his Stay in America, He never had Seen So good a Sort of Nutts, as those in France, I have Sent at all events Some Nutts of a very fine Sort, although the Season for Sowing them is over. There will be possibly Some one that will Spring up & will Produce a Tree, Provided there be Some Care taken of it, as Soon as Your Excellency will receive them, you must make them be Steep'd in Water, for the Space of Two or Three Days. Directly Sow them in Good Earth Mouldered, or Sifted, Water them very often, & keep them from the Excessive Burning heat of the Sun.[2] I am very happy of this opportunity to Offer my Respect, the most Profound, to the Hero of the World, who has Reunited, all the Virtues of Ancient Rome, with all the Politeness of the Grand World.

Translation, DLC:GW; ALS, DLC:GW.

Jean-Baptiste de Secondat de Montesquieu was the only son of Charles-Louis de Secondat, baron de La Brède et de Montesquieu, the famed author of *L'Esprit des Lois*, and the father of Charles-Louis de Secondat de Montesquieu (1749–1824), Chastellux's aide-de-camp in America during the American Revolution.

1. See the letter from Montesquieu fils to GW, 25 April; see also Thomas Ridout to GW, 1 May.

2. GW thanked Montesquieu père for the letter, wine, and walnuts on 20 August.

Resolutions of the Dismal Swamp Company

[Richmond, 2 May 1785]

That the money, which can at present be raised, be put into the hands of some proper person, and such person be empowered to engage as many German, or other labourers at Baltimore, or any other part of this continent, as the money will procure.[1]

That, if this scheme should prove wholly or in part abortive, the managers hire as many negroes as they may think proper, untill they can import from Holland, Germany, or some other Country of Europe, any number (not exceeding 300) labourers, acquainted with draining, and other branches of agriculture, which they are hereby required to do.

To carry the last resolutions into execution, Resolved that Mr Wm Anderson be, and ⟨he⟩ is hereby empowered to borrow ⟨the sum of⟩ £5,000. sterlg for ⟨a term not less than seven years at an interest not exceeding five pr Ct to be paid annually⟩ [for] the use of the company, and that the managers ⟨or any three of them⟩ be and are hereby authorized to execute a bond ⟨or bonds⟩ to secure the repayment of the ⟨principal & interest of the Sum so borrowed⟩ and the members ⟨of the sd Co. do hereby jointly⟩ and severally bind themselves, their heirs, executors &c. to indemnify the managers therein, in proportion to their respective interests.[2]

Dft (photocopy), DLC:GW. The first page (or pages) of the document is missing. See note 1. The words appearing here in angle brackets were inserted by GW; the draft itself is in someone else's hand. GW dockets the document: "Resolutions of the Dismal Swamp Company 1st May 1785." There is another copy of the resolution empowering William Anderson to borrow £5,000 in NcD: Dismal Swamp Land Company Papers; without GW's emendations, it is headed: "At a meeting of the dismal-swamp company at Richmond in Virginia this 2d May 1785."

1. In his letter to John de Neufville, 8 Sept. 1785, GW indicates what the laborers were to do, which undoubtedly was stated in the missing portion of this document. GW wrote de Neufville: "in May last the members [of the Dismal Swamp Company] (for the first time since the war) had a meeting, & resolved to prosecute the work with vigour: for this purpose they are inclined to borrow money on interest; & to import, if they can do it upon advantageous terms, a number of Hollanders, or Germans, as being best acquainted with the nature of the work; which is to drain & bank level, low & wet Land, which would from its situation, & the quality of its soil, be invaluable if accomplished."

2. There is a memorandum in GW's hand which is labeled by him: "List of Shares in the Great Dismal Swamp, 1st May 1785" (ViAlM). He lists a total of 10½ shares: GW, 1; Thomas Nelson, 1; Fielding Lewis (deceased), 1; Robert Tucker (deceased), 1; Francis Farley (deceased), 1; David and —— Mead, 1; Anthony Bacon, 1; Thomas Walker and Thomas Hornsby, 1; Nathaniel and William Nelson, 1; William Anderson and David Jameson, 1; and John Page, ½.

From Richard Henry Lee

Dear Sir,   New York May 3d 1785

I have long had a letter prepared for you in answer to your last favor which I have kept for the honorable Mr Sitgreaves to be the bearer of, as he proposed to visit you on his return to North Carolina;[1] and the more especially as his stay has been occasioned by the necessity of seeing the very important ordinance passed for selling the western lands, which I wished you to have in its perfected state[2]—The principal design of this letter is, to introduce to you Mr Graham, and his Lady the justly celebrated Mrs Macauley Graham, whose reputation in the learned world and among the friends to the rights of human nature is very high indeed. Her merit as an Historian is very great, and places her as an Author in the foremost rank of writers. I am well pleased to find that she, as well as all other judicious foreigners, think themselves when in America, however distant from Mount Vernon, obliged to pay their respects to you. I believe that this has been her only motive for going so far South as Virginia.[3] We are amused here with an account that does not indeed come officially to us, but however, in such a way as to merit attention—It is, a plan of the Emperor of Germany, which seems calculated to quiet his quarrel with Holland, altho perhaps it may not prevent a war in Europe—He is said to have made a treaty with the Elector of Bavaria, by which he exchanges his Netherland dominions for those of Bavaria, and transfers with the exchange, all his rights and claims upon Holland: reserving Namure and Luxembourg with a district of country around, as a douceur to France for obtaining the consent of that Court to the exchange. The Bavarian dominions being much more contiguous to the Austrian than those of the Netherlands, must greatly increase the Emperors power by a concentration of his force, heretofore so much divided, as to render the Netherlands of no great aid in case of war. This however, by increasing the Austrian power, must of course excite greatly the jealousy of Prussia in particular, whose King will probably risk a war rather than see his rival thus strengthened. Holland in the mean time will be relieved, by injurious claims being transferd from a strong to a weak hand, and the Emperor may find himself brought to a more equal contest by combating one, instead of three powers lately combined against him. What may be the issue of this new System, time must develope. I wish that I may be enabled by Mr Sitgreaves to furnish you with the final sense of Congress upon the momentous business of selling the western lands, in doing which, the first and greatest object seems to be, the discharging effectually the great weight of debt that the war has created, and which obstructs so effectually every arrangement for future security. I have the honor to be, with sentiments of the sincerest respect and esteem dear Sir Your most obedient and very humble servant

Richard Henry Lee

ALS, DLC:GW.

1. GW wrote to Lee on 15 March. Lee apparently finally sent this letter, with another letter to GW of 7 May, by John Sitgreaves (1757–1802), who did not arrive at Mount Vernon until 29 May. Sitgreaves was a member of Congress for North Carolina in 1784 and 1785. Robert Howe also wrote a letter introducing Sitgreaves, dated 4 May.

2. William Grayson sent GW a copy of the Land Ordinance of 1785 on 27 May, one week after its passage. For an earlier exchange between Grayson and GW about the terms of the ordinance, see Grayson to GW, 15 April, and GW to Grayson, 25 April. See also Grayson to GW, 4–8 May, 27 May, and GW to Grayson, 22 June.

3. The historian Catherine Macaulay Graham (1731–1791) and her young husband, William Graham, arrived at Mount Vernon on 4 June for a ten-day visit. Among the letters of introduction that they brought with them were letters from generals Benjamin Lincoln and Henry Knox, from the old radical Samuel Adams, from the lawyer and reformer John Gardiner (1737–1793), and from James Duane, mayor of New York. Lincoln wrote from Hingham, Mass., on 28 Mar. (a second copy is dated 30 Mar.): "This will be delivered to your Excellency by Mr Grayham whom with Mrs Maccaulay Grayham I do my self the honor of introducing to your acquaintance. The merit of this Gentleman is great and claims the attention of all—The reputation of the Lady extending through the literary world, I need but mention her name—The dignity of her character is already intimately known to your Excellency. . . . The sentiments of genuine republicanism, which this Lady has exhibited in her celebrated history of the Steuarts must render her an object of veneration and esteem to all such as have espoused the cause of America: with your Excellency she ardently wishes an acquaintance. . . ." Writing from Boston on 29 Mar., Henry Knox expressed his pleasure in introducing "the celebrated Mrs Macauley Graham and Mr Graham" and affirmed that "A glorious enthusiasm for the cause of general liberty and human happiness has impelled this Lady and her husband to visit the Country whose inhabitants have had the hardihood to encounter fordimable dangers, rather than submit to a principle of taxation, which though not grevious in

the first instance, would probably have terminated in a flagitious abuse of power." Adams, less fulsome than Knox, wrote on 14 April from Boston: "The Gentlemen who will honour me by delivering this Letter to your Excellency is Mr Graham, who with his Lady the celebrated Mrs M'Cauly Graham has favor'd this Town with their Residence for some Months past." In his letter of the same date and from the same place, John Gardiner showed himself more interested in reintroducing himself to "the Saviour of your Country" than in introducing the Grahams: "I must flatter myself, from the distinguished attention with which you were so condescending as to honor me, in June 1783 at Camp, when I came introduced to you from the Chevalier de la Luzerne, the minister of France, that I shall not be deemed too presumptous in attempting to introduce your Acquaintance that distinguished female Friend to the Liberties of mankind and our own Country Mrs Catharine Mac-Caulay Graham and her Consort Mr Graham—No part of my Life afforded me more Consolation or more real Satisfaction than that in which I was honored with the temporary Countenance and Protection of that fine Character of this or of any other Time, General Washington." James Duane, writing from New York on 5 May, began by thanking GW for his communications of 10 April (printed above): "I received with very great pleasure your Excellency's dispatches which have made a deep Impression on our Corporation. They beg leave to express, thro' me, the high sense they entertain of your goodness, in so kindly accepting their Testimonial of Affection Gratitude and Esteem for him whom they justly consider as the best Friend and the greatest benefactor of their Country!" Duane then introduced the Grahams in these terms: "This will be presented to you by Mrs Macaulay Graham and Mr Graham who come expresly to pay you a Visit. The high rank which this Lady sustained in the literary world, and the regard she has manifested for the Rights of human nature throughout her works, will secure her a welcome at Mount Vernon, and any other Recommendation must be superfluous." All of the letters are in DLC:GW.

Letter not found: to Thomas Marshall, 3 May. On 12 May Marshall wrote GW: "Your favor of the 3d Inst. I received by my Son."

From Thomas Bibby

Sir   New York 4th May 1785

The enclosed letter and a parcell which accompanies it was entrusted to my care by Sr Edward Newenham, to be delivered to Your Excellency;[1] I regret much the not having it in my power to present them myself, an honor which the situation of my affairs in this state deprives me of. I have hopes however before my return to Europe, to be enabled to receive in person any Commands Your Excellency may please to honor me with for that part of the World.² I have the honor to be with respect Your Excellency's most Obedient humble Servant

T: Bibby
Captn Royl Brit[is]h Fuzileers

ALS, DLC:GW.

Thomas Bibby earlier was a lieutenant in the 24th Regiment of Foot in Ireland, with date of rank 28 Jan. 1775. His present regiment was the 21st Regiment of Foot.

1. Newenham's letter was dated 3 Mar. and has not been found. The "parcell" probably contained the "Magazines, Gazettes &ca" for which GW thanked Newenham on 25 Nov. 1785.

2. See GW to Bibby, 10 Dec. 1785.

From William Grayson

Dear Sir.   New York [c.4–8] May 1785.

I have recieved your letter of the 25th of Aprill, for which I am much oblig'd to you; I am sorry for the melancholy occasion which has induc'd you to leave Mount Vernon, and for the affliction which the loss of such near relations must involve Mrs Washington in.

The Ordinance for disposing of the Western territory has been under consideration ever since I wrote you last & has underwent several alterations, the most considerable of which is that one half the land is to be sold by sections or lots, & the other half by intire Townships; & the dimension of each township is reduc'd to six miles; I *now* expect the Ordinance will be completed in a few days, it being the opinion of most gentlemen that it is better to pass it in it's present form nearly, than to delay it much longer & incur the risque of losing the country altogether. As soon as it is finished I shall do myself the honor to inclose you a copy,¹ and though it will be far from being the best that could be made, yet I verily believe it is the best that under present circumstances can be procured: There have appeared so many interfering interests, most of them imaginary, so many ill founded jealousies & suspicions throughout the whole, that I am only surpris'd the ordinance is not more exceptionable; indeed if the importunities of the public Creditors, & the reluctance to pay them by taxation either direct or implied had not been so great I am satisfyed no land Ordinance could have been procured, except under such disadvantages as would in a great degree have excluded the idea of actual settlements within any short length of time; This is not strange when we reflect that several of the states are averse to new votes from that part of the Continent & that some of them are now disposing of their own vacant lands, & of course wish to have their particular debts paid & their own countries settled in the first instance before there is any interference from any other quarter. With respect to the different places of sale, it is certainly open to the objections you mention, but it was absolutely necessary to accede to the measure, before we could advance a single step. Since the receipt of your letter I have hinted to some of the members the propriety of altering this part, but find that the idea of allowing the Citizens of each State an equal chance of buying the good lands at their own doors, was one of the strongest reasons with them for consenting to the Ordinance. As to the individual states interfering in the sale, it is guarded against; and in case the loan Officer who is responsible only to Congress, cannot dispose of the land in a limited time, it is to be return'd to the Treasury board: With respect to the fractional parts of Townships the Ordinance has now provided for all cases which can occur, except with respect to the Pensylvania line—The Course of the new state from the Ohio will be due North, and the dispute with Pensylvania will be open to discussion hereafter. I am sorry to observe that throughout this measure, there has been a necessity for sacrificing one's own opinion to that of other people for the purpose of getting forward. There has never been above ten States on the floor & nine of these were necessary to concur in one sentiment, least they should refuse to vote for the Ordinance on it's passage. The price is fix'd at a dollar the acre liquidated certificates, that is the land is not to be sold under that; The reason for establishing this sum was that a part of the house were for half a dollar, and another part for two dollars & others for intermediate sums between the two extremes, so that ultimately this was agreed upon as a central ground. If it is too high (which I am afraid is the case) it may hereafter be corrected by a resolution.

I still mean to move for some amendments which I think will not only advance the sale, but increase the facility of purchasing to foreigners, though from present appearances I own I have but little hopes of success.[2]

After this affair is over, the requisition for the current year will be brought forward The article of 30,000 dollars for the erection of fœderal buildings at Trenton I have already objected to, & shall continue to oppose by every means in my power, as I look upon the measure to be fundamentally wrong, & I am in hopes nine States cannot be found to vote for it; should those in opposition to the measure be able to put off the execution for the present year it is to be expected that the Southern States will open their eyes to their true interests & view this subject in a different light. What I at present fear is, that failing to get this article allowed in the requisition they will attempt to draw the money from Holland by a vote of seven States inasmuch as a hundred thousand dollars were voted at Trenton for that purpose although no particular fund was assigned. I own this matter has giv'n me some disgust, as I see an intemperate ardor to carry it into execution before the sense of the Union is know'n; and I have no doubt that some gentlemen have come into Congress expressly for that purpose.

I take the liberty of introducing Mr StGreave—a delegate from North Carolina a gentleman of great worth who is travelling through our state to his own Country: He will be very happy to communicate to you the news of this place.[3] I inclose you the report of a Comm[itte]e for altering the first paragraph of the 9[t]h article of the confederation, & which embraces objects of great magnitude, & about which there is a great difference of sentiment.[4] I have the honor to be with the highest respect yr Affect. frd & Most Obdt sert

Willm Grayson

ALS, DLC:GW. In the heading of the letter, Grayson leaves the day of the month blank, but the contents of the letter indicate that it was written before Congress suspended consideration of the land ordinance bill from 7 to 18 May and before Grayson offered his amendment of 6 May (see *JCC*, 28:341–65).

1. Grayson enclosed a copy of the Land Ordinance of 1785 in his letter to GW dated 27 May.

2. See *JCC*, 28:342–43.

3. GW probably received Grayson's letter when John Sitgreaves arrived at Mount Vernon on 29 May.

4. The proposed alteration in the first paragraph of article 10 of the Articles of Confederation was to alter it by giving Congress "the sole and exclusive right . . . of regulating the trade of the States, as well with foreign Nations, as with each other, and of laying such imposts and duties upon imports and exports as may be necessary for the purpose" (*JCC*, 28:201). The report of the committee, chaired by James Monroe, was presented and read on 28 Mar., and on 13 July the report was referred to the committee of the whole. Congress took no action on the proposal. See Grayson to GW, 25 July, James McHenry to GW, 1 Aug. 1785, and GW to James McHenry, 22 August.

From Robert Howe

My Dear Sir   New York 4th May 1785

The Bearer Mr Sitgreaves is a Delegate in Congress for the State of North Carolina, the Respect he has for your character induces him strongly to wish that he may know you personally, and being well assur'd that he is worthy of an introduction to you, I take the liberty to recommend him to your Civilities, I am sorry that inevitable Circumstances deprive the publick of the advantages which would result from his abilities at a juncture which I think Critical to America[1]—I have been *Compell'd* to wait the meeting of Congress at this place, they have dealt honourably by me & still mean to do more, they have consider'd the peculiarity of my Case, have Voted me a sum of money & have order'd the pay master general to settle my Accounts preparation to somthing more, added to the Releif this gives me, it saves me the trouble and Expence of attending the different states where I have serv'd, and brings my affairs to a speedier close.[2] I trouble you my Dear sir with these matters relative to my self because I know your Benevolent heart, and as I flatter my self your regard for me, will induce you to feel pleasure at the information. You will please make my very Respectful Compliments to Mrs Washington to whom with you I wish Every happiness. Tho I have not been honor'd by an answer to a letter written you long since, let me my Dear sir now hope ⟨mutilated⟩ you, for every ⟨mutilated⟩ be dear to my Remembrance. Direct for me to the Care of Abm Lott Esqr. ⟨Durkin⟩ Street—I am Dear Sir with the warmest Affection & freind ship your Excellencys most Obt servt

                                                  Robt Howe

ALS, DLC:GW.

Maj. Gen. Robert Howe (1732–1786), a rice planter in North Carolina, took command of the southern department of the Continental army in 1777. He was replaced by Benjamin Lincoln in 1778 and served in the North under GW for the rest of the war.

1. See Richard Henry Lee's letter of 3 May introducing John Sitgreaves. GW writes Howe on 15 June that Sitgreaves had delivered Howe's letter.

2. For the problem about Howe's unpaid salary and the actions Congress took regarding it, see Howe's petition of 10 Mar. 1785 and Congress's report of 5 April 1785 (DNA:PCC, items 160 and 19).

From William Grayson

Dear Sir   N. York May 5th 1785.

Mr King one of the delegates of Massachusets bay, & a gentleman of great worth has particularly requested me to introduce to you, Mr Prince & Mr Darby, the former a Clergyman of amiable character, the latter the son of a respectable Merchant: They are travelling to Virginia & have a desire of calling at Mount Vernon.[1]

I therefore hope you will excuse the liberty I take in presenting them to you. I have the honor to be with the highest respt Yr Affect. friend & Most Obedt Servt

Willm Grayson.

ALS, DLC:GW.

1. Rufus King (1755–1827), in 1787 one of the delegates to the Federal Convention from Massachusetts, was a member of Congress for Massachusetts from 1784 to 1786. John Prince (1751–1836) was minister of the First Church in Salem, Massachusetts. "Mr. Darby" was probably a son of Elias Hasket Derby, a prominent merchant in Salem. Prince and "Darby" had dinner at Mount Vernon on Sunday, 15 May. See *Diaries*, 4:139.

From Henry Knox

My dear Sir.   New York 5 May 1785

It has been my intention ever since I have been in this City which is fourteen days to have written to you, but my business has been such as to prevent this gratification.

Congress have directed 700 Men to be raised for three years, to be apportioned upon the states of Connecticut New York, New Jersey and Pennsylvania, for the protection of the Western frontiers, to defend the Settlers on the lands belonging to the united States from the depredations of the Indians, and to prevent unwarrantable intrusions thereon, and for guarding the public Stores.[1] As This Corps is to be under my direction as secretary at War, I should be extremely obliged by your Excellencys opinion, with respect to the posts they ought to occupy on the frontiers—I suppose about thirty or forty men and two officers will be retained at Westpoint for guarding the public Stores, and the remainder will be sent to the Westward. The nu⟨mber⟩s must be small at any point, but I imagine that circums⟨tances⟩ will hereafter dictate the necessity of Keeping up an efficient force in that Country.[2]

I expect to be at Boston about the first of June, and to return here again with my family by the first of July. I hope Mrs Washington and her grand Children are well, and I request that you would be pleased to present my best respects to her.

The celebrated Mrs McAuley Graham and her husband Mr Graham are now in this City on their way to visit you and Mrs Washington.[3] I am my dear Sir With the highest respect and affection Your most obedient humble Servant

H. Knox

ALS, DLC:GW.

1. For the text of the resolution of Congress of 12 April authorizing the raising of 700 men from the four states, see *JCC*, 28:247–48.

2. GW wrote to Knox on 18 June 1785 about stationing the troops, and Knox reported to GW on 22 Nov. on their disposition.

3. Knox wrote a letter to GW on 29 Mar. introducing the Grahams. See Richard Henry Lee to GW, 3 May, n.3.

From Ruthey Jones

Worthy Sir   Belfast Georgia may the 7—1785

Last December twelve months—I had the honour of receiveing your Excellencys' Letter by major Fishbourn being the first that ever Got safe to my hands.[1] I should have returned an earlier answer to it, had a Conveyance on which I Could have depended offered before the present—I am at a loss to express the Satisfaction I felt when major Fishbourn informed me he had a letter from You—it can be better felt then discribed, as I had long flattered my Self with the hope of seing you before I died, in preference to the Greatest Monarch on earth, had the Visit been ever so short: But how soon did that hope Vanish, when I perrused the Contents! The disappointment was the Greatest I ever met with, as I had ever been taught from my Infancy by the old People of South Carolina (where I was born) to consider you as a Relation. But if I have committed an Error in Claiming an affinity to you, I flatter myself you will forgive me, and be assured, my Dear Sir, that it was not done with a view of imposeing on you, had this been the case—was you to forgive me—I never shoud have forgiven myself—but as I always conceived you were acquainted with the circumstances that related to my Grand Father. Mr Jonathan Bryan, a Gentleman of Reputation and long standing here,[2] assures me that my Grand Father, Mr John Washington, and Mr James Washington were full Brothers, and that they Came to South Carolina together about the year 1707; that my Grand Father married, but his Brother remained single until he went to Virginia, that my Mother (who was the only Child of my Grand Father who lived to a mature age[)], She perfectly remembered my Grand uncle during his residence in Carolina, and that some time before my Grand Fathers Death he haveing been killed by his own waitingman—in the year 1714, his Brother left him and removed to Virgina where he married and had tow Sons, From this last Circumstance, you have ever been considered as one of them, as I am now in the decline of life, and find myself incapable of encountering much fatigue, I almost dispair of ever haaveing the happiness of seeing you, unless you should come to the southward. I beg therefore you will accept of my unfained Good wishes for your helth and prosperity, and I shall offer my Prayers to Heaven that you may long enjoy boath. I wish to prevent your Excellencys harbouring a suspicion that I had misrepresented matters to you, and have accordingly been particular, I earnesly beg your goodness will Pardon me should I be mistaken—in my opinion of your being a Decendant of my Grand uncles—Should I ever be so happy as to be honoured with a line from you again as nothing would offord me so much pleasure, as one *soft* word from you, which time nor Distance shall never efface the Greatfull rememberance of any thing you may be pleased to cummunicate, will come safe to me by being Sent to Mr John Habersham at Congress a worthy friend of mine, who takes Charge of this to you[3] I now beg leave to wish you all the happiness that this world can offord, and may Heaven Grant, that—happiness to be crowned with the best of Blessings is the Sincear and most Respectfull Sentiments of Dr Sir your affectionate Friend

Ruthey Jones

I cannot think of Sealing my Letter before I acquaint you of a most unfortuneate circumstance, a friend of mine had made me a compliment of your picture which I was to send for—but the house was burnt that night with every thing in it, which has been no Small disappointment to me, that has so Long wisht to se it in Vaine—I am my Dr Sir yours with the Greatest affection as before R. Jones

ALS, DLC:GW.

Ruthey Jones first wrote GW about what she supposed was their family relationship in a missing letter of April 1775. She wrote again on 15 Sept. 1776, from Belfast in Liberty County, Ga., advancing the same claims that she had in 1775 and restates here in 1785. When she wrote in 1776, she was a delicate young lady of 22 or 23 from South Carolina living in the house of a Mr. Maxwell (probably James Maxwell) whose mother had taken her in when Ruthey Jones's mother died. George Gilmer, a member of the Continental Congress from Georgia, was given the first letter for GW, and she entrusted the one of September 1776 to the care of Gen. Robert Howe. She seems to have written GW a number of other times on the same subject before writing again on 29 May 1783, pleading for a response to her letters. GW obliged on 25 Sept. 1783, saying: "The relationship which you seem to suppose there is betwn us does not exist of which you would have been clearly convinced if my former Letter had ever reached you." He then names the six children of his father's only brother and lists the grandchildren as well. He ends by saying: "I am not related to you in the degree you suppose, nor in any other that I can have the smallest conception of." All of the letters are in DLC:GW.

1. Ruthey Jones's letter of 29 May 1783 was conveyed to GW by Maj. Benjamin Fishbourn (Fishbourne), aide-de-camp to Gen. Anthony Wayne.

2. Jonathan Bryan (1708–1788), a rice planter and leading Revolutionary in Georgia, was released and returned to Georgia in 1781 after being a British prisoner for two years.

3. GW did not respond to this letter, but after his visit to Georgia during his southern tour of 1795, when Ruthey Jones did not see him, she wrote from Belfast on 12 May 1795: "I was always informed that you was, a son, or grand son, of my grand uncle Mr James Washington. . . ." John Habersham (1754–1799) was one of the sons of James Habersham (1715–1775), the first president of Georgia's royal council. In 1795 GW made John Habersham U.S. postmaster general. Habersham's covering letter to GW, dated at New York, 29 June 1785, reads: "I do myself the honor to inclose you a letter from Miss

Ruthey Jones, of Georgia; and shall be happy to forward any communications you may be pleased to make to that lady" (DLC:GW).

From Richard Henry Lee

Dear Sir,   New York May 7th 1785
This will be delivered to you by the honorable Mr Sitgreaves a very worthy delegate to Congress from N. Carolina; who has been long detained by his desire to see the Land Ordinance passed, but he is obliged at last to quit us before it is finally so— The reasons he can give you. I had some time ago written a letter for you in answer to your last faver & kept it to go by this Gentleman, whose detention has been so long as to render a new letter more fit.[1] I have now the honor to enclose you the Ordinance above alluded to, which meets the assent of nine States & every member of these Nine States, except one Man, who keeps the Ordinance from passing by the joint causes, as he alleges, of indisposition & dislike. I incline to think, however, that it will pass in the form you now receive it, with very little alteration, if any.[2] I think there is no doubt of the agreement having been made for change of dominions between the Elector of Bavaria & the Emperor as mentioned in my last, yet, altho we have letters from our Ministers in Europe of the 9th of february, we are yet in the dark upon the question whether there will be war between the Emperor & the Dutch, or whether it will settle finally between the former & the King of Prussia. The public papers, as you will see by the enclosed, make War very certain. I had lately the honor of writing to you by Mr Graham, & his Lady Mrs Macauley Graham the celebrated Historian of England, who go to Virginia, I believe solely to pay their respects to you.[3] I beg leave to refer you to Mr Sitgreaves for our foreign and domestic news, which indeed is not much.
My respects if you please to your Lady, whose health I hope is perfectly restored—I am, with the truest respect, esteem, and regard, dear Sir your most obedient and very humble servant
Richard Henry Lee.

ALS, DLC:GW.
 1. See Lee to GW, 3 May, n.1.
 2. See Lee to GW, 3 May, n.2.
 3. This is Lee's letter of 3 May.

From Jacob Read

Sir　　　　　　　　　　　　　Charles Ton [S.C.] May 8th 1785

Mr Charles Philips who does me the Honour to charge himself with the delivery of the present Letter is my most particular friend, permit me to introduce him to your Acquaintance and friendship as such—He is a Gentleman of very ample fortune in the West Indies and is now on his return to Europe after visiting his Estates—a very principal reason for Mr Philips's making a journey from this State to New York by land is to have the pleasure of Seeing and in person paying his respects to your Excellency, to which he is probably the more Strongly inclined from his being a native of York Town in your State. Tho' educated in Europe where he has Spent the greatest part of his life—I beg leave to assure you that I shall feel a particular obligation for any Attentions Shewn Mr Philips of whose virtues and merit I have the highest Sense and with whom I have had the honor to be on the most intimate terms of friendship for many years past.[1]

I did myself the honour of addressing a letter to you in the beginning of March from New York about which time my private affairs obliged me to make a visit to this State—Shall however return to Congress about the beginning of June.[2]

I unexpectedly Saw and only had the pleasure of transiently Seeing Major Washington in this City at the point of time when he was about to Embark on his return to Virginia and when the Excessive illness of my Mother prevented my having it in my power to pay him that Attention to which his own Merit entitled him and my wishes & Inclinations Strongly prompted me. a like situation will not I hope happen again and with great truth I assure you Sir, I Shall feel the utmost pleasure in tendering every Service in my power to any of your friends and much Satisfaction in Executing any Commands with which you may honour me either in this State or elsewhere.

I pray you'l do me the favour to present my most respectful Compliments to Mrs Washington and believe that I am with the greatest respect & regard Sir Your Excellency's most obedient and most Humble Servant

　　　　　　　　　　　　　　　　　　　　　　Jacob Read

ALS, DLC:GW.

1. Charles Philips spent the night of 26 June at Mount Vernon.

2. As a member of Congress from South Carolina, Read corresponded frequently with GW during much of 1784. His most recent letter to GW is dated 9 Mar. 1785.

From David Humphreys

My dear General   Paris May [10] 1785

Since I had the honor to receive by the last Packet your favor dated in Feby last I have been unwell with a slight fever, & tho recovered at this moment it has retarded my public business in such a manner, as will prevent me from writing so particularly as I wished to have done by the present opportunity.[1]

I am extremely concerned & mortified to find that you have been under the necessity of being so much occupied with unimportant & tedious applications. I hope you will have been able to procure some assistance before this time, and that you will not ultimately & altogether lose sight of the object I have more than once had the honor of suggesting to your Excellency.

For my own part I have not eat the bread of idleness—I have been pretty constantly employed in writings of one kind or another. Besides the correspondencies which have been opened with Russia, The Emperor, Prussia, Denmark, Sweden, Saxony, Sicily, Sardinia, Venice, the Pope, Tuscany, Spain, Portugal & England—and the reports which have been made in consequence to Congress, I have kept an accurate Record of the Proceedings of the Ministers, the minits of which have already more than half filled a large folio Volume—Tho' Treaties have proposed to be entered into with all the beforementioned Powers (except Sweden to whom a supplementary Treaty has been proposed) yet none of them appear to be near a completion except with the King of Prussia & the Grand Duke of Tuscany— Several of these Powers however, who have no commercial Treaties whatever, have declared that our vessels shall be recd in their ports in the most friendly manner & that we shall be upon equal terms with the most favored Nation.

I am happy to learn Congress have appointed Mr Adams their Minister at the Court of London, it was a measure which had become indispensably necessary to prevent growing trouble & perhaps an open rupture between the two Nations— I am pleased to find that the appointment of Secry has been given to one of your Aids de Camp.[2]

Upon my leaving America Mr Morris invested me with the power of procuring the several honorary presents which had been voted by Congress to different Officers in their service during the late War—The Royal Academy of Inscriptions & Belles Lettres to whom I addressed a Letter on the subject, have furnished me with the following device & inscriptions for the Gold Medal which is to be executed for your Excellency—"On one side the head of the General[,] Legend: Georgio Washington supremo Duci Exercituum adsertori Libertatis Comitia Americana. On the reverse: taken possession of Boston. The American Army advances in good order towards the Town, which is seen at a distance, while the British army flies with precipitation towards the shore to embark on board the vessels with which the harbour is covered. In the front of the American Army appears the General on horseback, in a groupe of officers, whom he seems to make observe the flight of the Enemy. Legend: hostibus primo fugatis. Exergue: Bostonium recuperatum die XVII Marti: MDCCLXXVI."

I think it has the character of simplicity & dignity which is to be aimed at in a memorial of this kind, which is designed to transmit the remembrance of a great event to posterity. You really do not know how much your name is venerated on this side the Atlantic.[3]

I have been fortunate in making several literary & noble acquaintances, by whom I have been treated with vastly more attention & hospitality than by any officers who served in America, & I except the Marquis la Fayette & one or two more.

It is pretty well decided now that there will be no war this summer.

We have had a remarkably long & distressing winter, many cattle have died for the want of forage, & the present want of rain threatens the most disastrous consequences. With my most respectful & affectionate regards to Mrs Washington & Complts to all the family I have the honor to be my Dr General Your sincere friend & hble Servt

D. Humphreys

ALS, DLC:GW. Humphreys does not give the day of the month that he wrote this letter, but on 1 Nov. he refers to his letter to GW of 10 May.

1. No letter from GW to Humphreys dated in February 1785 has been found. GW wrote Humphreys on 25 Nov. 1784.

2. William Stephens Smith was one of GW's aides-de-camp, from 1781 to 1783.

3. The gold medal for GW was voted by Congress on 25 Mar. 1776 and finally delivered to him by Thomas Jefferson in March 1790. For full details, see John Adams to GW, 1 April 1776, n.2, and Notes on American Medals Struck in France in Boyd, *Jefferson Papers*, 16:53–79.

From Christopher Richmond

Sir   Annapolis [Md.] 10th May 1785

Not having had any communication with the persons appointed by the Act of Assembly of Maryland to receive subscriptions for extending the Navigation of Potowmack, upon the Subject of advertising a Meeting; and being at a Loss how to proceed in the Business, I have taken the Liberty of addressing Your Excellency upon it.

It is but a few days since I saw the Act of Assembly for the first time—the Maryland Printer not having published, and delivered it, until the begining of the present Week—This circumstance has prevented Mr Davidson or myself from writing to the other Managers upon the subject; and as we are totally ignorant of the Ideas of the Gentlemen of Virginia, respecting the Meeting of the Subscribers; I have troubled you with this, to request your Advice thereon, and if you please direction how to proceed.[1] The Weather has been so indifferent for sometime past, that few People have left their Homes to come to this Place. Our General Court is now sitting—The Races will be next Week, and it is probable that some Subscriptions may be obtained during these Times. I have asked the advice of Major Jenifer and Mr Chase, and in consequence of it, have determined to keep the Subscription Book until the End of this Month; unless I have some directions to the contrary. Enclosed I send the present State of it; and shall esteem it as a favor that you will please to write me on the Subject by the next Post. It would have given me pleasure to have waited on the Subscribers on the 17th Instant, but my Health has so long been in a precarious State—and I have been so long unused to travelling; that I dare not undertake the Journey. Mr Davidson is also prevented by having lately received a Cargo of Goods which he is now opening.[2]

Should it be necessary that the original Subscription be had at the Meeting of the Subscribers, it shall be sent by Express. With the highest Respect I have the Honor to be Sir Your obedient hble Servant

Chrisr Richmond

ALS, DLC:GW.

1. Richmond and John Davidson, a member of the state's executive council, were the two managers at Annapolis for collecting subscriptions to the new Potomac River Company. The first meeting of the company was held in Alexandria on 17 May (see GW to Thomas Johnson and Thomas Sim Lee, 18 May, and notes).

2. Richmond's report on the subscriptions to the Potomac River Company has not been found, but see his earlier report in note 1, Richmond to GW, 8 April. See also note 2 of that document and GW to Richmond, 19 May.

From W. Symmes

Sir,   Fredericksburg [Va.] May 10. 1785.

I have considered well the terms your Excellency mentioned at your sisters as the best you could allow me, & find on comparing them with my present prospects in another line that I cannot with any justice to myself accept them. My views must be professional, or if I exchange them, 'tis natural to expect some compensation. The salary I receive from Mr Mercer, is perhaps the least advantage I derive from living in his family, & therefore should not, methinks, be made a rule in any other case where those additional advantages must all be given up, & perhaps the benefit I have already received thereby entirely lost.

My education, Sir, has been expensive, & I am now at that stage of it when 65£ is no equivalent for a year of my time. When your Excellency's wants were first made known to me, I conceived them to be such as would entitle me to an hundred guineas a year; & for this, with the improvement & satisfaction I made no doubt of finding in your Excellency's family, I predetermined to undertake the fatigues & application of the Office to which I had the honour to be invited. But I am certain that the sum your Excellency mentioned will not support me in the manner I should choose, though perhaps some other man may be found who can live within it. Of this, however, I am persuaded by experience, that no young man of a genteel character, I mean one who is received among persons of rank & distinction & would not appear unworthy that reception, ever can.

After what your Excellency said, I must suppose that the treaty will cease upon this declaration. However, I will mention at large the terms on which I will with pleasure obey your summons & exert myself to the utmost in your service. My first condition is that I shall have 120£ P. Annum, payable quarterly—with board, washing, & mending: my second that I shall be at liberty to attend the Gen. Court & Court of Appeals; & the last, that when I ride on your Excellency's business & am obliged to be out more than one day, I shall have a servant with me. If your Excellency should accede to these conditions, you will be sure of a person who will on all occasions consult & defend your interests committed to his care as if they were immediately his own.

I have only now to request that your Excellency will not think hardly of me for this proposal, which is the most moderate that I can possibly make. My views extend only to a bare support, & my professional interest, which I must not wholly abandon. Were it not for these two insuperable motives, I should esteem the honour of being in your family, & enjoying some part of your confidence, a compensation amply sufficient for all the services that I could render you. I have the honour to be, with' great respect, Sir, Your Excellencys most obedient humble servant

                                                              W. Symmes.

ALS, DLC:GW.
    Before leaving Richmond on 4 May, where he had attended a meeting of the Dismal Swamp Company, GW called on James Mercer of Fredericksburg, a judge of the Virginia General Court. On the next day, GW "Dined with my Sister [Betty] Lewis in Fredericksburgh" (*Diaries*, 4:134), at which time, it seems, he talked to Symmes about Symmes's coming to Mount Vernon as his secretary.

Letter not found: from Charles Vancouver, 10 May. GW wrote Vancouver on 30 June: "Your favor of the 10th of last month came safely to hand."

From Lafayette

My dear General   Paris May the 11th 1785

This is not the only letter You Will Get from me By this packet,[1] But as the opportunity is Safe, I will trust Young M. Adams With Some Matters Which I would not like to Be Ventured in the post offices of France.[2]

102 ⟨Protestants⟩ in 12 ⟨France⟩ are under intolerable 80 ⟨Despotism⟩—altho' oppen persecution does not now Exist, yet it depends upon the whim of 25 ⟨king⟩; 28 ⟨queen⟩, 29 ⟨parliament⟩, or any of 32 ⟨the Ministers⟩—marriages are not legal among them—their wills Have no force By law—their children are to Be Bastards—their parsons to Be Hanged—I Have put it into My Head to Be a 1400 ⟨Leader⟩ in that affair, and to Have their Situation changed—with that wiew I am Going, under other pretences to Visit their chief places of abode, With a Consent of 42 ⟨Castries⟩, and an other—I will afterwards Endeavour to Gain 39 ⟨Vergennes⟩ and 29 ⟨Parliament⟩, with the keeper of the Seals,[3] who acts as Chancellor—it is a Work of time, and of Some danger to me, Because none of them Would give me a Scrap of paper, or Countenance whatsoever—But I Run My chance—42 ⟨Castries⟩ Could only Receive the Secret from me, Because it is not in His departement—Don't Answer me about it, only that You Had my Ciphered letter By M. Adams—But when in the Course of the fall or winter You will Hear of Some thing that Way, I wanted You to know I Had an Hand in it.

100 ⟨Ireland⟩ are spent out, and Nothing for 73's ⟨liberty's⟩ Sake to do that Way—I was in Hopes Holland would offer some thing that Way—But I am affraîd not—I don't think 46's ⟨Calonne's⟩ political life May last long, unless He leaves 1600 ⟨finances⟩ for Some other Branch.

Before I arrived, a letter Had gone demanding Longchamps—Since which the Ministry were Satisfied with that Business and a letter went ordering to let it drop[4]—I Hope there Will Be no war in America—But if it Was Ever the Case, either to 840 ⟨South Spain⟩, to 590 ⟨Mississippy⟩, or to the fronteer posts and Canada, I depend Upon You, my dear General, to Be offered a Command, which in one Case my Situation as a french Man May Render personally a little ticklish for me,

But for which, in all Cases my Situation as Such, as well as my Roman Catholick Creed, or Supposed to Be So at least if any thing, and the Confidence You, and the public are pleased to Honour me with, may Render me a proper choice to propose[5]—But I Earnestly Hope it Will not Be the Case that You make War—particularly with Spain—altho' a Visit to Mexico and New orleans I would prefer to Any thing I know of—don't answer to me about it otherwise than in general terms. Adieu, My dear General, My Best Respects waît on Mrs Washington— Remember me to the family. Your filial and devoted friend

Lafayette

When You Arrange Your papers, my dear General, I Beg You Will Send me my letters to You, which I will Send Back a fortnight after I Have Received them—I Had no Copies kept of them—and wish to preserve some.[6]

ALS, PEL. Someone has written the encoded words in the letter above the code numbers, perhaps for GW, and these words are printed here in angle brackets.

1. Lafayette wrote on this date a letter of introduction for the comte de Doradour: "This letter will Be delivered By M. le Comte doradour of a Very Good family in Auvergne to whom I am Related and who is Going to look for a settlement in America—His fortune Has Been partly deranged By a law Suit, and what Remains of it He intends to fix in some of the United states—I Beg leave to Request Your Good Advice and Your patronage in His Behalf" (ALS, PEL). Thomas Jefferson at this time wrote similar letters for Doradour to James Madison and John Walker, among others (Boyd, *Jefferson Papers*, 8:145–52).

2. Written by Lafayette on the cover of the letter are these words: "favoured by M. [John Quincy] Adams, and particularly Recommended. LA-FAYETTE" (Idzerda, *Lafayette Papers*, 5:322–24).

3. Armand-Thomas Hué de Miromesnil (1723–1796) was keeper of seals.

4. For a brief description of the controversy arising out of the attack in Philadelphia in May 1784 by Charles-Julien de Longchamps on the French chargé d'affaires, Barbé-Marbois, see Jacob Read to GW, 29 June 1784, n.3.

5. The adventurer Sebastian Francisco de Miranda was in New York the first half of 1784. He may have talked at that time with Alexander Hamilton and Henry Knox of a plan for liberating Venezuela, and the names of GW and Lafayette may have come up as possible leaders of the enterprise. See Hamilton to Miranda, 23 Nov. 1784, in Syrett, *Hamilton Papers*, 3:585–87.

6. Bushrod Washington sent Lafayette's letters to him in 1817. They were not returned. See Bushrod Washington to Lafayette, 9 Jan. 1817 (PEL; see Idzerda, *Lafayette Papers*, 5:324).

From Jacquelin Ambler

Sir   Richmond [Va.] 12th May 1785

Still flattering ourselves with an expectation that some encouragement would be given here to the Scheme for opening and extending the navigation of Potowmack River, we were induced to delay closing the Subscription to the latest day which the Act admitted of: It is matter of real regret to us that our endeavours have proved unsuccessful.

My whole attention being necessarily engrossed by the duties of the Treasury, it will be impracticable for me, without manifest injury to that Department, to attend at Alexandria on Tuesday next; I am constrained, therefore, to adopt the alternative given me by the Act, and take the liberty to express my hope that you will be pleased to represent the State at the Meeting on that day:[1] when, most probably, Subjects of the greatest import to the Success of the Scheme will be discussed, and on which my knowledge and judgment are very inadequate to enable me to give a voice. Pardon this freedom, and believe me Sir, with the most grateful esteem, and most perfect respect, Your most obedient Servant

J: Ambler

ALS, DLC:GW.

Jacquelin Ambler (1742–1798), originally of Jamestown Island, was treasurer of the state of Virginia. In 1764 Ambler married Rebecca Burwell, daughter of Lewis Burwell, and in 1783 their daughter Mary Ambler married John Marshall, who was at this time a young lawyer in Richmond.

1. See GW to Thomas Johnson and Thomas Sim Lee, 18 May, n.1.

To La Serre

Sir,   Mt Vernon 12th May 1785.

The letter which you did me the honor to write to me the 20th of last month, I found at this place when I returned from Richmond a few days ago; but it had been previously lost in the high way, & came to me open & without a cover: by what means it met with this accident, I am unable to learn—a neighbour of mine picked it up in the condition I have mentioned, & sent it to me.[1]

I pray you to be assured Sir, that I should have great pleasure in presenting you with a letter to the Count de Vergennes if I cou'd suppose that my recommendation would have any weight at the Court of Versailles, & if I had ever opened a correspondence with the Minister thereof on a subject of this nature: but not having the vanity to suppose the first, & never having attempted the latter; I persuade myself I shall meet a ready excuse for not complying with your request in this instance.

Not being under such delicate circumstances with my intimate acquaintance & friend the Marqs de la Fayette, I have communicated your wishes to him; & as no language can do it more emphatically than your own, I have taken the liberty of enclosing your letter to me, to him.[2] I have the honor to be &c.

G: Washington

LB, DLC:GW.

Barbier, the chevalier de La Serre, served as an officer in the Saintonge Regiment in America. On 21 April 1784 he married Ann Dulany, the daughter of Daniel Dulany (1722–1797) of Maryland, and he was now making a trip to France "to do some business" (Miles King to Thomas Jefferson, 29 Aug. 1785, in Boyd, *Jefferson Papers*, 8:448–49).

1. The letter, which GW forwarded to Lafayette, has not been found.

2. GW wrote Lafayette on this day, to this effect: "The enclosed letter from the Chevr de la Serre conveys a strong expression of his wishes; & as you are well acquainted with his merits—his connexions, & his intention of remaining in America—I persuade myself it is unnecessary for me to add more to recommend him to your favourable notice in the line he wishes, & which he finds most convenient for himself to walk in, if the present Consul of France, at Baltimore, can be better provided for. I therefore submit his case and pretensions to that spirit which I know is ever ready to promote the happiness of others" (LB, DLC:GW).

La Serre wrote from Baltimore on 31 May: "I have had the Honour of receving your Excellency's very kind favor & beg in return you will Accept my best acknowledgments for your letter to the marquis delafayette, I have not the least doubt, but it will procure me the Entire Completion of my wishes" (DLC:GW).

From Thomas Marshall

Dear General   Fauquier [Va.] May the 12th 1785.

Your favor of the 3d Inst. I receiv'd by my Son & will with the greatest pleasure execute the small commission you are pleas'd to honor me with, by collecting & sending you the different seeds agreable to the list you inclos'd me. The Crown imperial—Tulip bearing Lawrel, & Cardinal flower, I am not acquainted with, but shall I dont doubt find them out by enquiry.[1]

In consiquence of a resolution of the last Assembly made in favor of such Officers as were in service in 79 & 80 and thereby deprived of the benefit of the act of Assembly allowing time for locateing Military Warrants, I have got your warrt as Assignee of Rootes, exchanged, shall carry it out with me & hope soon to give you a good account of it.[2] I have the honor to be with the most respectful esteem Dear General Your most obedt Servt
                                          T. Marshall

ALS, DLC:GW.

Thomas Marshall (1730–1802), the father of Chief Justice John Marshall and colonel of the 3d Virginia Regiment during the Revolution, was at the point of moving to Kentucky from Fauquier County, Va., where he was living when the county was created in 1759.

1. GW's letter has not been found. GW apparently knew of Marshall's impending move to Kentucky and had asked him to secure seed of these plants for Louis XVI's garden at Versailles. See Lafayette to GW, 17 Dec. 1784, and note 1 of that document, and GW to Lafayette, 25 July 1785.

2. The Virginia assembly in its session of May 1783 passed "An act for giving further time to enter certificates for settlement rights, and to locate warrants upon preemption rights, and for other purposes" (11 Hening 291–93), and it further extended the time in both its May and its October sessions in 1784 (ibid., pp. 376, 476).

From William Fitzhugh

Dear General   Maryl[an]d Millmont May 13th 1785
     This will be hand ⟨to⟩ You by Mr Bolton. The Person I recommended to Finish your Large Room—He is a masterly Hand, & I believe will Execute your work in an Elegant Manner at least equal to any in America—When I had the Honor to be with you & first Mention'd Mr Bolton, I told you His Foible as well as His Merrit & that I had lately discharg'd Him from my service, into which He Enterd in June last at a Dollar pr Day with two Negro Boys—& I to Find his Family in provission, Six in Number Inclusive—I Put under his direction four of my own Negro Carpenters—& the Scantlin Plank &c. was to be got from the woods—I did not remove to the—until the 4th of Janry last, when I found there had been Great Neglect. My Carpenters had done very Little and my work in every Part Backward. I then Expected my presence wou'd alter the Case, but

Mr Bolton His Wife & Family during my Absence had got such a Habit of Entertaining Idle Visitors, that I still found my work did not go on & that he had be Led rather into Excess of Drinking, which had not been his Custom & therfore Discharged Him—Indeed my work, considering that the whole was first to be taken from the woods, & that he had four Negro Carpenters of mine to Overlook, was by no means Sutable to him—Had it been otherwise He probably wou'd have gone on well with his work, as he is by no means an Idle Person, or subject to Liquor unless Tempted by Improper associates—His wife & Daughter too were fond of Company which often Occasioned their meeting—The wife is dead & the Daughter maried, & there is now only himself & one Negro apprentice.[1]

Mr Bolton carries an Invoice of Materials, of which you may have the marble Slabb, largest window Glass—Large Brass Spring Hinges, If wanting & one half of any or all the other Articles, as the other Half will be plenty for my Use, & I beg you will only Command such articles as you have Occasion for[2]—I hope you will Pardon this Scrawl & wish you may be able to read it—The morning is cloudy & my sight so defective, that it is with much Difficulty I can see to write.[3]

Mrs Fitzhugh joins with me in respectful Complts to you, your Lady & Family. I have the Honor to be with perfect Esteem & Respect your Excellencys Affect. & oblig'd H[umbl]e Sert

                         Willm Fitzhugh

ALS, DLC:GW. On the cover of the letter, Fitzhugh wrote: "Mr Poseys Ferry is the proper Line from Portobacco & opposite to General Washingtons on Potok. W. Fitzhugh."

1. See Fitzhugh to GW, 2 May and notes.

2. The enclosed invoice (DLC:GW) has been transcribed for CD-ROM:GW. The whole charges, coming to £87.3.5, included not only what Fitzhugh names here but also such things as paint, turpentine, paintbrushes, and nails.

3. Fitzhugh's handwriting is indeed far worse than in other letters that he presumably wrote on brighter days.

From John Harvie

Sir   Land office [Richmond, Va.] May 13th 1785

You will receive with this Letter a copy of the previous Title Law that pass'd in the year 1779[1]—I also Inclose you a Certificate of the loss of your Original Survey for the 2813 Acres of Land[2]—likewise a copy of the Grant that issued to you and General Lewis for the Burning Spring[3]—I do not Recollect that any application has been made for the Round Bottom by Cresups Heirs or any other person since your Grant Issued.[4] I have the Honour to be Sir Yr Most Obt Servt

John Harvie

ALS, DLC:GW.

1. This is the act that Harvie discusses in his letter to GW of 22 April.

2. Harvie wrote GW on 22 April that "the Original Survey upon which your patent issued [for the 2,813 acres on Millers Run] with a Number of other public papers fell into the Hands of the Enemy and were destroy'd by them."

3. For the purchase of the Burning Springs tract by GW and Andrew Lewis, see GW to Samuel Lewis, 1 Feb. 1784, n.3.

4. On 11 April GW wrote Thomas Freeman about securing renters for his Round Bottom tract on the Ohio, for which he had secured a patent in October 1784 after first laying claim to it in October 1770. See note 2 in his letter to Freeman. See also the references in GW to Thomas Lewis, 1 Feb. 1784, n.3, and William Crawford to GW, 2 Aug. 1771. Harvie wrote GW on 20 May 1785 that Cresap's heirs had applied for a grant to the Round Bottom and suggested that GW "enter a Caveat against a Grant issueing to them." GW sent Harvie his caveat on 31 May, in which he reviewed the history of his claims to the Round Bottom tract. See also Harvie's letter to GW of 5 August.

From Lafayette

My dear General   Paris May the 13th 1785

My Correspondance With You Will this time Be in two Volumes and Young Mr Adams, john Adams's Son, Has taken Care of a letter which I Hope He will Safely forward[1]—Your kind favour february the 15th only Came in the last Packet—I Need not telling You, My dear General, How Happy I was to Hear from You, and How Happy You will Make me By an Exact Correspondance and an Attention to Send the Letters in time for the Sailing of the Packets which now will Arrive in France at the Havre a place very Near paris at the Mouth of the Seine River—I am Very Glad to Hear Your Pottowmack Business Has Succeeded—it is Highly important, and I feel doubly Happy By Reflecting this Good is owing to the part You Have taken in the affair—the Compliment the State of Virginia Have paid You is No doubt perplexing—I feel for You, and With you, My dear General, on the Occasion—Your Reluctance to Receive

Such a present is the More pleasing to me, as I want it to Be Said in Your History—General Washington Got Every thing for His Country—and Would not Receive Any other Reward—But on the other Hand, You Certainly Wish to Avoid Every Step which Could appear a Slight, a want of proper Respect, or of Gratitude for the Compliment which a Nation pays to an Individual—You Better know what to do than I Can tell—But if it Can Be gently turned towards Some public popular Establishement, You May perhaps Avoid a deviation from Your plan, and the Appearance of Slight or ostentation[2]—I will look out for Subscribers when the Matter Comes to Be a little Better known—and will Have an Eye upon Your Recommendation Respecting the Engeneer.

There is not much News for the Present in this Country—Dutch affairs seem to Be in a Good train of Pacification—But if we Believe the Rumours that were Spread Yesterday, Baviera Would Be Invaded, or Rather, with the Consent of the Elector, taken Possession of By the Imperial troops—it is true that Elector is a Complete fool, and His Ministry are Bought By the Emperor—But I Cannot think the Report is true—altho' that Baviera, or the ottoman Empire are Now more probable Grounds of a future war than the provinces of Holland—duke de choiscuîl died a few days Ago—Some think He was not Without Hopes, and Worked pretty Hard to Reenter the Ministry.

French Hounds are not Now Very Easely got Because the king Makes use of English dogs as Being more Swift than those of Normandy—I However Have got Seven from a Normand Gentleman Called *Monsieur le Comte doilliamson* the Handsomest Bitch Among them Was a favourite with His lady who Makes a present of Her to You—as He was very active in procuring the Best Blooded dogs, I Beg leave to propose Your writing a line to Him, containing a thankfull notice of the Comtesse, who Seems to take much pride in Being mentionned to You.[3]

M[ar]quis de st Simon Has once writen a letter to You the Answer to which did not arrive—I think a Copy, or an Antidated letter would do the Business, and the Whole Will Be attributed to Naval Accidents.[4]

M. adams Has taken with Him Some proposals for a Contract about Whale oils which I think to Be Very advantageous to the Commerce of America, and will produce an Envoice of about 800,000 french livres. I Have Been very Busy in Bringing it on, and it is the Consolation I Had for failing in My Endeavours to obtain a General exemption of duties upon those oils[5]—You Have Been Very Right Not to purchase the spanish jack ass—the Best ones Come from the Isle of Maltha—Admiral Suffrein who goes there Has promised He would within these Six months Send me the Handsomest in the island with a female and the Whole Will not amount to more than fifty guineas.[6]

My wife, children, and myself are in perfect Health, and all join With me in Most affectionate Respects to You, to Mrs Washington, and we Send our love to the Young ones—I was very Happy to Hear George Arrived at Charlestown in a Better State of Health—Remember me to Him, to all your family, to my friends about you, or any of them you Happen to Meet—adieu, My dear General, I grieve to think we are Now Separated By this Immense Ocean—But my Heart is With You in Every Moment, My dear General, and I am Happy when I Can once more Mention to You the Sentiments of Respect, Gratitude, Unbounded affection which for Ever Render me, My Beloved general, Your Most devoted friend

lafayette

ALS, PEL.

1. See Lafayette to GW, 11 May.

2. GW had already decided to follow the course that Lafayette suggests here for dealing with the dilemma that the gift by the Virginia assembly of stock in the Potomac and James River companies posed. See, for instance, GW to William Grayson, 25 April 1785; see also Benjamin Harrison to GW, 6 Jan. 1785, n.1.

3. Lafayette wrote on 16 April of his intention to send by John Quincy Adams the hounds that GW had asked for. See note 3 of that document. GW wrote Lafayette on 1 Sept. to thank him for the hounds which had recently arrived, and he enclosed a letter to la comtesse Doilliamson.

4. For GW's explanation why Saint-Simon-Montbléru had not received an answer to his inquiry about membership in the Society of the Cincinnati, see GW to Lafayette, 1 Sept. 1785. Saint-Simon's letter, which has not been found, was enclosed in Lafayette's third letter to GW of 9 Mar. 1784. See GW to Saint-Simon-Montbléru, 10 May 1786.

5. Lafayette had arranged with Pierre Tourtille de Sangrain, who had a contract to provide lighting for a number of French cities, to buy New England whale oil. He also had persuaded Calonne, the comptroller general of French finances, to suspend certain duties on that oil. The New Englanders chose not to enter into a general agreement of this sort but to leave it to individual negotiations for the sale of their oil. See Lafayette to John Adams, 8 May 1785, in Idzerda, *Lafayette Papers*, 5:320–21, and Thomas Jefferson to Elbridge Gerry, 11 May 1785, and notes, in Boyd, *Jefferson Papers*, 8:142–45.

6. GW wrote Lafayette on 15 Feb. 1785 that he had told Robert Townsend Hooe not to get a Spanish jackass for him because of the cost. See the references in note 5 of that document for the saga of GW's Spanish jack.

From John Swan

Sir   Baltimore [Md.] May 13th 1785
When I was in England my friends Messrs Harrison Ansley & Co. of London gave me Charge of a power Attorney and several authentic papers from, and proving, the Heirs and legatees of Mr Thos Colvill of Fairfax County, who appears to have made a Will and died some time in October 1766, by which will You are appointed one of the Executors. I Shall esteem it a particular favor, If you will take the trouble of giving me any information respecting the Effects & Affairs of the said Thos Colvill, and the prospect the Heirs or Legatees have of receiving any part of his Estate and to what amount.[1]

I beg you will excuse me for this request—the Heirs are of Opinion they are intitled to some thing, which I assured them they would receive if any Property was bequeathed them and in any instance Came under Your Care I have the Honor to be with great respect and Esteem Your Excellencys most obedient and very Hble servant

John Swan

ALS, DLC:GW.
1. See GW to Swan, 23 May. For other references to the Colvill estate, see Henry Hollyday, 30 April, nn.1 and 2.

From Tench Tilghman

Sir   Baltimore [Md.] 14th May 1785.
I am desired by Mr Hollyday to transmit the inclosed to you, and to request the favor of an answer thro' my hands.[1] He has communicated the contents of his letter to me—That the Lady in question is the youngest Daughter of the late Capt. William Anderson of London, is well known to me and to many others; but if more regular proofs, than the bare assertions of Individuals, should be necessary to justify you in the payment of Colo. Collville's Legacy to *Miss Harriet Rebecca Anderson*, you will be pleased only to point out, to Mr Hollyday, the form you

would wish, and it will be complied with—The imprudence of a Brother, lately dead, has reduced the poor young Lady, now the last of her family, from affluence to intire dependance: so that what in time of her better fortunes was scarcely thought of by her, has now become an object of consequence.

I have almost the daily satisfaction of hearing by one or other of your (I fear too numerous) Visitors, of the health of Mrs Washington and yourself—Give me leave to assure you nothing affords me greater pleasure—Mrs Tilghman is upon a visit to her Friends upon the Eastern shore. I can safely take the freedom of joining her Respects to those of Dear Sir Your faithful and Affect: Hble Servt

Tench Tilghman

ALS, DLC:GW.
    1. See Henry Hollyday to GW, 30 April.

To Clement Biddle

Dear Sir,   Mount Vernon May 16th 1785.

I stand indebted to you for your several favors of the 7th of March, and 12th & 19th of April.

Believe me, Sir, the first was not productive of more surprize than real concern. The acct of your failure was as much regretted, as it was unexpected by me; and I feel for the causes of it—and for your present situation.[1]

You are sensible that my Commissions have been more troublesome than profitable to you; and as they are growing more trifling than ever, to continue them, might add to your embarrassments; otherwise, I do assure you, I should continue them with pleasure.

For the many friendly offices you have rendered me, I pray you to accept my thanks—The grass Seeds are all at hand (tho' late coming)—Mr Lewis has engaged me a Miller—The method you have taken to get the accts of the Indian Meal & Flour adjusted, is perfectly agreeable to me. and I approve of what you have done respecting my letter to Mr Lamont (the author of the Poems which were proposed to be dedicated to me).[2]

I have never received a paper from Messrs Claypool & Dunlap since your mention of their intention to forward them regularly; and think my self so ungenteelly treated by them, in this business, that I do not intend ever to take another of their Gazettes. If they had really sent them, I can conceive no reason why they should not have got to hand, as safe, as those from Carey—and others from Boston—&ca.

The Balle of your Acct Currt £2.3.0½ I have given to Genl Moylan who will pay it to you, or to your Assignees—I have done the same with respect to Claypools receipt, for £3.15.³— Cost of printing my advertisement. If you have not already paid his acct for the Gazettes, do me the favor, & justice to let him know (when it is done) that I am paying for what I have not had; and that it is my request that the acct may be finally closed between us; as I do not mean, unless I can be better satisfied than I am at present, to stand longer on their Books.

Mrs Washington joins me in every good wish for you, Mrs Biddle and family—and we both hope that fortune may be more propitious to you in future. If it should ever be in my way to render you any Services, I should have pleasure in doing it, being Dr Sir Yr Most Obedt Hble Servt

Go: Washington

ALS, NNC; LB, DLC:GW. GW wrote on the cover: "Favored by Genl Moylan."

1. In his letter of 7 Mar., Biddle informs GW of the failure of his business.

2. Biddle wrote GW on 12 April that upon Thomas Paine's advice he had made the decision not to deliver GW's letter of 31 Jan. giving Acneas Lamont permission to dedicate his collection of writings to GW. See GW to Biddle, 2 Feb., n.2.

3. Stephen Moylan (1737–1817) arrived at Mount Vernon with his wife on 27 April and left for Philadelphia on 16 May. He wrote from Alexandria on the day of his departure: "on looking over the Mem. you favord me with, I found a quarter of a dollar over, which Col. FitzGerald will be kind enough to return to you.

"permit me to return you my Sincere thanks for the polite attentions which Mrs Moylan and myself received from you & your good Lady during our agreeable Sojourn at Mount vernon—you may be assured it will be long rememberd with pleasure . . ." (ALS, DLC:GW).

To Francis Hopkinson

Dear Sir,   Mount Vernon May 16th 1785
In for a penny, in for a pound, is an old adage. I am so hackneyed to the touches of the Painters pencil, that I am *now* altogether at their beck, and sit like patience on a Monument whilst they are delineating the lines of my face.

It is a proof among many others, of what habit & custom can effect. At first I was as impatient at the request, and as restive under the operation, as a Colt is of the Saddle—The next time, I submitted very reluctantly, but with less flouncing. Now, no dray moves more readily to the Thill, than I do to the Painters Chair. It may easily be conceived therefore that I yielded a ready obedience to your request, and to the views of Mr Pine.

Letters from England, recommendatory of this Gentleman, came to my hand previous to his arrival in America—not only as an Artist of acknowledged eminence, but as one who had discovered a friendly disposition towards this Country—for which, it seems, he had been marked.[1]

It gave me pleasure to hear from you—I shall always feel an interest in your happiness—and with Mrs Washingtons compliments, & best wishes joined to my own, for Mrs Hopkinson & yourself, I am—Dr Sir, Yr Most Obedt & Affecte Hble Servant

Go: Washington

ALS, PWacD: Sol Feinstone Collection, on deposit PPAmP; LB, DLC:GW. Stephen Moylan took this letter and those cited in note 1 to Philadelphia. See GW to Biddle, 16 May, n.3.

1. For the letters introducing Robert Pine to GW, see Hopkinson to GW, 19 April, n.1. In his letter on this day thanking John Dickinson for his letter of introduction, GW repeats this third paragraph almost verbatim (ALS [photocopy], DLC:GW; LB, DLC:GW). In his letter to Thomas McKean, also of this day, GW varies his language somewhat: "I had the honor to receive your letter of the 23d Ulto by Mr Pine, whose character as a historical and Portrait Painter, and as a friend to the rights of America, has been very favorably represented to me from England before he made his appearance in this Country. His present design, if well executed, will do equal credit to his imagination and Pencil; and be interesting to America" (ALS, PHi: McKean Papers; LB, DLC:GW). Transcriptions of the letters are in CD-ROM:GW.

To Thomas Johnson and Thomas Sim Lee

Gentlemen   Alexa[ndria, Va.] 18th May 1785

At a meeting of the Subscribers to the Potowmac Navigation held yesterday agreeable to the Acts of Assembly of both States, a President and Directors were chosen, the former I have accepted of, & you two in conjunction with George Gilpin & John Fitzgerald Esqrs. were appointed Directors which I hope will be agreeable to you[.][1] As the Season begins to advance I have thought necessary that we should have a meeting as soon as it can be with convenience & have appointed Monday the 30th Inst. for that purpose.[2]

I have no doubt of your punctual attendance at that time the place I leave to you to fix upon, & request your answer by return of the Express, which is sent on this special Business[.] You'll also please mention the Hour you would wish to meet on.[3] I have the Honor to be &Ca

Signed G.W.

Copy, NIC.

Thomas Johnson (1732–1819) and Thomas Sim Lee (1745–1819) were both at this time living in Frederick, Maryland.

1. The following item appeared in the *Virginia Journal and Alexandria Advertiser* on 19 May: "Last Tuesday, being the Day appointed by the States of Virginia and Maryland, relative to opening the inland Navigation, of the River Potomack, a Meeting was held at Mr. Lomax's Tavern, consisting of a very numerous Assembly; of the first People in the respective States.—DANIEL CARROLL, Esq; President of the Assembly of Maryland, being appointed to the Chair, the Subscription Books were read as the Acts direct, when it appeared that Forty Thousand Three Hundred Pounds was subscribed, a Sum far beyond what was required to incorporate the Company.—The Company was of Course established, and proceeded to the Election of a President and Directors, when the following Gentlemen were appointed: His Excellency GEORGE WASHINGTON, President; GEORGE GILPIN, JOHN FITZGERALD, THOMAS JOHNSON, and THOMAS S. LEE, Esquires, Directors.

"The great and important Work is to be immediately begun —The vast Consequence that must derive to the Middle States when completed, cannot be elucidated but by Time, the Discoverer of all great Events.

"The next General Meeting is appointed to be held at George-Town on the first of August next."

John Lomax's tavern was on the corner of Princess and Water streets. Daniel Carroll (1730–1796), who lived in Montgomery County, Md., was a member of the Maryland senate. He was the brother of John Carroll (1735–1815), head of the Catholic church in America. George Gilpin (1740–1813), a native of Cecil County, Md., was a wheat merchant in Alexandria.

On 26 May the Alexandria paper printed the minutes of this first meeting of the Potomac River Company, held at "Alexandria, May 17, 1785": "THIS Day, and at this Town, pursuant to the Act of the General Assembly of the Commonwealth of Virginia for opening and extending the Navigation of Potomack River, and pursuant to the Act of the General Assembly of the State of Maryland for the same Purpose, there was a general Meeting of the Subscribers to the Undertaking, who proceeded to the Choice of a Chairman, and elected Daniel Carroll, Esq.; to that Office, and appointed Charles Lee, Esq.;

Clerk of the Meeting. The Books that had been opened for receiving Subscriptions at the City of Richmond, at the Towns of Alexandria and
Winchester, in Virginia; and at the City of Annapolis, at George-Town, and
Frederick-Town, in the State of Maryland, being produced and examined,
the Subscriptions therein appeared to be as follow, viz.

"In the Richmond Book[s], One Hundred Shares;

"In the Alexandria Books, One Hundred Thirty-Five Shares;

"In the Winchester Books, Thirty-One Shares;

"In the Annapolis Books, Seventy-Three Shares;

"In the George-Town Books, Forty-Two Shares;

"In the Frederick-Town Books, Twenty-Two Shares;

"Amounting in all to Four Hundred and Three Shares, which made a
Capital of Forty Thousand and Three Hundred Pounds, Sterling Money.

"On a Motion made and seconded, *Resolved,* That the Subscribers now
present in Person, together with those represented by Proxy, proceed to
the Choice of a President and Directors of the Potomack Company, and
that the President and Directors, now to be chosen, shall continue in Office
until the First Monday in the Month of August, which shall be in the Year One
Thousand Seven Hundred and Eighty-Six.

"*Resolved,* That at every General Meeting, in taking the Votes of the Proprietors, each Proprietor shall give in his Vote or Votes at the Clerk's Table in
Writing, and where the Vote or Votes shall be given by Proxy, that the Name
of each Constituent be also inserted.

"*Ordered,* That Charles Simms and James Keith be a Committee, to examine the Deputations to act and vote as Proxy, and to make Report thereof to
this Meeting; who having made Report accordingly,

"*Resolved,* That the Deputations from Thomas Blackburn to William
Brown, from Thomas Johnston to Abraham Faw, and from John Lynn to
Abraham Faw, to act and vote for them respectively, appearing to have been
executed before one Witness only, are illegal and insufficient, and that the
said Thomas Blackburn, Thomas Johnston, and John Lynn, be not admitted
to vote by their respective Proxies aforesaid.

"The Proprietors present in Person, as well as the absent Proprietors by
their respective Proxies, having given in their Votes in the Manner before
mentioned for the Choice of a President and Four Directors of the Potomack
Company, and the said Votes being duly examined and accounted, a Majority
of Votes as in Favor of his Excellency George Washington to be President, and
in Favor of Thomas Johnston, Thomas Sim Lee, John Fitzgerald, and George
Gilpin, Esquires, to be Directors; and thereupon his Excellency George Washington was declared by the Chairman to be elected President, and the said
Thomas Johnston, Thomas Sim Lee, John Fitzgerald and George Gilpin, Directors of the Potomack Company.

"*Ordered,* That the names of the Proprietors who were present in proper
Person, and also of those who voted and acted by Proxy at this Meeting, with
the Names of such Proxies respectively, be inserted on the Minutes.

"Present in proper Person. His Excellency George Washington, Daniel
Carroll, Robert Peter, Samuel Davidson, William Deakins, jun., Charles

Worthington, Thomas Beall of George, Henry Townsend, James M. Lingan, Benjamin Stoddert, John Boucher, Bernard O'Neill, Lyonel Bradstreet, Thomas Cramphin, George Digges, James Johnston, Abraham Faw, Horatio Gates, Peter B. Bruin, Edward Beeson, Edward Smith, Joseph Holmes, John Gunnell, Charles Little, Roger West, Lund Washington, William Hepburn, Henry Lyles, William Lowry, Benjamin Shreve, John Harper, William Scott, Daniel M'Pherson, William Brown, William Hartshorne, George Gilpin, Leven Powell, Charles Simms, Robert T. Hooe, William Ellzey, Samuel M. Brown, Joseph Janney, Daniel Roberdeau, John Allison, Baldwin Dade, Benjamin Dulany, James Lawrason, James Keith, Alexander Henderson, David Stewart, William Lyles, John Potts, jun. William Herbert, Dennis Ramsay, Richard Conway, John Fitzgerald and Charles Lee.

"*Present by Proxy.*—Jaquelin Ambler, Agent for the Commonwealth of Virginia, by his Excellency George Washington, Joseph W. Harrison by Dennis Ramsay, Richard Harrison by Robert T. Hooe, Thomas Lewis by Charles Simms, Robert Macky by Edward Smith, Henry Ridgely, jun. by William Deakins, jun. William Baley by William Deakins, jun. George Scott by Robert Peter, and James Rumsey by Peter B. Bruin.—Also, Baker Johnston, George Schnitzell, Thomas S. Lee, Joseph Chapline, Philip Thomas, Thomas Beaty, Joseph Sim, John F. Ameling, Thomas Gauntt, Thomas Hawkins and Patrick S. Smith, severally and respectively by Abraham Faw; also, Alexander White, Philip Pendleton, William Drew, Moses Hunter, William Bready, William M'Kewan, James Campbell, Henry Bedinger, George Scott, George Hite, Walter Baker, Abraham Shepherd, Benjamin Beiler, and Cornelius Wynkoop, severally and respectively by Horatio Gates.

"*Resolved*, That the Writings concerning the Deputations to act and vote as Proxy, be delivered, together with the Subscription Books and the Minutes of this Meeting, to the President and Directors; and that a general Meeting of the Potomack Company be held at George Town, in the State of Maryland, on the First Monday in August next. CHARLES LEE, Clerk of the Meeting."

2. At some point GW made a list of the powers and duties with which the Potomac River bill endowed the company's president and trustees. It would have been out of character for GW to have made this "Abstract from the Potomac Bill" before he was elected president of the company on 17 May; it would have been very much in character for him to make the abstract very soon after he took office. The text of the undated memorandum, in GW's hand and initialed by him, is: "The President and Directors to conduct the Undertaking & manage *all* the Company's business & concerns.

"Directors to agree on behalf of the Company with any person or persons to cut Canals, & open Locks, or perform other Works to the highest part of the No. Branch.

"Directors to appoint a treasurer, Clerk, Managers &ca &ca as they shall judge requisite & agree for & settle their Wages.

"Directors to establish rules of proceeding, and to transact *all* the business of the Company between the General Meetings.

"Directors to be allowed such a sum of money for their trouble as a Gen-[era]l Meeting shall direct.

"Treasurer to give Bond in such penalty and with such security as the Presidt & Directors shall direct.

"His allowances not to exceed three pounds in the hund[re]d for the disbursemts by him made.

"Directors have full power to call from time to time for money, as it shall be wanted. sign orders for that purpose—direct at what time—and in what proportion the Proprietors shall advance—giving 1 Months previous notice at least in the Virg[ini]a & Maryl[an]d Gazettes—To order the said sums to be *deposited* in the *hands* of the *Treasurer*.

"Treasurer to pay on the order of the President & Directors, or a Majority of them.

"If any of the Proprietors shall refuse, or neglect to pay their said proportions within one Month after the same is ordered & advertised as aforesaid— The Presidt & Directors or a majority of them may sell at Auction & convey to the Purchaser giving one Months notice of the Sale in the V. & M. Gazettes.

"President & Directors before they act to take an oath for the due execution of their Office.

"The President & Directors to make report to the Annual general Meeting of the Comp[an]y & render just & distinct accts of all their Proceedings & obtain a certificate thereof.

"Upon any emergency in the Intervals of the General Meetings the Directors may call a Genl Meeting giving a Months previous Notice in the V. & M. Gazettes.

"Presidt & Directors to agree with the owners of Land for passage through the same or to obtain a condemnation in case of disagreement.

"And the deficiency of the 500 Shares in whch Shares as first offered a certificate of which to be returned by them to the Genl Courts. Go: W———n" (ICU).

3. The following was added at the bottom of this copy of GW's letter of 18 May printed here: "Thomas Johnson Esqr. May 19th 85[.] Since the letter which accompanies this was wrote by Genl Washington I have found a private oppy (Mr Huff of this Town) who is to return immediately to this place & have to Save expence to the Company committed it to his care If you find it necessary to Send an express to Mr Lee the expence Shall be paid at the meeting."

To Richard Sprigg

Dear Sir,　　　　　　　　　　　Mount Vernon 18th May 1785.

I received the Grass-seeds which you sent me sometime since, & thank you for them.[1]

This Letter will be handed to you by Mr Pine, an Artist of acknowledged eminence; who, whilst it is yet possible is endeavouring to secure faithful representations of some of the interesting events of this War—As he proposes to take Annapolis on

his way to Philadelphia I pray you to allow me the liberty of introducing him to your civilities² at the sametime that I assure
you of the esteem & regard with which I am Dr Sir—Yr Most
Obedt Hble Servt

Go: Washington

ALS, MHi: Miscellaneous Bound Collection.

Richard Sprigg had fine gardens and orchards at his place, Strawberry
Hill, near Annapolis.

1. In his diary entry of 14 April GW recorded that he "Sowed 5 rows and a
small piece of the bird grass seed (sent me by Mr Sprig of Annapolis)" (*Diaries*,
4:119).

2. In GW's letter book (DLC:GW), there are letters of this day introducing
Robert Pine to two other men at Annapolis, Edward Lloyd (1744–1793) and
Gov. William Paca. The text of GW's letter to Lloyd is: "This letter will be presented to you by Mr Pine an eminent historical & portrait painter: he is now
by his drawings, representing some of the most memorable events of the late
war; & finding it necessary to call at Annapolis, I take the liberty of introducing him to your civilities." He wrote Paca: "Mr Pine who will deliver this letter
to your Excellency, is an artist of acknowledged eminence, & one who has
given the world many pleasing & forcible specimens of genius: he is engaged
in painting some of the most interesting events of the late war; in the prosecution of which he finds it necessary to call at Annapolis."

Index

Abridgement of the Gardener's Dictionary: Philip Miller, 174, 258, 384, 511–12
An Account of Washington College in the State of Maryland (1784), 38
An Act for Opening and Extending the Navigation of Potowmack River, 241–45
Adam, Robert & Co., 279
Adams, John: in London, 396, 416, 418, 424, 505, 545, 556; and negotiations for whale oil, 557–58; *letters from*: to Caleb Cushing, 305
Adams, John Quincy: id., 505; conveys letters, 550, 556, 557
Adams, Samuel: *letters from*: to GW, 534
Aitken, Robert: and Ebenezer Hazard, 251; prints Belknap's *History*, 3
Alexandria: and Potomac River Company, 313–14
Allegheny River, 90, 107, 169, 233
Allen, Zachariah, 276
Allison, John (*see* 1:310–11): holds shares in Potomac River Company, 565
Ambler, Jacquelin: and Potomac River Company subscriptions, 241; as a manager of Potomac River Company, 360–61, 552; id., 552; holds shares in Potomac River Company, 565; *letters from*: to GW, 552
Ambler, Rebecca Burwell: id., 552
Ameling, John F.: holds shares in Potomac River Company, 565
Andalusia (Pa.; house), 469
Anderson, Edward: and Harriot Rebecca Anderson's legacy, 527–28, 559–60; *letters from*: to GW, 528
Anderson, Harriot Rebecca: and Thomas Colvill's estate, 526–28, 559–60
Anderson, Robert: qualities of as husbandman, 113–14; *letters from*: to GW, 99; *letters to*: from GW, 113–14

Anderson, William: and Harriot Rebecca Anderson, 526, 559; and Dismal Swamp Company, 530, 531
Annapolis Convention, 250, 263
Ansley, Harrison, & Co.: and Thomas Colvill's estate, 559
Arbuthnot, Thomas: and French-Dulany tract, 373–74
Arell, David: id., 38; and Washington College lottery, 57
Ariss, John: id., 24; and lease of Bullskin land, 24–25, 26; and Warner Washington, 26; and land purchased from George Mercer, 27; *letters from*: to GW, 24–25; *letters to*: from GW, 27–28
Arkwright, Richard: and cotton manufactures, 205
Armstrong, James: id., 290
Armstrong, John: gives GW spiritual advice, 287–90; id., 290; *letters from*: to GW, 287–90
Armstrong, Mary Stevenson: id., 290
Articles of Confederation: and regulation of trade, 538. *See also* Congress
Artisans: joiners sought, 7–8, 14–15, 22, 337–38; joiners hired, 11–12, 15, 22, 23, 42, 337–38; bricklayers sought, 12, 22, 23, 42, 70, 337; millwright acquired, 23–24; Britain's bans on emigration of, 205; black apprenticed to joiner, 529
Asgill (play): Lebarbier, 406–7
Asgill, Charles: id., 407
Asgill, Sir Charles: id., 407
Asgill, Theresa Pratviel: id., 407
Asses. *See* Jackasses
Associate Presbyterian (Seceders') Church: members of on Millers Run tract, 340
Athawes, Edward: and the Corbin brothers, 441–42
Atkinson, J. (shipmaster), 337

Bacon, Anthony: and Dismal Swamp Company, 531

Baker, Walter: holds shares in Potomac River Company, 565

Balch, Stephen Bloomer: and schooling of GW's nephews, 61–62, 113, 138–39, 370–71, 495; *letters to*: from GW, 113

Baldridge, Matthew (*see* 1:484): hired as joiner, 337–38

Baley (Bayley; Bailey), William: holds shares in Potomac River Company, 565

Ball, Burgess, 371; id., 155

Ball, Frances Washington, 371; and death of child, 155; id., 155

Baltimore: opposes Potomac River Company, 166, 313

Bane, Robert, 62

Bank of England stock: attempted sale of, 13

Banks, John & Co.: and Nathanael Greene, 522–23

Barbé-Marbois (Barbé de Marbois), François (*see* 1:101), 247; and grapevines for GW, 148–49; and Longchamps, 550, 551; *letters to*: from Malesherbes, 148–49

Barnes & Ridgate, 424

Barrell, Joseph: *letters from*: to Samuel B. Webb, 104

Bartlett, Mary Crane: id., 45; leases Bullskin land, 46

Bartlett, William: leases Bullskin land, 46

Bassett, Burwell (*see* 1:57), 7, 14–15, 135, 258–59

Bassett, Frances (Fanny; *see* 1:251), 10, 32, 39, 284, 479, 491, 494–95, 504; visits friends, 65; illness of, 154, 258; portrait of by Robert Edge Pine, 509

Bath (Warm Springs; Berkeley Springs): and GW's houses at, 426–27, 428

Bauercraft, James: and GW's Millers Run ejectment suit, 354

Baylor, George: id., 518

Baylor, John (1708–1772): money owed Custis estate, 518, 519

Baylor, John (1750–1808): and Custis estate, 518, 519; id., 518; *letters from*: to GW, 518–19

Beall, Thomas (of George): holds shares in Potomac River Company, 565

Beatty, Charles: and Potomac River navigation, 131

Beaty, Thomas: holds shares in Potomac River Company, 565

Beckley, John (*see* 1:251–52), 263; and Potomac River Company, 241, 275, 322, 360–61; *letters from*: to GW, 360–61; *letters to*: from GW, 322–23

Bedinger, Henry: holds shares in Potomac River Company, 565

Beekman, James, 408; and grapevines for GW, 147–48, 149, 429; id., 149

Beeson, Edward: holds shares in Potomac River Company, 565

Beiler (Beeler), Benjamin, 138; holds shares in Potomac River Company, 565

Belknap, Jeremy: *The History of New Hampshire*, 3, 251; id., 3; *letters from*: to GW, 2–3; to Ebenezer Hazard, 3, 251; *letters to*: from Ebenezer Hazard, 3, 251; from GW, 251

Bell, Colonel ——, 83

Belvoir (house; *see* 1:435), 51, 118; ruinous state of, 387–88, 390

Benson, Egbert (*see* 1:53): and *Rutgers v. Waddington*, 189; as a commissioner of slave embarkation, 482

Berkeley Springs. *See* Bath

Bermuda, 31–32, 39; George Augustine Washington's arrival at, 10; prices in, 40

Berry Hill (house; later Cedar Lawn): id., 21

Bibby, Thomas: id., 535; *letters from*: to GW, 534–35

Biddle, Clement (*see* 1:20), 32; acts for GW, 22, 114–15, 115, 174, 259, 294, 298, 300, 306–8, 318–19, 334, 410–11, 480, 490–91, 507, 560–61; bankruptcy of, 410–11, 560; *letters from*: to GW, 298, 410–11, 490–91, 507; to William Thompson, 411; *letters to*: from GW, 14, 22, 114–15, 306–9, 318–19, 560–61

Biddle, Nicholas, 469
Biddle, Rebekah Cornell (*see* 1 : 20), 560
Big Beaver Creek (Pa.), 94, 97–98
Biggert, Thomas: settles on Millers Run tract, 354
Bingham, Anne Willing: travels to England, 498
Bingham, William: id., 498
Birks, Samuel & Co., 40
Blackburn, Thomas: appointed Virginia commissioner to secure Maryland Potomac River Company bill, 185–87, 195–96, 196, 223; id., 195; *letters from*: to GW, 196; *letters to*: from GW, 195
Blagge (Blaggs), John, 429
Blake, William: id., 259–60, 452; sends plants and seed, 451; *letters from*: to GW, 451–52
Blanchard, Jonathan: leaves Congress, 37
Bloxham, James: as farm manager at Mount Vernon, 114
Bomford, Sarah: and Margaret Savage's estate, 432–33; *letters from*: to GW, 84; *letters to*: from GW, 431–33
Bond, Jacob: id., 26
Bond, Thomas: and GW's Millers Run ejectment suit, 354
Booth, William: and schooling of GW's nephews, 138–39
Boucher, John (*see* 1 : 407): holds shares in Potomac River Company, 565
Boudinot, Elias (*see* 1 : 34): and grass seed for GW, 114–15, 115–16, 294, 298, 300, 306, 333–34, 410–11, 490, 507; *letters from*: to GW, 115, 180, 333–34; *letters to*: from GW, 115, 115–16, 294, 300
Boudinot, Hannah Stockton (*see* 1 : 34), 334
Boulton (Bolton), Richard: and Mount Vernon's New Room, 529, 554–55; id., 529–30; and William Fitzhugh, 554–55
Bowie, John: and biography of GW, 414–16, 496–97
Bowling Green (Va.): Lafayette and GW at, 145; id., 518
Boyle, John, Jr.: conveys Edward

Newenham's packages, 405–6, 430, 448, 452, 453–54; *letters from*: to GW, 405–6
Boyseau, Pierre de, 222
Brackenridge, Hugh Henry: id., 354; and GW's Millers Run ejectment suit, 354
Bradford, Charles, 19, 349
Bradford, Susan Vergereau Boudinot, 334; marriage of, 116, 294
Bradford, William, Jr., 294; id., 116
Bradstreet, Lyonel: conveys package, 15, 526; holds shares in Potomac River Company, 565; *letters from*: to GW, 526
Brady (Bready), William: holds shares in Potomac River Company, 565
Branning, ——: becomes indentured servant, 11–12
Brant, Joseph: and Treaty of Fort Stanwix, 36–37, 84, 105
Brent, George, 479
Brenton, Samuel: *letters from*: to GW, 276–77
Bristow, Mary (*see* 1 : 448): and Virginia property, 387
Bristow, Richard: and his patrimony in Virginia, 387
British debts: owed by Virginians, 183
British politics: news of, 16, 25–26, 29–30, 36, 53–54, 143, 176–77, 462
Britton, ——: and estate of Richard Richards, 316
Broglie, Victor-François, 335
Brown, John: id., 162; plans settlement along Potomac, 456–57; and gardener for GW, 457
Brown, Joseph: and Maj. James Keith, 359–60
Brown, Samuel M.: holds shares in Potomac River Company, 565
Brown, William: holds shares in Potomac River Company, 565
Bruce, Normand: argues for paper currency, 126–28; presents plans for a Potomac River company, 128–33; id., 131; *letters from*: to GW, 126–33
Bruce-Beatty report (1783): and Potomac River navigation, 131–33

Bruin, Peter B.: holds shares in Potomac River Company, 565
Bryan, John: leases Bullskin land, 46
Bryan, Jonathan: id., 542
Buchanan, James: and William Byrd's lottery, 4–5; id., 4–5
Bullskin land (*see* 1:114). *See* Lands of GW
Burning Springs tract: copy of grant for sent, 556. *See also* Lands of GW
Burwell, Lewis, 552
Burwell, Nathaniel: id., 69
Byrd, William, III: lottery of, 4–5

Cadwalader (Cadwallader), John: id., 179; and Maryland Potomac River Company bill, 236–40; *letters to*: from GW, 178–79
Caesar (ship), 337
Calonne, Charles-Alexandre de (*see* 1:30): and whale oil, 558
Campbell, James: holds shares in Potomac River Company, 565
Campbell, Matthew: and plaster of paris, 278–79, 402–3; id., 279; *letters to*: from GW, 278–79, 402–3
Campbell, Matthew (d. 1782): id., 279
Candles: manufacture of, 193–94
Cannon, John: and GW's Millers Run ejectment suit, 343, 347, 348, 353, 354
Captina Creek, 489–90
Caraman, Maurice Riquet, chevalier de, 44, 104, 176, 227, 336, 450; id., 85; visits Mount Vernon, 144–45
Carey, Christopher, 228
Carey, Mathew, 227, 561; and *Volunteer Journal* (Dublin), 227–28, 365; id., 228; and *Pennsylvania Herald* (Philadelphia), 228; and Lafayette, 434; GW's offers support to, 509; *letters from*: to GW, 472; *letters to*: from GW, 433–34, 509
Carleton, Sir Guy: sent to Canada, 30
Carlyle, John, 327; and John Ariss, 24
Carlyle & Adam, 279
Carmichael, William: and Spanish jackasses for GW, 2, 163–64, 165,
178, 460, 470; id., 164; *letters from*: to GW, 163–64, 460–61; to Thomas Jefferson, 178; *letters to*: from Floridablanca, 165; from Lafayette, 461
Carrington, Edward: and tribute to GW, 137
Carroll, Charles (of Annapolis; 1702–1782): and GW's purchase of Clifton's Neck, 266
Carroll, Charles (1723–1783; the barrister): id., 31
Carroll, Charles (of Carrollton; 1737–1832): id., 179; and Maryland Potomac River Company bill, 236–40; and GW's purchase of Clifton's Neck, 266; subscribes to Potomac River Company, 485; *letters to*: from GW, 178–79, 265–66
Carroll, Daniel: id., 563; and first meeting of Potomac River Company, 563; holds shares in Potomac River Company, 564
Carroll, John: id., 563
Carroll, Margaret Tilghman: and GW's greenhouse, 30–31, 42–44; id., 31
Carter, Charles (of Culpeper): transmits letter, 488
Carter, Landon, 423
Carter, Robert: acts for George Steptoe Washington and Lawrence Augustine Washington, 370–71
Cary, Robert & Co.: GW's account with, 12–13
Castries, Charles-Eugène-Gabriel de La Croix, maréchal de (*see* 1:449), 550
Cedar Lawn. *See* Berry Hill
Chamney, Christopher: id., 327; *letters from*: to GW, 326–27
Chapline, Joseph: holds shares in Potomac River Company, 565
Chapman, George: id., 184; *A Treatise on Education with a Sketch of the Author's Method of Instruction . . .*, 184; *letters to*: from GW, 183–84
Charles III of Spain: and jackasses for GW, 164, 165, 178
Charles Theodore, elector of Bavaria, 532, 543, 557
Chase, Hannah Kitty Giles, 253

Chase, Matilda, 253

Chase, Samuel, 354, 547; id., 179; and Maryland Potomac River Company bill, 252; and Mount Vernon conference, 297; *letters from*: to GW, 246; *letters to*: from GW, 178–79, 252–53, 272

Chastellux, François-Jean de Beauvoir, chevalier de (*see* 1:86): and Ducher, 492; and Montesquieu, 530; *letters from*: to GW, 45, 180, 484; *letters to*: from GW, 44–45, 401

Châteaufort, chevalier d'Aristay: id., 222; *letters to*: from GW, 222

Cheat River: and Potomac River navigation, 94, 238–39, 245–46, 250, 263, 294–95, 330, 455, 469

Chesterfield, earl of. *See* Stanhope, Philip

Choiseuil-Stainville, Etienne-François, duc de: death of, 557

Cider, 479

Cincinnati, Society of, 558; in Massachusetts, 10, 303; opposition to, 10, 59–60; and French officers, 22–23, 70–71; in Sweden, 48; and admission of French naval captains, 100–101; and diplomas of, 287, 319–20; and theft of diplomas of, 320, 512–13; in New Hampshire, 320–22; reforms of criticized, 320–22

Ciphers. *See* Codes

Claiborne, Richard: and John Filson, 169–70; id., 185; and western lands, 185; *letters from*: to GW, 139; *letters to*: from GW, 184–85

Clarke, Thomas: *letters to*: from GW, 290–91

Claypole, Abraham: and Society of Cincinnati diplomas, 287, 319–20

Claypoole, David C.: and *Pennsylvania Packet, and Daily Advertiser* (Philadelphia), 307–8, 507; GW's account with closed, 561

Clinton, Cornelia Tappen, 408–9; illness of, 146

Clinton, George: and GW's repayment of loan from, 146, 148, 463–64, 473–74, 477, 483, 510, 511–12; and purchase of New York land with GW, 146, 147–48, 408–9, 510, 512; and plants and seed for GW, 146–47, 148, 174, 224–26, 408–9, 429, 510; vouches for Charles Hay, 192; and Frederick Weissenfels, 439, 464–65; *letters from*: to GW, 125, 230, 408–9; *letters to*: from GW, 145–49, 174–75, 477, 509–12

Clinton, George Washington: accident of, 146

Codes: used by Lafayette and GW, 227, 336, 550–51

Colby, ——, 309; visits Mount Vernon, 250

Colquhoun, Patrick: id., 77

Colvill, Thomas: and Harriot Rebecca Anderson's legacy, 526–28, 559–60; estate of, 559

Condé, Louis-Joseph de Bourbon, prince de, 335

Congress: criticisms of, 25, 35–36, 142, 162, 301–2; location of, 230, 332, 365, 396, 418, 537; and land policy, 395–96; rejects Lady Huntingdon's scheme, 395; activities of, 424; memorials to, 471–72; and regulation of trade, 538; and the army, 539–40; and gold medal to GW, 546

Connecticut: politics in, 162

Constitutional Convention of 1787, 250

Continental loan certificates: GW's ownership of, 470, 473–74, 483, 484–85, 491, 501

Conway, Richard: holds shares in Potomac River Company, 565

Cook, James: *A Voyage to the Pacific Ocean*, 307, 411

Corbin, Francis: id., 441

Corbin, Richard (c.1714–1796): id., 442

Corbin, Richard (b. 1751): and squabble with Thomas Corbin, 441–42; id., 442

Corbin, Thomas: and squabble with Richard Corbin (b. 1751), 441–42; id., 442

Coxe, Tench: id., 296

Coxe & Frazier: and silverware for GW, 296

Coxeborough township (N.Y.): and GW's Mohawk Valley land, 147–48

Cragg, —— (shipmaster), 70
Craig, James: id., 456
Craig, John: id., 456; and western lands, 469; *letters from*: to GW, 455–56; *letters to*: from GW, 469
Craig, Margaret Craig: id., 469
Craigie, Andrew: id., 296
Craik, James (*see* 1:178), 2, 64; travels West with GW, 66, 82–83; *letters from*: to GW, 82–83
Craik, Nancy: id., 2
Craik, William: travels West with GW, 66, 83
Cramphin, Thomas: holds shares in Potomac River Company, 565
Crane, James: and Henry Whiting's account, 27; id., 45; and Bullskin land, 46; *letters to*: from GW, 45
Crawford, Valentine: and Millers Run tract, 347–48
Crawford, William, 284–85; and Millers Run tract, 338–39, 340–42, 443–46; and GW's Millers Run ejectment suit, 338–50, 353–54, 489; *letters from*: to GW, 338–39
Cresap, Michael: and claims to Round Bottom tract, 489–90, 556
Crèvecoeur, Michel-Guillaume St. Jean (John) de (*see* 1:433): and Lafayette, 194; forwards letter, 455; *letters from*: to GW, 455
Croghan, George: and Millers Run tract, 338–40, 353; *letters from*: to Joseph Wharton, 339
Crompton, Samuel: and cotton manufactures, 205
Cross, James: id., 435; *letters from*: to GW, 434–35
Cruikshank, Joseph: id., 38
Culpeper, Margaret, Lady: and sixth Lord Fairfax, 55
Cushing, Caleb: *letters to*: from John Adams, 305
Cushing, Thomas: and Spanish jackasses for GW, 164
Custis, Daniel Parke: estate of, 13, 519
Custis, Eleanor Parke, 155, 384; illness of, 116; schooling of, 183–84; and gift from Lafayette family, 502; portrait of by Robert Edge Pine, 509

Custis, George Washington Parke, 155, 176, 227, 384, 413, 450; and Jean Le Mayeur, 38, 65; illness of, 116; schooling of, 183–84; and William Gordon, 467; and gift from Lafayette family, 502; portrait of by Robert Edge Pine, 509
Custis, John Parke: estate of, 13, 519
Custis, Martha Parke, 450; estate of, 13, 519
Cuyahoga River, 94, 97–98

Dade, Baldwin: holds shares in Potomac River Company, 565
Dade, Parthenia: and George Steptoe Washington and Lawrence Augustine Washington, 62
Dana, Francis: leaves Congress, 37
Dandridge, Bartholomew (1737–1785; *see* 1:209): administers John Parke Custis's estate, 518, 519; death of, 521
Dandridge, Bartholomew, Jr.: and Potomac River Company papers, 275
Dandridge, Frances Jones: death of, 521
Darby, Elias Hasket: id., 539
Darley, George: draws plans for Mount Vernon piazza, 337–38
Dashiell, Joseph: and Maryland Potomac River Company bill, 236–40; id., 386; *letters from*: to GW, 385–86
Davenport, Joseph: hired as miller, 152, 318, 493–94; id., 480–81
Davidson, John: and Potomac River Company subscriptions, 547–48
Davidson, Samuel: holds shares in Potomac River Company, 564
Deakins, Francis: and Pennsylvania road, 245
Deakins, William, Jr.: holds shares in Potomac River Company, 564
Deane, Silas (*see* 1:277): and William Carmichael, 164
De Butts, John: and Maryland Potomac River Company bill, 236–40
Deer: to be sent by George William Fairfax, 390
De Hart, Sarah: silhouettes by, 411–13, 465–66

Deism, 289

De l'administration des finances de la France: Jacques Necker, 450

Delaware River, 231, 332

Detroit: distances from, 97–98, 106–7

Deux Ponts, Charles-Auguste-Christian, Count Palatine, duc de, 449

Dick, Samuel: leaves Congress, 37

Dickinson, John (*see* 1:321–22): *letters from*: to GW, 508; *letters to*: from GW, 562

Dickinson, Philemon: and James Duane, 189

Dickinson, Sylvanus: and GW's repayment of George Clinton's loan, 477; and GW's draft on, 483, 510, 511–12

Digges, Ann Atwood: id., 103

Digges, George: and Maryland Potomac River Company bill, 168, 236–40; holds shares in Potomac River Company, 565

Digges, Mary Carroll: and Clifton's Neck, 266

Digges, William: id., 103

Diriks, Jacob Gerhard: id., 286; *letters from*: to GW, 285–86; *letters to*: from GW, 435–36

The Discovery, Settlement, and Present State of Kentucke: John Filson, 169–70, 269–70, 327–28, 436

Dismal Swamp Company, 488–89; meeting of, 58, 62–63, 474–75, 518, 530–31; and foreign laborers, 530–31; resolutions of, 530–31

Dismal Swamp tract: owned by GW jointly, 62

Distance charts for Ohio country, 97–98

Dogs: sent from France, 504–5, 557–58; and superiority of English breeds, 504, 557

Dogue Creek: and French-Dulany tract, 374–75

Dohrman, Arnold Henry: id., 476–77

Doilliamson, comte de: and dogs for GW, 557–58 Doilliamson, comtesse de: and dogs for GW, 557–58

Dolphin (ship), 298, 411

Donald, Alexander: id., 410

Doradour, comte de: introduction of, 551

Dorset, John Frederick Sackville, third duke of, 467

Dow, Peter, 375

Dow tract, 375, 512

Drew, William (*see* 1:115), 264; and GW's Bullskin lands, 45–46; holds shares in Potomac River Company, 565; *letters to*: from GW, 45–46

Duane, James (*see* 1:321): and *Rutgers v. Waddington*, 189, 485; *addresses from*: to GW, 188–90; *letters from*: to GW, 187–90, 418–19, 534; *letters to*: from GW, 485–86, 487–88

Duane, Maria (Mary) Livingston, 419, 486

Duane, Maria (Mary; 1761–1813), 419, 486

Ducher, Gaspard-Joseph-Armand: id., 492–93

Dulany, Benjamin Tasker: and French-Dulany tract, 373–75, 565

Dulany, Daniel: id., 553

Dulany, Elizabeth French: and French-Dulany tract, 373–75

Dumfries: Lafayette and GW at, 145; GW's visit to, 281

Dunlap, John, 436; and *Pennsylvania Packet, and Daily Advertiser* (Philadelphia), 307–8, 411

Dunlap, William, 561

Dunmore, John Murray, fourth earl of, 444; and Proclamation of 1763, 123–24

Duportail (Du Portail), Louis Le Bègue (Le Bèque) de Presle (*see* 1:103): *letters to*: from GW, 46–47

Dupré, ———: and grapevines for GW, 149

Du Simitière, Pierre-Eugène: id., 413; and engravings of Revolution's leaders, 466

Dwight, Timothy (*see* 1:157): and David Humphreys, 33

East India Company: criticism of, 75–77

Elizabeth River: survey of ordered, 249
Elizabeth River Canal, 265, 330, 363, 380
Ellicott, Andrew: id., 429
Ellzey, William: holds shares in Potomac River Company, 565
Emigration: British restrictions on, 205, 497–98
Estaing, Charles-Hector, comte d' (*see* 1:21): and Society of Cincinnati, 71
European affairs: news of, 73, 124–25, 173, 176–77, 268–69, 271, 286, 335, 335–36, 367–68, 378–79, 396, 419, 423, 449, 462–63, 466–67, 503–4, 532–33, 543, 557
Evans, Lewis: *A General Map of the Middle Colonies in America*, 89, 106
Excise tax, 418
Experiments and Observations in Cement: Benjamin Higgins, 256

Fairfax, Bryan, 55; and the Savage affair, 276, 433
Fairfax, Catherine, Lady: and sixth Lord Fairfax, 55
Fairfax, George William, 45, 114; and dispute over quitrents, 51–55; and Battaile Muse, 73; and business affairs in Virginia, 117–18; and George Chapman, 184; and Lady Huntingdon, 209–10, 392; and wartime correspondence with GW, 388, 390, 441; and English deer, 390; and the Corbin brothers, 441–42; *letters from*: to GW, 51–55, 54–55, 441–42, 442; *letters to*: from GW, 55, 386–90
Fairfax, John: conducts jackass to Mount Vernon, 164; id., 403
Fairfax, Sarah Cary: greetings to, 387
Fairfax, William: id., 54
Fairfax of Cameron, Robert Fairfax, seventh Baron: succeeds to the title, 54
Fairfax of Cameron, Thomas Fairfax, sixth Baron: the will of, 51–52, 54–55; id., 54

Fairfield (house; *see* 1:164): id., 26
Farley, Francis (*see* 1:80): and Dismal Swamp Company, 531
Faw, Abraham: holds shares in Potomac River Company, 565
Fendall, Ann Steptoe Lee: id., 145
Fendall, Philip Richard: id., 145
Ferrers, Washington Shirley, Earl, 200
Filson, John: *The Discovery, Settlement, and Present State of Kentucke*, 169, 269–70, 327–28, 436; id., 169; *letters from*: to GW, 168–70, 170, 327–28; *letters to*: from GW, 269–70, 436
Fincastle County (Va.): and surveyor of, 124
Fishbourn (Fishbourne), Benjamin: conveys letters, 540, 541
Fitzgerald, John, 12, 23, 528, 561; acts as Potomac River Company commissioner, 88, 241, 273–75, 277–78, 280, 335; and diplomas of Society of Cincinnati, 319–20; made director of Potomac River Company, 562–63; holds shares in Potomac River Company, 565; *letters from*: to GW, 277–78, 335; *letters to*: from GW, 273–74
Fitzhugh, Ann Frisby Rousby (*see* 1:243), 529, 555
Fitzhugh, William (*see* 1:243): and George Steptoe Washington and Lawrence Augustine Washington, 61; and plaster of paris, 279; offers building material, 529, 555; and Richard Boulton, 529–30; *letters from*: to GW, 529–30, 554–55
Fitzwater, John, 298
Flax: grown by tenants, 324
Floridablanca, José Monino y Redondonde, conde de: and Spanish jackasses for GW, 164, 165, 178; id., 165; *letters from*: to William Carmichael, 165
Fontenille, Fremyn, marquis de: *letters from*: to GW, 141–42
Fort Cumberland, 238–39; and Pennsylvania road, 264
Fort Leboeuf, 369
Fort McIntosh, Treaty of. *See* Treaties

Fort Pitt, 94
Fort Stanwix, Treaty of. *See* Treaties
Fort Washington: GW describes surrender of, 267, 466; and papers relating to its capture, 412
Fox, Charles James, 462; and Anglo-American trade, 143
Fox, George Crocker & Sons: id., 484; *letters from*: to GW, 484
Franklin, Benjamin: and Pusignan, 100; and Sir Edward Newenham, 125; and Houdon's statue of GW, 177; and David Hartley, 442; and Jonathan Williams, 451
Franks, David S., 41; conveys peace treaty to Paris, 34
Fraunces, Samuel (*see* 1 : 165): sends gift to Martha Washington, 408
Frazier, George, 224
Frazier, Nalbro: id., 296
Frederick II of Prussia, 268, 396, 532, 543
Fredericksburg: Lafayette and GW at, 145
Free blacks: act as cooks, 14; act as apprentice, 529; wages of, 554
Freeman, Thomas: appointed agent of GW's western lands, 78–80; and GW's Millers Run ejectment suit, 341, 346; and GW's Round Bottom tract, 556; *letters to*: from GW, 78–80, 489–90
Freemasons. *See* Masons
French, Penelope Manley: and French-Dulany tract, 373–75
French Creek: courses of, 368–70
French-Dulany tract: GW's negotiations for, 373–75
Frontier forts: stationing of troops at, 539–40. *See also* Western posts
Frontiers: defensive forces for, 10–11

Galt's tavern, 63
Gardiner, John: id., 533; *letters from*: to GW, 534
Gardoqui, Diego Maria de, 424, 438; id., 362; sent to U.S., 461
Garvey, Robert & Charles: ships wine to GW, 247–48
Gates, Horatio (*see* 1 : 354), 225; as Virginia commissioner to secure

Maryland Potomac River Company bill, 185–87, 195–96, 196, 223, 229, 229–30, 235–40; GW's opinion of, 256; holds shares in Potomac River Company, 565; *letters from*: to GW, 229–30; to Virginia legislature, 235
Gaunt, John: id., 83
Gauntt, Thomas: holds shares in Potomac River Company, 565
A General Map of the Middle Colonies in America: Lewis Evans, 90, 106
Georgetown (Md.; *see* 1 : 105): and Potomac River Company, 313–14
Georgia: and Lady Huntingdon's scheme, 395
Gibbs, Caleb, 334
Gilmer, George: conveys letter, 542
Gilpin, ——: visits Mount Vernon, 250, 309
Gilpin, George: made director of Potomac River Company, 562–63; id., 563; holds shares in Potomac River Company, 565
Glaubeck, Baron: and Nathanael Greene's debts, 59, 61
Glenn, John: settles on Millers Run tract, 354
Gordon, James: and Charles Asgill, 407
Gordon, William (*see* 1 : 177–78): favors emancipation of slaves, 64; and GW's papers, 266–67, 466; requests portraits, 411–13; *letters from*: to GW, 63–65, 101, 266–67, 465–67; *letters to*: from GW, 28, 116–17, 196–97, 411–14
Graham, Catherine Sawbridge Macaulay, 533, 540, 543; *History of England, from the Accession of James I*, 65; id., 65
Graham, Richard: and plaster of paris for GW, 278–79, 402–3; id., 424
Graham, William, 65, 533, 540, 543
Graham, William (doctor): id., 424
Grandchain de Sémerville, Guillaume-Jacques-Constant Leberge de, 104, 144–45, 176, 227
Grayson, Elizabeth Smallwood: illness of, 420, 433; id., 424
Grayson, William, 261, 267, 275,

Grayson, William (*continued*)
322; and Potomac River Company
bill, 88, 157, 250; and GW's shares
in Potomac and James River companies, 280–81, 420–22; and
Land Ordinance of 1785, 498–
501, 535–37; *letters from*: to GW,
419–24, 498–501, 535–38, 539;
letters to: from GW, 280–82,
519–21
Great Britain: and posts on New
York's western frontier, 142–43;
and its relations with U.S., 461,
467. *See also* British politics
Great Kanawha Falls, 133
Great Kanawha tracts. *See* Western
landholdings
Green, Charles, 276
Greene, Catharine: petition of, 61
Greene, Nathanael (*see* 1 : 125), 225,
450; financial straits of, 59–61,
522–23; ill health of, 59; and
Society of Cincinnati, 59; criti-
cizes Congress, 162; vouches for
Charles Hay, 192; visits Lafayette
in New York, 227; and George
Augustine Washington, 383; and
surrender of Fort Washington,
413, 466; and James Gunn's chal-
lenge to a duel, 521–23; and
Henry Moyes, 525; *letters from*: to
GW, 59–61, 161–62, 521–23; to
John Jay, 61
Greenhouse at Mount Vernon:
building of, 30–31, 42–44; citrus
fruit plants for, 41; advice about,
42–44
Greenway Court (house): id., 54
Griffith, David (*see* 1 : 70): and
schooling of GW's nephews,
61–62, 138; *letters to*: from GW,
61–62
Gunn, James: id., 522
Gunnell, John: holds shares in Potomac River Company, 565
Gustavus (ship), 408
Gustavus III of Sweden: and Society
of Cincinnati, 48

Habersham, James: id., 542
Habersham, John: id., 542; *letters
from*: to GW, 542–43

Haines, ——: and estate of Richard
Richards, 316
Haldimand, Sir Frederick, 146; id.,
11; and Charles Hay, 191
Haley, George: id., 65
Haley, Mary: id., 65
Hall, ——, 431
Hamilton, Alexander: and
Nathanael Greene's public ac-
counts, 60–61; and *Rutgers v.
Waddington*, 190; and Sebastian
Francisco de Miranda, 551; *letters
from*: to GW, 424–25
Hamilton, Elizabeth Schuyler, 425
Hancock, John, 77; and Joseph Pal-
mer, 194
Hanksley & Rutherfoord, 454
Hanover Courthouse: Lafayette and
GW at, 145
Hanson, Samuel: and schooling of
GW's nephews, 62, 138
Hanway, Samuel: id., 295; *letters
from*: to GW, 294–95
Happy Retreat (house; *see* 1 : 164),
27; id., 21; GW's visit to, 67
Harewood (house), 495; id., 21; and
John Ariss, 24
Hargreaves, James: and cotton
manufactures, 205
Harmar, Josiah: id., 34
Harper, John: holds shares in Poto-
mac River Company, 565
Harris, Sir James, 77
Harrison, Benjamin (*see* 1 : 23), 170;
and Virginia state regiments, 5–6;
and James Rumsey, 69; and GW's
Potomac and James River com-
panies shares, 89, 282–84; elected
speaker, 134; and Potomac River
Company, 134; *letters from*: to GW,
77, 134–35, 256–57, 328–30;
letters to: from GW, 5–6, 85–98,
282–84
Harrison, Carter Henry: and tribute
to GW, 137; and Potomac River
Company bill, 157
Harrison, Elizabeth Bassett: id., 135;
illness of, 329
Harrison, Joseph W.: holds shares in
Potomac River Company, 565
Harrison, Nancy Craik. *See* Craik,
Nancy
Harrison, Richard: id., 2; and Span-

ish jackasses for GW, 2, 163–64, 178, 365; becomes consul in Cadiz, 227–28; holds shares in Potomac River Company, 565; *letters from*: to Robert Townsend Hooe, 470–71

Harrison, Robert Hanson (*see* 1:291), 227–28

Harrison & Hooe, 510; and Spanish jackasses for GW, 1–2, 164, 365; and GW's Continental loan certificates, 473–74, 483

Hartley, David: id., 442

Hartshorne, William: acts as Potomac River Company commissioner, 8, 241, 273–75, 277–78, 280; id., 226; holds shares in Potomac River Company, 565; *letters from*: to GW, 277–78; *letters to*: from GW, 273–74

Hartshorne & Lindley, 225

Harvey, Reuben (*see* 1:409): sends gift to GW, 55; *letters from*: to GW, 468; *letters to*: from GW, 55–56

Harvie, John (*see* 1:109), 435, 489–90; and John Filson, 169–70; and GW's Millers Run ejectment suit, 341, 350, 513–16; id., 446; sends land documents, 555–56; *letters from*: to GW, 495, 513–16, 555–56, 556; *letters to*: from GW, 442–47

Harwood, Thomas: and GW's Continental loan certificates, 398; id., 398

Haskell (Haskeill), W. (shipmaster), 325

Hastings, Warren: and East India Company, 77

Hawkins, Thomas: holds shares in Potomac River Company, 565

Hay, Charles: id., 191; arrest and imprisonment of, 191–92; and GW's certificate for, 300–301; and Udny Hay, 300–301

Hay, Udny (*see* 1:206): id., 191; vouches for Charles Hay, 192; *letters from*: to GW, 190–92; *letters to*: from GW, 300–301

Hayes, James, 474–75

Hayfield (house), 197

Hazard, Ebenezer (*see* 1:378): and Belknap's *History of New Hamp-*shire, 3, 251; *letters from*: to Jeremy Belknap, 3, 251; to GW, 226; *letters to*: from Jeremy Belknap, 3, 251

Henderson, Alexander (*see* 1:146–47), 267; represents Fairfax County, 140; id., 198; and Mount Vernon conference, 263, 297; and Dennis Ryan's note, 284; holds shares in Potomac River Company, 565; *letters from*: to GW, 267–68; *letters to*: from GW, 197–98

Henly, Samuel, 305; GW's certificate for, 399, 401

Henrico County: and William Byrd's lottery, 4–5

Henry, Patrick: and GW's Potomac and James River companies shares, 89, 391–92, 447–48; and tribute to GW, 137; elected governor, 186; and Lady Huntingdon's scheme, 395, 396; forwards packages, 405–6; and illness of grandson, 430, 452; *letters from*: to GW, 257, 323, 409–10, 430–31, 447–49, 476–77; to Congress, 396; *letters to*: from GW, 391–92, 452

Henry, Prince, of Prussia, 125; and GW's portrait, 71

Hepburn, William: holds shares in Potomac River Company, 565

Herbert, William (*see* 1:457), 101; and James Rumsey's debt to GW, 425–26; holds shares in Potomac River Company, 565; *letters to*: from James Rumsey, 426

Herbert & Potts: and James Rumsey, 101

Higgins, Benjamin: *Experiments and Observations in Cement*, 256

Hill, Henry: id., 55

Hillegas, Michael (*see* 1:171, 195), 358; and GW's Continental loan certificates, 398

Hillis, William: settles on Millers Run tract, 354

History of England, from the Accession of James I: Catherine Sawbridge Macaulay Graham, 65

The History of New Hampshire: Jeremy Belknap, 3, 251

Hite, Abraham, Jr.: id., 298–99; *letters from*: to GW, 298–99

Hite, Abraham, Sr.: id., 298–99
Hite, George: holds shares in Potomac River Company, 565
Hollyday (Holliday), Henry: id., 527; and Harriot Rebecca Anderson's legacy, 559; *letters from*: to GW, 526–28
Hollyday (Holliday), James: *letters to*: from John West, Jr., 527
Holmes, Joseph: holds shares in Potomac River Company, 565
Holmes, Kirkman, 77
Holroyd, John Baker. *See* Sheffield of Dunamore
Hooe, Robert Townsend (*see* 1:66, 469), 228, 490, 491, 501, 559; and Spanish jackasses for GW, 1–2, 2, 365, 470; and GW's Continental loan certificates, 470; holds shares in Potomac River Company, 565; *letters from*: to GW, 2, 470, 470–71, 474, 483; *letters to*: from GW, 1–2, 469, 474; from Richard Harrison, 470–71
Hooe, Robert & Co., 398. *See also* Harrison & Hooe
Hooe & Harrison. *See* Harrison & Hooe
Hooe's ferry (*see* 1:262), 252
Hope (ship), 70, 409, 429
Hopkinson, Ann Borden, 508
Hopkinson, Francis: id., 398; and Robert Edge Pine, 507–8, 562; and Henry Moyes, 525–26; *letters from*: to GW, 507–9; to Thomas Jefferson, 525–26; *letters to*: from GW, 561–62
Hornsby, Thomas: and Dismal Swamp Company, 531
Horses: transportation of from abroad, 454
Houdon, Jean-Antoine: id., 178
Hounds. *See* Dogs
Howe, Robert: id., 539; conveys letter, 542; *letters from*: to GW, 538–39
Howell, David: id., 457
Hudson, John, 327
Hughes, Hugh: id., 17, 18; *letters from*: to GW, 17–18; *letters to*: from GW, 18
Hughes, Samuel: and Maryland

Potomac River Company bill, 236–40
Hull, William: seeks evacuation of British forts, 10–11
Humphreys, David (*see* 1:15): poetry of, 33; and biography of GW, 80–82, 269; seeks to retain military rank, 430; duties in France, 545; *letters from*: to GW, 32–33, 41, 80–82, 124–25, 268–69, 545–47; to Richard Henry Lee, 430; *letters to*: from GW, 149
Hunter, Moses: holds shares in Potomac River Company, 565
Hunter, William (*see* 1:479): *letters to*: from GW, 458
Huntingdon, Selena Hastings, countess of: id., 200; scheme of, 211–15, 216–18, 330–32, 386, 392–94, 395, 396; *letters from*: to GW, 205–8, 208–10, 210–11; *letters to*: from GW, 392–94
Hutchins, Thomas (*see* 1:200): *A Topographical Description of Virginia, Pennsylvania, Maryland, and North Carolina*, 89–90, 106

Illnesses, 6, 146, 258, 300, 329, 420, 430, 452; colic, 9; effect of West Indies climate on, 39; pain in chest and side, 39; chest pains, 59, 383; diarrhea, 116; fall fever, 154; pulmonary complaints, 290; biliousness, 467; stomach gout, 479
Immigration: great value of, 218–22
Impost, 486
Inches, Samuel: and commissioners of slave embarkation (1783), 482
Indentured servants: acquired by GW, 11–12, 23–24, 337–38
Independent Chronicle (Boston), 414
Indian affairs: GW's views on, 119–20
Indians, 198–222. *See also* Treaties; Washington, George
Ireland: disturbances in, 29–30, 111, 125, 326–27, 450, 549; and Mathew Carey, 228; political situation in described, 468

Iroquois: negotiate with New York and United States, 36–37. *See also* Treaties

Irvine, William: and Christopher Ludwick, 471

Jackasses: sought by GW, 1–2, 2; to be sent from Spain, 163–64, 165, 178, 460, 470; GW countermands requests for, 365; and Lafayette's gift of, 504–5, 557

Jackson, William: and diplomas of Society of Cincinnati, 513

Jameson, David (*see* 1:79): and Dismal Swamp Company, 62, 531; *letters from*: to Thomas Walker, 62

James River Company, 248–50, 361, 379, 381, 389; establishment of, 88–89, 249, 260–61, 267, 273, 330, 339; tolls of, 232, 260–61, 309; GW's shares in, 256–57, 280–81, 328–30, 364–65, 381–82, 389, 391–92, 447–48; and the Ohio River, 264–65; and survey of river, 275; subscriptions for in France sought, 366

Jane & Diana (ship), 406, 452, 454

Janney, Joseph: holds shares in Potomac River Company, 565

Jay, Sir James, 392, 393; and Lady Huntingdon's scheme, 199–205, 207, 210, 217–22, 291–93, 331, 395; id., 200; circular letter from, 218–22; *letters from*: to GW, 200–205; *letters to*: from GW, 291–93

Jay, John, 200, 225, 227, 335, 378, 450, 461; arrives in New York, 16; and James Duane, 188; and Maine boundary dispute, 305; and slave embarkation lists, 418, 482; *letters to*: from Nathanael Greene, 61

Jefferson, Thomas, 41, 418; and Houdon's statue of GW, 177; and Spanish jackasses for GW, 178; and Lafayette, 227; and GW's shares in Potomac and James River companies, 381–82; and Alexander Donald, 410; and news from Europe, 466–67; delivers gold medal to GW, 547; and comte de Doradour, 551; *letters from*: to

GW, 176–78; *letters to*: from William Carmichael, 178; from GW, 379–82; from Francis Hopkinson, 525–26; from Miles King, 553

Jefferson County (Va.), 298

Jenifer, Daniel of St. Thomas, 547; id., 4; and Mount Vernon conference, 297; and GW's Continental loan certificates, 397–98, 470, 473–74, 483, 491, 501; and trees for GW, 397; *letters from*: to GW, 397–98, 473, 501; *letters to*: from GW, 491

Johns, John, 308

Johnson (Johnston), Baker: holds shares in Potomac River Company, 565

Johnson (Johnston), James: holds shares in Potomac River Company, 565

Johnson, Matthew: settles on Millers Run tract, 354

Johnson, Thomas: id., 51, 297; and Potomac River Company, 51; and Mount Vernon conference, 297; made director of Potomac River Company, 562–63; *letters to*: from GW, 273, 562–66

Jones, ——: killed by snakebite, 19

Jones, Gabriel (*see* 1:156), 442; visited by GW, 124

Jones, Joseph: and tribute to GW, 137; id., 156

Jones, Ruthey: claims kinship to GW, 540–41; *letters from*: to GW, 540–43, 542; *letters to*: from GW, 542

Joseph II of Austria, 124–25, 268, 367, 396, 449, 462, 503, 532, 543, 557; Jefferson's views of, 176

Joy & Hopkins, 112; and silverware for GW, 296; *letters from*: to Daniel Parker, 296

Kanawha. *See* Great Kanawha; Little Kanawha

Keith, James (of Massachusetts): court-martial of, 359–60; letter to forwarded, 400; *letters from*: to GW, 359–60; *letters to*: from GW, 404

Keith, James: (of Virginia): and Potomac River Company, 564; holds shares in Potomac River Company, 565

Kenmore (house), 24

Kennedy, David: leases Bullskin land, 67; debt of, 82; *letters to*: from GW, 67

Kentucky. *See* Filson, John

Kersaint, Armand-Guy-Simon de Coëtempren, comte de (*see* 1:499): visits America, 71–72; *letters from*: to GW, 71–72; *letters to*: from GW, 72

Key, Philip: and Maryland Potomac River Company bill, 236–40

King, Miles: *letters from*: to Thomas Jefferson, 553

King, Rufus: id., 539

Knight of Malta (jackass), 164

Knox, Henry (*see* 1:7), 225, 417, 429; and Maine boundary dispute, 10–11, 172, 302–3, 305; and Society of Cincinnati, 303, 319; and limestone for GW, 399–400, 458–59; and GW's Potomac and James River companies shares, 459; becomes secretary at war, 459–60; and manning of frontier forts, 539–40; and Sebastian Francisco de Miranda, 551; *letters from*: to GW, 10–11, 143–44, 295, 301–6, 458–60, 533–34, 539–40; *letters to*: from GW, 170–72, 253–56, 398–401

Knox, Lucy Flucker: gives birth to daughter, 144, 304; property of, 304, 460

Kosciuszko, Tadeusz Andrzej Bonawentura (*see* 1:527–28), 33

Lafayette, Anastasie-Louise-Pauline du Motier de (*see* 1:30), 336, 450; *letters to*: from GW, 150

Lafayette, Marie-Adrienne-Françoise de Noailles, marquise de (*see* 1:30), 176, 229, 336, 450, 460, 461; *letters from*: to GW, 502–3; *letters to*: from Lafayette, 28–29; from GW, 150–51

Lafayette, Marie-Joseph-Paul-Yves-Roch-Gilbert du Motier, marquis de (*see* 1:28), 41, 60, 105, 140, 162, 174, 196, 225, 333, 361, 362, 396, 397, 405, 434, 486, 546; and Society of Cincinnati, 22; arrives in Philadelphia, 28, 36; describes visit to Mount Vernon, 28–29; and George Augustine Washington, 40; and visit to Virginia, 44, 84–85, 86, 103–4, 135–36, 145, 172; and Chastellux, 45; conveys letters, 46, 48, 65, 149, 155, 378, 461; and abolition of slavery, 64; attends Iroquois peace congress, 84–85, 111; and visit to Boston, 103–4, 144; and Mesmer's "magnetism," 151; travels to Annapolis with GW, 157, 165, 167–68; and jackasses for GW, 164, 558, 559; and departure from America, 226–28, 231, 335, 460; and Mathew Carey, 226–28; views on U.S. politics, 227; invites Bushrod Washington to Paris, 227–28; made Maryland citizen, 229; warm reception of in America, 255; and Ducher, 492–93; and packages for GW, 504–5, 528; champions French Protestants, 550; asks for his letters to GW, 551; and Sebastian Francisco de Miranda, 551; and La Serre, 553; advises GW on gift of shares in Potomac and James River companies, 556–57; and hunting dogs for GW, 557–58; and whale oil, 557–58; *letters from*: to Adrienne Lafayette, 28–29; to GW, 28–29, 84–85, 103–4, 194, 226–28, 335–36, 449–51, 492, 503–5, 550–51, 551, 556–59; to William Carmichael, 461; *letters to*: from GW, 175–76, 228–29, 363–67, 492–93, 553

Lake Erie: and inland navigation, 94, 97–98, 368–70

Lake of the Woods, 123

La Luzerne, Anne-César-de La Luzerne de Beuzeville, chevalier de (*see* 1:128), 46, 57, 147; recommends Châteaufort, 222; and U.S. public debt, 367; gives views of U.S. policy, 462–63; *letters from*: to GW, 72–73, 222, 367–68,

461–63; *letters to*: from GW, 47–48, 172–74

Lamont, Aeneas: poetry of, 318–19, 411, 490, 560–61; *letters from*: to GW, 246; *letters to*: from GW, 319

Land. *See* Western landholdings; Lands of GW

Land Ordinance: terms of in Virginia, 513–16

Land Ordinance of 1785, 438, 532, 533, 543; drafting of, 498–501, 535–37; GW's opinion of, 519–21

Land policy: GW's views on, 119–20, 182–83, 437, 440. *See also* Congress; Land Ordinance of 1785

Lands of GW: Chesterfield [Henrico] County, 5; Berkeley County (Pendleton tract), 20–21; Berkeley County (Bullskin tract), 24–25, 26–27, 27–28, 45, 45–46, 67, 82, 117–18, 324; Frederick County (Mercer land), 27, 56, 67–68; Dismal Swamp tract, 62; and collection of rents, 73–74, 117–18; New York, 146–48, 408–9, 510, 512; Kentucky, 298–99. *See also* Western landholdings

Langdon (Langston), John: and Thomas Ogden, 77

Lapsley, Thomas: settles on Millers Run tract, 354

La Serre, Ann Dulany: id., 553

La Serre, Barbier, chevalier de: id., 553; *letters from*: to GW, 512, 553; *letters to*: from GW, 552–53

Latimer, Randolph B.: and Potomac River Company, 237

Laurel Hill, 294

Laurence, ——, 295

Laurens, Henry: reports from London, 25–26, 29–30; returns from London, 36; id., 291; conveys letter, 382

Laurens, John: GW's view of, 412; id., 413–14

La Vauguyon, Paul-François de Quélen de Stuer de Caussade, duc de, 450

Lawrason, James: holds shares in Potomac River Company, 565

Lear, Tobias: and Potomac River Company papers, 240

Lebarbier (the younger): id., 407; *letters from*: to GW, 406–8

Lebarbier, Jean-Jacques-François (1738–1826): id., 407

Lee, Ann Steptoe. *See* Fendall, Ann Steptoe Lee

Lee, Arthur, 487; and enmity to Thomas Paine, 7; and courtship of Sophia Sprigg, 16, 366; and Treaty of Fort Stanwix, 141; and Treaty of Fort McIntosh, 436–37; *letters from*: to GW, 141; *letters to*: from GW, 436–37

Lee, Charles (1731–1782): estate of, 102, 478; and surrender of Fort Washington, 466

Lee, Charles (1758–1815): and French-Dulany tract, 373–75; id., 374; elected clerk of Potomac River Company meeting, 563–64, 565; holds shares in Potomac River Company, 565; *letters to*: from GW, 373–75

Lee, Francis Lightfoot: and Mississippi Land Company, 76

Lee, Henry (of Leesylvania; *see* 1:485): sends plants and seed, 505; *letters from*: to GW, 505–6

Lee, Henry, Jr. (Light-Horse Harry; *see* 1:351): and Potomac River Company, 86–87, 139–41, 273; id., 140; invited to Mount Vernon, 144–45; sends plants to GW, 431; *letters to*: from GW, 144–45; *letters from*: to GW, 135, 139–41, 431

Lee, Margaret, 14

Lee, Matilda Lee, 505; id., 140

Lee, Philip Ludwell, 145

Lee, Richard Henry, 365, 501; and Thomas Paine, 6–7; id., 7; elected president of Congress, 181; and Lady Huntingdon's scheme, 199, 395; and GW's views of the West, 230; and Lebarbier's *Asgill*, 408; and Land Ordinance of 1785, 543; *letters from*: to GW, 6–7, 142–43, 230–31, 271–72, 361–62, 395–96, 532–34, 543; *letters to*: from Edmund Pendleton, 134; from James Madison, 157; from GW, 181–83, 330–33, 408, 437–38; from David Humphreys, 430

Lee, Sidney: and Charles Lee's estate, 102, 478; *letters from*: to GW, 478; *letters to*: from GW, 102
Lee, Thomas Sim: made director of Potomac River Company, 562–63; holds shares in Potomac River Company, 565; *letters to*: from GW, 562–66
Lee, William (Will, Billy; slave), 457; id., 14
Leet, Daniel, 348
Leland, John: *A View of the Principal Deistical Writers*, 289
Le Maire de Gimel, Jacques: id., 125
Le Mayeur, Jean-Pierre (*see* 1:64): describes visit to Mount Vernon, 38; *letters from*: to GW, 38–39; *letters to*: from GW, 65
L'Enfant, Pierre-Charles (*see* 1:29): and Society of Cincinnati, 22–23; and Society of Cincinnati diplomas, 287, 319; *letters from*: to GW, 22–23
L'Esprit des Lois: Charles-Louis de Secondat Montesquieu (the elder), 530
A Letter on the Subject of an Established Militia, and Military Arrangements . . . : Steuben, 157
Lewis, Andrew: and Burning Springs tract, 556
Lewis, Betty Washington (*see* 1:146), 548
Lewis, Fielding (*see* 1:146): and John Ariss, 24; and Dismal Swamp Company, 531
Lewis, John (*see* 1:78): and Millers Run tract, 340
Lewis, Robert. *See* Lewis, Robert & Sons
Lewis, Robert & Sons: finds miller (Joseph Davenport) for Mount Vernon, 152–53, 307, 317–18, 410, 480–82, 493–94, 560; *letters from*: to GW, 414, 480–82; *letters to*: from GW, 152–53, 317–18, 493–94
Lewis, Thomas (*see* 1:97), 368, 444; holds shares in Potomac River Company, 565
Limestone, 399–400; and Henry Knox, 254–56, 303–4; price of, 303–4

Lincoln, Benjamin (*see* 1:167), 539; and Maine boundary dispute, 10–11, 172, 302–3, 305; and Society of Cincinnati, 10; *letters from*: to GW, 101, 533; *letters to*: from GW, 323–24
Lindley, ——, 226
Lingan, James M.: holds shares in Potomac River Company, 565
Little, Charles (*see* 1:66): holds shares in Potomac River Company, 565
Little Hunting Creek: and French-Dulany tract, 373–74
Little Kanawha River, 295
Livingston, William, 225; code of, 366
Lloyd, Edward: id., 567; *letters to*: from GW, 567
Lomax, John, 563
Lomax's tavern, 86, 123, 140; id., 563
Longchamps, Charles-Julien de (*see* 1:473): and assault on Barbé-Marbois, 550, 551
Long Island, Battle of, 18
Lotteries: William Byrd's, 4–5; for Washington College, 37–38, 57
Louis XVI of France, 125, 462–63, 550; and Society of Cincinnati, 70–71; Houdon's statue of, 177; and American plants and seed, 194, 553–54
Love, Philip: id., 370
Love, Samuel: id., 370; *letters from*: to GW, 368–70
Lowell, John, 466–67
Lowry, William: holds shares in Potomac River Company, 565
Lowther, James: Irish titles of, 327
Loyalists: confiscation of property of in New York, 143
Loyanté, Anne-Philippe-Dieudonné de: id., 247
Ludwick, Christopher: certificates for, 471–72; id., 471–72; *letters from*: to GW, 471–72; *letters to*: from GW, 472
Lumber: cost of, 385–86, 458
Lyles, Henry: holds shares in Potomac River Company, 565
Lyles, William: holds shares in Potomac River Company, 565

McBride, James: settles on Millers Run tract, 354

McBride, Samuel: settles on Millers Run tract, 354

McCarmick (McCormack), George, 348; *letters to*: from GW, 352

McClean, —— (shipmaster), 507

McCormick (McCormack), James: and GW's Millers Run ejectment suit, 354

McDermott, Cornelius (McDermott Roe): acquired by GW, 24

McGeehon (McGeehan), Brice: settles on Millers Run tract, 354

McGeehon (McGeehan), Duncan: settles on Millers Run tract, 354

McHenry, James: id., 418

MacIver, Charles: and immigration scheme, 157–61; and GW's dealings with, 161; *letters from*: to GW, 157–61, 402; *letters to*: from GW, 161, 404–5

McKean, Thomas: and GW's Millers Run ejectment suit, 352; *letters from*: to GW, 509; *letters to*: from GW, 562

McKewan, William: holds shares in Potomac River Company, 565

Macky, Robert: holds shares in Potomac River Company, 565

McMechen, James: and James Rumsey's self-propelled boat, 371–72, 439

McPherson, Daniel: holds shares in Potomac River Company, 565

Macrac, Allan: id., 435

McWhir, Alexander: and schooling of GW's nephews, 62

Madison, James, 140, 276; and Thomas Paine, 7; and Potomac River Company bills, 86–89, 248–50, 260–61, 274; and tribute to GW, 137; and Mount Vernon conference, 263; and Pennsylvania road, 263–64; *letters from*: to Richard Henry Lee, 157; to GW, 178, 248–50, 260–61; *letters to*: from GW, 155–57, 165–68, 231–35

Magaw, Robert: and Fort Washington, 414

Magowan, Walter: id., 4; *letters to*: from GW, 3–4

Mahony, Thomas: acquired as joiner, 23–24

Maillebois, Yves-Marie-Desmarets, comte de: and French army, 268

Maine: dispute over boundary of, 10–11, 172, 231, 302–3, 305

Malesherbes, Chrétien-Guillaume Lamoignon de, 57; and grapevines for GW, 148–49; and Ducher, 493; id., 148; *letters from*: to Barbé-Marbois, 148–49

Manchester (Va.): and William Byrd's lottery, 4–5

Mandrillon, Joseph (*see* 1:441): *letters from*: to GW, 405

Manley, John: and French-Dulany tract, 374

Mann, George: id., 230

Mann's tavern, 229–30

Mannsfield (house), 24

Map of the British Colonies in North America: John Mitchell, 305

Maps, 90, 106, 168–70, 269–70, 305

Marie Antoinette, 504, 550

Marshall, John, 553–54; marries Mary Ambler, 552

Marshall, Mary Ambler: id., 552

Marshall, Thomas: and GW's land rights, 554; id., 554; *letters from*: to GW, 553–54; *letters to*: from GW, 534

Martin, Denny: id., 54

Martin, Thomas Bryan: and Lord Fairfax's estate, 54

Maryland legislature: and Potomac River Company, 87–89, 165–68, 168, 231–35, 235–36; and Potomac River navigation, 107–8, 131–33; and public education, 252; makes Lafayette a citizen, 449

Mason, ——: and Thomas Ogden, 77

Mason, George: and John Augustine Washington, 180; and Mount Vernon conference, 263, 297; sends gift, 479; *letters from*: to GW, 478–79; *letters to*: from GW, 180

Mason, John: and Potomac River Company papers, 239

Mason, Sarah Brent: id., 479

Mason, Thomson: and William Byrd's lottery, 4–5; id., 5

Mason and Dixon Line, 429

Masons: and King David's Lodge (Newport, R.I.), 277; and St. John's Lodge (Newport, R.I.), 277

Massie (Massey), Thomas, 265; id., 264

Matthews, Thomas: and Virginia Potomac River Company bill, 157

Maxwell, James: and Ruthey Jones, 542

May (ship), 325

Mead, ———: and Dismal Swamp Company, 531

Mead, David: and Dismal Swamp Company, 531

Mentges, Francis: id., 34; *letters from*: to GW, 34; *letters to*: from GW, 34

Mercer, George: land bought from, 27, 67–68

Mercer, James, 464, 549; and Battaile Muse, 74; *letters from*: to GW, 41; *letters to*: from GW, 56–57

Mercer, John Francis (*see* 1:489): marriage of to Sophia Sprigg, 16, 366; and the Mercer accounts, 56; and Battaile Muse, 74; *letters from*: to GW, 452; *letters to*: from GW, 366, 463–64

Mercer, Sophia Sprigg: marriage of, 16, 366. *See also* Sprigg, Sophia

Mesmer, Friedrich Anton (*see* 1:454): *letters to*: from GW, 151

Mifflin, Thomas (*see* 1:25), 36, 358; and Hugh Hughes, 18; and Jacob Diriks, 286; and Christopher Ludwick, 472; *letters from*: to GW, 509

Miller, Philip: *Abridgement of the Gardener's Dictionary*: referred to, 174, 258, 384, 511–12

Millers Run (Chartiers) tract, 6; GW's visit to, 19, 66, 166; settlers on, 116, 170–71; and GW's ejectment suit, 338–58, 442–47, 489, 513–16; certificate of survey of, 556

Mills: at Washington's Bottom tract, 79–80, 308–9; at Dogue Run, 152–53, 317–18, 480–82, 493–94, 496

Miralles, Don Juan de: id., 1

Miranda, Sebastian Francisco de: plans liberation of Venezuela, 551

Miromesnil, Armand-Thomas Hué de: id., 551

Mississippi Land Company, 74, 76

Mississippi River: GW's views on, 90–93; navigation of, 108–9, 230, 362, 378, 438, 450, 461, 504

Mitchell, John: *Map of the British Colonies in North America*, 305

Monongahela River: and Potomac River navigation, 94, 233, 238, 245–46, 250, 263, 295, 330, 455, 469

Monroe, James: and Indian relations, 143; and regulation of trade amendment, 538

Montesquieu, Charles-Louis de Secondat de: and Thomas Ridout, 523, 528; invited to Mount Vernon, 525; id., 530; *letters from*: to GW, 523–25; *letters to*: from GW, 524, 524–25

Montesquieu, Charles-Louis de Secondat, baron de La Brède et de (1749–1824; *see* 1:383): id., 530; *L'Esprit des Lois*, 530

Montesquieu, Jean-Baptiste Secondat de, 524–25; sends wine and walnuts, 528, 530; id., 530; *letters from*: to GW, 530

Montgomery, Richard, 191

Montgomery County (N.Y.), 147–48; and surveyor of, 124

Moore, Bernard: and Daniel Parke Custis's estate, 519; and John Baylor, 519

Moore, Francis, 401; and Margaret Savage's estate, 275–76, 431–32; *letters from*: to GW, 276; *letters to*: from GW, 276

Moore, Hanna: and Margaret Savage's estate, 275–76, 431–32; *letters from*: to GW, 275–76; *letters to*: from GW, 401–2

Moore, William (*see* 1:432): and Margaret Savage's estate, 275–76

Morgan, Charles: and GW's Millers Run ejectment suit, 348, 354

Morgan, Daniel (*see* 1:305): and David Kennedy, 67, 82; and GW's Millers Run ejectment suit, 489; *letters from*: to GW, 82; *letters to*: from GW, 67

Morgan, Zackwell, 295

Morris, Mary White (*see* 1:11), 506–7

Morris, Robert (*see* 1:11): and Alexander Donald, 410; and Charles Lee's estate, 478; and George C. Fox & Sons, 484; and Potomac River Company, 506; and gold medal for GW, 546; *letters from*: to GW, 250, 506–7, 508; *letters to*: from GW, 309–15

Morton, Mrs. Andrew: and Belvoir, 388

Morton, Andrew: and Belvoir, 390

Mount Airy (house), 24

Mount Clare (Md.; house): id., 31

Mount Vernon: visitors to, 9, 28–29, 38–39, 44, 60, 70, 103, 144–45, 162, 250, 258, 290, 397, 452, 457, 477, 482, 493, 526, 529, 533, 539, 544, 561; greenhouse at, 30–31, 40–42; and flooring for piazza, 70, 336–37; and French-Dulany tract, 373–75; and walkways at, 400, 459; overseers at, 403; gardener for sought, 456; and New Room, 529–30, 554–55

   goods and supplies for: wheat fan, 23–24, 42; silverware, 111–12, 223–24, 295–96; nails, 114; paint, 114, 529; Ticklenburg, 114; wine, 247–48, 528, 530; limestone, 254–56, 303–4, 399–400; cheese, 323; cranberries, 323; marble chimneypiece, 325, 326; wax work in glass case, 408; candles, 411; soap, 411; geese, 475; swans, 475; plaster of paris, 505–6; building materials, 529, 555; carpenter's tools, 529; glass, 529

   plants and seed for: clover, 114–15, 307; orchard grass, 114–15, 115–16, 294, 298, 300, 306, 334, 410–11, 490, 560; balsam, 146, 510; grapevines, 147–49, 408–9, 429, 511; linden, 148; nuts, 148, 224–26; peas, 148, 224–26, 429, 505–6, 510; corn, 224–26, 408–9, 510; trees, 224–26, 397; live oak, 258–60, 376–77, 384, 452; magnolia (*Magnolia grandiflora*), 258–59, 384–85, 452, 472; umbrella magnolia, 258–59, 384–85; water oak, 259; aspen, 281–82, 423–24;

hemlock, 281–82, 511; yew, 281–82, 423–24; English (goose, spear) grass, 298, 410–11; honeysuckle, 376–77; wild jessamine, 376; sweet bay, 384–85; boxwood cuttings, 431; cypress, 431; dwarf boxwood cuttings, 431, 475; holly, 431, 475; horse chestnut, 431; royal palm (palmetto royal), 452; sour orange, 452; watermelon, 479; cotton plants, 505–6; Italian barley, 505–6; grass, 507; hickory nuts, 510–11; lime trees, 510; spruce, 510; tulip laurel (poplar), 554; bird grass, 567. *See also* Greenhouse; Artisans; Dogs

Mount Vernon conference, 250, 452; id., 297

Moyes (Moyse), Henry: id., 525–26

Moylan, Mary Ricketts Van Horne, 561

Moylan, Stephen: id., 561; *letters from*: to GW, 561

Mules, 460. *See also* Jackasses

Munford, William Green: represents Charles City County, 134

Murray, John (*see* 1:140): *letters from*: to GW, 523

Murray, John & Co.: sends calico to GW, 523

Muse, Battaile: and Henry Whiting's account, 27–28; as GW's land agent, 73–74, 117–18, 324; and George William Fairfax, 117–18, 388, 390; *letters from*: to GW, 73–74, 293, 268; *letters to*: from GW, 117–18, 324

Muskingum River, 94, 98

Native Americans. *See* Indians

Necker, Jacques: *De l'administration des finances de la France*, 450

Nelson, Nathaniel: and Dismal Swamp Company, 531

Nelson, Thomas (1715–1787; *see* 1:80): and Dismal Swamp Company, 531

Nelson, Thomas (1738–1789; *see* 1:80), 264

Nelson, William (1754–1813; *see* 1:80): and Dismal Swamp Company, 531

Neufville, Jean de (*see* 1 : 18–19):
    letters from: to GW, 425, 438; *letters*
    to: from GW, 530
Newenham, Lady, 454
Newenham, Sir Edward (*see* 1 : 440):
    writes to Benjamin Franklin, 125;
    sends packages to GW, 405–6,
    430, 448, 452, 454, 534–35; *letters*
    from: to GW, 83, 98, 405; *letters to*:
    from GW, 453–54
Newmarket (house): id., 518
New Orleans, 438, 450
Newton, Thomas, Jr. (*see* 1 : 80): id.,
    260; *letters from*: to GW, 526
New York: negotiates with Iroquois,
    36–37, 142–43; and Treaty of
    Fort Stanwix, 36–37; and west-
    ward expansion, 107; and con-
    fiscation of Loyalist property, 143
New York City: pays tribute to GW,
    187–90, 487–88
Nicholas, George: and George
    William Fairfax, 51–52, 118, 390;
    id., 55
Nicholas, Robert Carter: and George
    William Fairfax, 55, 118, 390
Nolin, Abbé: and grapevines for
    GW, 148
Northern Neck Proprietary: and
    Fairfax family, 54–55
Nourse, James: and Thornton
    Washington, 20; and schooling of
    GW's nephews, 61; death of, 137
Nova Scotia: and Maine boundary
    dispute, 303, 305
Nymphe (ship): and Lafayette, 85,
    104, 105, 162, 174, 226, 229, 363

Observations on the Commerce of the
    American States: John Holroyd,
    Lord Sheffield, 143
Observations on the Importance of the
    American Revolution: Richard
    Price, 271, 325, 332, 361
Ogden, Amos, 77
Ogden, Robert, 77
Ogden, Thomas: and sale of wool,
    74–77; and David Parry, 77; *letters*
    from: to John Woddrop, 76–77
Ohio country: water courses of,
    368–70

Ohio River, 233; GW's lands on, 66;
    and Potomac River navigation,
    93–94, 97–98
Ohio River tracts. *See* Western
    landholdings
O'Neill, Bernard: holds shares in
    Potomac River Company, 565
Oriskany (N.Y.), 510, 512
Orr, John: id., 424
Osborne, Richard: and French-
    Dulany tract, 373–74
Oudinarde, M. & H., 425

Paca, William, 229, 274; and Wash-
    ington College lottery, 37; and Po-
    tomac River Company, 88–89,
    195–96, 223; and Potomac River
    navigation, 186; id., 195, 306; and
    Pennsylvania road, 245; subscribes
    to Potomac River Company, 485; *let-*
    ters to: from GW, 195–96, 306, 567
Page, John (of Rosewell), 328; id.,
    170; and John Filson, 436; and
    Dismal Swamp Company, 531
Page, Mann (c.1718–1781; *see* 1 : 80):
    and John Ariss, 24
Page, Mann (1749–1803; *see* 1 : 80):
    and Virginia Potomac River Com-
    pany bill, 250
Paine, Thomas (*see* 1 : 320–21):
    financial straits of, 6–7; and
    Aeneas Lamont, 246, 490, 561
Palmer, Joseph: id., 194; *letters from*:
    to GW, 192–94
Paper currency: merits of, 126–28;
    losses from, 375
Papers of George Washington. *See*
    Washington, George
Parker, Daniel (*see* 1 : 53, 467):
    and silverware for GW, 111–12,
    223–24, 296; *letters to*: from Joy &
    Hopkins, 296
Parker, Josiah: id., 259; sends
    plants, 376–77, 472; and George
    Augustine Washington, 385; *letters*
    from: to GW, 376–78, 472; *letters*
    to: from GW, 257, 326
Parry, David (*see* 1 : 306): and
    Thomas Ogden, 77
Partridge, George: and Maine
    boundary dispute, 10–11, 305

Passamaquoddy, Bay of: and Maine boundary dispute, 302–3, 305

Peale, Charles Willson: and portrait of GW, 71; receives payment from GW, 247; *letters from*: to GW, 247

Pearce, William: *letters from*: to GW, 482

Pendleton, Edmund (*see* 1:278): *letters from*: to Richard Henry Lee, 134

Pendleton, Philip (*see* 1:70): and land sold by GW, 20–21; holds shares in Potomac River Company, 565

Pennsylvania: and Potomac River navigation, 95–96, 168; and Potomac River Company, 262–63

Pennsylvania Herald (Philadelphia): and Mathew Carey, 228

Pennsylvania Packet, and Daily Advertiser (Philadelphia), 411; GW's complaints about, 307–8, 434

Pennsylvania Packet, and General Advertiser (Philadelphia): GW's complaints about, 307–8

Pennsylvania road: and navigation of Potomac, 238–39, 248–50. *See also* Potomac River Company

Peter, Robert: holds shares in Potomac River Company, 564

Peters, Thomas (*see* 1:530): and wheat fan, 23, 24, 42

Philip II of Spain: and his gift of jackasses, 461

Philips, Charles: and Jacob Read, 544

Pickawaxon vestry: and Walter Magowan, 3–4

Pickering, Timothy (*see* 1:300): and Hugh Hughes, 17, 18; mentioned as secretary at war, 225; and Christopher Ludwick, 471

Pierpont, John, 295

Pilgrim (ship), 147

Pine, Robert Edge (*see* 1:435), 566–67; recommendations of, 52–53, 508–9; and Robert Morris, 507; paints portraits at Mount Vernon, 509; and GW's portrait, 561–62

Pitt, William, the Younger (*see* 1:29), 462, 468

Plants: black alder or winterberry (*Prunus virginiana*), 194; buckeye or horse chestnut (*Aesculus hippocastanum*), 194; cardinal flower (*Lobelia cardinalis*), 194; crown imperial (*Imperiali coronata*), 194; Kentucky coffee tree (*Gymnoclaudus dioica*), 194; papaw (*Asimina triloba*), 194; tulip poplar (*Liliodendron tulipfera*), 194. *See also* Mount Vernon: plants and seed for

Plaster of paris, 278–79; GW's experiment with, 402–3

Plater, Elizabeth Frisby: id., 103

Plater, George: id., 103, 179; *letters from*: to GW, 102–3; *letters to*: from GW, 106–10, 178–79

Pocomoke River, 297

Poetry: by David Humphreys, 33; by Aeneas Lamont, 246, 318–19, 490, 560–61; by Wilhelmina van Winter, 472–73

Pollock, Oliver: and Walter Stewart, 111

Porter, Thomas, 224; id., 324

Porter & Ingraham, 324; and silverware for GW, 296

Posey, John: and Millers Run tract, 338, 341, 344, 346–47, 351, 444; and French-Dulany tract, 374; and GW's Millers Run ejectment suits, 513–16

Postal service: irregularity of, 300, 494; superiority of, 474; reliability of, 489; loses letter, 552

Potomac Company (1774), 51, 86

Potomac River Company, 556; origins of, 51, 121–22, 128–33; organizational meeting of, 86–87, 89, 123, 139–40, 155–57; and Virginia bills for its establishment, 86–89, 139–41, 155–57, 166–68, 231–35, 248–50, 260–61, 263, 272, 330, 399; and GW's shares in, 89, 256–57, 280–81, 328–30, 363–64, 381–82, 389, 391–92, 420–22, 447–48, 459, 521, 556–57; advantages of argued, 89–98, 102–3, 106–10, 309–15, 323, 363–65, 379–81, 389; and Maryland legislature, 99–100;

Potomac River Company (*continued*) and petition of organizational meeting, 156–57; Baltimore's opposition to, 166, 313; and cooperation between Virginia and Maryland assemblies, 167–68, 185–87, 195, 196, 223, 229–30, 235–40, 248–49; and enactment of Maryland bill, 231–35; tolls of, 231–35, 244–45, 309–10; and Pennsylvania roads, 232–33, 234–35, 245, 261–64, 272, 297, 310–12, 330; managers of, 241; opened to subscriptions, 241, 273, 274–75, 280, 360–61, 380–81, 547–48, 552; and papers relating to its founding, 273–75; and distribution of Virginia act creating it, 277–78, 280, 297, 306, 322, 323, 335; engineer for sought, 364–65, 379; subscriptions from abroad sought, 366, 380–81; and financing of, 380–81; and subscriptions to at Annapolis, 485; and election of officers, 562–63; and first meeting of subscribers, 563–66; minutes of first meeting of, 563–66; subscriptions to listed, 564. *See also* Washington, George

Potts, John, Jr.: id., 101; holds shares in Potomac River Company, 565

Powel, Elizabeth Willing (*see* 1:398), 525

Powel, Samuel (*see* 1:398): *letters from*: to GW, 525–26

Powell, Leven: holds shares in Potomac River Company, 565

Prager, Mark (*see* 1:532–33), 16

Preston, John: id., 124; *letters from*: to GW, 123–24; *letters to*: from GW, 82, 124

Preston, William: id., 124

Price, Benjamin, 414

Price, Richard: *Observations on the Importance of the American Revolution . . .* , 271, 325, 332, 361; *letters to*: from GW, 271–72

Priestley, Joseph, 289

Prince, John: id., 539

Principio Iron Company: and the Washingtons, 178–79

Pusignan (Surignan): and Society of Cincinnati, 100–101; *letters from*: to GW, 100–101; to Ségur, 101

Putnam, Israel: and surrender of Fort Washington, 466

Ramsay, Dennis: holds shares in Potomac River Company, 565

Randolph, Beverley: and Potomac River Company, 88, 223; and Houdon's statue of GW, 177; id., 186; *letters from*: to GW, 185–87; *letters to*: from GW, 223

Randolph, Edmund (*see* 1:110): and William Byrd's lottery, 4–5; and George William Fairfax, 52; and Mount Vernon conference, 263; and Dennis Ryan's note, 284, 451, 474, 479; and GW's Millers Run ejectment suit, 341, 351; *letters from*: to GW, 4–5, 479–80; *letters to*: from GW, 351–52, 451

Randolph, Richard (*see* 1:488): and William Byrd's lottery, 4–5; and William Skilling, 7, 14–15

Read, Jacob (*see* 1:101): advocates political reform, 35; goes to New England, 105; and slave embarkation lists, 482; *letters from*: to GW, 15–16, 25–26, 35–37, 104–5, 416–18, 418, 544–45; *letters to*: from GW, 29–30, 118–23

Read, Rebecca Bond: id., 26

Reed, David: settles on Millers Run tract, 354

Reed, John (*see* 1:64): settles on Millers Run tract, 354

Reed, Joseph: id., 498; *letters to*: from GW, 267

Religion: Virginia bill in support of deferred, 268; deism condemned, 289; treatment of French Protestants, 550

Revolutionary War: sufferings from, 192–94, 375–76, 411

Rhode Island: political unrest in, 60

Rice, —— (shipmaster), 298, 411

Rice, Nathan: id., 324

Richard, George: id., 275; prints Potomac River Act, 274, 277

Richards, Edmund (the elder): and claims to a Virginia estate, 315–16

Richards, Edmund (the younger):
and claims to a Virginia estate,
315–16; *letters from*: to GW,
315–16; *letters to*: from GW, 316
Richards, Richard, Jr.: and claims to
Virginia estate, 315–16
Richards, Richard, Sr.: and claims to
Virginia estate, 315–16
Richardson, Thomas (*see* 1:469), 490
Richmond (Va.): pays tribute to GW,
135–36
Richmond, Christopher: and GW's
Continental loan certificates,
473–74, 483, 484–85, 491, 501;
id., 483; and subscriptions to
Potomac River Company, 485,
547–48; *letters from*: to GW,
484–85, 547–48; *letters to*: from
GW, 483–84
Ridgely, Henry, Jr.: holds shares in
Potomac River Company, 565
Ridout, Thomas (shipmaster): con-
veys Lafayette gifts, 504–5, 528;
id., 524; *letters from*: to GW,
528–29
Rindfleisch, George: seeks to rent
land, 110; *letters to*: from GW, 110
Ritchie, Matthew, 348; and Millers
Run tract, 348, 353
Rittenhouse, David: id., 429
Roberdeau, Daniel (*see* 1:152–53):
holds shares in Potomac River
Company, 565
Roberts, William M.: id., 152–53;
discharged by GW, 317, 493–94;
character of, 493–94; seeks re-
instatement as miller, 496; *letters
from*: to GW, 151–53, 496
Rochambeau, Jean-Baptiste-Dona-
tien de Vimeur, comte de (*see*
1:29), 100; and Society of Cincinnati, 70–71; given GW's portrait,
71; *letters from*: to GW, 70–71,
378–79; *letters to*: from GW,
48–49, 71, 401; from Ségur, 71
Rolland & Co.: *letters from*: to
GW, 484
Rootes, John (*see* 1:99), 554
Rosewell (house), 170
Round Bottom tract, 338; and
Michael Cresap's claims to,
489–90; and Michael Cresap's
heirs, 556

Royal Gift (jackass), 164
Rumney, John: *letters from*: to GW,
336–38
Rumney, John, Jr. (*see* 1:484): and
flagstones for GW, 70, 336–37;
letters from: to GW, 70
Rumsey, James: and his self-
propelled boat, 69, 96, 101, 109,
364–65, 371, 427–29, 439–40;
and Richard Claiborne, 185; and
debt to GW, 198, 267, 284,
371–72, 425–26, 451, 474, 479;
and James McMechen, 371–72;
builds houses for GW at Bath,
426–27, 428; holds shares in Potomac River Company, 565; *letters
from*: to GW, 101, 425–29; to
William Herbert, 426; *letters to*:
from GW, 69, 376. *See also* Ryan,
Dennis
Rush, Benjamin (*see* 1:133), 418
Rutgers, Elizabeth: id., 190; and
Rutgers v. Waddington, 485
Rutgers v. Waddington, 485; id., 190
Rutherfoord, Thomas: id., 454
Rutland, Charles Manners, fourth
duke of, 228
Ryan, Dennis: id., 198; and his note
to GW, 198, 267, 284, 371–72,
425–26, 474, 479

St. Clair, Arthur (*see* 1:84): and
Christopher Ludwick, 471
St. Croix rivers: and Maine bound-
ary dispute, 302–3, 305, 399–400
St. Georges (Mass.): and limestone,
303–4
St. James Parish (Md.): and Walter
Magowan, 4
Saint-Simon Montbléru, Claude-
Anne-de Rouvroy, marquis de (*see*
1:187): application to Society of
Cincinnati, 557–58
Salt: manufacture of, 192–94
Salt springs: locations of, 193
Sanderson, Robert: and John
Rumney, Jr., 70
Sandy Hill (S.C.; house), 153
Sangrain, Pierre Tourtille de: and
whale oil, 558
Saratoga Springs: interest of GW
in, 146

Sargent, Winthrop (*see* 1 : 140): desires certificate of Revolutionary war service, 458

Savage, Margaret Green (*see* 1 : 135): and her will, 276, 401–2, 431–32

Savage, William: id., 276; and Savage affair, 433

Sayre, Stephen (*see* 1 : 426–27): and Potomac River navigation, 49–51, 65–66, 99–100; *letters from*: to GW, 49–51, 99–100; *letters to*: from GW, 65–66

Schnitzell, George: holds shares in Potomac River Company, 565

Schuylkill, 90, 107

Scioto River, 94

Scott, ——: visits Mount Vernon, 250, 309

Scott, George: holds shares in Potomac River Company, 565

Scott, Gustavus: and Maryland Potomac River Company bill, 236–40

Scott, James: id., 196; settles on Millers Run tract, 354; and GW's Millers Run ejectment suit, 354

Scott, Thomas, 354; id., 358

Scott, William: id., 196; holds shares in Potomac River Company, 565

Sears, Isaac: id., 409

Seaweed: and experiments with, 413–14

Secondat. *See* Montesquieu

Ségur, Philippe-Henri, maréchal de (*see* 1 : 60): and Society of Cincinnati, 70–71; *letters from*: to Rochambeau, 71; *letters to*: from Pusignan, 101

Seneca Falls: and Potomac River navigation, 49, 133, 457, 458

Sever (Seaver), James, 305–6; GW's certificate of service for, 399, 401; *letters to*: from GW, 399

Sharpe, Granville: political pamphlets of, 162

Shaw, Sarah Biddle Penmore (*see* 1 : 20): marriage of, 307

Shaw, William: becomes GW's secretary, 256

Shawnee, 142, 290, 437

Sheffield of Dunamore, John Baker Holroyd, Baron: *Observations on the Commerce of the American States*, 143; id., 143

Shenandoah Falls, 133

Shephard, David: and GW's Millers Run ejectment suit, 354

Shepherd, Abraham: holds shares in Potomac River Company, 565

Shippen, Edward, 358

Shippen, Nancy: and Henry Moyes, 526

Shockoe: id., 5

Shreve, Benjamin: holds shares in Potomac River Company, 565

Sills, Hannah: acts as cook, 14

Sills, Isaac: acts as cook, 14

Sim, Joseph: holds shares in Potomac River Company, 565

Simms, Charles: and Potomac River Company, 564; holds shares in Potomac River Company, 565; *letters to*: from GW, 352–53

Simpson, Gilbert, Jr. (*see* 1 : 118): 343, 348, 489; and Washington's Bottom tract, 18–19; partnership with GW ended, 80, 308–9; public certificates of, 307–9, 410–11, 560; and GW's visit to, 340; *letters from*: to GW, 18–19; *letters to*: from GW, 308–9

Sitgreaves, John: id., 533; introduction of, 537, 538, 543

Six Nations. *See* Iroquois

Skilling, William (*see* 1 : 488): offered employment at Mount Vernon, 7–8; and Richard Randolph, 14–15; *letters from*: to GW, 14–15; *letters to*: from GW, 7–8

Slattery, Farrell: acquired as millwright, 23–24

Slave embarkation lists (1783), 482; Congress's need for, 416–18

Slaves: and John Augustine Washington, 8; marriage of, 14; at Washington's Bottom tract, 19; owned by Lord Fairfax, 54; and abolition sentiment, 64; and lists of those embarking at New York City, 517; as carpenters, 554. *See also* Slaves of GW; Free blacks

Slaves of GW: William (Will, Billy) Lee, 14; marriage of, 14; wish for emancipation of, 64

Smith, Edward: and Potomac River Company subscriptions, 241;

holds shares in Potomac River Company, 565

Smith, Melancton: and silverware for GW, 111–12, 223–24, 295–96; id., 112; *letters from*: to GW, 111–12, 295–96; *letters to*: from GW, 223–24

Smith, Patrick S.: holds shares in Potomac River Company, 565

Smith, Thomas: and GW's Millers Run ejectment suit, 338–58, 442–47, 489, 513–16; *letters from*: to GW, 352, 354, 356–58

Smith, William (*see* 1:38, 372): and Washington College, 37–38; and Washington College lottery, 57; *letters from*: to GW, 37–38; *letters to*: from GW, 57

Smith, William Stephens (*see* 1:53), 429–30, 545; id., 418; as a commissioner of slave embarkation, 482

Smith & Wyckoff, 112; account with GW, 224; and silverware for GW, 296

Smiths (firm), 77

Snickers, Edward (*see* 1:393): as GW's land agent, 67–68; *letters to*: from GW, 67–69

Socinianism, 289

Southall, Henry: represents Charles City County, 134

Spain: and the American West, 90–93; and its relations with U.S., 461

Spencer, Nicholas, 373–74

Spencer-Washington tract: and French-Dulany tract, 373–74

Sprigg, Edward: id., 424

Sprigg, Richard, 464; and grass seed, 567; *letters to*: from GW, 566–67

Sprigg, Sophia: id., 16. *See also* Mercer, Sophia Sprigg

Stafford Courthouse: Lafayette and GW at, 145

Stanhope, Philip: id., 461

Stedham, Zachariah: and GW's Millers Run ejectment suit, 354

Stelle, Benjamin: and Gilbert Simpson's public certificates, 308, 411

Stephenson, John (*see* 1:119), 83,

343, 348; and GW's Millers Run ejectment suit, 489

Stephenson, Marcus, 344, 348; and GW's Millers Run ejectment suit, 354, 489

Steuben, Friedrich Wilhelm Ludolph Gerhard Augustin, Baron von (*see* 1:85), 225, 226, 247; and Frederick Haldimand, 146; *A Letter on the Subject of an Established Militia . . .* , 157; and his account with U.S., 429

Stevenson, George, 290

Stewart, ——: and Thomas Ogden, 77

Stewart, Andrew: and Potomac River Company papers, 239

Stewart, David: holds shares in Potomac River Company, 565

Stewart, Walter (*see* 1:82): settles accounts in Cuba, 58, 111; *letters from*: to GW, 110–11

Stewart, Mrs. Walter, 111

Stewart, William: settles on Millers Run tract, 354

Stickney, Enoch (shipmaster), 55

Stobo, Robert: and Fort Necessity, 57

Stoddert, Benjamin: holds shares in Potomac River Company, 565

Stone, Michael Jenifer: id., 464

Stone, Thomas: and Maryland Potomac River Company bill, 236–40, id., 297; and Mount Vernon conference, 297; *letters from*: to GW, 297

Stoney River, 238–39

Story (Storey), John: and Gilbert Simpson's public certificates, 308, 490, 507

Stratford Hall (house), 145; id., 140

Stuart, David (*see* 1:210), 64, 162, 197, 227, 504; translates for GW, 101, 148–49, 286, 407, 524

Stuart, Eleanor Calvert Custis, 39, 64, 155, 162, 197, 227, 336, 504

Suffren (Suffrein) Saint Tropez, Pierre-André de (*see* 1:21): and jackasses for GW, 558

Sullivan, John (*see* 1:207): opposes Society of Cincinnati reform, 320–22; id., 322; *letters from*: to GW, 320–22

Susquehanna River, 107, 166, 455, 469; as gateway to West, 90, 94–95, 107, 311–12
Swan, James: and Henry Knox, 304; id., 401
Swan, John: and Thomas Colvill's estate, 559; *letters from*: to GW, 559
Swearingen, Van, 348
Sweet Springs, 20, 290
Symmes, W.: responds to GW's offer to become secretary, 548–49; *letters from*: to GW, 548–49

Tannehill, John: id., 83
Taverns, 86, 123, 136, 140, 229, 563
Tayloe, John: and John Ariss, 24; id., 378
Temple, John: appointed British consul to U.S., 449
Tenants: John Ariss, 23–24, 26–27; Francis Whiting, 24–25; Henry Whiting, 24–25, 26–27, 117–18, 324; Mary Crane Bartlett, 45, 46; John Bryan, 46; William Bartlett, 46; David Kennedy, 67, 82; John Williams, 68–69; and collection of rents, 73–74, 117–18; and rent rolls, 118
Textiles: in Scotland, 74–77; and revolution in cotton manufactures, 205
Thomas, Margaret: and marriage to William Lee (slave), 14
Thomas, Philip: holds shares in Potomac River Company, 565
Thomas, Richard: and estate of Richard Richards, 316; *letters from*: to GW, 316; *letters to*: from GW, 316
Thompson, Daniel: acts as a messenger, 187, 223
Thompson, William: id., 298; *letters to*: from Clement Biddle, 411
Thomson, Charles, 67; and slave embarkation lists, 482, 517; *letters from*: to GW, 418, 508–9, 517–18; *letters to*: from John Woddrop, 76; from GW, 417–18, 482
Thoroughgood, John: id., 378
Thruston, Charles Mynn: conveys land to GW, 123–24

Tilghman, Anna Maria (*see* 1:232), 560
Tilghman, James: and Harriot Rebecca Anderson, 528; *letters from*: to GW, 528; *letters to*: from GW, 528
Tilghman, Tench (*see* 1:232): seeks artisans for GW, 11–12, 15, 22, 23–24; and GW's greenhouse, 30–31, 42–44; and George C. Fox & Sons, 484; and Harriot Rebecca Anderson's legacy, 527–28, 559–60; *letters from*: to GW, 11–12, 42–44, 528, 559–60; *letters to*: from GW, 15, 23–24, 30–31
Tobacco, 12, 55
Toby's Creek, 90, 107
A Topographical Description of Virginia, Pennsylvania, Maryland, and North Carolina: Thomas Hutchins, 90, 106
Townsend, Henry: holds shares in Potomac River Company, 565
Trade: GW's views on, 91–92, 121–22; with Great Britain, 396, 467
Treaties: of Paris (1783), 16, 34; of Fort Stanwix, 37, 84–85, 141, 142–47, 171, 173, 181; of Fort McIntosh, 173, 361–62, 372–73, 436–37, 437
A Treatise on Education with a Sketch of the Author's Method of Instruction . . . : George Chapman, 184
Trent, Alexander: and William Byrd's lottery, 4–5
Trenton: and location of Congress, 537
Trower's tavern, 136
Trumbull, Joseph: and Hugh Hughes, 17, 18
Tucker, Robert (d. 1779): and Dismal Swamp Company, 531
Turks Island (Bahamas): id., 153
Turner, George (*see* 1:271): and Society of Cincinnati diplomas, 287, 319, 512
Tygart Valley River, 295
Tyler, John: represents Charles City County, 134

United States: internal dissensions of, 187–90; abuses in states of, 301–2

Unzaga y Amézaga, Luis de (*see* 1:82), 110–11; *letters from*: to GW, 58

Van Berckel, Pieter Johan (*see* 1:42), 419, 486

Van Braam, Jacob: id., 57; *letters from*: to GW, 56–57

Vancouver, Charles: *letters from*: to GW, 549

Van Horne, David, 488

Van Horne, Mrs. David, 488

Van Maasdam, Count, 286, 435

Van Winter, Wilhelmina (*see* 1:280): *letters from*: to GW, 488; *letters to*: from GW, 472–73

Varick, Richard (*see* 1:2–3), 191; *letters from*: to GW, 163

Vaughan, Benjamin: and Richard Price, 271–72; and marble chimneypiece, 325, 326; *letters from*: to GW, 113; *letters to*: from GW, 325

Vaughan, Samuel (*see* 1:46): and marble chimneypiece, 325, 326; *letters to*: from GW, 326

Venango, 370

Venezuela: liberation of, 551

Vergennes, Charles-Gravier, comte de (*see* 1:30), 125, 449, 550, 553; and Charles Asgill, 407

A View of the Principal Deistical Writers: John Leland, 289

Virginia: British debts in, 143, 183; and its land laws, 513–16, 554

Virginia Gazette, or, the American Advertiser (Richmond), 140; runs Dismal Swamp Company advertisement, 474–75

Virginia house of delegates: *letters to*: from GW, 136–37

Virginia Journal and Alexandria Advertiser, 123, 140, 414; and Potomac River Company, 563

Virginia legislature: and Potomac River Company bills, 86–89, 156–57, 231–35, 248–50, 260–61; appoints Potomac com-

missioners to go to Maryland, 185–87; and bill to support teachers of Christian religion, 268; *letters to*: from GW, 257

Virginia land ordinances of 1776: and special tax, 284–85

Virginia state regiments: and fraudulent certificates, 5–6

Vogels, Gerard (*see* 1:195): and poetry of Wilhelmina van Winter, 472

Voltaire: Houdon's bust of, 177

Volunteer Journal (Dublin): and Mathew Carey, 227–28, 365

A Voyage to the Pacific Ocean: James Cook, 307, 411

Waddington, Joseph: and *Rutgers v. Waddington*, 190, 485

Wadsworth, Jeremiah: id., 498

Walker, Benjamin (*see* 1:138), 408, 409, 417; marriage of, 147, 225–26; and GW's New York land, 147–48; and George Clinton's gifts for GW, 224–25, 429; changes jobs, 225; *letters from*: to GW, 224–26, 429–30

Walker, Elizabeth, 62

Walker, Polly, 226

Walker, Thomas (*see* 1:77): and Dismal Swamp Company, 58, 62–63, 475, 488–89, 531; *letters from*: to GW, 62–63; *letters to*: from GW, 58, 488–89; from David Jameson, 62

Wallace, Johnson, & Muir: subscribes to Potomac River Company, 485

Ward, Artemas, 197

Ward, Edward, 338–39

Ward, Joseph: id., 197; marriage of, 197

Ward, Samuel (*see* 1:126): and Society of Cincinnati, 59

Washington, Anne Steptoe (*see* 1:70): id., 495

Washington, Augustine (1694–1743): and Principio Iron Company, 179

Washington, Augustine (1720–1762; *see* 1:262): and Principio Iron Company, 178–79

Washington, Bailey: id., 154
Washington, Bushrod, 154, 451, 476; travels west with GW, 8–9, 66, 83; visits Thornton Washington, 20; invited to Paris, 227–28, 365; and Dennis Ryan's note, 284, 474, 479; and GW's Millers Run ejectment suit, 341, 357, 358; and GW's letters from Lafayette, 551; *letters from*: to GW, 454; *letters to*: from GW, 284–85, 474–76
Washington, Charles (*see* 1:164), 83, 118, 154; moves to Berkeley County, 21; and Battaile Muse, 74; and schooling of George Steptoe Washington and Lawrence Augustine Washington, 137–39, 370–71, 495; and Potomac River Company, 495; *letters from*: to GW, 137–39, 370–71; *letters to*: from GW, 21, 494–95
Washington, Elizabeth Foote, 39, 64, 315; gives birth to daughter, 65; id., 197
Washington, George: tributes to, 2–3, 72–73, 80–81, 103–4, 135–36, 136–37, 141–42, 169–70, 187–90, 192, 271–72, 327, 472–73, 487–88; and William Byrd's lottery, 4–5; and tobacco cultivation, 12, 55; and Bank of England stock, 13; and Daniel Parke Custis estate, 13; and trip west, 19, 66, 67, 80, 82–83, 116, 118–19, 301; daily routine of, 29, 457–58; cancels trip to Niagara, 46–47; refers to disarray of personal affairs, 47, 388–89; and land purchased from George Mercer, 56; papers of, 56, 266–67, 388, 414–15, 466, 517–18; and Dismal Swamp Company, 58, 62, 474–75, 488, 518, 519, 531; and schooling of George Steptoe Washington and Lawrence Augustine Washington, 61–62, 113, 138–39, 370–71, 495; Joseph Wright's busts of, 66–67, 299, 307; and James Rumsey's self-propelled boat, 69, 371–72; French royal family's opinion of, 72–73; and Mississippi Land Company, 76; and Society of Cin-

cinnati, 100–101, 287, 319–20, 513; and Charles Lee's estate, 102, 478; seeks farm manager, 113–14; entertained in Richmond, 135–36; and his New York land, 146–48, 408–9, 510, 512; aids George Augustine Washington, 153, 155, 383–85; recommends road from headwaters of Potomac, 167–68; invited to contribute to Filson's *Kentucke*, 168–70, 269–70; Houdon's statue of, 178; asks George Mason for loan to brother, 180; advocates survey of the West, 182, 270; owns lots in Alexandria, 254, 256; seeks secretary, 256, 332, 388–89, 548–49; and purchase of Clifton's Neck, 266; describes surrender of Fort Washington, 267, 412–13; biographies of, 269; and the Savage affair, 276, 401–2, 431–32; receives spiritual counseling, 287–90; and Gilbert Simpson's public certificates, 307–9, 410–11, 560; and Millers Run ejectment suit, 338–58, 442–47, 489, 513–16; seeks seed for Versailles, 365, 553–54; and his use of code, 366; and acquisition of French-Dulany tract, 373–75; and rumors of his illness, 382–83; and wartime correspondence with George William Fairfax, 388, 390, 441; and his Continental loan certificates, 397–98, 470, 473–74, 483, 484–85, 491, 501; and French language, 407, 435; and his houses at Bath, 426–27, 428; refers to his financial straits, 447–48, 463, 495, 510; gives advice on traveling in U.S., 453–54; compared to Cincinnatus, 459; French opinion of, 463; and slave embarkation lists, 482, 517; and John Parke Custis's estate, 519; and George Baylor's estate, 519; and Thomas Colvill's estate, 528, 559; denies kinship to Ruthey Jones, 542; congressional medal for, 546; and Sebastian Francisco de Miranda, 551

gifts to: animals and fowl, 1–2,

2, 163–64, 165, 178, 460, 470, 475, 504–5; books, 2–3, 251, 318–19, 406–8, 450; prints, 52–53; food and wine, 55, 63, 65, 196–97, 323, 479, 528, 530; magazines, newspapers and pamphlets, 63, 162, 405–6, 430, 448, 452, 535; plants and seed, 146, 147–48, 148, 258–60, 408–9, 429, 431, 475, 479, 505–6; gold-headed cane, 290–91; marble chimneypiece, 325, 326

portraits of: by Charles Willson Peale, 71; by Sarah De Hart, 411–13, 465–66; by Pierre-Eugène Du Simitière, 413, 466; by Robert Edge Pine, 509, 561–62

and Potomac River Company: makes plans for, 51; advocates establishment of, 65–66, 85–89, 89–98, 106–9, 121–22; describes advantages of, 89–98, 102–3, 106–10, 121–22, 254, 309–15, 323, 363–65, 379–81, 389; made president of, 89, 562–63; negotiates with Maryland legislature, 99–100, 165–68, 265–66; and his negotiations with Virginia legislature, 134, 155–57; views on financing of, 156, 167; as commissioner to secure Maryland bill, 185–87, 195, 195–96, 196, 223, 229, 229–30, 231–35, 248–50, 252; and his shares in Potomac and James River companies, 256–57, 280–81, 282–84, 328–30, 363–64, 381–82, 389, 391–92, 399, 420–23, 447–48, 459, 521, 556–57; and papers relating to its founding, 273–75; seeks foreign subscriptions, 366, 380–81; seeks engineer for, 389; sets first meeting of directors, 562–63

views on: jackasses, 1; pay for workers, 7; Britain's intentions, 29–30; slavery, 64; tenants, 68; navigation of Mississippi, 90–93, 108–9, 438; European powers in American West, 90–94, 108–9, 121, 171–72; foreign trade, 91–92; interstate rivalries, 91, 91–92, 107–8, 145–46, 172, 272,

400; ties with the West, 91–96, 106–8, 121–22, 170–71, 310–14; James River navigation, 95; education, 113, 183–84, 252; Britain's retention of western posts, 119, 121, 145–46, 181–82; Indian affairs, 119–20, 170–71; land speculation, 119–20; western land policy, 119–20, 182–83, 437, 440; political dissension, 145–46, 171; weakness of Congress, 171–72, 181; friendship with Lafayette, 175; his own life, 175; public ownership of western minerals, 182; public schools, 252; conducting correspondence, 253; exercise, 253, 332; Horatio Gates, 256; gift of shares in Potomac and James River companies, 282–84, 364–65, 381–82, 389; writing to dignitaries unknown to him, 286, 435–36, 553; American Indians, 291, 293, 437; Lady Huntingdon's scheme, 291–93, 330–32, 393–94; style of living, 325, 326; location of U.S. capital, 332–33; accepting gifts, 391; reversing court-martials, 404; Lebarbier's play, 408; John Laurens, 412; biographies of himself, 414–16; James Rumsey's self-propelled boat, 439–40; New York politics, 485–86; decadence of Europe, 486; Land Ordinance of 1785, 519–21; sitting for portraits, 561–62

Washington, George Augustine (*see* 1:30, 164), 39, 85, 324, 377–78, 544, 558; complains of Barbados, 9; visits Bermuda, 10, 31–32, 39; illness of, 21, 147, 154; visits William Washington, 41, 153, 155, 258–59, 371, 382–85, 513; letter of forwarded, 494; *letters from*: to GW, 9–10, 31–32, 39–41, 85, 382–83; *letters to*: from GW, 154–55, 176, 258–60

Washington, George Steptoe (*see* 1:70): schooling of, 61–62, 113, 138–39, 370–71; visits his mother, 494

Washington, Hannah Fairfax, 55

Washington, James (of South Carolina): and Ruthey Jones, 541

Washington, Jane Elliott (*see* 1:271), 153, 513

Washington, John (b. 1756), 373–74; id., 154

Washington, John (of South Carolina): and Ruthey Jones, 541, 542

Washington, John Augustine, 476; and schooling of George Steptoe Washington and Lawrence Augustine Washington, 137–38; seeks loan, 180; sends swan, geese, and holly berries, 475; *letters from*: to GW, 8–9, 180

Washington, Lawrence (1728–1752): and Principio Iron Company, 179

Washington, Lawrence Augustine (*see* 1:70): schooling of, 61–62, 113, 138–39, 370–71

Washington, Lund (*see* 1:30), 39, 64, 85, 227, 298, 327, 336, 504; and GW's Bullskin lands, 46; reimburses James Craik, 83; and schooling of GW's nephews, 138; and William Roberts, 151–53; id., 197; and plaster of paris, 278–79; and GW's Continental loan certificates, 398, 473–74, 501; holds shares in Potomac River Company, 565; *letters from*: to GW, 46, 118, 152

Washington, Martha, 104; greetings to, 10, 11, 16, 21, 28, 32, 36, 38, 41, 53, 60, 64, 85, 103, 104, 105, 111, 134, 141, 142, 143, 144, 162, 177, 188, 193, 205, 210, 211, 225, 227, 231, 271, 334, 336, 337, 371, 379, 384, 397, 409, 417, 419, 425, 430, 431, 450, 451, 452, 457, 460, 463, 467, 479, 480, 497, 501, 504, 506–7, 508, 513, 517, 523, 525, 529, 538, 540, 543, 546, 551, 558; greetings from, 21, 47, 48, 65, 109, 116, 122, 147, 151, 172, 176, 259, 284, 294, 300, 301, 307, 315, 326, 366, 387, 390, 437, 438, 454, 464, 473, 477, 486, 491, 511, 562; and Joseph Wright's busts of GW, 66–67, 299; gifts from, 70; illness of, 116, 300, 467; and Margaret Savage's will, 276; requests flax from tenants, 324; goes to Alexandria, 375; given wax grotto, 408, 429, 502; and loan to John Mercer, 464; De Hart's silhouette of, 465–66; invited to France, 502; portrait of by Robert Edge Pine, 509; grief of, 535; letter to, 406

Washington, Mary Ball: greetings to, 503

Washington, Mary Whiting: id., 26

Washington, Mildred Thornton, 154

Washington, Samuel (*see* 1:70), 61, 495; and land sold to Thornton Washington, 20; and John Ariss, 24

Washington, Thornton: and land bought from, 20; id., 21; *letters from*: to GW, 20–21

Washington, Warner (*see* 1:114), 55; id., 26; visited by James Craik, 83; *letters from*: to GW, 26–27

Washington, Warner, Jr.: id., 26

Washington, William (*see* 1:271), 259; and George Augustine Washington's visit, 41, 155, 382–85, 513; id., 153; sends acorns and magnolia seed, 259–60; *letters from*: to GW, 513; *letters to*: from GW, 153–54

Washington, William Augustine (1757–1810; *see* 1:262): and Principio Iron Company, 178–79

Washington College, 57, 252; lottery for, 37–38; subscriptions for, 37–38

Washington County (Pa.): and GW's Millers Run ejectment suit, 338–58

Washington's Bottom mill: and Gilbert Simpson's public certificates, 410–11

Washington's Bottom tract (*see* 1:118): state of, 18–19; GW's visit to, 66. *See also* Western landholdings

Watson, Elkanah: id., 162; describes GW's character and routine, 457–58; *letters from*: to GW, 456–58

Wax grotto. *See* Washington, Martha

Wayne, Anthony, 541; and Christopher Ludwick, 471

Webb, Samuel B.: *letters to*: from Joseph Barrell, 104

Webster-Ashburton Treaty, 305

Weissenfels, Frederick: id., 375–76; and depreciation of public certificates, 438–39; military service of described, 465; *letters from*: to GW, 375–76, 464–65; *letters to*: from GW, 438–39, 465

Welch, Wakelin: id., 13; *letters to*: from GW, 12–13, 13

Wesley, Charles: and Lady Huntingdon, 200

Wesley, John: and Lady Huntingdon, 200

West, John, Jr.: and Thomas Colvill's estate, 527; *letters from*: to James Hollyday, 527

West, Roger: holds shares in Potomac River Company, 565

West, Thomas: represents Fairfax County, 140

West, William: id., 528

Western landholdings: Millers Run tract, 6, 66, 116, 170–71, 338–58, 442–47, 489, 513–16, 555–56; Washington's Bottom tract, 18–19, 66, 78–79, 342; Great Kanawha tracts, 66, 78–79, 123–24, 393–94; Ohio River tracts, 66, 78–79, 393–94; Great Meadows tract, 78, 342; and terms of leases, 78–80; Thomas Freeman made agent of, 78–80; advertisement of, 80; Round Bottom tract, 338, 489–90, 556; and offer to Lady Huntingdon, 393–94; Burning Springs tract, 556

Western posts: British occupation of, 10–11, 29–30, 47, 93, 119, 121, 143, 145–46, 181, 230, 462

West Point, 540

Whale oil: and Lafayette's negotiations, 557–58

Wharton, Joseph: *letters to*: from George Croghan, 339

Wheat, 55

White, Alexander (*see* 1:401): and Charles Lee's estate, 102, 478; holds shares in Potomac River Company, 565

Whitefield, George: and Lady Hunt-

ingdon, 200; and orphanage in Georgia, 201

Whiting, Anne Carlyle, 24

Whiting, Francis, 118; leases Bullskin land, 24–25, 27–28

Whiting, Henry: id., 24–25; leases Bullskin land, 24–25, 26–27, 27–28, 117–18, 324

Whiting, Mary. *See* Washington, Mary Whiting

Willett, Marinus (*see* 1:255): sells land to GW and George Clinton, 146–48

Williamos, Charles (*see* 1:275): and grapevines for GW, 147–48, 149, 408–9, 429

Williams, John: leases Bullskin land, 68–69

Williams, Jonathan: id., 451

Williams, Otho Holland (*see* 1:24): and Society of Cincinnati diplomas, 287, 319–20, 512–13; *letters from*: to GW, 287, 512–13; *letters to*: from GW, 319–20

Williamson, Hugh: and Elizabeth River Canal, 62; and James McMechen's petition to Congress, 371–72; and public land policy, 438; *letters from*: to GW, 371–73; *letters to*: from GW, 439–40

Willing, Thomas: *letters to*: from GW, 315

Willoughby, John: id., 378

Wilson, James (of Pennsylvania): id., 358

Wilson, James (of Virginia): id., 279

Wilson, William: id., 279

Wine: Mountain Red, 247; champagne, 247–48; Moussaux, 247–48; and salubrious effects of port, 467; white Bordeaux, 528, 530

Witherspoon, John: and John Bowie, 414–15, 497–98; id., 497; and settlers for GW's western lands, 497–98; *letters from*: to GW, 496–98; *letters to*: from GW, 414–16

Woddrop, John: and textile trade, 74–77; *letters from*: to GW, 74–77; to Charles Thompson, 76; *letters to*: from Thomas Ogden, 76–77

Woddrop, Robert: id., 74, 76
Wolcott, Oliver: and Indian rela-
    tions, 142
Women: as cooks, 14; as historians,
    65; and childbirth, 144, 155; as
    artists, 411–13, 465–66; as poets,
    473; travel with husbands, 498
Worthington, Charles: holds shares
    in Potomac River Company,
    564–65
Wright, Joseph (*see* 1 : 32–33): and
    busts of GW, 66–67, 299, 307;
    letters from: to GW, 66–67; *letters*
    to: from GW, 299
Wright, Patience Lovell (*see* 1 : 32): id.,
    300; *letters to*: from GW, 299–300

Wright, Patrick: and William
    Wright, 434–35
Wright, William: id., 435
Wyckoff, Henry: and Melancton
    Smith, 112
Wynkoop, Cornelius: holds shares
    in Potomac River Company, 565

Yeates, Jasper: id., 358
Youghiogheny River: and Potomac
    River navigation, 82–83, 94, 232,
    238, 245, 330; and Pennsylvania
    roads, 264
Younger, Peter How, 337–38